Lecture Notes in Computer Science 15728

The series Lecture Notes in Computer Science (LNCS), including its subseries Lecture Notes in Artificial Intelligence (LNAI) and Lecture Notes in Bioinformatics (LNBI), has established itself as a medium for the publication of new developments in computer science and information technology research, teaching, and education.

LNCS enjoys close cooperation with the computer science R & D community, the series counts many renowned academics among its volume editors and paper authors, and collaborates with prestigious societies. Its mission is to serve this international community by providing an invaluable service, mainly focused on the publication of conference and workshop proceedings and postproceedings. LNCS commenced publication in 1973.

Michael Leuschel · Fuyuki Ishikawa
Editors

Rigorous State-Based Methods

11th International Conference, ABZ 2025
Düsseldorf, Germany, June 10–13, 2025
Proceedings

Springer

Editors
Michael Leuschel
Heinrich-Heine-Universität Düsseldorf
Düsseldorf, Nordrhein-Westfalen, Germany

Fuyuki Ishikawa
National Institute of Informatics
Chiyoda-ku, Tokyo, Japan

ISSN 0302-9743 ISSN 1611-3349 (electronic)
Lecture Notes in Computer Science
ISBN 978-3-031-94532-8 ISBN 978-3-031-94533-5 (eBook)
https://doi.org/10.1007/978-3-031-94533-5

This Springer imprint is published by the registered company Springer Nature Switzerland AG
The registered company address is: Gewerbestrasse 11, 6330 Cham, Switzerland

In memory of Jean-Raymond Abrial

Preface

ABZ 2025, the 11th International Conference on Rigorous State Based Methods, was held in Düsseldorf, Germany, from June 10 to June 13, 2025.

The ABZ conference series is dedicated to the cross-fertilization of state-based and machine-based formal methods. Abstract State Machines (ASM), Alloy, B, TLA, VDM, and Z are examples of these methods. They share a common conceptual foundation and are widely used in both academia and industry for the rigorous design and analysis of hardware and software systems. The ABZ conferences aim to be a forum for the vital exchange of knowledge and experience among the research communities around different formal methods.

ABZ 2025, which this volume is dedicated to, follows the success of the nine ABZ conferences from its first edition organized in London (UK) in 2008, where the acronym ABZ was invented to merge, into a single event, the ASM, B, and Z conference series. The Alloy community joined the event at the second ABZ 2010 conference, which was held in Orford (Canada). The VDM community joined the event at ABZ 2012, which was held in Pisa (Italy). ABZ 2014, held in Toulouse (France), brought the inclusion of the TLA+ community and the idea of proposing at each ABZ an industrial case study as a common problem for the application of different formal methods. The ABZ 2016 conference was held in Linz, Austria, and ABZ 2018 in Southampton, UK. In 2018 the steering committee decided to retain the acronym ABZ and add the subtitle 'International Conference on Rigorous State-Based Methods' to make more explicit the intention to include all state-based formal methods. The two successive ABZ events were organized in Ulm (Germany) as virtual events, while ABZ 2023 was held in Nancy, France and ABZ 2024 in Bergamo, Italy.

ABZ 2025 received 33 submissions. At least three program committee members reviewed each submission, and 21 papers were accepted for publication in this volume and presentation at the conference: 10 long papers covering a broad spectrum of research, from fundamental to applied work, 4 short papers of work in progress, industrial experience reports and tool development, 2 papers of PhD students working on topics related to state-based formal methods, and 5 papers on the ABZ 2025 case study, which was dedicated to the specification and analysis of how to control autonomous vehicles on a highway. A paper in this volume is dedicated to describing the case study.

The ABZ program included three invited talks: Michael Butler, Thierry Lecomte, and Nils Jansen.

ABZ 2025 hosted two workshops, one on the Rodin Platform, an Eclipse-based toolset for Event-B, and the other on formal modelling for UAVs.

Organizing and running this event required a lot of effort from several people. We are grateful to all the authors who submitted their work to ABZ 2025. We wish to thank all members of the Program Committee and all the additional reviewers for their precise, careful evaluation of the papers, and for their availability during the discussion period which considered each paper's acceptance. Furthermore, we thank Claudia Kiometzis for the local organization, Fabian Vu for managing the case study for ABZ 2025, Jan Gruteser and Fabian Vu for their valuable work in advertising this event and managing the conference website, Alexander Raschke for setting up the ABZ conference web sites, Asieh Fathabadi and Philipp Körner for taking care of the doctoral symposium, and Elvinia Riccobene for useful advice on difficult issues.

We wish to express our deepest gratitude to the Heinrich Heine University of Düsseldorf, which provided organizational support.

For readers of these proceedings, we hope that you find these proceedings useful, interesting, and challenging for future research.

April 2025

Michael Leuschel
Fuyuki Ishikawa

Organization

Program Chairs

Michael Leuschel	Heinrich-Heine-Universität Düsseldorf, Germany
Fuyuki Ishikawa	National Institute of Informatics, Japan

Case Study Chair

Fabian Vu	Heinrich-Heine-Universität Düsseldorf, Germany

Doctoral Symposium Chairs

Asieh Salehi Fathabadi	University of Southampton, UK
Philipp Körner	Heinrich-Heine-Universität Düsseldorf, Germany

Publicity/Social/Web Chairs

Jan Gruteser	Heinrich-Heine-Universität Düsseldorf, Germany
Fabian Vu	Heinrich-Heine-Universität Düsseldorf, Germany

Local Chair

Michael Leuschel	Heinrich-Heine-Universität Düsseldorf, Germany

Registration Chair

Claudia Kiometzis	Heinrich-Heine-Universität Düsseldorf, Germany

Program Committee

Yamine Aït Ameur	IRIT/INPT-ENSEEIHT, France
Toshiaki Aoki	JAIST, Japan
Paolo Arcaini	National Institute of Informatics, Japan
Richard Banach	University of Manchester, UK
Silvia Bonfanti	University of Bergamo, Italy
Chiara Braghin	Università degli Studi di Milano, Italy
Maximiliano Cristia	CIFASIS-UNR, Argentina
Alcino Cunha	University of Minho, Portugal
Catherine Dubois	ENSIIE-Samovar, France
Guillaume Dupont	Institut de Recherche en Informatique de Toulouse, France
Marie Farrell	University of Manchester, UK
Flavio Ferrarotti	Software Competence Centre Hagenberg, Austria
Marc Frappier	Université de Sherbrooke, Canada
Angelo Gargantini	University of Bergamo, Italy
Uwe Glässer	Simon Fraser University, Canada
Stefan Hallerstede	Aarhus University, Denmark
Thai Son Hoang	University of Southampton, UK
Akram Idani	Laboratoire d'Informatique de Grenoble, France
Fuyuki Ishikawa	National Institute of Informatics, Japan
Eunsuk Kang	Carnegie Mellon University, USA
Tsutomu Kobayashi	Japan Aerospace Exploration Agency, Japan
Philipp Körner	Heinrich-Heine-Universität Düsseldorf, Germany
Igor Konnov	Informal Systems, Austria
Regine Laleau	Paris-East Créteil University, France
Thierry Lecomte	CLEARSY, France
Michael Leuschel	University of Düsseldorf, Germany
Frédéric Mallet	Université Côte d'Azur, France
Atif Mashkoor	Johannes Kepler University Linz, Austria
Dominique Mery	Université de Lorraine, LORIA, France
Stephan Merz	Inria Nancy, France
Alexander Raschke	Ulm University, Germany
Elvinia Riccobene	University of Milan, Italy
Asieh Salehi Fathabadi	University of Southampton, UK
Patrizia Scandurra	University of Bergamo, Italy
Gerhard Schellhorn	Universität Augsburg, Germany
Klaus-Dieter Schewe	Zhejiang University, China
Emil Sekerinski	McMaster University, Canada
Neeraj Kumar Singh	INPT-ENSEEIHT/IRIT, University of Toulouse, France

Maurice ter Beek	CNR, Italy
Laurent Voisin	Systerel, France
Fabian Vu	Heinrich Heine University Düsseldorf, Germany
Hillel Wayne	Windy Coast Consulting, USA

Invited Talks

The Role of Abstraction and Refinement in Safety of Intelligent Systems

Michael Butler

University of Southampton, UK

Abstract. Rapid developments in artificial intelligence (AI) and robotics pose challenges to conventional methods of safety assurance. Machine learning is a very different programming approach to algorithm design, and notions of correctness for machine learning systems are still evolving. Increasing levels of autonomy being deployed in robotic systems means weaker concepts of control and predictability, increasing risk of accidents, and challenging conventional safety assurance methods. The role of abstraction/refinement formal methods, such as Event-B, is quite well established for traditional safety-critical systems, but it remains an open question whether and how such methods are applicable to systems with autonomy and learning-based control.

Recent ideas on *guaranteed safe AI* from leading formal methods researchers propose the use of three components to ensure safe AI systems: a *safety specification*, a *world model*, and a *verifier*. At a high level this represents a systems approach to safety analysis which aligns well with common usage of Event-B in conventional system design. Constructing specifications and world (or environment) models for complex systems remains challenging, and abstraction and refinement approaches are aimed at addressing system complexity through incremental modelling and verification. Systematic approaches to analysis of (informal) requirements and of safety hazards also play in important role. We explore how existing work on hierarchical analysis and verification could be extended and relaxed to deal with autonomy and machine learning. The focus is on physical safety rather than broader issues of influences of AI on human behaviours and ethics.

The ideas are influenced by collaboration with Asieh Salehi Fathabadi, Colin Snook, Dana Dghaym, Fahad Alotaibi, Haider Al-Shareefy, and Thai Son Hoang.

Neurosymbolic Learning Systems: Artificial Intelligence and Formal Methods

Nils Jansen

Ruhr-University Bochum, Germany
Chair of Artificial Intelligence and Formal Methods
n.jansen@rub.de
https://nilsjansen.org

Abstract. Artificial Intelligence (AI) has emerged as a disruptive force in our society. Increasing applications in healthcare, transport, military, and other fields underscore the critical need for a comprehensive understanding and the robustness of an AI's decision-making process. Neurosymbolic AI aims to create robust AI systems by integrating neural and symbolic AI techniques. We highlight the role of formal methods in such techniques, serving as a rigorous and structured backbone for symbolic AI methods.

Moreover, as a specific machine learning technique, we look at deep reinforcement learning (RL) with the promise that autonomous systems can learn to operate in unfamiliar environments with minimal human intervention. However, why haven't most autonomous systems implemented RL yet? The answer is simple: there are significant unsolved challenges. One of the most important ones is obvious: Autonomous systems operate in unfamiliar, unknown environments. This lack of knowledge is called uncertainty. This talk will explore why making decisions that account for this uncertainty is essential to achieving trustworthiness, reliability, and safety in RL.

Keywords. Artificial Intelligence · Formal Methods · Machine Learning · Formal Verification · Markov Decision Process · Decision-Making Under Uncertainty

References

1. Badings, T., Junges, S., Marandi, A., Topcu, U., Jansen, N.: Efficient sensitivity analysis for parametric robust markov chains. In: CAV (2023)
2. Badings, T., Simão, T.D., Suilen, M., Jansen, N.: Decisionmaking under uncertainty: beyond probabilities. Challenges and perspectives. Int. J. Softw. Tools Technol. Transf. (STTT) (2023)
3. Badings, T.S., et al.: Robust control for dynamical systems with nongaussian noise via formal abstractions. J. Artif. Intell. Res. **76**, 341–391 (2023)
4. Bovy, E., Suilen, M., Junges, S., Jansen, N.: Imprecise probabilities meet partial observability: Game semantics for robust pomdps. In: IJCAI (2024)

5. Köprülü, C., Simão, T.D., Jansen, N., Topcu, U.: Safety-prioritizing curricula for constrained reinforcement learning. In: ICLR (2025). To appear
6. Krale, M., Simão, T.D., Tumova, J., Jansen, N.: Robust active measuring under model uncertainty. In: AAAI (2024)
7. Suilen, M., Badings, T.S., Bovy, E.M., Parker, D., Nils Jansen: Robust markov decision processes: a place where AI and formal methods meet. In: Principles of Verification (2025)
8. Suilen, M., Simao, T.D., Parker, D., Jansen, N.: Robust anytime learning of markov decision processes. In: NeurIPS (2022)
9. Wienhöft, P., Suilen, M., Simão, T.D., Dubslaff, C., Baier, C., Jansen, N.: More for less: safe policy improvement with stronger performance guarantees. In: IJCAI (2023)
10. Zubia, M., Simão, T.D., Jansen, N.: Robust transfer of safety-constrained reinforcement learning agents. In: ICLR (2025). To appear

Contents

Case Study Papers

Short Papers

Invited Talks

Mathematical Proofs and Moving Trains: The Double Life of Atelier B

Thierry Lecomte(✉)

CLEARSY, Aix en Provence, France
thierry.lecomte@clearsy.com

Abstract. Atelier B has played a crucial role in ensuring the safety of critical systems for more than three decades. This presentation explores the recent evolution of Atelier B, from the last keynote in 2016 in Linz to its current, expanded role in system engineering across industries. We will revisit key milestones, such as the modeling of complex systems, the development and programming of the CLEARSY Safety Platform, and its use in educating students and engineers. The session will also showcase how the versatility of Atelier B has been harnessed to model, prove, and implement robust systems - from automated metros to industrial control. Through these advancements, Atelier B continues to shape the landscape of high-integrity software development, merging mathematical rigor with practical, real-world applications.

Keywords: Formal proof · Safety critical · B

1 Introduction

Atelier B will soon be celebrating its 30th anniversary. The keynote "Atelier B has turned 20", presented in Linz for ABZ 2016, summarised the work carried out in Atelier B in support of the B Method and Event-B since his first public appearance. These 20 years have been synonymous with technical and application wandering. For example:

- B has been extended to real and floating-point numbers to prove code embedded in the inertial units of airliners.
- Event-driven B generates proof obligations specific to the modelling of microelectronic components.
- B models without refinement have been used to generate maintenance documentation and for multiplexed vehicle diagnostics.

Over the last 10 years, a certain maturity has been reached, as development work and applications have found a framework for use that benefits the vast majority of the human community. In some cases, the state of the art has advanced. The aspects that were part of the keynote perspectives for ABZ 2016 have materialised or are in the process of materialising. This article presents the main aspects that have taken on real scientific or industrial substance. The

M. Leuschel and F. Ishikawa (Eds.): ABZ 2025, LNCS 15728, pp. 3–11, 2026.
https://doi.org/10.1007/978-3-031-94533-5_1

remainder of this paper is organised as follows. Section 2 presents the use of Atelier B for software and system modeling. Section 3 describes the CLEARSY Safety Platform. Section 4 presents the formal data validation with B and ProB, before concluding.

2 Atelier B for Software and System Modeling

Software and system modeling are supported by three versions of Atelier B. For each version, we indicate the specific features, the work carried out and the practical applications.

2.1 Atelier B Community Edition

It is a fully functional version of Atelier B, updated every 2 years, developed in C/C++ and with Qt framework. It can be downloaded free of charge[1] and is free to use. During the last academic year, it has been downloaded more than 10,000 times from all continents. It supports Windows, Linux and MacOS operating systems, even if last years we have been meeting portability issues with Qt for the Apple platform.

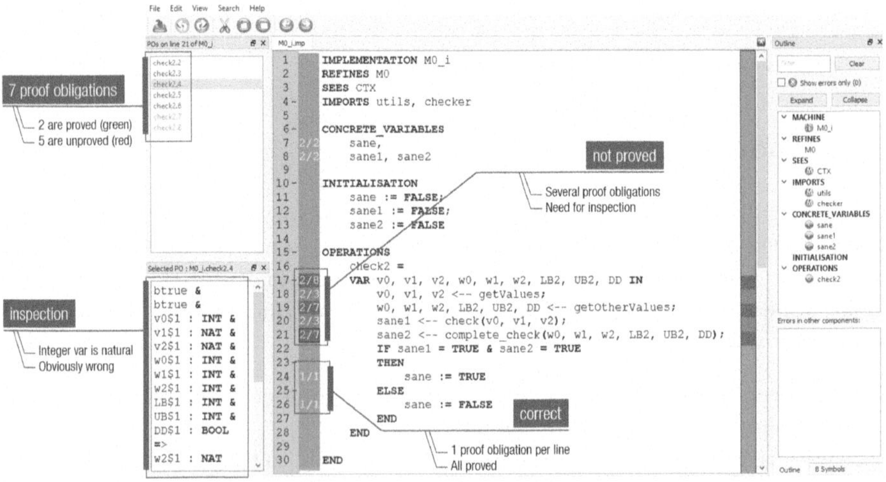

Fig. 1. Proof information integrated with B model editor.

Proof. It is a tool for formally developing and proving software. The integration of proof information within the B model editor (Fig. 1) provides immediate feedback on the complexity and provability of models.

The improvement of the proof performances is a never ending subject. The connection with external provers has been added over the time [2].

[1] https://www.atelierb.eu.

The Atelier Main Prover is also packaged as a plugin for the Rodin platform, to improve proof performances of this platform.

An open proof obligation database is available for benchmark on GitHub[2]. It contains a very large number of proof obligations stored in POG files, and a translation to SMTLib-2.6 of these proof obbligations, stored as SMTLIB-2.6 files.

Research and Development. Improving proof performance has been studied in several French and European collaborative research projects:

- ICSPA (Interoperable and Confident Set-based Proof Assistants) focuses on the set-based specification formalisms B, Event-B, and TLA+ that have been adopted for industrial development projects, for applications where correctness is critical. It aims at reinforcing the confidence in proofs carried out mechanically using them.
- BLaSST (Enhancing B Language Reasoners with SAT and SMT Techniques) targets bridging combinational and symbolic techniques in automatic theorem proving and validating the results for proof obligations generated from B models. Work is carried out on SAT-based encodings and optimized resolution techniques for proof, model generation, and lemma suggestion, as well as on encoding and reasoning techniques for expressive SMT-based formalisms.
- DISCONT (Correct Integration of DIScrete and CONTinous models) was aimed at providing efficient and easy to use refinement and proof-based techniques and tools that scale to complex systems and offer more convenient and automatic proof platforms centered around B and Event-B, with Atelier-B and Rodin. The main theoretical challenge is in how to better formalize the verification of the transition from the real to the discrete models, using refinement.
- AIDOaRt (AI-augmented automation supporting modelling, coding, testing, monitoring and continuous development in Cyber-Physical Systems) was aimed at using AIOps to automate proof activity by pre-selecting best proof tool during automatic proof and by suggesting proof tactics during interactive proof.

Code Generation. The generic C code generator offers the possibility of translating most of the syntactic constructs of B0, B's implementation language. The production of ACSL assertions from B models is being studied at IMD (UFRN, Brazil) for the verification with Frama-C of generated C code. Assertions are produced from specifications. This feature would improve the level of confidence in the generated code for applications below SIL3 when there is no application redundancy.

A Rust code generator has recently been added experimentally to extend the range of target languages.

[2] https://github.com/CLEARSY/apero.

Education. A Workbook on B is under construction. It will be freely available on the CLEARSY GitHub from the start of the 2025–2026 academic year (i.e. in September 2025). It is covering formal modelling with B, mathematical proofs and their automation, code generation (C, Rust) and integration with other programs and libraries, animation of B models using ProB[3]. It is aimed at helping everyone develop and enhance their skills in formal methods [4], while demonstrating how the B Method (and its support in Atelier B) can be applied to increasingly complex, real-world examples.

2.2 Atelier B Professional Edition

Compared to the Community Edition, it is updated several times per year and includes exclusive features such as an Ada translator, a Project Checker, and tools to prove mathematical rules. It can be used in industrial settings requiring close support, as well as in academic environments. It is available on request through a maintenance contract.

Software Development. For years, Alstom and Siemens have been using Atelier B Professional Edition for their most safety-critical software [1,3]. Their product lines, respectively Urbalis and Trainguard equip more than 100 metros in the world, representing 1250 km of lines and 30% of the CBTC market (Radio communication based train control). In particular, B has been used for some of the automated safety systems on Paris's automatic metro lines, i.e. L1, L4, L13, and L14 (which has been extended for the 2024 Olympics).

Systerel has developed an open-source Safe and Secure Open Platform Communications (S2OPC) solution for OPC UA (standard for industrial communications). This development incorporates B modelling of dynamic memory management, including memory allocation, deallocation and pointer validity. This OPC UA implementation confirms that software development using the B method with EAL4 and SIL2 certification capabilities is feasible and well-founded.

Event-B System Modeling. Since the early 2000s, Atelier B and Event-B have been used to demonstrate that the security policy for smart cards is correct by modelling the hardware and software elements of components such as MPUs (Memory Protection Units). This proven modelling is mandatory for EAL6+ certification according to the Common Criteria, which is currently the only standard to impose the use of formal methods beyond a certain level of security. Over the last 10 years, several Event-B models, reaching up to twenty levels of refinement, have been produced for certification by ANSSI, the French agency for information systems security, of microcircuits from different brands.

The Formal Proof of System Level Specification is here an approach to obtain a formal proof for the main safety properties of the system which are in the railways synonymous of "no collision and no over-speeding". The methodology is in two steps and mixes natural language and formal modelling in Event-B. It is not

[3] https://prob.hhu.de/.

a structural model containing all parts and associated behaviours. It is a model of the safety reasoning used to design the system. Atelier B is used to validate the model. The model is usually compact, without refinement, and contains up to 1000 proof obligations in total. The methodology for ensuring good correspondence between Event-B models and the "natural language proof" relies on checking mathematical objects for each notion used in the proof precursor, and checking events for each possible evolution of these notions.

This approach has been used to build the safety proof [8] of the OCTYS CBTC deployed in Paris on metro lines L3, L5, L9, L6, and L11. With the project Haute performance Marseille Vintimille (HPMV), the Marseille - Ventimiglia line will be the pilot project for the deployment of ERTMS Level 3 Hybrid on the conventional network. It will implement ERTMS level 3 Hybrid for the first time in Europe on a conventional line, without any other signalling, without any cohabitation phase between the old and new systems, and on a line in dense operation that it will only be possible to close for migration for a very short time. The French railways (SNCF) have decided to apply the formal proof of system level specification to demonstrate irrefutably that the Control-Command-Signalling system meets its safety requirements, based on the guarantees expected of the various sub-systems: new signalling stations ARGOS and MISTRAL, a new RBC, new generation axle counters, a high-performance GSM-R, and fibre-optic telecommunications network architecture with high-resilience redundancy. This activity will be a complementary element of the evidence to be produced by the HPMV Project for certification by the body in charge of qualification, and will enable the French Railway Safety Authority (EPSF) to agree to the direct switchover between the two railway signalling worlds.

2.3 Atelier B T2 Certified Edition

With its T2 certification jointly obtained by CLEARSY, Alstom, RATP and Siemens Mobility, it enables the development of critical software compliant with EN 50128 and the validation of system properties compliant with EN 50129 for SIL4 applications. A replay tool, Certifier, guarantees that projects developed with a recent Atelier B comply with standards. It is available on request for industrial applications and offers the same exclusive features as the Atelier B Professional Edition.

It should soon be used for the first time for an on-board application to ensure train safety.

3 CLEARSY Safety Platform

The CLEARSY Academic Safety Platform[4] is a simplified version of the industrial platform[5] allowing the development and deployment of critical applications

---

[4] Safety refers to the control of recognized hazards to achieve an acceptable level of risk.

[5] Certified as SIL4 T3, with applications for platform screen-doors, braking systems, and autonomous trains, https://www.clearsy.com/en/tools/clearsy-safety-platform/.

up to SIL4 level. It provides an introduction to formal modeling and programming for the control of critical functions within a simplified framework suitable for a training session of about ten hours.

The CLEARSY Academic Safety Platform [7] is a fail-safe computer capable of performing a self-assessment to check if it can safely complete its mission. The self-assessment is based on various hardware and software features to detect, for example, memory corruption, clock drift, or leakage current.

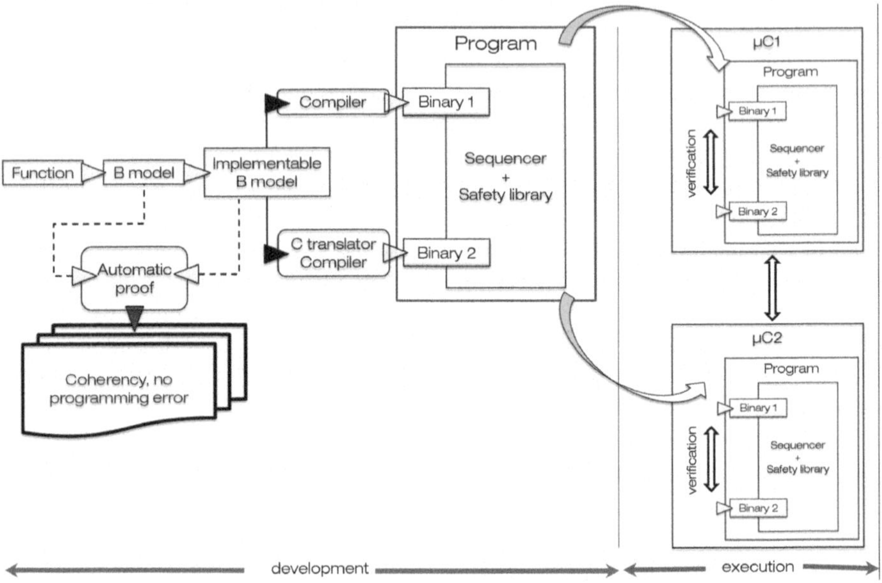

Fig. 2. CLEARSY Safety Platform architecture.

The main architecture (Fig. 2) relies on 2 microcontrollers executing the same program while regularly checking that they can communicate with each other. Digital outputs are electrical relays requiring both microcontrollers to agree to activate. If the self-assessment fails, the computer deactivates its outputs and enters an infinite loop doing nothing. The executed program consists of two parts:

- One part developed in C and MIPS assembly language, called non-replicated code, containing the main loop, interrupt processing, and some non-safety-related functions.
- One part developed with B (specification and implementation), called replicated code, which contains the critical application.

Binary codes are produced from the B implementation using two different code generators (C + gcc on one hand, an in-house B to binary compiler on the other). During each iteration of the main loop, the two binaries are executed in sequence, and their memory spaces containing the safety variables must have exactly the same content. Verifications are programmed once and for all in the safety library provided with Atelier B. The safety properties of the platform are out of the developer's reach and cannot be altered.

The Atelier B CSP Educational Version is a special version of the Atelier B Community Edition, which allows you to program the CLEARSY Safety Platform integrated into a demonstration circuit board. Developed during the COVID, a simulator version allows to program and verify the functional aspects of the modeling. It is being used for teaching formal methods [6] in several universities and engineering schools in Belgium, Brazil, France, Italy, and UK. Recently the Atelier B CSP Educational Version was manipulated by hundred students for a firefighting drone case-study during a robotic summer-school[6] organized with Robostar[7]

4 Formal Data Validation

In the railways, safety critical software applications are usually developed and validated independently from the parameters or constant data that fine-tune their behavior. For example, the track topology, signal and point positions, kilometer points, etc. are constant data used by an automatic pilot to compute braking curves and to determine when to trigger the emergency brake. So, each part must be safe at the same level, i.e. SIL4. Data validation process consists in ensuring that the data set is correct. For example: in ERTMS standard, tracks are equipped with signals and beacons. Rules to verify are related to the topology: each signal should have an associated beacon group, distance between signal and its beacon group should be less than 2 m, beacons should be less than 2 m apart from each other's. Other rules to verify are related to the content of the messages sent by the beacons to the trains (distances, gradients, speeds...). Manual data validation process used to be entirely human, leading to painful, error-prone, long-term activities (requiring several months to check manually up to 100,000 items of data against 1,000 rules).

Formal data validation process (Fig. 3) is the natural evolution of this human-based process into a secure one. A formal DSL has been defined to specify the constant data model. This data model is instantiated with the constant values and saved as a B machine. The ProB model-checker [5] is applied to verify that the model is correct. If not, all the counterexamples are listed. The tool, CLEARSY Data Solver[8], has been applied and specialized to several projects for both metros and mainlines (including ERTMS) for Alstom, Atkins, RATP, Siemens SNCF, and Thales.

[6] Robotics Applications and Innovation 2025, Third Summer School on Robotic Mission Engineering, https://rome.gesaduece.com.br/.

[7] Centre of excellence dedicated to research and technology transfer in the area of Software Engineering for Robotics, https://robostar.cs.york.ac.uk/.

[8] https://www.clearsy.com/en/tools/data-solver/.

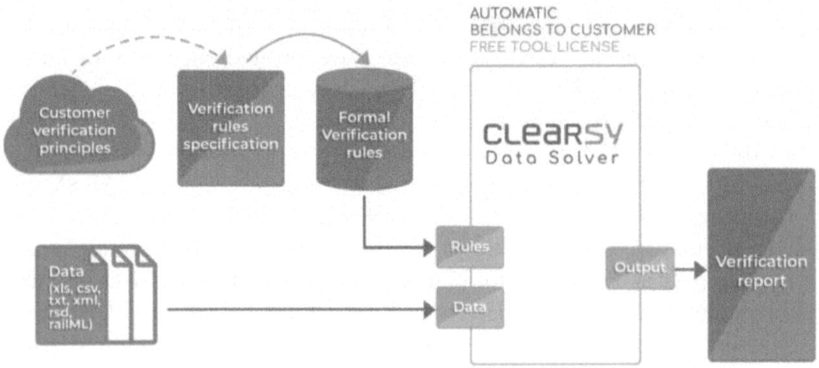

Fig. 3. Formal Data Validation Process.

5 Conclusion and Perspectives

The last 10 years have confirmed the value of B and Atelier B for the development and verification of critical applications, mainly in the rail sector. The use of B for the future automation of the metro lines L15, L16, L17 and L18 in Paris is a perfect example.

Atelier B is a living product that is regularly enriched with scientific results and new techniques, helping to advance the state of the art. The formal validation of data and the formalisation of safety reasoning, unknown 20 years ago, are now regularly mentioned in call for tenders.

The CLEARSY Safety Platform, programmable with B, is a generic tool to formally solve industrial control and command problems. The educational version makes the use of formal methods more concrete and allows them to be learned by a wider audience. Work to develop the educational tools, including the addition of remote inputs/outputs, should make it possible to tackle themes other than command control, such as cryptography, and other areas such as autonomous mobility on land, at sea and in the air.

Acknowledgements. The work and results described in this article were partly funded by:

– ECSEL JU under the framework H2020. as part of the project AIDOaRt (AI-augmented automation supporting modelling, coding, testing, monitoring and continuous development in Cyber-Physical Systems).

– ANR under the framework "appel à projets générique 2020". as part of the projects ICSPA (Interoperable and Confident Set-based Proof Assistants) and BLaSST (Enhancing B Language Reasoners with SAT and SMT Techniques).

References

1. ter Beek, M.H., et al.: Formal methods in industry. Form. Asp. Comput. 37(1) (2024). https://doi.org/10.1145/3689374
2. Burdy, L., Deharbe, D., Prun, E.: Interfacing automatic proof agents in atelier b: Introducing iapa. Electron. Proc. Theor. Comput. Sci. **240** (2017)
3. Butler, M., et al.: The first twenty-five years of industrial use of the b-method. In: ter Beek, M.H., Ničković, D. (eds.) Formal Methods for Industrial Critical Systems, pp. 189–209. Springer, Cham (2020)
4. Carvalho, G.: Teaching formal methods for 10 years: reflections on theories, tools, materials, and communities. In: Sekerinski, E., Ribeiro, L. (eds.) Formal Methods Teaching, pp. 58–74. Springer, Cham (2024)
5. Hansen, D., Schneider, D., Leuschel, M.: Using B and ProB for data validation projects. In: Butler, M., Schewe, K.-D., Mashkoor, A., Biro, M. (eds.) ABZ 2016. LNCS, vol. 9675, pp. 167–182. Springer, Cham (2016). https://doi.org/10.1007/978-3-319-33600-8_10
6. Lecomte, T.: Teaching and training in formalisation with b. In: Dubois, C., San Pietro, P. (eds.) Formal Methods Teaching, pp. 82–95. Springer, Cham (2023)
7. Lecomte, T., et al.: Low cost high integrity platform. In: ERTS 2020 - 10th European Congress on Embedded Real Time Systems. Toulouse, France (2020). https://hal.archives-ouvertes.fr/hal-02446132
8. Sabatier, D.: Using formal proof and B method at system level for industrial projects. In: Lecomte, T., Pinger, R., Romanovsky, A. (eds.) RSSRail 2016. LNCS, vol. 9707, pp. 20–31. Springer, Cham (2016). https://doi.org/10.1007/978-3-319-33951-1_2

Regular Papers

Behavioural Theory of Reflective Parallel Algorithms

Klaus-Dieter Schewe[1(✉)] and Flavio Ferrarotti[2]

[1] Institut Nationale Polytechnique de Toulouse / ENSEEIHT, Toulouse, France
kd.schewe@gmail.com
[2] Software Competence Center Hagenberg, Hagenberg, Austria
flavio.ferrarotti@scch.at

Abstract. We develop a behavioural theory of reflective parallel algorithms (RAs), i.e. synchronous parallel algorithms that can modify their own behaviour. The theory comprises a set of postulates defining the class of RAs, an abstract machine model, and the proof that all RAs are captured by this machine model. RAs are sequential-time, parallel algorithms, where every state includes a representation of the algorithm in that state, thus enabling linguistic reflection. Bounded exploration is preserved using multiset comprehension terms as values. The abstract machine model is defined by reflective abstract state machines (rASMs), which extend ASMs using extended states that include an updatable representation of the main ASM rule to be executed by the machine in that state.

Keywords: adaptivity · abstract state machine · linguistic reflection · behavioural theory · tree algebra

We dedicate this article to our former colleague, collaborator and friend Qing Wang (1972–2025). She will live on in our memories and our sincere appreciation for her personality and her inspiring research contributions.

1 Introduction

A *behavioural theory* in general comprises an axiomatic definition of a class of algorithms or systems by means of a set of characterising postulates, and an abstract machine model together with the proof that the abstract machine model captures the given class of algorithms or systems. The proof comprises two parts,

The research of Flavio Ferrarotti has been funded by the Federal Ministry for Climate Action, Environment, Energy, Mobility, Innovation and Technology (BMK), the Federal Ministry for Digital and Economic Affairs (BMDW), and the State of Upper Austria in the frame of the COMET Module Dependable Production Environments with Software Security (DEPS) within the COMET - Competence Centers for Excellent Technologies Programme managed by Austrian Research Promotion Agency FFG.

M. Leuschel and F. Ishikawa (Eds.): ABZ 2025, LNCS 15728, pp. 15–30, 2026.
https://doi.org/10.1007/978-3-031-94533-5_2

one showing that every instance of the abstract machine model satisfies the postulates (*plausibility*), and another one showing that all algorithms stipulated by the postulates can be step-by-step simulated by an abstract machine model instance (*characterisation*).

The ur-instance of a behavioural theory is Gurevich's sequential ASM thesis [11], which clarifies what a sequential algorithm is, and proves that sequential algorithms are captured by sequential Abstract State Machines (ASMs). Extensions of this thesis are the behavioural theories of parallel, recursive and concurrent algorithms [5,6,8] and further variations of these.

Adaptivity refers to the ability of a system to change its own behaviour. In the context of programming this concept is known as *(linguistic) reflection* since the 1950s. A brief survey of the development of reflection over the decades is contained in [14]. The recently increased interest in adaptive systems raises the question of their theoretical foundations. Such foundations are needed to achieve a common understanding of what can be gained by reflection, what the limitations of reflection are, and how reflection can be captured by state-based rigorous methods. This also constitutes the basis for the verification of properties of adaptive systems.

A first step towards answering this question was made by means of a behavioural theory of reflective sequential algorithms [12] and an extension of the logic of ASMs to a logic for reflective ASMs [14]. This theory provides the axiomatic definition of reflective sequential algorithms (RSAs), the proof that RSAs are not yet captured by Gurevich's postulates for sequential ASMs, the definition of reflective sequential ASMs (rsASMs), by means of which RSAs can be specified, and the proof that RSAs are captured by rsASMs, i.e. rsASMs satisfy the postulates of the axiomatisation, and any RSA stipulated by the axiomatisation can be defined by a behaviourally equivalent rsASM.

This article is dedicated to an extension of the theory to a behavioural theory of reflective, parallel algorithms (RAs), so the starting point is the (simplified) parallel ASM thesis developed in [8]. Concerning the postulates it is crucial that abstract states of RAs must contain a representation of the algorithm itself, which can be interpreted as an executable rule that is to be used to define the successor state. This gives rise to generalised *sequential time* and *abstract state* postulates analogous to those for reflective sequential algorithms [12].

Concerning a modified *bounded exploration* postulate we claim that while there cannot exist a fixed set of terms determining update sets in all states by simple interpretation, there is nonetheless a finite bounded exploration witness, provided a double interpretation is used: the first interpretation may result in multiset comprehension terms over the standard subsignature, which then can again be interpreted to define the values needed in the updates. Phrased differently, the first interpretation can be seen as resulting in a bounded exploration witness for the represented algorithm, and we obtain the terms that determine update sets by interpretation of (generalised) terms. Finally, these postulates involve some assumptions about the background, which are made explicit in a *background* postulate analogous to all other behavioural theories.

Concerning the definition of rASMs, this is straightforward, as only a concrete representation of a (parallel) ASM is required, for which we can choose a self-representation by means of trees and exploit the tree algebra from [15] to manipulate tree values as well as partial updates [16] to minimise clashes. The self-description comprising signature and rule can be stored in a dedicated location *pgm*. Instead of defining update sets for a fixed rule, the rule to be considered is obtained by *raising* the value stored in the state representing the rule into an executable rule.

For the plausibility and characterisation proofs the former one requires a rather straightforward construction of a bounded exploration witness from an rASM, for which the representation using *pgm* is essential, while the latter one will be accomplished by a sequence of lemmata, the key problem being that there is a theoretically unbounded number of different algorithms that nonetheless have to be handled uniformly. In essence we have to integrate the parallel ASM thesis [8] and the reflective sequential ASM thesis [12].

The remainder of this article is organised as follows. Section 2 is dedicated to the first part of the behavioural theory, the axiomatic definition of RAs. The key problems concern the self-representation in abstract states and the extension of bounded exploration. In Sect. 3 we introduce rASMs, which are based on ASMs with the differences discussed above and a background structure capturing tree structures and tree algebra operations. In Sect. 4 we first sketch that rASMs satisfy our postulates, thus they define RAs, then we outline the more difficult part of the theory, the proof that every RA as stipulated by the postulates can be modelled by a behaviourally equivalent rASM. In this article we focus on the motivation of the postulates and the definition of rASMs. Due to length restrictions detailed proofs have been omitted; they are available in [13]. We conclude with a summary and outlook in Sect. 5.

2 Axiomatisation of Reflective Algorithms

We assume familiarity with the basic concepts of ASMs [7] and partial updates [16]. We will modify the postulates of (synchronous) parallel algorithms [8] to capture the requirements of linguistic reflection.

2.1 Sequential Time and Abstract States

Reflective algorithms proceed in sequential time, though in every step the behaviour of the algorithm may change. As argued in [12] it is always possible to have a finite representation of a sequential algorithm, which follows from the sequential ASM thesis in [11]. This does not change, if parallel algorithms (as defined in [8]) are considered, which is a consequence of any of the parallel ASM theses [1,2,8], so the crucial feature of reflection can be subsumed in the notion of state, while the sequential time postulate can remain unchanged.

Postulate 1 (Sequential Time Postulate). A *reflective algorithm* (RA) comprises a set $\mathcal{S}$ of *states*, a subset $\mathcal{I} \subseteq \mathcal{S}$ of *initial states*, and a *one-step transition* *function* $\tau : \mathcal{S} \to \mathcal{S}$. Whenever $\tau(S) = S'$ holds, the state S' is called the *successor state* of the state S.

A *run* of a reflective algorithm $\mathcal{A}$ is then given by a sequence $S_0, S_1, \dots$ of states $S_i \in \mathcal{S}$ with an initial state $S_0 \in \mathcal{I}$ and $S_{i+1} = \tau(S_i)$.

A *signature* Σ is a finite set of function symbols, and each $f \in \Sigma$ is associated with an *arity* $\mathrm{ar}(f) \in \mathbb{N}$. A *structure* over Σ comprises a *base set* B and an *interpretation* of the function symbols $f \in \Sigma$ by functions $f_S : B^{\mathrm{ar}(f)} \to B$. An *isomorphism* σ between two structures is given by a bijective mapping $\sigma : B \to B'$ between the base sets that is extended to the functions by $\sigma(f_B)(\sigma(a_1), \dots, \sigma(a_n)) = \sigma(f_B(a_1, \dots, a_n))$ for all $a_i \in B$ and $n = \mathrm{ar}(f)$. For convenience to capture partial functions we assume that base sets contain a constant *undef* and that each isomorphism σ maps *undef* to itself. Note that an isomorphism also extends naturally to terms defined over Σ.

In order to capture reflection it will be necessary to modify the abstract state postulate such that we capture the self-representation of the algorithm by a subsignature and the signature is allowed to change. Furthermore, we need to be able to store terms as values, so the base sets need to be extended as well. For initial states we apply restrictions to ensure that the algorithm represented in an initial state is always the same. This gives rise to the following modification of the abstract state postulate.

Postulate 2 (Abstract State Postulate). States of an RA $\mathcal{A}$ must satisfy the following conditions:

(i) Each state $S \in \mathcal{S}$ of $\mathcal{A}$ is a structure over some finite signature Σ_S, and an extended base set B_{ext}. The extended base set B_{ext} contains at least a *standard base set* B and all terms defined over Σ_S and B.
(ii) The sets $\mathcal{S}$ and $\mathcal{I}$ of states and initial states of $\mathcal{A}$, respectively, are closed under isomorphisms.
(iii) Whenever $\tau(S) = S'$ holds, then $\Sigma_S \subseteq \Sigma_{\tau(S)}$, the states S and S' of $\mathcal{A}$ have the same standard base set, and if σ is an isomorphism defined on S, then also $\tau(\sigma(S)) = \sigma(\tau(S))$ holds.
(iv) For every state S of $\mathcal{A}$ there exists a subsignature $\Sigma_{alg,S} \subseteq \Sigma_S$ for all S and a function that maps the restriction of S to $\Sigma_{alg,S}$ to a parallel algorithm $\mathcal{A}(S)$ with signature Σ_S, such that $\tau(S) = S + \Delta_{\mathcal{A}(S)}(S)$ holds for the successor state $\tau(S)$.
(v) For all initial states $S_0, S_0' \in \mathcal{I}$ we have $\mathcal{A}(S_0) = \mathcal{A}(S_0')$.

Condition (iv) makes use of the unique consistent update set $\Delta(S)$ defined by the algorithm in state S. This requires some explanation. A *location* ℓ in state S is a pair $(f, (v_1, \dots, v_n))$ with a function symbol $f \in \Sigma_S$ of arity n and values $v_1, \dots, v_n$ in the (extended) base set. If the interpretation defines $f_S(v_1, \dots, v_n) = v_0$, then the value $v_0 \in B_{ext}$ is called the *value* of location ℓ in S, which we denote as $\mathrm{val}_S(\ell)$. An *update* is a pair (ℓ, v) comprising a location and a value. An *update set* is a set Δ of updates. An update set is *consistent* iff $(\ell, v_1) \in \Delta$ and $(\ell, v_2) \in \Delta$ imply $v_1 = v_2$. We define the state $S' = S + \Delta$ resulting from the *application of a consistent* Δ *to* S by $val_{S'}(\ell) = v$ for $(\ell, v) \in \Delta$ and $val_{S'}(\ell) = \text{val}_S(\ell)$ else. For inconsistent Δ we set $S + \Delta = S$.

Concerning a state S and its successor $\tau(S)$ we obtain a set $\mathit{Diff} = \{\ell \mid \text{val}_{\tau(S)}(\ell) \neq \text{val}_S(\ell)\}$ of those locations, where the states differ. Then $\Delta(S) = \{(\ell, v) \mid \ell \in \mathit{Diff} \wedge v = \text{val}_{\tau(S)}(\ell)\}$ is a consistent update set with $S + \Delta(S) = \tau(S)$ and furthermore, $\Delta(S)$ is minimal with this property.

2.2 Background

We need to formulate minimum requirements for the *background*, which concern the reserve, truth values, tuples, as well as functions *raise* and *drop*, but they leave open how algorithms are represented by structures over $\Sigma_{alg,S}$.

As backgrounds are defined by background structures, it is no problem to request that the set $\mathcal{D}$ of base sets contains an infinite set *reserve* of reserve values and the set $\mathbb{B} = \{\mathbf{true}, \mathbf{false}\}$ of truth values. As we need to define arities for function symbols, $\mathcal{D}$ must further contain the set $\mathbb{N}$ of natural numbers. Note that truth values and natural numbers can be defined by hereditarily finite sets as in [3]. Then the usual connectives on truth values need to be present as background function symbols.

Furthermore, as in the parallel ASM thesis the background must contain constructors for tuples and multisets and the usual functions on them. As we leave the specific way of representing algorithms open, there may be further constructors and functions in the background, but they are not fixed.

We emphasised that we must be able to store terms as values, so instead of using an arbitrary base set B we need an extended base set. For a state S we denote by B_{ext} the union of the universe U defined by the background class $\mathcal{K}$ using B, $\mathbb{N}$, $\mathbb{B}$, and a subset of the reserve, and the set of all terms defined over Σ_S. We further denote by $\mathbb{T}_S$ the set of all terms defined over Σ_S. Note that with the presence of tuple and multiset cobstructors the set $\mathbb{T}_S$ contains also multiset comprehension terms as used in the parallel ASM thesis [8]. These are essential for obtaining bounded exploration witnesses.

In doing so we can treat a term in $\mathbb{T}_S$ as a term that can be evaluated in the state S or simply as a value in B_{ext}. We use a function *drop* : $\mathbb{T}_S \rightarrow B_{ext}$ that turns a term into a value of the extended base set, and a partial function *raise* : $B_{ext} \rightarrow \mathbb{T}_S$ turning a value (representing a term) into a term that can be evaluated. In the same way we get a function *drop* : $\mathcal{P}_S \rightarrow B_{ext}$ that turns an algorithm that can be executed in state S into a value in the extended base set B_{ext}. Again, *raise* : $B_{ext} \rightarrow \mathcal{P}_S$ denotes the (partial) inverse. We overload the function *drop* to also turn function symbols into values, i.e. we have *drop* : $\Sigma_S \rightarrow B_{ext}$, for which *raise* : $B_{ext} \rightarrow \Sigma_S$ denotes again the (partial) inverse. The presence of functions *raise* and *drop* is essential for linguistic reflection [17].

Postulate 3 (Background Postulate). The *background of a RA* is defined by a background class $\mathcal{K}$ over a background signature V_K. It must contain an infinite set *reserve* of reserve values, the equality predicate, the undefinedness value *undef*, truth values and their connectives, tuples and projection operations on them, multisets with union and comprehension operators on them, natural numbers and operations on them, and constructors and operators that permit the representation and update of parallel algorithms.

The background must further provide partial functions: $drop : \mathbb{T}_S \cup \mathcal{P}_S \cup \Sigma_S \rightarrow B_{ext}$ and $raise : B_{ext} \rightarrow \mathbb{T}_S \cup \mathcal{P}_S \cup \Sigma_S$ for each base set B and extended base set B_{ext}, and an *extraction function* $\beta : \mathbb{T}_S \rightarrow \bar{\mathbb{T}}$, which assigns to each term defined over a signature Σ_S and the extended base set B_{ext} a set of terms in $\bar{\mathbb{T}}$, which is defined over B, $\Sigma_S - \Sigma_{alg}$ and the tuple and multiset operators.

For instance, constructors for trees as well as operations on trees, e.g. for the extraction of subtrees or the composition of new trees must be defined in the background structures. We also need a set of constants such as `if`, `forall`, `par`, `let`, `assign` and `partial` by means of which we can label nodes in trees. Then expressions such as $tr = \langle \texttt{par}, \langle \texttt{assign}, c, \texttt{term}\langle f, t \rangle \rangle, t_2 \rangle$ are elements of B_{ext} as well as executable algorithms in $\mathcal{P}_S$. While tr itself is just a value, $raise(tr)$ is a rule that can be executed on the state S. In this case $\beta(tr)$ is the set of multiset terms defined by the terms $c, f(t), t$ occurring in the value tr.

2.3 Bounded Exploration

Finally, we need a generalisation of the bounded exploration postulate. As in every state S we have a representation of the actual parallel algorithm $\mathcal{A}(S)$, this algorithm possesses a bounded exploration witness W_S, i.e. a finite set of multiset comprehension terms in $\bar{\mathbb{T}}$ such that $\Delta_{\mathcal{A}(S)}(S_1) = \Delta_{\mathcal{A}(S)}(S_2)$ holds, whenever states S_1 and S_2 coincide on W_S. We can always assume that W_S just contains terms that must be evaluated in a state to determine the update set in that state. Thus, though W_S is not unique we may assume that W_S is contained in the finite representation of $\mathcal{A}(S)$. This implies that the terms in W_S result by interpretation from terms that appear in this representation, i.e. W_S can be obtained using the extraction function β. Consequently, there must exist a finite set of terms W such that its interpretation in a state yields both values and terms, and the latter ones represent W_S. We will continue to call W a *bounded exploration witness*. Then the interpretation of W and the interpretation of the extracted terms in any state suffice to determine the update set in that state. This leads to our *bounded exploration postulate* for RAs.

If S, S' are states of an RA and W is a set of multiset comprehension terms over the common signature $\Sigma_S \cap \Sigma_{S'}$, we say that S and S' *strongly coincide* over W iff the following holds:

- For every $t \in W$ we have $\text{val}_S(t) = \text{val}_{S'}(t)$.
- For every $t \in W$ with $\text{val}_S(t) \in \mathbb{T}_S$ and $\text{val}_{S'}(t) \in \mathbb{T}_{S'}$ we have $\text{val}_S(\beta(t)) = \text{val}_{S'}(\beta(t))$.

We may further assume that the complex values representing an algorithm are updated by several operations in one step, i.e. shared updates defined by an operator and arguments [16] may be used to define updates. If operators are compatible [16], such shared updates are merged into a single update. In order to capture this merging we extend the bounded exploration witness W as follows: A term indicating a shared update takes the form $op(f(t_1, \dots, t_n), t'_1, \dots, t'_m)$, where op is the operator that is to be applied, $f(t_1, \dots, t_n)$ evaluates in every state S to a value $\text{val}_S(\ell)$ of some location $\ell = (f, (\text{val}_S(t_1), \dots, \text{val}_S(t_n)))$, and $t'_1, \dots, t'_m$ evaluate to the other arguments of the shared update. If $op_1(f(t_1, \dots, t_n), t'_{11}, \dots, t'_{1m_1}), \dots, op_k(f(t_1, \dots, t_n), t'_{k1}, \dots, t'_{km_k})$ are several terms occurring in W or in $\beta(W)$, then the term

$$op_1(\dots(op_k(f(t_1, \dots, t_n), t'_{k1}, \dots, t'_{km_k}), \dots, t'_{21}, \dots, t'_{2m_2}), t'_{11}, \dots, t'_{1m_1})$$

will be called an *aggregation term over* $f(t_1, \dots, t_n)$, and the tuple $(\text{val}_S(\hat{t}), \text{val}_S(t_1), \dots, \text{val}_S(t_n))$ will be called an *aggregation tuple*. Then we can always assume that the update set $\Delta_{\mathcal{A}}(S)$ is the result of collapsing an update multiset $\ddot{\Delta}_{\mathcal{A}}(S)$.

Postulate 4 (Bounded Exploration Postulate). For every RA $\mathcal{A}$ there is a finite set W of multiset comprehension terms such that $\ddot{\Delta}_{\mathcal{A}}(S) = \ddot{\Delta}_{\mathcal{A}}(S')$ holds (hence also $\Delta_{\mathcal{A}}(S) = \Delta_{\mathcal{A}}(S')$) whenever the states S and S' strongly coincide over W.

Furthermore, $\ddot{\Delta}_{\mathcal{A}}(\text{res}(S, \Sigma_{alg})) = \ddot{\Delta}_{\mathcal{A}}(\text{res}(S', \Sigma_{alg}))$ holds (and consequently also $\Delta_{\mathcal{A}}(\text{res}(S, \Sigma_{alg})) = \Delta_{\mathcal{A}}(\text{res}(S', \Sigma_{alg}))$) whenever the states S and S' coincide over W. Here, $\text{res}(S, \Sigma_{alg})$ is the structure resulting from S by restriction of the signature to Σ_{alg}.

Any set W of terms as in the bounded exploration postulate 4 will be called a *(reflective) bounded exploration witness* (R-witness) for $\mathcal{A}$. The four postulates capturing sequential time, abstract states, background and bounded exploration together provide an axiomatic definition of the notion of a reflective algorithm.

2.4 Behavioural Equivalence

According to the definitions in [1,11] two algorithms are *behaviourally equivalent* iff they have the same sets of states and initial states and the same transition function τ. If we adopted without change this definition of behavioural equivalence from [11], then the substructure over Σ_{alg} would be required to be exactly the same in corresponding states. However, the way how to realise such a representation was deliberately left open in the axiomatisation. Therefore, instead of claiming identical states it suffices to only require identity for the restriction to $\Sigma_S - \Sigma_{alg}$, while structures over Σ_{alg} only need to define behaviourally equivalent algorithms.

However, this is still too restrictive, as behavioural equivalence of $\mathcal{A}(S)$ and $\mathcal{A}(S')$ would still imply identical changes to the self-representation. Therefore, we can also restrict our attention to the behaviour of the algorithms $\mathcal{A}(S)$ on states over $\Sigma_S - \Sigma_{alg}$. If $\mathcal{A}(S)$ and $\mathcal{A}(S')$ produce significantly different changes to the represented algorithm, the next state in a run of the reflective algorithm will reveal this.

Therefore, two RAs $\mathcal{A}$ and $\mathcal{A}'$ are *behaviourally equivalent* iff there exists a bijection Φ between runs of $\mathcal{A}$ and those of $\mathcal{A}'$ such that for every run $S_0, S_1, \dots$ of $\mathcal{A}$ we have that for all states S_i and $\Phi(S_i)$

(i) their restrictions to $\Sigma_{S_i} - \Sigma_{alg}$ are the same, and
(ii) the restrictions of $\mathcal{A}(S_i)$ and $\mathcal{A}'(\Phi(S_i))$ to $\Sigma_{S_i} - \Sigma_{alg}$ represent behaviourally equivalent algorithms.

3 Reflective Abstract State Machines

In this section we define a model of reflective ASMs, which uses a self representation of an ASM as a particular tree value that is assigned to a location *pgm*. For basic operations on this tree we exploit the tree algebra from [12]. Then in every step the update set will be built using the rule in this representation, for which we exploit *raise* and *drop* as in [17].

3.1 Tree Structures

We now provide the details of the tree structures and the tree algebra. An *unranked tree structure* is a structure $(\mathcal{O}, \prec_c, \prec_s)$ consisting of a finite, non-empty set $\mathcal{O}$ of node identifiers, called tree domain, and irreflexive relations $\prec_c$ (child relation) and $\prec_s$ (sibling relation) over $\mathcal{O}$ satisfying the following conditions:

- there exists a unique, distinguished node $o_r \in \mathcal{O}$ (root) such that for all $o \in \mathcal{O} - \{o_r\}$ there is exactly one $o' \in \mathcal{O}$ with $o' \prec_c o$, and
- whenever $o_1 \prec_s o_2$ holds, then there is some $o \in \mathcal{O}$ with $o \prec_c o_i$ for $i = 1, 2$ and vice versa.

For $x_1 \prec_c x_2$ we say that x_1 is the *parent* of x_2 and x_2 is a *child* of x_1. For $x_1 \prec_s x_2$ we say that x_2 is the *next sibling* of x_1, and x_1 is the *previous sibling* of x_2. In order to obtain trees from this, we add labels and assign values to the leaves. For this we fix a finite, non-empty set L of *labels*, and a finite family $\{\tau_i\}_{i \in I}$ of data types. Each data type τ_i is associated with a *value domain* $dom(\tau_i)$. The corresponding *universe* U contains all possible values of these data types, i.e. $U = \bigcup_{i \in I} dom(\tau_i)$.

A *tree* t over the set of labels L with values in the universe U comprises an unranked tree structure $\gamma_t = (\mathcal{O}_t, \prec_c, \prec_s)$, a total label function $\omega_t : \mathcal{O}_t \to L$, and a partial value function $v_t : \mathcal{O}_t \to U$ that is defined on the leaves in γ_t.

Let T_L denote the set of all trees with labels in L, and let $root(t)$ denote the root node of a tree t. A sequence $t_1, ..., t_k$ of trees is called a *hedge*, and a multiset $\{\!\{t_1, ..., t_k\}\!\}$ of trees is called a *forest*. Let ϵ denote the empty hedge, and let H_L denote the set of all hedges with labels in L. A tree t_1 is a *subtree* of t_2 (notation $t_1 \sqsubseteq t_2$) iff the following properties are satisfied:

(i) $\mathcal{O}_{t_1} \subseteq \mathcal{O}_{t_2}$,
(ii) $o_1 \prec_c o_2$ holds in t_1 for $o_1, o_2 \in \mathcal{O}_{t_1}$ iff it holds in t_2,
(iii) $o_1 \prec_s o_2$ holds in t_1 for $o_1, o_2 \in \mathcal{O}_{t_1}$ iff it holds in t_2,
(iv) $\omega_{t_1}(o') = \omega_{t_2}(o')$ holds for all $o' \in \mathcal{O}_{t_1}$, and
(v) for all leaves $o' \in \mathcal{O}_{t_1}$ we have $\upsilon_{t_1}(o') = \upsilon_{t_2}(o')$.

t_1 is the *largest subtree* of t_2 (denoted as $\widehat{o}$) at node o iff $t_1 \sqsubseteq t_2$ with $root(t_1) = o$ and there is no tree t_3 with $t_1 \neq t_3 \neq t_2$ such that $t_1 \sqsubseteq t_3 \sqsubseteq t_2$.

The *set of contexts* C_L over L is the set $T_{L \cup \{\xi\}}$ of trees with labels in $L \cup \{\xi\}$ ($\xi \notin L$) such that for each tree $t \in C_L$ exactly one leaf node is labelled with ξ and the value assigned to this leaf is *undef*. The context with a single node labelled ξ is called trivial and is simply denoted as ξ. Contexts allow us to define substitution operations that replace a subtree of a tree or context by a new tree or context. This leads to the following four kinds of substitutions:

Tree-to-tree substitution. For a tree $t_1 \in T_{L_1}$, a node $o \in \mathcal{O}_{t_1}$ and a tree $t_2 \in T_{L_2}$ the result $subst_{tt}(t_1, o, t_2) = t_1[\widehat{o} \mapsto t_2]$ of substituting t_2 for the subtree rooted at o is a tree in $T_{L_1 \cup L_2}$.

Tree-to-context substitution. For a tree $t_1 \in T_{L_1}$, a node $o \in \mathcal{O}_{t_1}$ the result $subst_{tc}(t_1, o, \xi) = t_1[\widehat{o} \mapsto \xi]$ of substituting the trivial context for the subtree rooted at o is a context in C_{L_1}.

Context-to-context substitution. For contexts $c_1 \in C_{L_1}$ and $c_2 \in C_{L_2}$ the result $subst_{cc}(c_1, c_2) = c_1[\xi \mapsto c_2]$ of substituting c_2 for the leaf labelled by ξ in c_1 is a context in $C_{L_1 \cup L_2}$.

Context-to-tree substitution. For a context $c_1 \in C_{L_1}$ and a tree $t_2 \in T_{L_2}$ the result $subst_{ct}(c_1, t_2) = c_1[\xi \mapsto t_2]$ of substituting t_2 for the leaf labelled by ξ in c_1 is a tree in $T_{L_1 \cup L_2}$.

As a shortcut we write $subst_{tc}(t_1, o, c_2)$ for $subst_{cc}(subst_{tc}(t_1, o, \xi), c_2)$, which is a context in $C_{L_1 \cup L_2}$.

To provide manipulation operations over trees at a level higher than individual nodes and edges, we need constructs to select arbitrary tree portions. For this we provide two selector constructs, which result in subtrees and contexts, respectively. For a tree $t = (\gamma_t, \omega_t, \upsilon_t) \in T_L$ these constructs are defined as follows:

- *context* : $\mathcal{O}_t \times \mathcal{O}_t \to C_L$ is a partial function on pairs (o_1, o_2) of nodes with $o_1 \prec_c^+ o_2$ and $context(o_1, o_2) = subst_{tc}(\widehat{o}_1, o_2, \xi) = \widehat{o}_1[\widehat{o}_2 \mapsto \xi]$, where $\prec_c^+$ denotes the transitive closure of $\prec_c$.
- *subtree* : $\mathcal{O}_t \to T_L$ is a function defined by $subtree(o) = \widehat{o}$.

The *set* $\mathbb{T}$ *of tree algebra terms* over $L \cup \{\epsilon, \xi\}$ comprises label terms, hedge terms, and context terms, i.e. $\mathbb{T} = L \cup \mathbb{T}_h \cup \mathbb{T}_c$, which are defined as follows:

- The set $\mathbb{T}_h$ is the smallest set with $T_L \subseteq \mathbb{T}_h$ such that (1) $\epsilon \in \mathbb{T}_h$, (2) $a\langle h \rangle \in \mathbb{T}_h$ for $a \in L$ and $h \in \mathbb{T}_h$, and (3) $t_1 \dots t_n \in \mathbb{T}_h$ for $t_i \in \mathbb{T}_h$ $(i = 1, \dots, n)$.

- The set of context terms $\mathbb{T}_c$ is the smallest set with (1) $\xi \in \mathbb{T}_c$ and (2) $a\langle t_1, \dots, t_n\rangle \in \mathbb{T}_c$ for $a \in L$ and terms $t_1, \dots, t_n \in \mathbb{T}_h \cup \mathbb{T}_c$, such that exactly one t_i is a context term in $\mathbb{T}_c$.

With these we now define the operators of our tree algebra as follows (see [12]):

label_hedge. The operator *label_hedge* turns a hedge into a tree with a new added root, i.e. $label\_hedge(a, t_1 \dots t_n) = a\langle t_1, \dots, t_n\rangle$.
label_context. Similarly, the operator *label_context* turns a context into a context with a new added root, i.e. $label\_context(a, c) = a\langle c\rangle$.
left_extend. The operator *left_extend* integrates the trees in a hedge into a context extending it on the left, i.e. $left\_extend(t_1 \dots t_n, a\langle t'_1, \dots, t'_m\rangle) = a\langle t_1, \dots, t_n, t'_1, \dots, t'_m\rangle$.
right_extend. Likewise, the operator *right_extend* integrates the trees in a hedge into a context extending it on the right, i.e.
$right\_extend(t_1 \dots t_n, a\langle t'_1, \dots, t'_m\rangle) = a\langle t'_1, \dots, t'_m, t_1, \dots, t_n\rangle$.
concat. The operator *concat* simply concatenates two hedges, i.e.
$concat(t_1 \dots t_n, t'_1 \dots t'_m) = t_1 \dots t_n t'_1 \dots t'_m$.
inject_hedge. The operator *inject_hedge* turns a context into a tree by substituting a hedge for ξ, i.e. $inject\_hedge(c, t_1 \dots t_n) = c[\xi \mapsto t_1 \dots t_n]$.
inject_context. The operator *inject_context* substitutes a context for ξ, i.e. $inject\_context(c_1, c_2) = c_1[\xi \mapsto c_2]$.

3.2 Self Representation Using Trees

For the dedicated location storing the self-representation of an ASM it is sufficient to use a single function symbol *pgm* of arity 0. Then in every state S the value $\mathrm{val}_S(pgm)$ is a complex tree comprising two subtrees for the representation of the signature and the rule, respectively. The signature is just a list of function symbols, each having a name and an arity. The rule can be represented by a syntax tree.

Thus, for the tree structure we have a root node o labelled by `pgm` with exactly two successor nodes, say o_0 and o_1, labelled by `signature` and `rule`, respectively. So we have $o \prec_c o_0$, $o_0 \prec_s o_1$ and $o \prec_c o_1$. The subtree rooted at o_0 has as many children $o_{00}, \dots, o_{0k}$ as there are function symbols in the signature, each labelled by `func`. Each of the subtrees rooted at o_{0i} takes the form $\mathtt{func}\langle\mathtt{name}\langle f\rangle\ \mathtt{arity}\langle n\rangle\rangle$ with a function name f and a natural number n. The subtree rooted at o_1 represents the rule as a tree. Trees representing rules are inductively defined as follows:

- An assignment rule $f(t_1, \dots, t_n) = t_0$ is represented by a tree of the form $label\_hedge(\mathtt{update}, \mathtt{func}\langle f\rangle\mathtt{term}\langle t_1 \dots t_n\rangle\mathtt{term}\langle t_0\rangle)$.
- A partial assignment rule $f(t_1, \dots, t_n) \leftleftarrows^{op} t'_1, \dots, t'_m$ is represented by a tree of the form
$label\_hedge(\mathtt{partial}, \mathtt{func}\langle f\rangle\mathtt{func}\langle op\rangle\mathtt{term}\langle t_1 \dots t_n\rangle\mathtt{term}\langle t'_1 \dots t'_m\rangle)$.

- A branching rule $\texttt{IF}\ \varphi\ \texttt{THEN}\ r_1\ \texttt{ELSE}\ r_2\ \texttt{ENDIF}$ is represented by a tree of the form $label\_hedge(\texttt{if}, \texttt{bool}\langle\varphi\rangle\texttt{rule}\langle t_1\rangle\texttt{rule}\langle t_2\rangle)$, where t_i (for $i = 1, 2$) is the tree representing the rule r_i.
- A forall rule $\texttt{FORALL}\ x\ \texttt{WITH}\ \varphi\ \texttt{DO}\ r\ \texttt{ENDDO}$ is represented by a tree of the form $label\_hedge(\texttt{forall}, \texttt{term}\langle x\rangle, \texttt{bool}\langle\varphi\rangle, \texttt{rule}\langle t\rangle)$, where t is the tree representing the rule r.
- A parallel rule $\texttt{PAR}\ r_1 \dots r_k\ \texttt{ENDPAR}$ is represented by a tree of the form $label\_hedge(\texttt{par}, \texttt{rule}\langle t_1\rangle\ \dots\ \texttt{rule}\langle t_k\rangle)$, where t_i (for $i = 1, \dots, k$) is the tree representing the rule r_i.
- A let rule $\texttt{LET}\ x = t\ \texttt{IN}\ r$ is represented by a tree of the form $label\_hedge(\texttt{let}, \texttt{term}\langle x\rangle\texttt{term}\langle t\rangle\texttt{rule}\langle t'\rangle)$, where t' is the tree representing the rule r.
- An import rule $\texttt{IMPORT}\ x\ \texttt{DO}\ r$ (which imports a fresh element from the reserve) is represented by a tree of the form $label\_hedge(\texttt{import}, \texttt{term}\langle x\rangle\ \texttt{rule}\langle t\rangle)$, where t is the tree representing the rule r.

3.3 The Background of an rASM

Let us draw some consequences from this tree representation. As function names in the signature appear in the tree representation, these are values. Furthermore, we may in every step enlarge the signature, so there must be an infinite reserve of such function names. Since ASMs have an infinite reserve of values, new function names can naturally be imported from this reserve. Likewise we require natural numbers in the background for the arity assigned to function symbols, though operations on natural numbers are optional. Terms built over the signature and a base set B must also become values. This includes tuple and multiset terms. Concerning the subtree capturing the rule, the keywords for the different rules become labels, so we obtain the set of labels

$$\begin{aligned} L = \{&\texttt{pgm}, \texttt{signature}, \texttt{rule}, \texttt{func}, \texttt{name}, \texttt{arity}, \texttt{update}, \texttt{term}, \texttt{if},\\ &\texttt{bool}, \texttt{forall}, \texttt{par}, \texttt{let}, \texttt{partial}, \texttt{import}\}. \end{aligned}$$

Consequently, we must extend a base set B by such terms, i.e. terms will become values. For this let Σ be a signature and let B be the base set of a structure of signature Σ. An *extended base set* is the smallest set B_{ext} that includes all elements of B, all elements in the reserve, all natural numbers, all terms t_i of signature $\Sigma \cup \Sigma_{ext}$ such that Σ_{ext} is some finite subset of $\{raise(v_i) \mid v_i \text{ is an element of the reserve}\}$ and each function symbol of Σ_{ext} has some arbitrary fixed arity, and all terms of the tree algebra over all possible signatures Σ_{ext} with labels in L as defined above. As B is closed under the operators in the background, also tuples and multisets are included in B and hence in B_{ext}.

In an extended base set terms are treated as values and thus can appear as values of some locations in a state. This implies that terms now have a dual character. When appearing in an ASM rule, e.g. on the right-hand side of an assignment, they are interpreted in the current state to determine an update. However, if they are to be treated as a value, they have to be interpreted by themselves. Therefore, we require a function *drop* turning a term into a value, and inversely a function *raise* turning a value into a term. Over elements of the (non-extended) base set B, elements imported from the reserve and natural numbers, i.e. over elements that do not represent terms, both functions can be thought of as the identity. Thus, if we raise an element a of B, then the result is a nullary function symbol named a. Such a function symbol a can be seen as a constant in the sense that it is always interpreted by itself, i.e. by $a \in B$. As discussed in [17], functions *drop* and *raise* capture the essence of linguistic reflection.

For instance, when evaluating *pgm* in a state S the result should be a tree value, to which we may apply some tree operators to extract a rule associated with some subtree. As this subtree is a value in B (and thus in B_{ext}) we may apply *raise* to it to obtain the ASM rule, which could be executed to determine an update set and to update the state. Analogously, when assigning a new term (e.g. a Boolean term in a branching rule) to a subtree of *pgm* the value on the right-hand side must be the result of the function *drop*, otherwise the term would be evaluated and a Boolean value would be assigned instead.

The functions *drop* and *raise* can be applied to function names as well, so they can be used as values stored within *pgm* and used as function symbols in rules. In particular, if $\mathcal{O}$ denotes the set of nodes of a tree, then each $o \in \mathcal{O}$ is a value in the base set, but $raise(o)$ denotes a nullary function symbol that is bound in a state to the subtree $\hat{o}$. However, as it is always clear from the context, when a function name f is used as a value, i.e. as $drop(f)$, this subtle distinction can be blurred.

Finally, the self-representation as defined above involves several non-logical constants such as the keywords for the rules, which are labels in L. For a theoretical analysis it is important to extract from the representation the decisive terms defined over Σ and B. That is, we further require an *extraction function* $\beta : \mathbb{T}_{ext} \to \bar{\mathbb{T}}$, which assigns to each term included in the extended base set B_{ext} a tuple of terms in $\bar{\mathbb{T}}$ defined over Σ, B and the background operators. This extraction function β on rule terms is easily defined as follows:

$$\begin{aligned}
&\beta(\mathit{label_hedge}(\texttt{update}, \texttt{func}\langle f\rangle\texttt{term}\langle t_1 \dots t_n\rangle\texttt{term}\langle t_0\rangle)) = \\
&\qquad (\{\!\!\{t_0, t_1, \dots, t_n \mid \text{true}\}\!\!\}) \\
&\beta(\mathit{label_hedge}(\texttt{partial}, \texttt{func}\langle f\rangle\texttt{func}\langle op\rangle\texttt{term}\langle t_1 \dots t_n\rangle\texttt{term}\langle t_1' \dots t_m'\rangle)) = \\
&\qquad (\{\!\!\{(t_1, \dots, t_n, op(f(t_1, \dots, t_n), t_1', \dots, t_m')) \mid \text{true}\}\!\!\}) \\
&\beta(\mathit{label_hedge}(\texttt{par}, \texttt{rule}\langle t_1\rangle \ \dots \ \texttt{rule}\langle t_k\rangle)) = \\
&\qquad (t_1^1, \dots, t_1^{n_1}, \dots, t_k^1, \dots, t_k^{n_k}) \\
&\qquad\qquad \text{for } \beta(t_i) = (t_i^1, \dots, t_i^{n_i}) \ (1 \le i \le k)
\end{aligned}$$

$$\beta(\textit{label\_hedge}(\texttt{if}, \texttt{bool}\langle\varphi\rangle\texttt{rule}\langle t_1\rangle\texttt{rule}\langle t_2\rangle)) =$$
$$(\{\!\{\varphi, \mid \text{true}\}\!\}, \dots, \{\!\{(t^1_{i,1}, \dots, t^1_{i,n_i}) \mid \varphi_i \wedge \varphi\}\!\}, \dots,$$
$$\dots, \{\!\{(t^2_{j,1}, \dots, t^2_{j,n'_j}) \mid \psi_j \wedge \neg\varphi\}\!\}, \dots)$$
$$\text{for } \beta(t_1) = (\dots \{\!\{(t^1_{i,1}, \dots, t^1_{i,n_i}) \mid \varphi_i\}\!\}, \dots)\ (1 \le i \le m_1)$$
$$\text{and } \beta(t_2) = (\dots \{\!\{(t^2_{j,1}, \dots, t^2_{j,n'_j}) \mid \psi_j\}\!\}, \dots)\ (1 \le j \le m_2)$$
$$\beta(\textit{label\_hedge}(\texttt{forall}, \texttt{term}\langle x\rangle, \texttt{bool}\langle\varphi\rangle, \texttt{rule}\langle t\rangle)) =$$
$$(\dots, \{\!\{(t_{i,1}, \dots, t_{i,n_i}) \mid \varphi_i \wedge \varphi\}\!\}, \dots,$$
$$\dots, \{\!\{(t_{i,1}, \dots, t_{i,n_i}) \mid \varphi_i \wedge \neg\varphi\}\!\}, \dots)$$
$$\text{for } \beta(t) = (\dots \{\!\{(t_{i,1}, \dots, t_{i,n_i}) \mid \varphi_i\}\!\}, \dots)\ (1 \le i \le k)$$
$$\beta(\textit{label\_hedge}(\texttt{let}, \texttt{term}\langle x\rangle\texttt{term}\langle t\rangle\texttt{rule}\langle t'\rangle)) =$$
$$(t, t_1, \dots, t_n) \text{ for } \beta(t'[x \mapsto t]) = (t_1, \dots, t_n)$$
$$\beta(\textit{label\_hedge}(\texttt{import}, \texttt{term}\langle x\rangle\texttt{rule}\langle t\rangle)) = \beta(t)$$

Then the *background of an rASM* is defined by a background class $\mathcal{K}$ over a background signature V_K. It must contain an infinite set *reserve* of reserve values, the equality predicate, the undefinedness value *undef*, and a set of labels $L = \{\texttt{pgm}, \texttt{signature}, \texttt{rule}, \texttt{func}, \texttt{name}, \texttt{arity}, \texttt{update}, \texttt{if}, \texttt{term}, \texttt{bool}, \texttt{forall}, \texttt{par}, \texttt{let}, \texttt{partial}, \texttt{import}\}$.

The background class must further define truth values and their connectives, tuples and projection operations on them, multisets with union and comprehension operators natural numbers and operations on them, trees in T_L and tree operations, and the function $\mathbf{I}$, where $\mathbf{I}x.\varphi$ denotes the unique x satisfying condition φ.

The background must further provide functions: $\textit{drop} : \hat{\mathbb{T}}_{ext} \to B_{ext}$ and $\textit{raise} : B_{ext} \to \hat{\mathbb{T}}_{ext}$ for each base set B and extended base set B_{ext}, as well as the derived *extraction function* β defined above.

In the previous definition we use $\hat{\mathbb{T}}_{ext}$ to denote the union of:

(i) The set $\mathbb{T}_{ext}$ of all terms included in B_{ext};
(ii) The set of all ASM rules which can be formed together with the terms included in B_{ext};
(iii) The set of all possible signatures of the form signature $\Sigma \cup \Sigma_{ext}$ such that Σ_{ext} is a finite subset of $\{\textit{raise}(v_i) \mid v_i \text{ in the reserve}\}$ and each function symbol of Σ_{ext} has some arbitrary fixed arity.

3.4 Reflective ASMs

A *reflective ASM* (rASM) $\mathcal{M}$ comprises an (initial) signature Σ containing a 0-ary function symbol *pgm*, a background as defined above, and a set $\mathcal{I}$ of initial states over Σ closed under isomorphisms such that any two states $I_1, I_2 \in \mathcal{I}$ coincide on *pgm*. If S is an initial state, then the signature $\Sigma_S =$

$raise(signature(\mathrm{val}_S(pgm)))$ must coincide with Σ. Furthermore, $\mathcal{M}$ comprises a state transition function $\tau(S)$ on states over the (extended) signature Σ_S with $\tau(S) = S + \Delta_{r_S}(S)$, where the rule r_S is defined as $raise(rule(\mathrm{val}_S(pgm)))$ over the signature $\Sigma_S = raise(signature(\mathrm{val}_S(pgm)))$.

Here we use extraction functions *rule* and *signature* defined on the tree representation of a parallel ASM in *pgm*. These are simply defined as $signature(t) = subtree(\mathbf{I}o.root(t) \prec_c o \wedge label(o) = \texttt{signature})$ and $rule(t) = subtree(\mathbf{I}o.root(t) \prec_c o \wedge label(o) = \texttt{rule})$.

4 The Reflective Parallel ASM Thesis

Our first main result is that each rASM satisfies the defining postulates, i.e. each rASM defines an RA. This constitutes the plausibility part of our reflective parallel ASM thesis. A full proof is given in [13].

Theorem 1. *Every reflective ASM $\mathcal{M}$ defines a RA.*

Proof (sketch). In every initial state $S_0 \in \mathcal{I}$ we have a unique rule $r_{S_0} = raise(rule(\mathrm{val}_{S_0}(pgm)))$ using the rule extraction function *rule* defined in Subsect. 3.2. Furthermore, the state transition function is built into the definition of an rASM. This easy implies the satisfaction of the sequential time postulate. As the background requirements are also built into the definition of an rASM, we easily get the satisfaction of the background postulate.

Concerning the abstract state postulate all required conditions except (iv) are easily verified, and for (iv) we have $\Sigma_{alg} = \{pgm\}$, so the restriction of a state S is simply given by $\mathrm{val}_S(pgm)$. Applying the functions *rule* and *signature* from Subsect. 3.2 to this tree value yield the rule r_S and the signature Σ_S, which define the algorithm $\mathcal{A}(S)$ with the desired properties.

This leaves the task to show the satisfaction of the bounded exploration postulate, for which we can take $W = \{pgm\}$. If S and S' are two states that strongly coincide on W, we have $r_S = raise(rule(\mathrm{val}_S(pgm))) = r_{S'}$ with signature $\Sigma_S = raise(signature(\mathrm{val}_S(pgm))) = \Sigma_{S'}$. Also, applying the extraction function β gives $\beta(\mathrm{val}_S(pgm)) = \beta(\mathrm{val}_{S'}(pgm))$. If this tuple of terms is $(t_1, \dots, t_n)$, $\{t_1, \dots, t_n\}$ is a bounded exploration witness for the ASM defined by Σ_S and r_S, hence $\mathrm{val}_S(raise(t_i)) = \mathrm{val}_{S'}(raise(t_i))$ holds for all $i = 1, \dots, n$, so the states S and S' coincide on a bounded exploration witness, and further $\ddot{\Delta}_{\mathcal{A}}(S) = \ddot{\Delta}_{r_S}(S) = \ddot{\Delta}_{r_{S'}}(S') = \ddot{\Delta}_{\mathcal{A}}(S')$ must hold, which shows the satisfaction of the bounded exploration postulate. □

Our second main result is the converse of Theorem 1, i.e. every RA $\mathcal{A}$ can be step-by-step simulated by a behaviourally equivalent rASM $\mathcal{M}$. Hence rASMs capture all RAs regardless how algorithms are represented by terms. This constitutes the characterisation part of the reflective parallel ASM thesis. A full proof, which is longer than this whole article, is given in [13].

Theorem 2. *For every RA $\mathcal{A}$ there is a behaviourally equivalent rASM $\mathcal{M}$.*

5 Conclusion

In this article we investigated a behavioural theory for reflective parallel algorithms (RAs) extending our previous work on reflective sequential algorithms (RSAs) in [12]. Grounded in related work concerning a behavioural theory for (synchronous) parallel algorithms [8] we developed a set of abstract postulates defining RAs, extended ASMs to reflective abstract state machines (rASMs), and sketched that any RA as stipulated by the postulates can be step-by-step simulated by an rASM. The key contributions are the axiomatic definition of RAs and the proof that RAs are captured by rASMs. Full proofs are given in [13].

With this behavioural theory we lay the foundations for rigorous development of reflective algorithms and thus adaptive systems. So far the theory covers only reflective sequential and parallel algorithms, but not non-deterministic algorithms nor (asynchronous) concurrent algorithms. So in view of the behavioural theory for concurrent algorithms the next step of the research is to extend also this theory to capture reflection. We envision a part III on reflective concurrent algorithms. The latter one would then lay the foundations for the specification of distributed adaptive systems in general.

Concerning non-determinism, however, there is not yet a behavioural theory available, except for the case of bounded non-determinism in connection with bounded parallelism, which is a simple add-on to the sequential ASM thesis [7,11]. Therefore, first such a theory has to be developed before thinking about an extension covering reflection.

Furthermore, for rigorous development extensions to the refinement method for ASMs [4] and to the logic used for verification [9,10] will be necessary. These will also be addressed in follow-on research.

References

1. Blass, A., Gurevich, Y.: Abstract state machines capture parallel algorithms. ACM Trans. Comput. Logic **4**(4), 578–651 (2003)
2. Blass, A., Gurevich, Y.: Abstract state machines capture parallel algorithms: correction and extension. ACM Trans. Comp. Logic **9**(3) (2008)
3. Blass, A., Gurevich, Y., Shelah, S.: Choiceless polynomial time. Ann. Pure Appl. Logic **100**, 141–187 (1999)
4. Börger, E.: The ASM refinement method. Formal Aspects Comput. **15**, 237–257 (2003)
5. Börger, E., Schewe, K.-D.: Concurrent abstract state machines. Acta Informatica **53**(5), 469–492 (2016)
6. Börger, E., Schewe, K.-D.: A behavioural theory of recursive algorithms. Fund. Inform. **177**(1), 1–37 (2020)
7. Börger, E., Stärk, R.: Abstract State Machines. Springer, Heidelberg (2003)
8. Ferrarotti, F., Schewe, K.-D., Tec, L., Wang, Q.: A new thesis concerning synchronised parallel computing - simplified parallel ASM thesis. Theor. Comp. Sci. **649**, 25–53 (2016)

9. Ferrarotti, F., Schewe, K.-D., Tec, L., Wang, Q.: A complete logic for database abstract state machines. Logic J. IGPL **25**(5), 700–740 (2017)
10. Ferrarotti, F., Schewe, K.-D., Tec, L., Wang, Q.: A unifying logic for non-deterministic, parallel and concurrent abstract state machines. Ann. Math. Artif. Intell. **83**(3–4), 321–349 (2018)
11. Gurevich, Y.: Sequential abstract-state machines capture sequential algorithms. ACM Trans. Comp. Logic **1**(1), 77–111 (2000)
12. Schewe, K.-D., Ferrarotti, F.: Behavioural theory of reflective algorithms I: reflective sequential algorithms. Sci. Comput. Program. **223**, 102864 (2022)
13. Schewe, K.-D., Ferrarotti, F.: Behavioural theory of reflective algorithms II: reflective parallel algorithms (2025). arxiv.org
14. Schewe, K.-D., Ferrarotti, F., González, S.: A logic for reflective ASMs. Sci. Comput. Program. **210**, 102691 (2021)
15. Schewe, K.-D., Wang, Q.: XML database transformations. J. UCS **16**(20), 3043–3072 (2010)
16. Schewe, K.-D., Wang, Q.: Partial updates in complex-value databases. In: Heimbürger, A., et al. (eds.) Information and Knowledge Bases XXII. Frontiers in Artificial Intelligence and Applications, vol. 225, pp. 37–56. IOS Press (2011)
17. Stemple, D., et al.: Type-safe linguistic reflection: a generator technology. In: Atkinson, M., Welland, R. (eds.) Fully Integrated Data Environments. Esprit Basic Research Series, pp. 158–188. Springer, Berlin Heidelberg (2000)

Using Symbolic Model Execution to Detect Vulnerabilities of Smart Contracts

Chiara Braghin[1], Giuseppe Del Castillo[2], Elvinia Riccobene[1(✉)], and Simone Valentini[1]

[1] Computer Science Department, Università degli Studi di Milano, via Celoria 18, Milan, Italy
{chiara.braghin,elvinia.riccobene,simone.valentini}@unimi.it
[2] Munich, Germany
giuseppedelcastillo@acm.org

Abstract. Smart contracts are programs that automate agreements between parties without the need for intermediaries. Embedded in a blockchain, they ensure transparency, immutability, and trustworthiness. While efficient, their immutable nature and reliance on internet-connected nodes make them susceptible to attacks. Identifying vulnerabilities before deployment is critical to mitigate risks, prevent catastrophic events, and avoid significant financial losses. This paper introduces a method for detecting vulnerabilities in smart contracts written in Solidity and deployed on the Ethereum blockchain. The approach models a smart contract as an Abstract State Machine (ASM), where the absence of specific vulnerabilities is encoded as invariants. An existing symbolic execution technique for ASM models was extended and improved to enable the processing of the ASM models of the smart contracts. By symbolically executing the ASM, the method identifies faulty execution paths that violate these invariants, exposing potential vulnerabilities in the contract's behavior. Vulnerable execution scenarios of the smart contract can be generated using the symbolic execution results.

As a proof of concept, we show the approach on a running case study, the *Auction* smart contract. Furthermore, we discuss the results of applying the technique to a number of Solidity smart contracts.

Keywords: Blockchain · Ethereum · Solidity · Smart contract vulnerabilities · Abstract State Machines · Symbolic execution

1 Introduction

Blockchain technology has emerged as a fundamental component in applications ranging from finance to supply chain management and beyond, enabling secure,

This work was partially supported by project SERICS (PE00000014) under the MUR National Recovery and Resilience Plan funded by the European Union - NextGenerationEU.

G. DelCastillo — Independent Researcher.

M. Leuschel and F. Ishikawa (Eds.): ABZ 2025, LNCS 15728, pp. 31–51, 2026.
https://doi.org/10.1007/978-3-031-94533-5_3

transparent, and decentralized transaction management without the need for trusted intermediaries. Through cryptographic techniques and distributed consensus mechanisms, it ensures data integrity and trust. In addition, the introduction of smart contracts has made it possible to automate agreements between parties without intermediaries, enhancing efficiency and reducing costs. However, despite their benefits, they remain vulnerable to attacks, as they are publicly accessible to all network nodes and often handle significant amounts of cryptocurrency. For instance, the notorious DAO hack [27] on the Ethereum blockchain [31] resulted in the loss of $70 million worth of Ether due to a vulnerable smart contract that lacked proper verification [25]. Addressing vulnerabilities before (permanent) deployment is essential for mitigating risks, preventing catastrophic incidents, and avoiding substantial financial losses. Moreover, high-cost vulnerabilities and exploits can severely impact the trust and acceptance of the blockchain ecosystem.

Formal verification can play a crucial role in advancing the maturity and adoption of blockchain technology by providing a rigorous approach to ensuring the accuracy and reliability of smart contracts. However, while formal verification for smart contracts has made significant advancements [19,29], several challenges remain. Existing tools have notable limitations: (a) bytecode-based tools generate results that are challenging to trace back to code-level vulnerabilities; (b) tools operating at a higher level, rely on complex notations that require a strong mathematical background, making them less accessible to many developers, and (c) some tools produce vulnerability reports that are difficult to interpret, often failing to accurately locate the exact code segment containing the issue or clearly identify the type of vulnerability detected [24].

In [10,11], we explored the potential of using the Abstract State Machines (ASMs) [7,8] to model Ethereum smart contracts written in Solidity. Thanks to the pseudo-code format of an ASM model, which allows for an easy comprehension by practitioners and not-experts, and the tool support of this formal method [6], our long-term vision [30] is to develop a practical verification framework, leveraging ASMs as the foundational formalism for specifying and analyzing smart contract vulnerabilities. Thus, we formalized the Ethereum Virtual Machine (EVM) and introduced key language primitives that enable a straightforward translation of Solidity smart contracts into ASMETA models. ASMETA provides a toolset for model editing, validation, and verification, including a translator to the NuSMV model checker for formal verification. However, as model size increases, we encountered the state space explosion problem, a common challenge in model checking. To address this, in this paper, we explore the potential of a recently developed symbolic execution tool [14] for ASMs. Unlike model checking, symbolic execution does not require exhaustive state searching, mitigating state explosion and allowing it to manage infinite domains more effectively. While model checking is better suited for exhaustively proving correctness properties, symbolic execution excels in detecting concrete bugs and vulnerabilities. On the other hand, compared to traditional testing approaches, symbolic execution offers significant advantages in vulnerability detection by systematically exploring execution paths and achieving higher coverage than random or manually designed test cases. Additionally, it identifies exact inputs that trigger bugs, whereas fuzzing often detects crashes without providing precise failure conditions.

In our approach, we express the absence of specific vulnerabilities as model invariants within an ASMETA smart contract model. The symbolic execution engine is then employed to uncover faulty execution paths that lead to invariant violations. To achieve this, we significantly enhanced the symbolic executor, adapting it to ASMETA models and improving its ability to detect invariant violations. The insights provided by the symbolic execution tool can also be used to generate execution scenarios, helping to identify and analyze vulnerabilities within the smart contract. We demonstrate our approach using a case study, the *Auction* smart contract, and discuss the results of applying our vulnerability detection method to a good broad set of Solidity smart contracts.

The rest of the paper is organized as follows: in Sect. 2, we provide a background description of Ethereum smart contracts, and we introduce the Auction smart contract. In Sect. 3, we briefly present the ASM-based modeling of the Ethereum virtual machine and of smart contracts. In Sect. 4, we present the tool for symbolic execution of ASMETA models, its improvement and features. In Sect. 5, we show the application of our vulnerability detection strategy to the running example, while in Sect. 6 we report results to evince the effectiveness of the approach and discuss the potential limitations and threats of our contribution. In Sect. 7, we compare our results with existing approaches. Section 8 concludes the paper and outlines future research directions.

2 Blockchain and Solidity Smart Contracts

A blockchain is a decentralized and distributed ledger that records transactions across a network of computers. It comprises data blocks, each containing a set of transactions, a unique cryptographic hash of the previous block, and a timestamp. These blocks are linked together, forming an immutable chain: once a block is added, its contents cannot be altered without modifying all subsequent blocks, making retroactive tampering virtually impossible.

Ethereum [31] is an open-source blockchain platform designed for developers to create and deploy decentralized applications. It offers the Ethereum Virtual Machine (EVM) as a decentralized runtime environment for executing smart contracts, self-executing programs that automate agreements with the terms directly coded into them. They are written in high-level languages like Solidity and compiled into bytecode that the EVM can run.

The EVM operates on every node within the Ethereum network, guaranteeing decentralized execution of smart contracts. Additionally, it upholds the state of the Ethereum blockchain, encompassing account balances, smart contract code, and storage. Two types of accounts have an Ether (ETH) balance and can interact with the blockchain by sending transactions on the chain: *externally owned accounts* (EOA) and *smart contract accounts*. EOA are humans-managed accounts identified by a public key, which serves as the account address, and controlled by a corresponding private key. These accounts use the private key to sign transactions, proving ownership and authorization through an elliptic curve digital signature algorithm. Contract accounts, on the other hand, are special accounts that contain associated code and data storage. They have unique addresses but do not have private keys. When a smart contract transaction is initiated, the EVM processes the bytecode linked to the contract and executes it. This execution modifies the blockchain's state by updating account balances or storage values. A special global variable called `msg` is employed to capture transaction-related information, including `msg.sender` representing the address that initiated the function call, and `msg.value` yielding the liquidity sent with the message.

2.1 Running Case Study

The code in Listing 2.1 reports the *Auction* smart contract written in Solidity [9]. This contract is commonly encountered in real-world blockchain applications to guarantee greater transparency and avoid cheating auctioneers.

```
contract Auction {
  address currentFrontrunner;
  address owner;
  uint currentBid;

  function destroy() {
    selfdestruct(owner);
  }
  function bid() payable {
    require(msg.value > currentBid);
    if (currentFrontrunner != 0) {
      require(currentFrontrunner.send(currentBid));
      }
    currentFrontrunner = msg.sender;
    currentBid         = msg.value;
  }
}
```

Listing 2.1. Solidity code of the Auction smart contract

The contract keeps track of the current highest bidder (`currentFrontrunner`) and the highest bid amount (`currentBid`). Participants can submit bids through the `bid()` function, which takes payment in Ether. The function `requires` that (1) the submitted bid value (`msg.value`) is greater than the current highest bid, and that (2) if there is an existing highest bidder (`currentFrontrunner != 0`), the contract must refund his/her bid amount before assigning the new bid. The `payable` keyword is required for a function to receive Ether. In Solidity, the `send` function, used as `address.send(amount)`, returns true if the transfer to the specified `address` succeeds; otherwise, it returns false.

The contract also defines a `destroy` function, which invokes Solidity's built-in `selfdestruct(recipientAddress)` function to terminate the contract and transfer any remaining Ether to a specified recipient. This function reveals a vulnerability that falls under the category of *unprotected function vulnerability*, where a smart contract exposes a critical functionality without enforcing access control, thus allowing unauthorized users to execute sensitive operations. In this case, without a restriction ensuring that only the contract owner can disable the contract and withdraw its remaining balance, an attacker could exploit the function to force the contract to self-destruct, resulting in a denial-of-service (DoS) attack.

3 Modeling Solidity Smart Contracts

In [11,30], we demonstrated how to model the EVM and Solidity smart contracts in ASMETA [4]. Our approach supports all the core features of smart contracts, except for the *gas* mechanism.[1] In the sequel, regarding the used formalism and notation, we refer the non-expert reader to [6–8] for a very short introduction.

An ASMETA library, `EVMlibrary`, provides functions and rules to model both the EVM behaviour and Ethereum accounts. Specifically, the library defines the EVM stack structure, representing the execution stack through the `StackLayer` domain and the `current_layer` function, which tracks the stack frame of the method currently being executed (i.e., the top of the stack). To manage execution flow, the library includes functions such as `executing_function` and `instruction_pointer`, which track the currently running function and the instruction being executed. Each stack layer is enriched with additional functions - `sender`, `receiver`, `amount` - that store essential transaction details, including the initiating account's address, the recipient, and the amount of ether transferred. Two library rules, `r_Transaction` and `r_Ret` are defined to move along the stack. The rule `r_Transaction` simulates a transaction execution with an Ether transfer (due to a call to either a `send` or `transfer` function); it increases the stack size and stores relevant execution details within the stack layer, such as the executing contract and instruction pointer; it also updates the caller's instruction pointer accordingly. The rule `r_Ret` stops the execution by decreasing the stack size and restoring the previous execution frame. Additionally, the library provides rules corresponding to predefined Solidity functions. Specifically, `require` is modeled by the r_Require rule, which increments the `instruction_pointer` on the true value of a given condition, or stops the execution otherwise; `selfdestruct` is modeled by the r_Selfdestruct rule, which stops the execution and sends the whole contract balance to the User (passed as parameter). Table 1 presents a structured mapping of Solidity smart contracts to ASMETA models, written in `AsmetaL`, the model editing textual notation of the ASMETA toolset.

In addition to the special *global* variables msg.sender and msg.value, which are defined in the `EVMlibrary`, a Solidity contract includes two main types of variables: *state* variables, which are permanently stored in the contract's storage, and *local* variables, which exist only during the execution of a function. Furthermore, Solidity provides the `mapping` keyword, a reference type used to store data as key-value pairs.

---

[1] *Gas* is the unit used to measure computational effort in Ethereum: each operation in the EVM consumes a certain amount of gas, and users must pay gas fees to execute transactions and smart contracts.

Table 1. Schema for mapping a Solidity contract to an ASMETA model

Solidity contract	ASMETA model
contract `SCName`	create a model asm SCName and add `scname` to domain User to identify the contract
for each *state* variable `type p`	add a function p: Type
for each *local* variable `type v`	add a function v: StackLayer → Type
for each mapping *state* variable `mapping(keyType => valueType)`	add a function p: KeyType → ValueType
for each mapping *local* variable `mapping(keyType => valueType)`	add a function p: StackLayer x KeyType → ValueType
for each function `f()`	add static f: Function and a rule r_F[]
for the body of function `f()`	add the body of the rule r_F[]
if the `fallback` function is present	add a corresponding rule r_fallback
if the `fallback` function is absent	add the *default* rule r_fallback
if the contract is executed in isolation	add the rule r_main calling in parallel all rules r_F[] and set the initial state
if two or more contracts are co-executed	add the rule r_main orchestrating the rules r_contractName$_i$ of all the contracts and set the initial state

In the mapping schema, particular attention deserves the translation of a Solidity function into an ASMETA rule. The latter mainly consists of a `case` rule on the value of the instruction_pointer(current_layer), which refers to the Solidity instruction within the function body, and allows the instruction pointer to jump to a specific instruction when needed.

A special handling applies to the Solidity `fallback` function, which is executed when a contract receives Ether with a call to a function that does not exist in the contract, or when no data is provided in the transaction. While including a `fallback` function is generally recommended, it is not mandatory. If absent, the contract raises an exception and halts execution. To model this behavior, we introduce a *default version* of the r_Fallback rule. If no contract function is invoked, this rule calls r_Require with a false value to raise an exception, followed by r_Ret to handle termination. A version of this r_Fallback rule for the Auction contract is shown in Listing 3.2.

3.1 Model of the Auction Contract

Based on the Solidity contract code in Listing 2.1, we define the corresponding ASMETA model Auction.asm following the mapping schema outlined in Table 1. The complete model is available at [12].

Listing 3.1 presents the functions that model the contract's state variables. Additionally, constants are added to the predefined library domains `User` and `Function` to include the contract-specific functions and users.

```
signature:
/* contract's arguments */
  dynamic controlled owner : User
  dynamic controlled currentFrontrunner : User
  dynamic controlled currentBid : MoneyAmount

/* initializing library domains for the specific contract*/
  static auction : User
  static bid : Function
  static destroy : Function
```

Listing 3.1. Signature of the ASMETA Auction Model

Listing 3.2 reports the specification of the three rules corresponding to the three functions of the contract. The rule `r_Bid` is triggered when `bid()` is the currently executing function in the current layer. The `switch` statement in the rule manages the execution flow based on the instruction pointer's value in the current layer. Initially, in case 0, the rule ensures that the amount specified in current_layer exceeds the currentBid. Next, in case 1, if the current front-runner for the bid is defined, the instruction pointer increments to the next case; otherwise, it jumps to case 4. In case 2, a transaction is initiated, sending the current bid to the current front-runner.[2] After the transaction is performed, case 3 requires that the response from the previous transaction is successful. Cases 4 and 5 update the current front-runner with the transaction sender and the current bid with the transaction amount. The last case invokes the rule r_Ret since the execution of function `bid()` terminates.

Listing 3.2 also includes the rule for the Auction function `destroy()`, which calls the `r_Selfdestruct` rule from the library (not shown here) on the contract owner. This rule mirrors the behavior of Solidity `selfdestruct` function by setting a predefined boolean variable, `disabled` to true. Defined within the `Users` domain, this variable indicates whether the user associated with the given contract has been disabled.

4 Symbolic Execution of ASMETA Models

The ASE Tool. To symbolically execute the smart contract models, the prototype ASM symbolic execution tool ("ASE tool") presented in [14] and available at [16] was used. The main feature of the ASE tool is the ability to transform a sequential composition of ASM rules into a semantically equivalent parallel ASM rule that has a simpler structure and is easier to reason about. Such a rule is essentially a decision tree, i.e. a rule consisting of nested conditionals (inner nodes of the decision tree) and blocks of parallel updates of individual, unambiguously identified locations (leaves of the decision tree). The running example throughout the other sections shows examples of these rules and how

[2] The argument `none` in the r_Transaction rule is because the function `bid()` implies money transfer and no nested function calls.

```
rule r_Bid =
    if executing_function(current_layer) = bid then
      switch instruction_pointer(current_layer)
        case 0 :
          r_Require[amount(current_layer) > currentBid]
        case 1 :
          if currentFrontrunner != undef then
            instruction_pointer(current_layer) := instruction_pointer(current_layer) + 1
          else
            instruction_pointer(current_layer) := 4
          endif
        case 2 :
          r_Transaction[auction, currentFrontrunner, currentBid, none]
        case 3 :
          r_Require[exception]
        case 4 :
          par
            currentFrontrunner := sender(current_layer)
            instruction_pointer(current_layer) := instruction_pointer(current_layer) + 1
          endpar
        case 5 :
          par
            currentBid := amount(current_layer)
            instruction_pointer(current_layer) := instruction_pointer(current_layer) + 1
          endpar
        case 6 :
          r_Ret[]
      endswitch
    endif

rule r_Destroy =
    if executing_function(current_layer) = destroy then
      switch instruction_pointer(current_layer)
        case 0 :
          r_Selfdestruct[owner]
      endswitch
    endif

rule r_Fallback =
    if executing_function(current_layer) != bid and executing_function(current_layer) != destroy then
        r_Require[false]
    endif
```

Listing 3.2. Model of the `bid()`, `destroy()` and `fallback()` functions

the tool is used. For details on the formal definition of the transformation and its implementation, see [14,15].

To meet the needs of the vulnerability analysis of the models presented in this paper, the tool had to be enhanced in various ways. The following subsections describe these enhancements.

AsmetaL Support. The ASE tool had to be made compatible with `AsmetaL`, the source language of the ASMETA toolset [4] that was used to specify the smart contract ASM models (including the Auction example). For this purpose, an `AsmetaL` parser was added to the ASE tool and support for symbolic execution of the required subset of `AsmetaL` was implemented, including ASM constructs such as `forall` that were not implemented in the initial version of the ASE tool. In particular, the tool has been extended to support enumerated and (non-dynamic) abstract domains, function definitions and initializations, macro rule definitions, `forall` rules and quantifiers over finite domains.

The implementation of these constructs is rather straightforward, mostly consisting of some form of syntactic expansion followed by symbolic execution. For example, a universally quantified Boolean term "`forall` x `in` A `with` t" (where A is a finite set $\{a_1, \ldots, a_n\}$) is expanded into a term "$t[x/a_1] \wedge \ldots \wedge t[x/a_n]$", which is then symbolically evaluated. Similarly, a `forall` rule over the same set A is expanded into a `par` rule "$R[x/a_1]$ `par` ... `par` $R[x/a_n]$", which is then symbolically executed according to the rules given in [14] for `par`.[3]

Symbolic Execution of Basic ASMs. The symbolic execution scheme, which was introduced in [14] to transform ASM rules including the sequential composition rules `seq` and `iterate` into basic ASM rules, has been adapted to symbolically execute regular sequential ASMs.

The state S_n of a sequential run $S_0, S_1, \ldots$ starting in the initial state S_0 can be seen as $S_0 \oplus P^n$, where P^n is the main rule (*program*) P of the ASM iterated n times. As such iteration can be defined as $P^0 :=$ `skip`, $P^{i+1} := P^i$ `seq` P $(i \geq 0)$, the transformation rules of [14] for `seq` can be applied repeatedly to obtain S_n.

The ASE tool now provides a `-steps` n option that constructs an ASM rule equivalent to P^n using symbolic execution. This rule can be inspected to understand the system behavior and the root causes of any identified invariant violation, if it is found that an invariant is violated in state S_n (see "Invariant Checking" below). In Sect. 6, we show a concrete use of this option for the Auction contract vulnerability analysis.

Nested Non-static Functions. A limitation of the symbolic execution method presented in [14] is its inability to process rules containing terms of the form $f(t_1, \ldots, g(s_1, \ldots, s_m), \ldots, t_n)$, $m \geq 0$, where f is a non-static function and g is an uninitialized non-static function[4], when no value has yet been assigned to the relevant location $(g, (x_1, \ldots, x_m))$ (where $x_1, \ldots, x_m$ are the values of terms

---

[3] A `forall` Boolean term is used for example in the definition of invariant E3 in the KotET model. A `forall` rule is used for example in the `r_Main` rule of the Auction model, see the GitHub repository [12].

[4] Non-static functions are all functions that are not static, i.e. all functions that can have a different interpretation in different states of an ASM run (such as controlled and monitored functions). In the Auction model, unary functions executing_contract and balance are examples of (uninitialized) non-static functions; nullary function current_layer, instead, is an initialized non-static function. Even though the only non-static functions supported by the ASE tool at the time of writing are controlled functions (no monitored functions), the remarks of this subsection apply in principle to all nested non-static functions. The essential difference is that static functions have a fixed interpretation, while non-static functions can be (at least partially) uninterpreted.

$s_1, \ldots, s_m)$. The problem is that, as the location $(g, (x_1, \ldots, x_m))$ does not hold a concrete value, the term $f(t_1, \ldots, g(s_1, \ldots, s_m), \ldots, t_n)$ cannot be mapped to an unambiguously identified location $(f, (y_1, \ldots, y_n))$.

Due to this limitation, none of the smart contract models presented here could be symbolically executed using the initial ASE tool introduced in [14]. This problem can be illustrated using the Auction example. For example, the `r_Selfdestruct` rule contains an update rule

```
balance(executing_contract(current_layer)) := 0
```

While the initialized non-static function current_layer always evaluates to a concrete value, so that the subterm executing_contract(current_layer) unambiguously identifies a location of the executing_contract function, this is not the case for the whole term. Indeed, the uninitialized (i.e., uninterpreted) non-static function executing_contract occurs as an argument of non-static function balance, so that it is not clear which location of balance is to be updated.

However, it was observed that, in all the smart contract models presented in this paper, the range of the problematic "inner terms" (such as the $g(s_1, \ldots, s_m)$ above, or the executing_contract(current_layer) in the example) is always finite. Accordingly, terms can be transformed by making a case distinction over the elements of the range of g:

$$\frac{[\![g(s_1, \ldots, s_m)]\!]_{S,C} \neq \langle \text{val } x \rangle \qquad \text{range}(g) = \{x_1, \ldots, x_p\} \qquad f, g \text{ not static}}{\begin{array}{l} [\![\, f(t_1, \ldots, g(s_1, \ldots, s_m), \ldots, t_n) \,]\!]_{S,C} = \\ \quad [\![\, \texttt{if } g(s_1, \ldots, s_m) = x_1 \texttt{ then } f(t_1, \ldots, x_1, \ldots, t_n) \\ \quad \ldots \\ \quad \texttt{else if } g(s_1, \ldots, s_m) = x_{p-1} \texttt{ then } f(t_1, \ldots, x_{p-1}, \ldots, t_n) \\ \quad \texttt{else } f(t_1, \ldots, x_p, \ldots, t_n) \,]\!]_{S,C} \end{array}}$$

The above rule is applied for all subterms t_i of $f(t_1, \ldots, t_n)$ that cannot be fully evaluated to a value $\langle \text{val } x \rangle$. Further transformation rules similar to those defined in [14] are then applied to the terms and rules that include $f(t_1, \ldots, t_n)$ to "move out" the introduced conditional terms until the main ASM rule has been transformed into the "decision tree" form mentioned above.[5] A complete specification of the transformation rules and algorithm is outside the scope of this paper and may be provided elsewhere, but the basic technique should be clear from the above explanation in combination with [14].

Invariant Checking. The last addition to the ASE tool is a feature to check whether the invariants specified in the ASMETA model are met within the first

[5] This may appear to be a prohibitively expensive transformation, but in practice it turned out that in many cases, with the help of the SMT solver and taking into account the path condition that holds in the given context, the conditionals generated by the case distinction are simplified (even to a single branch, resulting in the elimination of the conditional) and/or lead to the generation of further path conditions for their subrules that cause considerable simplifications in the subrules.

n steps of the symbolic ASM run (command line option `-invcheck` n, which is shown in action in Sect. 6 on the running example). The invariant checking is carried out by symbolically evaluating each Boolean term inv_j defining the j-th invariant ($0 \leq j \leq m$) in the appropriate state S_i ($0 \leq i \leq n$) as follows:

1. each invariant j is checked in the initial state by evaluating $[\![inv_j]\!]_{S_0,\emptyset}$, where S_0 is the initial state and $\emptyset$ is the empty path condition;
2. for each $i \in \{1, \ldots, n\}$:
   (a) a decision tree rule equivalent to P^i is built using symbolic execution, as explained in "Symbolic Execution of Basic ASMs" above;
   (b) the decision tree rule for P^i is traversed and, at each leaf of the tree, the invariants are checked by evaluating $[\![inv_j]\!]_{S_0 \oplus U,C}$, where U is the symbolic update set found at that leaf (see "The ASE Tool" above) and C is the path condition corresponding to the path from the root to the leaf (C is constructed starting with $\emptyset$ at the root and adding, at each inner conditional node with guard G, either G or $\neg G$ depending on whether the "then" or the "else" branch is taken);
   (c) note that there are three possible outcomes for $[\![inv_j]\!]_{S_0 \oplus U,C}$:
      i. **true**: the invariant inv_j is *met* on the given path;
      ii. **false**: the invariant inv_j is *definitely violated* on the given path (by this terminology we mean that, based on the specification of the initial state S_0, it can be established that the invariant is violated);
      iii. a Boolean term ϕ_j, which is more or less simplified in comparison to inv_j, but neither **true** nor **false**, and depends on one or more non-static functions that are uninterpreted in S_0: in this case, we say that inv_j is *possibly violated* on the given path, i.e. it is violated when the relevant locations of those uninterpreted functions have certain values, specifically the values for which $\neg\phi_j \wedge C$ is satisfied.[6]

5 Vulnerabilities Detection of Solidity Smart Contracts

Here, we explain our strategy for detecting vulnerabilities in smart contracts through the symbolic execution of ASMETA models.

Given an ASMETA model of a contract such as the Auction case study, we define model invariants to represent the absence of vulnerabilities as safety properties. These invariants are based on either the intended contract behavior or, as explained in Sect. 6, on known unsafe operations. The vulnerabilities we consider here relate to contract-intrinsic issues, rather than those arising from interactions with malicious smart contracts designed to exploit weaknesses. They can result from coding errors, design flaws, or misunderstandings of the blockchain platform's functionality. In the models we consider for the purposes of this paper, we

[6] By inspecting the simplified invariant $[\![inv_j]\!]_{S_0 \oplus U,C} = \phi_j$ and the path condition C, both of which are displayed by the tool, it is possible to identify which values lead to the invariant violation. A possible future improvement is the automatic generation of a counterexample with concrete values that lead to the violation of the invariant.

```
// A_1 - The destroy function can only be called by the owner of the contract
invariant over sender : (current_layer = 0 and executing_contract(1) = auction and executing_function
    (1) = destroy and not exception and destroyed(auction)) implies (sender(1) = owner)
// A_2 - If a call is made to the bid function and a current_frontrunner already
    exists, the previously deposited money is returned to it
invariant over balance : (current_layer = 1 and instruction_pointer(1) = 6 and executing_contract(1) =
    auction and executing_function(1) = bid and old_frontrunner != undef_user and not exception
    and old_frontrunner = user and sender(1) = user) implies (old_balance(user) + old_bid =
    balance(user)
// A_3 - If the bid function is called with a msg.value greater than current_bid then
    the caller become the new current_frontrunner
invariant over balance : (current_layer = 0 and executing_contract(1) = auction and
    executing_function(1) = bid and amount(1) > old_bid and not exception) implies (
    currentFrontrunner = sender(1))
// A_4 - If the destroy function is called, all the money in the contract go to the
    owner
invariant over balance : (current_layer = 0 and executing_contract(1) = auction and
    executing_function(1) = destroy and not exception) implies (old_balance(user2) + old_balance(
    auction) = balance(user2))
```

Listing 5.1. Invariant specification for the Auction model

model a slightly simplified exception-handling mechanism with no full rollback, without affecting the analysis results.

For the Auction contract, we defined four invariants, with their informal descriptions and their ASMETA specification in Listing 5.1. We expect that two of them, A_1 and A_4, would be violated, while the other two should hold as true safety properties. Specifically, A_1 checks for the absence of an unprotected function vulnerability by stating that if the destroy function is executed and the auction contract is *destroyed*, then the transaction sender must be the contract owner. However, this invariant can be violated because the `r_Selfdestruct` rule is not protected since there is no restriction on the sender(current_layer) value. A_4 states that if the destroy function executes successfully (without raising an exception), all the contract's funds are transferred to the owner. However, since the r_Selfdestruct rule uses the transaction sender as the recipient instead of the contract owner, this invariant is likely to be violated. We included them to show that ASE does not generate false positives within the explored state space (see Sect. 6).

Note that some invariants compare the correct value of a location with its value in the previous state; this requires adding, for that specific location, an auxiliary function declaration recording such previous value. Listing 5.2 presents the additional auxiliary functions used in the Auction model to evaluate almost all the invariants in Listing 5.1. Moreover, before executing the ASE tool on the contract's model, a slight modification of the model is needed to deal with:

- *Monitored functions*: ASE does not deal with monitored values, so the transformation monitored foo: $D_1 \rightarrow D_2$ in controlled foo: Integer $\times$ $D_1 \rightarrow D_2$ is required for each monitored function foo of the model signature, and foo(i,d) yields the monitored value of foo(d) at state i.
- *Number of steps*: a new function controlled stage: Integer is added to the model to index the current execution state during the symbolic execution (it also

```
signature:
.....
/* functions to save previos values of contract's arguments */
  controlled old_frontrunner : User
  controlled old_bid : MoneyAmount
  controlled old_balance : User −> MoneyAmount
```

Listing 5.2. Signature of the ASMETA Auction Model

```
1  -- this path is taken when the following conditions hold in the initial state:
2  not ((random_sender (0) = auction))
3  not ((random_sender (0) = undef_user))
4  (random_receiver (0) = auction)
5  not ((random_function (0) = bid))
6  ((random_amount (0) >= 0) and ((3 >= random_amount (0)) and not ((random_amount (0) > 0))))
7  (random_sender (0) = user)
8  (random_function (0) = destroy)
9  ...
10 --- S_2 summary:
11 '_inv_1': met on 62 paths / definitely violated on 1 paths / possibly violated on 0 paths
12 '_inv_2': met on 63 paths / definitely violated on 0 paths / possibly violated on 0 paths
13 '_inv_3': met on 63 paths / definitely violated on 0 paths / possibly violated on 0 paths
14 '_inv_4': met on 61 paths / definitely violated on 2 paths / possibly violated on 0 paths
```

Listing 5.3. Faulty path and invariants violation summary for the Auction model

yields the current depth of the symbolic execution tree). Initialized to 0, it is incremented by 1 in parallel with all the other rules by r_main rule.

- *Undef value*: the current version of ASE does not support the predefined ASM *undef* value (while ASMETA does). This requires replacing each occurrence of undef with a suitable undef_value upon adding to the signature the declaration static undef_value: D, being D the domain of the model function that could take value *undef*. For example, the guard in line 7 of Listing 3.2 is replaced with currentFrontrunner != undef_user and the declaration static undef_user : User is added to the signature.

These model transformations are currently performed manually but can be automated, and future tool improvements will incorporate this automation. The modified version of the Auction model is available at [12]. When the model, augmented with the four invariants in Listing 5.1, is symbolically executed, ASE identifies violation of invariants A_1 and A_4, as shown in Listing 5.3: invariants are violated in two execution steps (see stage S_2 in line 10), on one out of 62 paths for A_1 and two out of 63 paths for A_4. At this stage S_2, invariants A_2 and A_3 are true and are never violated within the state space ASE constructs. This, of course, does not guarantee their truth at subsequent stages.

Examining ASE's detailed reports on the violated invariants, consider inv_1, which corresponds to A_1. The report provides information on the *initial state conditions* required to trigger the faulty execution path (lines 2-8 of Listing 5.3). These initial values for the monitored functions can be used to generate an ASMETA scenario, shown in Listing 5.4.[7] The scenario begins by assigning values to the monitored functions (lines 4-7) ensuring these values adhere to the conditions outlined in Listing 5.3: the value `user` is assigned to `random_sender`, as stated by the condition at line 7; `auction` is assigned to `random_receiver`, following the condition at line 4; `random_amount` is set to 0, as at line 6; `random_function` is set to `destroy`, as in the condition at line 8. From this initial configuration, after two model steps, both invariants A_1 and A_4 are violated.

```
1 scenario inv_1
2 load ../Auction.asm
3
4 set random_sender := user;
5 set random_receiver := auction;
6 set random_amount := 0;
7 set random_function := destroy;
8 step
9 step
```

Listing 5.4. Generated scenario violating `inv_1` in Auction contract

Based on the model analysis results, we refined the contract model by introducing appropriate rule guards to prevent the violation of invariants A_1 and A_4. The symbolic execution of this revised version, *Auction v2* in Table 2 and available at [12], does not violate any invariant, at least within the state space ASE constructs for the given input stage value.

6 Analysis Results

To assess the effectiveness of our vulnerability detection strategy, we applied the approach described in Sect. 3 to model a set of smart contracts. Some of these contracts were inspired by existing repositories [5,20], while others were either widely used or specifically developed for this evaluation.

For each modeled contract, we defined invariants asserting the absence of vulnerabilities, either based on the original contract's repositories or crafted specifically for the given contract. To rigorously test the tool's ability to detect invariant violations and assess false positives or false negatives, all invariants in this dataset were intentionally designed to be false. A detailed list of the smart contracts and their corresponding invariants, described in natural language, is provided in Table 2.

Each smart contract was then slightly modified to enable symbolic execution, following the method described in Sect. 5 for the Auction contract (all models are available at [12]). Multiple versions of each contract were produced, with the same invariants applied across versions. The purpose of these variations was to stress the tool's ability to detect invariant violations, particularly as the number of execution paths and monitored functions increased. This process involved progressively increasing the contract's complexity (such as adding more users or imposing additional conditions on state variables), thereby making symbolic execution increasingly difficult.

Symbolic execution was conducted on each model, exploring a state space of up to 30 stages, with a maximum runtime of 3600 s. These limits were set

[7] `set` is the command to provide monitored values; `step` induces a model step.

Table 2. The list of proposed invariants for each smart contract

Contracts		Invariants
Auction	A_1	The `destroy` function can only be called by the owner of the contract
	A_2	If a call is made to the `bid` function and a `current_frontrunner` already exists, the previously deposited money is returned to it
	A_3	If a call is made to the `bid` function with a `msg.value` greater than `current_bid` then the caller becomes the new `current_frontrunner`
	A_4	If a call is made to the `destroy` function, all the money in the contract goes to the owner
StateDao	B_1	If there was no exception and the contract is not running, the contract's state is INITIALSTATE
	B_2	If a call to `deposit` is made with a `msg.sender` value greater than 0 then it does not raise an exception
	B_3	An exception is not raised even if a call to `deposit` is made and the balance of `state_dao` is greater or equal than 12
	B_4	There is always at least one balance that is greater than the corresponding `customer_balance`
	B_5	If there was no exception and the contract is not running, the balance of `state_dao` is less than 12
Airdrop	C_1	Even if a call to `receive_airdrop` is made and no exceptions are raised, the value for `msg.sender` of `received_airdrop` remains false
	C_2	If a call to `receive_airdrop` is made from an account with `received_airdrop` set to 0, an exception is not raised
	C_3	Not all users received the airdrop
Crowdfund	D_1	If a call to `donate` is made, and no exceptions have been raised, then `donors(msg.sender)` is greater than 0
	D_2	Even if a call to donate is made and the donation phase is over, an exception is not raised
	D_3	If a call to `withdraw` completes without any exceptions being raised, then the sender was the owner of the contract
	D_4	After a call to `reclaim`, if no exceptions are raised, then the value of donors for the sender is 0
KotET	E_1	Every time a user becomes king it must be a different user from the previous king
	E_2	It is not possible for the balance of the contract to reach 0
	E_3	`claim_price` cannot be greater than all user balances
	E_4	If a call to the Kotet `fallback` is made with an amount greater than or equal to `claim_price` an exception is not raised
Baz	F_1	Not all the states are set to true

using the tool's `-invcheck` n parameter and `gtimeout` command. The results are summarized in Table 3, which allows for an effective comparison of the tool performance across different contracts and their versions.

Table 3. Symbolic Execution results

Contracts	EV	FV	Invariant Results														
			A_1	s	t	A_2	s	t	A_3	s	t	A_4	s	t			
Auction v1	2	2	✓	2	1.5	×			×			✓	2	1.5			
Auction v2	0	0	×			×			×			×					
			B_1	s	t	B_2	s	t	B_3	s	t	B_4	s	t	B_5	s	t
StateDao v1	5	5	✓	13	1.0	∽	8	0.6	✓	4	0.2	∽	1	0.1	✓	13	1.0
StateDao v2	5	4	×			∽	8	0.6	✓	4	0.2	∽	1	0.1	∽	7	0.3
			C_1	s	t	C_2	s	t	C_3	s	t						
Airdrop v1	3	3	✓	5	0.3	✓	3	0.2	✓	4	0.2						
Airdrop v2	3	3	✓	5	21	✓	3	3.4	✓	9	1214						
Airdrop v3	3	2	×			✓	5	25	✓	9	1396						
			D_1	s	t	D_2	s	t	D_3	s	t	D_4	s	t			
Crowdfund v1	4	4	∽	5	2.9	✓	4	2.0	✓	7	6.8	✓	10	20			
Crowdfund v2	4	4	∽	4	1.5	✓	4	1.5	✓	7	5.6	∽	13	62			
			E_1	s	t	E_2	s	t	E_3	s	t	E_4	s	t			
Kotet v1	4	4	✓	12	9.2	∽	0	0	∽	0	0	✓	3	0.3			
Kotet v2	4	3	×			∽	0	0	∽	0	0	✓	3	1.9			
			F_1	s	t												
Baz	1	1	✓	29	515												

Table 3 is structured into several horizontal sub-tables, each corresponding to a specific contract and its versions. The first column, labeled *Contracts*, lists the contract names and versions. The second column, (EV), represents the number of *expected violations*, i.e., the number of invariant violations the tool ideally should find. The third column, *FV*, indicates the number of invariant violations actually found by the tool. Ideally, the *FV* value should closely match the *EV* value, reflecting the tool's accuracy. The final section of Table 3 presents the aggregated execution results. Each row in this section corresponds to an individual invariant and includes three key evaluation metrics: the *invariant ID* (e.g., A_1, ..., A_n), the stage s at which the invariant was violated (representing the depth of the state in the execution), and the time t in seconds taken to reach that stage.

While the values for s and t are straightforward, the *invariant ID* column may contain one of three different symbols:

- ✓: the tool confirmed that the corresponding invariant is always violated on at least one path at stage s ("*definitely violated*", see Sect. 4, item 2c);
- ∽: the tool found that the corresponding invariant is violated in some cases on at least one path at stage s ("*possibly violated*", see Sect. 4, item 2c);
- ×: the tool did not detect any violation within the defined state space, which is bounded by the time and stage limits.

Note that, in our context, even if a property is possibly violated, it can be counted as a violation, since a dangerous system configuration exists. Therefore, observing the results in Table 3, we note that ASE was able to identify all invariant violations in the initial versions of each contract (i.e., those corresponding to Solidity deployed contracts), as we expected. Indeed, for these versions, the number of find violations FV is the same as the number of the expected violations EV. However, performance tends to decline for later versions, with increased execution times or failure to detect violations. In these cases, the value of FV is less than that of EV.

Despite the promising results, the approach suffers from the well-known limitation of symbolic execution path explosion. In the ASE tool, this is exacerbated by the sequential execution logic of an ASM. This limitation also affects the symbolic execution of multi-agent ASMETA models (not used here, but in [10,11]) useful to model *good* contracts operating in combination with *bad* contracts, namely those that try to exploit the vulnerability to make an attack. Ideas on how to overcome this limitation are to be addressed in future work.

However, compared to the model checking approach employed in [10,11,30] to guarantee the safety properties of Solidity contracts, by using the symbolic execution-based strategy we can deal with infinite domains, and the encountered path explosion problem is very limited with respect to the state explosion problem of the model checker.

7 Related Work

Numerous automated tools exist for analyzing, testing, and debugging Ethereum smart contracts. However, as demonstrated by [32], current tools fail to detect a significant majority (approximately 80%) of exploitable bugs found in real-world smart contracts.

An analysis of several surveys and reviews, including [1,32], and [5], was conducted to identify some of the most widely used and effective smart contract analysis tools.

Several tools address the challenge of identifying vulnerable behavior in smart contracts, employing techniques such as formal methods, theorem proving, model checking, runtime verification, and fuzzing to specify and verify properties and invariants. Certora [22] is a commercial tool offering a proprietary cloud-based platform for verification, where property specifications are separated from the contract code. Properties are expressed in the Certora Verification Language (CVL), an extension of Solidity incorporating metaprogramming primitives. While the verification process is effective, using Certora requires learning CVL and the tool works as a black box. Similarly, Halmos [3] offers a Certora like workflow, by exploiting a combination of symbolic execution and testing. It allows to execute Solidity tests providing all possible inputs.

The work presented in [28] utilizes the K-Framework [13], enabling smart contract analysis through runtime verification of bytecode, rather than Solidity, subsequently, many other tools try to improve K-Framework usability and effectiveness, like KEVM [21] or Kontrol [26]. Isabelle/HOL is employed to verify the

EVM bytecode of smart contracts. This process involves partitioning contracts into basic blocks, with the properties of each block proven using Hoare triples. Similarly TLA+ [23] is used in [17] to analyze different security-critical smart contracts. They have been able to detect bugs, including reentrancy. These aforementioned approaches often demand a strong mathematical and logical background, employing complex mathematical notations.

SolCMC [2] is a symbolic model checker integrated into the Solidity compiler since 2019. Developers specify properties using assert statements within the contract code. Similarly, HEVM [18] is a symbolic EVM written in Haskell language. However, these approaches are limited to the verification of assertions placed at specific positions in the code.

Finally, Echidna [20] is a Haskell program for fuzzing and property-based testing of Ethereum smart contracts. It automatically generates inputs and verifies user-defined invariants. However, fuzzing necessitates substantial computational power and resources.

ASM/ASMETA offers a more accessible alternative for smart contract verification. Models appear as high-level programs, use a simple notation and basic control flow constructs, are executable and supported by other lightweight validation techniques. This allows for immediate feedback on model reliability, providing a preliminary assessment before resorting to more complex verification methods. In [10,11,30], we employed the *code to model* translation schema outlined in Sect. 3 and used the NuSMV model checker to verify CTL properties, facing the classical limitations of state explosion and domain size.

8 Conclusion

In this paper, we presented a new strategy for vulnerability detection in Solidity smart contracts through the symbolic execution of ASMETA models. This approach required enhancements to the ASE tool, mainly to adapt it to the ASMETA model notation and to deal with model invariant checking. The preliminary results shown here and obtained on (different versions of) various contracts, confirm that the method is promising for design-time detection of vulnerabilities. However, the current focus is on contract-intrinsic issues and does not yet address interactions with other smart contracts. Some work is planned in the future: (1) optimizing the ASE tool, improving its consistency with ASMETA (e.g., handling *undef* values and monitored functions) and developing a more user-friendly interface; (2) exploring partial order reduction techniques to mitigate the path explosion problem in multi-agent models; (3) automating some key steps, such as mapping Solidity code to ASMETA models, preparing models for ASE execution, and generating execution scenarios from the initial states identified in invariant violations; (4) expanding the approach to a broader range of concrete smart contracts, particularly those with unknown vulnerabilities; (5) evaluating the method on contract models with a fully specified exception-handling mechanism.

References

1. Almakhour, M., Sliman, L., Samhat, A.E., Mellouk, A.: Verification of smart contracts: a survey. Pervasive Mob. Comput. **67**, 101227 (2020). https://doi.org/10.1016/j.pmcj.2020.101227
2. Alt, L., Blicha, M., Hyvärinen, A.E., Sharygina, N.: SolCMC: solidity compiler's model checker. In: 34th International Conference on Computer Aided Verification, CAV 2022, pp. 325–338. Springer, Cham (2022). https://doi.org/10.1007/978-3-031-13185-1_16
3. Andreessen Horowitz VC: Halmos (2025). https://github.com/a16z/halmos
4. Arcaini, P., Gargantini, A., Riccobene, E., Scandurra, P.: A model-driven process for engineering a toolset for a formal method. Softw. Pract. Experience **41**(2), 155–166 (2011). https://doi.org/10.1002/spe.1019
5. Bartoletti, M., Fioravanti, F., Matricardi, G., Pettinau, R., Sainas, F.: Towards benchmarking of solidity verification tools. In: 5th International Workshop on Formal Methods for Blockchains (FMBC 2024). Open Access Series in Informatics (OASIcs), vol. 118, pp. 6:1–6:15. Schloss Dagstuhl – Leibniz-Zentrum für Informatik (2024). https://doi.org/10.4230/OASIcs.FMBC.2024.6
6. Bombarda, A., Bonfanti, S., Gargantini, A., Riccobene, E., Scandurra, P.: ASMETA tool set for rigorous system design. In: Formal Methods, vol. 14934, pp. 492–517. Springer, Cham (2025). https://doi.org/10.1007/978-3-031-71177-0_28
7. Börger, E., Raschke, A.: Modeling Companion for Software Practitioners. Springer, Cham (2018). https://doi.org/10.1007/978-3-662-56641-1
8. Börger, E., Stärk, R.: Abstract state machines: a method for high-level system design and analysis. Springer (2003). https://doi.org/10.1007/978-3-642-18216-7
9. Braghin, C., Cimato, S., Damiani, E., Baronchelli, M.: Designing smart-contract based auctions. In: Security with Intelligent Computing and Big-data Services, SICBS 2018, pp. 54–64. Springer, Cham (2020). https://doi.org/10.1007/978-3-030-16946-6_5
10. Braghin, C., Riccobene, E., Valentini, S.: An ASM-based approach for security assessment of ethereum smart contracts. In: Proceedings of the 21st International Conference on Security and Cryptography, SECRYPT 2024, pp. 334–344. SCITEPRESS (2024). https://doi.org/10.5220/0012858000003767
11. Braghin, C., Riccobene, E., Valentini, S.: Modeling and verification of smart contracts with abstract state machines. In: Proceedings of the 39th ACM/SIGAPP Symposium on Applied Computing, SAC 2024, pp. 1425–1432. Association for Computing Machinery, New York (2024). https://doi.org/10.1145/3605098.3636040
12. Braghin, C., Riccobene, E., Valentini, S.: Ethereum Via ASM (2025). https://github.com/smart-contract-verification/ABZ2025
13. Ştefănescu, A., Park, D., Yuwen, S., Li, Y., Roşu, G.: Semantics-based program verifiers for all languages. In: Proceedings of the 31th Confernce on Object-Oriented Programming, Systems, Languages, and Applications, OOPSLA 2016, pp. 74–91. ACM (2016). https://doi.org/10.1145/2983990.2984027
14. Del Castillo, G.: Using symbolic execution to transform turbo abstract state machines into basic abstract state machines. In: 10th International Conference on Rigorous State-Based Methods, ABZ 2024. Lecture Notes in Computer Science, vol. 14759, pp. 215–222. Springer, Cham (2024). https://doi.org/10.1007/978-3-031-63790-2_15

15. Del Castillo, G.: Using symbolic execution to transform turbo abstract state machines into basic abstract state machines (extended version) (2024). https://github.com/constructum/asm-symbolic-execution/blob/main/doc/2024--Del-Castillo--extended-version-of-ABZ-2024-paper.pdf
16. Del Castillo, G.: ASM symbolic execution (2025). https://github.com/constructum/asm-symbolic-execution. version used for the experiments presented in this paper: https://github.com/constructum/asm-symbolic-execution/tree/32251c45d43b41f39cdbff061ddd64914976c244
17. Dfinity: Eliminating smart contract bugs with TLA+ (2023). https://medium.com/dfinity/eliminating-smart-contract-bugs-with-tla-e986aeb6da24
18. Dxo, Soos, M., Paraskevopoulou, Z., Lundfall, M., Brockman, M.: Hevm, a fast symbolic execution framework for EVM bytecode. In: International Conference on Computer Aided Verification, pp. 453–465. Springer, Cham (2024)
19. Fekih, R.B., Lahami, M., Jmaiel, M., Bradai, S.: Formal verification of smart contracts based on model checking: an overview. In: IEEE International Confernce on Enabling Technologies: Infrastructure for Collaborative Enterprises, WETICE 2023, pp. 1–6 (2023). https://doi.org/10.1109/WETICE57085.2023.10477834
20. Grieco, G., Song, W., Cygan, A., Feist, J., Groce, A.: Echidna: effective, usable, and fast fuzzing for smart contracts. In: Proceedings of the 29th ACM SIGSOFT International Symposium on Software Testing and Analysis, pp. 557–560 (2020). https://doi.org/10.1145/3395363.3404366
21. Hildenbrandt, E., et al.: KEVM: a complete formal semantics of the ethereum virtual machine. In: 2018 IEEE 31st Computer Security Foundations Symposium (CSF), pp. 204–217. IEEE (2018)
22. Jackson, D., Nandi, C., Sagiv, M.: Certora technology white paper. https://docs.certora.com/en/latest/docs/whitepaper/index.html
23. Lamport, L.: The temporal logic of actions. ACM Trans. Program. Lang. Syst. (TOPLAS) **16**(3), 872–923 (1994)
24. Marmsoler, D., Ahmed, A., Brucker, A.D.: Secure smart contracts with isabelle/solidity. In: Madeira, A., Knapp, A. (eds.) Software Engineering and Formal Methods, pp. 162–181. Springer, Cham (2025)
25. New Alchemy: A short history of Smart Contract hacks on Ethereum: A.k.a. why you need a smart contract security audit (2018). https://medium.com/new-alchemy/a-short-history-of-smart-contract-hacks-on-ethereum-1a30020b5fd
26. Runtime Verification Inc.: Kontrol (2025). https://github.com/runtimeverification/kontrol
27. Siegel, D.: Understanding The DAO Attack (2016). https://www.coindesk.com/learn/understanding-the-dao-attack/
28. Sotnichek, M.: Formal verification of smart contracts with the K framework (2019). https://www.apriorit.com/dev-blog/592-formal-verification-with-k-framework
29. Tolmach, P., Li, Y., Lin, S.W., Liu, Y., Li, Z.: A survey of smart contract formal specification and verification. ACM Comput. Surv. **54**(7) (2021). https://doi.org/10.1145/3464421
30. Valentini, S., Braghin, C., Riccobene, E.: A modeling and verification framework for ethereum smart contracts. In: 10th International Confernce on Rigorous State-Based Methods, ABZ 2024. Lecture Notes in Computer Science, vol. 14759, pp. 201–207. Springer, Cham (2024). https://doi.org/10.1007/978-3-031-63790-2_13

31. Wood, G., et al.: Ethereum: a secure decentralised generalised transaction ledger. Ethereum Proj. Yellow Paper **151**(2014), 1–32 (2014)
32. Zhang, Z., Zhang, B., Xu, W., Lin, Z.: Demystifying exploitable bugs in smart contracts. In: 2023 IEEE/ACM 45th International Conference on Software Engineering, ICSE, pp. 615–627. IEEE (2023). https://doi.org/10.1109/ICSE48619.2023.00061

Safely Encoding B Proof Obligations in SMT-LIB

Vincent Trélat(✉)

Université de Lorraine, CNRS, Inria, LORIA, Nancy, France
vincent.trelat@inria.fr

Abstract. This paper presents an encoding of B proof obligations in SMT-LIB 2.7, leveraging the recent extensions of SMT-LIB to higher-order logic. Our encoding improves upon previous approaches by eliminating uninterpreted membership predicates and by avoiding the complexity of encoding functions as relations. Through SMT-LIB's support for higher-order constructs, we achieve a more natural representation of B's set theory, while ensuring soundness of the translation. Preliminary experimental results are promising and indicate that our encoding allows certain proof obligations that previously failed to be discharged.

Keywords: B Proof Obligations · SMT-LIB · Higher-Order Logic · Set Theory

1 Introduction

Formal specification techniques like the B method [1] have been increasingly used in the development of high-assurance software systems, particularly in safety-critical domains such as transportation. Verifying properties of B models has been facilitated by integrated development environments such as Atelier B [8] and Rodin [3], which provide a framework for development and verification. Proof obligations are systematically generated from B components and translated into machine-verifiable formats to be fed into automated solvers [10]. While automated theorem proving has made steady progress over the past decades, a small but significant proportion of applications still require human intervention for verification in practice. Recent advances in automated reasoning have opened the door to higher-order logic [4] and have led to the introduction of higher-order constructs in SMT-LIB 2.7, thus creating new opportunities for the encoding.

This paper presents a novel approach to encoding B proof obligations that leverages higher-order logic, addressing limitations in previous translation methods and offering a more natural and computationally efficient encoding. Background context on B and SMT is provided in Sect. 2, followed by the formalization of both languages with their respective type systems in Sect. 3 and Sect. 4. Section 5 introduces an encoding that leverages SMT-LIB 2.7's higher-order features to represent sets and functions. Preliminary experimental results are shown in Sect. 6.

This work is supported by the ANR project BLaSST (ANR-21-CE25-0010).

M. Leuschel and F. Ishikawa (Eds.): ABZ 2025, LNCS 15728, pp. 52–69, 2026.
https://doi.org/10.1007/978-3-031-94533-5_4

2 Background

This section provides an overview of the B method and SMT-LIB, focusing on the aspects relevant to the encoding of B proof obligations.

2.1 The B Method

The B Method is a formal approach to software development, enabling the specification of abstract machines that can be progressively refined into concrete, implementable code while preserving correctness through proof obligations. From specification to implementation, all artifacts are expressed in a single formalism, the B language. At its core, the B language uses set theory [13,18], treating all objects—including relations and functions—as sets.

This theoretical basis enables rigorous reasoning about software properties while remaining practical for industrial use. Notable applications include various Communication-Based Train Control (CBTC) systems worldwide such as the Métro Line 14 in Paris, which generated about 27,800 proof obligations, among which 2,250 required manual intervention [15].

Atelier B and Rodin provide tools for generating proof obligations from B components and interacting with external provers [12], which involves translating proof obligations into machine-verifiable formats such as SMT-LIB. Atelier B's Proof Obligation Generator (POG) derives proof obligations from refinement steps, well-formedness and consistency checks on B components.

Example 1. Refining a set to an array would generate obligations ensuring that (a) the array bounds can accommodate the maximum set size, (b) array operations preserve the abstract set's properties and (c) the invariant linking abstract and concrete representations is maintained. □

These obligations are stored in an XML-based format [9], essentially representing B expressions in a structured way.

2.2 Satisfiability Modulo Theories

The Satisfiability Modulo Theories (SMT) problem extends Boolean satisfiability by incorporating background theories such as arithmetic, arrays, and uninterpreted functions. SMT solvers determine whether a formula is satisfiable with respect to these theories. Such formulas are written in the SMT-LIB language, which provides a standard interface for interacting with SMT solvers. The expressiveness of SMT-LIB was recently extended from multi-sorted first-order logic to higher-order logic in version 2.7 [6]. In particular, the introduction of the arrow type for functions and the lambda binder significantly enhances the expressiveness of the language, allowing for more direct representations of higher-order constructs.

Solvers are gradually adapting to these new features. Thanks to recent advances in higher-order instantiation [4,20,21], the cvc5 solver [5] now provides partial support for higher-order reasoning, as shown in the following example.

Example 2. Consider the following SMT-LIB 2.7 script, which declares a higher-order predicate `P` that takes functions from integers to integers as arguments—notice the directive `(set-logic HO_ALL)`, which enables higher-order reasoning. The script asks for a satisfiability check of the formula asserting the existence of a function `f` such that `P(f)` is true.

```
(set-logic HO_ALL)
(declare-const P (-> (-> Int Int) Bool))
(assert (exists ((f (-> Int Int))) (= (P f) true)))
(check-sat)
```

cvc5 returns `sat` and provides the following model for `P`:

```
(define-fun P ((f (-> Int Int))) Bool (= (lambda ((x Int)) 0) f))
```

□

3 Formalizing B Proof Obligations

The following section formalizes the B language and its type system.

3.1 Syntax

The grammar formalized below is intentionally simplified compared to the full syntax of the B language, though it is not minimal, to avoid overly complex definitions for simple constructs. Let $\mathcal{V}$ represent a collection of variables. A term t is then defined inductively as one of these constructs:

- literals, where v is a variable in $\mathcal{V}$, n is an integer, and b is a Boolean:

$$v \mid n \mid b \mid \mathbb{Z} \mid \mathbb{B}$$

- arithmetic operations:

$$t +^{\mathrm{B}} t \mid t -^{\mathrm{B}} t \mid t *^{\mathrm{B}} t \mid t \leq^{\mathrm{B}} t \mid t =^{\mathrm{B}} t$$

- Boolean operations:

$$t \wedge^{B} t \mid \neg^{B} t$$

- set operations:

$$t \mapsto^{\mathrm{B}} t \mid t \in^{\mathrm{B}} t \mid \mathcal{P}^{\mathrm{B}}(t) \mid t \times^{\mathrm{B}} t \mid t \cap^{\mathrm{B}} t \mid t \cup^{\mathrm{B}} t$$

- partial functions, application, minimum, maximum, and cardinality:

$$t \nrightarrow^{\mathrm{B}} t \mid t(t) \mid \min t \mid \max t \mid |t|^{\mathrm{B}}$$

– binders, where $v_1, \ldots, v_n$ are variables in $\mathcal{V}$:

$$\{v_1, \ldots, v_n \in t \mid t\}^{\mathrm{B}} \mid \lambda^{\mathrm{B}} v_1, \ldots, v_n \cdot (t \mid t) \mid \forall^{\mathrm{B}} v_1, \ldots, v_n \in t \cdot t$$

Additional syntax constructs are defined in terms of these base constructs, such as disjunction ($\vee^{\mathrm{B}}$), implication ($\Rightarrow^{\mathrm{B}}$), existential quantifier ($\exists^{\mathrm{B}}$), and a variety of interrelated constructs defining specific classes of functions, encompassing all combinations of partial and total functions with injective, surjective and bijective properties.

3.2 Type System

Strictly speaking, the B language does not require a type system to be well-defined, as it is grounded in set theory. While the B-Book [2] introduces a relation associated with a typing judgment, this relation is fundamentally part of the language semantics rather than a separate type system layer and should not be misconstrued as a type system. Its purpose is to ensure well-definedness of terms and should be understood as a membership constraint forming the foundation for the generation of proof obligations. Formally, the B language is therefore untyped since there is no explicit type system provided within the language. However, to make the language practical for software specification and development, it is necessary to introduce facilities for manipulating well-defined expressions, machine integers and implementable objects that cannot be easily represented within pure set theory, as illustrated in the following example.

Example 3. If the integer 3 is to be treated as an immediate value, in set theory it is represented as follows:

$$3 \stackrel{\text{def}}{=} \{\varnothing, \{\varnothing\}, \{\varnothing, \{\varnothing\}\}, \{\varnothing, \{\varnothing\}, \{\varnothing, \{\varnothing\}\}\}\} \tag{1}$$

Moreover, even a seemingly simple statement such as $3 = 2 + 1$ requires a non-trivial proof involving extensionality and case analysis. □

That being said, the B language can indeed be equipped with a type system, which serves to enforce the well-formedness of expressions. Atelier B includes a well-formedness checker that computes variable domains and verifies that expressions conform to the well-formedness rules of the B language, as shown in the following example.

Example 4. In ZFC set theory, the expression $1 + \top$ is well-formed and definitionally equal to the set $\mathbb{B}$ of Booleans, or the natural number 2, but it is not a valid expression in B. □

The fact that integer and Boolean literals are assigned distinct constructs in the syntax motivates the introduction of distinct types for integers and Booleans, as mentioned in the last two examples.

Additional constructs, such as the minimum, maximum, and cardinality functions were included in the syntax. While these could theoretically be defined

$$\frac{\Gamma \vdash^{\mathrm{B}} A : \mathtt{set}(\alpha) \qquad \Gamma \vdash^{\mathrm{B}} B : \mathtt{set}(\beta)}{\Gamma \vdash^{\mathrm{B}} A \mathrel{+\!\!\!\rightarrow}^{\mathrm{B}} B : \mathtt{set}(\mathtt{set}(\alpha \times^{\mathrm{B}} \beta))} \ \textbf{(pfun)}$$

$$\frac{\Gamma \vdash^{\mathrm{B}} x : \alpha \qquad \Gamma \vdash^{\mathrm{B}} f : \mathtt{set}(\alpha \times^{\mathrm{B}} \beta)}{\Gamma \vdash^{\mathrm{B}} f(x) : \beta} \ \textbf{(app)}$$

$$\frac{\forall i \in [\![1,n]\!],\ \Gamma \vdash^{\mathrm{B}} D_i : \mathtt{set}(\alpha_i) \qquad \Gamma, v_1 : \alpha_1, \ldots, v_n : \alpha_n \vdash^{\mathrm{B}} P : \mathtt{bool}}{\Gamma \vdash^{\mathrm{B}} \{v_1, \ldots, v_n \in^{\mathrm{B}} D_1 \times^{\mathrm{B}} \ldots \times^{\mathrm{B}} D_n \mid P\} : \mathtt{set}(\alpha_1 \times^{\mathrm{B}} \ldots \times^{\mathrm{B}} \alpha_n)} \ \textbf{(collect)}$$

Fig. 1. Typing rules for partial functions, function application and set comprehension. In the last rule, variables $v_1, \ldots v_n$ are fresh variables and must not appear in Γ.

using more fundamental constructs, it would complicate the encoding unnecessarily. Contrary to the rules presented in the B Book, in our setting they are simply typed as functions into integers, and the premises for their correct application—for instance, that the cardinal is applied to finite sets—is handled at the semantics level.

It is therefore sufficient to consider a type system with four base types: integers, Booleans, (power) sets, and (cartesian) products.

$$\tau ::= \mathtt{int} \mid \mathtt{bool} \mid \mathtt{set}\ \tau \mid \tau \times^{B} \tau$$

Remark 5. This type system could be extended to also model user-defined sets, which can be used as type parameters for functions and relations. For the moment, such sets, along with enumerations, are assimilated to sets of integers. Note that the typing rule for set comprehension is slightly more restrictive than the corresponding well-definedness rule in the B-Book since it enforces the cartesian product to be explicit. Also, Boolean values and propositions are considered to be on the same level in this framework, although they are distinct syntactical categories in B.

3.3 Typing Rules

Typing is then naturally defined inductively on terms within a typing context, which is a map associating variables with their representive types. The typing rules are formally expressed judgments $\Gamma \vdash^{\mathrm{B}} t : \tau$, indicating that term t has type τ in context Γ. A selection of three such rules is illustrated in Fig. 1, covering partial functions, function application, and set comprehension.

Remark 6. A POG file always represents closed terms: therefore, any proof obligation *PO* must verify the judgment with any typing context, and in particular, the empty context:

$$\vdash^{\mathrm{B}} PO : \mathtt{bool}$$

4 Formalizing a Subset of SMT-LIB

Similarly, a subset of the SMT-LIB language is formalized, based on the official language specification [6], with simplifications.

4.1 Syntax

Let $\mathcal{V}$ be a collection of variables. A term t is then defined inductively as one of these constructs:

- literals, where v is a variable in $\mathcal{V}$, n is an integer, and b is a Boolean:

$$v \mid n \mid b$$

- arithmetic operations:

$$t +^{\mathrm{S}} t \mid t -^{\mathrm{S}} t \mid t *^{\mathrm{S}} t$$

- Boolean operations:

$$t \wedge^{\mathrm{S}} t \mid t \vee^{\mathrm{S}} t \mid \neg^{\mathrm{S}} t \mid t =^{\mathrm{S}} t \mid t \leq^{\mathrm{S}} t \mid t \Rightarrow^{\mathrm{S}} t \mid \text{if } t \text{ then } t \text{ else } t$$

- binders, where $v_1, \ldots, v_n$ are variables in $\mathcal{V}$ and $\alpha_1, \ldots, \alpha_n$ are SMT-LIB types (which are defined below in Sect. 4.2):

$$\lambda^{\mathrm{S}} v_1 : \alpha_1, \ldots, v_n : \alpha_n, t \mid \forall^{\mathrm{S}} v_1 : \alpha_1, \ldots, v_n : \alpha_n, t \mid \exists^{\mathrm{S}} v_1 : \alpha_1, \ldots, v_n : \alpha_n, t$$

- other constructs, where α is an SMT-LIB type:

$$t(t) \mid \text{as } t\ \alpha \mid \text{some } t \mid \text{none} \mid \text{the } t \mid \text{pair } t\ t \mid \text{fst } t \mid \text{snd } t$$

Remark 7. Note that the some, none, the, pair, fst and snd constructs are not part of the official SMT-LIB language, but are introduced here to simplify the encoding of certain constructs. They are formally defined as constructors of a polymorphic datatype in the following section.

4.2 Type System

We formalize a simplified version of SMT-LIB's type system covering the restricted syntax defined in the previous section. Recalling that SMT-LIB functions are total, a standard approach to representing partial functions within this framework involves encoding them as total functions whose codomain includes an additional element denoting the absence of value, as commonly achieved via the so-called `Option` type. The type system of SMT-LIB is simplified to a minimal form that accommodates the requirements of the formalization as follows:

$$\tau ::= \texttt{Int} \mid \texttt{Bool} \mid \texttt{Unit} \mid \tau \rightarrow^{\mathrm{S}} \tau \mid \texttt{Option}\ \tau \mid \texttt{Pair}\ \tau\ \tau$$

$$\frac{\Gamma \vdash^{\mathsf{S}} x : \alpha}{\Gamma \vdash^{\mathsf{S}} \textbf{some } x : \texttt{Option } \alpha}\ \textbf{(some)} \qquad \frac{}{\Gamma \vdash^{\mathsf{S}} \textbf{as none } \alpha : \texttt{Option } \alpha}\ \textbf{(none)}$$

$$\frac{\Gamma \vdash^{\mathsf{S}} x : \alpha \qquad \Gamma \vdash^{\mathsf{S}} y : \beta}{\Gamma \vdash^{\mathsf{S}} \textbf{pair } x\ y : \texttt{Pair } \alpha\ \beta}\ \textbf{(pair)} \qquad \frac{\Gamma, v_1 : \alpha_1, \ldots, v_n : \alpha_n \vdash^{\mathsf{S}} P : \texttt{bool}}{\Gamma \vdash^{\mathsf{S}} \forall^{\mathsf{S}} v_1 : \alpha_1 \ldots, v_n : \alpha_n, P : \texttt{Bool}}\ \textbf{(forall)}$$

Fig. 2. Typing rules for options, pairs and forall. In the last rule, variables $v_1, \ldots v_n$ are fresh variables and must not appear in Γ.

Remark 8. The `Option` and `Pair` types, along with the `some`, `none`, and `pair` constructors are included as terms of the syntax to circumvent unnecessary complexity in the formalization of the language. Formally, they are defined as the following polymorphic datatypes:

```
(declare-datatype Pair (par (T1 T2) ((pair (fst T1) (snd T2)))))
(declare-datatype Option (par (T) ((some (the T)) (none))))
```

The judgment $\Gamma \vdash^{\mathsf{S}} t : \tau$, denotes that term t has type τ in context Γ. Four of the complete set of typing rules are presented in Fig. 2, covering the `some`, `none`, `pair`, and `forall` constructs.

Similarly to the B language, the semantics of SMT-LIB is defined in a set-theoretic setting for type-correct terms, but is out of the scope of this paper.

5 Encoding B in SMT-LIB

With the formalizations of B and SMT-LIB established, the encoding rules can now be formulated. The translation of POG files in SMT-LIB format has historically been handled by the tool *ppTransSMT* [12]. This approach requires complex encodings, particularly for set-theoretic constructs and functions [16]. The limitations of this encoding strategy, along with the new possibilities offered by SMT-LIB 2.7's higher-order features, are presented in the following. The encoding rules are then detailed, followed by a discussion on soundness.

5.1 Prior Approach

Versions of SMT-LIB prior to 2.7 were limited to multi-sorted first-order logic; therefore higher-order elements required encoding through first-order reductions, leaving certain components uninterpreted and only partially specified. The encoding performed by *ppTransSMT* was therefore based on a first-order reduction and monomorphization of polymorphic constructs like membership, leaving any higher-order terms uninterpreted. The set-theoretic constructs of the B language were encoded using two distinct sorts: a unary sort `P` representing the powerset operator, and a binary sort `C` encoding the cartesian product.

```
(declare-sort P 1)
(declare-sort C 2)
```

This formalization approach, while operational, presents two limitations. The first limitation stems from its conflation of set-theoretic concepts (specifically the powerset and cartesian product operations) with type-theoretic notions, two paradigms that are based on divergent foundational principles [7]: *collections* and *constructions* respectively.

Example 9. To visualize this theoretical divergence in practice, consider the type of integers that are equal to their successor and the type of prime numbers between 13 and 17, which are both uninhabited. For the sake of readability, they can be informally expressed as:

$$\{x\colon \texttt{int} \mid x = x + 1\} \quad \text{and} \quad \{x\colon \texttt{int} \mid x \in \mathbb{P} \wedge 13 < x < 17\}$$

where $\mathbb{P}$ denotes the set of prime numbers. For these to be definitionally equal, their constructions must be definitionally equal as well:

$$\forall x\colon \texttt{int}, x = x + 1 \overset{\text{def}}{=} x \in \mathbb{P} \wedge 13 < x < 17$$

This clearly does not hold, showing that both of these uninhabited types are not definitionally equal, despite being propositionally equal (since both sides of the equation are logically equivalent to $\perp$). □

The second limitation arises from the necessity to declare distinct uninterpreted membership predicates for each sort combination. These predicates must then be axiomatically specified to define concrete sets.

Example 10. Let $S := \{a, b, c\}$ be an enumeration of three sets.[1] The encoding of S via the unary sort **P** is as follows:

```
(declare-const a (P (Int)))
(declare-const b (P (Int)))
(declare-const c (P (Int)))
(declare-const S (P (P (Int))))
(declare-const ∈_1 ((P (Int)) (P (P (Int)))) Bool)
(assert (forall ((x (P (Int))))
  (= (∈_1 x S) (or (= x a) (= x b) (= x c)))))
```

With such a definition, the claim "$a \in S$" is not true by definition but is an assertion to be proven; it is relevant to the specification of S which is not a definition. □

These limitations motivate an alternative encoding approach that capitalizes on SMT-LIB 2.7's support for higher-order logic to achieve a more faithful and direct representation of set-theoretic constructs.

[1] Note that the constants a, b, c are not assigned a specific type *a priori* and are encoded as sets of integers for simplicity. Alternatively, they could be declared as sets of an abstract nullary sort.

5.2 Sets as Characteristic Predicates

The primary notable distinction in the design of this new encoding is the representation of sets as predicates, i.e., total functions that evaluate to the truth value of any element being a member of a set. Note that this approach is only feasible thanks to the support of higher-order constructs brought by SMT-LIB 2.7, since sets of sets are encoded as higher-order functions.

Definition 11 (Characteristic predicate). *Let S be a set. The characteristic predicate $\hat{S}$ of S is defined as the following total function:*

$$\forall x, \hat{S}(x) \stackrel{def}{=} x \in S$$

Lemma 12 (Existence and uniqueness). *In any set theory embedding extensional reasoning on sets, the characteristic predicate of a set as defined above describes the set correctly and is unique up to logical equivalence.*

Proof. Any set S is extensionally equal to $\{x \mid \hat{S}(x)\}$. Let then P be a predicate such that the following holds:

$$\forall x,\ x \in S \Leftrightarrow P(x)$$

Then by definition of $\hat{S}$, $\forall x, \hat{S}(x) \Leftrightarrow P(x)$. ■

It follows that for any type α, any type representing homogeneous sets containing elements of type α is isomorphic to the type $\alpha \rightarrow^{\mathrm{S}}$ `Bool`. Note that B types can be inductively embedded into SMT-LIB types in an axiomatic way, via the following mapping ξ:

$$\xi(\texttt{int}) = \texttt{Int} \qquad \xi(\texttt{bool}) = \texttt{Bool}$$
$$\xi(\texttt{set}\ \alpha) = \xi(\alpha) \rightarrow^{\mathrm{S}} \texttt{Bool} \qquad \xi(\alpha \times^{\mathrm{B}} \beta) = \texttt{Pair}\ \xi(\alpha)\ \xi(\beta)$$

where α and β are B types. This implies that B integers (resp. Booleans) can be semantically interpreted as SMT-LIB integers (resp. Booleans). For instance, B sets of integers are represented as functions mapping integers to Booleans. This is the basis of the encoding of sets in SMT-LIB. Moreover, the mapping ξ can be extended to accommodate uninterpreted sorts, as in the example below.

Example 13. A set `S` of elements of type `A` is declared in SMT-LIB as follows:

```
(declare-sort A 0)
(declare-const S (-> A Bool))
```

□

Note that thanks to the `lambda` binder, any concrete set may be defined either via a specification or directly as a function.

Example 14. The encoding of the set of natural numbers, first specified, then inlined, yields:

```
(declare-const Nat (-> Int Bool))
(assert (forall ((x Int)) (= (Nat x) (>= x 0))))
```

```
(define-const Natλ (-> Int Bool) (lambda ((x Int)) (>= x 0)))
```

□

The latter option is chosen, so that set membership can be verified through definitional equality with one β-reduction.

Example 15. Revisiting the set $S = \{a, b, c\}$ from Example 10, its encoding using characteristic predicates is as follows:

```
(declare-const a (-> Int Bool))
(declare-const b (-> Int Bool))
(declare-const c (-> Int Bool))
(define-const S (-> (-> Int Bool) Bool)
  (lambda ((x Int)) (or (= x a) (= x b) (= x c))))
```

□

This encoding offers the advantage of being more direct: it eliminates the need to declare membership predicates, reducing membership to function application, which is polymorphic. It suffers from a notable drawback, as it erases the structure of sets, which can be a hindrance when attempting proof reconstruction.

5.3 Functions as Functions

Another notable distinction in our encoding is the direct representation of functions in B as actual SMT-LIB functions rather than encoding them as functional relations, i.e., sets of pairs. This is achieved by leveraging the inherent function type (->) introduced in SMT-LIB 2.7 and allowing for a more natural representation of functions. This approach not only simplifies the encoding but also reduces the burden on SMT solvers by avoiding the overhead of quantifiers that would be necessary when encoding functions as relations. Quantifier elimination and instantiation are among the most significant challenges in SMT solving, motivating the choice of avoiding them whenever feasible.

Functions in B, being rooted in set theory, are fundamentally represented as relations rather than natively as found in similar languages such as TLA$^+$ [17] or Alloy [14]. In particular, they are characterized as binary relations satisfying some property, as defined below.

Definition 16 (Partial function). *Let f be a binary relation over two arbitrary sets S and T, i.e. $f \subseteq S \times T$. f verifies the functional property if:*

$$\forall x \in S, y \in T, z \in T, (x \mapsto y \in f \wedge x \mapsto z \in f) \Rightarrow y = z$$

In this case, f is said to be a partial function, denoted by $f \in S \nrightarrow T$.

Remark 17. In the case of a functional relation f, the notation $x \mapsto y \in f$ should be understood as $f(x) = y$. The definition above simply states that each element from the domain of f is mapped to at most one element in its codomain.

Example 18. The overhead of encoding functions as relations can be readily grasped by examining the encoding of the B expression `FINITE(S)`, where `S` is an arbitrary set. For improved readability, the superscript annotations of the B operators are omitted in this example only and all expressions below are written in B syntax.

By definition of the `FINITE` predicate in B, the expression expands to:

$$\forall a \in \mathbb{Z} \cdot (\exists b, f \in \mathbb{Z} \times (\mathtt{S} \leftrightarrow \mathbb{Z}) \cdot f \in \mathtt{S} \rightarrowtail a..b)$$

This expresses that the set `S` can be injectively mapped onto a finite interval of integers, i.e., it can be enumerated. Unfolding all definitions yields the following:

$$\begin{array}{ll} \forall a \in \mathbb{Z} \cdot \exists b, f \in \mathbb{Z} \times (\mathtt{S} \leftrightarrow \mathbb{Z}) \cdot & \\ \quad (\forall x, y \in \mathtt{S} \times \mathbb{Z} \cdot x \mapsto y \in f \Rightarrow a \leq y \land y \leq b) & \land \\ \quad (\forall x, y, z \in \mathtt{S} \times \mathbb{Z} \times \mathbb{Z} \cdot x \mapsto y \in f \land x \mapsto z \in f \Rightarrow y = z) & \land \\ \quad (\forall z \in \mathtt{S} \cdot \exists w \in \mathbb{Z} \cdot z \mapsto w \in f) & \land \\ \quad (\forall x, y, z \in \mathtt{S} \times \mathbb{Z} \times \mathbb{Z} \cdot x \mapsto z \in f \land y \mapsto z \in f \Rightarrow x = y) & \end{array}$$

Encoding this expression with *ppTransSMT* yields the following SMT-LIB script, where τ is the SMT-LIB type of the elements in the set `S`:

```
(assert (forall ((a Int)) (exists ((b Int) (f (P (C τ Int)))) (and
  (forall ((x τ) (y Int)) (=> (mem2 x y f) (and (<= a y) (<= y b))))
  (forall ((x τ) (y Int) (z Int))
    (=> (and (mem2 x y f) (mem2 x y f)) (= y z)))
  (forall ((z τ)) (exists ((w Int)) (mem2 z w f)))
  (forall ((x τ) (y τ) (z Int))
    (=> (and (mem2 x z f) (mem2 y z f)) (= x y)))))))
```

It can be seen that the encoding obtained via a first-order reduction produces a large expression with many quantifiers. In particular, the variable f bound under the existential quantifier has the SMT-LIB type `P (C \inlinealttext{\detokenize{\\t}}{τ} Int)`, which is already a complex type and depends on τ. □

With the arrow type, B functions can be directly encoded as SMT-LIB functions, thereby avoiding the need to rely on relations satisfying some property.

Example 19. Returning to the B expression `FINITE(S)` from Example 18, let τ denote an SMT-LIB type representing the type of the elements in the set `S`. By directly encoding the function f as a function from τ to `Option Int`, the expression is encoded as follows in SMT-LIB, omitting the superscript annotations for readability:

$$\begin{aligned}\exists N\colon \texttt{Int}, f\colon \tau \to \texttt{Option Int}\cdot \\ &(\forall x\colon \tau, (\neg f(x) = \texttt{none}) = \hat{S}(x)) && \wedge \\ &(\forall x\colon \tau, y\colon \tau, z\colon \texttt{Int} \cdot f(x) = \texttt{some}\ z \wedge f(y) = \texttt{some}\ z \Rightarrow x = y) && \wedge \\ &(\forall x\colon \tau \cdot \hat{S}(x) \Rightarrow 0 \leq \texttt{the}\ f(x) \wedge \texttt{the}\ f(x) < N)\end{aligned}$$

□

Ultimately, expressions involving operators such as FINITE or CARD, which rely on functions embedded within their definitions, can be encoded in a more direct and efficient manner.

This idea can be systematically extended to all B terms involving functions, rather than being restricted solely to those derived from fixed definitions. To ensure the soundness of the proof obligations generated by the encoding, it is essential to establish the conditions under which the encoding remains valid. This is safe in the particular case of invariants enforcing functional properties on terms. These properties are indeed easily broken in other contexts, as illustrated in the following example.

Example 20. Consider the following B operation:

```
op (x, y) =
PRE
  x : INTEGER & y : INTEGER        // x ∈ᴮ ℤ ∧ y ∈ᴮ ℤ
THEN
  f := f \/ {x |-> y}              // f := f ∪ᴮ {x ↦ᴮ y}
END
```

and assume f has been initialized to the partial function $\{0 \mapsto^{\mathrm{B}} 1, 1 \mapsto^{\mathrm{B}} 2\}$.

After a call to op(2, 3), the value of f is $\{0 \mapsto^{\mathrm{B}} 1, 1 \mapsto^{\mathrm{B}} 2, 2 \mapsto^{\mathrm{B}} 3\}$, which is still a partial function. After another call to op(2, 4) however, the value of f is $\{0 \mapsto^{\mathrm{B}} 1, 1 \mapsto^{\mathrm{B}} 2, 2 \mapsto^{\mathrm{B}} 3, 2 \mapsto^{\mathrm{B}} 4\}$, which is no longer a partial function, as it maps 2 to both 3 and 4. Encoding f as a function in SMT-LIB would be unsound.

Now, consider that the operation op occurs within the following B machine:

```
VARIABLES
  f
INVARIANT
  f : INTEGER +-> INTEGER          // f ∈ᴮ ℤ ⇸ᴮ ℤ
INITIALISATION
  f := {0 |-> 1, 1 |-> 2}          // f := {0 ↦ᴮ 1, 1 ↦ᴮ 2}
```

This machine requires f to be a partial function as an invariant. In this case, two proof obligations are generated, one for the initialization and one for the invariant preservation. Written using the syntax defined in Sect. 3.1, they are:

$$\{0 \mapsto^{\mathrm{B}} 1, 1 \mapsto^{\mathrm{B}} 2\} \in^{\mathrm{B}} \mathbb{Z} \mathrel{+\!\!\!\rightarrow}^{\mathrm{B}} \mathbb{Z} \quad \text{(init)}$$
$$f \in^{\mathrm{B}} \mathbb{Z} \mathrel{+\!\!\!\rightarrow}^{\mathrm{B}} \mathbb{Z} \Rightarrow^{\mathrm{B}} \forall^{\mathrm{B}} x, y \in^{\mathrm{B}} \mathbb{Z} \times^{\mathrm{B}} \mathbb{Z} \cdot f \cup^{\mathrm{B}} \{x \mapsto^{\mathrm{B}} y\} \in^{\mathrm{B}} \mathbb{Z} \mathrel{+\!\!\!\rightarrow}^{\mathrm{B}} \mathbb{Z} \quad \text{(invariant)}$$

The first proof obligation is trivially satisfied. However, the second one is false: consider the counterexample $f := \{0 \mapsto^{\mathrm{B}} 1, 1 \mapsto^{\mathrm{B}} 2, 2 \mapsto^{\mathrm{B}} 3\}$, $x := 2$, and $y := 4$. Then $f \cup^{\mathrm{B}} \{x \mapsto^{\mathrm{B}} y\}$ is not a partial function.

As will be shown in the following section, the encoding of relation-related operations must vary depending on whether neither, one, or both operands are encoded as functions. In this example, the union $f \cup^{\mathrm{B}} \{x \mapsto^{\mathrm{B}} y\}$ of a partial function and a singleton has to be encoded.[2] Since no additional constraints are provided on variables x and y, a safe choice is to encode it as a relation, based on the following consideration:

$$\begin{aligned} &f \cup^{\mathrm{B}} \{x \mapsto^{\mathrm{B}} y\} =^{\mathrm{B}} \\ &\qquad \{p \in^{\mathrm{B}} \mathbb{Z} \times^{\mathrm{B}} \mathbb{Z} \mid p =^{\mathrm{B}} x \mapsto^{\mathrm{B}} y \vee^{\mathrm{B}} \exists^{\mathrm{B}} a \in^{\mathrm{B}} \mathbb{Z} \cdot p =^{\mathrm{B}} a \mapsto^{\mathrm{B}} f(a)\} \end{aligned}$$

The SMT-LIB encoding of $f \cup^{\mathrm{B}} \{x \mapsto^{\mathrm{B}} y\}$ is then:

$$\begin{aligned} &\lambda^{\mathrm{S}} p : \texttt{Pair Int Int}, \\ &\qquad \big(\exists^{\mathrm{S}} a : \texttt{Int}, b : \texttt{Int},\ p =^{\mathrm{S}} \texttt{pair}\ a\ b \wedge^{\mathrm{S}} f(a) =^{\mathrm{S}} \texttt{some}\ b\big) \vee^{\mathrm{S}} p =^{\mathrm{S}} \texttt{pair}\ x\ y \end{aligned}$$

Using this expression in the encoding of the proof obligation, stating that this relation is a partial function, would then result in an SMT-LIB expression that can be proven to be false; however the semantics of the B expression would be preserved by the encoding. □

5.4 Encoding Rules

With these foundational considerations established, the encoding rules can be defined. To establish a sound encoding, it is imperative to formalize the source and target languages, thereby enabling rigorous reasoning about their structure and properties. While the scope of this paper is confined to encoding B proof obligations in SMT-LIB, it is noteworthy that a POG file encapsulates typing information that can be checked at runtime. Soundness of the encoding is therefore contingent upon correctness of the typing and well-definedness of the encoding rules, among other factors.

Literals, Arithmetic and Boolean Operations. Literal values are encoded directly, associating B types with SMT-LIB types via the mapping ξ. Since

[2] The fact that the proof obligation encodes the fact that $f \cup^{\mathrm{B}} \{x \mapsto^{\mathrm{B}} y\}$ is a partial function is a semantic property of the expression, and has nothing to do with how the encoding is done.

arithmetic and Boolean operations are natively supported in both B and SMT-LIB, they can be directly encoded, namely $\odot^{\mathrm{B}}$ is encoded as $\odot^{\mathrm{S}}$, where $\odot$ is one of the operators $+, -, *, =, \wedge, \vee, \Rightarrow$ and $\neg$. Binders are also encoded directly, the only difference being that the SMT-LIB types of the bound variables must be computed from the domain of the B quantifier.

Set Operations. Maplets are encoded as pairs, i.e. $\mapsto^{\mathrm{B}}$ is encoded as `pair`, and membership is encoded as function application, benefiting from the encoding of sets as characteristic predicates. Powerset is encoded as the set of all subsets. Cartesian product is encoded with pairs as follows: let S and T be B terms such that $\Gamma \vdash^{\mathrm{B}} S : \mathtt{set}\ \alpha$ and $\Gamma \vdash^{\mathrm{B}} T : \mathtt{set}\ \beta$ for some context Γ and types α and β. Let $\hat{S}$ and $\hat{T}$ be their respective encodings. The expression $S \times^{\mathrm{B}} T$ is encoded as:

$$\lambda^{\mathrm{S}} p \colon \mathtt{Pair}\ \xi(\alpha)\ \xi(\beta), \hat{S}(\mathtt{fst}\ p) \wedge^{\mathrm{S}} \hat{T}(\mathtt{snd}\ p)$$

More complex operations like union are trickier to encode and are discussed later.

Partial Functions. Let $f, \mathcal{A}$ and $\mathcal{B}$ be B terms. The expression $f \in^{\mathrm{B}} \mathcal{A} \mathrel{+\!\!\!\rightarrow}^{\mathrm{B}} \mathcal{B}$, assuming it is well-typed in the type system of B, is encoded in SMT-LIB as follows:

- the symbol f is declared with the type $\alpha \rightarrow^{\mathrm{S}} \mathtt{Option}\ \beta$,
- the following assertion is added:

$$(\forall^{\mathrm{S}} x \colon \alpha, f\ x \neq \mathtt{none} \Rightarrow^{\mathrm{S}} \hat{\mathcal{A}}\ x)\ \wedge^{\mathrm{S}} (\forall^{\mathrm{S}} x \colon \alpha, f\ x \neq \mathtt{none} \Rightarrow^{\mathrm{S}} \hat{\mathcal{B}}\ (\mathtt{the}\ f\ x))$$

  where α (resp. β) is the SMT-LIB type corresponding to the B type of elements of $\mathcal{A}$ (resp. $\mathcal{B}$), and $\hat{\mathcal{A}}$ (resp. $\hat{\mathcal{B}}$) is the encoding of $\mathcal{A}$ (resp. $\mathcal{B}$) as a characteristic predicate.

This rule is, in fact, quite straightforward: the characterization of a function is determined by two components—its domain and codomain—such that each element in the domain is associated with exactly one corresponding element in the codomain.

Example 21. Returning to the B expression from Example 18, the SMT-LIB code obtained from encoding the expression `FINITE(S)` where `S` is a set of integers is as follows:

```
(declare-const S (-> Int Bool))
(assert (exists ((N Int) (f (-> Int (Option Int)))) (and
  (forall ((x Int) (y Int)) (=>
    (and (S x) (S y) (= (f x) (f y)))
    (= x y)))
  (forall ((x Int)) (= (not (= (f x) none)) (S x)))
  (forall ((x Int)) (=> (S x) (and (<= 0 (f x)) (<= (f x) N)))))))
```

□

Union. As mentioned in Example 20, the main challenge stemming from juggling relations and functions is to ensure that operations dealing with relations are correctly handled in the case of functions.

Let f, g be two B terms and $\tilde{f}, \tilde{g}$ their respective encoding in SMT-LIB such that $\Gamma \vdash^{\mathrm{S}} \tilde{f} : \alpha$ and $\Gamma \vdash^{\mathrm{S}} \tilde{g} : \beta$ for some context Γ and SMT-LIB types α and β. The expression $f \cup^{\mathrm{B}} g$ is encoded as follows, distinguishing between the following cases on α and β:

- if $\alpha = \beta = \sigma \rightarrow^{\mathrm{S}} \mathtt{Bool}$,

$$\lambda^{\mathrm{S}} x \colon \sigma, \tilde{f}(x) \vee^{\mathrm{S}} \tilde{g}(x)$$

- if $\alpha = \beta = \sigma \rightarrow^{\mathrm{S}} \mathtt{Option}\ \gamma$,

$$\lambda^{\mathrm{S}} p \colon \mathtt{Pair}\ \sigma\ \gamma,\ (\tilde{f}(\mathtt{fst}\ p) =^{\mathrm{S}} \mathtt{some}\ (\mathtt{snd}\ p)) \vee^{\mathrm{S}} (\tilde{g}(\mathtt{fst}\ p) =^{\mathrm{S}} \mathtt{some}\ (\mathtt{snd}\ p))$$

- if $\alpha = \mathtt{Pair}\ \sigma\ \gamma \rightarrow^{\mathrm{S}} \mathtt{Bool}$ and $\beta = \sigma \rightarrow^{\mathrm{S}} \mathtt{Option}\ \gamma$ (the symmetric case is omitted),

$$\lambda^{\mathrm{S}} p \colon \mathtt{Pair}\ \sigma\ \gamma,\ \tilde{f}(p) \vee^{\mathrm{S}} (\tilde{g}(\mathtt{fst}\ p) =^{\mathrm{S}} \mathtt{some}\ (\mathtt{snd}\ p))$$

The rules described above cover the subset of the B language formalized in Sect. 3.1 while ensuring type correctness of the SMT-LIB translation under the assumption that the B input is well typed. While additional B operators can be encoded following similar principles by relying on the base constructs we have defined, new encoding rules may be established to handle more complex constructs in a more efficient manner.

5.5 Towards Soundness

Establishing soundness—i.e., proving that the SMT-LIB encoding preserves the semantics of B proof obligations—is a non-trivial task and remains future work. However, the key ideas of the proof are outlined, without formally defining semantics, for the more intricate rules: partial functions and unions. The non-trivial aspect of these rules is that the SMT-LIB types must be correctly computed from the B types. The notations used in the rules detailed in Sect. 5.4 are kept.

Partial Functions. The idea is to reason by induction on B terms. Assuming that $f \in^{\mathrm{B}} \mathcal{A} \nrightarrow^{\mathrm{B}} \mathcal{B}$ is well-typed in B, there exists a context Γ such that:

$$\Gamma \vdash^{\mathrm{B}} f \in^{\mathrm{B}} \mathcal{A} \nrightarrow^{\mathrm{B}} \mathcal{B} : \mathtt{bool}$$

By definition of the typing rules, this implies that there exist two B types α' and β' such that:

$$\Gamma \vdash^{\mathrm{B}} f : \mathtt{set}\ (\alpha' \times^{\mathrm{B}} \beta') \quad \text{and} \quad \Gamma \vdash^{\mathrm{B}} \mathcal{A} : \mathtt{set}\ \alpha' \quad \text{and} \quad \Gamma \vdash^{\mathrm{B}} \mathcal{B} : \mathtt{set}\ \beta'$$

Consequently, $\mathcal{A}$ (resp. $\mathcal{B}$) is encoded to $\hat{\mathcal{A}}$ (resp. $\hat{\mathcal{B}}$) via its characteristic predicate and the type α (resp. β) is shown to be equal to $\xi(\alpha')$ (resp. $\xi(\beta')$) where ξ is the mapping embedding B types into SMT-LIB types defined in Sect. 5.2. This encoding rule is therefore well-defined. ∎

Union. The cases listed in the encoding rule are shown to be exhaustive. Assuming that $\Gamma \vdash^{\mathrm{B}} f \cup^{\mathrm{B}} g : \mathtt{set}\ \tau'$, for some context Γ and B type τ', the typing rules of B imply that:

$$\Gamma \vdash^{\mathrm{B}} f : \mathtt{set}\ \tau', \quad \Gamma \vdash^{\mathrm{B}} g : \mathtt{set}\ \tau'$$

If $\tau' = \sigma' \times^{\mathrm{S}} \gamma'$, then f and g can be encoded either as functions or relations, which constitutes the different cases. We only consider the case where only one operand is encoded as a function—suppose it is f—as the other cases are similar. By induction, the types α and β of $\tilde{f}$ and $\tilde{g}$ are shown to be such that:

$$\alpha = \sigma \to^{\mathrm{S}} \mathtt{Option}\ \gamma \quad \text{and} \quad \beta = \mathtt{Pair}\ \sigma\ \gamma \to^{\mathrm{S}} \mathtt{Bool} \quad \text{for some types } \sigma \text{ and } \gamma$$

which are shown to be equal to $\xi(\sigma')$ and $\xi(\gamma')$ respectively. ∎

6 Evaluation

Although our encoding currently covers only a limited subset of the B language, it can already be tested against real-world B proof obligations. An executable version of the encoding, developed in Lean 4.15.0, is available at [22] with instructions and example proof obligations. A publicly available dataset of B proof obligations [11] from industrial applications was used to compare our encoding to *ppTransSMT*.

For the evaluation, 133 POG files that fall within the subset of the syntax that can be handled by our encoding were selected from the dataset and encoded into SMT-LIB using both our encoding and *ppTransSMT*, yielding a total of 2,195 proof obligations. These proof obligations were processed using cvc5 [5], with model-based quantifier instantiation enabled and a timeout of 3 s per proof obligation. Table 1 indicates that, on average, cvc5 discharges proof obligations encoded using our approach twice as fast as those encoded with *ppTransSMT*, likely due to the more direct encoding of functions. As shown in Table 2, the solver exhibits consistent behavior across both encodings, except for 64 proof obligations. Among these, 28 are successfully solved with our encoding but not with *ppTransSMT*, which is a promising result. However, 14 proof obligations are solved by *ppTransSMT* but not by our encoding, suggesting that our approach may still overwhelm the solver in certain cases, especially when dealing with complex lambda expressions that cannot be reduced. Finally, 22 proof obligations remain unsolved by both encodings, indicating that further work is needed to address these challenges. Inspection of these proof obligations reveals that they are large and complex, involving multiple nested quantifiers that are difficult to simplify in either encoding. It could be beneficial to consider splitting these proof obligations into smaller, more manageable parts and it requires a good understanding of the internal workings of the solvers.

Table 1. Total time taken by cvc5 to solve the proof obligations encoded using *ppTransSMT* (PP) and our encoding (HO).

	Time (s)	Time/PO (ms)
PP	296	135
HO	116	53

Table 2. Results of the proof obligations on both encodings, where r denotes either `sat` or `unsat` and u denotes `unknown`.

	(u, u)	(r, u)	(u, r)
#PO	22	14	28

7 Conclusion

This paper introduces an encoding of B proof obligations into SMT-LIB, laying the groundwork for formal verification. The encoding rules are carefully designed to guarantee soundness and are evaluated against a dataset of real-world B proof obligations. The results are promising, demonstrating that our encoding is efficient. However, further work is required to resolve the remaining challenges.

The encoding is being implemented in the Lean theorem prover [19], along with a formalization of the B language and SMT-LIB semantics to ensure the correctness of the encoding and to facilitate the verification of further properties. Future work will focus on proving the soundness of the encoding in Lean, on extending the encoding to cover more constructs of the B language, and on improving the efficiency of the encoding, both in terms of solving time and number of discharged proof obligations.

Acknowledgments. I thank Stephan Merz, Sophie Tourret and Ghilain Bergeron for providing valuable feedback on my work, and David Déharbe for discussions on the B method and ppTransSMT.

References

1. Abrial, J.R., Lee, M., Neilson, D.S., Scharbach, P.N., Sørensen, I.H.: The B-method. In: Prehn, S., Toetenel, H. (eds.) VDM '91 Formal Software Development Methods, pp. 398–405. Springer, Heidelberg (1991)
2. Abrial, J.R.: The B-Book: Assigning Programs to Meanings. Cambridge University Press, USA (1996)
3. Abrial, J.R., Butler, M., Hallerstede, S., Hoang, T.S., Mehta, F., Voisin, L.: Rodin: an open toolset for modelling and reasoning in Event-B. Int. J. Softw. Tools Technol. Transfer **12**(6), 447–466 (2010). https://doi.org/10.1007/s10009-010-0145-y
4. Barbosa, H., Reynolds, A., Ouraoui, D.E., Tinelli, C., Barrett, C.: Extending SMT solvers to higher-order logic. In: Fontaine, P. (ed.) Proceedings of the 27th International Conference on Automated Deduction (CADE 2019). Lecture Notes in Artificial Intelligence, vol. 11716, pp. 35–54. Springer (2019). http://theory.stanford.edu/~barrett/pubs/BREO+19.pdf

5. Barbosa, H., et al.: cvc5: a versatile and industrial-strength SMT solver. In: Fisman, D., Rosu, G. (eds.) Tools and Algorithms for the Construction and Analysis of Systems - 28th International Conference, TACAS 2022, Held as Part of the European Joint Conferences on Theory and Practice of Software, ETAPS 2022, Munich, Germany, 2–7 April 2022, Proceedings, Part I. Lecture Notes in Computer Science, vol. 13243, pp. 415–442. Springer (2022). https://doi.org/10.1007/978-3-030-99524-9_24
6. Barrett, C., Fontaine, P., Tinelli, C.: The SMT-LIB standard: version 2.7. Technical report, Department of Computer Science, The University of Iowa (2025). www.SMT-LIB.org
7. Bruijn, de, N.: On the roles of types in mathematics, pp. 27–54. Cahiers du centre de logique, Academia-Erasme (1995)
8. Clearsy: Atelier B. https://www.atelierb.eu
9. Clearsy: PO XML Format Documentation (2023). https://www.atelierb.eu/wp-content/uploads/2023/10/pog-1.0.html
10. Déharbe, D.: Integration of SMT-solvers in B and Event-B development environments. Sci. Comput. Program. **78**, 310–326 (2013). https://doi.org/10.1016/j.scico.2011.03.007
11. Déharbe, D.: Proof obligations from the B formal method (2022). https://doi.org/10.5281/zenodo.7050797
12. Déharbe, D., Fontaine, P., Guyot, Y., Voisin, L.: Integrating SMT solvers in Rodin. Sci. Comput. Program. **94** (2014). https://doi.org/10.1016/j.scico.2014.04.012
13. Fraenkel, A.A., Bar-Hillel, Y.: Foundations of Set Theory. Elsevier, Atlantic Highlands (1973)
14. Jackson, D.: Alloy: a logical modelling language. In: Bert, D., Bowen, J.P., King, S., Waldén, M. (eds.) ZB 2003: Formal Specification and Development in Z and B, Third International Conference of B and Z Users, Turku, Finland, 4–6 June 2003, Proceedings. Lecture Notes in Computer Science, vol. 2651, p. 1. Springer (2003). https://doi.org/10.1007/3-540-44880-2_1
15. Jacquel, M.: Automatisation des preuves pour la vérification des règles de l'Atelier B. Theses, Conservatoire national des arts et metiers - CNAM (2013). https://theses.hal.science/tel-00840484
16. Konrad, M.: Translation from set-theory to predicate calculus. Technical report, ETH Zurich (2012)
17. Lamport, L.: Specifying Systems: The TLA+ Language and Tools for Hardware and Software Engineers. Addison-Wesley Longman Publishing Co., Inc., USA (2002)
18. Mendelson, E., Fraenkel, A.A.: Axiomatic set theory. J. Symb. Log. **24** (1958). https://doi.org/10.2307/2963801
19. de Moura, L., Kong, S., Avigad, J., van Doorn, F., von Raumer, J.: The lean theorem prover (system description). In: Felty, A.P., Middeldorp, A. (eds.) Automated Deduction - CADE-25, pp. 378–388. Springer, Cham (2015)
20. Reynolds, A., Barbosa, H., Fontaine, P.: Revisiting enumerative instantiation, pp. 112–131 (2018). https://doi.org/10.1007/978-3-319-89963-3_7
21. Tourret, S., Fontaine, P., El Ouraoui, D., Barbosa, H.: Lifting congruence closure with free variables to λ-free higher-order logic via SAT encoding. In: SMT 2020 - 18th International Workshop on Satisfiability Modulo Theories. Online COVID-19, France (2020). https://hal.science/hal-03049088
22. Trélat, V.: Safely encoding B proof obligations in SMT-LIB (2025). https://doi.org/10.5281/zenodo.14870543

On Writing Alloy Models: Metrics and a New Dataset

Soaibuzzaman(✉), Salar Kalantari, and Jan Oliver Ringert

Bauhaus-University Weimar, Weimar, Germany
soaibuzzaman@uni-weimar.de

Abstract. Alloy is a modeling language that combines relational first-order logic and temporal logic while providing powerful automated analyses via the Alloy Analyzer. Recent efforts in tool development and teaching of Alloy have contributed the Alloy4Fun dataset enabling many analyses of fine-grained model editing histories.

We present a smaller, but complementary dataset $\mathsf{FMP_{als}}$ of similar editing granularity. While the Alloy4Fun dataset captures users filling in predefined predicates, our dataset is more diverse and users develop all parts of Alloy models including signatures, fields, facts, and commands.

We illustrate the differences between the datasets, define a Halstead metric to measure the difficulty of models, and evaluate model edit paths from both datasets on various metrics.

Keywords: Alloy · evolution · metrics · dataset

1 Introduction

Alloy [13] is a modeling language that combines relational first-order logic and temporal logic while providing powerful automated analyses via the Alloy Analyzer. Alloy has been applied to modeling software designs [23,40], code testing, debugging, and repair [9,28,38], and to analyze security properties [1,37].

Recent efforts in tool development and teaching of Alloy have contributed the Alloy4Fun platform [18] and dataset [17]. Alloy4Fun provides a web-based editor with selected Alloy models and tasks inside these models. The platform generates feedback in terms of Alloy instances for each user attempt. The Alloy4Fun dataset [17,18] has attracted research interest [2,14,41] as it provides fine-grained model editing histories previously not available.

Alloy4Fun [18] focuses on writing expressions inside predefined predicates that are then semantically evaluated against an instructor's solution. This limits the insight one could obtain about how novice users use Alloy, as the Alloy language also provides elements like signatures, fields, and commands (all briefly introduced in Sect. 2.1), which instructors provide and are not expected to be written or modified by users in the Alloy4Fun dataset. We present a smaller but complementary dataset with similar editing granularity. Our $\mathsf{FMP_{als}}$ dataset is more diverse, and users develop all parts of Alloy models, including signatures, fields, facts, and commands.

M. Leuschel and F. Ishikawa (Eds.): ABZ 2025, LNCS 15728, pp. 70–87, 2026.
https://doi.org/10.1007/978-3-031-94533-5_5

We illustrate the differences between the datasets, define a Halstead metric to measure the difficulty of models, and evaluate model edit paths from both datasets on various metrics.

The remainder of this work is structured as follows. Section 2 briefly presents the foundations of our work. Section 3 lists our research questions, Sect. 4 presents our dataset and data processing. Section 5 presents the evaluation of our research questions on the datasets. We discuss related work in Sect. 6 and conclude in Sect. 7.

2 Preliminaries

We now give a brief overview of the Alloy language, the Alloy4Fun platform, the Formal Methods Playground, and Halstead metrics.

2.1 Alloy

Alloy [12,13] is a textual modeling language based on relational first-order logic. An example Alloy model is shown in Listing 1.1 consisting of signature declarations (ll. 1–3) with fields, e.g., field `link` in signature `File` (l. 1). Intuitively, the semantics of an Alloy model are instances consisting of atoms and relations over atoms where each signature is a set (unary relation) of atoms, and each field is an n-ary relation, e.g., the field `link` defines a binary relation that relates each `File`-atom with an arbitrary number of `File`-atoms (multiplicity `set` in l. 1). Facts, predicates, and assertions may contain expressions in relational as well as temporal logic, e.g., the expression `no Trash` in predicate `inv1` (l. 5) states that the set `Trash` is empty in all instances satisfying predicate `inv1`. Alloy models can be automatically analyzed [13] by the Alloy Analyzer in a bounded scope (bounding number of atoms) via a reduction to SAT [36].

```
1 sig File { link : set File }
2 sig Trash in File {}
3 sig Protected in File {}
4
5 pred inv1 { /* The trash is empty. */ /* solution: */ no Trash }
6 pred inv2 { /* All files are deleted. */ }
7 pred inv3 { /* Some file is deleted. */ }
```

Listing 1.1. An example Alloy model from [17] with three out of 10 predicates for the user to complete, e.g., as attempted in predicate `inv1`.

2.2 Alloy4Fun

Alloy4Fun [18] is a web application for writing and analyzing Alloy models intended for teaching Alloy. Alloy4Fun offers automated assessment and feedback by requiring users to fill in predefined predicates (see the predicates in Listing 1.1, ll. 5–7). Each predicate is independent of the others to avoid "distracting problems corresponding to failures of other properties" [18].

Interactions with Alloy4Fun are captured and published in the Alloy4Fun dataset [17] collected mainly from master students' submissions at the University of Minho and the University of Porto between Fall 2019 to Spring 2023.

2.3 Formal Methods Playground

The Formal Methods Playground[1] is a web application for writing and analyzing models in various modeling and specification languages. We have developed this application mainly for teaching, e.g., slides in our Formal Methods for Software Engineering lecture [33] contain permalinks to example models on the Formal Methods Playground for direct analysis in the browser. Currently, the Formal Methods Playground supports Limboole[2], Z3 [21], Alloy [13], nuXmv [3] and Spectra [20] specifications.

2.4 Halstead Metrics (also *Theory of Software Science*)

Halstead [11] introduced various measures for software, e.g., the effort related to the time required to write the program or the difficulty D of understanding a program when reading or writing it. Halstead metrics are computed based on the numbers of unique operators η_1 and operands η_2, and the total numbers of occurrences of operators N_1 and operands N_2. Halstead difficulty is defined as

$$D = \frac{\eta_1}{2} \times \frac{N_2}{\eta_2}, \text{ i.e., } \frac{\#\text{ unique operators}}{2} \times \frac{\#\text{ occurrences of operands}}{\#\text{ unique operands}} \quad (1)$$

Shen et al. [30] have summarized early critical assessment of Halstead metrics as well as some "tentative support" [30] from empirical studies. Shepperd [31] criticizes three representative metrics (including Halstead's) based on their definition and general (ab-)use. We reflect on this criticism in Sect. 4.4 and Sect. 5.6.

3 Research Questions

We aim to understand better the differences between the existing Alloy4Fun dataset and our new dataset and how Alloy models evolve in these.

We define the following research questions:

- **RQ1**: In what characteristics do the two datasets differ?
- **RQ2**: What is the Halstead difficulty for typical Alloy Models?
- **RQ3**: How does Halstead difficulty evolve in Alloy modeling tasks?
- **RQ4**: Is Halstead difficulty related to making and fixing errors?
- **RQ5**: How large are editing steps in Alloy modeling tasks?

[1] See https://play.formal-methods.net and https://www.youtube.com/playlist?list=PLGyeoukah9NYq9ULsIuADG2r2QjX530nf.

[2] See https://fmv.jku.at/limboole/.

4 Data Processing and Metrics Computation

4.1 Experimental Data

In this study, we utilize two datasets: the publicly accessible Alloy4Fun (A4F) dataset [17] and our new Formal Methods Playground Alloy ($\mathsf{FMP_{als}}$) dataset [34].

Our $\mathsf{FMP_{als}}$ dataset contains Alloy models executed on the Formal Methods Playground from November 2023 to January 2025. Unlike with Alloy4Fun, users usually initiate their work with a blank canvas rather than a starter model, and there are no fixed predicates to encode. Students at Bauhaus-University Weimar use this platform as part of our Formal Methods for Software Engineering [33] module. Based on user activity and the models authored, at least one additional university uses the platform. We capture models with their analyses, timestamps, and historical derivations structured in a parent-child relationship.

The A4F dataset includes a total of 97,755 models. However, 1,358 of these models only serve as starting points for users and do not include user edits or lack an executed command (cmd_i). The remaining A4F dataset consists of 96,397 Alloy models. In contrast, the $\mathsf{FMP_{als}}$ dataset contains 8,219 Alloy models.

4.2 Edit Paths

Both the A4F and $\mathsf{FMP_{als}}$ datasets maintain records of the previous revision of each Alloy model. Each revision is a user submission [17], i.e., the current model whenever the user executes an analysis. We utilize this information to reconstruct the *edit path*[3], allowing us to capture the sequences of edits/submissions made by users (these edits are typically small, see Sect. 5.5).

The A4F dataset comprises a total of 5,268 unique edit paths, whereas the $\mathsf{FMP_{als}}$ dataset consists of 747 unique edit paths. In particular, the top 25% of the edit paths have a length greater than 28 for A4F and 22 for $\mathsf{FMP_{als}}$, with median lengths of 11 and 8, respectively. The edit paths in the A4F dataset are all derived from 19 distinct models[4] that each define multiple tasks. In contrast, the $\mathsf{FMP_{als}}$ dataset has 392 unique initial models[5] within the edit paths.

4.3 Alloy4Fun Edit Paths Partitioning (from A4F to A4FpT)

The Alloy4Fun platform offers a variety of starter models, each defined by unique signatures and empty predicates that describe distinct tasks. Users may solve these tasks across multiple edits in any order as the tasks are independent [18] of each other. Thus, analyzing entire edit paths might lead to wrong conclusions when trying to understand how individual tasks are solved. We, therefore, partitioned the original edit paths of the A4F dataset. In addition to the

[3] We adopt the terminology of [14] although *interaction paths* might be more fitting as shown in Table 3.

[4] "original: the first ancestor with secrets (always the same within an exercise)" [17].

[5] While most edit paths start from scratch, some edit paths share initial models provided by instructors [33].

executed commands, Alloy4Fun provides information about the predicates that users evaluated. We utilized this information to develop new edit paths that capture users' efforts per task and refer to this dataset as A4FpT (Alloy4Fun per Task). Technically, we remove the task predicates for unrelated tasks from these models. They all remain stand-alone Alloy models with the common signatures and facts defined in their 19 starter models. For more information, readers can refer to our replication package [32].

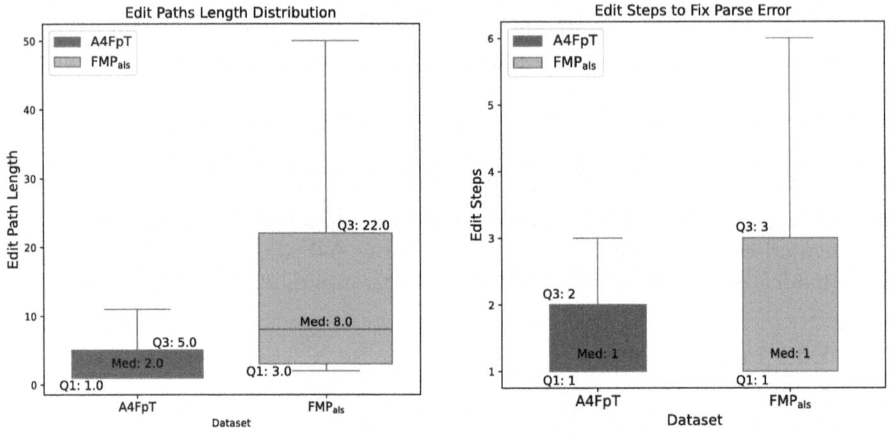

(a) (b)

Fig. 1. (a) Distribution of the edit paths length and (b) Edit steps required to fix errors in edit paths

Figure 1a illustrates the distribution of edit paths of the A4FpT dataset. The partitioning process resulted in a total of 24,592 edit paths. The box plot reveals that 75% of the edit paths have lengths of ≤ 5 for A4FpT and ≤ 22 for $\mathsf{FMP_{als}}$, with median lengths of 2 and 8, respectively (outliers excluded from box plot).

4.4 A Halstead Metric for Alloy

The Halstead metrics, while offering an intuitive static analysis framework, have received various criticism [30,31] on practical challenges associated with the methodology of counting operators and operands. Halstead [11] does not provide explicit definitions for these terms but instead characterizes their meanings as "intuitively obvious". Paige [24] defines operators as "all language elements which must be used to allow the operands to be operated on". As suggested by Salt [27] we document our counting strategy by definitions of operators and operands and provide an implementation in [32].

Table 1. Counting strategy of operators and operands of a model from Listing 1.1

Operator	Frequency	Operand	Frequency
sig	3	inv1	1
no	1	inv2	1
set	1	inv3	1
in	2	Protected	1
pred	3	File	4
		link	1
		Trash	2

Counting Strategy. Our counting strategy roughly follows the Alloy grammar [12, App. B] extended with temporal operators added in Alloy 6 as described in the Alloy Language Reference[6].

1. Only parts of the current model are considered; the contents of imported (operator `open`) models, and comments are ignored.
2. Operators are:
   - Keywords: `abstract`, `extends`, `var`, `enum`, `steps`, `sig`, `fun`, `pred`, `assert`, `check`, `run`, `but`, `else`, `module`, `open`, `disj`, `as`, `let`, `for`, `fact`, `exactly`
   - Multiplicity and quantifiers: `lone`, `some`, `one`, `all`, `sum`, `no`
   - Unary operators: `!`, `not`, `no`, `set`, `#`, `~`, `*`, `^`, `always`, `eventually`, `after`, `before`, `historically`, `once`, `'`
   - Binary operators: $\vee$, `or`, $\wedge$, `and`, $\Longleftrightarrow$, `iff`, $\Longrightarrow$, `implies`, `&`, `+`, `-`, `++`, `<:`, `:>`, `.`, `until`, `releases`, `since`, `triggered`, `;`, `in`, $=$, $<$, $>$, $\leq$, $\geq$, `->`, `[]` (box join)
3. Operands are:
   - literals of `Int` and `String`; and constants: `none`, `univ`, `iden`
   - names of modules, signatures, fields, variables, predicates, functions, and asserts
   - names and types of parameters and types of predicates and functions
4. Overloaded elements (fields, predicates, or functions) are counted once.
5. Parentheses and curly brackets are neither operators nor operands.

Table 1 illustrates an example of counting operators and operands for the Alloy model presented in Listing 1.1, following our established counting strategy. The unique counts of operators and operands are 5 (η_1) and 7 (η_2), respectively, while the total occurrences of operators and operands are 10 (N_1) and 11 (N_2), respectively. Utilizing Eq. 1, we can calculate the Halstead difficulty as

$$D = \frac{5}{2} \times \frac{11}{6} = 4.58$$

An implementation of this counting strategy is available from [32].

[6] https://alloytools.org/spec.html.

5 Evaluation

We now present data to answer the research questions defined in Sect. 3.

5.1 RQ1: Dataset Characteristics

We evaluate characteristics of the A4F and the FMP_{als} datasets along (slightly modified) research questions from [14], a recent, thorough analysis of the A4F dataset. We had to slightly modify the research questions of [14] as detailed below and omit replication of RQs 4, 6, and 7 due to the absence of an oracle/fixed task for models from FMP_{als}, which would allow for deciding correct, under-, or over-specified attempts, in this more open dataset.

Errors Users Make. We build on the research questions from [14], which examine the classification of correct and incorrect user submissions ([14], RQ1) and mistakes in writing formulas ([14], RQ5). We modify and extend these to identify top-level language constructs where errors are made.

Approximately two-thirds of the models are syntactically correct, at 70.9% for A4F and 66.3% for the FMP_{als} dataset. Conversely, around one-third are syntactically incorrect, with 29.1% for A4F and 33.7% for the FMP_{als} dataset.

The syntactically incorrect models include both syntax and type errors. As shown in Table 2, these error types are evenly distributed in the A4F dataset. In contrast, the FMP_{als} dataset has a significant prevalence of syntax errors at 77.6%, with type errors making up just 22.4%.

Finally, Table 2 indicates top-level language constructs where users face the greatest challenges. In A4F, nearly all errors are found within predicates, which is expected since users must only complete these. Conversely, the FMP_{als} dataset indicates that users similarly struggle with writing predicates and facts (25.7% and 31.6% of errors), but also with signatures (15.5%) and commands (15.5% + 3.6%). This shows the importance of additional datasets like ours as users also make errors in parts not assessed by the A4F dataset.

Table 2. Error category and location of the errors for A4F and FMP_{als} dataset

Dataset		Type	Syntax	sig	pred	fact	assert	fun	run	check
A4F	#	13 657	13 734	72	27 202	26	1	52	22	11
	%	49.9	50.1	0.002	99.3	≈ 0.0	≈ 0.0	0.001	≈ 0.0	≈ 0.0
FMP_{als}	#	566	1 962	376	625	769	101	97	378	87
	%	22.4	77.6	15.5	25.7	31.6	4.2	4.0	15.5	3.6

Submission Similarity. RQ2 from [14] examines the prevalence of syntactically and semantically unique submissions. We focus on syntactic similarity as a semantic comparison is easy on the predicate-level (sufficient for A4F), but more complex on the model-level [26] (as it would have been required for FMP_{als}).

Table 3. Syntactically unique models in the A4FpT and FMP_{als} datasets

	A4FpT		FMP_{als}	
	#	%	#	%
Syntactically Unique Models	57 777	59.9	3 513	42.7
Syntactically Correct Models (in unique models)	37 024	64.1	1 880	53.5
Syntax Error (in unique models)	20 753	35.9	1 633	46.5
Models within single edit paths:				
Consecutive Identical Models	4 664	4.64	3 174	25.58
Non-Consecutive Identical Models	5 758	5.73	667	5.38

Table 3 demonstrates that many user submissions comprise syntactically unique models. Specifically, the A4F dataset reveals that 59.9% of models maintain syntactic uniqueness, in contrast to 42.7% observed within the FMP_{als} dataset. Among these submissions, 64.1% of models in the A4F dataset are syntactically correct, whereas 35.9% are incorrect. Conversely, the FMP_{als} dataset indicates a syntactic correctness rate of 53.2% among the unique models, with 46.4% of the models being incorrect. The A4F dataset demonstrates significantly more unique models than the FMP_{als} dataset. Further analysis reveals (Table 3, bottom) that for FMP_{als} 25.6% of consecutive models in edit paths are identical (only 4.6% in A4FpT). We believe that users repeatedly browse instances and thus analyze the same model again. The Formal Methods Playground, as the official Alloy Analyzer, only allows showing the next instances, whereas Alloy4Fun also allows for navigating previous ones. It might be worthwhile implementing this backward navigation feature in the Formal Methods Playground and the Alloy Analyzer as well. Additional contributors to this difference might be that instances displayed on the Alloy4Fun platform are usually counterexamples that come with semantic classifications. This task-specific information might reduce the amount of instances users choose to inspect.

Fixing Errors. We adapt RQ3 from [14], which examines invalid submissions and the effectiveness of Alloy's compiler-based error reporting, by focusing specifically on how users fix errors over multiple edit steps.

Approximately one-third of the models are deemed invalid in both the A4FpT and FMP_{als} datasets. To gain further insights into how users address these issues, we analyze the presence of errors within the edit paths associated with the models. The results are summarized in Table 4. In the A4FpT dataset, 39.24% of the edit paths contain at least one erroneous model, with 3.80% consisting entirely of erroneous models. In comparison, the FMP_{als} dataset reveals that 54.08% of the edit paths include at least one erroneous model, and 6.55% are comprised entirely of erroneous models.

Figure 1b depicts the edit steps necessary to correct the errors, i.e., the numbers of consecutive, syntactically invalid models until reaching a syntactically correct one. In the A4FpT dataset, users generally require a median of 1 revision

Table 4. Details of syntactically invalid models in edit paths

	A4FpT	$\mathsf{FMP_{als}}$
Edit paths (#)	24 592	747
With Invalid Models (%)	39.24	54.08
Without Valid Models (%)	3.80	6.55
Edit Path Length ≥ 5 (%)	25.93	64.79
Max Edit Path Length	107	211

to resolve errors, with 75% needing less than or equal to two revisions for complete correction. Likewise, in the $\mathsf{FMP_{als}}$ dataset, users also show a median of 1 revision; however, 75% of them need less than or equal to 3 revisions to address the errors. This could point to more complex errors experienced by users within the $\mathsf{FMP_{als}}$ dataset. A distinction between specific error types might be helpful for future analyses.

5.2 RQ2: Halstead Metrics for Typical Models

We aim to assess modeling difficulty using Halstead difficulty as defined in Sect. 4.4. As an intuitive baseline, we analyze the sample models provided with the Alloy Analyzer to assess the Halstead difficulty of well-known Alloy models. These ca. 80 models comprise four categories: Algorithm, Book, Case Study, and Temporal. Figure 2a presents the Halstead difficulty for each category.

The Book category comprises example models from [12]. Most of these models exhibit a difficulty rating ranging from 11.9 to 60.4, with a median difficulty of 27.2. In contrast, the Case Studies category includes Alloy case studies, e.g., analyses of the Firewire [8] and Chord [39] protocols, and exhibits much higher Halstead difficulties between 130.8 and 176.4, with a median value 140.8.

We selected the final submitted Alloy model from each edit path to compare the Halstead difficulty of the A4FpT and $\mathsf{FMP_{als}}$ datasets with typical Alloy models. Figure 2b presents a box plot of the Halstead difficulty for these final submissions across both datasets. The results indicate that the A4FpT and $\mathsf{FMP_{als}}$ datasets exhibit similar Halstead difficulty levels to the Book category of typical Alloy models shown in Fig. 2a. This is no surprise, as both platforms are mainly used in teaching contexts. However, the $\mathsf{FMP_{als}}$ dataset demonstrates greater Halstead difficulty than A4FpT, with median values of 20.3 and 16.3, respectively. Furthermore, the plot suggests that the $\mathsf{FMP_{als}}$ dataset demonstrates greater variability in Halstead difficulty compared to A4FpT.

5.3 RQ3: Evolution of Halstead Difficulty

We analyzed both datasets using clustering and standard deviation to examine how Halstead difficulty evolves during Alloy modeling tasks.

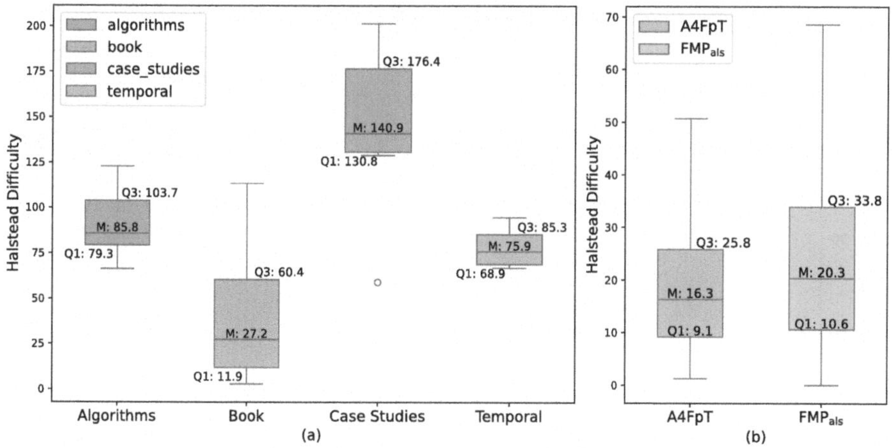

Fig. 2. Halstead difficulty of (a) typical Alloy models from the sample models of Alloy Analyzer and (b) last submitted models of the A4FpT & $\mathsf{FMP_{als}}$ edit paths

We performed KMeans clustering on the Halstead difficulty scores of models in both datasets. The clustering allowed us to group edit paths with similar difficulty levels, revealing how difficulty changes over time across different revisions of the models. We identified eight distinct clusters in the A4FpT dataset, while the $\mathsf{FMP_{als}}$ dataset revealed three clusters. This variation reflects the differing complexity and characteristics of the models within each dataset.

In addition, we incorporated standard deviation into our analysis to assess the consistency of difficulty levels within each cluster. It offers insights into whether the evolution of difficulty is stable or erratic across edit paths within a cluster.

Figure 3 and Fig. 4 demonstrate the evolution of Halstead difficulty for the A4FpT and $\mathsf{FMP_{als}}$ datasets, respectively. These plots illustrate the mean difficulty scores for each cluster over time, spanning across edit path steps. Shaded regions represent the standard deviation, offering insights into how the difficulty of models within each cluster varies as users refine their Alloy models.

In our analysis of Halstead difficulty within the A4FpT dataset, we found that the standard deviation for seven of the eight clusters was relatively low, ranging from 0 to 20. This indicates that the models within these clusters display consistent difficulty levels throughout their revisions.

Cluster 4 is the largest, comprising 9,675 edit paths, and is characterized by relatively low difficulty levels, with fewer than 20 revision steps required. Other significant clusters with larger model counts include Clusters 1, 3, 5, and 8, each containing thousands of edit paths. These clusters typically involve less than 30 revision steps, suggesting that the tasks in these groups are generally less complex requiring fewer edits.

Cluster 6, which consists of only 24 edit paths, displays significantly higher difficulty levels, ranging from 30 to 50. Further investigation revealed that most of the models in this cluster originate from the Train Station modeling problem

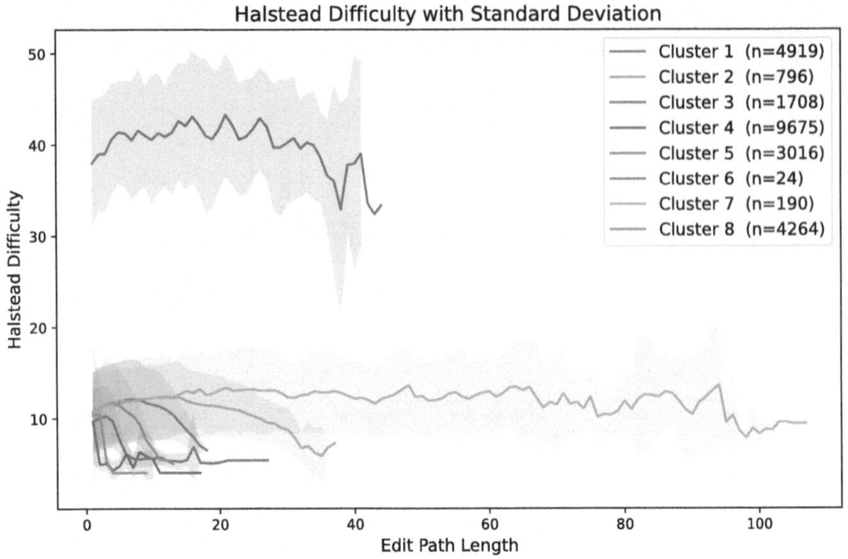

Fig. 3. Clustered Halstead difficulty of A4FpT dataset. The shaded region represents the standard deviation for each cluster

from the EM 20/21 dataset. This suggests that this particular task may be inherently more complex than others in the dataset.

```
always all f:File | (f not in Protected and f not in Trash) implies f in
    ↪ Protected'
always all f:File | always f not in Protected implies f in Protected'
always all f:File | eventually f not in Protected implies f in Protected'
always all f:File | f not in Protected implies after f in Protected
always all f:File | f not in Protected implies f in Protected'
```

Listing 1.2. An example investigation on the decline of difficulty over edit paths

A common observation across nearly all clusters of the A4FpT dataset is a noticeable decrease in difficulty at the end of the editing process, accompanied by a narrow standard deviation. We investigated this trend and discovered that the decline may be linked to users making significant changes, such as removing entire constraints to fix errors in their models. Users often begin with a more complex constraint and gradually simplify it over time. Listing 1.2 provides an example of this revision strategy where each line is a separate edit. Note that Listing 1.2 shows the predicate body only while the Halstead difficulty is always computed for the whole model.

In the $\mathsf{FMP}_{\mathsf{als}}$ dataset, we identified three clusters of Halstead difficulty. The largest cluster, Cluster 1, with 592 edit paths, demonstrates a broad range of Halstead difficulty values, spanning from 0 to 50, which indicates variability in model complexity within this group. Cluster 2 is noteworthy due to its elevated difficulty levels, ranging from 25 to 175. Upon further analysis, we discovered

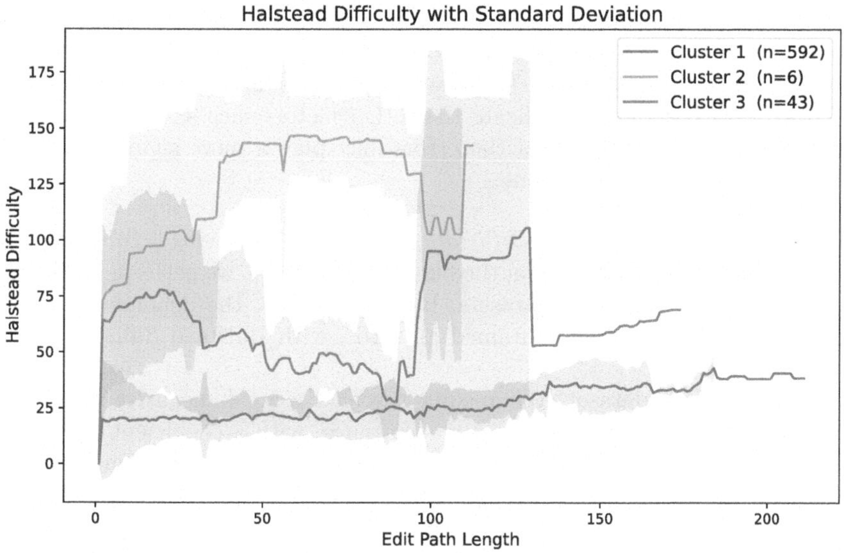

Fig. 4. Clustered Halstead difficulty of $\mathsf{FMP_{als}}$ dataset. The shaded region represents the standard deviation for each cluster

that most of the models in this cluster were generated automatically[7] rather than being crafted by users, which may account for the higher difficulty levels observed. Cluster 3, consisting of only 43 edit paths, is the most diverse regarding difficulty, reflecting a broad spectrum of complexity. This diversity suggests that the models in this cluster embody a broad array of challenges.

5.4 RQ4: Metrics Related to Errors/Fixing

Correlation Between Halstead Difficulty and Time to Fix Errors. To investigate whether higher Halstead difficulty is linked to error-fixing times, we calculated the Spearman correlation coefficient between the Halstead difficulty of each first syntactically incorrect model and the total time required to rectify its errors. We focused our analysis on models that underwent at least one revision and excluded cases where the time difference exceeded 600 s to concentrate on active revision sessions.

For the A4FpT dataset, the Spearman correlation coefficient was −0.032 ($p = 0.006$). This negative correlation indicates a weak association, suggesting that higher Halstead difficulty is correlated with slightly shorter error-fixing times. However, the small effect size and low correlation strength imply that this relationship is likely not practically significant.

Conversely, for the $\mathsf{FMP_{als}}$ dataset, the Spearman correlation coefficient was 0.236 ($p < 0.0001$), revealing a weak yet statistically significant positive correlation between Halstead difficulty and the time taken to correct errors. This

[7] The models were generated as part of a student project based on [29].

suggests that in the $\mathsf{FMP_{als}}$ dataset, models with higher Halstead difficulty tend to require more time for error correction. Although this correlation is stronger than that observed in the A4FpT dataset, it still remains relatively weak.

These weak correlations indicate that other factors-such as model structure, user expertise, or the nature of the errors-may play a more significant role in determining error resolution time.

Correlation Between Halstead Difficulty and Error Occurrence. To explore the impact of Halstead's Difficulty on the likelihood of errors, we performed a logistic regression analysis on both datasets. In this analysis, the dependent variable indicated whether a model contained an error, with Halstead difficulty as the independent variable.

For the A4FpT dataset, the results revealed a weak negative correlation between Halstead difficulty and error occurrence, with a coefficient of -0.0167 ($z = -10.84, p < 0.001$). Although this finding is statistically significant, the effect size is minimal, as demonstrated by the low $pseudo - R^2$ value of 0.0010 and the Point-Biserial correlation of -0.0339.

This suggests that models with higher Halstead difficulty are slightly less likely to contain errors. However, this difference is negligible, suggesting that factors beyond difficulty have a more pronounced influence on error occurrence.

In contrast, the $\mathsf{FMP_{als}}$ dataset indicates a weak positive correlation between Halstead difficulty and error occurrence, with a coefficient of 0.0034 ($z = 6.28, p < 0.001$). While this relationship is statistically significant, it remains small, as indicated by the $pseudo - R^2$ value of 0.0027 and a Point-Biserial correlation of 0.0587. This suggests that models with higher Halstead difficulty are slightly more likely to experience errors in the $\mathsf{FMP_{als}}$ dataset.

In summary, while the statistical analysis suggests a modest association between Halstead difficulty and error occurrence, the effect sizes in both datasets are petite.

5.5 RQ5: Edit Distance and Difficulty Delta

To better understand how users evolve Alloy models, we have computed Levenshtein distances [15] between consecutive models, i.e., the minimal number of characters modified to transform one into the other. We show box plots of Levenshtein distances between consecutive, non-identical models for both datasets in Fig. 5a. The median and 75th percentile of the edit distance in the A4FpT dataset are relatively small, with 10 and 28. They are significantly larger in the $\mathsf{FMP_{als}}$ dataset with 25 and 123. This is expected for the A4FpT dataset, as most edits are confined to a single line in a predicate. It also shows that users typically analyze their models frequently, not only when solving predefined tasks.

In addition to Levenshtein distances, we have also computed and aggregated changes in Halstead difficulty in Fig. 5b. Note that Fig. 5b aggregates the difference not in absolute terms and thus also shows decreases in Halstead difficulty, e.g., for both datasets more than 25% of the edit steps decrease the model's Halstead difficulty. This is no surprise as we have seen negative trends in particular

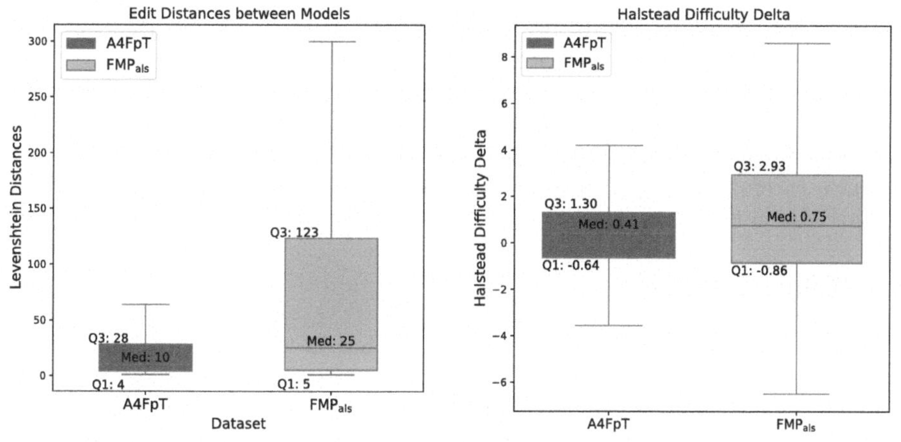

(a) (b)

Fig. 5. (a) Distribution of the edit distance (Levenshtein distance) and (b) Halstead difficulty differences in edit chain

for the A4FpT dataset already in Fig. 3 and Fig. 4. Again, the median values and 75th percentile show that larger change sizes in the $\mathsf{FMP}_{\mathsf{als}}$ are also reflected in larger differences of Halstead difficulty between edited models.

5.6 Threats to Validity

We now identify and discuss various threats to the validity of our analyses.

First, we have processed the A4F dataset from [17] to obtain edits per task as described in Sect. 4.3. To ensure correctness we have performed manual inspection of the resulting edit paths as the excerpt shown in Listing 1.2. In addition, for transparency and reproducibility we provide the implementation of our processing in [32].

Second, we assume that the use of the Formal Methods Playground across the dataset is similar to that of our students, i.e., small models are created and analyzed. However, we have no control over how other users use the publicly available platform, e.g., it could be used for teaching with very narrow task definitions. To assess this uncertainty, we have assessed unique initial nodes of edit paths in Sect. 4.2, giving some confidence in the models' variability (392 in $\mathsf{FMP}_{\mathsf{als}}$ vs. 19 in A4FpT). In addition, we have manually inspected the edit paths' clusters as described in Sect. 5.3, identifying a small number of (partially) generated models inside the dataset.

Third, existing resources on Halstead metrics do not contain formal definitions of operators and operands and we are not aware of previous applications of the metrics to Alloy. Following best practices suggested by Salt [27] we have clearly defined our counting strategy in Sect. 4.4 and provide an implementation for reproducibility and inspection at [32]. We cannot rule out that different counting strategies would change the data presented across Sect. 5.

Finally, the use of metrics like the Halstead difficulty has been criticized for being employed as indicators when they show low or no evidence of correlation with various phenomena [30,31]. Our use of the metrics is rather descriptive, and we have carefully analyzed possible correlations with errors and times required to fix these in Sect. 5.4.

6 Related Work

In recent years, an increasing amount of work has been invested to understand how novice users use formal methods and, in particular, the Alloy language. Mansoor et al. [19] performed an exploratory study where users fix Alloy models and also create them from scratch. They report that users (both novices and non-novices) find it hard to start Alloy models from scratch [19]. Our new $\mathsf{FMP}_{\mathsf{als}}$ dataset [34] exhibits these challenges.

Many works have analyzed the popular Alloy4Fun dataset [17,18]. Zheng et al. [41] and Cerqueira et al. [4] use it to evaluate their model repair approaches. Our analysis in Sect. 5.1 shows that the $\mathsf{FMP}_{\mathsf{als}}$ dataset is complementary in locations and kinds of issues exposed and might be beneficial for works on model repair. Barros et al. [2] used the Alloy4Fun dataset to generate suggestions for the next edits based on similar models written by other users. This approach relies on fixed tasks and known goals of edits, which are not given for our dataset.

Cunha et al. [6] have assessed what kind of hints best support novice users in fixing faulty Alloy models. Datasets like ours and platforms like Alloy4Fun and the Formal Methods Playground would allow large-scale comparative analyses of the strategies suggested above on diverse models and modeling tasks.

Another line of work has focused on improving instance generation for Alloy models [16,22,25,35] and understanding how different strategies support users in understanding Alloy models [5,10]. These and the ambitious early user study by Danas et al. [7] highlight the difficulty of setting up controlled studies and evaluating data from multiple sources, e.g., interviews and tool instrumentation. While our dataset is much more diverse, we are only able to make general observations due to absent task descriptions and characteristics of individual users.

Closest to our current work is the analysis of the Alloy4Fun dataset by Jovanovic and Sullivan [14]. They extensively analyze user edits syntactically as well as semantically, i.e., whether predicates are over- or under- constrained. We adapt their research questions as described in Sect. 5.1 to compare our new dataset to the one of Alloy4Fun. In addition, our analysis introduces and investigates a Halstead difficulty measure for Alloy models and strongly focuses on edits performed on edit paths.

7 Conclusion

We have presented the Formal Methods Playground Alloy ($\mathsf{FMP}_{\mathsf{als}}$) dataset and compared it to the well-known Alloy4Fun (A4F) dataset. Our comparison shows that additional datasets are worthwhile as the A4F dataset is limited to user edits in predicates while our $\mathsf{FMP}_{\mathsf{als}}$ dataset shows challenges in writing other language constructs as well.

Our analysis focused on the evolution of model complexity as characterized by the Halstead difficulty metric we adapted for Alloy models. The $\mathsf{FMP}_{\mathsf{als}}$ dataset exhibits more stable growth of the Halstead difficulty of models in edit paths, while the A4FpT shows interesting dips as edit paths terminate. These trends indicate iteratively growing models in the $\mathsf{FMP}_{\mathsf{als}}$ dataset and debugging behavior in the A4FpT dataset. Interestingly, the Halstead difficulty shows only a (very) weak correlation with error prevalence and fixing times in both datasets, i.e., it does not seem to be suitable indicator for the difficulty of fixing errors in Alloy models.

Finally, an observation on repeated analyses of identical models in the $\mathsf{FMP}_{\mathsf{als}}$ dataset suggests for tool improvements and for further analyses of how users interact with generated instances.

Data Availibility Statement. We have made the Formal Methods Playground Alloy ($\mathsf{FMP}_{\mathsf{als}}$) dataset publicly available on Zenodo as [34]. As the use of the Formal Methods Playground increases, we plan to follow the example of [17] and provide updates to this dataset.
In addition, to support reproducibility of our metrics computations and the preprocessing of the A4FpT dataset, we have made the implementation used for our analyses available in a GitHub repository as [32].

References

1. Bagheri, H., Kang, E., Malek, S., Jackson, D.: A formal approach for detection of security flaws in the android permission system. Formal Aspects Comput. **30**(5), 525–544 (2018). https://doi.org/10.1007/S00165-017-0445-Z
2. Barros, A., Neto, H., Cunha, A., Macedo, N., Paiva, A.C.R.: Alloy repair hint generation based on historical data. In: FM 2024. LNCS, vol. 14934, pp. 104–121. Springer, Cham (2024). https://doi.org/10.1007/978-3-031-71177-0_8
3. Cavada, R., et al.: The nuXmv symbolic model checker. In: Biere, A., Bloem, R. (eds.) CAV 2014. LNCS, vol. 8559, pp. 334–342. Springer, Cham (2014). https://doi.org/10.1007/978-3-319-08867-9_22
4. Cerqueira, J., Cunha, A., Macedo, N.: Timely specification repair for alloy 6. In: SEFM 2022. LNCS, vol. 13550, pp. 288–303. Springer, Cham (2022). https://doi.org/10.1007/978-3-031-17108-6_18
5. Cornejo, C., et al.: An analysis of the impact of field-value instance navigation in alloy's model finding. In: ABZ 2024. LNCS, vol. 14759, pp. 141–159. Springer, Cham (2024). https://doi.org/10.1007/978-3-031-63790-2_9
6. Cunha, A., Macedo, N., Campos, J.C., Margolis, I., Sousa, E.: Assessing the impact of hints in learning formal specification. In: SEET@ICSE 2024, pp. 151–161. ACM (2024). https://doi.org/10.1145/3639474.3640050
7. Danas, N., Nelson, T., Harrison, L., Krishnamurthi, S., Dougherty, D.J.: User studies of principled model finder output. In: SEFM 2017. LNCS, vol. 10469, pp. 168–184. Springer, Cham (2017). https://doi.org/10.1007/978-3-319-66197-1_11

8. Devillers, M., Griffioen, W., Romijn, J., Vaandrager, F.W.: Verification of a leader election protocol: formal methods applied to IEEE 1394. Formal Methods Syst. Des. **16**(3), 307–320 (2000). https://doi.org/10.1023/A:1008764923992
9. Dini, N., Yelen, C., Alrmaih, Z., Kulkarni, A., Khurshid, S.: Korat-api: a framework to enhance korat to better support testing and reliability techniques. In: SAC 2018, pp. 1934–1943. ACM (2018). https://doi.org/10.1145/3167132.3167339
10. Dyer, T., Nelson, T., Fisler, K., Krishnamurthi, S.: Applying cognitive principles to model-finding output: the positive value of negative information. Proc. ACM Program. Lang. **6**(OOPSLA1), 1–29 (2022). https://doi.org/10.1145/3527323
11. Halstead, M.H.: Elements of Software Science. Operating and Programming Systems, Elsevier Science Inc (1977)
12. Jackson, D.: Software Abstractions - Logic, Language, and Analysis. MIT Press (2006). http://mitpress.mit.edu/catalog/item/default.asp?ttype=2&tid=10928
13. Jackson, D.: Alloy: a language and tool for exploring software designs. Commun. ACM **62**(9), 66–76 (2019). https://doi.org/10.1145/3338843
14. Jovanovic, A., Sullivan, A.: Right or wrong - understanding how users write software models in alloy. In: SEFM 2024. LNCS, vol. 15280, pp. 309–327. Springer, Cham (2024). https://doi.org/10.1007/978-3-031-77382-2_18
15. Levenshtein, V.I.: Binary codes capable of correcting deletions, insertions, and reversals. In: Proceedings of the Soviet Physics Doklady (1966)
16. Macedo, N., Cunha, A., Guimarães, T.: Exploring scenario exploration. In: FASE 2015. LNCS, vol. 9033, pp. 301–315. Springer, Cham (2015). https://doi.org/10.1007/978-3-662-46675-9_20
17. Macedo, N., Cunha, A., Paiva, A.C.R.: Alloy4fun dataset for 2022/23 (2023). https://doi.org/10.5281/zenodo.8123547
18. Macedo, N., et al.: Experiences on teaching alloy with an automated assessment platform. Sci. Comput. Program. **211**, 102690 (2021). https://doi.org/10.1016/J.SCICO.2021.102690
19. Mansoor, N., Bagheri, H., Kang, E., Sharif, B.: An empirical study assessing software modeling in alloy. In: FormaliSE 2023, pp. 44–54. IEEE (2023). https://doi.org/10.1109/FORMALISE58978.2023.00013
20. Maoz, S., Ringert, J.O.: Spectra: a specification language for reactive systems. Softw. Syst. Model. **20**(5), 1553–1586 (2021). https://doi.org/10.1007/S10270-021-00868-Z
21. de Moura, L.M., Bjørner, N.S.: Z3: an efficient SMT solver. In: TACAS 2008. LNCS, vol. 4963, pp. 337–340. Springer, Cham (2008). https://doi.org/10.1007/978-3-540-78800-3_24
22. Nelson, T., Saghafi, S., Dougherty, D.J., Fisler, K., Krishnamurthi, S.: Aluminum: principled scenario exploration through minimality. In: ICSE 2013, pp. 232–241. IEEE Computer Society (2013). https://doi.org/10.1109/ICSE.2013.6606569
23. Nelson, T., Barratt, C., Dougherty, D.J., Fisler, K., Krishnamurthi, S.: The margrave tool for firewall analysis. In: LISA 2010. USENIX Association (2010). https://www.usenix.org/conference/lisa10/margrave-tool-firewall-analysis
24. Paige, M.: A metric for software test planning. In: Conference Proceedings of COMPSAC, vol. 80, pp. 499–504 (1980)
25. Ringert, J.O., Sullivan, A.: Abstract alloy instances. In: FM 2023. LNCS, vol. 14000, pp. 364–382. Springer, Cham (2023). https://doi.org/10.1007/978-3-031-27481-7_21
26. Ringert, J.O., Wali, S.W.: Semantic comparisons of alloy models. In: MoDELS 2020, pp. 165–174. ACM (2020). https://doi.org/10.1145/3365438.3410955

27. Salt, N.F.: Defining software science counting strategies. ACM SIGPLAN Not. **17**(3), 58–67 (1982). https://doi.org/10.1145/947912.947916
28. Samimi, H., Aung, E.D., Millstein, T.D.: Falling back on executable specifications. In: ECOOP 2010. LNCS, vol. 6183, pp. 552–576. Springer, Cham (2010). https://doi.org/10.1007/978-3-642-14107-2_26
29. Schnabel, T., Weckesser, M., Kluge, R., Lochau, M., Schürr, A.: Cardygan: tool support for cardinality-based feature models. In: VaMoS 2016, pp. 33–40. ACM (2016). https://doi.org/10.1145/2866614.2866619
30. Shen, V.Y., Conte, S.D., Dunsmore, H.E.: Software science revisited: a critical analysis of the theory and its empirical support. IEEE Trans. Softw. Eng. **9**(2), 155–165 (1983). https://doi.org/10.1109/TSE.1983.236460
31. Shepperd, M.J., Ince, D.C.: A critique of three metrics. J. Syst. Softw. **26**(3), 197–210 (1994). https://doi.org/10.1016/0164-1212(94)90011-6
32. Soaibuzzaman, Kalantari, S., Ringert, J.O.: Alloy metrics replication package (2025). https://github.com/se-buw/alloy-metrics
33. Soaibuzzaman, Ringert, J.O.: Introducing github classroom into a formal methods module. In: FMTea 2024. LNCS, vol. 14939, pp. 25–42. Springer, Cham (2024). https://doi.org/10.1007/978-3-031-71379-8_2
34. Soaibuzzaman, Ringert, J.O.: Formal methods playground alloy dataset (2025). https://doi.org/10.5281/zenodo.14865553
35. Sullivan, A.: Hawkeye: user-guided enumeration of scenarios. In: ISSRE 2021, pp. 569–578. IEEE (2021). https://doi.org/10.1109/ISSRE52982.2021.00064
36. Torlak, E., Jackson, D.: Kodkod: a relational model finder. In: TACAS 2007. LNCS, vol. 4424, pp. 632–647. Springer, Cham (2007). https://doi.org/10.1007/978-3-540-71209-1_49
37. Trippel, C., Lustig, D., Martonosi, M.: Security verification via automatic hardware-aware exploit synthesis: the checkmate approach. IEEE Micro **39**(3), 84–93 (2019). https://doi.org/10.1109/MM.2019.2910010
38. Zaeem, R.N., Khurshid, S.: Contract-based data structure repair using alloy. In: ECOOP 2010. LNCS, vol. 6183, pp. 577–598. Springer, Cham (2010). https://doi.org/10.1007/978-3-642-14107-2_27
39. Zave, P.: Using lightweight modeling to understand chord. Comput. Commun. Rev. **42**(2), 49–57 (2012). https://doi.org/10.1145/2185376.2185383
40. Zave, P.: Reasoning about identifier spaces: how to make chord correct. IEEE Trans. Software Eng. **43**(12), 1144–1156 (2017). https://doi.org/10.1109/TSE.2017.2655056
41. Zheng, G., et al.: ATR: template-based repair for alloy specifications. In: ISSTA 2022, pp. 666–677. ACM (2022). https://doi.org/10.1145/3533767.3534369

On Quantitative Solution Iteration in QAlloy

Pedro Silva[1,3(✉)], Nuno Macedo[2,3], and José N. Oliveira[1,3]

[1] Univ. do Minho, Braga, Portugal
jno@di.uminho.pt
[2] Faculdade de Engenharia, Univ. Porto, Porto, Portugal
nmacedo@fe.up.pt
[3] INESC TEC, Porto, Portugal
pedro.d.silva@inesctec.pt

Abstract. A key feature of model finding techniques allows users to enumerate and explore alternative solutions. However, it is challenging to guarantee that the generated instances are relevant to the user, representing effectively different scenarios.

This challenge is exacerbated in quantitative modelling, where one must consider both the qualitative, structural part of a model, and the quantitative data on top of it. This results in a search space of possibly infinite candidate solutions, often infinitesimally similar to one another. Thus, research on instance enumeration in qualitative model finding is not directly applicable to the quantitative context, which requires more sophisticated methods to navigate the solution space effectively.

The main goal of this paper is to explore a generic approach for navigating quantitative solution spaces and showcase different iteration operations, aiming to generate instances that differ considerably from those previously seen and promote a larger coverage of the search space.

Such operations are implemented in QAlloy – a quantitative extension to Alloy – on top of Max-SMT solvers, and are evaluated against several examples ranging, in particular, over the integer and fuzzy domains.

Keywords: Quantitative Modelling · Scenario Exploration · Model Finding · Alloy · Max-SMT Solvers

1 Introduction

Alloy [9] is a successful, lightweight formal modelling language supported by a model finding and model checking tool-set. The language finds its semantic foundations in relation algebra [26], abstracting as much as possible over concrete data so as to make model checking feasible. Such use of uninterpreted symbols is very welcome in abstract modelling but less handy wherever models involve concrete (e.g. numeric) data types behaving as measures, metrics or quantities. This led to the development of QAlloy [21,22], a quantitative extension to standard Alloy that allows reasoning about quantitative models (e.g. fuzzy).

M. Leuschel and F. Ishikawa (Eds.): ABZ 2025, LNCS 15728, pp. 88–105, 2026.
https://doi.org/10.1007/978-3-031-94533-5_6

A key feature of model discovery techniques is to allow users to explore alternative model instances. However, generating instances that are helpful to the user is challenging [4], and research has focused on providing instances that represent truly different and illustrative scenarios [11,15,29]. This challenge becomes more difficult when considering quantitative models, where not only the qualitative and structural component of a model must be considered, but also its quantitative data.

In fact, quantities introduce a new layer of complexity in model finding because of possible infinite solution spaces. The main contributions of this paper are: *i*) the formalization of iteration operations in the context of quantitative model finding; *ii*) their implementation in QAlloy using its SMT-based backend; *iii*) an evaluation of the approach in terms of performance and diversity of generated instances.

The rest of the paper is structured as follows. Section 2 motivates the work through a couple of examples. Section 3 formalizes the iteration operations, whose implementation in QAlloy is presented in Sect. 4. Section 5 presents the evaluation of the approach proposed. Lastly, Sect. 6 presents related work, followed by conclusions and directions for future work in Sect. 7.

2 Quantitative Enumeration by Example

This section demonstrates the issues related with the iteration over quantitative relational instances and why previously proposed approaches for (qualitative) instance iteration are inadequate in this context. Then we briefly show how the enumeration approach proposed in this paper would result in more varied, and possibly more useful, instance exploration sessions.

We will consider two examples from distinct quantitative domains, one requiring *integer* quantities and another *fuzzy* values (reals between 0 and 1). This will help highlight the challenges that arise in domains that are inherently infinite, the former on its upper and lower bounds, and latter for the infinite number of reals in any interval. For illustration purposes we rely on QAlloy[1], although the discussion applies to quantitative model finding in general.

Example 1: Supermarket Self-Checkout System. Consider a self-checkout system operating in a supermarket: there are *products*, that have a certain `stock` available, and *bags* processed by the system, each `contains` varying amounts of the available products. The system is expected to find inconsistencies, for instance, regarding the products in the bags and available stock. We consider a section of the supermarket handling *tea*, *coffee* and *milk* products. These are packaged in containers of varying sizes, whose *weight* is measured in *oz*, subject to some restrictions guaranteed by the suppliers. Model finding techniques are useful not only to explore scenarios that satisfy certain properties, but also to explore counterexamples that violate certain properties. Consider the verification of the constraint *"if a bag weights more than another, it means that it contains more*

[1] The full QAlloy models used in this section are publicly available [20].

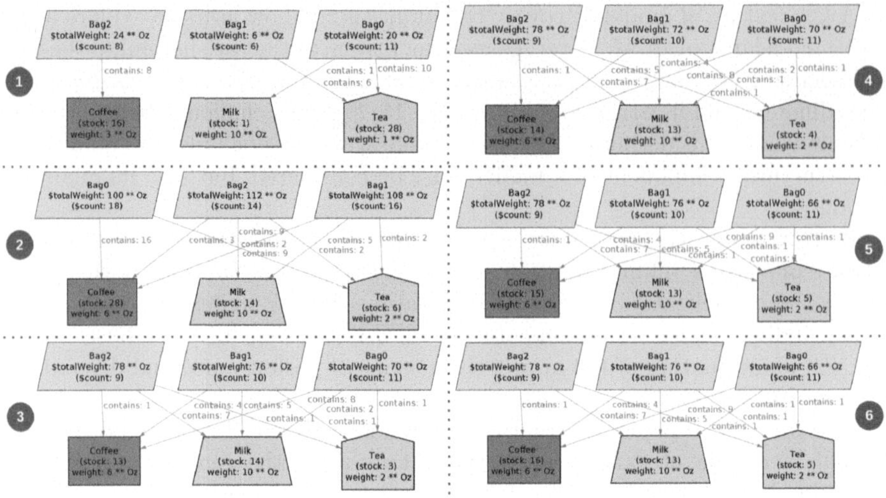

Fig. 1. Naive solution iteration on the supermarket example.

products", which naturally does not hold in general. We modelled this problem in QAlloy [22], and wish to explore its counterexamples.

Naive Iteration. The most basic enumeration in model finding is to remove the current instance from the solution space by negating the current valuation of the model's variables. This is the technique used in Alloy 5 and the current QAlloy. Figure 1 shows the first counterexamples found through this approach.[2]

Two kinds of changes can be identified: in the first two steps there is a change in the *structure* of the instance, albeit a minimal change in the 2nd one. Additionally, in every step there are arbitrary changes in the quantities assigned to the model's elements.[3] After the two first steps, there are no longer any changes in the structure, and only quantities are being changed. This persists through the first 100 instances, with only occasional changes of an edge, while often getting "stuck" for dozens of instances changing the stock of a single item. These instances are valid counterexamples, but they are so similar that the user can easily miss relevant instances evidencing important issues within the model, resulting in a frustrating experience and reduced effectiveness for validation.

Separation of Concerns. The two kinds of change mentioned above are quite different in nature: one affects the structural aspects of the instance and is similar to traditional (qualitative) iteration; the other affects the quantities assigned to

[2] Recall that model finding is often backed by off-the-shelf solvers, so different solvers or configuration may result in a different sequence of instances.

[3] `$totalWeight` and `$count` are not part of the instance, but helper functions showing derived information, respectively the total weight and product count of a bag.

each element of the instance. Mixing these two concepts may result in modifications that may be too difficult for the user to interpret. We propose to factor iteration across two distinct axes: (a) *structure-level methods* will focus in finding instances that are structurally distinct, providing a different support on which to assign quantities, and (b) *quantity-level methods* will focus on finding alternative quantities for a fixed structure. This dichotomy will allow the user to first search for an interesting structure to examine, and then explore alternative quantities over that structure in a more predictable and controlled way; once validated, the user can ask for another structure and repeat the process. Since model finders act on a bounded domain of discourse, iteration over structures is necessarily finite and can be exhausted. This is similar in nature to the approach taken in Alloy 6 when the dynamic aspect was introduced: iteration over the static elements of the instance (its configuration) is distinct from trace iteration over a fixed configuration; likewise, the number of valid configurations is finite, but traces are potentially infinite (if no upper bound is imposed on trace prefix length).

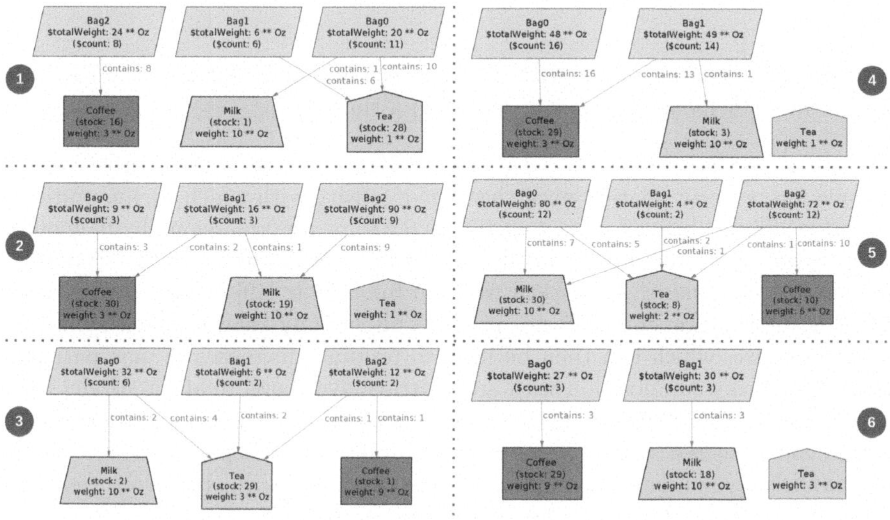

Fig. 2. Structure-level solution iteration on the supermarket example.

The sequence of solutions presented in Fig. 2 was obtained by employing an iteration approach focusing on structural changes. Notice how the instances clearly change shape, illustrating more varied scenarios, with different number of bags and contained products. Once the user finds an instance that requires further analysis, quantities can be varied for that structure. If the 3rd instance in Fig. 2 piqued the interest of the user, the iteration over quantity values only would result in the instances shown in Fig. 3. From one instance to another, there are noticeable changes between variants of the same solution structure-wise, that violate the property. For example, the 1st instance has two bags containing the

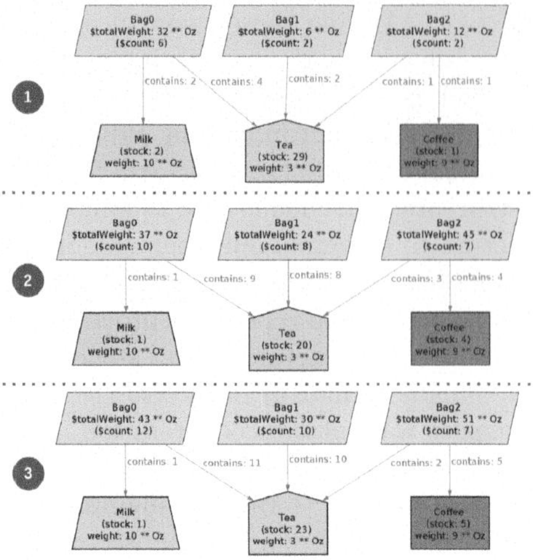

Fig. 3. Quantity-level solution iteration on the supermarket example.

same number of elements but with different weight, while in 2nd two of the bags contain more elements but weight less than a third one.

Example 2: Synthesis of Medical Diagnoses. Consider that medical professionals compile into a fuzzy relation `symptoms` the intensity with which each monitored *patient* is afflicted by each *symptom*. These patients are professionally diagnosed, the information thereof being encoded in a fuzzy relation `diagnostic` from each patient to each *disease*. A classical work on fuzzy logic [19] proposed to synthesize this information into a fuzzy relation `pathology` relating each symptom to each disease, which can then be used to produce diagnoses of new patients, through its fuzzy composition with an arbitrary `symptoms` relation. Model finding can be used to validate relation `pathology` by searching for patients with certain combinations and intensities of symptoms. Given a pre-determined relation `pathology`, suppose one wishes to explore scenarios where *"two patients do not share any common symptoms, but are diagnosed with the same diseases"*.

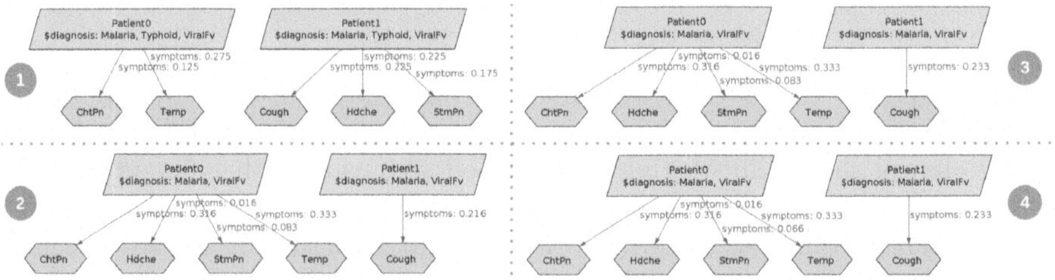

Fig. 4. Naive solution iteration for the medical diagnosis example.

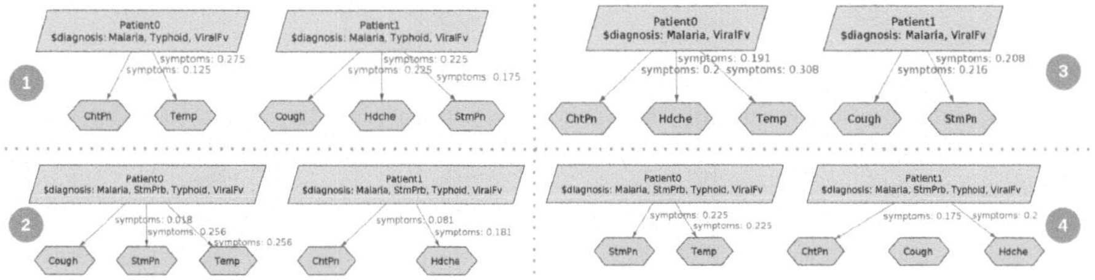

Fig. 5. Structure-level solution iteration for the medical diagnosis example.

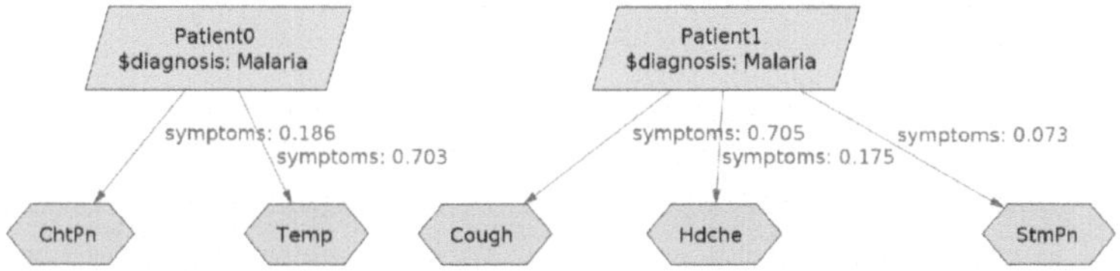

symptoms

Patient^0	ChtPn^0	0.1861572265625
	Temp^0	0.7029052734375
Patient^1	Cough^0	0.7056396484375
	Hdche^0	0.1752197265625
	StmPn^0	0.0733154296875

symptoms

Patient^0	ChtPn^0	0.18624267578125
	Temp^0	0.70316162109375
Patient^1	Cough^0	0.70555419921875
	Hdche^0	0.17530517578125
	StmPn^0	0.07340087890625

symptoms

Patient^0	ChtPn^0	0.186285400390625
	Temp^0	0.703118896484375
Patient^1	Cough^0	0.705596923828125
	Hdche^0	0.175347900390625
	StmPn^0	0.073443603515625

symptoms

Patient^0	ChtPn^0	0.186306762695312 5
	Temp^0	0.7030975341796875
Patient^1	Cough^0	0.7055755615234375
	Hdche^0	0.1753265380859375
	StmPn^0	0.0734649658203125

Fig. 6. Naive quantity-level solution iteration for the medical diagnosis example.

Guided Iteration. Having modelled this problem in QAlloy [21], Fig. 4 depicts the first instances obtained using the naive iteration approach. Similarly to example 1, only the 1st and 2nd solutions vary significantly, both patients showing the same symptoms thereafter, in very similar intensities. Therefore, the resulting diagnosis is always the same.[4] Let us apply the structure/quantity-level operations discussed previously. The former, shown in Fig. 5, leads to different combinations of symptoms under the imposed restrictions (patients with the same diagnosis). Meanwhile, quantity iterations show change in symptom intensity and a possible change in the diagnosis outcome. However, after a few more iterations, the process "converges" into the one presented in Fig. 6, producing solutions which are infinitesimally different from one another. Tabular information is shown since they are indistinguishable in the graphic representation due to rounding.

Clearly, naive quantity-level iteration is still insufficient, for such iteration operations should ensure more "vectorial distance" among instances. This problem, already explored in the qualitative setting [11], is more complex in quantitative domains: one cannot ask for instances that are furthest away from the *current* instance, because this would result in a "ping-pong" between two sets of marginally different instances. Instead, to guarantee a good coverage of the search space, one must generate instances that are far from all previously seen instances. Figure 7 displays one such enumeration, starting from the 1st solution

[4] Relation `$diagnosis` is a derived relation selecting the most likely disease(s).

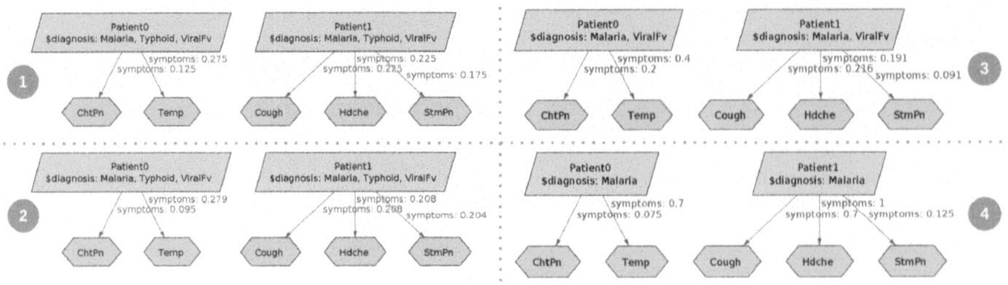

Fig. 7. Guided quantity-level solution iteration for the medical diagnosis example.

found, from which three different diagnosis were quickly found. These varied scenarios may be essential for field experts to validate and refine the diagnosis relation, unlike the very similar scenarios resulting from naive iteration operations.

In summary, our main insights for this work are that *i*) iteration over structural and quantitative aspects must be provided as separate operations, and that *ii*) the latter must be guided in order to guarantee sufficiently varied instances.

3 Solution Iteration

Quantitative Relational Model Finding. A quantitative, relational model finding *problem* Q is a tuple $\langle \mathcal{M}, L, U, \phi, \mathcal{S} \rangle$, where:

- $\mathcal{M}$ is a tuple $\langle \mathbb{D}, \mathcal{U}, L_0, U_0 \rangle$ containing the static information of the problem, namely the quantitative domain (such as integers, fuzzy values, or reals) $\mathbb{D}$, the universe of atoms $\mathcal{U}$, and the original lower- and upper-bounds L_0 and U_0, which are qualitative bindings $\mathcal{R} \to \mathcal{P}(\mathcal{T_U})$ where $\mathcal{T_U}$ is the set of atom tuples from $\mathcal{U}$, setting the upper- and lower-bounds of free relations $\mathcal{R}$;
- $L, U : \mathcal{R} \to \mathcal{P}(\mathcal{T_U})$ are the current lower- and upper-bounds such that, for any $r \in \mathcal{R}$, $L(r) \subseteq U(r)$;
- ϕ is a relational formula over variables from $\mathcal{R}$;
- $\mathcal{S}$ a set of bindings from which the instance is to be distanced.

An *instance* is a quantitative binding $I : \mathcal{R} \to \mathcal{T_U} \to \mathbb{D}$ that, for each relation $r \in \mathcal{R}$, assigns a quantity from $\mathbb{D}$ to each tuple from $\mathcal{T_U}$. The support of I is a qualitative binding supp $I : \mathcal{R} \to \mathcal{P}(\mathcal{T_U})$, such that for each relation $r \in \mathcal{R}$, $t \in$ supp $I(r)$ iff $I(r)(t) \neq 0$. An instance I is a *solution* to a problem $Q = \langle \mathcal{M}, L, U, \phi, \mathcal{S} \rangle$, denoted by $I \models Q$, if for any relation $r \in \mathcal{R}$, $L(r) \subseteq$ supp $I(r) \subseteq U(r)$, and ϕ holds. Additionally, the solver will try to optimize the distance of the newly generated solution from the set $\mathcal{S}$. We will allow $\mathcal{S}$ to contain both qualitative and quantitative bindings, and assume that the model finder adapts the distance measures accordingly. (More about this in Sect. 4.)

As a simple example, consider a problem with 3 relations declared with the following lower- and upper-bounds: unary (i.e., sets) $\{\} \subseteq X \subseteq \{(x), (y)\}$ and

$\{\} \subseteq Y \subseteq \{(w), (z)\}$, and binary $\{\} \subseteq R \subseteq \{(x, w), (x, z), (y, w), (y, z)\}$, and a constraint ϕ imposing $R \subseteq X \times Y$. A possible valid solution for $\mathbb{D} = \mathbb{Z}$ would be the following, omitting the zero-valued tuples:

$$\begin{aligned} I =& \{X \mapsto (x) \mapsto 1, Y \mapsto (w) \mapsto 1, Y \mapsto (z) \mapsto 2, \\ & R \mapsto (x, w) \mapsto 5, R \mapsto (x, z) \mapsto 7\} \quad . \end{aligned}$$

An *iteration* is an operation that, given a problem Q and a solution (quantitative binding) I, returns a new problem to generate a new solution. For instance, the naive iteration, denoted by next, is simply defined as:

$$\mathsf{next}(\langle \mathcal{M}, L, U, \phi, \_ \rangle, I) = \langle \mathcal{M}, L, U, \phi \wedge \neg [\![I]\!], \emptyset \rangle$$

where $[\![I]\!]$ produces a formula that exactly represents I, which is excluded as a possible solution by being negated into ϕ. $\mathcal{S}$ is set to $\emptyset$ since there is no distance goal in next. This guarantees that no identical instance is returned, i.e.:

$$\forall I' \cdot I' \models \mathsf{next}(Q, I) \Rightarrow I \neq I'$$

Subsequent applications of next accumulate negated solutions in ϕ, so no two identical instances are ever returned.

Structure-Level Iteration. These iterations, which we shall denote as variants of a next_S operation for different optimization goals, are expected to produce a new solution with a different structure, i.e., abiding to the following property:

$$\forall I' \cdot I' \models \mathsf{next}_S(Q, I) \Rightarrow \text{supp } I \neq \text{supp } I'$$

Without a distance goal, this operation essentially removes the current structure from the search space:

$$\mathsf{next}_S^{\emptyset}(\langle \mathcal{M}, \_, \_, \phi, \_ \rangle, I) = \langle \mathcal{M}, L_0, U_0, \phi \wedge \neg [\![\text{supp } I]\!], \emptyset \rangle$$

Note the abuse of notation in denoting by $[\![\text{supp } I]\!]$ the translation of a qualitative binding into a formula that just determines whether tuples are present in the solution, regardless of the associated quantity (i.e., whether their value is zero). Notice how the bounds must be reset by this operation: the quantitative-level iterations (presented next), force a particular structure by tightening the bounds, which must be reset whenever a new structure is requested.

Without any optimization goal, $\mathsf{next}_S^{\emptyset}$ behaves essentially like a qualitative iteration, ignoring the quantities. If we wish to explore more varied structures, a distance goal must be set. This is similar to target-oriented operations proposed for the qualitative context [11]. As an example, consider an operation next_S^{B} that tries to produce maximally different structures.

$$\mathsf{next}_S^{B}(\langle \mathcal{M}, \_, \_, \phi, \_ \rangle, I) = \langle \mathcal{M}, L_0, U_0, \phi \wedge \neg [\![\text{supp } I]\!], \{\text{supp } I\} \rangle$$

The distance goal is simply the support of the previous instance, so that the structure of the next solution is as distinct as possible. Notice that the previous goal is ignored, including any instances accumulated by the quantitative-level iterations (presented next).

Quantity-Level Iteration. Enumerating over quantities of a particular structure, a class of operations to be denoted by variants of next_Q, must satisfy two invariants: that the solutions preserve the specified structure throughout such enumeration steps (or until there are no more solutions of this kind respecting the model's constraints), and that some quantity changes:

$$\forall I' \cdot I' \models \mathsf{next}_Q(Q, I) \Rightarrow \text{supp } I = \text{supp } I' \wedge I \neq I'$$

The naive quantitative-level iteration $\mathsf{next}_Q^{\emptyset}$ will allow quantities to change arbitrarily. Formally:

$$\mathsf{next}_Q^{\emptyset}(\langle \mathcal{M}, \_, \_, \phi, \_ \rangle, I) = \langle \mathcal{M}, \text{supp } I, \text{supp } I, \phi \wedge \neg [\![I]\!], \emptyset \rangle$$

Note how the lower- and upper-bounds are fixed with the support of I, forcing the exact same tuples to exist in the next solution.

To produce solutions that are maximally distinct, note that one cannot simply ask for quantities further away from the current I, because in dense domains such as the fuzzy one, this could result in a "ping-pong" behaviour between two sets of similar solutions. Thus, we must accumulate all previously seen solutions as the distance goal. Structure-level iterations always reset $\mathcal{S}$, so these operations only consider the distance to solutions for the currently fixed structure.

$$\mathsf{next}_Q^{\mathcal{S}}(\langle \mathcal{M}, \_, \_, \phi, \mathcal{S} \rangle, I) = \langle \mathcal{M}, \text{supp } I, \text{supp } I, \phi \wedge \neg [\![I]\!], \mathcal{S} \cup \{I\} \rangle$$

4 Quantitative Iteration in QAlloy

The authors have previously proposed an extension to Alloy to allow quantitative relational modelling – QAlloy—which currently supports both the integer and fuzzy domains. This section describes how the iteration operations from the previous section were integrated into the model finding backend of QAlloy, briefly introducing the QAlloy infrastructure as needed.[5] For a more detailed description of QAlloy, the interested reader is redirected to [21,22].

QAlloy and its Analyzer. At the language level, the key extension of QAlloy is the introduction of n-ary quantitative relations through special keywords, whose tuples will be assigned values from the selected domain ($\mathbb{Z}$ for **int** and $[0, 1] \subseteq \mathbb{R}$ for **fuzzy**), the 0 quantity representing the tuple's absence from the relation. The semantics of the relational operators (e.g. relational composition) were adapted accordingly, preserving the bulk of the language and retro-compatibility in case only Boolean relations are used. A particularity is that numerical constants cannot be declared standalone, but rather associated with an element from $\mathcal{U}$, i.e., they are "typed" and thus benefit from the Alloy's type system. This promotes a more rigorous usage of *units*, which are often the source of issues in software (e.g., combining two quantities of "incompatible units" throws a type error).

[5] QAlloy is an extension to Alloy 5; migration into Alloy 6 is underway, but currently the temporal aspect introduced in this latest release is not supported.

Both the Alloy Analyzer and the underlying Kodkod [27] relational model finder have been extended to handle quantitative relational models. Kodkod's Boolean structures managing relations and operations between them were extended to numerical ones, namely representing quantitative relations through numerical matrices. Relational operations are thus defined by linear algebra. To actually solve a model finding problem, Kodkod's SAT solver backend was switched to one that relies on off-the-shelf SMT solvers. The results are then provided back to the Analyzer whose visualizer and evaluator were adapted to the quantitative context, as shown in the examples of Sect. 2.

The two new classes of iterations, whose implementation is detailed next, are provided to the user in the visualizer's toolbar with buttons "`Next Structure`" and "`Next Quantity`", in contrast to the single "`Next`" of Alloy 5.

Quantitative iteration in Kodkod As highlighted in Sect. 2, Kodkod's iteration (operation next) is not effective in quantitative problems. Thus, the alternative iteration methods proposed in Sect. 3 were implemented at the Kodkod level. Since these require optimization capabilities, we rely on Max-SMT solvers [16] which allow the definition of optimization goals.

The SMT specification for a given quantitative model finding problem Q defines its primary variables through *function symbols*. When $\mathbb{D} = \mathbb{Z}$, the function symbols are declared as integer-valued, with the solving process being executed according to the *Theory of Integers* using the logical fragment `QF_NIA`; for $\mathbb{D} = [0, 1] \subseteq \mathbb{R}$, the function symbols are specified as reals and the `QF_NRA` of the *Theory of Reals* is used instead. Each free n-ary relation $r \in \mathcal{R}$ is encoded as a $|\mathcal{U}|^n$ matrix; each matrix element gives origin to a free variable at SMT-level, denoting the value of an n-ary tuple t in r. Let `r_t` be such a primary SMT variable. If a tuple t is in the lower-bound of $L(r)$, `r_t` is forced is be non-zero; if it is outside the upper-bound of $U(r)$, it is forced to be zero.

Table 1. SMT encoding of bindings for n_i-ary relations $r_i \in \mathcal{R}$ and tuples $t_j^{n_i} \in \mathcal{T}_\mathcal{U}$

Binding	SMT encoding	$f(r,t)$
$\neg[\![B]\!]$	`(assert (or` $f(r_0, t_0^{n_0})$ $f(r_0, t_1^{n_0})$ ... $f(r_k, t_{\lvert\mathcal{U}\rvert^{n_k}}^{n_k})$`)))`	`(not (= r_t 0))` if $B(r)(t) = 0$ `(= r_t 0)` otherwise
$\neg[\![I]\!]$	`(assert (or` $f(r_0, t_0^{n_0})$ $f(r_0, t_1^{n_0})$ ... $f(r_k, t_{\lvert\mathcal{U}\rvert^{n_k}}^{n_k})$`)))`	`(not (= r_t v))` where $v = I(r)(t)$

Constraints over function symbols are imposed through *assertions*, which are managed in the solver's **Assertion Stack**. This structure supports *push* and *pop* operations to manage assertions at different levels, and commands such as e.g. `(check-sat)`—which is used to determine the satisfiability of the model—take into account every declaration and assertion up to the level of the stack where it is being called. Thus, although formally a new problem is generated whenever an iteration is applied, for performance issues we actually preserve the SMT problem running between iterations and update the stack accordingly. The problem's constraint ϕ is set at the base level of the assertion stack, meaning that it is always considered; meanwhile, temporary constraints might be considered in a new level through *push*, and later on may be disregarded using *pop*, enabling the application of different iteration operations. Two kinds of additional constraints can occur in a problem Q: (a) imposing additional lower- or upper-bounds adds constraints to the primary variables, which are popped when reset into L_0 and U_0; and (b) introducing additional constraints $\neg[\![B]\!]$ and $\neg[\![I]\!]$ for qualitative and quantitative bindings, respectively, whose translation is shown in Table 1. These assertions are pushed after every solution is found and are never popped, so the removal of a solution from the search space is permanent.

Table 2. SMT incremental goals for n_i-ary relations $r_i \in \mathcal{R}$ and tuples $t_j^{n_i} \in \mathcal{T}_\mathcal{U}$

Goal	SMT encoding	$d(r,t)$

B	`(assert-soft` $d(r_0, t_0^{n_0})$`)`
	`(assert-soft` $d(r_0, t_1^{n_0})$`)`
	...
	`(assert-soft` $d(r_k, t_{\lvert\mathcal{U}\rvert^{n_k}}^{n_k})$`)`
		`(not (= r_t 0))` if $B(r)(t) = 0$
		`(= r_t 0)` otherwise

I_{SDST}	`(maximize (+` $d(r_0, t_0^{n_0})$`)` $d(r_0, t_1^{n_0})$ `...` $d(r_k, t_{\lvert\mathcal{U}\rvert^{n_k}}^{n_k})$`)))`	`(ite (> r_t v) (- r_t v) (- v r_t))` where $v = I(r)(t)$

I_{VDST}	`(maximize` $d(r_0, t_0)$`)`
	`(maximize` $d(r_0, t_1)$`)`
	...
	`(maximize` $d(r_k, t_{\lvert\mathcal{U}\rvert^{\lvert r_k\rvert}})$`)`	

Max-SMT solvers provide optimization commands such as `(maximize t)`, which signal the solver to maximize the value of term `t` according to the stack's assertions; and `(assert-soft a)` to declare soft-constraints, whose validity is not required, but the solver will attempt to maximize the number of soft-constraints which can hold. These features can be used to implement different goals in guided iterations. The goal is to generate a solution that is as further away from a set of bindings $\mathcal{S}$, but since $\mathcal{S}$ grows incrementally with each new instance, we can also incrementally accumulate goals in the assertion stack (until it is reset by a structure-level operation, in which case the goals must be popped). Table 2 shows the encoding for single qualitative and quantitative bindings. It should be noted that the shown encoding implements the Manhattan distance between bindings (i.e., the sum of differences), rather than the more classical Euclidean distance. Our early experiments showed that the latter weighted heavily on the underlying solvers, due to the usage of exponentiation and square root operations. Evaluation in the next section will show that this still produced reasonable results with acceptable performance.

Two alternative encodings are shown for a quantitative binding I: one maximizes the distance to the instance (SDST), the other the distance to each tuple of the instance individually (VDST). Although these are semantically equivalent, Max-SMT solvers perform differently in multi-objective optimization problems. In order to further mitigate this issue, we explore alternative goal implementations that reduce the number of objectives by considering the average of all seen

Table 3. SMT batch goals for n_i-ary relations $r_i \in \mathcal{R}$ and tuples $t_j^{n_i} \in \mathcal{T}_\mathcal{U}$

Goal	SMT encoding	$d(r,t)$
I_{SAvg}	`(maximize (+` $d(r_0, t_0^{n_0})$ $d(r_0, t_1^{n_0})$ ... $d(r_k, t_{\lvert\mathcal{U}\rvert^{n_k}}^{n_k})$`)))`	`(ite (> r_t v) (- r_t v) (- v r_t))` where $v = \frac{\sum_{I \in \mathcal{S}} I(r)(t)}{\lvert\mathcal{S}\rvert}$

I_{VAvg}	`(maximize` $d(r_0, t_0^{n_0})$`)`
	`(maximize` $d(r_0, t_1^{n_0})$`)`
	...
	`(maximize` $d(r_k, t_{\lvert\mathcal{U}\rvert^{n_k}}^{n_k})$`)`	

bindings (SAvg and VAvg, respectively). The trade-off is that these averages are updated in each iteration, so these objectives must be popped from the stack at each iteration. Their encoding is shown in Table 3 (focusing on quantitative cases, since structure-level goals consider a single previous binding). Max-SMT solvers use different **priorities** towards which the goals should be optimized, including a *lexicografic* order; an *independent box objective* that attempts to find a solution where every goal is maximal; or through *pareto fronts*. These vary in performance and may reach different solutions; we evaluate these alternatives in the next section.

Unbounded Domains. As one might expect, when using optimization goals for problems which are neither implicitly nor explicitly bounded, the optimization goal may be infinitely valued. In these situations Max-SMT solvers report that a goal is unbounded, alongside a non-optimal solution. Our current implementation reports this to the user, but still providing the valid, but not-optimal, solution. The user is nonetheless advised to restrict the quantitative model with additional constraints to bound the values of the quantitative relations.

5 Evaluation

This section evaluates the proposed quantitative solution-iterations and their implementation in a Max-SMT backend through QAlloy. We shall be interested in assessing not only performance but also how varied the generated solutions are. While we are aware that assessing the quality of the generated instances requires proper user studies, we consider their variety to be a prerequisite for useful iteration sessions, this leading to the following research questions:

RQ1 How efficient is the SMT implementation of the quantitative iterations?
RQ2 Which iterations produce more varied solutions within their class?
RQ3 How efficient is the detection of infinitely-valued optimization goals?

To answer these questions, we consider several QAlloy examples. We consider a very simple model of a point in the Cartesian plane in both the integer and fuzzy domains, which proved useful to visualize the impact of the iterations in the solution space. In the integer domain, these include the supermarket self-checkout system addressed in Sect. 2; a model of quantitative properties over vertex-labelled graphs; a model for a simple electronic purse and the transference operations between them; two variants of flow networks, with the flow that passes through the network being untyped in the first example, and explicitly typed as *litres* in the second. In the fuzzy domain, problems include the QAlloy medical diagnosis showcased in Sect. 2, as well as an *intuitionistic* variant [5]; fuzzy clustering applied to grouping portraits based on visual similarity [25]; two distinct models of fuzzy controllers, one an automatic heater using the Mamdani fuzzy inference system, and the other a tipping system according to the service and food appraisal, modelled as a Sugeno fuzzy inference system [12,18,24].

We selected 19 commands for these models, all satisfiable in order to allow for iteration (i.e., either run commands generating instances or check commands generating counterexamples).[6] To answer **RQ1** and **RQ2**, all these commands acted on variables bounded by the model. To answer **RQ3**, variants of 4 commands were considered that left some variables unbounded. The ν_Z [2] (v4.8.12) Max-SMT solver was used at the backend.[7] All commands were run with the alternative distance measures presented in Sect. 4, and with alternative priority strategies in multi-objective problems. All tests were run in a machine equipped with a deca-core Intel Core i7-1355U @ 1.30 GHz with 16 GB of RAM. QAlloy ran with 8192 MB maximum memory and 8192k of maximum stack size. For all commands, each iteration operation was applied up to 30 times or until unsatisfiable (i.e., no more solutions). For the initial execution of a command, a timeout of 10 min was considered, while a timeout of 1 min was set for every iteration step. All QAlloy models, the benchmark script and the execution results, as well as summary tables, are publicly available [20].

Table 4. Aggregated results for the first 10 applications of next_S variants.

Operation	$\mu_{min}(ms)$	$\mu_{max}(ms)$	μ_N	σ_N	$t_{out}(\%)$	$\mu_{<1}(\%)$	$\mu_{<10}(\%)$	μ_D	σ_D
next	2	1928	4	24	0.0	94.74	100.0	5	67
$\mathsf{next}_S^{\emptyset}$	1	848	13	47	5.26	94.74	94.74	66	22
next_S^{B}	3	5812	100	65	10.53	68.42	89.47	100	57

Tables 4 and 5 summarize the results for the first 10 instances produced with structure- and quantity-level iterations, respectively. Each G_P in column "Goal" of Table 5 represents running operation I_G (see Tables 2 and 3), employing the priority P for those implementing multiple optimization goals (either "LEXicographic order", "independent BOX objective" or "PAReto fronts"). Regarding execution time, μ_{min} and μ_{max} show the lowest and highest (excluding timeouts) response times produced by each method, in milliseconds; columns

[6] For fuzzy problems, the popular Gödelian t-norm was selected.

[7] We focused on ν_Z as the most popular and stable Max-SMT solver, but it could be easily swapped by others conforming to SMT-LIB.

Table 5. Aggregated results for the first 10 applications of next_Q variants.

Operation	Goal	$\mu_{min}(ms)$	$\mu_{max}(ms)$	μ_N	σ_N	$t_{out}(\%)$	$\mu_{<1}(\%)$	$\mu_{<10}(\%)$	μ_D	σ_D
$\text{next}_Q^{\emptyset}$	NA	2	187	0	0	0.0	100.0	100.0	11	15
next_Q^S	SDSTBOX	18	3934	74	74	21.05	47.37	78.95	17	45
	SDSTLEX	14	4352	33	23	15.79	78.95	84.21	12	42
	SDSTPAR	7	34	13	4	57.89	42.11	42.11	21	26
	VDSTBOX	22	6773	73	77	31.58	52.63	68.42	26	24
	VDSTLEX	13	5969	30	17	10.53	78.95	89.47	9	37
	VDSTPAR	15	33	16	4	68.42	31.58	31.58	13	17
	VAVGBOX	8	11512	25	13	21.05	73.68	73.68	51	31
	VAVGLEX	7	1706	16	2	10.53	84.21	89.47	74	69
	VAVGPAR	9	37	43	6	68.42	31.58	31.58	33	29
	SAVG	5	7082	26	6	10.53	84.21	89.47	76	63

μ_N and σ_N display the response times after normalization between commands (ranging from 0 to 100, the lower the better); t_{out} measures the % of commands which reached a timeout, and $\mu_{<1}$ and $\mu_{<10}$ show the % of commands whose response time was lower than 1 and 10 seconds on average, respectively. Regarding the variety of the produced solutions, μ_D and σ_D evaluate the average distance between every pair of generated solutions, also normalized for each command. For structure-level iterations, quantities are disregarded when measuring distances, amounting to the set difference of the supports. For quantity-level iterations, although the implementation relied on the Manhattan distance, for evaluation we consider the ideal Euclidean distance. In order for the comparison to be fair, only commands that do not hit a timeout are considered in these metrics (since a smaller number of instances is more likely to be varied). For example, VDST$_{\text{PAR}}$, shows low response times, but a high timeout rate of $\sim 70\%$; the times measured refer only to the $\sim 30\%$ commands where it did *not* timeout. Table 4 also presents the results for the naive approach as a baseline, but this comparison must be made with care since next was not designed to produce varied solutions.

RQ1 and RQ2. Focusing first on the performance of structure-level iterations (**RQ1**), $\text{next}_S^{\emptyset}$ finds solutions in line with the naive approach next (its response time, bar timeouts, does not exceed $0.9s$ (seconds) on average), while next_S^B is an order of magnitude slower but without exceeding $6s$ on average. Moreover, both methods are overall consistent in finding answers without hitting timeout, with a low rate of $\sim 5\%$ and $\sim 10\%$, respectively. Regarding **RQ2**, the difference in variety from the baseline next to both methods is large, as expected; moreover, next_S^B consistently produces the most varied set of solutions for almost every command. When extending the analysis to the first 30 solutions (full data available at [20]), there is a slight increase of timeouts for the naive approach and

$\mathsf{next}_S^{\emptyset}$, but not for next_S^{B}, without significant changes in the normalized variety of solutions.

Moving on to quantity-level iterations, we consider $\mathsf{next}_Q^{\emptyset}$ as a baseline, since it fixes the structure of the solution but changes quantities arbitrarily (next can change the structure, making the comparison more complicated). Regarding response time (**RQ1**), it is apparent that in multi-objective encodings the pareto (PAR) priority results in timeouts for most commands (57–69%). At the other end of the spectrum, VDST$_{\text{LEX}}$, VAVG$_{\text{LEX}}$ and SAVG display the lowest amounts of timeouts ($\sim$ 10%), while VAVG$_{\text{LEX}}$, SAVG and VAVG$_{\text{BOX}}$ have the best performance (lowest average mean and average standard deviation); when these methods do not timeout, they do not exceed $12s$ on average. Focusing on the distance metrics (**RQ2**), the same configurations overall show significant improvements in the solution variety. VAVG$_{\text{BOX}}$ (high mean and low variance), VAVG$_{\text{LEX}}$ (high mean and highest variance) and SAVG (highest mean and high variance) are the quantity-level iterations generating solutions in a richer way. Note that higher values of mean and standard deviation indicate larger differences between the solutions produced. When considering the first 30 solutions, there is a noticeable decrease in solution distance (which is expected, since more of the search space has been covered), but VAVG$_{\text{BOX}}$, VAVG$_{\text{LEX}}$ and SAVG still show the best variety. SDST$_{\text{BOX}}$ and VDST$_{\text{BOX}}$ suffer from an increase in timeouts (of $\sim$ 20% and $\sim$ 10%, respectively) and their average response times are on the higher end. This is perhaps not surprising, as both methods cumulatively add assertions to the stack in each iteration, so while the initial solutions may be found faster and be varied, it will be harder for the solver to find varied solutions while meeting every optimization goal. Besides these, SDST$_{\text{LEX}}$ shows an increase of $\sim$ 5% timeouts, while the rate for the remaining quantity-level methods is unaffected.

Table 6. Examples which lead to infinite optimization goals.

Operation	Goal	$\mu_{min}(ms)$	$\mu_{max}(ms)$	μ_N	σ_N	$i_{tout}(\%)$	$t_{out}(\%)$	$\mu_{<1}(\%)$	$\mu_{<10}(\%)$	μ_D	σ_D
$\mathsf{next}_Q^{\emptyset}$		2	29	0	6	0	0	100	100	0	2
next_Q^{S}	SDST$_{\text{BOX}}$	7	5975	76	75	0	0	75	100	54	52
	SDST$_{\text{LEX}}$	4	119	14	14	0	0	100	100	10	8
	SDST$_{\text{PAR}}$	*NA*	*NA*	*NA*	*NA*	0	100	0	0	*NA*	*NA*
	VDST$_{\text{BOX}}$	6	947	87	90	25	50	50	50	50	50
	VDST$_{\text{LEX}}$	5	60	21	9	0	0	100	100	5	2
	VDST$_{\text{PAR}}$	*NA*	*NA*	*NA*	*NA*	100	100	0	0	*NA*	*NA*
	VAVG$_{\text{BOX}}$	4	29	13	0	0	50	50	50	59	51
	VAVG$_{\text{LEX}}$	3	46	7	6	0	0	100	100	33	28
	VAVG$_{\text{PAR}}$	*NA*	*NA*	*NA*	*NA*	100	100	0	0	*NA*	*NA*
	SAVG	3	48	7	0	0	0	100	100	31	26

RQ3. Table 6 addresses iterations that make use of Max-SMT optimization capabilities, for commands that lead to unbounded optimization goals, resulting in an infinite outcome (a special case of a satisfiable outcome). It has an extra column i_{tout} presenting the % of commands that reached a timeout on the *first* iteration, representing cases where the user is not informed of the unbounded nature of the command; t_{out} still identifies the cases where a timeout was *eventually* reached. Column i_{tout} shows three cases where the user is not properly informed. Notice also that there are now no methods on the higher-end of the distance metric; since solutions are no longer optimal, results are much less predictable.

6 Related Work

There is considerable literature on controlling how solutions are generated in *qualitative* model finding. The authors of [11] introduce the concept of weighted target-oriented model finding, which was subsequently used in solution enumeration operations [11]. These relied on (partial) maximum satisfiability (Max-SAT) solvers, as do subsequent approaches, namely Aluminum [15] and Bordeaux [13]. REACH [10] enumerates solutions ordered by size (smallest to largest). At the GUI-level, HawkEye [23] allows the user to control the next solutions by manipulating the instance in the visualizer. Few works have tried to effectively measure the impact of the different provided solutions through user studies [3,4].

Focusing on SMT solvers, path exploration work (e.g. [28]), inspired by testing techniques, tries to generate instances that cover different valuations of SMT formulas; SMT sampling approaches focus on generating stimuli to ensure "good coverage" (e.g. according to user-defined criteria) of the solution space. They include SMTSampler [7] and GuidedSampler [8], which only support theories of bit-vectors, arrays, and uninterpreted functions, and MeGASampler [17], that provides an heuristic using a theory of intervals to support the theory of integer arithmetic (without division). However, it remains unclear how iteration at the SMT-level would reflect at more abstract level of model finding problems. In contrast, similarly to qualitative approaches based on Max-SAT, we took advantage of Max-SMT solvers to achieve diverse quantitative enumeration, whose distance goals are provided at the model finding problem level. Moreover, many of these approaches require further user input, while we believe that, at model finding level operations should be provided with "push-button" simplicity.

Another technique employed by model finders is symmetry breaking, to avoid the generation of isomorphic solutions, which Kodkod in particular implements at the SAT level [27]. There is some work on symmetry breaking at the SMT level. SyMT [1] provides an approach centered in building coloured graphs from SMT formulas and finding said graphs' automorphisms, representing the problem's symmetries. CVC4-SymBreak [6] makes use of the SyMT tool, but rather to exploit the symmetries of the SAT module of the SMT solving process.

7 Conclusions and Future Work

This paper proposes a formalization of solution enumeration operations in quantitative relational model finding, considering distinct operations for changes to the structure and to the quantities. An implementation of these operations on top of Max-SMT solvers is provided, whose evaluation shows to be performant and capable of generating solutions with a high degree of variability.

There are a few directions along which this work may evolve. Symmetry breaking is still unaddressed at the quantitative model finding level, despite works at the SMT level. Our formalization could be extended with further information, such as providing different weights to the relations, or considering user information provided through the instance visualizer. More advanced operations may require information from the problem's constraints (e.g., to satisfy different properties regardless of the distance to the seen solutions). Relevant insights may come from data-driven search-based techniques [14] used in software engineering, for instance, for test case generation.

QAlloy is also being migrated to the most recent Alloy 6 release, whose temporal dimension introduces an additional layer of complexity in iteration.

Last but not least, and perhaps most important: to effectively assess the quality of the generated solutions, thorough user studies must be performed.

Acknowledgements. This work is financed by National Funds through the Portuguese funding agency, FCT - Fundação para a Ciência e a Tecnologia, within project LA/P/0063/2020 (DOI 10.54499/LA/P/0063/2020). J.N. Oliveira is also supported by project FCT: PTDC/CCI-COM/4280/2021 and P. Silva holds FCT grant 2023.01186.BD.

References

1. Areces, C., Déharbe, D., Fontaine, P., Ezequiel, O.: SyMT: finding symmetries in SMT formulas. In: SMT Workshop (2013)
2. Bjørner, N.S., Phan, A.: νz-maximal satisfaction with Z3. In: SCSS. EPiC Series in Computing, vol. 30, pp. 1–9. EasyChair (2014)
3. Cunha, A., Macedo, N., Campos, J.C., Margolis, I., Sousa, E.: Assessing the impact of hints in learning formal specification. In: SEET@ICSE, pp. 151–161. ACM (2024)
4. Danas, N., Nelson, T., Harrison, L., Krishnamurthi, S., Dougherty, D.J.: User studies of principled model finder output. In: Cimatti, A., Sirjani, M. (eds.) SEFM 2017. LNCS, vol. 10469, pp. 168–184. Springer, Cham (2017). https://doi.org/10.1007/978-3-319-66197-1_11
5. De, S.K., Biswas, R., Roy, A.R.: An application of intuitionistic fuzzy sets in medical diagnosis. Fuzzy Sets Syst. **117**(2), 209–213 (2001)
6. Dingliwal, S., Agarwal, R., Mittal, H., Singla, P.: Advances in symmetry breaking for SAT Modulo Theories (2020). https://arxiv.org/abs/1908.00860
7. Dutra, R., Bachrach, J., Sen, K.: SMTSampler: efficient stimulus generation from complex SMT constraints. In: ICCAD, p. 30. ACM (2018)
8. Dutra, R., Bachrach, J., Sen, K.: GUIDEDSAMPLER: coverage-guided sampling of SMT solutions. In: FMCAD, pp. 203–211 (2019)

9. Jackson, D.: Alloy: a language and tool for exploring software designs. Commun. ACM **62**(9), 66–76 (2019)
10. Jovanovic, A., Sullivan, A.: REACH: refining Alloy scenarios by size (tools and artifact track). In: ISSRE, pp. 229–238. IEEE (2022)
11. Macedo, N., Cunha, A., Guimarães, T.: Exploring scenario exploration. In: Egyed, A., Schaefer, I. (eds.) FASE 2015. LNCS, vol. 9033, pp. 301–315. Springer, Heidelberg (2015). https://doi.org/10.1007/978-3-662-46675-9_20
12. Mamdani, E., Assilian, S.: An experiment in linguistic synthesis with a fuzzy logic controller. Int. J. Man-Mach. Stud. **7**(1), 1–13 (1975)
13. Montaghami, V., Rayside, D.: Bordeaux: a tool for thinking outside the box. In: Huisman, M., Rubin, J. (eds.) FASE 2017. LNCS, vol. 10202, pp. 22–39. Springer, Heidelberg (2017). https://doi.org/10.1007/978-3-662-54494-5_2
14. Nair, V., et al.: Data-driven search-based software engineering. CoRR **abs/1801.10241** (2018)
15. Nelson, T., Saghafi, S., Dougherty, D.J., Fisler, K., Krishnamurthi, S.: Aluminum: principled scenario exploration through minimality. In: ICSE, pp. 232–241. IEEE Computer Society (2013)
16. Nieuwenhuis, R., Oliveras, A.: On SAT modulo theories and optimization problems. In: Biere, A., Gomes, C.P. (eds.) SAT 2006. LNCS, vol. 4121, pp. 156–169. Springer, Heidelberg (2006). https://doi.org/10.1007/11814948_18
17. Peled, M., Rothenberg, B., Itzhaky, S.: SMT sampling via model-guided approximation. In: FM. LNCS, vol. 14000, pp. 74–91. Springer, Cham (2023)
18. Reznik, L.: Fuzzy Controllers Handbook: How to Design Them, How They Work. Elsevier (1997)
19. Sanchez, E.: Solutions in composite fuzzy relation equations: application to medical diagnosis in brouwerian logic. In: Readings in Fuzzy Sets for Intelligent Systems, pp. 159–165. Morgan Kaufmann (1993)
20. Silva, P.: QAlloy repository – quantitative solution iteration (2025). https://github.com/pf7/QAlloy-QSI
21. Silva, P., Cunha, A., Macedo, N., Oliveira, J.N.: Alloy goes fuzzy. In: ABZ. LNCS, vol. 14759, pp. 61–79. Springer, Cham (2024)
22. Silva, P., Oliveira, J.N., Macedo, N., Cunha, A.: Quantitative relational modelling with QAlloy. In: ESEC/SIGSOFT FSE, pp. 885–896. ACM (2022)
23. Sullivan, A.: HawkEye: user-guided enumeration of scenarios. In: ISSRE, pp. 569–578. IEEE (2021)
24. Takagi, T., Sugeno, M.: Fuzzy identification of systems and its applications to modeling and control. IEEE Trans. Syst. Man Cybern. **15**(1), 116–132 (1985)
25. Tamura, S., Higuchi, S., Tanaka, K.: Pattern classification based on fuzzy relations. IEEE Trans. Syst. Man Cybern. **1**(1), 61–66 (1971)
26. Tarski, A., Givant, S.: A Formalization of Set Theory without Variables. AMS, vol. 41. AMS Colloquium Publications (1987)
27. Torlak, E., Jackson, D.: Kodkod: a relational model finder. In: Grumberg, O., Huth, M. (eds.) TACAS 2007. LNCS, vol. 4424, pp. 632–647. Springer, Heidelberg (2007). https://doi.org/10.1007/978-3-540-71209-1_49
28. Wu, H.: Generating metamodel instances satisfying coverage criteria via SMT solving. In: MODELSWARD, pp. 40–51. SciTePress (2016)
29. Zhang, C., et al.: AlloyMax: bringing maximum satisfaction to relational specifications. In: ESEC/SIGSOFT FSE, pp. 155–167. ACM (2021)

Proof Semantics of Railway Interlocking

Linas Laibinis[1(✉)], Alexei Iliasov[2], and Alexander Romanovsky[2,3]

[1] Institute of Computer Science, Vilnius University, Vilnius, Lithuania
linas.laibinis@mif.vu.lt
[2] The Formal Route Ltd., London, UK
[3] School of Computing, Newcastle University, Newcastle upon Tyne, UK

Abstract. SafeCap is a modern toolkit for modelling, simulation and formal verification of railway networks, focused on fully-automated scalable safety verification of Solid State Interlocking (SSI) programs – a technology at the heart of many railway signalling solutions worldwide. In this paper, we elaborate on the formal foundations of the employed method by presenting the formal proof semantics of the modelled systems and the properties we are interested in verifying. We discuss the composite nature of this semantics, namely, interrelationships between signalling programs, signalling plan data, and the safety principles we need to ensure. The main focus is to formally justify the derivation of a number of proof obligations that a specific interlocking solution must satisfy. The semantic definitions, properties, and inference rules are formalised with the Coq proof assistant.

1 Introduction

Railway interlockings are the core of ensuring the safe operation of modern railway systems. The increasing demands for railway efficiency, including capacity, punctuality, and energy consumption, lead to the increasing complexity of interlocking designs. This makes it harder to ensure their safety. Modern interlocking includes complex software that controls the side track equipment and interacts with trains and operating centers. From our experience, modern interlockings can have up to 80K–110K lines of code. This complexity calls for an extensive use of formal methods in the development of such systems and, especially, in ensuring their safety.

Formal verification by proofs has been successfully used in the design of complex control systems in the railway domain, starting with the groundbreaking development of the METEOR metro (L14) using the B method and the Atelier-B prover by Siemens Mobility France (formerly Matra Transport) in 1998 [1]. Since 2020 we have been commercially using the SafeCap toolkit for fully automated formal verification of railway interlockings by theorem proving [2–4]. SafeCap uses a custom rewriting-based prover for a language based on first-order logic and set theory. This paper takes this work further by introducing a composite proof semantics of interlocking programs and formalising (a part of) it in the Coq proof assistant [5].

M. Leuschel and F. Ishikawa (Eds.): ABZ 2025, LNCS 15728, pp. 106–123, 2026.
https://doi.org/10.1007/978-3-031-94533-5_7

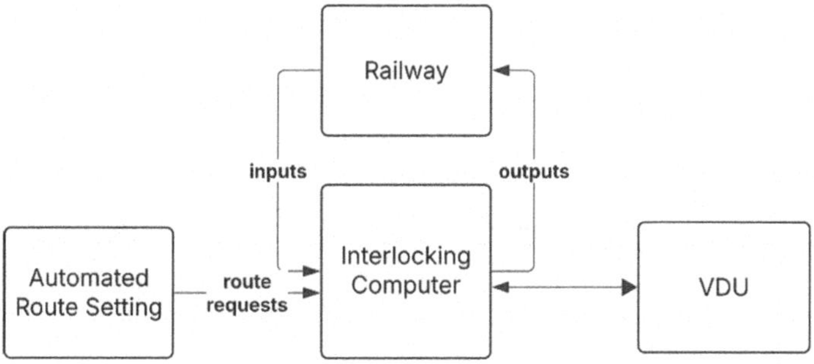

Fig. 1. Digital interlocking

After introducing the context of this work in the next section, in Sect. 3 we discuss the underlying semantics of the interlocking design language that SafeCap targets, namely, Solid State Interlocking (SSI) [6]. Section 4 formalises and extends this semantics with formal safety constraints, preparing the foundation for defining the proof semantics of the SSI programs. Section 5 discusses the contributions of this work, and looks at possible directions for future research.

2 Background: Ensuring Safety in the Railway Domain

Digital railway interlocking is a typical example of a safety-critical control system. It comprises a computer executing control logic (in an endless loop from power on) that reads in inputs from environment (railway track-side equipment such as track occupation circuits, signals and points), calculates the internal state update, and sends out outputs to command controlled equipment (see the diagram in Fig. 1).

Interlocking also interfaces with other, less safety critical subsystems such as automated route setting, which uses a combination of train location sensors and timetables to automatically issue route setting requests ahead of a train, and Visual Display Unit (VDU), which displays track layouts, train positions, and signal status and also offers manual triggering of route requests. In relation to such systems, interlocking plays the role of a gatekeeper or a safety kernel protecting trains and track-side equipment.

In this work, we focus on Solid State Interlocking (SSI), fully computerised interlocking technology developed in the UK in the 1980s [6]. SSI is the predominant interlocking technology used on the UK mainline railways. It also has applications overseas, including in Australia, New Zealand, France, Egypt, India and Belgium. Running on bespoke hardware based on real or emulated Motorola 68K or PowerPC CPUs, SSI software consists of a generic application (common to all signalling plans) and site specific geographic data. The latter configures a signalling area by defining site specific rules concerning the signalling and other equipment that the interlocking must obey.

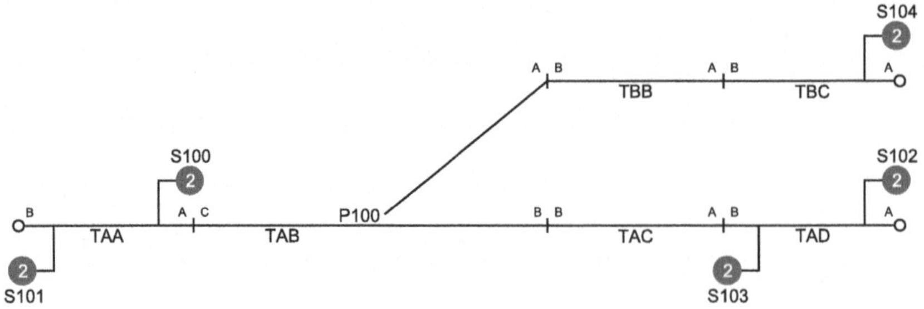

Fig. 2. Sample signalling plan. Three routes are defined: R100A from S100 to S104, R100B from S100 to S102 and R103 from S103 to S101.

Despite being referred to as data, an interlocking configuration is a program written in a simple imperative programming language. The language has boolean and integer variables, assignments, conditional execution, and subroutines. It does not feature complex data types, pointers, recursion, and iteration. Thus, while interlocking programs can be quite large (in tens of thousands of lines of code), they are structurally and algorithmically quite simple.

Code review and scenario-based testing are the traditional and still dominant validation techniques. However, after a flurry of incidents related to configuration errors (that is, errors in interlocking programs), Network Rail has mandated [7] an automated tool check prior their commissioning. We have developed a Network Rail approved tool, called SafeCap [2], able to carry out such checks using theorem proving and applied it commercially to nearly 100 interlockings.

In the process, we have devised a formal semantics for interlocking programs focusing on their safety properties. Since we rely solely on theorem proving, it is what may be called a proof semantics – interpretation of the interlocking source code as a collection of proof conjectures which, once discharged, demonstrate that certain safety properties are satisfied by the interlocking.

To give an intuition of how interlocking operates, we shall consider a very small example as depicted in Fig. 2 (we had to omit many details that would be found in a real interlocking). The example is a junction with one point `P100`, six track sections, five signals, and three routes. The point is a movable part of the track that allows traveling in left (diagram top) or right (diagram straight) directions. Track sections serve to detect occupancy. At the first approximation, they are boolean flags that indicate the presence of a train axle. Signals, which may be any combination of physical and virtual, indicate the limits of routes and also the permissible train speed. In this example, all signals are two aspect colour signals (as indicated by "2" in circle), with the red aspect for no proceed and the green aspect for proceed and be prepared to stop at the exit signal.

Not shown directly on the diagram but deducible from it, there are *sub routes* – directed paths corresponding to possible traversals of track sections. The linear section `TAA` can be traversed in both directions and these paths are called `BA` and `AB` (as marked on track section borders) for left-to-right and right-to-left directions. Sub routes are typically named by replacing leading `T` in track section name with `U` and adding path names, e.g., `UAA-BA`, `UAA-AB`. For instance, the section `TAB` has sub routes `UAB-CA`, `UAB-AC`, `UAB-CB` and `UAB-BC` but not, e.g., `UAB-AB`.

In the example, we shall consider solely the route setting part of interlocking logic, thus omitting the logic processing inputs and outputs. Let us consider the following interlocking code fragment:

```
*QR100A if R100A a   / route is available
          UAB-CA f, UBB-BA f, UBC-BA f  / route sub routes free
          UAB-BC f  / opposing locking check
          P100 crf  / point P100 can be put in reverse
        then
          R100A s  / mark the route as set
          P100 cr  / command point P100 reverse
          UAB-CA l, UBB-BA l, UBC-BA l  / lock required sub routes
        \
*QR100B if R100B a   / route is available
          UAB-CB f, UAC-BA f, UAD-BA f  / route sub routes free
          UAB-BC f  / opposing locking check
          P100 cnf  / point P100 can be put in normal
        then
          R100B s  / mark the route as set
          P100 cn  / command point P100 normal
          UAB-CB l, UAC-BA l, UAD-BA l  / lock required sub routes
        \
*QR103 if R103 a   / route is available
          UAC-AB f, UAB-BC f, UAA-BA f  / route sub routes free
          UAC-BA f  / opposing locking check
          P100 cnf  / point P100 can be put in normal
        then
          R103 s  / mark the route as set
          P100 cn  / command point P100 normal
          UAC-AB l, UAB-BC l, UAA-BA l  /  lock required sub routes
        \
```

It defines three code blocks for route requests, one for each route. A route request block is implicitly predicated on the state of the eponymous request flag, which is set either by the automated route setting system or via VDU by a signaller. Let us consider the first block in more detail.

The clause `R100A a` is a predicate $a($`R100A`$)$ written in a postfix notation, where the function a stands for *route available*. The function f in `UAB-CA f` (and other two cases) stands for *sub route free*. The expression `P100 cnf` (`P100 crf`) stands for *point P100 is either already commanded normal (reverse) or free to be commanded normal (reverse)*. The part *free to be commanded* is a reference to a separately defined predicates that take the following form in our example:

```
*P100N   if TAB c, UAB-CA f, UAB-AC f / free to be commanded normal
*P100R   if TAB c, UAB-CB f, UAB-BC f / free to be commanded reverse
```

Finally, the clause `R100A s` is a command setting the boolean flag `R100A` to true (i.e., the function s stands for *set route*). Similarly, `P100 cr` commands point to reverse, and `UAB-CA l` (and other two cases) locks a given sub route.

3 Formal Semantics of the SSI Language

There are three main parts to an interlocking control system:

- a signalling plan, which in our case is a *digital* representation of a particular railway layout,
- a signalling logic, i.e., an interlogic program written in the SSI notation,
- signalling principles, i.e., formally encoded safety requirements.

A signaling plan is a simpler artifact than a signaling logic, and its correctness is presumed from the position of commercial signalling production practices. Therefore, we verify the signalling logic against the plan and highlight any discrepancies or inconsistencies in the logic, while fully trusting the plan. Whereas the signalling logic and the plan vary from area to area, the principles stay the same and are formulated once and for all.

The aim of our SSI semantics is to combine the three ingredients in an effective verification procedure. Before we can arrive at such a procedure, we need more details on the meaning of each of the parts. We use set theory as a mathematical notation of choice.

3.1 Semantics of a Signalling Plan

A digital signalling plan is a graph with a number of annotations capturing the track topology, route paths, signal positions, etc. We represent such a graph as a collection of constant relations. Naturally, the definition of every possible signalling plan adheres to the same template, so, where necessary, we can reason about signalling plans in general, operating with abstract constants.

Formally, a signalling plan is a combination of axioms introducing constant relations encoding the signalling plan graph, and, optionally, axioms providing values to these relations.

For instance, the constant *route_subroutes* defines all sub routes of a route. For our example, we define it as follows:

$$\begin{aligned}&\mathit{route\_subroutes} \subseteq \mathrm{Route} \times \mathrm{SubRoute}\\&\mathit{route\_subroutes} = \{(\mathtt{R100A}, \mathtt{UAB\text{-}CA}), (\mathtt{R100A}, \mathtt{UBB\text{-}BA}), (\mathtt{R100A}, \mathtt{UBC\text{-}BA}), \ldots\}\end{aligned}$$

We shall later refer to the relation $\mathit{point\_tracks} \subseteq \mathrm{Point} \times \mathrm{Track}$ defining the correspondence between points and their parent track sections. In our example it simply defined as:

$$\mathit{point\_tracks} = \{(\mathtt{P100}, \mathtt{TAB})\}.$$

Another relation we refer to later is *route_opposing_subroutes* $\subseteq$ Route $\times$ SubRoute defining all the opposing sub routes of a route. For our example, it is defined as:

$$route\_opposing\_subroutes = \{(\texttt{R100B}, \texttt{UAB-BC}), (\texttt{R103}, \texttt{UAC-BA})\}$$

From now on, we will denote the set of all the possible values of signalling plan constants (i.e., their different combinations) as C. In other words,

$$C \;=\; C_1 \times C_2 \times \cdots \times C_n,$$

where C_i, $i \in 1..n$, are the carrier sets of the corresponding constants.

3.2 Semantics of a Signalling Logic

The signalling logic in SSI is defined in a restricted form of an imperative programming language notation. It is initialized by some predetermined state Q_I and proceeds executing in an endless control cycle, which is a characteristic of control systems. Each iteration of the cycle is split into three stages: processing of inputs from environment by reading in and reacting to input telegrams, processing of the internal logic dealing with route and point requests as well as some other controls and, finally, the formation of output telegrams encoding output commands to various trackside equipment such as signals and points.

Each stage consists of a number of code blocks executed sequentially. Block execution cannot be interrupted midway or interleaved with any other activity. From the viewpoint of an observer, it forms an atomic step of interlocking control.

Let Q be the signalling program state space such that $Q = A_0 \times A_1 \times ...A_j$ where A_i is the type of i-th signalling program variable, i.e., $v_i \in A_i$. In other words, a variable is simply the corresponding projection of a program state.[1]

The execution stages (dealing with reading input telegrams, executing the internal logic, and producing output telegrams respectively) can be represented as next-state relations, depending on the predefined constant values C, i.e., $SI_C \subseteq Q \times Q$, $SL_C \subseteq Q \times Q$, $SO_C \subseteq Q \times Q$. Moreover, each stage consists of separate code blocks $SI_i \subseteq Q \times Q$, $SL_i \subseteq Q \times Q$, and $SO_i \subseteq Q \times Q$, such that $SI_C = \bigcup_{i \in 0..k} SI_i$, $SL_C = \bigcup_{i \in 0..m} SL_i$, and $SO_C = \bigcup_{i \in 0..n} SO_i$.

In practice, each iteration cycle executes code blocks in some order. We can write this as a signal iteration transition $T_C \subseteq Q \times Q$ defined as relational composition of all the possible blocks:

$$T_C = SI_0; SI_1; ...; SI_k; SL_0; SL_1; ...SL_m; SO_o; SO_1, ..., SO_n.$$

Each such SI_i, SL_i, and SO_k must be automatically derived from the imperative interlocking source code. Due to the absence of nondeterminism, this relational composition may be replaced with functional composition of the corresponding state update functions.

[1] We will make the connection between signalling variables and the state space more precise in Sect. 4, where we define variables as functions from variable names and the current state to variable values.

Assuming Q_I stands for the initial state, a state trace of a complete signalling program is then a sequence

$$\{Q_I\},\ T[Q_I],\ T^2[Q_I],\ ...,$$

where $R[S]$ is the relational image operator.

3.3 Signalling Data State Space Model

An interlocking program uses thousands of variables, with larger ones running over 8,000 variables. Majority of variables are Booleans, the rest are 8-bit unsigned integers. For instance, for each route there would be a dedicated flag in the interlocking computer memory stating whether the route is set, available to be set, being requested and so on.

Fortunately, the SSI notation is so limited that any given variable appears as an argument to a small number of functions and commands. For instance, the route set flag can only be used in conjunction with the route set predicate and the route setting command. If one wanted to copy the state of one flag into another, in most cases the only way to accomplish this is by using the IF-ELSE clause, e.g., `IF R100A s then R100B s else R100B xs` to copy the state of `R100A` into `R100B` (the command `xs` here sets its argument flag to false).

Such a rigid specialisation of variables enables a rather compact model of the signalling data state space based on the set theory and used in the formulation of next-state relations and signalling principles.

In this model, the states of all boolean flags concerning the same interlocking function (e.g., route setting) are combined into a single set variable of the form $v : \mathbb{P}(\mathbb{A})$ where $\mathbb{A}$ is a carrier (typically enumerated) set of the function argument and $\mathbb{P}(..)$ is the power set operator. For instance, for the route setting function, we define $route\_s \in \mathbb{P}(\mathsf{Route})$, where Route is the predefined set of all routes.

To model a route set check predicate such as `R123 s`, we use the set membership test `R123` $\in route\_s$. For route set command `R123 s`, we use set union to update the variable $route\_s$: $route\_s' = route\_s \cup \{R123\}$.

Sets like Route are interpreted as abstract sets, when there is no concrete signalling plan in the context, or as concrete, enumerated sets with their values derived from a specific signalling plan.

3.4 Semantics of Signalling Principles

The level of granularity associated with an atomic code block forms a convenient basis for the reasoning about signalling data correctness. Considering properties of a whole iteration or even multiple iterations is, in principle, more expressive, however, it presents no practical advantages since a signalling program is developed in stages and aggregated from many smaller parts with the implicit assumption that each block performs its assigned function completely. At the same time, iteration-level reasoning is vastly more expensive and is, perhaps, outside the realms of automated static verification.

We interpret signalling safety principles P as a *maximal safe signalling data* defined as a next-state relation over signalling program state and dependent on signalling plan, i.e., $P_C \subseteq Q \times Q$. Typically, safety principles or properties are represented as invariant properties of state transition systems, defining the set of safe states that the system must stay within. To express safety principles in signalling, however, we need, in general, to consider a pair of the previous (history) and current states. That allows to represent these principles as state relations expressing the safe behaviour. The point locking principle SAF-2 given below is one example of reasoning about transition between states.

Such P_C defines all possible safe signalling logic implementations for a given signalling plan. That is, for some signalling program iteration step T to be safe with respect to the given signalling plan d, it would be necessary that $T \subseteq P_d$; this equally applies to individual atomic blocks: $SI_k \subseteq P_d, SL_j \subseteq P_d, ...$

The whole verification process can be defined inductively. We start with the test of membership for the first initial state(s) Q_I which must belong to the domain of P_d and then check that every possible block SI_i, SL_j and SO_k defines a transition relation that, when started in a state satisfying P_d, is compatible with (i.e., included into) P_d:

$$Q_I \in \text{dom}(P_d)$$
$$\text{ran}(P_d) \lhd S_k \subseteq P$$

Here S_k stands for any block of the iteration T, dom and ran are functions returning relation domain and range respectively, and $\lhd$ is the domain restriction operator, restricting the given relation (S_k) by the set of starting states ($\text{ran}(P_d)$). Note that $\text{ran}(P_d)$ is used in the second conjecture instead $\text{dom}(P_d)$, because the latter would refer to possible previous states satisfying P_d.

It is convenient to partition principles P_d into a collection P_{d_i} such that $P_d = \bigcap_i P_{d_i}$ and proceed with a test of one principle at a time:

$$Q_I \in \text{dom}(P_{d_i})$$
$$\text{ran}(P_d) \lhd S_k \subseteq P_{d_i}$$

Examples of Safety Principles. There is a large number of safety principles encoded in standards and working papers on SSI, while the SafeCap tool checks over 140 of such principles. As examples, we shall consider only three following ones:

SAF-1: *All sub routes of a set route must be locked*: when a route is set, all the sub routes on the path of the route must be locked.

$$\mathit{route\_subroutes}[\mathsf{routes\_set}] \subseteq \mathsf{subroutes\_locked}$$

Here $\mathsf{routes\_set} \subseteq \text{Route}$ and $\mathsf{subroutes\_locked} \subseteq \text{SubRoute}$ are model variables defining all currently set routes and locked sub routes, while $R[S]$ is the relational image operator.

SAF-2: *Point movements should be protected*: while a point is moving to a new direction, the containing track section must be clear.

$$\mathit{point\_tracks}[\mathbf{commanded}] \cap \mathsf{track\_c} = \varnothing,$$

where the set **commanded** is defined as

$$(\mathsf{point\_c'}^{-1}[\{\mathrm{NOR}\}] \setminus \mathsf{point\_c}^{-1}[\{\mathrm{NOR}\}]) \cup$$
$$(\mathsf{point\_c'}^{-1}[\{\mathrm{REV}\}] \setminus \mathsf{point\_c}^{-1}[\{\mathrm{REV}\}])$$

Here $\mathsf{track\_c}$ is a model variable defining the set of currently clear track sections, $\mathsf{point\_c} \in \mathrm{Point} \rightarrow \{\mathrm{NOR}, \mathrm{MID}, \mathrm{REV}\}$ is a function defining the point commanded state (i.e., normal, undefined, or reversed), and , finally, $\mathsf{point\_c'}$ defines a new point commanded state (as produced, for instance, by an assignment statement).

SAF-3: *Opposing movement protection*: on route setting, last opposing sub routes of all opposing routes must be checked free and locked.

$$\mathit{route\_opposing\_subroutes}[\mathsf{routes\_set}] \subseteq \mathsf{subroutes\_locked'} \setminus \mathsf{subroutes\_locked}$$

Here $\setminus$ is the set difference operator.

In all the presented formalisation examples we heavily rely on set theory, where various interconnections between values (defined as relations or various kinds of functions) are represented as sets of pairs.

4 Building the Proof Semantics in Coq

In the previous section we presented a high-level view of the formal SSI semantics currently employed in the SafeCap verification framework. Many practical details describing the verification process were omitted here and discussed earlier in our previous papers [2–4]. In addition, we have started building an alternative formalisation of the same semantics using the Coq proof assistant [5]. The main goals of this exercise are to give us extra assurance in the correctness of the verification process as well as to provide an alternative way using an external tool to replicate formal verification of safety properties for concrete SSI systems. Our choice of Coq as the theorem-proving assistant, in preference to systems such as Isabelle/HOL or LEAN, is predicated on its highly programmable proof techniques and its capacity for verified code extraction from completed proofs, thus making it well-suited for software verification and more integrable into the SafeCap automated processes.

In this section we introduce a formal semantics of SSI systems using the Coq proof assistant. As explained in the previous sections, the semantics of SSI programs is composite and essentially represents that of a control system. In simple terms, since there is no non-determinism occurring within each cycle describing the SSI system reaction to external stimuli, each simple system reaction can easily be formalised as a function between states, which in turn can be represented as functions mapping variables to their values.

The main purpose of the attempted formalisation exercise, however, is to guarantee safety properties derived from safety principles. These properties are formalised as safety invariant properties that should be verified for each control system cycle as well as each atomic SSI code block occurring within a cycle. As explained in Sect. 3, this results in a number of proof obligations (conjectures) that need to be proved for specific code fragments in order to formally guarantee the overall safety of the system. Formally defining the process of generating necessary proof obligations gives us the extended proof semantics focusing on ensuring system safety properties.

4.1 Building Proof Semantics for Safety Verification

We start by formalising the main notions necessary to define the semantics of SSI programs as state transition (control) systems. Then we extend it by introducing the notion of safety invariants and proving the theorems or inference rules for generating all the necessary proof obligations. We are going to present fragments of the corresponding Coq theories, defining the main notions as well as proved essential theorems. The full theories (including the proofs for all theorems) are available from [8].

A standard approach to define program variables (based on the existing Coq definitions [9]) is to interpret them as total maps from the variable names to the associated values.

```
Definition total_map (A : Type) := string → A.

Definition t_empty {A : Type} (v : A) : total_map A :=
  (fun _ ⇒ v).

Definition t_update {A : Type} (m : total_map A) (x : string) (v : A) :=
  fun x' ⇒ if String.eqb x x' then v else m x'.
```

Safety properties will be represented as safety invariants. As explained earlier, a safety invariant for SSI programs is a predicate (relation) defined on the previous (history) and current states. We can assume that such a relation satisfies reflexivity and transitivity properties (like preorder relations). We will need these properties for our essential result later on, so we formulate them as separate definitions.

```
Definition Reflexive {A : Type} (r : A → A → Prop) :=
  ∀ a : A, r a a.

Definition Transitive {A : Type} (r : A → A → Prop) :=
  ∀ (a : A) b c, r a b → r b c → r a c.

Definition Preorder {A : Type} (r : A → A → Prop) :=
  Reflexive r ∧ Transitive r.
```

The collective type **Val** represents all the values that program variables can take. They can be natural numbers, booleans, or sets of predefined constant values.

The latter can also have structure and represent relations or functions between respective values.

```
Inductive Val : Type :=
  | Nval (n : nat)
  | Bval (b : bool).
  | Sval (s : FinSet).
```

In addition, we introduce the essential types that we will rely on to define necessary pieces of the SSI semantics, namely, state variables, states, state predicates, state functions, state relations, state expressions, state conjectures, and state invariants. Note the difference between state predicates (state relations) and state conjectures (state invariants). In the first case, the resulting value is a boolean, in the second one – a proposition we need to prove.

```
Definition SVar := string.

Definition State := total_map Val.

Definition SPred := State → bool.

Definition SFun := State → State.

Definition SRel := State → State → bool.

Definition SExpr := State → Val.

Definition SPr := State → Prop.

Definition SInv := State → State → Prop.
```

On the syntactic level, we have three layers of an SSI system. On the lowest, a particular variable is updated as a result of an assignment statement. In the middle, we have a code block containing a sequential composition of assignments and conditional statements. We call such a block a state transition since it is considered atomic with respect to the safety properties we want to guarantee. These properties can be, however, broken in intermediate states of a transition. Finally, on the top, state transition system level we have a collection (a list) of transitions that can be executed within one cycle of an SSI control system. Each such transition (independently of their execution order) must preserve the predefined safety invariants.

```
Inductive SAssign : Type :=
  | Assign (v : SVar) (e : SExpr).

Inductive Trans :=
  | Asgn (a : SAssign)
  | Cond (p : SPred) (t1 : Trans) (t2 : Trans)
  | Seq (t1 : Trans) (t2 : Trans).

Definition STS := list Trans → SFun.
```

Semantically, we associate these system elements with the corresponding state functions. Note that SemAssign a function is directly associated with a single state update. The displayed syntax is syntactic sugaring for t_update st v (e st)). SemTrans builds a state function for an arbitrary number of nested conditionals, assignments, and sequential compositions. Finally, SemSTS just defines one cycle of the SSI control system as a functional composition of all the system transitions.

```
Definition SemAssign (a : SAssign) (st : State) :=
  match a with
  | Assign v e ⇒ (v !-> (e st) ; st)
  end.

Fixpoint SemTrans (t : Trans) (st : State) : State :=
  match t with
  | Asgn a ⇒ SemAssign a st
  | Cond p a1 a2 ⇒ if p st then SemTrans a1 st else SemTrans a2 st
  | Seq a1 a2 ⇒ SemTrans a2 (SemTrans a1 st)
  end.

Fixpoint SemSTS (tlist : list Trans) (st : State) : State :=
  match tlist with
  | nil ⇒ st
  | t :: tl ⇒ SemSTS tl (SemTrans t st)
  end.
```

Now, relying on the above semantic definitions, we can easily define program correctness (e.g., Hoare correctness triples) for each of these layers. In all three cases, the corresponding state functions (on different levels of system execution) are constructed and checked against the given precondition and postcondition.

```
Definition CorrectAssign (pre : SPr) (a : SAssign) (post : SPr) (st : State) :
Prop :=
  pre st → post (SemAssign a st).

Definition CorrectTrans (pre : SPr) (t : Trans) (post : SPr) (st : State) : Prop
:=
  pre st → post (SemTrans t st).

Definition CorrectSTS (pre : SPr) (sts : list Trans) (post : SPr) (st : State) :
Prop :=
  pre st → post (SemSTS sts st).
```

The invariant preservation property (on the state transition system level) can be easily expressed as a special kind of program correctness. A separate lemma shows how we can move from one kind of correctness to another. Note how the invariant property (defined on both previous and current states) is adjusted or shifted in the corresponding state transition by partial function application.

```
Definition InvSTS (inv : SInv) (sts : list Trans) (pre_st : State) (st : State) :
Prop :=
  inv pre_st st → inv st (SemSTS sts st).
```

Lemma InvSTSCorrect:
  ∀ (*inv* : SInv) (*sts* : **list Trans**) (*pre_st* : State) (*st* : State),
    InvSTS *inv sts pre_st st* ↔ CorrectSTS (*inv pre_st*) *sts* (*inv st*) *st*.

The same correspondence can be shown on the single transition level.

Definition InvTrans (*inv* : SInv) (*t* : **Trans**) (*pre_st* : State) (*st* : State) : Prop :=
  inv pre_st st → *inv st* (SemTrans *t st*).

Lemma InvTransCorrect:
  ∀ (*inv* : SInv) (*t* : **Trans**) (*pre_st* : State) (*st* : State),
    InvTrans *inv t pre_st st* ↔ CorrectTrans (*inv pre_st*) *t* (*inv st*) *st*.

Finally, on the single assignment level, the respective state function is incorporated.

Definition InvSAssign (*inv* : SInv) (*a* : **SAssign**) (*pre_st* : State) (*st* : State) : Prop :=
  inv pre_st st → *inv st* (SemTrans (Asgn *a*) *st*).

Lemma InvAssignCorrect:
  ∀ (*inv* : SInv) (*a* : **SAssign**) (*pre_st* : State) (*st* : State),
    InvSAssign *inv a pre_st st* ↔ CorrectAssign (*inv pre_st*) *a* (*inv st*) *st*.

To derive the proof semantics of the SSI system, we need a number of inference rules (Coq theorems) that allow us to split the proof task of invariant preservation for the whole system into a collection of simpler proof obligations that collectively are sufficient to prove the main system property which stipulates that all the safety properties must hold. To achieve that, we formulate and prove the theorem that proving safety invariant invariant for each transition (SSI block), independently of the order of their execution, allows us to prove the main goal. The proof requires an additional assumption, stating that the given safety invariant is a preorder relation between states.

Lemma STSCorrectTrans:
  ∀ (*inv* : SInv) (*sts* : **list Trans**) (*pre_st* : State) (*st* : State),
    Preorder *inv* →
    (∀ *t pre_st' st'*, In *t sts* → InvTrans *inv t pre_st' st'*) →
    InvSTS *inv sts pre_st st*.

Since we know the structure and semantics of SSI transitions, we can continue this process. For a single assignment, we just rely on its semantic definition, i.e. unfold the underlying state function.

Lemma AsgnTransInv:
  ∀ (*inv* : SInv) (*a* : **SAssign**) (*pre_st* : State) (*st* : State),
    inv pre_st st → *inv st* (SemAssign *a st*) →
    InvSFun *inv* (SemTrans(Asgn *a*)) *pre_st st*.

For a conditional statement, we require invariant preservation for both its branches.

```
Lemma CondTransInv:
  ∀ (inv : SInv) (p : SPred) (t1 : Trans) (t2 : Trans) (pre_st : State) (st : State),
     InvTrans inv t1 pre_st st →
     InvTrans inv t2 pre_st st →
     InvTrans inv (Cond p t1 t2) pre_st st.
```

For a sequential composition, we compose two semantical state functions into one and the require invariant preservation in a post state. In order to do that, we introduce the notion of invariant preservation for an arbitrary state function and rely on the standard Coq definition of function composition (compose). Note that here the invariant in question can be broken in an intermediate state.

```
Definition InvSFun (inv : SInv) (f : SFun) (pre_st : State) (st : State) : Prop
:=
  inv pre_st st → inv st (f st).
```

```
Lemma SeqTransInv:
  ∀ (inv : SInv) (p : SPred) (p : SPred) (t1 : Trans) (t2 : Trans) (pre_st : State)
(st : State),
     InvSFun inv (compose (SemTrans t2) (SemTrans t1)) pre_st st →
     InvTrans inv (Seq t1 t2) pre_st st.
```

4.2 Reasoning at the Expression Level

The generated proof conjectures will refer to system variables and attributes, most of which are defined as particular kinds of finite sets (including relations, functions, etc.). The safety proof conjectures SAF1, SAF2, SAF3, presented in Sect. 3 are examples of such properties to be verified. Please note the abundance of various set and relational and set operators (relational image, inverse, etc.) that are used to express various relationships between state variables.

To make efficient automated reasoning involving such structures and their properties, a separate Coq theory was created. The theory is generic (i.e., parameterised over an arbitrary element type supporting the equivalence relation) and facilitates more efficient inductive reasoning over such finite structures.

```
Section FinSets.

Variable U : Type.

Variable equiv : U → U → bool.

Axiom equiv_comm : ∀ (x:U) y, equiv x y = equiv y x.

Axiom equiv_trans : ∀ (x:U) y z, equiv x y = true → equiv y z = true  → equiv x
z = true.
```

```
Axiom equiv_refl : ∀ (x:U), equiv x x = true.
Axiom Axiom equiv_extensionality: ∀ (x : U) y, equiv x y = true ↔ x = y.
```

The base type for finite sets is then introduced by the following inductive definition.

```
Inductive FinSet : Type :=
  | Empty_set
  | Add (x : U) (A : FinSet).
```

The main notions and standard operations of a set theory can be easily introduced based on the above definitions. Some instances of those (a singleton set, membership, a subset, etc.) are given below.

```
Definition Singleton (x : U) : FinSet := Add x Empty_set.

Fixpoint Union (A : FinSet) (B : FinSet) :=
  match A with
  | Empty_set ⇒ B
  | Add y A0 ⇒ Add y (Union A0 B)
  end.

Fixpoint mem (x : U) (A : FinSet) : bool :=
  match A with
    | Empty_set ⇒ false
    | Add y B ⇒ (equiv x y) || mem x B
  end.

Definition Full_set (A : FinSet) : Prop :=
  ∀ (x : U), mem x A = true.

Definition Subset (A : FinSet) (B : FinSet) : Prop :=
  (∀ x:U, mem x A = true → mem x B = true).

Definition Same_set (A : FinSet) (B : FinSet) : Prop :=
  Subset A B ∧ Subset B A.
```

Most of the employed data structures express various relationships between predefined sets of values, i.e., are defined as sets of pairs representing relations or functions. The above definitions of finite sets can be easily instantiated and then extended to introduce finite relations and various useful operators for them.

```
Section FinRelations.

Variable T: Type.
Variable U: Type.

Definition Relation T U := FinSet (T × U).
```

In a similar manner, we can inductively introduce all the relational operators used in the safety properties (such as domain, range, inverse and so on).

```
Fixpoint dom (R : Relation T U) : FinSet T :=
```

```
  match R with
  | Empty_set _ ⇒ Empty_set _
  | Add _ (x,y) R0 ⇒ Add _ x (dom R0)
  end.
Fixpoint ran (R : Relation T U) : FinSet U :=
  match R with
  | Empty_set _ ⇒ Empty_set _
  | Add _ (x,y) R0 ⇒ Add _ y (ran R0)
  end.
Fixpoint inverse (R : Relation T U) : Relation U T :=
  match R with
  | Empty_set _ ⇒ Empty_set _
  | Add _ (x,y) R0 ⇒ Add _ (y,x) (inverse R0)
  end.
```

Following the same approach, different types of finite functions can be introduced as special kinds of relations. Once all the definitions are in place, many essential properties have been proven by induction to be used for simplifying and rewriting expressions, and thus facilitating automated reasoning about SSI safety properties. The Coq sources of this theory are available from [8].

5 Discussion and Conclusions

This paper presents the proof semantics of SSI signalling programs focusing on generation of necessary proof conjectures to ensure safety properties of such systems. The core underlying semantics of a SSI program as a control system is quite simple and can be easily represented as a state transition system, where each transition in turn can be expressed as a state function or a state relation. The complexities arise when we have to include into consideration the other composite parts of the overall semantics – a signalling plan and signalling (safety) principles. Because of such a composite nature, the traditional denotational semantics becomes insufficient and should be upgraded to the proof semantics determining what proof conjectures must be proven for atomic code blocks to ensure the predefined safety properties (safety invariants) with respect to the given signalling plan and the signalling logic (SSI code).

The benefits of creating such proof semantics are twofold. First, it gives us extra assurance in correctness of the SafeCap verification process (based on such formalised semantics) in general, as well as in a number of the employed internal tactics, inference rules, and other simplification techniques. Second, it provides us with an alternative way to replicate formal verification of actual safety properties for concrete SSI systems, i.e., to diversify the automated verification procedure of SafeCap by using a well-established theorem proving system such as Coq. Both aspects are also important for the ongoing work on tool certification.

The proof semantics formalises the process of decomposing the overall correctness verification for the whole system until the lowest atomicity level (i.e., sequential composition of assignments) with respect to the verified safety properties is reached. The described process is rather straightforward. The only complication is the treatment of safety properties as invariant properties defined on the previous (history) and current states. Another important aspect is the possibility of exploiting the fact that all data structures (sets, relations, functions) used to represent variable or constant values are finite sets. Induction over finite sets can ultimately lead to an efficient combination of theorem proving (for general properties) and functional programming computations (by unfolding and traversing given finite structures) to improve automation and efficiency of formal verification of concrete safety proof conjectures.

There have been a number of research studies focusing on formal verification of SSI programs [10–15]. The majority of works use various forms of model-checking in an attempt to verify safety of *train run scenarios*, with interlocking rules derived manually or via an automated translation from SSI data. With few exceptions, the proposed techniques actually scale up to only toy examples, or cover a small subset of functionalities, or both. Even if our proposed SSI semantics does not achieve any major theoretical breakthroughs, it serves pragmatic purposes to support practical full scale automated verification of SSI programs.

In [16,17], the authors present a new modelling and verification framework (EB4EB) for the Event-B formal language and its possible extensions, relying on a defined trace-based semantics for Event-B as well as deep and shallow instantiation mechanisms based on metamodelling techniques. The framework allows for the introduction of new properties, data types, and proof rules for the extended language. The approach presented in this paper is much more straightforward, targeted, and pragmatic. However, its future enhancements might adopt some elements of the proposed techniques.

This is still work in progress. To fully realise the benefits mentioned above, we plan to further extend the theory of finite data structures (such as relations, various kinds of functions, etc.) and their inductive properties, to allow us to make full use of combining theorem proving and automated computations over concrete finite data structures. Moreover, we are going to investigate how the automated reasoning based on the proposed semantics can be integrated within the existing SafeCap framework, providing an alternative and independent way of verifying concrete safety properties of SSI signalling systems.

References

1. Behm, P., Desforges, P., Meynadier, J.: Météor: an industrial success in formal development. In: Bert, D. (ed.) B 1998: Recent Advances in the Development and Use of the B Method, Second International B Conference, Montpellier, France, 22–24 April 1998, Proceedings. Lecture Notes in Computer Science, vol. 1393, p. 26. Springer (1998). https://doi.org/10.1007/BFB0053352
2. Iliasov, A., Taylor, D., Laibinis, L., Romanovsky, A.: Practical verification of railway signalling programs. IEEE TDCS **20**(Jan-Feb), 695–707 (2023)
3. Iliasov, A., Laibinis, L., Taylor, D., Lopatkin, I., Romanovsky, A.: Safety invariant verification that meets engineers' expectations. In: Dutilleul, S.C., Haxthausen,

A.E., Lecomte, T. (eds.) Proceedings of Reliability, Safety, and Security of Railway Systems (RSSRail 2022). LNCS, vol. 13294, pp. 20–31. Springer (2022)

4. Iliasov, A., Laibinis, L., Taylor, D., Lopatkin, I., Romanovsky, A.: The SafeCap trajectory: industry-driven improvement of an interlocking verification tool. In: Milius, B., Dutilleul, S.C., Lecomte, T. (eds.) Proceedings of Reliability, Safety, and Security of Railway Systems (RSSRail 2023). LNCS, vol. 14198, pp. 117–127. Springer (2023)
5. Bertot, Y., Castran, P.: Interactive Theorem Proving and Program Development Coq'Art: The Calculus of Inductive Constructions, 1st edn. Springer, Incorporated (2010)
6. Cribbens, A.H.: Solid State Interlocking (SSI): an integrated electronic signalling system for mainline railways. Proc. IEE **134**(3), 148–158 (1987)
7. NR/L2/SIG/11201/MOD B11. Signalling Design Handbook: Interlocking Guidelines. Network Rail, 20 p. (2018)
8. Source archive for two Coq theories used in the paper (Transitions.v - for state transition systems and proof semantics, FinSets.v - for finite sets and relations). https://www.dropbox.com/scl/fi/kjh3lhdd3k0qlqk100q43/SafeCap_B.zip?rlkey=fdu9j72ivo7xp4cami3oz4lu8&st=fmef1yqi&dl=0
9. Coq Standard Library. https://coq.inria.fr/doc/V8.20.0/stdlib/
10. Morley, M.J.: Safety assurance in interlocking design. Ph.D. thesis, University of Edinburgh (1996)
11. James, P., et al.: Verification of solid state interlocking programs. In: SEFM 2013 Workshops. LNCS, vol. 8368, pp. 253–268. Springer (2014)
12. Huber, M., King, S.: Towards an integrated model checker for railway signalling data. In: Proceedings of FME 2002: Formal Methods Europe. LNCS, vol. 2391, pp. 204–223. Springer (2002)
13. Cappart, Q., Limbrée, C., Schaus, P., Quilbeuf, J., Traonouez, L.M., Legay, A.: Verification of interlocking systems using statistical model checking. In: Proceedings of HASE – High Assurance Systems Engineering, pp. 61–68 (2017)
14. Busard, S., Cappart, Q., Limbrée, C., Pecheur, C., Schaus, P.: Verification of railway interlocking systems. In: Proceedings of ESSS 2015, pp. 19–31 (2015)
15. Cappart, Q., Schaus, P.: A dedicated algorithm for verification of interlocking systems. In: Proceedings of Computer Safety, Reliability, and Security - 35th International Conference, SAFECOMP 2016. Lecture Notes in Computer Science, vol. 9922, pp. 76–87. Springer (2016). https://doi.org/10.1007/978-3-319-45477-1_7
16. Rivière, P., Singh, N.K., Aït-Ameur, Y.: Reflexive Event-B: semantics and correctness the EB4EB framework. IEEE Trans. Reliab. **73**(2), 835–850 (2024). https://doi.org/10.1109/TR.2022.3219649
17. Rivière, P., Singh, N.K., Aït-Ameur, Y., Dupont, G.: Extending the EB4EB framework with parameterised events. Sci. Comput. Program. **243**, 103279 (2025). https://doi.org/10.1016/J.SCICO.2025.103279

Translating Event-B Models and Development Proofs to TLA+

Anne Grieu, Jean-Paul Bodeveix, and Mamoun Filali(✉)

IRIT, Université de Toulouse, Toulouse, France
{anne.grieu,jean-paul.bodeveix,mamoun.filali}@irit.fr

Abstract. Event-B and TLA^+ are two formal languages based in set theory. It is thus natural to exchange models between them. The work presented in this paper has been partly supported by the French ANR ICSPA project, which focuses on studying formal methods based on set theory (B, Event-B, TLA+) and by the ANR EBRP project which focus on enhancements of the Event-B method. It aims at translating Event-B models, proof obligations, and their corresponding proofs to the TLA^+ environment. While the translation of models has been previously studied in [9], we extend this work by generating various proof obligations in TLA^+. Finally, we address the translation of proofs interactively constructed in the Rodin platform into the TLA^+ proof script language.

Keywords: formal methods · B/Event-B · TLA^+ · set theory · proof systems · model translation

1 Introduction

Event-B and TLA^+ are widely used in the formal method community and share the same theoretical basis, that of set theory. It is thus quite natural to try exchanging developments between them. Event-B brings more automation (proof obligations generation, proof construction) and a development method based on refinement that can be shared with TLA^+. We thus focus on the transfer of Event-B developments to TLA^+ and present our work on translating Event-B models, proof obligations, and their corresponding proofs scripts into the TLA^+ environment. The translation of B models has already been explored in [9] for the B method. Here, we propose a new translation integrated to the Rodin platform [3] and extend the previous work by also generating proof obligations related to well-formedness, feasibility, and invariant preservation in $^+$. Finally, we demonstrate how to translate proofs interactively constructed in the Rodin platform into the TLA^+ proof language. To illustrate the translation of Event-B models and proofs into $^+$, we consider a simple example (Fig. 1) specifying the mutual exclusion problem. Data structures needed to specify the problem are introduced in a context (Fig. 1a). Two abstract sets are declared: `Proc` for processes and `State` for their states. They are constrained by two labeled axioms:

M. Leuschel and F. Ishikawa (Eds.): ABZ 2025, LNCS 15728, pp. 124–142, 2026.
https://doi.org/10.1007/978-3-031-94533-5_8

```
context cMutex1
sets Proc State
constants In Out
axioms
  @fin  finite (Proc)
  @State partition (State,
      {In},{Out})
end
```

(a) Event-B Context

```
machine mMutex1 sees cMutex1
variables state
invariants
  @state_ty state ∈ Proc → State
  @mutex ∀p1,p2· state(p1)=In ∧ state(p2)=In
                         ⇒ p1 = p2
events
  event INITIALISATION then
    @i state := Proc × {Out} end
  event Enter any p where
      @p_ty p ∈ Proc
      @mutex ran(state) = {Out}
    then @pIn state(p) := In end
  event Exit any p where
      @pIn state(p) = In
    then @pOut state(p) := Out end
end
```

(b) Event-B machine

Fig. 1. The Mutex example in Event-B

`@fin` declares `Proc` to be a finite set and `@State` that `State` can be partitioned in to singletons, which means it consists of the two elements `In` and `Out`.

The machine `mMutex1` (Fig. 1b) defines two events responsible for entering and exiting a critical section while ensuring the preservation of the `mutex` invariant. An event can have parameters (here `p`) constrained by guards following the `where` clause and makes actions updating the machine state defined here by the `state` variable. The events should preserve the machine invariants, which is checked through the generation of proof obligations that must be discharged by the user when not automatically proved.

2 Translating Event-B Models

An Event-B [2] model is defined as a single machine that describes the dynamics of a system using a symbolic labeled transition system. Its state is represented by variables and invariants, while its behavior is governed by parameterized events that must preserve these invariants. A machine can reference contexts, which define static information such as carrier sets, constants, and axioms, organized hierarchically. Translating a machine involves recursively translating its referenced contexts first, followed by the translation of the machine's internal components. Both machines and contexts are mapped to separate TLA$^+$ modules [13].

2.1 TLA$^+$ Modules

A TLA$^+$ module can extend other modules. It plays the role of an Event-B context through the declaration of constants, axioms (assumptions) and theorems and also the role of an Event-B machine through the declaration of variables and actions that correlate current and next (primed) values of variables.

```
---- MODULE time ----
EXTENDS Naturals
CONSTANTS N
VARIABLES t
ASSUME N_ty N ∈ Nat \ {0}
Init ≜ t = 0
Next ≜ t' = IF t = N−1 THEN 0 ELSE t+1
======================
```

2.2 Translating Contexts

Event-B contexts are translated hierarchically, with each context generating a corresponding TLA$^+$ module. In this module, each Event-B set or constant is represented by a CONSTANT declaration, each axiom by an ASSUME declaration, and each theorem by a THEOREM declaration. For example, translating the context shown in Fig. 1a produces the following:

```
------- MODULE cMutex1 -------
EXTENDS Naturals, Integers, TLAPS, Relations, Partitions, FiniteSets
CONSTANTS State, Proc, In, Out
ASSUME In_ty ≜ In ∈ State // type synthesized by Rodin
ASSUME Out_ty ≜ Out ∈ State // type synthesized by Rodin
ASSUME fin ≜ IsFiniteSet(Proc)
ASSUME State ≜ Partition(State, ⟨{In}, {Out}⟩)
=====================================
```

2.3 Translating Event-B Machines

An Event-B machine is translated into a TLA$^+$ module (see Fig. 2 and Annex A for a full translation) that extends the modules corresponding to its referenced contexts. State variables are mapped to TLA$^+$ VARIABLES (line 3), with an additional variable (`event`) introduced to store the name of the executed event. Invariants are translated as TLA$^+$ definitions (lines 5 and 6). Each Event-B event is translated into three TLA$^+$ macros (lines 11, 12, 13). Given an event of the form: `ev = any p where G then A`, we get:

- `EVT_ev(p) ==` $\langle\langle "ev", p\rangle\rangle$ defines the Event-B transition label as an ordered pair consisting of the event name and its parameters.
- `GRD_ev(p) ==` $\overline{G}$ represents the conjunction of the TLA$^+$ translations of the Event-B guards G.

– `ACT_ev(p)` == $\overline{BA(A)}$ encodes the TLA$^+$ translation of the before-after relation $BA(A)$ associated with the event's actions A.

The complete translation of the event `ev` is then defined as the conjunction of these three components (line 14): _ev(p) ≜ EVT_ev(p) ∧ GRD_ev(p) ∧ ACT_ev(p).

Then, the TLA$^+$ `Next` operator can be defined as usual as the disjunction of existentially quantified operators associated to each event, as well as the specification of the system `Spec` (lines 15–16).

```
1  -------- MODULE mMutex1 --------
2  EXTENDS Naturals, Integers, TLAPS, Relations, Partitions, FiniteSets , cMutex1
3  VARIABLES event, state
4  vars ≜ ⟨event, state⟩
5  Inv_state_ty ≜ (state ∈ TotalFunctions(Proc, State))
6  Inv_mutex ≜ (∀ p1 ∈ Proc, p2 ∈ Proc: ((FunImage(state, p1) = In) ∧
7                        (FunImage(state, p2) = In)  ⇒ (p1 = p2)))
8  Invariant ≜ Inv_state_ty ∧ Inv_mutex
9
10 Init ≜ event = ⟨"INITIALISATION"⟩ ∧ ⟨state⟩ = ⟨(Proc × { Out})⟩
11 EVT_Enter(p) ≜ event = ⟨"Enter", p⟩
12 GRD_Enter(p) ≜ (p ∈ Proc)  ∧ (Ran(state) = { ut})
13 ACT_Enter(p) ≜ ⟨state'⟩ = ⟨Overwrite(state, {⟨p, In⟩})⟩
14 _Enter(p) ≜ EVT_Enter(p) ∧ GRD_Enter(p) ∧ ACT_Enter(p)
15 Next ≜ (∃ p ∈ Proc : _Enter(p)) ∨ (∃ p ∈ Proc : _Exit(p))
16 Spec ≜ Init ∧ [□][Next]_vars
17 ========================================
```

Fig. 2. TLA$^+$ translation of mMutext1

2.4 Translating Event-B Formulas

The Event-B mathematical language is based on a typed set theory. In the Rodin environment, types are inferred and assigned to each declared identifier, including constants, variables, event parameters, and quantifiers. An Event-B type is either a user defined carrier set, the Integer and Boolean types, or a Cartesian product of types or a powerset of a type:

$$t ::= \mathcal{S} \mid \mathbb{Z} \mid \mathbb{B} \mid t \times t \mid \mathbb{P}(t)$$

Although TLA$^+$ is an untyped language, type information is essential for translating Event-B formulas, as it defines the bounds for quantified variables. For instance, the formula: $\forall E \cdot 0 \in E \wedge (\forall x \cdot x \in E \Rightarrow x + 1 \in E) \Rightarrow \mathbb{N} \subseteq E$ is first type-checked by Rodin which provides type annotations for all its quantified variables. It becomes: $\forall E ⦂ \mathbb{P}(\mathbb{Z}) \cdot 0 \in E \wedge (\forall x ⦂ \mathbb{Z} \cdot x \in E \Rightarrow x + 1 \in E) \Rightarrow \mathbb{N} \subseteq E$ where terms on the right of the ⦂ operator are expressed in Event-B type language. The formula is then translated to TLA$^+$ by using the synthesized type information to bound the quantifiers:

```
∀ E ∈ SUBSET(Int): 0 ∈ E ∧ (∀ x ∈ Int: x ∈ E ⇒ x+1 ∈ E) ⇒ Nat ⊆ E
```

Rodin also infers type information for constants (based on context axioms), machine variables (derived from invariants), and event parameters (determined by event guards).

Formulas are classified into three categories: expressions, predicates, and actions. Expressions are assigned types.

Expressions. The primary challenge in translating Event-B expressions lies in the fact that most operators are relational, with no direct counterparts in TLA$^+$. Therefore, a library of TLA$^+$ operators, designed to define all Event-B relational operators, must be provided (the `Relation` module). A subset of these operators is presented here (close to the library provided by [9])[1].

```
-------------------- MODULE Relations ------------------
Rel(A,B) ≜ SUBSET (A × B)
Id(S) ≜ {r ∈ Rel(S,S) : ∀ c ∈ r: c[1] = c[2]}
Dom(R) ≜ {xy[1] : xy ∈ R }
Ran(R) ≜ {xy[2] : xy ∈ R }
Rev(R) ≜ {xy ∈ Ran(R) × Dom(R): ⟨xy[2],xy[1]⟩ ∈ R}
RestrictDom(R,D) ≜ { xy ∈ R : xy[1] ∈ D}
AntirestrictDom(R,D) ≜ { xy ∈ R : xy[1] ∉ D}
RestrictRan(R,D) ≜ { xy ∈ R : xy[2] ∈ D}
AntirestrictRan (R,D) ≜ { xy ∈ R : xy[2] ∉ D}
Overwrite(R,S) ≜ S ∪ AntirestrictDom(R,Dom(S))

PartialFunctions (D,R) ≜ {r ∈ Rel(D,R): ∀ e,x,y: ⟨e,x⟩∈ r ∧ ⟨e,y⟩∈ r ⇒ x=y}
TotalFunctions(D,R) ≜ {r ∈ PartialFunctions(D,R): Dom(r) = D}
PartialInjections (D,R) ≜ {r ∈ PartialFunctions(D,R): Rev(r) ∈ PartialFunctions(R,D)}
TotalInjections (D,R) ≜ TotalFunctions(D,R) ∩ PartialInjections (D,R)
```

We emphasize the `Overwrite(R,S)` operator, which takes two relations as arguments and returns a relation that includes pairs from S as well as pairs from R where the first projection has no corresponding image in S. The `Overwrite` operator is crucial for defining the semantics of function updates in machine actions. For instance, the Event-B assignment `f(x) := y` is translated into the following TLA$^+$ action: `f' = Overwrite(f, {⟨x,y⟩})`.

The second point concerns partial functions (and by extension, total, injective, and surjective functions), which are encoded in TLA$^+$ as specific relations, similar to their representation in Event-B. As a result, TLA$^+$ functions are not used. While it would be possible to identify relations that are actually functions and represent them using TLA$^+$ functions, which would lead to a more efficient translation to SMT, this approach would also require duplicating relational operators based on the nature of their arguments or introducing conversions during

[1] We uses TLA$^+$ tuples $x = \langle x_1, \ldots, x_n \rangle$ where fields are accessed through $x[i]$.

the translation process. Such an approach would also complicate the translation of Event-B proof scripts to TLAPS [6].

Given this encoding, functional application in TLA$^+$ is defined using the `CHOOSE` operator, which means that the TLA$^+$ function call notation `f[x]` is not used. Instead, Event-B `f(x)` is encoded as follows:

```
RImage(R,S) ≜ {y ∈ Ran(R): ∃ x ∈ S: ⟨x,y⟩ ∈ R}
FunImage(R,c) ≜ CHOOSE i ∈ RImage(R,{c}): TRUE
```

However, this definition is not explicitly expanded to make the TLA$^+$ proof as close as possible to the Rodin proof. It is only used on leaves of the TLA$^+$ proof tree supposed to be resolved by SMT calls. Otherwise, derived properties are used instead, such as the following, which can be proven in TLA$^+$:

```
THEOREM FunImageSingleton ≜
  ASSUME NEW S, NEW i PROVE ∀ c ∈ S: FunImage(S × {i},c) = i
```

In fact, it would be necessary to create a TLA$^+$ library containing all the theorems used by Event-B proof rules.

Predicates. The translation of the predicate language is straightforward, as quantifier bounds are available through Rodin's type synthesis. However, Event-B built-in predicates (such as `finite` and `partition`) need to be defined in TLA$^+$, for instance, `partition` is defined as follows:

```
Partition (S,s) ≜ S = UNION {s[i] : i ∈ DOMAIN s}
                  ∧ ∀ i ∈ DOMAIN s, j ∈ DOMAIN s: i ≠ j ⇒ s[i] ∩ s[j]= ∅
```

Actions. Event-B actions are translated into TLA$^+$ actions, which are predicates that relate the current state to the next (primed) state of the module. Unchanged variables must be identified and explicitly declared. The four types of Event-B actions are transformed as follows:

- The multi-assignment action $x_1, \ldots, x_n := e_1, \ldots e_n$ becomes $\langle x'_1, \ldots, x'_n \rangle = \langle \overline{e_1}, \ldots, \overline{e_n} \rangle$ where $\overline{e}$ denotes the translation of the expression e.
- Function update actions `f(e) := e'` are transformed by Rodin into single variable assignments `f := f` $\Leftarrow\!\!\!+$ {e $\mapsto$ e'} using the overwrite operator.
- The non-deterministic multi-assignment $x_1, \ldots x_n :| \; P(x_1, \ldots, x_n, x'_1, \ldots x'_n)$ where P is the before-after predicate of the action becomes the TLA$^+$ translation of P
- The non-deterministic assignment to a set element $x :\in E$ becomes $x' \in \overline{E}$

Finally, the translation of all individual Event-B actions within an event is conjoined with the TLA$^+$ `UNCHANGED(V)` action, where `V` represents the tuple of state variables that are not syntactically modified by any Event-B action.

In our example, the deterministic assignment `state(p) := In` is translated into

```
ACT_Enter(p) ≜ ⟨state'⟩ = ⟨Overwrite(state,{⟨p, In⟩})⟩
```

Note that initialization actions are transformed differently; instead of generating an action that relates the current and next states, a predicate over the current state is produced.

3 Generation of Proof Obligations in TLA$^+$

In addition to translating the Event-B model, our plugin also generates proof obligations corresponding to Event-B ones [10] as TLA$^+$ theorems. The Event-B proof obligation generator provided by the Rodin platform [3] is not used here. Our plugin generates statements specific to TLA$^+$ that use named predicates (for example `Invariant` instead of the conjunction of individual formulas making the invariant) or the next-state operator. Furthermore, we generate generic proof scripts for TLAPS to facilitate automatic proof attempts.

WD Proof Obligations. Well-definedness proof obligations arise from the use of partially defined constructs, such as treating a relation as a function, calculating the cardinality of a set, or taking the minimum of a set. The most common case involves function calls. The proof obligation ensures that the relation belongs to a function space and that its argument is within the domain of the relation. These checks are performed based on the hypotheses inherited from referenced contexts, previous axioms (within contexts), invariants (within machines), prior guards, and quantified parameters (within events).

We illustrate these principles with the TLA$^+$ translation of the well-definedness (WD) proof obligation generated for the guard `state(p) = In` in the event `Exit(p)`. The synthesized type for `p`, provided by the Rodin environment, is `Proc`, which is used to bound the TLA$^+$ universal quantifier.

```
THEOREM Exit_pst_WD ≜ Invariant ⇒ (∀ p ∈ Proc :
  p ∈ Dom(state) ∧ state ∈ PartialFunctions(Proc, State))
```

Feasibility Proof Obligations. Proof obligations are generated to ensure that when the invariants and guards hold, non-deterministic actions are feasible. Specifically, this means that the before-after predicate must have at least one solution, and the corresponding set must be non-empty.

Theorem Proof Obligations. Theorems derived from axioms, invariants, and guards are translated into TLA$^+$ theorems, with the hypotheses consisting of seen axioms, previous theorems, and, in the case of guards, previous guards. For guards, the hypotheses are quantified by typed event parameters. Outside of contexts, seen axioms are directly included in the TLA$^+$ model and do not need to be added to the theorem's hypotheses.

Invariant Preservation Proof Obligations. A proof obligation is generated for each declared invariant and event, ensuring that the invariant is preserved by the event actions.

For example, the preservation of the `mutex` invariant by the `Enter(p)` event results in the following theorem, where the TLA$^+$ prime operator is used to express that the invariant must be satisfied in the next state. Additionally, we assume that the previous invariants (such as `Inv_state_ty`) are preserved, as the corresponding theorem has already been established.

```
THEOREM PO_Next_Enter_mutex ≜ ∀ p ∈ Proc:
  Invariant ∧ Inv_state_ty' ∧ _Enter(p) ⇒ Inv_mutex'
```

Variant-Related Proof Obligations. We also generate proof obligations for set-based or integer-based non-lexicographic variants. Events declared as `convergent` must ensure that the variant strictly decreases, while `anticipated` events should not cause the variant to increase.

In the following example, the `exit` event is declared as convergent with respect to the variant `state` ▷ `In`. This leads to two proof obligations: one asserting the strict decrease of the variant, and the other confirming its finiteness. Note the use of the TLA$^+$ prime operator, which ensures that the left argument of the $\subset$ operator is evaluated in the next state.

```
THEOREM Exit_vv_VAR ≜ Invariant ⇒ (∀ p ∈ Proc:  _Exit(p) ⇒
  RestrictRan({In}, state)' ⊂ RestrictRan({In}, state))
THEOREM Exit_vv_FIN ≜ Invariant ⇒ (∀ p ∈ Proc:  _Exit(p) ⇒
  IsFiniteSet(RestrictRan({In}, state))
```

Deadlock-Freedom. We also generate a proof obligation not typically produced by Event-B: deadlock-freedom. This obligation asserts that the disjunction of guards is implied by the invariant. It is important to note that in Event-B, an action is always considered feasible when its guard is true, thanks to the feasibility proof obligations.

```
THEOREM NoDeadlock ≜ Invariant ⇒
  (∃ p ∈ Proc : GRD_Enter(p)) ∨ (∃ p ∈ Proc : GRD_Exit(p))
```

Automatic Proof of Proof Obligations. Automatically proving obligations in TLAPS is often challenging because the user must provide all necessary theorems and definitions. While TLAPS implicitly injects the definitions and theorems related to standard TLA$^+$ modules (such as `Naturals`, `Sequences`, `FiniteSets`, etc.), Event-B operators are fundamentally defined using relational operators. As a result, all these operators must be explicitly defined in TLA$^+$ and provided to TLAPS.

If we supply the prover with the complete list of definitions, the resulting statement transmitted to SMT solvers is often too complex and difficult to prove.

In contrast, Event-B employs numerous domain-specific rewrite and deduction rules, which are applied before invoking specialized set theory-based solvers or SMT solvers (after first-order reduction). Additionally, the Rodin user may need to guide the prover interactively to ultimately build the proof.

As a consequence, in case the automatic proof fails, we have explored how to translate Event-B proofs to TLA$^+$.

4 Translating Event-B Proof Trees

Since automatically proving generated proof obligations is challenging, we attempt to generate TLAPS proof scripts from the Rodin proof trees, utilizing the hints contained within them. To keep the TLA$^+$ proof synchronized with the Rodin proof, the translation of Event-B proof trees is performed through a recursive traversal of the tree. Each node leads to a corresponding TLA$^+$ proof script schema, where the proofs of the subtrees are inserted. The subgoals (and their hypotheses) are extracted from the Rodin proof tree and translated into TLA$^+$. Then, TLA$^+$ should prove that the node goal follows from the conjunction of the sub-node goals.

However, this general approach fails if the proof, which expresses the correctness of the rule instance, cannot be automated (through SMT calls performed by TLA$^+$). In such cases, additional information-such as dedicated theorems, definitions to be unfolded, or intermediate goals-must be provided. These depend on the specific rule and its parameters, as indicated by the Rodin proof tree.

4.1 TLA$^+$ Proof Language

TLA$^+$ defines a textual proof script language [12]. A proved statement is characterized by an identifier, a formula or an assume-prove statement, and a tree structure[2]. The leaves of the tree are composed of definitions and/or facts (e.g., theorems) that are used to support the proof. A subtree represents a sequence of steps that ends with a `QED` step. Each step is associated with its own proof. TLA$^+$ provides proof constructs for building these steps. Figure 3 shows a simplified view of the TLA$^+$ proof structure. The entry point is the `Proof` class. A proof is either direct (classes `Obvious` and `By`) or needs several steps (class `Steps`) ending with a `qed` step. Some of the basic proof steps (specified by subclasses of the class `Step`) include:

- The construct `WITNESS E` (class `Witness`) provides a value (E) for proving an existential goal.
- The construct `HAVE P` (class `Have`) introduces a lemma stating the property `P`
- The construct `ASSUME H PROVE G` (class `SubProof`) introduces a TLA$^+$ sequent, where `H` represents a sequence of either a variable declaration (using the `NEW` keyword) or a hypothesis. This construct can be viewed as a forward proof mechanism, as it allows for assuming `H` and proving `G` based on that assumption.

[2] The tree structure is optional; in such cases, the proof consists of a named statement.

- The `SUFFICES` construct (class `Suffices`) introduces an intermediary step to discharge the current goal. After justifying this step, the proof continues with the newly introduced goal. Thus, `SUFFICES` can be viewed as a backward proof mechanism, as it helps to derive the goal by working backwards from the current step.

We illustrate the use of these constructs with the following excerpt, which is taken from the translation of the Rodin proof tree.

```
<1>3. SUFFICES ∀ p1 ∈ Proc, p2 ∈ Proc :
          FunImage(Overwrite(state, {⟨p, In⟩}), p1) = In
          ∧ FunImage(Overwrite(state, {⟨p, In⟩}), p2) = In ⇒ p1 = p2
  OBVIOUS
<1>4. SUFFICES
        ASSUME NEW CONSTANT p1 ∈ Proc, NEW CONSTANT p2 ∈ Proc
        PROVE  FunImage(Overwrite(state, {⟨p, In⟩}), p1)=In ∧ FunImage(Overwrite(state, {⟨p, In⟩}), p2)=In ⇒
               p1 = p2
  OBVIOUS
<1>5. SUFFICES
        ASSUME FunImage(Overwrite(state, {⟨p, In⟩}), p1)=In , FunImage(Overwrite(state, {⟨p, In⟩}), p2)=In
        PROVE p1 = p2
  OBVIOUS
```

4.2 Structure of Rodin Proof Trees

A property to be proven is represented as a sequent, which consists of hypotheses and a goal. A proof is structured as a tree of such sequents, as depicted in the (simplified) UML diagram in Fig. 4. A non-terminal sequent (class `Sequent`) is resolved by a rule (class `Rule`), which may take input parameters (class `Input`) provided by the user, such as expressions for quantifier instantiation, the position of a subterm to be transformed, and so on. The application of a rule generates new sequents, which may introduce new identifiers (derived from universal goals or existential hypotheses) (class `Identifier`) or create new hypotheses (subclasses of `Action`) by applying actions (e.g., deduction, rewriting) to the parent hypotheses.

This tree structure will be illustrated in the next section by considering a concrete proof tree. It represents, together with the structure of formulas, the main data structure to be traversed for transforming a Rodin proof.

4.3 A Rodin Proof Tree

Figure 5 illustrates the tree representation of the Rodin proof for the preservation of the `mutex` invariant by the `Exit` event. The key points to note are the following:

- Some rules (such as ∀ goal) introduce new variables, corresponding to the universally quantified rules at the head of the goal. These new variables are found by following the `newIdents` link of Fig. 4.
- Some rules (such as ⇒ goal) introduce new hypotheses, corresponding to the conjuncts in the left part of the implication goal. They are found by following the link `actions` of Fig. 4.

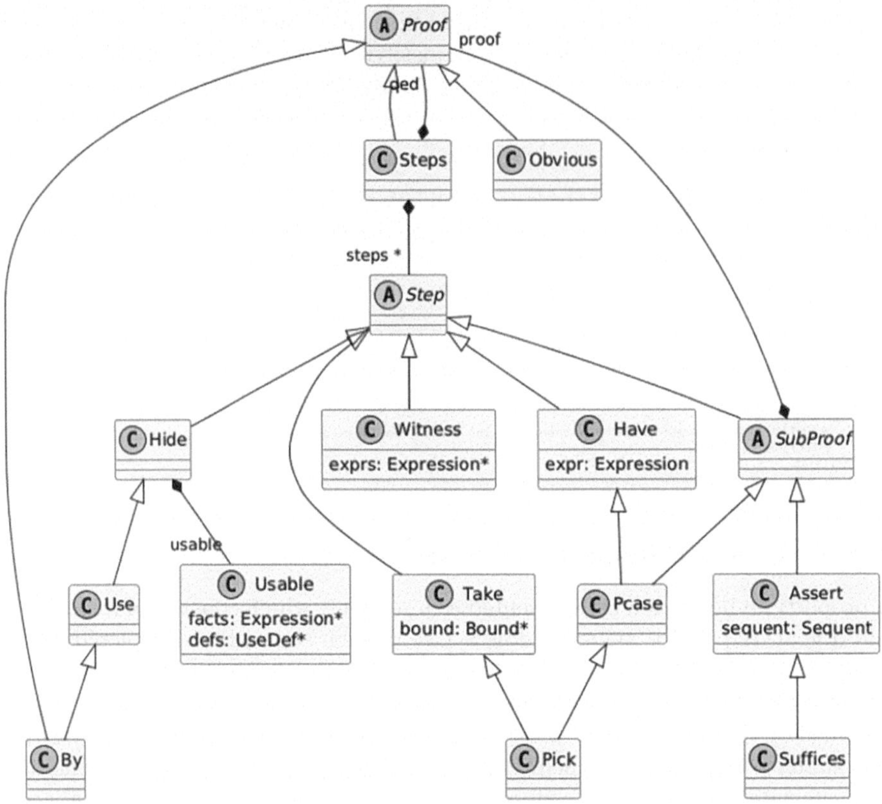

Fig. 3. Simplified view of the TLA$^+$ proof tree structure

- Certain rules create multiple sub-trees. For example, the overwrite rule `ovr` creates one when the argument of the function is the overwritten point, and another when it is not. They are found by following the `sequents` link of Fig. 4.
- Some rules (such as `ovr`) apply to specific terms, which can be specified by the user during the proof development process. They are found by following the link `input` of Fig. 4.
- Deduction rules (e.g., `MP` for *Modus Ponens*) and rewrite rules (e.g., `he`, for *reverse equality in hypothesis*) generate new hypotheses from existing ones. The corresponding actions are instances of the `ForwardInfHypAction` or `RewriteHypAction` classes of Fig. 4.

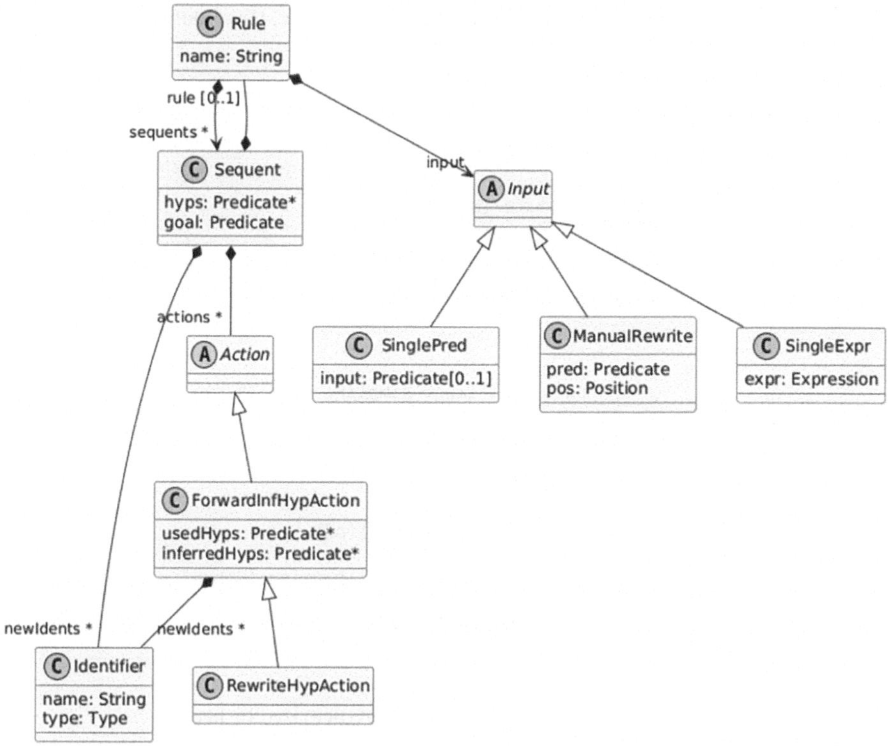

Fig. 4. Simplified view of Rodin Proof Tree Structure

4.4 Translating Proofs of Rodin Proof Obligations

The following TLA$^+$ theorem is a direct translation of the proof tree built by the Rodin user for the proof obligation stating the preservation of the invariant `mutex` by the `Enter` event of the `Mutex1` machine. It is important to note that Rodin produces a self-contained proof obligation, i.e. it includes identifiers and axioms declared in the seen contexts (such as `Proc`, `State`, `In`, `Out`, etc.) and variables of the machine (`state` here). Additionally, we observe that the state of the machine after the event is expressed using the Event-B `Overwrite` operator (lines 12–13).

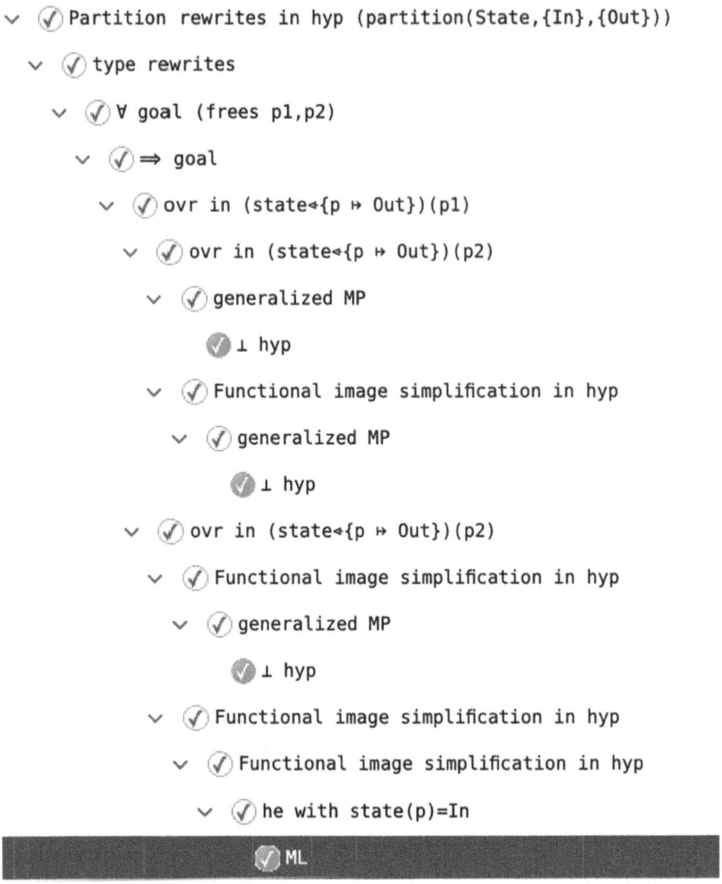

Fig. 5. A Rodin proof

```
THEOREM Mutex1_Enter_mutex_INV_po ≜
  ASSUME NEW CONSTANT Proc, NEW CONSTANT State,
         NEW CONSTANT p ∈ Proc, NEW CONSTANT In ∈ State,
         NEW CONSTANT state ∈ SUBSET Proc × State,
         NEW CONSTANT Out ∈ State,
         RImage(Rev(state), {In}) = ∅ ,
         state ∈ TotalFunctions(Proc, State) ,
         ∀ p1 ∈ Proc, p2 ∈ Proc :
            FunImage(state, p1) = In ∧ FunImage(state, p2) = In ⇒ p1 = p2 ,
         Partition(State, ⟨{In}, {Out}⟩)
  PROVE  ∀ p1 ∈ Proc, p2 ∈ Proc :
            FunImage(Overwrite(state, {⟨p, In⟩}), p1) = In
            ∧ FunImage(Overwrite(state, {⟨p, In⟩}), p2) = In ⇒ p1 = p2
```

4.5 Translating Rodin Proof Structure

Translating an Event-B proof tree involves recursively generating a TLAPS proof schema for each node. A node representing an Event-B proof rule is structured as follows:

$$\frac{C_1 : T_1, nH_1, H \vdash G_1 \quad \ldots \quad C_k : T_k, nH_k, H \vdash G_k}{H \vdash G}\ R(p)$$

which says that applying the rule R with input parameters p on the goal $H \vdash G$ generates k new sequents, each of them using new constants C_i of type T_i and new hypotheses nH_i to solve the goal G_i. The generated TLAPS proof schema is then the following:

```
<N> ASSUME H PROVE G (* current goal *)
   <N+1>1 ASSUME NEW CONSTANT C1 ∈ T1, H1 PROVE G1
        ... (* proof of G1 *)
   <N+1>k ASSUME NEW CONSTANT Cn ∈ Tk, Hk PROVE Gk
        ... (* proof of Gk *)
   <N+1>k+1 QED BY <N+1>1 ... <N+1>k (* try to prove H⇒G from subgoals *)
```

which means that given a proof for the k subgoals (marked with ...), we get a proof for the initial goal. TLA$^+$ will attempt to automatically prove the QED step.

In order to simplify the proof structure, the generated schema is different when we only have one subgoal ($k = 1$):

```
ASSUME H PROVE G
SUFFICES ASSUME NEW CONSTANT C1 ∈ T1, H1 PROVE G1
  OBVIOUS (* try to prove H⇒G from the subgoal *)
... (* proof of G1 *)
```

This rule can be read: it suffices to prove G_1 using the new constants and hypotheses to get a proof of the initial goal. As previously, TLA$^+$ tries to prove automatically the correctness of the rule, i.e. that the subgoal is really a sufficient condition for the goal to hold.

The example of Sect. 4.1 is the translation of steps $\forall goal$ and $\Rightarrow goal$ of the Rodin proof tree of Fig. 5. The first step introduces the two typed quantified variables that are referred to by the `newIdents` role of Fig. 5. The second step moves the left hand side of the $\Rightarrow$ connector to the assumptions.

The two script schemas aim to automatically verify the correctness of rule instances, ensuring that the conjunction of subgoals imply the initial goal. This automation typically succeeds for propositional and basic set reasoning. For more complex cases managed by Rodin through the use of domain-specific rules or theorems, we provide dedicated techniques in Sect. 5. They avoid trying to prove set-related formulas by reducing them to (often complex) first-order formulas.

4.6 Taking into Account Rodin Proof Rules

The general schema we have presented does not consider the specific nature of the proof rule referenced in the Rodin Proof Tree. Instead, it attempts to automatically verify that the conjunction of subgoals implies the initial goal—that is, to establish the correctness of the proof rule instance. In most cases, this approach succeeds when the deduction relies on propositional logic or set-theoretic arguments, thanks to TLA$^+$'s internal transformations and its use of SMT solvers. However, it fails when the proof requires specific theorems or definitions.

5 Translating Rodin Tactics

As mentioned in the introduction, this work is preliminary, and achieving full coverage of the Event-B framework is a long-term effort. The Event-B framework has evolved over many years, incorporating more than 50 proof rules and over 500 simplification rules. Addressing these is essential to accurately preserve the structure of Event-B proofs.

5.1 Proof Rules

Here, we highlight two proof rules that illustrate the inherent challenges of translating Event-B proofs to TLA$^+$: Generalized Modus Ponens, which encapsulates a complex reasoning process, and Overwrite Right Subset, which functions as a rule schema rather than a single rule.

- The reasoner `GeneralizedModusPonens` uses many modus ponens-like rules such as the two following:

  $$\frac{P, \varphi(\top) \vdash G}{P, \varphi(P) \vdash G} \qquad \frac{\varphi(\top) \vdash \neg G}{\varphi(G) \vdash \neg G}$$

  where P is a predicate present in the list of hypotheses (left rule), $\varphi(\_)$ the list of (remaining for the left rule) hypotheses and G the current goal. Predicates of this list may contain P (left rule) or G (right rule) as a subformula. Applying one of these rules replaces P by $\top$ or G by $\bot$ in all the hypotheses. These rule applications are not explicitly traced, so the approach to handling this tactic is to let TLA$^+$ attempt to prove the resulting goal automatically.
- The OVR_RIGHT_SUBSET: This rule facilitates the proof of a relational overwrite statement in the presence of another overwrite. However, it cannot be directly expressed as a single rule, as it functions more as a rule schema. Therefore, applying this rule requires supplying TLA$^+$ with the necessary elementary theorems to support the proof and relying on automatic verification.

  $$f \mathbin{\lhd\!\!\!+} \cdots \mathbin{\lhd\!\!\!+} g \mathbin{\lhd\!\!\!+} \cdots \mathbin{\lhd\!\!\!+} h \subseteq A \vdash g \mathbin{\lhd\!\!\!+} \cdots \mathbin{\lhd\!\!\!+} h \subseteq A$$

  In this case, providing the binary variant of the mentioned rule along with a theorem stating the associativity of the overloading operator should be sufficient. In the next section, we present an example to illustrate this idea.

5.2 Simplification Rules

An Event-B proof rule triggers a simplification procedure that applies numerous rewriting rules to the current goal and its hypotheses. However, the order in which these rules are applied is only available in debug mode via standard output, and the transformed sub-formulas are not specified. Even when the final formula is known, expecting an automatic proof in TLA$^+$ remains challenging. Therefore, it is essential to identify as many applied rules as possible to assist the TLA$^+$ prover. To illustrate potential approaches to this problem, we have selected two specific rules as examples.

- The rule `SIMP_MULTI_BINTER` removes duplicates in an intersection. It is specified as follows: $S \cap \ldots \cap T \cap \ldots \cap T \cap \ldots \cap U = S \cap \ldots \cap T \cap \ldots \cap U$. It cannot be directly expressed as a TLA$^+$ theorem as it is in fact a rule schema. However, since we know the left and right terms, and the $\cap$ operator is a built-in TLA$^+$ operator, we can state the expected goal and expect an automatic proof[3].

```
THEOREM ints_SIMP_MULTI_BINTER ≜
    ASSUME NEW S, NEW T, NEW I, NEW U
    PROVE S ∩ T ∩ I ∩ T ∩ U = S ∩ T ∩ I ∩ U
    OBVIOUS
```

- Simplifications rules may also concern relational operators that are not built-in. For example, a duplication inside a chain of overwrite operators can be removed: $r_1 \lessdot\!\!+ \ldots \lessdot\!\!+ r_n = r_1 \lessdot\!\!+ \ldots \lessdot\!\!+ r_{i-1} \lessdot\!\!+ r_{i+1} \ldots \lessdot\!\!+ \ldots \lessdot\!\!+ r_n$ if $\exists k > 0 : r_{i+k} = r_i$. The corresponding theorems (associativity of overwrite, binary and ternary instances of the previous rule) must be provided through the `BY` clause to get an automatic proof of the following theorem provided as an example[4].

```
R <: S ≜ Overwrite(R,S) (* an infix notation for Overwrite *)
THEOREM MULTI_OVERWRITE ≜
    ASSUME NEW S, NEW T, NEW I1, NEW I2, NEW U
    PROVE S <: T <: I1 <: I2 <: T <: U = S <: I1 <: I2 <: T <: U
    BY Ovr_ASSOC, Ovr_IDEMP, Ovr_IDEMP_GAP
```

The given information must be well chosen to avoid an overload of the underlying SMT's and thus chosen on a case by case basis.

5.3 Architecture of the Generated TLA$^+$ Development

As seen in Sect. 4.4, Event-B proof trees are self-contained and thus do not depend the Event-B model. Links are only provided for traceability. Consequently, the TLA$^+$ proofs generated from Event-B proof trees are currently

[3] It is indeed the case!.
[4] The whole module `OVERWRITE` is given in Appendix B.

self-contained also. However, the TLA$^+$ language allows a module containing a proof script to import a module containing a model. Establishing this connection remains an open task and involves two key steps: first, eliminating proof assumptions that duplicate information already present in the model, and second, expanding TLA$^+$ macros (such as invariants, event guards, and actions) used in the direct generation of proof obligations in TLA$^+$ (Sect. 3), so that the obtained statements match those of the Rodin proof tree.

6 Conclusion

A conclusion of our study is that Event-B and TLA$^+$ are more closely related than they might initially seem. While Event-B is based on relations and TLA$^+$ on functions, both rely on Zermelo-Fraenkel (ZF) set theory, and the syntax of their formula languages are nearly identical. However, Event-B relies heavily on relations while TLA$^+$ introduces functions. It would be interesting to distinguish Event-B relations which behave as functions and are not mixed with other relations. Then, such relations could be encoded as TLA$^+$ functions. Moreover, since Event-B lacks a textual proof language, it could potentially benefit from TLA$^+$'s approach. Our initial experiments suggest that this integration is promising. Conversely, regarding proof obligations, Event-B's methodology could enhance TLA$^+$ by standardizing the way proof statements for properties such as safety are formulated. Such uniformity would improve model readability and comprehension while facilitating intuitive translations between models or entire developments.

A closely related work is EB4EB [15], which also explores Event-B semantics. However, we believe EB4EB is better suited for addressing meta-level issues, such as defining the semantics of new constructs not currently supported by Event-B-e.g., liveness [13] or scheduling properties [11]. In contrast, our work is more focused on verification, specifically at the proof level. Other research efforts, such as the BWare project [7], have explored the translation of B-system proof obligations. However, those efforts primarily use proof obligations generated by Atelier B [1,4,14] and do not take underlying proofs into account. Additionally, the Why3 tool [8] has been employed as an interface to various provers to facilitate proof discovery.

For future work, we plan to explore machine refinement and the syntactic extensions introduced by Event-B, which aid in refinement proofs. In particular, witness declarations serve as valuable hints for existential proofs. Finally, we aim to define a TLA$^+$ translation semantics for Event-B context instantiation [5,16].

Acknowledgments. The authors greatly thank the reviewers for their helpful and insightful comments.

A mMutex in TLA$^+$

```
-------- MODULE mMutex1 --------
EXTENDS Naturals, Integers, TLAPS, Relations, Partitions, FiniteSets , cMutex1
VARIABLES event, state
vars ≜ ⟨event, state⟩
Inv_state_ty ≜ (state ∈ TotalFunctions(Proc, State))
Inv_mutex ≜ (∀ p1 ∈ Proc, p2 ∈ Proc: ((FunImage(state, p1) = In) ∧
                 (FunImage(state, p2) = In)  ⇒ (p1 = p2)))
 Invariant ≜ Inv_state_ty ∧ Inv_mutex

 Init ≜ event = ⟨"INITIALISATION"⟩ ∧ ⟨state⟩ = ⟨(Proc × { Out})⟩
EVT_Enter(p) ≜ event = ⟨"Enter", p⟩
GRD_Enter(p) ≜ (p ∈ Proc)  ∧ (Ran(state) = { ut})
ACT_Enter(p) ≜ ⟨state'⟩ = ⟨Overwrite(state, {⟨p, In⟩})⟩
_Enter(p) ≜ EVT_Enter(p) ∧ GRD_Enter(p) ∧ ACT_Enter(p)

EVT_Exit(p) ≜ event = ⟨"Exit", p⟩
GRD_Exit(p) ≜ (FunImage(state, p) = In)
ACT_Exit(p) ≜ ⟨state'⟩ = ⟨Overwrite(state, {⟨p, Out⟩})⟩
_Exit(p) ≜ EVT_Exit(p) ∧ GRD_Exit(p) ∧ ACT_Exit(p)

Next ≜ (∃ p ∈ Proc : _Enter(p)) ∨ (∃ p ∈ Proc : _Exit(p))
Spec ≜ Init ∧ [□][Next]_vars
========================================
```

B Simplification of Overwrite

```
R <: S  Overwrite(R,S) ( an infix notation for Overwrite )
THEOREM MULTI_OVERWRITE
ASSUME NEW S, NEW T, NEW I1, NEW I2, NEW U
PROVE S <: T <: I1 <: I2 <: T <: U = S <: I1 <: I2 <: T <: U
BY Ovr_ASSOC, Ovr_IDEMP, Ovr_IDEMP_GAP
```

References

1. Abrial, J.R.: The B-Book: Assigning Programs to Meanings. Cambridge University Press, New York (1996)
2. Abrial, J.R.: Modeling in Event-B: System and Software Engineering, 1st edn. Cambridge University Press, New York (2010)
3. Abrial, J.R., Butler, M., Hallerstede, S., Hoang, T.S., Mehta, F., Voisin, L.: Rodin: an open toolset for modelling and reasoning in Event-B. Int. J. Softw. Tools Technol. Transf. **12**(6), 447–466 (2010). https://doi.org/10.1007/s10009-010-0145-y
4. Berkani, K., Dubois, C., Faivre, A., Falampin, J.: Validation des règles de base de l'atelier B. Tech. Sci. Informatiques **23**(7), 855–878 (2004). https://doi.org/10.3166/TSI.23.855-878
5. Bodeveix, J.-P., Filali, M.: Event-B formalization of Event-B contexts. In: Raschke, A., Méry, D. (eds.) ABZ 2021. LNCS, vol. 12709, pp. 66–80. Springer, Cham (2021). https://doi.org/10.1007/978-3-030-77543-8_5
6. Cousineau, D., Doligez, D., Lamport, L., Merz, S., Ricketts, D., Vanzetto, H.: TLA$^+$ proofs. In: Giannakopoulou, D., Méry, D. (eds.) FM 2012. LNCS, vol. 7436, pp. 147–154. Springer, Heidelberg (2012). https://doi.org/10.1007/978-3-642-32759-9_14
7. Delahaye, D., Dubois, C., Marché, C., Mentré, D.: The BWare project: building a proof platform for the automated verification of b proof obligations. In: Ait Ameur, Y., Schewe, K.D. (eds.) ABZ 2014. LNCS, vol. 8477, pp. 290–293. Springer, Heidelberg (2014). https://doi.org/10.1007/978-3-662-43652-3_26
8. Filliâtre, J.-C., Paskevich, A.: Why3—where programs meet provers. In: Felleisen, M., Gardner, P. (eds.) ESOP 2013. LNCS, vol. 7792, pp. 125–128. Springer, Heidelberg (2013). https://doi.org/10.1007/978-3-642-37036-6_8
9. Hansen, D., Leuschel, M.: Translating B to TLA+ for validation with TLC. Sci. Comput. Program. **131**, 109–125 (2016). https://doi.org/10.1016/J.SCICO.2016.04.014
10. Hoang, T.S.: An introduction to the Event-B modelling method. In: Romanovsky, A., Thomas, M. (eds.) Industrial Deployment of System Engineering Methods, pp. 211–236. Springer, Heidelberg (2013). http://www.springer.com/computer/swe/book/978-3-642-33169-5
11. Hudon, S., Hoang, T.S., Ostroff, J.S.: The Unit-B method: refinement guided by progress concerns. Softw. Syst. Model. **15**(4), 1091–1116 (2016). https://doi.org/10.1007/S10270-015-0456-2
12. Lamport, L.: TLA$^+$ version 2 a preliminary guide. https://lamport.azurewebsites.net/tla/tla2-guide.pdf. Accessed 18 Feb 2025
13. Lamport, L.: Specifying Systems: The TLA$^+$ Language and Tools for Hardware and Software Engineers. Addison-Wesley Longman Publishing Co., Inc., USA (2002)
14. Lecomte, T., Déharbe, D., Fournier, P., Oliveira, M.: The CLEARSY safety platform: 5 years of research, development and deployment. Sci. Comput. Program. **199**, 102524 (2020). https://doi.org/10.1016/J.SCICO.2020.102524
15. Rivière, P., Singh, N.K., Aït-Ameur, Y.: Reflexive Event-B: semantics and correctness the EB4EB framework. IEEE Trans. Reliab. **73**(2), 835–850 (2024). https://doi.org/10.1109/TR.2022.3219649
16. Verdier, G., Voisin, L.: Context instantiation plug-in: a new approach to genericity in Rodin (2021). https://eprints.soton.ac.uk/449887/1/proceedings.pdf. Accessed 19 Feb 2025

The Proved Construction of a Protocol with an Example Inspired by the Paxos Protocol

Dominique Cansell[1(✉)] and Jean-Raymond Abrial[2]

[1] Lessy, France
dominique.cansell@gmail.com
[2] Marseille, France

Abstract. This paper present a complete proved development of a protocol inspired by the Lamport's Paxos protocol. Our protocol is not fault-tolerant. This work was carried out at the end of 2019.

1 Informal Description

This document contains the description of the formally proved construction of a protocol. Such a description is not so different from that of the formally proved construction of a loop program as this one:

$$A; \textbf{while } G \textbf{ do } S \textbf{ end}$$

with loop initialisation A, loop guard G and loop body S. Such a program can be specified by means of a pre-condition PRE and a post-condition $POST$. In order to demonstrate that this program achieves $POST$, one has to prove the following:

$$\neg G, I \vdash POST$$

where I stands for some invariant predicates (to be discovered) in the loop body, invariants to be proved as follows:

$$PRE \vdash [A]I$$
$$G, I \vdash [S]I$$

where $[A]I$ and $[S]I$ stand for the establishment of invariant I by the loop initialisation A and the loop body S. Another proof is needed, namely that the loop terminates. This can be done by exhibiting a variant that is decreased by the loop body S.

In the case of the loop program, the initialisation A, the guard G and the body S are executed by a single computing entity. In the case of a protocol, we have also a kind of loop, but the initialisation A, the guard G and the body S are executed concurrently by several (sometimes many) computing entities communicating with one another by means of messages. We still have some pre- and post-conditions specifying our protocol and we have a kind of proof similar to the one proposed for the loop program above.

D. Cansell and J.-R. Abrial—Independent authors.

M. Leuschel and F. Ishikawa (Eds.): ABZ 2025, LNCS 15728, pp. 143–160, 2026.
https://doi.org/10.1007/978-3-031-94533-5_9

As for the loop program, we need to propose some invariants. We have also to prove the termination of our protocol. It might be a little more complicated than in the case of the loop program as we might have now several loops involved. An additional demonstration is needed to prove that the concurrent execution of the body does not deadlock while our protocol execution is not terminated. This has to be done under the implicit assumption that the communication between the computing entities do not fail.

In this paper, we illustrate what has been just said. For this, we choose a terminating variant of part of the protocol Paxos [3] proposed by Leslie Lamport. In our protocol, besides the basic behaviour, it is also supposed that the communication between the computing entities does not fail. Our intention is to write later an extension of this document taking account of the communication failure.

In the present section, we present first a general background in Sect. 1.1. Then we propose an informal description of our protocol in Sect. 1.2. In Sect. 2, we propose two approaches to formally proving our protocol: a direct approach and a constructive approaches. Details of the direct approach are given in Sect. 3 while details of the constructive approach are given in Sect. 4. Related works are given in Sect. 5. In Sect. 6, we have a short conclusion.

1.1 Background

We are given a set V of values. The purpose of our protocol is to distribute elements in the set V to elements of a finite set A of entities called "acceptors". One value only will be distributed to each acceptor. We suppose that each acceptor is ignorant of the presence of other acceptors.

At the end of our protocol all acceptors must have received the same value. *This is the goal of our Protocol.*

There exists another finite set, P, of entities, called "proposers". As is the case for acceptors, each proposer ignores the presence of other proposers. Some of the elements of the set V of values are spread over proposers. In other words, each proposer p owns a value $val(p)$, which is a member of the set V. Notice that several proposers may own the same value. Moreover, the only values able to be distributed to acceptors are those owned by proposers. This distribution is made possible through messages sent by proposers to acceptors as is explained in the next paragraph.

Although each proposer ignores other proposers, each proposer knows all acceptors. Thus a proposer is able to send messages to all acceptors. Conversely, an acceptor receiving a message from a proposer p is able to reply to this message from the proposer p. Messages between proposers and acceptors and vice versa are sent concurrently.

In this document, we suppose that the communication between proposers and acceptors is safe (reliable). That is, we suppose that messages sent from proposers to acceptors and vice versa always reach their destination, and this without being modified. Notice that the general Paxos protocol handles the case where the communication is not safe (although general Paxos assumes that messages reaching their destination are not modified). Again, we do not consider this case in the present document.

It is clearly not possible to achieve the main goal of our protocol (i.e. all acceptors receive the same value) with the previous data we mentioned. This is so because the only information to be transmitted from a proposer p to acceptors is the value $val(p)$

owned by the proposer p. All acceptors might receive the same value only if the set A contains a single element or if all elements in the set P own the same value.

In order to solve the problem, another data structure is needed. In fact, each proposer p is given a unique *positive* natural number $num(p)$ not shared by other proposers. Proposers are thus organised as a strict hierarchy.

From the point of view of each proposer, our protocol is decomposed into two phases:

In a first phase, each proposer p sends $num(p)$ to all acceptors. Such a message from a proposer to an acceptor is called a "prepare" message. This not done at once, only gradually by each proposer concurrently with other proposers.

In a second phase, when a proposer p has sent a prepare message to all acceptors and has received the associated reply (called a "promis" message, whose contents is defined below in Sect. 1.2) from each of them, the proposer p sends, again gradually, its value $val(p)$ (or a substitute of it, $store(p)$) to all acceptors. Such a message from a proposer to all acceptors is called an "accept" message.

We have similar phases for acceptors.

In order to finalise the description of our protocol, more data structures are needed. Each acceptor a can record numbers sent by proposers (in a prepare message) in a variable called $the\_num(a)$. Initially, $the\_num(a)$ is equal to 0 (remember that $num(p)$ is a *positive* natural number). Moreover, each acceptor contains a variable $The\_val(a)$. Initially, $The\_val(a)$ contains any value. At the end of our protocol, each variable $The\_val(a)$ must contain the same value for all acceptors a. Finally, each acceptor has a boolean variable $val\_bool(a)$. Initially, $val\_bool(a) = FALSE$. When $val\_bool(a) = TRUE$, it means that acceptor a received a value from a proposer (in an accept message), and that this value has been recorded in $The\_val(a)$.

Each proposer p can record values to be sent to acceptors not only in the initial constant $val(p)$ but also in a variable $store(p)$ which is local to each proposer. Initially, $store(p)$ is equal to $val(p)$, but, during the execution of our protocol, $store(p)$ is modified in order to send the same value to all acceptors.

1.2 Informal Description of Our Protocol

Here is the informal description of our protocol. It is made of the following six numbered actions:

(1) Each proposer p sends a prepare message containing $num(p)$ to all acceptors.

(2) When receiving a prepare message from a proposer p, an acceptor a compares the $num(p)$ contained in the prepare message with its local variable $the\_num(a)$. If $num(p) > the\_num(a)$, then the value of $the\_num(a)$ is updated with $num(p)$.

(3) Whatever the comparison between $num(p)$ and $the\_num(a)$, a promise message is send by acceptor a as a reply to the processor p which sent the prepare message to acceptor a. This promise message contains $val\_bool(a)$ and $The\_val(a)$

(4) When a proposer p receives a promise message from an acceptor a containing $TRUE$ and $The\_val(a)$, the proposer p updates $store(p)$ with $The\_val(a)$ contained in the promis message, otherwise proposer p does nothing.

(5) Once a proposer p has received replies from all acceptors, it sends an accept message to all acceptors. This message contains $num(p)$ and $store(p)$.

(6) When an acceptor a receives an accept message from a processor p, this message is discarded if the $num(p)$ contained in the message is smaller than $the\_num(a)$ or if a has already received a value (that is, if $val\_bool(a)$ = TRUE). Otherwise, $The\_val(a)$ is updated with the $store(p)$ contained in the accept message and $val\_bool(a)$ is set to $TRUE$.

Our protocol ends when each acceptor has received a value, that is when, for each acceptor a, we have $val\_bool(a) = TRUE$.

As can be seen, the behaviour of this protocol is highly non-deterministic and *it is not at all obvious that all acceptors get the same value at the end of it*. In fact, model checking is absolutely impossible even with small sets P and A. A proof can only be convincing in this case.

We want to prove three things: (1) at the end of the execution of our protocol, all acceptors receive the same value, (2) the execution of our protocol comes eventually to an end (notice that the general Paxos protocol might fail to terminate), (3) there is no deadlock in the execution of our protocol.

2 Approaches to Proofs

We tried two different approaches: a direct approach and a constructive approach. We started with the direct approach but we had, after adding many invariants only one unproved proof obligation. We were stuck so we started the constructive approach (till model M4) . In the meantime (but after a long time) the missing invariant was discovered for the direct approach. After that we were able to finish the constructive approach easily.

2.1 A Direct Approach

In this approach, we encode directly our protocol with Event-B [1] on the Rodin toolset [7] (see below in Sect. 3). For doing this, each kind of messages (prepare, promis, accept) is encoded by at least two events: one corresponding to the sending of the message, and at least one corresponding to the reception and reactions to the message. Note that this reaction can be the sending of another message.

In order to perform the proof of (1) defined in the previous Section, we had to introduce some invariants. It was not an easy task. It took us a long time until we had the proper set of invariants. During this approach, we used the model checker ProB [5,6] a lot in order to find some invariant counter examples.

The conclusion was that this approach was not satisfactory at all, due to the main difficulty to discover good invariants.

2.2 A Constructive Approach

In this approach, we define a sequence of models, each of which being a refinement of the one before it in the sequence (see below in Sect. 4). The first models are very abstract containing some global variables able to be seen by proposers or acceptors. As refinements progress, these abstract variables are removed so that we reach in the final model our genuine protocol. In each model, some invariants are introduced and proved far more easily than in the direct approach.

3 Details of the Direct Approach

In this section, we describe how the informal description of our protocol defined in Sect. 1.2 can be encoded in terms of various events. Besides the data presented in Sect. 1.1 (the_num, The_val, val_bool and $store$), we use six technical variables. Three variables define the three kinds of messages: $prepare\_msg \in (P \times A) \nrightarrow \mathbb{N}1$, $promis\_msg \in (P \times A) \nrightarrow (\text{bool} \times V)$ and $accept\_msg \in (P \times A) \nrightarrow (\mathbb{N}1 \times V)$. Three more variables are used to control loops in the proposers: $loop\_prepare \in P \rightarrow \mathbb{P}(A)$, $loop\_accept \in P \rightarrow \mathbb{P}(A)$ and $loop\_promis \in P \rightarrow \mathbb{P}(A)$.

For reasons of space, we will only give the names of the events; the reader can see them (guards and action) in the Subsect. 4.10:

- Event send_prepare corresponds to a proposer sending a *prepare* message to an acceptor (this corresponds to action (1) of the informal description of our protocol in Sect. 1.2):
- The two events rcv_prepare_1 and rcv_prepare_2 correspond to the reactions of an acceptor receiving a *prepare* message from a proposer. Notice that a *promis* message is sent back to the proposer (this corresponds to actions (2) and (3)):
- The two events rcv_promis_1 and rcv_promis_2 correspond to the reactions of a proposer receiving a *promis* message (this corresponds to action (4)):
- When a proposer has received reactions from all acceptors, this proposer can send an *accept* message to all acceptors (this corresponds to action (5)). It's the event send_accept.
- The two events rcv_accept_1 and rcv_accept_2 correspond to the reactions of an acceptor receiving an *accept* message (this corresponds to action (6)):

The main property to prove is the following. It says that at the end of our protocol (when all acceptors have received a value), all acceptors received the same value:

$$(val\_bool = A \times \{\text{TRUE}\}) \Rightarrow (\exists v \cdot v \in V \wedge The\_val = A \times \{v\})$$

This property is quite difficult to prove at this point because many invariants have to be introduced. Nevertheless it is important to have defined these events as it is then possible to validate the constructing approach defined in Sect. 4: at the end of the constructing approach we must obtain exactly the same set of events as defined in this section except the event final. To prove our invariant we have to add the two (abstract) variables $init\_acc$ and $init\_p$. Two other properties have to be proved at the next level: ending property and no deadlock property. In this first refinement $init\_acc$ and $init\_p$ disappear. Again, some invariants are needed to perform such proofs. The no deadlock is a little different. Since event final is not present we prove that the negation of the disjunction of all guards implies that the protocol is finished.

$$
\begin{array}{l}
\neg((\exists p, a \cdot a \notin loop\_prepare(p)) \ \vee \\
\quad (\exists p, a, n \cdot (p \mapsto a) \mapsto n \in prepare\_msg \ \wedge \ the\_num(a) < n) \ \vee \\
\quad (\exists p, a, n \cdot (p \mapsto a) \mapsto n \in prepare\_msg \ \wedge \ the\_num(a) \geq n) \ \vee \\
\quad (\exists p, a, v \cdot (p \mapsto a) \mapsto (\text{FALSE} \mapsto v) \in promis\_msg) \ \vee \\
\quad (\exists p, a, v \cdot (p \mapsto a) \mapsto (\text{TRUE} \mapsto v) \in promis\_msg) \ \vee \\
\quad (\exists p, a \cdot loop\_promis(a) = A \ \wedge \ a \notin loop\_accept(a)) \ \vee \\
\quad (\exists p, a, n, v \cdot (p \mapsto a) \mapsto (n \mapsto v) \in accept\_msg \ \wedge
\end{array}
$$

$$val\_bool(a) = \text{FALSE} \wedge n \geq the\_num(a)) \vee$$
$$(\exists p, a, n, v \cdot (p \mapsto a) \mapsto (n \mapsto v) \in accept\_msg \wedge$$
$$(n < the\_num(a) \vee val\_bool(a) = \text{TRUE})))$$
$$\Rightarrow$$
$$(val\_bool = A \times \{\text{TRUE}\})$$

4 Details of the Constructive Approach

4.1 Context C1 and Model M1

Before describing model M1 in this section, we have to define the most abstract *pre-condition* of our protocol. Such a pre-condition is defined by means of some constants in the context C1: the set V (the set of values) and the finite set A (the set of acceptors): finite(A).

In model M1, we have a unique variable the_val. This variable is supposed to record values sent to acceptors during the execution of our protocol. It is a partial function from A to V: $the\_val \in A \nrightarrow V$. It is initialised to the empty set $\varnothing$.

The *post-condition* of our protocol is defined in the guard of the special event final with no action. This post-condition states that, at the end of our protocol, each acceptor receives the same value. We have an additional event, chg_val, that, non-deterministically, states that the variable the_val can be modified. This event will be made more precise in the next model:

```
final
  when
    ∃v·v ∈ V ∧ the_val = A × {v}
  then
    skip
  end
```

```
chg_val
  then
    the_val :∈ A ⇸ V
  end
```

The event chg_val is *anticipated*. It means that we do not prove now that this event does not take control for ever. This will be done in the next model where the event chg_val will be refined by two convergent events.

4.2 Model M2

In this model, we add the variable $init\_val$. It is a member of the set V that is, supposedly, the value distributed to all acceptors. Of course, in this abstract model, we do not know how this value is chosen. This will be made clear in further models. The event final is refined as follows:

```
final
  when
    dom(the_val) = A
  then
    skip
  end
```

In order to prove that this new version of the event final refines the more abstract version proposed in the previous section, we have to prove that the guard of this concrete version implies the guard of the abstract version, that is the following:

$$(\mathrm{dom}(the\_val) = A) \Rightarrow (\exists v \cdot v \in V \wedge the\_val = A \times \{v\})$$

In order to do so, we need the following invariant:

$$\mathrm{ran}(the\_val) \subseteq \{init\_val\}$$

The abstract event chg_val is refined by the two events first_val and next_val. The event first_val corresponds to the first time a value v is ever sent to an acceptor a. In this event, the variable $init\_val$ is updated to v. The event next_val corresponds to the case where a variable is not sent for the first time to an acceptor. In fact, $init\_val$ is used in this case:

first_val
any
v, a
where
$the\_val = \varnothing$
$v \in V$
$a \in A$
then
$the\_val(a) := v$
$init\_val := v$
end

next_val
any
a
where
$the\_val \neq \varnothing$
$a \notin \mathrm{dom}(the\_val)$
then
$the\_val(a) := init\_val$
end

These events are *convergent*. This means that we have to prove that they cannot take control for ever. For proving this, we must define a decreasing variant. In this case, the variant is the following finite set:

$$A \setminus \mathrm{dom}(the\_val)$$

4.3 Context C2 and Model M3

In this model, proposers enter into the scene. For this, we extend the context C1 by the context C2. The finite set P is defined in this context: finite(P). This is done together with the total constant function val defining the value owned by each proposer: $val \in P \rightarrow V$. In model M3, we remove the variable $init\_val$. We replace it by the new variable $init\_acc$, which is the first acceptor receiving $init\_val$. The two events first_val and next_val are refined as follows:

first_val
any
a, p
where
$the\_val = \varnothing \ \wedge \ a \in A \ \wedge \ p \in P$
with
$v = val(p)$
then
$the\_val(a) := val(p) \ \|\| \ init\_acc := a$
end

next_val
any
a
where
$the\_val \neq \varnothing$
$a \notin \mathrm{dom}(the\_val)$
then
$the\_val(a) := the\_val(init\_acc)$
end

In order to prove the correct refinement of these events, we have to introduce the following invariant:

$$the\_val \neq \varnothing \Rightarrow init\_acc \in \mathrm{dom}(the\_val) \wedge the\_val(init\_acc) = init\_val$$

4.4 Context C3 and Model M4

Here, we introduce the new constant num. It defines a unique positive natural number for each proposer. The constant num is thus an injective function from P to $\mathbb{N}1$: $num \in P \rightarrowtail \mathbb{N}1$. This is done in a context C3, extending context C2.

In this model, we add the new variable a_met_p. It is a relation between A and P: $a\_met\_p \in A \leftrightarrow P$. If $a \mapsto p \in a\_met\_p$, it means that acceptor a met proposer p in the past. This variable is initialised to the empty set $\varnothing$. The event first_val is refined as follows. Notice the guard $A \times \{p\} \subseteq a\_met\_p$: it means that all acceptors met proposer p. The last guard means that $num(p)$ has the greatest number among other similar proposers. These two guards correspond to what is done in the concrete protocol.

```
first_val
  any
    a, p
  where
    the_val = ∅
    a ∈ A
    A × {p} ⊆ a_met_p
    ∀q · a ↦ q ∈ a_met_p ⇒ num(q) ≤ num(p)
  then
    the_val(a) := val(p)
    init_acc := a
  end
```

Notice that several acceptors can trigger this event. However, the proposer p is unique. This is due to the fact that the number $num(p)$ associated with each proposer p is unique. More precisely, if we have the following according to the guards of the event first_val with parameters $a1$, $p1$ and $a2$, $p2$:

$$\begin{array}{l} A \times \{p1\} \subseteq a\_met\_p \\ \forall q \cdot a1 \mapsto q \in a\_met\_p \Rightarrow num(q) \leq num(p1) \\ A \times \{p2\} \subseteq a\_met\_p \\ \forall q \cdot a2 \mapsto q \in a\_met\_p \Rightarrow num(q) \leq num(p2) \end{array}$$

we can deduce $num(p2) \leq num(p1)$ and $num(p1) \leq num(p2)$, that is $num(p1) = num(p2)$, that is $p1 = p2$ since the function num is injective.

We have a new abstract event modifying the variable a_met_p:

```
chg_a_met_p
  any
    a, p
  where
    a ∈ A
    a ↦ p ∉ a_met_p
  then
    a_met_p := a_met_p ∪ {a ↦ p}
  end
```

This event is convergent. Here is the corresponding finite set variant:

$$(A \times P) \setminus a\_met\_p$$

4.5 Model M5

In this model, we introduce the variable the_num. It is a total function: $the\_num \in A \rightarrow \mathrm{ran}(num) \cup \{0\}$. It is initialised to $A \times \{0\}$. When $the\_num(a) \neq 0$, it means that acceptor a knows at least the number of one proposer. The event first_val is refined as follows:

```
first_val
  any
    a, p
  where
    the_val = ∅
    A × {p} ⊆ a_met_p
    num(p) = the_num(a)
  then
    the_val(a) := val(p)
    init_acc := a
  end
```

To prove this refinement, we need the following invariant:

$$\forall a, p \cdot a \mapsto p \in a\_met\_p \;\Rightarrow\; num(p) \leq the\_num(a)$$

The abstract event chg_a_met_p is refined by the following events:

```
chg_the_num
  any
    a, p
  where
    a ↦ p ∉ a_met_p
    num(p) > the_num(a)
  then
    a_met_p := a_met_p ∪ {a ↦ p}
    the_num(a) := num(p)
  end
```

```
no_chg_the_num
  any
    a, p
  where
    a ↦ p ∉ a_met_p
    num(p) ≤ the_num(a)
  then
    a_met_p := a_met_p ∪ {a ↦ p}
  end
```

4.6 Model M6

So far, we did not introduce messages. This is quite normal in a constructive approach: messages are part of an implementation. In this model M6, we introduce the last kind of messages involved in our protocol: *accept* messages. For this, we define the following variable: $accept\_msg \in (P \times A) \twoheadrightarrow (\mathbb{N}1 \times V)$. Events first_val and next_val are refined as follows:

```
first_val
  any
    a, p, n, v
  where
    the_val = ∅
    (p ↦ a) ↦ (n ↦ v) ∈ accept_msg
    n ≥ the_num(a)
  then
    the_val(a) := v
    init_acc := a
    accept_msg := accept_msg \
                  {(p ↦ a) ↦ (n ↦ v)}
  end
```

```
next_val
  any
    a, p, n, v
  where
    the_val ≠ ∅
    a ∉ dom(the_val)
    (p ↦ a) ↦ (n ↦ v) ∈ accept_msg
    n ≥ the_num(a)
  then
    the_val(a) := v
    accept_msg := accept_msg \
                  {(p ↦ a) ↦ (n ↦ v)}
  end
```

For proving the guards of the event first_val, we need the following invariant:

$$\forall p, a, n, v \cdot (p \mapsto a) \mapsto (n \mapsto v) \in accept\_msg \;\Rightarrow\; A \times \{p\} \subseteq a\_met\_p$$

For proving the actions of the event first_val , we need the following invariant:

$$\begin{array}{ll}\forall p, a, n, v \cdot & (p \mapsto a) \mapsto (n \mapsto v) \in accept\_msg \;\wedge \\ & the\_val = \varnothing \;\wedge \\ & n \geq the\_num(a) \\ & \Rightarrow \\ & v = val(p)\end{array}$$

For the event next_val, we need the following invariant:

$$\begin{array}{ll}\forall p, a, n, v \cdot & (p \mapsto a) \mapsto (n \mapsto v) \in accept\_msg \;\wedge \\ & the\_val \neq \varnothing \;\wedge \\ & n \geq the\_num(a) \\ & \Rightarrow \\ & v = the\_val(init\_acc)\end{array}$$

In order to deal with these invariants, we define the following event sending an *accept* message. Before presenting this new event, we must introduce the new variable $already\_accept \in P \leftrightarrow A$. When $p \mapsto a \in already\_accept$, it means equivalently that proposer p already sent an *accept* message to acceptor a:

```
send_accept
  any
    a, p, v
  where
    p ↦ a ∉ already_accept
    A × {p} ⊆ a_met_p
    the_val(a) = ∅ ⇒ v = val(p)
    the_val(a) ≠ ∅ ∧ num(p) ≥ the_num(a) ⇒ v = the_val(init_acc)
  then
    accept_msg := accept_msg ∪ {(p ↦ a) ↦ (num(p) ↦ v)}
    already_accept := already_accept ∪ {p ↦ a}
  end
```

The following event explains under which circumstances the accept message is ignored:

```
ignore_accept
  any
    a, p, n, v
  where
    (p ↦ a) ↦ (n ↦ v) ∈ accept_msg
    n < the_num(a)  ∨  a ∈ dom(the_val)
  then
    accept_msg := accept_msg \ {(p ↦ a) ↦ (n ↦ v)}
  end
```

The last two events are convergent. This can be proved by means of the following lexicographic variant:

$$(P \times A) \setminus send\_accept$$
$$\mathrm{dom}(accept\_msg)$$

4.7 Model M7

In this model, we introduce other messages. Here is the event sending a *prepare* message:

```
send_prepare
  any
    p, a
  where
    p ↦ a ∉ already_prepare
  then
    prepare_msg := prepare_msg ∪ {(p ↦ a) ↦ num(p)}
    already_prepare := already_prepare ∪ {p ↦ a}
  end
```

The next invariant makes precise the contents of a *prepare* message:

$$\forall p, a, n \cdot (p \mapsto a) \mapsto n \in prepare\_msg \;\Rightarrow\; n = num(p)$$

Events chg_the _num and no_chg_the _num are refined as follows (notice the changes of name):

```
rcv_prepare_1
  refines
    chg_the_num
  any
    a, p, b, v, m
  where
    (p ↦ a) ↦ m ∈ prepare_msg
    m > the_num(a)
    a ∈ dom(the_val) ⇒
                 b = TRUE ∧
                 v = the_val(init_acc)
    a ∉ dom(the_val) ⇒
                 b = FALSE ∧ v ∈ V
  then
    the_num(a) := m
    prepare_msg := prepare_msg \
                 {(p ↦ a) ↦ m}
    promis_msg := promis_msg ∪
                 {(p ↦ a) ↦ (b ↦ v)}
  end
```

```
rcv_prepare_2
  refines
    no_chg_the_num
  any
    a, p, b, v, m
  where
    (p ↦ a) ↦ m ∈ prepare_msg
    m ≤ the_num(a)
    a ∈ dom(the_val) ⇒
                 b = TRUE ∧
                 v = the_val(init_acc)
    a ∉ dom(the_val) ⇒
                 b = FALSE ∧ v ∈ V
  then
    prepare_msg := prepare_msg \
                 {(p ↦ a) ↦ m}
    promis_msg := promis_msg ∪
                 {(p ↦ a) ↦ (b ↦ v)}
  end
```

When a proposer p receives a $promis$ message with TRUE and value v, it means that the value v is the one that is chosen. The proposer p will save this value in a variable $store(p)$ where $store \in P \to V$ is initialised to val. When a proposer p receives a $promis$ message with FALSE and value v, it means that the value v is not the one that is chosen. Here are the two corresponding events rcv_promis_1 and rcv_promis_2:

```
rcv_promis_1
  any
    a, p, v
  where
    (p ↦ a) ↦ (TRUE ↦ v) ∈ promis_msg
  then
    promis_msg := promis_msg \
          {(p ↦ a) ↦ (TRUE ↦ v)}
    already_promis := already_promis ∪
          {p ↦ a}
    store(p) := v
  end
```

```
rcv_promis_2
  any
    a, p, v
  where
    (p ↦ a) ↦ (FALSE ↦ v) ∈ promis_msg
  then
    promis_msg := promis_msg \
          {(p ↦ a) ↦ (FALSE ↦ v)}
    already_promis := already_promis ∪
          {p ↦ a}
  end
```

The variable a_met_p can be removed thanks to the following invariant:

$$a\_met\_p^{-1} = \mathrm{dom}(promis\_msg) \cup already\_promis$$

The event send_accept can now be refined as follows:

```
send_accept
  any
    a, p
  where
    p ↦ a ∉ already_accept
    {p} × A ⊆ already_promis
  with
    v = store(p)
  then
    accept_msg := accept_msg ∪ {(p ↦ a) ↦ (num(p) ↦ store(p))}
    already_accept := already_accept ∪ {p ↦ a}
  end
```

Only two proof obligations were unproved for the refinement of send_accept. The case of the guard

$$the\_val = \varnothing \Rightarrow store(p) = val(p)$$

is easy using the following invariant:

$$the\_val = \varnothing \;\Rightarrow\; (\forall p \cdot\; store(p) = val(p))$$

The case of the guard:

$$the\_val(a) \neq \varnothing \wedge num(p) \geq the\_num(a) \;\Rightarrow\; store(p) = the\_val(init\_acc)$$

is more difficult. For doing it, we introduce the variable $init\_p$. This variable stands for the proposer whose value is to be distributed to all acceptors. It is initialised by the event first_val as follows:

```
first_val
  any
    a, p, n, v
  where
    the_val = ∅
    (p ↦ a) ↦ (n ↦ v) ∈ accept_msg
    n ≥ the_num(a)
  then
    the_val(a) := v
    init_acc := a
    init_p := p
    accept_msg := accept_msg \ {(p ↦ a) ↦ (n ↦ v)}
  end
```

We have the following invariant concerning $init\_p$:

$$the\_val \neq \varnothing \;\Rightarrow\; \{init\_p\} \times A \subseteq already\_promis$$

Four more invariants are needed to prove the refinement of the event send_accept:

$$store(init\_p) = val(init\_p) \qquad the\_val \neq \varnothing \;\Rightarrow\; val(init\_p) = the\_val(init\_acc)$$

$$\begin{array}{l} \forall p \cdot\; the\_val \neq \varnothing \wedge \\ \quad \text{FALSE} \in \\ \quad \mathrm{dom}(promis\_msg[\{p \mapsto init\_acc\}] \\ \quad \Rightarrow \\ \quad num(p) \leq num(init\_p) \end{array} \qquad \begin{array}{l} \forall p \cdot\; the\_val \neq \varnothing \wedge \\ \quad p \mapsto init\_acc \in already\_promis \\ \quad \wedge\, num(p) > num(init\_p) \\ \quad \Rightarrow \\ \quad store(p) = the\_val(init\_acc) \end{array}$$

The proof of the second guard can be managed by cases:

- $p = init\_p$ then $store(init\_p) = val(init\_p) = the\_val(init\_acc)$
- $p \neq init\_p$ then $num(p) > num(init\_p)$ since $num(init\_p) \leq the\_num(a) \leq num(p)$ and $num(p) \neq num(init\_p)$ because num is injective. Then we can conclude $store(p) = the\_val(init\_acc)$ using the last invariant.

The three new events send_prepare, rcv_promis_1 and rcv_promis_2 are all convergent. This is proved by means of the following finite set variant:

$$(P \times A \setminus already\_prepare) \cup \mathrm{dom}(promis\_msg)$$

The two convergent events rcv_promis_1 and rcv_promis_2 are the last ones to be introduced. As a consequence, we have thus proved that our system in indeed convergent.

4.8 Model M8

In this model, we eliminate variables $init\_p$ and $init\_acc$. Notice that these variables were used in the model M7 for the definitions of some important invariants, this was their only purpose.

The eliminations of $init\_p$ and $init\_acc$ makes actions of events first_val and next_val becoming identical. Consequently, both events will be merged in the next model. Here are the actions of these events:

then
  $the\_val(a) := v$
  $accept\_msg := accept\_msg \setminus \{(p \mapsto a) \mapsto (n \mapsto v)\}$
end

4.9 Model M9

In this model we put together events first_val and next_val in the following event:

```
rcv_accept_1
  refines
    first_val
    next_val
  any
    a, p, n, v
  where
    a ∉ dom(the_val)
    (p ↦ a) ↦ (n ↦ v) ∈ accept_msg
    n ≥ the_num(a)
  then
    the_val(a) := v
    accept_msg := accept_msg \ {(p ↦ a) ↦ (n ↦ v)}
  end
```

We also change the name of the event ignore_accept:

```
rcv_accept_2
  refines
    ignore_accept
  any
    a, p, n, v
  where
    (p ↦ a) ↦ (n ↦ v) ∈ accept_msg
    n < the_num(a) ∨ a ∈ dom(the_val)
  then
    accept_msg := accept_msg \ {(p ↦ a) ↦ (n ↦ v)}
  end
```

We have the following invariant. It helps proving deadlock freeness:

$$\begin{array}{ll} \forall p, a \cdot & (\forall x \cdot num(x) \leq num(p)) \land \\ & p \mapsto a \in already\_accept \land \\ & p \mapsto a \notin \mathrm{dom}(accept\_msg) \\ & \Rightarrow \\ & a \in \mathrm{dom}(the\_val) \end{array}$$

4.10 Model M10

In this model, we localise the variables. Concerning acceptors, we replace the variable the_val by the total function The_val and the boolean variable val_bool. Both new variables are formally defined by means of the following invariants:

$$\begin{array}{l} The\_val \in A \rightarrow V \\ the\_val \subseteq The\_val \\ val\_bool \in A \rightarrow \mathrm{bool} \\ \forall a \cdot val\_bool(a) = \mathrm{TRUE} \Leftrightarrow (a \in \mathrm{dom}(the\_val)) \end{array}$$

The event final is refined as follows:

```
final
  when
    val_bool = A × {TRUE}
  then
    skip
  end
```

Concerning proposers, the variables $already\_prepare$, $already\_promis$ and $already\_accept$ are replaced by the variables $loop\_prepare$, $loop\_promis$ and $loop\_accept$ defined by the following invariants:

$$\begin{array}{l} loop\_prepare \in A \rightarrow \mathbb{P}(A) \\ \forall p \cdot loop\_prepare(p) = already\_prepare[\{p\}] \\ loop\_promis \in A \rightarrow \mathbb{P}(A) \\ \forall p \cdot loop\_promis(p) = already\_promis[\{p\}] \\ loop\_accept \in A \rightarrow \mathbb{P}(A) \\ \forall p \cdot loop\_accept(p) = already\_accept[\{p\}] \end{array}$$

The introduction of the new variables implies the following modifications of the remaining events:

```
send_prepare
  any
    p, a
  where
    a ∉ loop_prepare(p)
  then
    prepare_msg := prepare_msg ∪ {(p ↦ a) ↦ num(p)}
    loop_prepare(p) := loop_prepare(p) ∪ {a}
  end
```

rcv_prepare_1
any
p, a, n
where
$(p \mapsto a) \mapsto n \in prepare\_msg$
$n > the\_num(a)$
then
$the\_num(a) := n$
$promis\_msg := promis\_msg \cup \{(p \mapsto a) \mapsto (val\_bool(a) \mapsto The\_val(a))\}$
$prepare\_msg := prepare\_msg \setminus \{(p \mapsto a) \mapsto n\}$
end

rcv_prepare_2
any
p, a, n
where
$(p \mapsto a) \mapsto n \in prepare\_msg$
$n \leq the\_num(a)$
then
$promis\_msg := promis\_msg \cup \{(p \mapsto a) \mapsto (val\_bool(a) \mapsto The\_val(a))\}$
$prepare\_msg := prepare\_msg \setminus \{(p \mapsto a) \mapsto n\}$
end

rcv_promis_1
any
p, a, v
where
$(p \mapsto a) \mapsto (\mathrm{TRUE} \mapsto v) \in promis\_msg$
then
$store(p) := v$
$loop\_promis(p) := loop\_promis(p) \cup \{a\}$
$promis\_msg := promis\_msg \setminus \{(p \mapsto a) \mapsto (\mathrm{TRUE} \mapsto v)\}$
end

rcv_promis_2
any
p, a, v
where
$(p \mapsto a) \mapsto (\mathrm{FALSE} \mapsto v) \in promis\_msg$
then
$loop\_promis(p) := loop\_promis(p) \cup \{a\}$
$promis\_msg := promis\_msg \setminus \{(p \mapsto a) \mapsto (\mathrm{FALSE} \mapsto v)\}$
end

send_accept
any
p, a
where
$loop\_promis(p) = A$
$a \notin loop\_accept(p)$
then
$accept\_msg := accept\_msg \cup \{(p \mapsto a) \mapsto (num(p) \mapsto store(p))\}$
$loop\_accept(p) := loop\_accept(p) \cup \{a\}$
end

rcv_accept_1
any
p, a, n, v
where
$(p \mapsto a) \mapsto (n \mapsto v) \in accept\_msg$
$n \geq the\_num(a)$
$val\_bool(a) = \mathrm{FALSE}$
then
$The\_val(a) := v$
$val\_bool(a) := \mathrm{TRUE}$
$accept\_msg := accept\_msg \setminus \{(p \mapsto a) \mapsto (n \mapsto v)\}$
end

rcv_accept_2
any
p, a, n, v
where
$(p \mapsto a) \mapsto (n \mapsto v) \in accept\_msg$
$n < the\_num(a) \lor val\_bool(a) = \mathrm{TRUE}$
then
$accept\_msg := accept\_msg \setminus \{(p \mapsto a) \mapsto (n \mapsto v)\}$
end

4.11 Model M11

In this last model, we prove that the system is deadlock free while it is not terminated. Here is the theorem we proved:

$$
\begin{array}{l}
(val\_bool = A \times \{\text{TRUE}\}) \vee \\
(\exists p, a \cdot a \notin loop\_prepare(p)) \vee \\
(\exists p, a, n \cdot (p \mapsto a) \mapsto n \in prepare\_msg \ \wedge \ the\_num(a) < n) \vee \\
(\exists p, a, n \cdot (p \mapsto a) \mapsto n \in prepare\_msg \ \wedge \ the\_num(a) \geq n) \vee \\
(\exists p, a, v \cdot (p \mapsto a) \mapsto (\text{FALSE} \mapsto v) \in promis\_msg) \vee \\
(\exists p, a, v \cdot (p \mapsto a) \mapsto (\text{TRUE} \mapsto v) \in promis\_msg) \vee \\
(\exists p, a \cdot loop\_promis(a) = A \ \wedge \ a \notin loop\_accept(a)) \vee \\
(\exists p, a, n, v \cdot (p \mapsto a) \mapsto (n \mapsto v) \in accept\_msg \wedge \\
\qquad\qquad val\_bool(a) = \text{FALSE} \ \wedge \ n \geq the\_num(a)) \vee \\
(\exists p, a, n, v \cdot (p \mapsto a) \mapsto (n \mapsto v) \in accept\_msg \wedge \\
\qquad\qquad (n < the\_num(a) \vee val\_bool(a) = \text{TRUE}))
\end{array}
$$

For proving this theorem, we need the following invariant (to be proved in model M7) stating that the sets $\text{dom}(prepare\_msg)$, $\text{dom}(promis\_msg)$, and $already\_promis$ partition the set $already\_prepare$.

4.12 About the Proofs

For the direct approach the overall proving effort required 194 proofs, among which 164 were proved automatically by the Rodin Toolset (that is , 84.5%). The 30 interactive proofs are more complicated than the constructive approach but not difficult. There is only one variant (non lexicographic) and their proofs are more long but technical (9 interactive proofs). We can have less with a lexicographic variant. For the deadlock freeness theorem the proof is the same in both approach..

For the constructive approach the overall proving effort required 253 proofs, among which 244 were proved automatically by the Rodin Toolset (that is , 96.4%). The 9 interactive proofs are not complicated except one for the refinement of event send_accept in model M7 and one for the deadlock freeness theorem in model M11 (technical proof). There are only 2 interactive proofs (on 95!) in M7 (heart of the protocol) and 1 for M10 (implementation).In the first version we have 11 interactive proofs: one was proved by an updated SMT solver (5 years after!) and one was proved automatically when we changed the variant to a lexicographic one in the model M6. Thanks to the reviewer who suggested a lexicographic variant.

Remark: Numbers of interactive proof can change using a specific profile. For this development we used the profile:

$withZ3\_with\_PP\_with\_EqualHyp\_with\_CVC3\_with\_CVC4$.

Using the profile SMT (predefined in Rodin) we have more interactive proofs 34 for the direct approach and 38 for the constructive one.

5 Related Works

Our work is very closed to the Lamport's Paxos protocol [3], same variables almost same events, but it's not fault tolerant. Like in Lamport's Bakery algorithm [4] where each process has an unique number here each *proposer* has also an unique number to decide. There are also many protocols developed in [1] using Event-B (on trees, rings, ...). In [2] authors added liveness properties in Event-B and used the Peterson (mutual exclusion) algorithm as example. In our case although our protocol is more complicated we don't have to prove fairness properties like in the Bakery's or Peterson's one. We never thought of using temporal logic to model our protocol: invariants and variants are sufficient to express what we want.

6 Concluding Remarks

In this document, we presented two approaches to control the basic behaviour of a protocol : a direct approach and a constructive approach. The direct approach was not successful. This approach is not sufficient to find the missing invariant. We were extremely lucky to have find it. Only the constructive approach allowed us to derive a significant an simpler proof. At this point, we want to point out the importance of refinement in the constructing development of this protocol: better explanation, simpler proofs as usual using the refinement process. We can notice that the fundamental invariants in model M7 were defined by means of two abstract variables : $init\_acc$ and $init\_p$.

As usual the correctness of this protocol is ensured by refinement: the last model behaves like the first (thanks to invariants). The variant and the deadlock freeness assure that the event final in the last model will be triggered.

Event-B models can be found on http://perso.numericable.fr/cansell.dominique.

References

1. Abrial, J.-R.: Modeling in Event-B: System and Software Engineering. Cambridge University Press, Cambridge (2010)
2. Hoang, T.S., Abrial, J.-R.: Reasoning about liveness properties in event-B. In: Qin, S., Qiu, Z. (eds.) ICFEM 2011. LNCS, vol. 6991, pp. 456–471. Springer, Heidelberg (2011). https://doi.org/10.1007/978-3-642-24559-6_31
3. Lamport, L.: Byzantizing paxos by refinement. In: DISC 2011, pp. 211–224 (2011)
4. Lamport, L.: A new solution of Dijkstra's concurrent programming problem. Commun. ACM **17**(8) (1974)
5. Leuschel, M., Butler, M.: ProB: A Model Checker for B. In: FME 2003, pp. 855–874 (2023)
6. The ProB Animator and Model Checker. https://prob.hhu.de
7. Rodin Platform. http://www.event-b.org

Insider Threat Simulation Through Ant Colonies and ProB

Akram Idani(✉), Aurélien Pepin, and Mariem Triki

Univ. Grenoble Alpes, Grenoble INP, CNRS, 38000 Grenoble, France
akram.idani@univ-grenoble-alpes.fr,
{aurelien.pepin,mariem.triki}@grenoble-inp.org

Abstract. In cyber-security, insider threats are particularly challenging to prevent because they are carried out by individuals who already have legitimate access to the information system (IS). In fact, insiders exploit their privileges to perform malicious actions. In previous works we proposed to tackle this problem via a backward symbolic search built on a formal B specification of the IS. Unfortunately this approach is not performant because many proof obligations and constraints must be solved interactively. In this paper, we provide a heuristic-based forward search built on the ant colony optimization algorithm called *API* (Ant-based Path Identification) that we implemented using ProB. We show how API can be used to search for malicious scenarios and we present the results of our experiments in comparison with other approaches.

Keywords: B Method · Access Control · Ant colonies · Insider attacks

1 Introduction

Cyber-attacks known as insider attacks are difficult to tackle because they are perpetrated by trusted users, *i.e.* persons who already have legitimate access to the Information System (IS). These attackers exploit their privileges to perform malicious actions, such as data theft, privilege escalation, or system sabotage. Unlike external threats, insider attacks do not rely on breaching network defenses but instead misuse of authorized access, making prevention less effective. In this paper, authorized access is represented via the Role Based Access Control pattern. In practice, insider threats are not violations of the access control policy, but authorized actions that may lead to unwanted situations. To address this challenge, we developed a formal model-driven framework on top of UML and the B method [1]. The approach is suitable to deal with the dynamic evolution of an IS thanks to the composition mechanism of the B method. The platform, named B4MSecure [10], translates UML and SecureUML [17] models into B and then applies the model-checking facilities of ProB [16] to exhibit malicious scenarios [11].

Detecting an insider attack can be reduced to searching for a specific critical state in the system's state space. If this state is reachable, it means that a sequence of legitimate operations can lead to a security breach. However, a major

M. Leuschel and F. Ishikawa (Eds.): ABZ 2025, LNCS 15728, pp. 161–179, 2026.
https://doi.org/10.1007/978-3-031-94533-5_10

limitation of model-checking is the combinatorial explosion of states. As systems grow in complexity, the number of possible states increases exponentially, making exhaustive search impractical for real-world applications. A naive brute-force approach would require examining millions or even billions of states, leading to excessive computational costs and long processing times. To circumvent this limitation, we proposed in our previous works [23] a backward symbolic search built on theorem proving and constraint solving. Unfortunately, this approach is not performant because many proof obligations and constraints must be solved interactively. In this paper, we propose to employ a forward search strategy based on ant colony optimization [6], implemented in the API (Ant-based Path Identification) algorithm [7]. Instead of exploring all states blindly [11], like in pure model-checking, or interactively [23], like in symbolic search, API guides the search using a quality-based heuristic, prioritizing paths that are more likely to lead to a given situation.

Ant colony optimization [6,7] (ACO) is a bio-inspired algorithm that mimics the behavior of ants searching for food. In nature, ants deposit pheromones along paths they take, reinforcing routes that lead to successful outcomes. Similarly, in API, artificial ants explore the state space and leave digital pheromones on promising paths. Over multiple iterations, these pheromones accumulate, guiding subsequent ants towards more relevant states. Instead of checking all states, the algorithm prioritizes highly relevant paths, reducing the number of evaluations. The pheromone system allows the algorithm to dynamically adjust and refine its search strategy based on past findings. This work is an attempt to evaluate the efficiency of API for the identification of insider threats, and its capability to find attack scenarios faster than exhaustive search or symbolic search. By combining formal verification with heuristic search, we hope to improve the detection of insider attacks while mitigating the limitations of state-space explosion.

Section 2 presents the B4MSecure platform and the formal modeling of secure IS. Section 3 introduces the API algorithm. Section 4 shows how ProB and API are combined to deal with the insider threat problem and presents the obtained results. Section 5 situates this work within the state of the art. Finally, Sect. 6 concludes the paper and outlines future work.

2 B for Modeling Secure Information Systems

2.1 Functional and Security Modeling

To illustrate our approach we consider a simplified model of a bank IS that is inspired by [2]. The UML class diagram of Fig. 1 defines functional concerns: customers (class *Customer*) and their accounts (class *Account*). A bank account has a balance (attribute *balance*), an authorized overdraft (attribute *overdraft*) and a unique identifier (attribute *IBAN*). Operations of class *Account* (*e.g. transferFunds*, *withdrawCash* and *depositFunds*) allow one to transfer an amount of money from an account to another, to withdraw and to deposit cash on a given account. A customer is associated with at least one bank account that he does not share. Transferring the ownership of the account or carrying out fraudulent financial operations are examples of insider attacks to prevent. Before searching for these scenarios, it is necessary to define users together with their permissions.

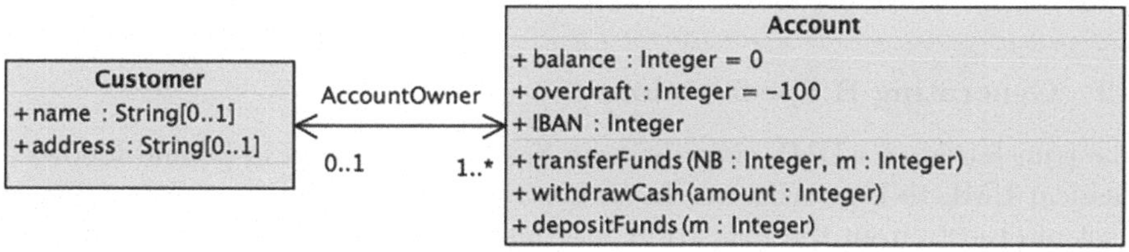

Fig. 1. Functional *UML* class diagram

Figure 2 is a SecureUML model associated to our class diagram. This model defines two roles: *CustomerUser* and *AccountManager*. They respectively represent the customer of the system and the account manager in charge of the bank's customers.

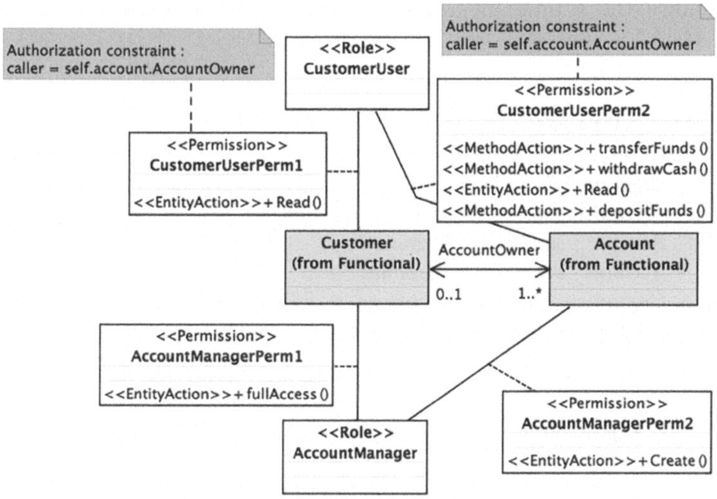

Fig. 2. Security modeling with SecureUML

In this IS, customers have the ability to read their personal data (permission *CustomerUserPerm1*) and perform financial operations such as transfer money, deposit, and withdraw cash (permission *CustomerUserPerm2*). Account managers have full access to *Customer* class (permission *AccountManagerPerm1*), allowing them to create, read, and modify customer data. However, their rights on the *Account* class are restricted to the creation of new accounts; which is ensured by permission *AccountManagerPerm2*. An authorization constraint is associated with permissions *CustomerUserPerm1* and *CustomerUserPerm2*, ensuring that only the account holder can perform the corresponding actions on their account. Under this security policy, the account manager has no read or write access to the attributes of the *Account* class.

2.2 Generating B Specifications

The translation of a UML class diagram has been discussed in [9] and follows a classical UML-to-B translation. In B, abstract sets represent an abstraction of a set of objects from the real world. As this definition is close to the notion of class in UML, it is used by all UML-to-B approaches to formalize UML classes. Attributes are translated into functions that map the set of existing instances to the attribute's type. The result depends on the attribute's characteristics: mandatory or optional, unique or non-unique, single-valued or multi-valued. For instance, attribute *IBAN* of class *Account* is single-valued, mandatory, and unique; it is therefore translated into $Account\_IBAN \in \text{Account} \rightarrowtail \mathbb{N}$, which is a total injection. Associations are translated similarly into functional relations depending on multiplicities. For example, association *AccountOwner* is translated into a partial surjective function due to multiplicities `0..1` and `1..*`. Figure 3 shows the typing invariants generated by B4MSecure from our class diagram.

INVARIANT
$Account \subseteq ACCOUNT$
$\wedge\ Customer \subseteq CUSTOMER$
$\wedge\ AccountOwner \in Account \twoheadrightarrow\!\!\!\!\!\!+\ Customer$
$\wedge\ Account\_balance \in Account \rightarrow \mathbb{Z}$
$\wedge\ Account\_overdraft \in Account \rightarrow \mathbb{Z}$
$\wedge\ Customer\_name \in Customer \mathrel{+\!\!\!\!\rightarrow} STRING$
$\wedge\ Customer\_address \in Customer \mathrel{+\!\!\!\!\rightarrow} STRING$
$\wedge\ Account\_IBAN \in Account \rightarrowtail \mathbb{N}$

Fig. 3. Structural invariants produced by B4MSecure

The SecureUML model is translated by B4MSecure into a B machine that enforces permissions for functional operations based on the roles assigned to a user. For instance, if a user *Paul* is assigned to role *CustomerUser*, he is permitted to read his personal data through the getters of class *Customer*, while other operations such as modification or creation are restricted. The tool produces for every functional operation, a secured operation that verifies (using a security guard) whether the current user is allowed to call the functional operation. The secure operation also verifies the authorization constraints, if they are defined in the underlying permissions, and updates the assignment of roles when required.

Figure 4 shows the secure operation associated to *Account_transferFunds*. The security guard is defined in clause *SELECT*. It verifies that the functional operation belongs to set *isPermitted*[*currentRoles*], where definition *currentRoles* refers to the roles activated by *currentUser* (in a session) as well as their super-roles. The security guard of *secure_Account_transferFunds* is strengthened with the authorization constraint of permission *CustomerUserPerm2*. For a permission p associated to a role r and a constraint c, the tool adds guard ($r \in currentRoles \Rightarrow c$) to all operations that are concerned with p. In this case the constraint is: *AccountOwner* (*aAccount*) = *currentUser*.

```
secure_Account_transferFunds(aAccount, NB, m) =
PRE
    aAccount ∈ Account ∧ NB ∈ ℕ ∧ m ∈ ℕ1 [∧...]
THEN
  SELECT
    Account_transferFunds_ ∈ isPermitted[currentRoles]
    ∧ (CustomerUser ∈ currentRoles ⇒ AccountOwner(aAccount) = currentUser)
  THEN
    Account_transferFunds(aAccount, NB, m)
  END
END;
```

Fig. 4. Secured operation

The B specifications generated by B4MSecure from a given class diagram are designed to be animated using ProB [16]. This enables the observation of the IS's evolution and the impact of execution scenarios on its functional state. B4MSecure generates all basic operations, including the creation/deletion of class instances, creation/deletion of links between instances, and getters/setters for attributes and links. Integrity constraints can be introduced using B invariants and proof of correctness for invariant preservation can be done via a proof assistant such as AtelierB.

2.3 Malicious Behaviors

To identify malicious behaviors, we analyze the set of finite observable traces of our B specification. The latter can be represented using trace semantics, which consist of an initialization substitution *init*, a set of operations $\mathcal{O}$, and a set of state variables $\mathcal{V}$. A functional behavior is an observable sequence $\mathcal{Q}$ defined as:

$$\mathcal{Q} \hat{=} init \; ; \; op_1 \; ; \; op_2 \; ; \; \ldots \; ; \; op_m$$

such that $\forall i.(i \in 1..m \Rightarrow op_i \in \mathcal{O})$ and there exists a sequence $\mathcal{P}$ of states that do not violate invariant properties:

$$\mathcal{P} \hat{=} s_0 \; ; \; s_1 \; ; \; \ldots \; ; \; s_{m-1}$$

where s_0 is an initial state, and each op_i is enabled from state s_{i-1}, leading to state s_i. $\mathcal{P}$ is called a path.

The security model filters functional behaviors by analyzing access control premises, which are triplets (u, R, c) where u is a user, R is a set of roles assigned to u, and c is an authorization constraint. An observable secure behavior is a sequence $\mathcal{Q}$, where for every step i, the premise (u_i, R_i, c_i) is valid (expressed as $(u_i, R_i, c_i) \models true$). This means that the roles R_i activated by user u_i grant the right to execute operation op_i, and any constraint c_i must be satisfied. The following sequence of premises must be valid for $\mathcal{Q}$:

$$(u_1, R_1, c_1) \ ; \ (u_2, R_2, c_2) \ ; \ \dots \ ; \ (u_m, R_m, c_m)$$

The search for a malicious scenario reduces to finding a specific state in the state space. The path from the initial state to this target state represents the sequence of operations required to execute the attack. Therefore, a malicious behavior, done by a user u, considering an access control policy, is an observable path $\mathcal{P}$ with m steps such that:

- op_m is a critical operation associated with an authorization constraint c_m.
- State s_{m-1} is called malicious and enables op_m.
- User u is malicious and aims to execute op_m by exploiting his roles R_u.
- s_0 is an initial state where $(u, R_u, c_m) \models false$.
- For every step i ($i \in 1..m$), the premise $(u, R_u, c_i) \models true$.

In other words, malicious user u is not initially allowed to execute the critical operation, but he is able to run a sequence of operations leading to a state from which he can execute this operation. Suppose that s_0 is as follows:

$$\begin{array}{l} s_0 \hat{=} \\ \quad Account = \{cpt_1, cpt_2\} \\ \quad Customer = \{Paul, Martin\} \\ \quad Account\_balance = \{(cpt_1 \mapsto 300), (cpt_2 \mapsto -100)\} \\ \quad AccountOwner = \{(cpt_1 \mapsto Paul), (cpt_2 \mapsto Martin)\} \\ \quad Account\_IBAN = \{(cpt_1 \mapsto 111), (cpt_2 \mapsto 222)\} \\ \quad Account\_overdraft = \{(cpt_1 \mapsto -100), (cpt_2 \mapsto -100)\} \end{array}$$

In this state, *Paul* is a customer and owns account cpt_1 with a balance of 300. *Bob*, as an *AccountManager*, cannot execute operations like *transferFunds* or *withdrawCash* on cpt_1. A static query such as "Is Bob able to transfer funds from Paul's account?" would return NO, since the permission granted to a manager on the *Account* class only allows instance creation. The more pertinent question is, "Is there a sequence of operations that Bob can execute to gain the ability to transfer funds from Paul's account?". To answer this, one naive approach is to use ProB's model-checking feature to exhaustively explore the state space and find states that satisfy property: $AccountOwner(cpt_1) = \text{Bob}$. We are looking for a sequence of operations executed by Bob that allows him to become the owner of cpt_1, thereby granting him the permission to execute an action he initially could not. Sequence $\mathcal{Q}$ that we want to exhibit is represented in Fig. 5.

```
/* step 1: create customer Bob */
    Connect(Bob, {AccountManager}) ;
    setCurrentUser(Bob) ;
    secure_Account_NEW(cpt3, 333) ;
    secure_Customer_NEW(Bob,{cpt3}) ;
/* step 2: get the ownership of Paul's Account */
    secure_Account_NEW(cpt4, 444) ;
    secure_Customer_AddAccount(Paul,{cpt4}) ;
    secure_Customer_RemoveAccount(Paul,{cpt1}) ;
    secure_Customer_AddAccount(Bob,{cpt1}) ;
/* step 3: attack */
    disConnect(Bob) ;
    Connect(Bob, {CustomerUser}) ;
    secure_Account_transferFunds(cpt1, 333, 100) ;
```

Fig. 5. Malicious scenario

The attacker (Bob) creates a fictitious customer profile and associates it with a newly created bank account. To gain control over an existing customer account (cpt_1), Bob first assigns another dummy account (cpt_4) to Paul. Then, Bob removes the ownership link between Paul and cpt_1, and assigns cpt_1 to himself. Bob logs in the system as a customer in order to transfer funds from cpt_1. In this example, ProB reached a timeout after exploring millions of transitions, indicating that the state space is too large to be explored efficiently. To solve this issue, we proposed in [11] a CSP||B that helps ProB searching in a subset of the state space. ProB was able to exhibit the sequence above after exploring about 70,000 states and 200,000 transitions. We also proposed a more generic technique based on a backward symbolic search [23]. This approach follows a two-step process: it first identifies symbolic functional executions that could potentially lead to a malicious scenario using theorem proving, and then checks their feasibility against the security model using constraint solving. While this method is particularly useful for understanding the origin and structure of attack scenarios, its main drawback lies in its low performance and interactive nature, as many proofs and constraints require manual intervention. In the example discussed, this approach required 38 min to identify the attack sequence.

3 Ant Colony Optimization – ACO

Ant colony algorithms [6,7] are a class of heuristic search algorithms inspired by the foraging behavior of ants. Developed in the 1990s, these algorithms have proven to be highly effective in solving combinatorial optimization problems, where exhaustive search methods are often computationally prohibitive. Different species of ants exhibit various behaviors, which have been modeled into a range of algorithms with different objectives.

3.1 Ant-Based Path Identification with Pachycondyla Apicalis

This algorithm has been formalized by N. Monmarché in 2000 [20,21]. It is inspired by *Pachycondyla apicalis*, a species of ants present in South America. In most ant colony algorithms, the global solution is the one that attracts the most individuals, this is called *stigmergy*. The search space is divided into several regions, each of which is explored by a group of ants. The ants of a group are attracted by the pheromones left by their congeners. The pheromones are a way to communicate the quality of the solutions found. The more a region is visited, the more the pheromones are deposited and the more the region is attractive. The algorithm is iterative: ants explore regions, pheromones are deposited, regions are updated and ants are attracted to regions with most pheromones.

The particularity of API species is that they live in small colonies (a few dozen individuals), with an unstable habitat that is likely to evolve often, and little direct communication between individuals. These characteristics have been transcribed into the algorithmic that we are experimenting in this work. The colony sends n ants $a_1, \ldots, a_n$ (called *foragers*) around the nest. Each ant creates and then stores in memory p hunting sites. In parallel with the other ants, the ant randomly chooses one of its hunting sites, denoted S, and begins a local exploration. If the exploration is successful, it replaces S with its new hunting site S'. Otherwise, it counts an additional failure for the site S. If the number of failures of S exceeds a threshold called *local patience*, it is forgotten and replaced by a new random site. Patience allows to dig a track for a few turns rather than abandoning it immediately. The colony regularly recalls its foragers and looks at their results. If a hunting site of an ant is better than those of the other ants and the current position of the nest, the whole nest moves and the memory of all the ants starts from scratch. The procedure then starts again: the ants are scattered around the nest again.

3.2 Algorithm

The *API* algorithm uses the following notations:

- $\mathcal{S}$ is a search space;
- $N \in \mathcal{S}$ is the position of the nest, initialized with the random operator $\mathcal{O}_{\text{rand}}$;
- $\mathcal{O}_{\text{explo}}$ returns a point S' in the neighborhood of a point $S \in \mathcal{S}$;
- $f : \mathcal{S} \to \mathbb{R}$ is the objective function to minimize;
- $n_s(a_i)$ is the number of hunting sites of ant a_i;
- A_{site} and A_{locale} are the maximum amplitudes to create hunting sites;
- e_j is the number of failures associated with hunting site s_j for a given ant;
- P_{locale} is the threshold of failures before an ant abandons a site.

The algorithm is presented in Fig. 6. First, it chooses the nest location N using an operator $\mathcal{O}_{\text{rand}}$, which represents a random initialization function. A variable T is initialized to keep track of the number of explorations and the loop runs until the stopping condition is reached.

Algorithm 1: API()

Choose the initial nest location : $N := \mathcal{O}_{\text{rand}}$;
$T := 0$; `// Number of ant explorations`
while *The stopping condition is not met* **do**
  foreach *ant* a_i **do**
    API-FORAGING(a_i);
  if *The nest must be moved* **then**
    $N := S^+$; `// Best solution found by an ant`
    Clear the memory of all ants;
  $T := T + 1$
return $(S^+, f(S^+))$

Fig. 6. API Main Algorithm

The stopping condition can be based on a maximum number of iterations, convergence to an optimal solution, or performance metrics, etc. Each ant performs an exploration process (API-FORAGING) searching for better solutions and using pheromone updates. If a better solution (S^+) is found, the nest is moved to this new location and the memory of all ants is cleared so that they can start fresh from the new nest. The algorithm returns the best solution found (S^+) along with its objective function value ($f(S^+)$). Algorithm of Fig. 7 simulates the behavior of a single ant a_i in the search space. The ant has a memory of p hunting sites. If the memory is not full, the ant creates a new hunting site around the nest. Otherwise, it explores the neighborhood of the last site visited. If the exploration is successful, the ant moves to the new site. Otherwise, it counts a failure and may abandon the site if the number of failures exceeds a threshold. The algorithm returns the best solution found by the ant.

3.3 Discussion

API has been applied in many optimization problems such as the traveling salesman problem, the quadratic assignment problem, and the job-shop scheduling problem. It has also been used in various applications such as data mining [18], image processing [8], and network routing [5]. In this work we use it to search for malicious scenarios in the execution of a formal model of an IS. The application of the algorithm requires only the knowledge of the exploration operators $\mathcal{O}_{\text{explo}}$ and $\mathcal{O}_{\text{rand}}$. The exploration operator $\mathcal{O}_{\text{explo}}$ is specific to the problem to be solved. It is a function that generates a new solution in the neighborhood of a given solution. The random operator $\mathcal{O}_{\text{rand}}$ is used to initialize the search space.

In our opinion, *API* is a good solution to identify insider threats because the behavior of the ant colony is somehow close to that of an attacker. Attackers first try to identify critical states of the software and then he/she concentrates his/her efforts to find security flaws starting from these critical states. Similarly, API ants focus on the most promising sites to find the best possible solution. Both

Algorithm 2: API-FORAGING(a_i)

if $n_s(a_i) < p$ **then**
  // The ant's memory is not full
  $n_s(a_i) := n_s(a_i) + 1$;
  Creation of a foraging site around the nest: $s_{n_s(a_i)} := \mathcal{O}_{\text{explo}}(N, A_{\text{site}})$;
  Initialization of the failure counter for the site: $e_{n_s(a_i)} := 0$;
else
  Let s_j be the last site explored by the ant ;
  if $e_j > 0$ **then**
    // The last exploration was unsuccessful.
    Randomly select a foraging site $s_j (j \in \{1, \ldots, p\})$
  Local exploration around s_j : $s' := \mathcal{O}_{\text{explo}}(s_j, A_{\text{locale}})$;
  if $f(s') < f(s)$ **then**
    $s_j := s'$;
    $e_j := 0$;
  else
    $e_j := e_j + 1$;
    if $e_j > P_{locale}$ **then**
      Delete site s_j from the ant's memory ;
      $n_s(a_i) := n_s(a_i) + 1$;

Fig. 7. Simulation of a given ant a_i

API ants and attackers adopt an incremental, exploratory approach. Indeed, API ants begin by randomly exploring potential paths, but over time, they reinforce the most promising routes based on pheromone trails (here function f). Insiders follow a similar strategy: they first explore the system, looking for weaknesses; once they find a critical state (*e.g.*, a vulnerability or misconfiguration), they focus their efforts on exploiting it. Furthermore, in API, ants are designed to focus on highly probable paths that lead to optimal solutions, much like how real ants reinforce the best paths to a food source. In cybersecurity, attackers prioritize high-value targets, such as privileged data (*e.g.*, account cpt_1). They start from accessible points and progressively refine their approach. Finally, API ants adjust their search behavior dynamically, reacting to previous successes. Attackers do the same by adapting their attack strategies based on the system's defenses, security policies, and feedback from failed attempts.

4 API and ProB to Exhibit Insider Threats

The API algorithm is a generic algorithm. It only specifies how the ants are organized. Here, we propose a modeling of our optimization problem for the API algorithm based on the state space discovered by ProB.

4.1 State Evaluation Functions

The *state evaluation function*, denoted f, formalizes what is an "interesting state" of the state space with regard to an insider attack. This function can be a binary function that checks if a current state strictly approaches the malicious one. A drawback is that a path can stagnate on few states or slightly regress before being considered interesting. An evaluation in $\{0, 1\}$ rejects all states that do not advance. Our idea is to have a refined evaluation function. In the API algorithm, the local patience of the ants allows to visit states that are not immediately fruitful, that's why we propose an evaluation function f with values in $[0, 1]$.

Considering our formal B specification, $\mathcal{S}$ is simply the state space discovered by ProB during the exploration process. We denote by s^* the malicious state and by $s(v)$ the value of variable v ($v \in \mathcal{V}$) in a given state s. Let $w_v \in \mathbb{R}$ be a weight associated with variable v to ponder its impact on the exploration. We define the evaluation function as:

$$f\colon \mathcal{S} \rightarrow [0, 1]$$

$$f(s) = \frac{\sum_{v \in \mathcal{V}} w_v \cdot \delta(s^*(v), s(v))}{\sum_{v \in \mathcal{V}} w_v}$$

Function f is an objective function. It defines a weighted average of the distance between the current values of the variables (in state s) and the desired ones (in state s^*). Intuitively, a desired path $\mathcal{P}$ is a sequence of states whose variables look more and more like those of the target state, until they match completely. In our approach, the malicious state s^* is a state that enables a critical operation (*e.g.*, *transfer_Funds*) and satisfies security premises of the attacker (*i.e.*, Bob). Note that we generate state s^* using the constraint-solving feature of ProB, with various strategies not detailed here for space reasons. State s^* is:

$$\begin{aligned}
s^* \mathrel{\hat{=}}&\\
&Account = \{cpt_1, cpt_2, cpt_3, cpt_4\}\\
&Customer = \{Paul, Martin, Bob\}\\
&Account_balance = \{(cpt_1 \mapsto 300), (cpt_2 \mapsto -100), (cpt_3 \mapsto 0), (cpt_4 \mapsto 0)\}\\
&AccountOwner = \{(cpt_1 \mapsto Bob), (cpt_2 \mapsto Martin)(cpt_3 \mapsto Paul), (cpt_4 \mapsto Bob)\}\\
&Account_IBAN = \{(cpt_1 \mapsto 111), (cpt_2 \mapsto 222), (cpt_3 \mapsto 333), (cpt_4 \mapsto 444)\}\\
&Account_overdraft\\
&\quad = \{(cpt_1 \mapsto -100), (cpt_2 \mapsto -100), (cpt_3 \mapsto -100), (cpt_4 \mapsto -100)\}
\end{aligned}$$

A state s_i where $Account = \{cpt_1, cpt_2, cpt_3\}$ is less distant from s^* than a state s_j where $Account = \{cpt_4\}$. This distance between s^*, s_i and s_j is measured with the evaluation function f. The similarity δ between two values is defined according to the type of the variable. The objective is to minimize f as much as possible and if $f(s) = 0$, then s is the target state. To this purpose we apply the following measures, which are adapted from Jaccard's Index of Similarity [12]:

- For a variable derived from a class or an association, we measure the distance between two sets (A and A). Specifically, we compute 1 minus the ratio of the size of their intersection to the size of their union. As a result, $\delta(A, A) = 0$ when $A = A$, and $\delta(A, A) = 1$ when $A \cap A^* = \emptyset$.

$$\delta(A^*, A) = 1 - \frac{\text{card}(A \cap A^*)}{\text{card}(A \cup A^*)}$$

- For an integer variable, the comparison is bounded in an interval. The distance is defined as the difference between the two values divided by the amplitude of the interval. Interval $[A_{\text{min}}, A_{\text{max}}]$ is chosen such that it covers all values of A and A^*.

$$\delta(A^*, A) = 1 - \frac{|A - A^*|}{|A_{\text{min}} - A_{\text{max}}|}$$

- For a boolean variable, the distance is 0 if the variable values are equal and 1 otherwise.

$$\delta(A^*, A) = \begin{cases} 0 \text{ if } A = A^* \\ 1 \text{ if } A \neq A^* \end{cases}$$

Function f computes a weighted average. Indeed, weights $w_v \in \mathbb{R}$ depend on the search strategy. By default, they are equal to 1. They are useful to limit the impact of some variables compared to others during the search. For example, a transition leading to a state where δ becomes 0 for a boolean variable decreases f much more than the inclusion of a new value for a class variable of type set. This can unbalance the search of the ants. One solution is to reduce the weight of the boolean variable in comparison with a class variable.

4.2 Search Heuristics

The movement of ants requires two operators: $\mathcal{O}_{\text{rand}}$ to give an initial location to the nest; and $\mathcal{O}_{\text{explo}}$ to guide the ants in the search space. Since the search space $\mathcal{S}$ is that of ProB, a natural choice for the nest is the root of the state space. This choice removes randomness in the initial position of the nest.

Operator $\mathcal{O}_{\text{explo}}$ is a heuristic for moving in the search space. It generates a point s' in the neighborhood of a point $s \in \mathcal{S}$. Here, a point is a state explored by the *model-checker*. The neighborhood corresponds to all the states that can be reached in one transition from a given state. A chosen solution for $\mathcal{O}_{\text{explo}}$ is to return a random transition among those evaluated by `ProB`. All transitions have the same probability of being chosen. Since transitions go in one direction, ants may get stuck in a sub-search space that corresponds to a local minimum. To address this issue, we add an artificial "backtracking" transition. Figure 8 represents a simplified `ProB` state space. Red arrows are transitions between states already explored by the ants. Dashed red arrows represent the backtracking transitions that allow the ant to go back. Blue nodes are states that become accessible to the ant due to the backtracking transitions. This mechanism leads to the creation of a spanning tree for the already visited states.

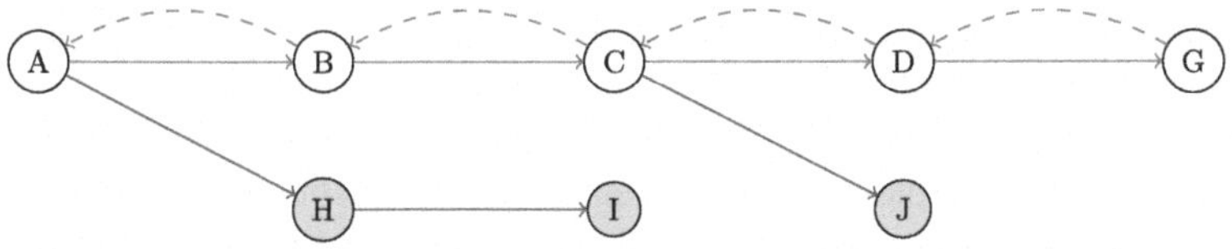

Fig. 8. Backtracking activation on a simplified state space of *ProB*. (Color figure online)

The *API* algorithm does not define any condition on the number of explorations. At any time during execution, it may provide a valid solution in $\mathcal{S}$. To stop it, several strategies are possible. One may define a fixed number of explorations $T_{\max}$, meaning as long as $T < T_{\max}$, a new exploration is started. This solution has the disadvantage of not taking into account the number of ants. Thus, for the same $T_{\max}$, an algorithm with ten ants will take twice as long to execute as an algorithm with five ants. An other idea is to stop when the ants find a solution that no longer improves. If the current solution does not change after a certain number of explorations, the algorithm stops. In the same idea one can stop when the algorithm reaches a solution *close enough* to the optimal $(f(S^+) < \varepsilon)$. This corresponds to the case where state S^+ is close to s^* without being identical. If only a few operations are missing to reach the optimal state, a *deterministic* search algorithm can take over. This stopping condition should only be triggered after a certain number T of iterations. Otherwise, *API* will never reach the optimal state.

Another solution would be to define a maximum number of visited states. In this solution, a common counter for all ants is added and when a state is visited for the first time, the counter is incremented. An advantage of this solution is that the execution time is less dependent on the number of ants. Also, the number of visited states is an important criterion in *model-checking* algorithms. `ProB` includes this data when animating a model. This choice therefore facilitates comparisons between algorithms. For the example of this paper the stopping criterion we use is the maximum number of state evaluations (in which a distance is computed). As for the maximum number of visited states, a global counter is added. We count the number of times a state is evaluated, whether for the first time or not. The execution time is independent of the number of ants, making it a good performance measure. Moreover, it is a relevant measure for animating models in *ProB*. Indeed, evaluating a state is a very costly operation. It represents 60% of the computation time in the implementation of *API*. The δ functions presented in Sect. 4.1 are first translated into the *B* syntax, and then sent to `ProB` during exploration, evaluated, and returned back to the algorithm. This criterion is combined with an option that allows the algorithm to stop immediately if the final state is found $(f(s) = 0)$. The state count is kept to compare various executions of the *API* algorithm.

The nest movement criterion adjusts the frequency at which the colony recalls its ants to check their solutions. If this delay between explorations is too long, the ants may forget satisfactory solutions. Conversely, if it is too short, the ants do not have time to explore the search space and the colony does not progress. Based on local search, it is possible to use a patience factor for the nest, denoted P_N. Let p be the size of an ant's memory and P_{locale} its local patience. In [20], the nest's patience is: $P_N = 2 \times (P_{\text{locale}} + 1) \times p$. The evaluation function f can have significant variations with a few number of variables. For the example in this article, we adapt the initial formula with: $P_N = (P_{\text{locale}} + 1) \times p$.

Amplitudes define the neighborhood area of a state during exploration. The global amplitude, denoted A_{site}, provides an area to place the ants around the nest at the beginning of the exploration. The local amplitude, denoted A_{locale}, provides an area where the ants choose their hunting sites. The amplitude is normally defined as a proportion relative to the search space ($A \in [0, 1]$). Since the state space is discovered by ProB during exploration, its size is not known in advance. Therefore, we represent the amplitude by a maximum number of transitions ($A \in \mathbb{N}$) between the starting state and the state to be explored. Our experiments apply the following parameters:

- Number of ants: $n = 5$;
- Ant memory: $p = 3$;
- Amplitudes (local and global): $A_{\text{locale}} = 3$, $A_{\text{site}} = 15$;
- Patience (local and global): $P_{\text{locale}} = 3$, $P_{\text{N}} = (P_{\text{locale}} + 1) \times p = 12$;
- Maximum number of evaluations: 1000;

4.3 Results and Discussion

The *API* algorithm is non-deterministic, as its efficiency depends on the random exploration performed by the ants in the state space. Consequently, the number of states visited before identifying a critical state can vary significantly between executions. Table 1 presents the results of 20 independent executions of the *API* algorithm on the example of this paper.

Table 1. Summary of 20 runs.

Run	Nb of evaluations	Length of critical path	Transitions (total)	Transitions (unique)	States	Time (s)
1	322	21	764	442	135	41.69
2	214	22	477	295	81	27.35
3	154	23	524	279	55	23.77
4	423	24	1006	708	187	59.57
5	323	22	821	564	158	51.58
6	426	29	1089	522	140	46.91
7	406	28	844	601	188	57.74
8	246	24	517	311	95	31.20
9	176	19	421	266	80	26.17
10	284	17	672	456	125	41.21
11	302	25	748	508	137	46.49
12	566	25	1270	900	242	75.30
13	282	20	761	490	111	39.65
14	298	20	772	523	139	46.30
15	420	19	1054	655	168	54.59
16	318	22	715	499	147	45.67
17	308	18	804	506	125	41.86
18	413	19	912	629	182	56.36
19	393	23	818	511	164	49.27
20	286	23	683	452	124	40.15
	Avg: 321.4	**21.6**	**782.0**	**518.8**	**134.7**	**44.62**

These results are fully reproducible. The implementation, along with the B models and automation scripts used in the experiments, is open-source and publicly available at https://github.com/meeduse/insider_threats. Each row corresponds to a complete run of the algorithm. The table reports: the number of calls to the evaluation function f (even when a state is visitied several times), the length of the reconstructed critical path, the total and unique number of transitions executed, the total number of visited states, and the total execution time in seconds. The last row shows the average value for each metric over the 20 runs. The execution traces reveal that the algorithm's performance may fluctuate, but remains consistently effective. In 100% of these executions, API successfully reconstructs a path reaching the expected critical state.

Compared to exhaustive methods such as pure model-checking or the CSP||B approach [11], API demonstrates a significant reduction in the number of visited states. On average, only 321 states are explored per run to find the attack scenario, whereas CSP||B required up to 70,000 states and 200,000 transitions. We have also applied our symbolic search approach [23] to this simple example. Since the method relies on symbolic states rather than concrete ones, it is difficult to compare it directly using criteria such as the number of states or transitions. However, in terms of performance, the symbolic search proved inefficient, requiring 38 min to discover a single attack scenario, whereas the

API-based approach achieved the result in an average of 44 s. This shows the benefit of API's exploration strategy, which leverages heuristic search instead of systematic enumeration or constraint solving and symbolic proofs. The length of the critical path also varies, ranging from 17 to 29 actions. The minimal length of 17 (highlighted in Table 1) is close to the optimal path of 11 operations identified manually. On average, 22 actions are needed to reach a critical state.

These results support the conclusion that API has the potential to outperform traditional approaches by substantially reducing state-space exploration and improving overall execution time. We experimented our approach on many case studies: Medical IS [14], Meeting scheduler [3], Bank IS [2], Conference Review [25]. API is more than 500x more efficient than pure model-checking. However, the algorithm's random nature introduces variability in the number of steps required to reach the critical state. Furthermore, API parameters are crucial in obtaining good results but there are no predefined rules for choosing their values. Finding an optimal set of parameter values requires extensive testing. The selected values provided a good balance between exploration and convergence in our case study. In particular, setting the number of ants to $n = 5$ allowed sufficient coverage of the state space while keeping the number of evaluations per ant high enough for each to reach relevant areas. Interestingly, increasing the number of ants does not always improve performance. For instance, setting $n = 50$ while keeping the evaluation limit at 1000 drastically reduces the number of evaluations available to each ant. In such settings, none of the ants may explore deeply enough to discover the critical path. Finding the optimal parameter configuration remains an open question. Our experiments show that performance improves when the number of ants is increased moderately. For example, using $n = 10$ ants yields better results than $n = 5$, without compromising the depth of exploration too severely. More systematic parameter tuning could further enhance the algorithm's efficiency.

5 Related Works

As far as we know, works that addressed access control together with a formal method did not deal with the insider threat problem such as discussed in this paper. However, we can assume that this kind of threat is a typical reachability problem. In [25], the authors proposed a plain model-checking approach built on security strategies. A similar approach is proposed in [13] to validate access control in web-based collaborative systems. Even though their experiments show that they achieve better results compared to [25], the approach still has a partial coverage of realistic policies. In [19], the authors proposed two approaches to prove reachability properties in a B formal information system modelling, but unlike our work, they do not search sequences leading to a goal state.

Ant Colony Optimization has also been successfully applied to software testing problems. Several surveys explore this connection, including the work of Suri and Singhal [24], which provides a classification of ACO-based techniques for test case generation, test suite minimization, and prioritization. More recent surveys, such as [4], further expand on the role of ACO and other metaheuristics in automated test data generation. While these applications share with our approach the principle of guided search in large input spaces, they differ in their objectives and representations: our work focuses on local exploration guided by a Jaccard-based distance metric, derived from formal specifications and evaluated dynamically using the ProB model checker.

Another relevant line of research concerns directed model checking. In the context of the B method and ProB, Leuschel and Bendisposto [15] introduced heuristic-guided search strategies to steer the exploration toward goal states. The ProB tool supports this approach through the `HEURISTIC_FUNCTION` feature, which allows users to define custom heuristics to influence transition prioritization during state space exploration [22]. Although this technique shares with our ant-based method the use of heuristic guidance, the two approaches differ fundamentally in their mechanisms. API is a population-based, stochastic metaheuristic that relies on memory and pheromone reinforcement to guide exploration over time. In contrast, directed model checking in ProB follows a deterministic or best-first strategy driven by a fixed heuristic function-either statically defined or dynamically computed for each state.

6 Conclusion

Insider threats represent a major challenge in cybersecurity due to the legitimate privileges and trust inherently granted to internal users. Formal methods, and in particular model checking, have long been used to rigorously analyze system behavior. However, the state-space explosion problem often limits their scalability, especially for realistic or evolving information systems. This paper shows that combining formal verification with ant colony optimization offers a promising direction for identifying malicious scenarios more efficiently.

We proposed an original method based on the API variant of ACO [21], applied to formal models expressed in the B method and analyzed using the ProB model checker [16]. To our knowledge, this is the first application of ACO to the insider threat detection problem in a formal setting. Our experiments confirm that the API algorithm can guide the exploration toward critical states using a fitness function tailored to a target configuration. Compared to exhaustive or symbolic search, our approach significantly reduces the number of visited states while still reconstructing full attack paths.

Beyond the specific case study, the proposed method is more generally applicable. The algorithm can be extended to handle more complex attacker models, including coalitions of insiders. In this setting, the search would aim to discover coordinated sequences of actions performed by multiple users that lead to policy violations. Regarding the specification of critical states, our current implementation assumes a known target state (e.g., a policy breach where a security constraint is violated). Another approach could be to detect when an authorization constraint becomes unsatisfied. Such dynamic assertion checking could serve as a trigger to automatically mark a state as "critical".

Future work will focus on these extensions: (1) integrating collaborative attacker models and verifying multi-user attack strategies, (2) exploring automatic generation of target states based on the negation of authorization constraints, and (3) improving the scalability of the algorithm through parallel search and adaptive pheromone strategies. We believe this opens a new path for bridging formal policy analysis and heuristic-driven attack simulation.

References

1. Abrial, J.-R.: The B-Book: Assigning Programs to Meanings. Cambridge University Press, Cambridge (1996)
2. Bandara, A., et al.: Security Patterns: Comparing Modeling Approaches. IGI Global (2010)
3. Basin, D., Clavel, M., Doser, J., Egea, M.: Automated analysis of security-design models. Inf. Softw. Technol. **51** (2009)
4. Chhillar, M., Bhatia, R.: A systematic literature review on metaheuristic test data generation techniques. ACM Comput. Surv. **54**(2), 1–37 (2021)
5. Debbat, F., Bendimerad, F.T.: Assigning cells to switches in cellular mobile networks using hybridizing API algorithm and tabu search. Int. J. Commun Syst **27**(12), 4028–4037 (2013)
6. Dorigo, M., Middendorf, M., Stützle, T. (eds.) ANTS'2000 - From Ant Colonies to Artificial Ants: Second International Workshop on Ant Algorithms. Brussels, Belgium (2000)
7. Dorigo, M., Stützle, T.: Ant Colony Optimization. MIT Press, Cambridge (2004)
8. Hannane, A.M., Fizazi, H.: Supervised images classification using metaheuristics. Comput. Modell. New Technol. **20**(3), 17–23 (2016)
9. Idani, A.: The B method meets MDE: review, progress and future. In: Guizzardi, R., Ralyté, J., Franch, X. (eds.) 16th International Conference on Research Challenges in Information Science (RCIS 2022). LNCS, vol. 446, pp. 495–512. Springer, Spain (2022)
10. Idani, A., Ledru, Y.: B for modeling secure information systems - the B4MSecure platform. In: Butler, M.J., Conchon, S., Zaïdi, F. (eds.) 17th International Conference on Formal Engineering Methods. LNCS, vol. 9407, pp. 312–318. Springer (2015)
11. Idani, A., Ledru, Y., Vega, G.: A process-centric approach to insider threats identification in information systems. In: 18th International Conference on Risks and Security of Internet and Systems (CRiSIS 2023). LNCS, vol. 14529, pp. 231–247. Springer (2023)
12. Jaccard, P.: The probabilistic basis of Jaccard's index of similarity. Syst. Biol. **45**(3), 380–385 (1996)
13. Koleini, M., Ryan, M.: A knowledge-based verification method for dynamic access control policies. In: 13th International Conference on Formal Engineering Methods, ICFEM 2011. LNCS, vol. 6991, pp. 243–258. Springer (2011)
14. Ledru, Y., et al.: Validation of IS security policies featuring authorisation constraints. Int. J. Inf. Syst. Model. Design (IJISMD) (2014)
15. Leuschel, M., Bendisposto, J.: Directed model checking for B: an evaluation and new techniques. In: SBMF 2010: Formal Methods. LNCS, vol. 6527, pp. 1–16. Springer (2010)

16. Leuschel, M., Butler, M.: ProB: an automated analysis toolset for the B method. Int. J. Softw. Tools Technol. Transfer **10**(2), 185–203 (2008)
17. Lodderstedt, T., Basin, D., Doser, J.: SecureUML: a UML-based modeling language for model-driven security. In: Proceedings of the 5th International Conference on The Unified Modeling Language, UML 2002. Springer, London (2002)
18. Luh, G.C., Lin, C.Y.: Optimal design of truss structures using ant algorithm. Struct. Multidiscip. Optim. **36**(4), 365–379 (2008)
19. Mammar, A., Frappier, M.: Proof-based verification approaches for dynamic properties: application to the information system domain. Formal Asp. Comput. **27**(2), 335–374 (2015)
20. Monmarché, N.: Algorithmes de fourmis artificielles: applications à la classification et à l'optimisation. Ph.D. thesis, Université François Rabelais, Tours (2000)
21. Monmarché, N., Venturini, G., Slimane, M.: On how Pachycondyla apicalis ants suggest a new search algorithm. Futur. Gener. Comput. Syst. **16**(8), 937–946 (2000)
22. ProB. Tutorial: Directed model checking. https://prob.hhu.de/w/index.php?title=Tutorial_Directed_Model_Checking. Accessed 09 Apr 2025
23. Radhouani, A., Idani, A., Ledru, Y., Rajeb, N.B.: Symbolic search of insider attack scenarios from a formal information system modeling. LNCS Trans. Petri Nets Other Models Concurr. **10**, 131–152 (2015)
24. Suri, B., Bawa, S.: Literature survey of ant colony optimization in software testing. Int. J. Comput. Appl. **45**(14), 1–6 (2012)
25. Zhang, N., Ryan, M., Guelev, D.P.: Synthesising verified access control systems through model checking. J. Comput. Secur. **16**(1), 1–61 (2008)

Developing Safe Exception Recovery Mechanisms for CHERI Capability Hardware Using UML-B Formal Analysis

Colin Snook(✉), Asieh Salehi Fathabadi, Thai Son Hoang, Robert Thorburn, Michael Butler, Leonardo Aniello, and Vladimiro Sassone

School of Electronics and Computer Science (ECS), University of Southampton, Southampton, UK
{cfs,a.salehi-fathabadi,t.s.hoang,robert.thorburn, m.j.butler,l.aniello,vsassone}@soton.ac.uk

Abstract. While detection of suspicious or erroneous CPU behaviour can be achieved by generic mechanisms such as memory-safe processors, recovering safely from the resulting exceptions is an application-specific problem. The challenge is to ensure that a complex closed system including the controller and its environment remain in a safe state while undertaking abnormal state changes in the controller as part of its exception recovery process. Handling exceptional error events is a complex task that requires insight and domain expertise to ensure that a process is designed to recover from abnormal conditions and return the system to a safe state. Exception handling relies on a notion of *transactions* in order to identify how the system can be systematically returned to a consistent state. Formal methods can address this complexity, by supporting the analysis of transactions and exception handling at the abstract design stages utilising mathematical modelling and proofs. Event-B is a state-based formal method for modelling and verifying the consistency of discrete systems; however, it lacks explicit support for analysing the handling of exceptions. UML-B is a diagrammatic front-end for Event-B modelling which allows models to be constructed using class diagrams and state machines. In this paper, we use UML-B state machines to support the modelling of normal behaviour, with a notion of consistency and augment this with a technique for modelling 'transactions' which may either complete to reach a consistent state or encounter exceptional errors that have to return the system to a consistent state despite the non-completion of the transaction. We also discuss an implementation of the modelled exception handling in the 'C' programming language as a first stage towards automatic code generation of exception handlers.

Keywords: Exception handling · Formal methods · Event-B · UML-B

M. Leuschel and F. Ishikawa (Eds.): ABZ 2025, LNCS 15728, pp. 180–199, 2026.
https://doi.org/10.1007/978-3-031-94533-5_11

1 Introduction

Our work is influenced by considering implementations on *capability hardware* which provides hardware-level protection against incorrect memory access [17]. Capability hardware blocks unauthorised memory access at runtime, raising hardware exceptions that should be handled by application code. Unauthorised memory access might be caused by unintentional coding errors, such as out of bounds array access, or malicious attacks, such as buffer overflow exploitation. In principle, code that is developed formally will be free from incorrect memory access. However, we assume the applications we develop will operate in software environments where vulnerabilities remain, e.g., through use of untrusted libraries.

Mechanisms for detecting exceptional erroneous behaviour are often generic since they flag unusual activity in the underlying low-level machinery. An example is the CHERI memory safe capability approach which is implemented within general purpose electronic computing devices. In contrast, the design of a suitable recovery response to the detected exception is usually application specific, or at least domain specific. In some cases a safe response might be to halt, but this could play into the hands of a malicious attacker by providing an easy vector to achieve denial of service attacks. In many cases, it is not safe for a critical service to halt. Therefore, we believe that generic memory protection mechanisms such as CHERI are only useful if they are complemented by tools and techniques for application engineers to design and implement safe recovery strategies that allow the system to continue its service as much as possible.

We already use formal modelling tools to support the rigorous analysis of systems, ensuring that they meet important (e.g., safety and security) properties. In the HDSEC project[1] we have adapted these formal analysis tools to show how they can be used to design and analyse exception recovery responses and verify that they recover the system to a condition that satisfies the important system properties. We focus on designing a safe recovery after an exception and abstract away from the mechanisms that detect the exception.

We have also implemented the modelled system in order to demonstrate the recovery responses in a real system running on a CHERI Morello PC[2]. The implementation is a demonstrator that also contains a simulation of the environment and the user interfaces. The code is seeded to allow a capability exception to be detected so that the recovery can be demonstrated.

Programming languages provide a framework for detection, notification and handling of exceptions. Exception handling is a complex and error-prone activity, and systematic reasoning is needed to identify and characterise exceptions. Formal analysis of the exceptional control flow provides a means to validate the design of the exception handling recovery [4]. However, support for exceptions in formal methods is less mature. This paper proposes an approach to systematic

[1] https://hd-sec.github.io/.

[2] www.cl.cam.ac.uk/research/security/ctsrd/cheri/cheri-morello.html.

reasoning about exception handling at the design level using the UML-B and Event-B formal method.

Event-B [2] is a formal method to model and verify correctness of safety/security critical systems. While exception handling can be modelled within the existing features of the Event-B toolkit, there is no explicit support for it. We use UML-B [14] and Event-B to visualise and verify the normal expected behaviour of a system and then add support for handling exceptions in safety/security systems from the design level to the implementation. The encoding of state machine states provides (i) a mechanism for detecting where the exception occurred and hence choosing the appropriate recovery, and (ii) for going into a suitable recovery state. We propose extensions to the UML-B state machine notation to facilitate the automatic deduction of which transitions represent exception recovery and how system variables should be rolled back during a recovery. The Event-B model generated by UML-B already has sufficient features to express the recovery behaviour and does not need to be extended.

We illustrate our approach using a Smart Ballot System (SBB) [7], an integral part of some modern voting systems. Earlier research work [6] presented a correct-by-construction secure SBB system using Event-B. Our proposed approach can address the robustness of SBB against exceptions in [6].

This work follows on from previous work presented at ABZ2024 [12]. We have revised the way that we model and verify exception recovery so that it is better integrated with the UML-B development of normal behaviour and is modelled using state machine transitions. We have introduced a notion of transactions and model these with superstates. This enables us to formally verify that exception recovery correctly rolls back any partially completed transaction behaviour. We have also added a demonstration implementation which runs on a CHERI Morello memory-safe PC.

The paper is structured as follows. Section 2 introduces the CHERI architecture, POSIX signals, Event-B and the SBB case study. Our proposed approach is described using the case study, firstly by modelling the normal behaviour in Sect. 3, then by adding a concept of transactions in Sect. 4 and finally by adding the exception recovery in Sect. 5. Section 6 summarises an overview of the complete approach, Sect. 7 describes the implementation of the case study on a Cheri Morello machine as a demonstration. In Sect. 8, we review existing literature and research, highlighting key methodologies, findings, and gaps that our study aims to address. Finally Sect. 9 discusses our plans for the next steps and Sect. 10 summarises related works and concludes.

2 Background

Memory Safety and Capability-Based Hardware: Capability-based architectures have shown promise in enhancing memory safety and preventing unauthorized access at the hardware level. The CHERI (Capability Hardware Enhanced RISC Instructions) architecture is a notable approach that provides fine-grained memory safety guarantees by embedding capabilities into processor instructions. Watson et al. [17] present CHERI as a hybrid capability-system architecture that allows scalable compartmentalization, enhancing the security of software through pointer integrity and memory access control. Further refinements to CHERI's instruction set, as detailed in the technical report by Sewell et al. [13], enable efficient enforcement of memory safety in complex, high-assurance systems. These foundational works provide a hardware-level basis for secure exception handling, which our approach extends by focusing on application-specific recovery mechanisms and maintaining system consistency after exceptions.

Signals are a mechanism for asynchronous event notification used in Unix-based (POSIX-compliant) operating systems. Signals are used by the kernel to interrupt (e.g. suspend, terminate or kill) a process. When an event occurs, the operating system interrupts the target process' normal flow of execution to handle the signal. If the process has registered a signal handler, that routine is executed. Otherwise, the default signal handler is executed. The CHERI-BSD operating system [16] running on Morello hardware adds a new signal SIGPROT which is used to notify the active process that the Morello hardware has detected a memory protection error. In our example case study, we also use the standard signal SIGALRM, which is used to notify that a timeout set by a process has expired.

Event-B [2] is a refinement-based formal method for system development. The mathematical language of Event-B is based on set theory and first order logic. An Event-B model consists of two parts: *contexts* for static data and *machines* for dynamic behaviour. Contexts contain carrier sets, constants, and axioms that constrain the carrier sets and constants. Machines contain variables, invariant predicates that constrain the variables, and events. In Event-B, a machine corresponds to a transition system where *variables* represent the states and *events* specify the transitions. An event comprises a guard denoting its enabling-condition and an action describing how the variables are modified when the event is executed. Event-B is supported by the Rodin tool set [3], an extensible open source toolkit which includes facilities for modelling, verifying the consistency of models using theorem proving and model checking techniques. In this paper we make extensive use of the UML-B plug-in [15] which provides a diagrammatic modelling notation for Event-B in the form of state machines and class diagrams that automatically generate Event-B models. The diagrammatic models relate to an Event-B machine and generate or contribute to parts of it. For example, a state machine will automatically generate the Event-B data elements (sets, constants, axioms, variables, and invariants) to implement the states. Transitions contribute further guards and actions representing their state change, to the events that they elaborate.

SBB (Smart Ballot Box) [7] is a computerised system to automate election voting. The SBB system inspects a ballot paper by detecting a barcode and decrypting it to evaluate whether the ballot is valid. If the ballot is valid, then a vote can be cast, spoiled or cancelled by the user and the ballot paper is sorted accordingly into the storage boxes. If the ballot is not valid, the SBB rejects the paper. The key function of the SBB is to ensure that only valid ballot documents are included in the ballot boxes.

3 Modelling Normal-Behaviour and Verifying Safety Invariants

Utilising UML-B, we model the SBB normal behaviour (without exceptions) as a state-machine[3]. The normal-behaviour SBB case, presented in Fig. 1on the following page,, starts in the Waiting state and, in the case of accepting the ballot, progresses through the following sequence of states: Waiting, BarcodeReading, BarcodeProcessing, UserSelection, PrepareAccepting, Accepting, Waiting. There are several functional variables (not shown in the state-machine diagram) which are manipulated by actions of the transitions. They are

- paper_count- a count of the papers input to the roller (incremented by the transition ROLLER_paper_in),
- accepted_count- a count of the papers categorized as accepted by the roller (incremented by the transition ROLLER_accept_paper),
- spoilt_count- a count of the papers categorized as spoilt by the roller (incremented by the transition ROLLER_spoil_paper),
- rejected_count- a count of the papers categorized as rejected by the roller (incremented by the transition ROLLER_reject_paper),
- cast_count- a count of the votes cast by the user (incremented by the transition USER_cast),

The Waiting state contains two desired *safety* properties that are expected to hold when the SBB has completed the processing of any papers and is in the Waiting state:

- The count of votes cast by the user (cast_count) should be the same as the count of papers categorized as accepted by the roller (paper_count).
- The count of papers input to the roller should be the same as the sum of papers categorized as accepted, spoilt or rejected by the roller.

In general, a system may have important properties that are expected to hold whenever the system is quiescent, but that are temporarily violated while the system is engaged in active processing. We refer to properties that are expected to hold in *quiescent states* as *quiescent invariants* and states that are not quiescent as *active states*. Active states may contain *intermediate invariants* that describe the expected progress during the activity. In fact, intermediate invariant properties are needed in the active states to help the provers prove the quiescent invariants are re-established. This is because the prover considers one transition at a time and attempts to infer the invariants of the post-state (e.g. the desired quiescent invariants) from the known pre-state (e.g. intermediate invariants) as

[3] The example models described in this paper are available here: https://doi.org/10.5258/SOTON/D3452.

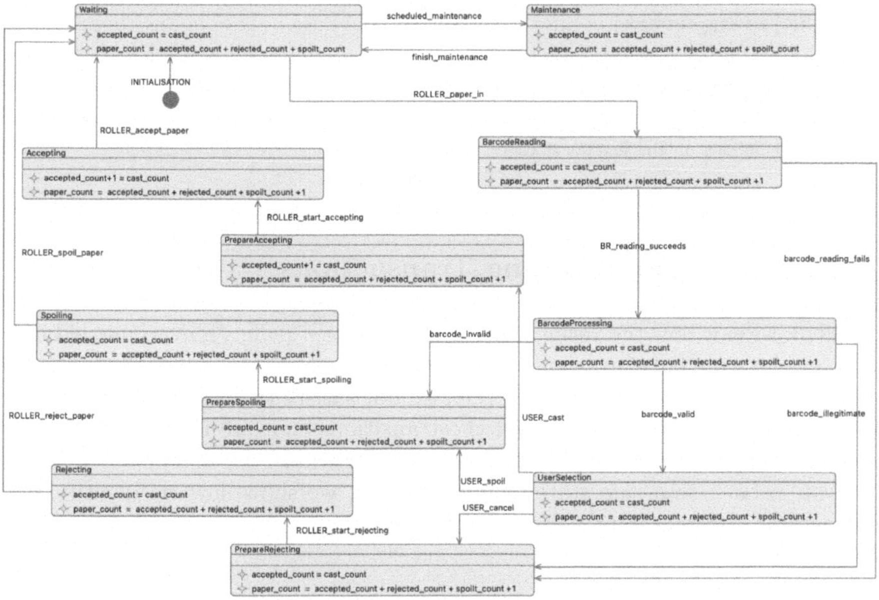

Fig. 1. State Machine, normal-behaviour SBB.

well as any guards of the transition. Hence, since the prover cannot 'see' back up the sequence of transitions, we have to provide this sight via the intermediate invariants in the active states. Once this is done, the proofs are automatically discharged by the Rodin provers. Notice how the intermediate invariants document where the counts are out of step and by how much. For example in the Accepting state, cast_count is one ahead of the accepted_count because it has been incremented by the transition User_cast, but the Roller has yet to finish categorizing the paper as accepted.

The UML-B tools automatically generate sets, constants and axioms in a newly generated context component in order to represent the UML-B state machines using Event-B syntax. The SBB states are an enumeration of a carrier set where each state (Waiting, BarcodeReading, ...), is specified as a *constant* and the set of states, SBB_STATES, are specified as an axiom using *carrier sets*. The enumeration is then specified as a partition via the following axiom:

```
@axm1: partition(SBB_STATES, {Waiting}, {BarcodeReading},{BarcodeProcessing},
    {UserSelection}, {Accepting}, {Spoiling}, {Rejecting}, {PrepareRejecting},
    {PrepareSpoiling}, {PrepareAccepting})
```

The dynamic behaviour of the state machine (Fig. 1), is generated as part of the containing machine component. Each event that represents a transition, checks, within its guards, that the current state of the SBB is the transition source state, and changes the state to the transition target state, within its actions. For example:

```
event BR_reading_succeeds
when
    @grd1: SBB =BarcodeReading
    <other guards about the functional vars>
then
    @act1: SBB :=BarcodeProcessing
    <other actions on the functional vars>
end
```

4 Identifying and Adding Transactions

In Sect. 3, we saw how the verification of the quiescent (safety) invariants led us to introduce intermediate invariants that document where (i.e., in which states) the functional variables are out of step (i.e., do not satisfy the quiescent invariants). We could think of these states and the transitions that are involved in passing through them as a process or *transaction* which must be completed to bring the system back to a safe state. In this section, we show how we identify such transactions and represent them in the model.

4.1 Adding Transactions to the State Machine Model

In UML-B we can arrange state machine states hierarchically by nesting a state machine within a superstate. We use this superstate structure here to represent the transactions. We introduce a transaction superstate to contain all the states that have a similar same intermediate invariant. Some of the contained states may have other intermediate invariants that differ within them.

For example in Fig. 1, all of the states, i.e., BarcodeReading, BarcodeProcessing, UserSelection, PrepareAccepting, Accepting, PrepareSpoiling, Spoiling, PrepareRejecting and Rejecting, have the same invariant:

$$\text{paper\_count} = \text{accepted\_count} + \text{rejected\_count} + \text{spoilt\_count} + 1.$$

This is because a paper has been fed in to the roller but since its processing is not complete, none of the accepted, rejected or spoilt counts has been increased yet. Hence this group of states form a transaction and we wrap them in a superstate Paper_in_transaction. A useful feature of superstates is that they can contain invariants that apply throughout all of their contained sub-states. Therefore we can move the intermediate invariant that we used to identify the transaction up to the superstate and remove all the repetitions of it in the sub-states.

The modified model is shown in Fig. 2.

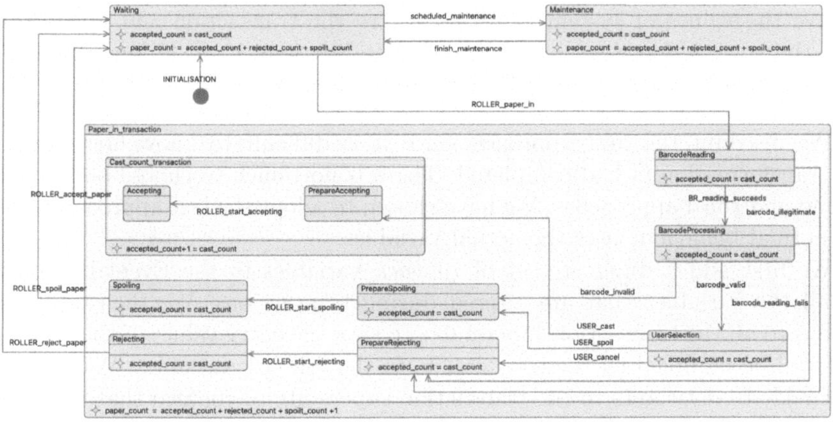

Fig. 2. State Machine, SBB with transactions.

Notice that another intermediate invariant: accepted_count+1 = cast_count identifies a transaction consisting of the states Prepare_Accepting and Accepting (but not the other sub-states of the previous transaction). Hence we have a nested transaction and can introduce a further transaction superstate Cast_count_transaction to contain those two sub-states and move the transaction intermediate invariant into it.

As soon as we re-generate the Event-B for the UML-B model, the automatic provers re-prove the model and verify that the quiescent invariants are still satisfied. The changes are superficial notational ones which do not change the semantic.

4.2 Adding Rollback Caching to Transactions

Our model so far only deals with successful outcomes of transactions (even if it is a successful rejection response by the controller). However, the aim of identifying transactions is to consider failure cases where the transaction does not complete, which, by definition, leaves the system in an invalid condition requiring some recovery process. There are several possible approaches to recovering a safe and valid condition:

1. design specific compensation actions for each recovery (rollback is $V = G(V')$, where V' is the state of the variables V that may be altered in the transaction and G is the transformation that had completed before the exception occurred),
2. modify temporary copies of the variables and only commit their values to the real system variables when the transaction completes (no rollback is needed, but there is a pre-transaction action $V' = V$ to make temporary copies of V and there is a commit action $V = V^T$ where V^T is the value of the temporary copies of V),

3. save the values of system variables before the transaction and revert them if the transaction does not complete. (Rollback is $V = V'$ and there is a pre-transaction action $V' = V$ to make temporary copies of V),

We discount the first approach since it is difficult to know how much of the transformation G had completed. There is not much to choose between the second and third approaches. We have chosen to adopt the last approach so that the normal behaviour uses the actual variables.

We first add a duplicate set of *rollback* variables to the Event-B machine for all the variables that are altered during transactions. We then add entry actions to all the transaction superstates to save the entry values of the variables that will be modified by the transaction, in the rollback variables. We then add intermediate invariants to the transaction superstate to confirm that the values in the rollback variables, satisfy the quiescent invariant. That is, we make a copy of the quiescent invariants and replace the variables with the rollback variables used by that transaction.

For example, in SBB, we add the invariant:

$$\text{paper\_in\_rollback} = \text{accepted\_count} + \text{rejected\_count} + \text{spoilt\_count}$$

to Paper_in_transaction, and

$$\text{cast\_count\_rollback} = \text{accepted\_count}$$

to the Cast_count_transaction. These will be needed in the next step to prove that exceptions establish the quiescent invariants when they use the rollback variables to restore the values of variables that have been changed in the transaction.

This process of adding rollback variables is done for each of the transactions, including nested ones. Note that the rollback variable should be used by the lowest level transaction possible. For example, in the SBB model, cast_count is saved as rollback_cast_count by Cast_count_transaction, not by Paper_in_transaction.

5 Adding Exception Handling to Transactions

Having prepared by identifying transactions and their associated rollback requirements, in the next step we identify where exceptions could occur and how the system should recover from them. The model should be analysed state by state to identify negative outcomes that could prevent the activities within the state from completing successfully. Since the model abstracts away from the details of these state activities, identification of exceptions is a subjective assessment of the concepts represented by the state. As we are interested in the memory safety provided by CHERI hardware, we might consider certain states to be particularly untrusted (whether malicious or accidental). We may also wish to consider failures due to external system components such as user mis-actions and machinery failures. For example, Table 1 outlines the potential exceptions and their recovery strategy in the SBB system:

Table 1. Exceptions handled by the SBB system

Exception	Recovery
memory capability violation in barcode software library	if occasional, reject the ballot, if persistent, external maintenance
user does not enter selection within timeout	reject the ballot
roller does not complete within timeout	external maintenance

The first exception is a memory capability violation in the barcode processing software. This could be due to a simple software error or it could be due to a security attack via virus software which is trying to use memory accesses to create an attack vector. We could react by disabling the service immediately to ensure that the SBB does not record invalid results. However, this could play into the hands of an attacker trying to create denial of service attack. Therefore, we decided to adopt a two-phase recovery strategy. For occasional exceptions, the paper is rejected and the user can try again. It is the best we can do since the paper cannot be processed without a barcode. If several exceptions are detected consecutively, then the service is aborted and the system awaits external intervention.

The second exception is a timeout on the user choosing either to cast, spoil or cancel their vote. In this case the recovery strategy is to default to rejecting the paper. The third exception is a breakdown in the roller machinery that sorts the physical papers into their respective categories. If the roller does not complete within a timeout, it is assumed that manual maintenance will be required to fix the roller machinery. (Note that we are not interested in quantifying intervals of time; only in an ordinal arrangement of events and therefore, we do not need to model the tick of a clock).

Figure 3 shows the UML-B model with exception handling transitions added. The first exception can occur either in the BarcodeReading or BarcodeProcessing states and can result in two different exception handlers. If an exception counter (which is not shown in the diagram) is below a threshold, exception_handler1a recovers to the PrepareRejecting state. This does not leave the transaction Paper_in_transaction so does not need to use the rollback mechanism. However, the exception count is incremented as part of the exception handling. If the exception count reaches the threshold the exception is handled by exception_handler1b which exits the Paper_in_transaction and recovers to the Maintenance state. In this case the paper_count is rolled back by the action paper_count := paper_count_rollback which is attached to the transition exception_handler1b. The second exception can occur in the state UserSelection and is handled by the transition exception_handler2 which recovers to PrepareRejecting without any rollback actions. The third exception can occur in Accepting, Spoiling or Rejecting and always recovers to Maintenance with the same paper_in rollback

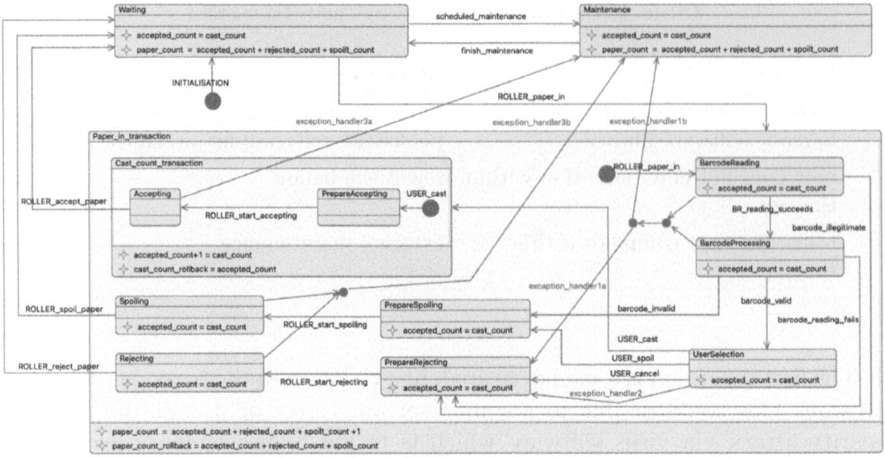

Fig. 3. State Machine, SBB with exception handling.

action as the first exception. However, in the case where it occurs in Accepting, the exception also exits the nested Cast_count_transaction and therefore must also roll back the cast_count via an action cast_count := cast_count_rollback which is attached to the transition exception_handler3a. (Note that, in Event-B, conditional actions are only possible using different guarded events for each condition hence the need for separate transitions for exception_handler3a and exception_handler3b).

6 Overview of the Method of Modelling Transactions and Exceptions in UML-B

The generic technique for modelling transactions and exceptions and analysing their recovery using UML-B state-machines and Event-B verification is summarised in this section.

1. Model the normal behaviour as a UML-B state-machine.
   - Construct a UML-B state-machine to model the control modes (states) and mode changes (transitions) of the system.
   - In the containing machine, add additional variables involved in the functionality. The variables may be used to control (guard) the firing of transitions and be altered when transitions fire (actions).
   - Add quiescent invariants to the states to express desired safety properties about the expected values of the variables in particular quiescent states[4].

[4] We refer to these invariants as *safety* properties, however, we use *safety* in a very broad way to represent any properties the modeller would like to remain true in this model.

  - Verify the model using the Rodin provers, adding intermediate invariants to states in order to achieve the proofs.
2. Identify and represent any transactions in the model.
   - Where intermediate invariants indicate that variables are out of step in a sequence of states (i.e. are different from the quiescent invariants) a superstate should be introduced to represent the transaction.
   - The sequence of states containing the intermediate invariants is then contained in a nested state-machine within the transaction superstate.
   - The transition that enters the parent transaction superstate will contain an action that alters the variable that is out of step (i.e. introduces the difference from the quiescent invariant).
   - The intermediate invariants expressing the difference from the quiescent invariant are replaced by a single intermediate invariant in the parent transaction superstate.
   - Transactions may be nested within other transactions where a variable is changed in a sub-transaction.
   - Check that the model can still be verified by the Rodin provers. The changes are superficial/structural so should not affect the validity of the proofs.
3. Add rollback caching of variables to support the transactions.
   - In the containing machine, add rollback variables to store the entry state of all of the ancillary variables that are altered during the transaction.
   - Add entry actions to the transaction superstate to cache the value of the variables that will be changed by the transaction, in their corresponding rollback variables.
   - Add intermediate invariants to the transaction superstate to confirm that the quiescent invariants, with variables replaced by rollback variables, obey the quiescent properties. These will be needed in the next step to prove that exceptions re-establish the quiescent invariants when they use the rollback variables to restore the values of variables that have been changed in the transaction.
   - Check that the model can still be verified by the Rodin provers. The proofs should be straightforward.
4. Add exception handling to the model.
   - Consider each state in turn and identify any potential exceptions that could occur in that states actions.
   - Add transitions to represent exceptions that can occur from states within the transaction.
   - Their target (recovery) states can be within the transaction or external to the transaction.
   - Junctions can be used to merge transitions when the same exception handler can handle an exception occurring in several source states. (The transition can fire from either of the source states)
   - Junctions can also be used to split a transition into several outcomes and hence model alternative exception handlers (with different recovery target states) of the same exception. In this case, guards on the final segments

of the transition, can be used to distinguish the cases and they can have different rollback actions.
- For exceptions that exit a transaction, add actions to the transition to roll back the variables that have been changed (i.e. v := rv where rv is the rollback variable for variable v).
- Exceptions must add rollback actions for each of the nested transaction superstates that are exited.
- Verify the model using the Rodin provers.

7 Demonstration Implementation

We have implemented the modelled system in order to demonstrate recovery responses from an exception signal in a real system running on a CHERI Morello PC. The implementation is a demonstrator that also contains a simulation of the SBB environment (the roller machine) and the user interfaces. An invalid memory access is seeded in the barcode processing simulation so that a SIGPROT signal can be induced as part of the demonstration. The user simulation asks the tester to supply the expected user responses and if this is delayed sufficiently, a SIGALRM is induced for demonstration purposes. Although this is just a demonstrator program, we can envision the controller code, including the exception handling, being generated automatically from the UML-B model. In the following we use pseudo-code to illustrate the generic abstract structure of the envisioned automatically generated code.

The processing of a state-machine state and firing of transitions, is wrapped in a conditional sigsetjmp which acts as a kind of 'try'. The following pseudocode shows the generic structure of the controller code where 'try' is implemented with sigsetjmp.

```
do forever {
    try {
        set alarm timeout for the new state
        repeat until the statemachine state changes
            progress the environment
            progress the statemachine }
    //any exception handler will return to here}
```

The hand-constructed C code for the SBB example corresponding to the pseudocode above is in Fig. 4 on the next page.

The function that progresses the statemachine selects the case based on the current statemachine state and tests to see whether it has the necessary conditions to fire any of its outgoing transitions. The conditions may involve trigger events from the environment, user inputs, internal system variables or may be always true (i.e. the next transition fires immediately).

```
switch state
case STATE1:
    if can fire TRANSITION1
        fire TRANSITION1
    else if can fire TRANSITION2
        fire TRANSITION2
    etc.
case STATE2:
    fire TRANSITION3
    etc.
```

```
void SBB_statemachine(){
    bool  changedState=false;
    while (true){
        if (sigsetjmp(SBB_abort_step,true) ==0) {   // TRY
            if (sbb_control.state==SBB_Null){
                printf("Something went wrong! SBB_state is Null\n");
            }else{
                alarm(getAlarm());      //set the timeout for the current state
                changedState = false;
                printCurrentState();
                do {
                    ROLLER_step();                      //progress the roller simulation
                    changedState = SBB_checkState(); //see if we can change the state
                } while (!changedState);            //repeat until can change state
            }
        }   //SBB_abort_step - exit point for handled exceptions
        sbb_control.trigger = NULL_TRIGGER;
    }
}
```

Fig. 4. Code for the main SBB state-machine execution showing 'sigsetjmp'.

When fired, transition functions take any transition actions such as changing system variables and then update the statemachine state to the new (target) state. If the source state has any exit actions or the target state has any entry actions, these are also added as transition actions.

If there is an exception (which could be any POSIX signal but we use SIGPROT and SIGALRM as examples) the exception handler will be called to intervene with any roll back actions and change the state to the appropriate recovery action. The exception handler then exits (using a siglongjmp), to the end of the main try (sigsetjmp) conditional block. This is also where main loop ends up after a normal transition in order to enter a new state. Therefore the exception handler sets up the next state variables to enter the designated recovery state depending on the exception that was raised and the state that was executing when the exception occurred.

The exception handling is set up at intialisation using sigaction which is a facility built in to POSIX signals library for this purpose. The sigaction assigns our exception handler to the handled signals (see Fig. 5).

```
void SBB_setup_exception_handling(){
    //set up mask to only allow further interrupts
    //from exceptions other than the ones we handle
    sigemptyset(&SBB_sa.sa_mask);
    sigaddset(&SBB_sa.sa_mask, SIGPROT);
    sigaddset(&SBB_sa.sa_mask, SIGALRM);
    //assign the exception handler routine
    SBB_sa.sa_handler = (void *)SBB_Handler;
    //assign the sigaction to SIGALRM and SIGPROT
    sigaction(SIGALRM, &SBB_sa, &SBB_SIGALRM_oldsa);
    sigaction(SIGPROT, &SBB_sa, &SBB_SIGPROT_oldsa);
}
```

Fig. 5. Code for setting up the exception handler using 'sigaction'.

Note that we use a single exception handler routine for both signals. The different exception transitions of the UML-B model map to different condition branches within the handler. (Event-B does not support conditional execution within an event).

The exception handler, (see SBB example in Fig. 6 on the facing page), contains a switch case for each type of signal that is handled and each case contains conditional branches for the state(s) that the signal has a defined recovery. The choice of recovery state can also be conditional for a particular signal source state combination and recovery may or may not require rolling back system variables.

```
switch signal type
case SIGNAL 1:
    if current state = STATE1
        if condition for recovery 1
            change current state to recovery state 1
            //possibly no rollback is needed for some recovery states
        if condition for recovery 2
            change current state to recovery state 2
            rollback system variables to saved pre−transaction values
case SIGNAL 2: ... etc. ...
exit to end of main try block (using siglongjmp)
```

Of course the signal could occur in a state for which we did not model a recovery. In this case the signal is ignored. The recovery for a particular signal and state may also depend on further conditions. For example, *exception 1* of the SBB depends on a count and takes a different recovery of the exception occurs several times (which may be a persistent attack). Each branch sets the appropriate recovery state in the state machine control data structure and also rolls back any variables that were part of a transaction where the recovery leaves that transaction.

To demonstrate the code and signal handling we have executed it on a CHERI Morello PC. The code for the barcode reading and processing states is 'seeded' with an invalid memory access (using a data value as a pointer) so that a SIGPROT exception can be generated. SIGALRM timeouts are easily simulated by not responding to the user interface simulation code. The console output provided by the demonstration program provides a record of the occurrence of exceptions.

8 Related Work

This section reviews relevant research on exception handling and fault recovery mechanisms, the application of formal methods in safety-critical systems, and recent advances in code generation for safe exception handling.

Exception Handling and Fault Recovery in Safety-Critical Systems. Exception handling is essential for robust system behaviour in safety-critical applications, where maintaining a safe state during abnormal conditions is paramount. Julliand and Perrouin [8] discuss the complexities of exception handling in formal methods, emphasising the challenges of fault tolerance when designing for systems that must adhere to stringent safety standards. This work underscores the importance of domain expertise in designing tailored recovery mechanisms that respond effectively to error events. Unlike general-purpose error handling, safety-critical applications require a transactional approach to return systems to a consistent state, even under exceptional conditions. Our work builds on this by incorporating formal methods to model transactional behaviour that can systematically manage exceptions in a capability-based hardware environment.

Formal Methods for Exception Handling and Safety Assurance. Formal methods, particularly Event-B, have proven valuable in the verification of safety-critical systems by enabling mathematical rigour in system design and error detection. However, traditional Event-B lacks explicit support for exception handling and fault recovery. Snook and Butler's [14] UML-B framework extends Event-B with UML-like state machines, allowing high-level modelling of system behaviour while maintaining consistency in the presence of exceptions. Abdallah et al. [1] further adapt Event-B for handling exceptions, proposing a model for safe exception handling that ensures safety-critical systems can reliably transition to safe states. Our approach builds on these advancements by using UML-B to model system consistency and integrating exception-handling transactions that respond to non-completions and error states, contributing to the formal analysis of capability-based hardware systems.

Transactional Models and Consistency Recovery. Maintaining a consistent system state is crucial for safe exception handling in transactional models, particularly in distributed and embedded systems. Lamport's [9] classic work on distributed systems provides a foundational understanding of time and event ordering, which underpins transactional recovery in complex systems. Lynch and Tuttle [10] introduce the input/output automata model, highlighting the importance of input/output synchronization for achieving reliable consistency in safety-critical applications. These foundational models inform our approach by providing a theoretical basis for handling transactions and error states within closed systems, which we implement in our UML-B framework to manage exception recovery effectively.

```
void SBB_Handler(int sigtype, siginfo_t *info, void *context) {
    printf("\n>>SBB Handler - sigtype: %d while in state ", sigtype);
    printCurrentState();
    record_exception(info);
    switch (sigtype) {

        case SIGPROT:   //capability  violation
            if (    sbb_control.paper_in_state == SBB_BarcodeReading ||
                    sbb_control.paper_in_state == SBB_BarcodeProcessing) {
                //Exception 1  has conditional recovery targets
                if (sbb_control.attack_count<ATTACK_LIM){  //Exception1a
                        printf(">>> attack counter < attack limit\n");
                        sbb_control.state = SBB_Paper_in;
                        sbb_control.paper_in_state = SBB_PrepareRejecting;
                        sbb_control.attack_count++;
                        printf(">>> inc attack counter to %d\n", sbb_control.attack_count);
                }else if (sbb_control.attack_count>=ATTACK_LIM){  //Exception1b
                        printf(">>> attack limit EXCEEDED\n");
                        sbb_control.state = SBB_Maintenance;
                        sbb_control.paper_in_state = SBB_Paper_in_Null;
                        sbb_control.attack_count = 0;
                        printf(">>> reset attack counter to %d\n", sbb_control.attack_count);
                        //roll back paper count as exiting transaction Paper_in
                        sbb_data.papers = sbb_rollback.papers;
                        printf(">>> rolled  back papers to %d\n", sbb_data.papers);
                }else{
                    printf(">>> no handling defined for this signal-state-condition... ignoring\n");
                }
            }else{
                printf(">>> no handling defined for this signal-state... ignoring\n");
            }
            break;

        case SIGALRM:   //timeout
            if (sbb_control.paper_in_state == SBB_UserSelection){   //Exception2
                sbb_control.state = SBB_Paper_in;
                sbb_control.paper_in_state = SBB_PrepareRejecting;
            //Exception 3 has 2 different cases due to Accepting being within a nested transaction
            }else if (sbb_control.cast_count_state == SBB_Accepting){   //Exception3a
                sbb_control.state = SBB_Maintenance;
                sbb_control.paper_in_state = SBB_Paper_in_Null;
                sbb_control.cast_count_state = SBB_Cast_count_Null;
                //roll back paper count as exiting transaction Paper_in
                sbb_data.papers = sbb_rollback.papers;
                //roll back cast count as exiting transaction Cast_count
                printf(">>> rolled  back papersto %d\n", sbb_data.papers);
                sbb_data.cast = sbb_rollback.cast;
                printf(">>> rolled  back cast to %d\n", sbb_data.cast);
            }else if (sbb_control.paper_in_state == SBB_Spoiling ||
                        sbb_control.paper_in_state == SBB_Rejecting){   //Exception3b
                sbb_control.state = SBB_Maintenance;
                sbb_control.paper_in_state = SBB_Paper_in_Null;
                //roll back paper count as exiting transaction Paper_in
                sbb_data.papers = sbb_rollback.papers;
                printf(">>> rolled  back papers to %d\n", sbb_data.papers);
            }else{
                printf(">>> no handling defined for this signal-state... ignoring\n");
            }
            break;

        default:
            printf(">>> no handling defined for this signal... ignoring\n");
            return;
    }
    //Console message about state change
    printf(">>> recover to: ");
    printCurrentState();
    printf(">>> aborting the step that caused the exception\n");
    //jump back to the 'catch' clause  (end of sigsetjmp condition)
    siglongjmp(SBB_abort_step, 1);
}
```

Fig. 6. Code for the common exception handler.

Automatic Code Generation for Safe Exception Handling. Finally, translating formal models into executable code is a significant step toward implementing safe exception handling in practice. Abrial [2] outlines techniques for generating code from Event-B models, which can facilitate a direct path from formal design to application. Dalvandi [5] proposes SEB-CG tool for extensible automatic code generation from Scheduled Event-B (SEB), an extension of Event-B that augments models with control structures, to executable code in a target language. Mendes and Bensalem [11] extend this to safety-critical applications, demonstrating that automated code generation can preserve the integrity of exception-handling logic across various system states. Our work contributes to this body of research by developing an implementation of our UML-B model in C, with the goal of enabling future automatic code generation for exception handlers in CHERI-based systems.

Summary. The existing literature demonstrates the feasibility of using formal methods for exception handling in safety-critical systems, though there remains a gap in capability-specific recovery models that address the unique needs of memory-safe hardware like CHERI. By leveraging UML-B state machines and transactional recovery modelling, our approach advances the formal analysis of exception handling mechanisms tailored for capability-based systems, ultimately contributing to safer, more reliable embedded applications.

9 Future Work

We intend to develop a code generation tool that will convert our UML-B models into C code with the exception handling functions automatically produced and populated based on the transaction and exception transition detail in the models. In previous work we have developed more general Event-B to C code generation tools based on our Eclipse/Rodin plug-in tool framework. These tools can be extended to be more specific to UML-B state-machines with exception handling. We would also like to develop better tool support for the modelling proposed here. For example, special features within UML-B to model transaction states and exception transitions would make the modelling easier as well as providing better support for the code generation.

The methods discussed here assume the use of POSIX signals and associated Unix-based exception-handling infrastructure. The target hardware for the case study was a CHERI Morello PC running a variant of the BSD operation system. We would also like to support embedded systems which run on smaller real-time operating systems. We are now investigating a new case study using the Sonata development board which is based on an FPGA implementation of the CHERIoT processor running CheriRTOS. A significant difference is that the POSIX signal infrastructure is not present in such systems and the exception handling concepts are closer to hardware device level.

So far we have not considered compartmentalisation in our methods. CHERI compartments enhance the memory-safe capabilities of the hardware providing better detection of suspicious behaviours. Compartmentalisation may require further modelling features/techniques and improved code generation. Compartments also provide the basis of a hierarchical unwinding of un-handled exceptions (analogous to unwinding of the call stack in some typical exception handling languages). We imagine that this could be modelled using hierarchical statemachines.

10 Conclusions

Whereas the focus in hardware design is on generic mechanisms for detecting unusual potentially erroneous or suspicious behavior, the design of safe exception handling after the detection, is application or domain specific and therefore generic solutions are unattainable. Application engineers need supporting methods and tools to help them design and verify that recovery mechanisms do not violate the safety or security of the system. We provide a formal model-based analysis approach to achieve this by first modelling and verifying the system in the absence of exceptions and then adding the exceptional behaviour and appropriate recovery mechanisms. The modelling approach is based on discovering transactions which then suggest the necessary rollback of variables that were involved in the transaction. Usually we promote the use of safety-preserving refinement to incrementally develop the details of a system. However, a limitation of the approach is that exceptions cannot be added as a refinement stage and instead must be seen as a second stage within a single refinement. However, the first and second stages are a relatively simple/methodical progression of the same refinement level and therefore the consequences in terms of verifiability are not excessive. Furthermore, the detail of the system can be expanded as several refinements that each contain the two-stage approach. We have also demonstrated that an implementation can be derived from the formal models. While this is handwritten for now, it would be relatively straightforward to write a tool to automatically generate the code using our Eclipse-based code generation frameworks.

Acknowledgement. This work is supported by HD-Sec project, which was funded by the Digital Security by Design (DSbD) Programme delivered by UKRI to support the DSbD ecosystem.

References

1. Abdallah, A., et al.: A formal model for safe exception handling in safety-critical systems using Event-B. Int. J. Crit. Comput.-Based Syst. **7**(1), 64–85 (2017)
2. Abrial, J.R.: Modeling in Event-B: System and Software Engineering. Cambridge University Press (2010)
3. Abrial, J.R., Butler, M., Hallerstede, S., Hoang, T.S., Mehta, F., Voisin, L.: Rodin: an open toolset for modelling and reasoning in Event-B. Int. J. Softw. Tools Technol. Transf. **12**(6), 447–466 (2010)
4. Brito, P., de Lemos, R., Rubira, C., Martins, E.: Architecting fault tolerance with exception handling: verification and validation. J. Comput. Sci. Technol. **24**(2), 212–237 (2009)
5. Dalvandi, M., Butler, M., Salehi Fathabadi, A.: SEB-CG: code generation tool with algorithmic refinement support for Event-B. In: Sekerinski, E., et al. (eds.) FM 2019, Part I. LNCS, vol. 12232, pp. 19–29. Springer, Cham (2020). https://doi.org/10.1007/978-3-030-54994-7_3

6. Dghaym, D., Hoang, T.S., Butler, M., Hu, R., Aniello, L., Sassone, V.: Verifying system-level security of a smart ballot box. In: Raschke, A., Méry, D. (eds.) ABZ 2021. LNCS, vol. 12709, pp. 34–49. Springer, Cham (2021). https://doi.org/10.1007/978-3-030-77543-8_3
7. Galois and Free & Fair: The BESSPIN Voting System. https://github.com/GaloisInc/BESSPIN-Voting-System-Demonstrator-2019. Accessed 07 Feb 2024
8. Julliand, J., Perrouin, G.: Exception handling and fault tolerance in formal methods: from theory to practice. Formal Aspects Comput. **27**(3), 497–509 (2015)
9. Lamport, L.: Time, clocks, and the ordering of events in a distributed system. Commun. ACM **21**(7), 558–565 (1978)
10. Lynch, N.A., Tuttle, M.R.: An introduction to input/output automata. CWI Q. **2**(3), 219–246 (1989)
11. Mendes, M., Bensalem, S.: Automatic code generation for safety-critical applications. IEEE Trans. Softw. Eng. **42**(7), 650–666 (2016)
12. Salehi Fathabadi, A., et al.: Designing exception handling using Event-B. In: Bonfanti, S., Gargantini, A., Leuschel, M., Riccobene, E., Scandurra, P. (eds.) ABZ 2024. LNCS, vol. 14759, pp. 270–277. Springer, Cham (2024). https://doi.org/10.1007/978-3-031-63790-2_22
13. Sewell, P., et al.: CHERI instruction-set architecture. Technical report, University of Cambridge (2019)
14. Snook, C.F., Butler, M.J.: UML-B: formal modeling and design aided by UML. ACM Trans. Softw. Eng. Methodol. **15**(1), 92–122 (2006)
15. Snook, C., Butler, M.: UML-B: a plug-in for the Event-B tool set. In: Börger, E., Butler, M., Bowen, J.P., Boca, P. (eds.) ABZ 2008. LNCS, vol. 5238, p. 344. Springer, Heidelberg (2008). https://doi.org/10.1007/978-3-540-87603-8_32
16. SRI International and the University of Cambridge: CheriBSD website. https://www.cheribsd.org/. Accessed 20 Feb 2025
17. Watson, R.N.M., et al.: CHERI: a hybrid capability-system architecture for scalable software compartmentalization. In: 2015 IEEE Symposium on Security and Privacy, SP 2015, San Jose, CA, USA, pp. 20–37. IEEE Computer Society (2015)

Case Study Papers

Case Study: Safety Controller for Autonomous Driving on Highways

Michael Leuschel, Fabian Vu(✉), and Kristin Rutenkolk

Faculty of Mathematics and Natural Sciences, Institute of Computer Science, Heinrich-Heine-Universität Düsseldorf, Düsseldorf, Germany
{leuschel,fabian.vu,kristin.rutenkolk}@uni-duesseldorf.de

Abstract. This requirements document presents the case study for the ABZ conference 2025. The case study is about a safety controller for autonomous driving on a highway. The description contains two variations of the case study. First, in the simpler setting, we just consider a single-lane highway where each vehicle can accelerate and brake. The goal is to keep a safe distance to the preceding car. Second, we consider a multi-lane highway where each vehicle can also change lanes.

The challenge is to model the system and its environment, derive assumptions, and model a controller that guarantees safety. The challenge is also to present the safety case in such a way that it is convincing to readers not entirely familiar with the formal method employed.

The case study is designed so that the formal model can be used as a safety shield within a highway simulation environment. We provide pre-trained (unsafe) AI agents for experimental purposes. This part of the case study is optional.

Keywords: Formal Methods · Autonomous Driving · Case Study · Highway · Artificial Intelligence

1 Introduction and Motivation

This requirement document presents the case study for the ABZ conference 2025, which is about a safety controller for driving vehicles on a highway (motorway in UK English). In practical use, the safety controller could be employed as an assistant for a human driver, or can also be added to an artificial intelligence (AI) component to obtain a safe autonomous driving system.

In practice, the vehicle contains cameras and sensors to observe its environment. In the case study, the perception system is abstracted away, i.e., the controller has access to the vehicle's position and the positions of all cars in the vicinity. There are no other obstacles on the highway. The challenge of the case

The work of Fabian Vu is part of the KI-LOK project funded by the "Bundesministerium für Wirtschaft und Energie"; grant # 19/21007E, and the IVOIRE project funded by "Deutsche Forschungsgemeinschaft" (DFG) and the Austrian Science Fund (FWF) grant # I 4744-N.

M. Leuschel and F. Ishikawa (Eds.): ABZ 2025, LNCS 15728, pp. 203–211, 2026.
https://doi.org/10.1007/978-3-031-94533-5_12

study is to model the driving system with appropriate safety rules that guarantee safety, i.e., the absence of collisions.

For demonstration and empirical evaluation purposes, the case study is combined with a simulated highway environment along with trained reinforcement learning AI agents based on [6]. We consider two environments specifically: a single-lane highway where each vehicle can accelerate and brake, and a multi-lane highway where each vehicle can also change lanes.

With this case study, we ask the following questions:

- Which strategy and assumptions do we need for safe driving?
- Under which conditions is it possible to guarantee complete safety?
- How can we implement those conditions on an autonomous driving system, and verify and validate the safety?

2 Requirements

This section presents the details of the vehicles, the (single-lane and multi-lane) environments, and the safety requirements that are considered for this case study. We build on the highway environment presented by Leurent [6] and configure it accordingly. The technical details and configuration of the parameters correspond to [6] as well.

2.1 Vehicles

In the following, we provide environmental requirements for the vehicles.

- **VEH1:** Every vehicle has a length of l meters.
- **VEH2:** Every vehicle has a width of w meters.
- **VEH3:** A vehicle has a maximum speed of v_{max} m/s
- **VEH4:** A vehicle has a minimum speed of 0 m/s, i.e., it cannot move backwards.
- **VEH5:** A vehicle has a maximum acceleration of a_{max} m/s^2.
- **VEH6:** A vehicle has a maximum braking deceleration of b_{max} m/s^2.
- **VEH7:** A vehicle has a minimum guaranteed braking deceleration of b_{min} m/s^2, i.e., if it is braking, then the braking deceleration will be between b_{min} and b_{max}, until the point it stops.

Concluding from **VEH3**, **VEH4**, and **VEH5**, the range for the speed is thus $[0, v_{max}]$ m/s. Concluding from **VEH6** and **VEH7**, the range of the acceleration is thus $[-b_{max}, a_{max}]$ m/s^2, with $b_{max} > 0$ and $a_{max} > 0$.

Note that there are edge cases where the acceleration can be in $[-b_{min}, 0]$ as well, e.g., when the difference between a full stop (0 m/s) and the current speed is less than b_{min}. For all other cases, the acceleration is in $[-b_{max}, b_{min}]$ when braking and $[0, a_{max}]$ when accelerating.

When using the highway environment from [6], the concrete values for the parameters above are:

- **VEH1-ENV:** Each vehicle has a length l of 5 m.
- **VEH2-ENV:** Each vehicle has a width w of 2 m.
- **VEH3-ENV:** Each vehicle has a maximum speed v_{max} of 40 m/s (= 144 km/h).
- **VEH4-ENV:** Each vehicle has a minimum speed of 0 m/s.
- **VEH5-ENV:** Each vehicle has a maximum acceleration of 5 m/s^2.
- **VEH6-ENV:** Each vehicle has a maximum braking deceleration of 5 m/s^2.
- **VEH7-ENV:** Each vehicle has a minimum guaranteed braking deceleration of 3 m/s^2.

In the following, we describe actions a controller can perform to control one or multiple vehicles in the environment. We will use the term *cycle* as a time interval in which a vehicle observes its environment and performs an action until reaching the next cycle, i.e., until the next observation and decision.

- **ACT1:** Accelerate (`FASTER`): This action increases the speed (up to v_{max}) with an acceleration up to a_{max} m/s^2. Once the car reaches the v_{max}, the acceleration is 0 m/s^2.
- **ACT2:** Brake (`SLOWER`): This action brakes with a braking deceleration of b_{min} up to b_{max} m/s^2. Once the car stops, the braking deceleration is 0 m/s^2.
- **ACT3:** Idle (`IDLE`): This action reduces the (braking) acceleration close to 0 m/s^2.
- **ACT4:** Change lane to left (`LANE_LEFT`): This action changes the current lane of the vehicle to the lane directly left of it within the current cycle. The acceleration behaves like `IDLE`.
- **ACT5:** Change lane to right (`LANE_RIGHT`): This action changes the current lane of the vehicle to the lane directly right of it within the current cycle. The acceleration behaves like `IDLE`.

Note that the other vehicles also perform these actions but at different times. For example, another vehicle could brake for the first half of the cycle and accelerate in the second half. In Sect. 3, we provide trained agents configured as single agents. Instead/additionally, one can also train and configure multi-agents.

Also, note that there is no guarantee that `FASTER` will use the maximal acceleration a_{max}.

Regarding the controller, the following requirement applies:

- **CON1:** All controlled vehicles observe the environment in a specific time interval of t, i.e., the response time is t seconds.

Concerning the environment, the requirement is:

- **CON1-ENV:** All controlled vehicles observe the environment every second, i.e., the response time is 1 s.

2.2 Single-Lane Environment

Figure 1 shows a visualization of a single-lane environment. Regarding the environment, the following assumption can be made:

- **ENV1:** At any time, there are n_{ve} vehicles on the highway with $n_{ve} \geq 1$.
- **ENV2:** All vehicles drive in the same direction.

In the single-lane environment, the relevant actions are `FASTER`, `SLOWER`, and `IDLE`.

Fig. 1. Visualization of Single-Lane Environment; figure is created while simulating in [6].

2.3 Multi-lane Environment

Figure 2 shows a visualization of a multi-lane environment (with 4 lanes). **ENV1** and **ENV2** also apply to the multi-lane environment. Additionally, the following assumption can be made about the environment:

- **ENV3:** The multi-lane environment consists of a fixed number of lanes n_{la} with $n_{la} \geq 2$.

This means that the number of lanes does not change over time. In addition to `FASTER`, `SLOWER`, and `IDLE`, actions to change lanes to the left (`LANE_LEFT`) or the right (`LANE_RIGHT`) are also relevant.

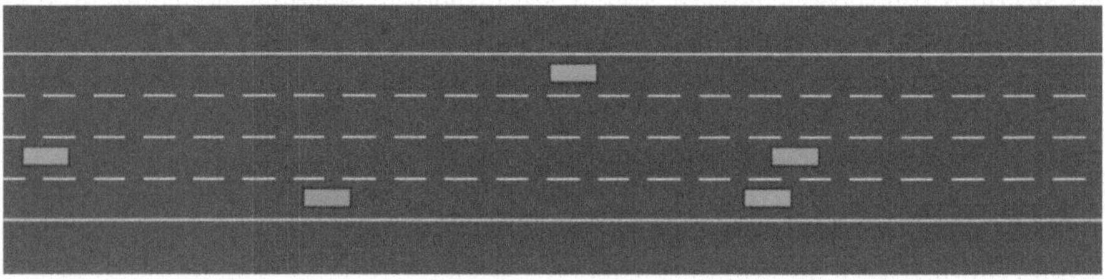

Fig. 2. Visualization of Multi-Lane Environment (with 4 lanes); figure is created while simulating in [6].

2.4 Safety Requirement

This section presents the main safety requirement and a formula to maintain the safety distance. The safety requirement for the case study is:

- **SAF:** All controlled vehicles must avoid collisions.

One could achieve **SAF** by maintaining a safety distance. For the single-lane environment, one must consider the distance to the vehicle behind and the vehicle in front. For the multi-lane environment, one has to consider lane changes and possibly even more rules. A model to maintain safety distances is Responsibility-Sensitive Safety (RSS) [10].[1]. In particular, the first rule [10] of RSS defines the computation of the safety distance as:

$$d_{min} = [v_r * \rho + \frac{1}{2} * a_{max} * \rho^2 + \frac{(v_r + \rho * a_{max})^2}{2 * \beta_{min}} - \frac{v_f^2}{2 * \beta_{max}}]_+$$

using the notation $[x]_+ := max\{x, 0\}$ and with

- ρ - response time
- v_r - speed of rear vehicle
- v_f - speed of front vehicle
- a_{max} - maximum acceleration of rear vehicle before braking
- β_{max} - maximum braking acceleration of front vehicle
- β_{min} - braking acceleration of rear vehicle (reaction to braking of front vehicle)

This formula was, for example, used in [2] with Isabelle to prove safety or combined with goals in [3,4]. For the case study, one can also consider other formulas or assumptions (additionally or instead of RSS) for computing the safety distance.

3 Simulation in AI Environment

This section provides additional material, in case you wish to use and evaluate your safety controller as a safety shield [5] for an AI system. As such, we provide several reinforcement learning (RL) agents trained in the highway environment [6]. The requirements above were designed in such a way that the formal model integrates with the abstraction provided by this highway environment.

3.1 Overview

Figure 3 depicts using a safety controller for an autonomous driving system. In practice, the perception is done by cameras and sensors; this is abstracted away in our case study. We suppose we obtain position and speed information about vehicles in the vicinity (see Sect. 3.3 below).

[1] More details available here: https://www.mobileye.com/technology/responsibility-sensitive-safety/.

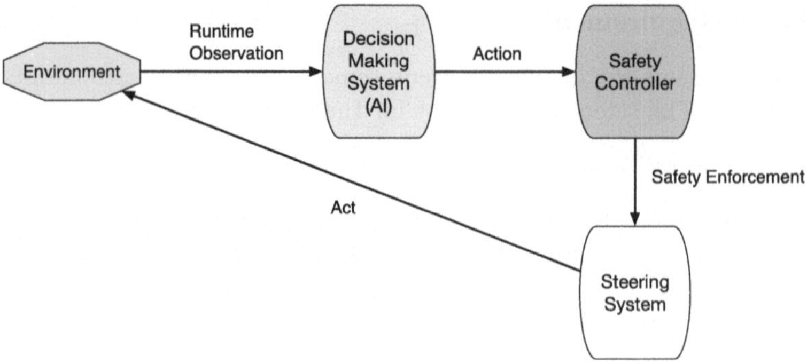

Fig. 3. Components of Autonomous Driving System

Based on the observations, the decision-making system decides which actions to execute next. The safety controller checks whether the actions made by the decision-making system are safe and intervenes/corrects the decisions accordingly. The corrected action is then provided to the steering system for execution.

3.2 Trained Agents

We trained agents for both the single-lane and the multi-lane environment with Deep Q-learning (DQN) [7]. For both environments, we present two agents: an agent trained with penalties for collisions, and another agent which behaves adversarially, i.e., it is rewarded for collisions.

The trained agents are available here: https://github.com/hhu-stups/abz2025_casestudy_autonomous_driving.

Single-Lane Environment. For the single-lane environment, we use the standard configuration for training and modify them for both agents as follows:

- The first agent, called BASE, is trained with a penalty for collisions and a reward v_{cur}/v_{max} for the current speed (the faster the better).
- The second agent, called ADVERSARIAL, is trained with a reward for collisions and again a reward depending on the current speed.

Multi-Lane Environment. For the multi-lane environment, we also use the standard configuration for training and modify them for both agents as follows:

- The first agent, called BASE, is trained with a penalty for collisions, a right-lane reward (i.e., the agent is rewarded if it drives on the right to let other cars pass), and again a reward for the current speed.
- The second agent, called ADVERSARIAL, is trained with a reward for collisions, again a reward for the current speed, and no right-lane reward but a lane change reward.

3.3 Observing and Controlling Vehicles in Highway Environment

In the following, we provide information that are only relevant to implement Fig. 3, i.e., to implement an adapter between the agents' observations and the safety controller. The details relate to how a controlled vehicle observes its environment.

An agent observes the environment in each cycle (1 s by default) and performs an action (**ACT1**–**ACT5** from Sect. 2.1). Each observation contains the presence, the positions, and the speeds of all vehicles. The position and speed of the controlled vehicle are absolute, while the positions and speeds of the other vehicles are relative to the controlled vehicle. Each vehicle's position is defined by its center. A controlled vehicle can observe other vehicles up to 200 m, but reliable perception is only guaranteed up to 100 m.

$$
\begin{array}{l} \\ ControlledVehicle \\ Vehicle_2 \\ Vehicle_3 \\ Vehicle_4 \\ Vehicle_5 \end{array}
\begin{array}{c} \begin{array}{ccccc} Presence & x & y & v_x & v_y \end{array} \\ \begin{pmatrix} 1.0 & 0.89 & 0.50 & 0.31 & 0.0 \\ 1.0 & 0.09 & -0.50 & -0.04 & 0.0 \\ 1.0 & 0.21 & 0.00 & -0.02 & 0.0 \\ 1.0 & 0.33 & 0.00 & -0.04 & 0.0 \\ 1.0 & 0.43 & -0.25 & -0.04 & 0.0 \end{pmatrix} \end{array}
$$

Fig. 4. Example: Observation in Highway Environment

Such an observation for a single agent is shown in Fig. 4. The observations in the provided agents (and thus also Fig. 4) are normalized. More details about the environment are available here[2]:

https://highway-env.farama.org/observations/.

3.4 Metrics

In the validation process, one can consider more metrics to evaluate the quality of an autonomous driving system: the accident rate, the expected time until collision, the distance traveled, the speed, the cumulative reward (of the reinforcement learning agent), the time spent on right-most lane according to the *keep right requirement* in many countries. Some metrics are described in [12]; they are only relevant when the safety controller is adapted to the RL agents.

3.5 Some Related Works

The idea of using a simple system to control a complex system was introduced by Sha [9], and later expanded to reinforcement learning applications [11] in the neural simplex architecture [8]. Figure 3 works similarly to post-shielding [1], where the AI's decisions are corrected. Another approach is pre-shielding [1], which provides safe actions for the AI to choose.

[2] There is also a multi-agent setting to control multiple vehicles where the state is represented by an array of observations: https://highway-env.farama.org/multi_agent/.

4 Summary

We expect contributions which

- formalise the behaviour of the vehicles and the effect of the different control actions (FASTER, SLOWER, ...),
- derive a set of assumptions and rules for which the system is safe,
- formally show the safety for the system under these rules and assumptions.

For this case study, we would like to put particular emphasis on a clear exposition of the models and the safety argument. Ideally, your argument should convince somebody who is not familiar with the particular formal method used for the safety of the system.

Your solution can target one or both of these settings:

- a single line setting without lane changes,
- a multi-lane setting with possible lane changes.

Another motivation for our case study is applying formal methods to AI to improve the safety. The main goal here is to develop a formal model that can supervise an existing AI system. To this end, we provide trained AI agents for our case study, which can be run in a highway simulation environment and combined with your formal model (or code generated from your formal model). We thus encourage you to develop a solution

- that can be used as a safety shield for an AI agent in the highway environment,
- thereby improving safety or even guaranteeing safety,
- while achieving good practical performance (e.g., in terms of total distance travelled).

Acknowledgements. We thank Amel Mammar, Atif Mashkoor, and Nico Pellegrinelli for useful feedback.

References

1. Alshiekh, M., Bloem, R., Ehlers, R., Könighofer, B., Niekum, S., Topcu, U.: Safe reinforcement learning via shielding. In: Proceedings AAAI, pp. 2669–2678. AAAI Press (2018). https://doi.org/10.1609/aaai.v32i1.11797
2. Crisafulli, P., Taha, S., Wolff, B.: Modeling and analysing cyber-physical systems in HOL-CSP. Robot. Auton. Syst. **170**, 104549 (2023). https://doi.org/10.1016/J.ROBOT.2023.104549
3. Hasuo, I., et al.: Goal-aware RSS for complex scenarios via program logic. IEEE Trans. Intell. Veh. **8**(4), 3040–3072 (2023). https://doi.org/10.1109/TIV.2022.3169762
4. Kobayashi, T., Bondu, M., Ishikawa, F.: Formal modelling of safety architecture for responsibility-aware autonomous vehicle via event-b refinement. In: Proceedings FM 2023, pp. 533–549 (2023). https://doi.org/10.1007/978-3-031-27481-7_30

5. Könighofer, B., Lorber, F., Jansen, N., Bloem, R.: Shield synthesis for reinforcement learning. In: Margaria, T., Steffen, B. (eds.) ISoLA 2020. LNCS, vol. 12476, pp. 290–306. Springer, Cham (2020). https://doi.org/10.1007/978-3-030-61362-4_16
6. Leurent, E.: An environment for autonomous driving decision-making (2018). https://github.com/eleurent/highway-env
7. Mnih, V., et al.: Human-level control through deep reinforcement learning. Nature **518**(7540), 529–533 (2015). https://doi.org/10.1038/nature14236
8. Phan, D.T., Grosu, R., Jansen, N., Paoletti, N., Smolka, S.A., Stoller, S.D.: Neural simplex architecture. In: Lee, R., Jha, S., Mavridou, A., Giannakopoulou, D. (eds.) NFM 2020. LNCS, vol. 12229, pp. 97–114. Springer, Cham (2020). https://doi.org/10.1007/978-3-030-55754-6_6
9. Sha, L.: Using simplicity to control complexity. IEEE Softw. **18**(4), 20–28 (2001). https://doi.org/10.1109/MS.2001.936213
10. Shalev-Shwartz, S., Shammah, S., Shashua, A.: On a formal model of safe and scalable self-driving cars. CoRR abs/1708.06374 (2017). http://arxiv.org/abs/1708.06374
11. Sutton, R.S., Barto, A.G.: Reinforcement Learning: An Introduction. MIT Press (2018)
12. Vu, F., Dunkelau, J., Leuschel, M.: Validation of reinforcement learning agents and safety shields with ProB. In: Benz, N., Gopinath, D., Shi, N. (eds) NFM 2024. LNCS, vol. 14627, pp. 279–297. Springer, Cham (2024). https://doi.org/10.1007/978-3-031-60698-4_16

Safety Enforcement for Autonomous Driving on a Simulated Highway Using Asmeta Models@run.time

Andrea Bombarda(✉), Silvia Bonfanti, Angelo Gargantini, Nico Pellegrinelli, and Patrizia Scandurra

University of Bergamo, Bergamo, Italy
{andrea.bombarda,silvia.bonfanti,angelo.gargantini,nico.pellegrinelli,patrizia.scandurra}@unibg.it

Abstract. Mission-critical systems, such as autonomous vehicles, operate in dynamic environments where unexpected events should be managed while guaranteeing safe behavior. Ensuring the safety of these complex systems is a major open challenge and requires robust mechanisms to enforce correct behavior during runtime. This paper illustrates a runtime safety enforcement framework for the *output sanitization* of an autonomous driving agent on a highway. The enforcement mechanism is based on a (formally validated and verified) Asmeta model representing the enforcement rules and used at run-time to eventually steer the driving agent to behave safely and avoid collisions. We demonstrate both efficacy and efficiency of the proposed enforcement approach by conducting an experimental evaluation. We connected our safety enforcer with the highway simulation environment and co-executed it with the pre-trained (unsafe) AI agents as provided by the ABZ 2025 case study. We consider the single-lane case with the safety requirement and one scenario of the multi-lane case about preferring the right-most lane.

Keywords: ASMs · Asmeta · Runtime Safety Enforcement · Safety shield

1 Introduction

Mission-critical self-adaptive systems, like autonomous vehicles (AVs), are capable of adapting their behavior at runtime in complex environments with little to no human intervention. Given the critical roles these systems play, they are expected to safely adapt to changes in their execution environment. Runtime adaptation mechanisms of these systems can leverage formal models, referred to as *formal models@run.time* [10]. The applicability of formal analysis techniques can be extended to runtime environment to support adaptation decision-making and applying safety assurance approaches in adaptive systems [2,24].

Leveraging our previous approach in [7], in this paper, we present a safety enforcement framework for the sanitization of the output control action of an AI-based driving agent in a simulated highway [17]. The proposed enforcement

M. Leuschel and F. Ishikawa (Eds.): ABZ 2025, LNCS 15728, pp. 212–230, 2026.
https://doi.org/10.1007/978-3-031-94533-5_13

mechanism works as a *safety controller* (or *safety shield*): it observes the environmental changes and the action decided by the controlled AV (referred to as the *ego vehicle* or the *controlled vehicle* throughout the text) that might lead to potential safety violation (i.e., a collision), and then proactively elaborates and actuates a *proper answer* to replace the AV control action (*output sanitization*). The enforcement strategies are formally specified and served at runtime by an *Abstract State Machine* (ASM) [8,9] , developed using the `Asmeta` tool set [6].

Precisely, we validate and verify the correctness of the enforcement strategies, as specified in the `Asmeta` *enforcement model*, against the safety requirement (see Sect. 3). We keep this pre-analysis separated as an *offline phase*, where we can execute demanding analysis activities (including model checking for the verification of behavioral properties) without interfering with the system operation. For the runtime execution of this `Asmeta` model within the enforcement framework and its connection with the simulated highway environment and driving agents (*online phase*), we use the simulation engine `AsmetaS@run.time`. The latter was recently adapted for its use at run-time and for providing *simulation-as-a-service* exposed via a REST API [2] of `Asmeta` models. We connect our safety enforcer software with the pre-trained (unsafe) AI agents to work as a safety shield. We consider the single-lane case, where agents can accelerate and brake and the enforcement strategy is to *maintain a safe distance without slowing down too much*, and one scenario of the multi-lane case where the enforcement goal is to promote virtuous driving behavior by *preferring the rightmost lane* as required in many countries. To demonstrate the efficacy and efficiency of our approach, we conducted an experimental campaign using the highway simulation environment as provided by the ABZ 2025 case study [18].
The main contributions of this paper are the following:

- The application of the Runtime Safety Enforcement (RSE) approach [7] to the ABZ 2025 case study *Safety Controller for Autonomous Driving* [18];
- A RSE framework implemented using the Python programming language, and causally connected and co-executing with the simulated highway and driving AI-based agents;
- The evaluation of the RSE framework and of the `Asmeta` enforcement model in terms of soundness and computational overhead.

This paper is organized as follows. Section 2 provides some preliminary concepts. Section 3 illustrates the safety enforcement approach for AVs (including addressed requirements and assumptions, details of the RSE framework and of the `Asmeta` enforcement models). Section 4 reports the results of our evaluation experiments, conducted both offline and online. Section 5 highlights related work, and Sect. 6 concludes the paper.

2 Background

This section briefly introduces a mathematical model for AV safety, the `Asmeta` tool set, and the runtime safety enforcement approach.

2.1 Responsibility-Sensitive Safety for Autonomous Driving

Responsibility-Sensitive Safety (RSS) by Shalev-Shwartz et al. [21] is a mathematical model suggested by the specification document of the ABZ 2025 case study [18]. The RSS formula for calculating the (longitudinal) safety distance is:

$$d_{RSS} = \left[v_r \cdot \rho + \frac{1}{2} \cdot a_{max} \cdot \rho^2 + \frac{(v_r + \rho \cdot a_{max})^2}{2 \cdot \beta_{min}} - \frac{v_f^2}{2 \cdot \beta_{max}} \right] +$$

where ρ is the response time, v_r is the speed of the rear (the ego) vehicle, a_{max} is the maximum acceleration of the rear vehicle before braking, β_{max} is the maximum braking acceleration of the front vehicle, β_{min} is the braking acceleration of the rear vehicle (reaction to braking of front vehicle), and the notation $[x]+$ denotes $\max\{x, 0\}$. Collisions can be avoided by maintaining this safety distance.

2.2 ASMs and the Asmeta Tool Set

In this work, we adopt Abstract State Machines (ASMs) to devise the system. They are an extension of Finite State Machines (FSMs) that replaces unstructured control states with states capable of handling arbitrarily complex data represented with dynamic functions. The basic transition rules of ASMs consist of guarded parallel function updates. Specifically, we leverage the features provided by the `Asmeta` framework [2,6], which supports a comprehensive specification and analysis process encompassing the system life-cycle with three main stages: design, development, and operation. Each stage is supported by a variety of tools.

This work combines the design and operation phases, by exemplifying the applicability of `Asmeta` models produced at design time to the runtime environment [2]. In particular, we use the simulator `AsmetaS@run.time` to deploy the `Asmeta` enforcement model as runtime model of the enforcement framework, executing in tandem with the simulated highway environment.

2.3 Runtime Safety Enforcement (RSE)

A promising approach to managing complexity in runtime environments is to develop adaptation mechanisms that leverage software models, known as *models@run.time* [4]. A model@run.time is a causally connected self-representation of the associated system (its structure and behavior) or goals of the system from a problem-space perspective. In this work, we use an ASM as *enforcement model* to specify the strategies/policies to apply at runtime to assure safety. Essentially, we implemented an enforcement mechanism from the framework presented in [7] for the *output sanitization* of the ego vehicle's control action before it is actuated. The ego vehicle is simulated by a trained AI-based driving agent as provided by the ABZ 2025 case study [18] for the driving simulation environment [17].

Borrowing the terminology used in [7], we apply a *black-box enforcement* mechanism E, which treats the target system S as a black-box (indeed, the AI agent is a black box) by observing only the input (I) and output (O). Formally: we denote by $\delta(I, O)$ an operational change made by S producing output O in response to the input I. We denote by Σ the system state space and by $\Sigma \setminus A(\Sigma)$ the subset of *unsafe states* where safety assertions A may be violated[1]. If $(\sigma, \delta(I, O), \sigma')$ is a state change of S from σ to σ' with $\sigma' \in \Sigma \setminus A(\Sigma)$, then E try to sanitize O in $O' = E(I, O)$ such that $(\sigma, \delta(I, O'), \sigma'')$ is an operational change with $\sigma'' \in A(\Sigma)$.

Note that in practice E may take more than one corrective step to effectively bring back the system S to the safe region $A(\Sigma)$. Moreover, at runtime there is no guarantee that a safe state is always reached in all situations; the enforceable properties are impacted by uncertain environmental factors or uncontrolled variables that may make not timely and ineffective the enforcer adjustment. These factors include, for example, the monitoring frequency that may not be high enough for having fresh observations of the surrounding environment (see experiments in Sect. 4), and the abruptness with which the target entities in the system environment change their behavior or appear/disappear.

To apply the RSE approach [7] to a target system, the following key steps are to be carried out throughout the phases of the system life cycle:

1. **Enforcement Strategies Definition**. This involves defining safety assertions, I/O interfaces, and enforcement goals and strategies (@design.time).
2. **Formal Specification and Analysis**. The enforcement model is formally specified, validated and verified to ensure the safety assertions are correctly enforced over the global state of the runtime model (@design.time).
3. **RSE Framework Development and Binding**. An enforcer framework is developed, instantiated and connected to the target system, with the runtime model for safety enforcement (@development.time).
4. **Deployment and Running**. The enforced system is deployed, set up, and put into operation in its runtime environment (@run.time).
5. **Runtime Model Evolution**. Adaptation of safety assertions and enforcement rules to accommodate new requirements (@design.time or @run.time).

The next sections illustrate these steps, except step 5, for the ABZ case study.

3 Safety Modeling and Enforcement Approach

In this section, we describe the requirements we have chosen to model in our `Asmeta` specification, our assumptions, and the RSE framework.

3.1 Considered Requirements and Assumptions

We consider the following goals (**step 1** of the RSE process) in order to guarantee the safety requirement `SAF` of the specification document (i.e., no collisions) [18], good performance, and a virtuous driving behavior:

[1] E.g., driving without maintaining the RSS safety distance may lead to a collision.

- **G1**: *Maintain a safety distance*;
- **G2**: *Achieve a high total distance traveled safely*;
- **G3**: *Keep to the right-most free lane.*

The enforcement strategies adopted by the enforcer to achieve such goals are reported in Table 1. These strategies are examples of compensation actions that the enforcer can put in place to achieve the prefixed goals. In order to achieve all goals, more than one strategy must be used and combined. Note that for the same goal G1 two alternative strategies can be adopted. Strategy *Go super safe* is the most prudent; it aims to maintain an upper bound of the distance as calculated by the RSS formula in the *worst case scenario*. Such an upper bound is calculated using both the maximum speed and the maximum acceleration, and assuming that the front vehicle speed is zero. Strategy *Go safe*, instead, maintains the safety distance as calculated by the RSS formula (see Sect. 2.1).

Table 1. Enforcement goals, strategies and rules

Goal	Strategy name	Enforcement rule
G1	Go super safe	Brake if the worst case safety distance is violated
G1	Go safe	Brake if the safety distance is violated
G2	Go fast safely	Increase speed if *far away*, i.e. the distance to the front vehicle is $x\%$ (e.g., 70%) greater than the required safety distance
G3	Take the rightmost free lane	Change lane to right if the lane directly right is free

To concretely implement these enforcement strategies in the simulated highway, we had to make some assumptions. Specifically, we considered all assumptions contained in the specification document: `VEH1-ENV`–`VEH7-ENV` for the concrete values of the vehicle parameters (length, width, maximum speed, etc.), `CON1` (all controlled vehicles observe the environment every t seconds), `ENV1` (there is at least one vehicle on the highway), `ENV2` (all vehicles drive in the same direction), and `ENV3` (the number of lanes does not change over time). We also adhere to the *cycle*-based execution semantics of the specification document: every time interval t (also called *response time*) a controlled vehicle observes its environment, and decides to perform an action until reaching the next cycle ; the other vehicles may actuate actions at different times instead.[2]

In addition, we considered also the following assumptions, due in part to constraints of the provided simulation environment [17] and its configuration for agent training [18], as obtained by code inspection and direct and extensive experimentation:

1. Within the simulation environment, the response time t of the controlled vehicle depends on the *policy frequency* (expressed in Hz). Whereas, the time interval between decisions made by other vehicles is determined by the *simulation frequency* (expressed in Hz).

[2] E.g., a vehicle braking in the first half of the cycle can accelerate in the second half.

2. The runtime observation interface allows us to observe presence, positions, and speeds of the controlled vehicle and of its four closest front vehicles up to a range of 200 m.
3. As required by ML models for a better accuracy, the observed features are normalized (using the min-max method) in range [–1, 1] and are relative to the controlled vehicle, while those of the controlled vehicle are absolute. Note that the RSS formula requires absolute values, therefore, the observations are de-normalized before they are used by the enforcement model.
4. The maximum observable distance from the front vehicle may be smaller than the safety distance, even with an infinitesimally small response time.
5. When calculating the safety distance RSS, three cases could be considered: (i) the speed of the controlled vehicle is less than the maximum speed and, after accelerating with the maximum acceleration during the response time, it is still less than the maximum speed; (ii) the speed of the controlled vehicle is less than the maximum speed, but when accelerating with the maximum acceleration it reaches the maximum speed before the response time has elapsed; (iii) the speed of the controlled vehicle is equal to the maximum speed. In the first case, the RSS formula is used as it is. In the second case, the RSS formula could be adapted to be more specific, but we use it as it is; therefore, a higher RSS value is used, making the model more stringent. In the last case, the RSS formula is used by setting the maximum acceleration to 0 m/s^2.
6. In the multi-lane case, when considering which vehicles are occupying a lane, the following assumptions are made:
   - All vehicles traveling straight ahead in the lane occupy the lane;
   - All vehicles leaving the lane but not yet traveling straight on the other lane occupy the lane;
   - All vehicles leaving another lane and just entering the lane but not yet traveling straight on occupy the lane.

   Consequently, it is possible for a vehicle to occupy multiple lanes.
7. In the multi-lane case, we consider a vehicle proceeding straight on a lane when its y position is close enough to the y_{lane} position associated to a lane with a given tolerance Θ (default 0.1 m):

$$y_{lane} - \Theta < y < y_{lane} + \Theta$$

8. When calculating the distance between two vehicles, the vehicle dimensions, particularly the length, are considered. The x and y coordinates when observing a vehicle refer to its center. Therefore, when considering the distance between two vehicles, it is necessary to consider the front half of the length for the rear vehicle and the rear half of the length for the front vehicle, i.e. the full length of a vehicle must be removed from the observed distance between two vehicles.
9. If there is no observable front vehicle (either because it is further than the maximum observable distance or there are four closest vehicles in the other lanes), the enforcer is not activated since not necessary. The enforcer is not

activated also when the controlled vehicle is changing lane until the maneuver is complete; this steady state ensures that any adaptation made by the enforcement is based on a stable snapshot of the controlled vehicle's status[3].
10. The RSS safety distance refers only to longitudinal (X-axis) positions and speeds. The lateral position (on the Y-axis) is used to determine which lane each vehicle is in, while the lateral speed is not used. The Y-axis position and speed could be used in some formulas such as the one defined in Lemma 4 in [21] to calculate the lateral (Y-axis) safety distance, but some variables (e.g., the maximum lateral acceleration) required by this formula are not provided.
11. We say that the lane directly right is free if no front vehicles would be observed by the ego vehicle once changed lane to right maintaining the same X-position.

3.2 Enforcement Model Details

We here illustrate excerpts of the Asmeta models specifying the enforcement strategies reported in Table 1 (specification task of **step 2** of the RSE process). We incrementally defined various models to achieve all the three goals (goals G1 and G2 for both the single-lane and multi-lane cases, and G3 for the multi-lane case only). A replication package containing these models, all software artifacts, and data sets used in the evaluation of our approach is available online at [5].

For this case study, the enforcement rules are extremely intuitive and take the form of an ASM conditional rule ***if*** *cond* ***then*** *updates*. They are actually aimed at correcting the output (0-ary) function `outAction` representing the final decision, i.e. the control action (chosen from the set `{FASTER, SLOWER, IDLE, LANE_LEFT, LANE_RIGHT}`) that replaces the one chosen by the AI agent and is actuated on the ego vehicle until the next observation and decision.

Case Single-lane. To achieve G1, first we introduced the Asmeta model for the *Go super safe* strategy. Essentially, to promote a super safe policy we introduced the threshold `dRSS_upper_bound` denoting an upper bound on the safest distance observable in the worst-case scenario and calculated setting v_r to v_{max} and v_f to 0:

$$d_{RSS\_upper\_bound} = \left[v_{max} \cdot \rho + \frac{1}{2} \cdot a_{max} \cdot \rho^2 + \frac{(v_{max} + \rho \cdot a_{max})^2}{2 \cdot \beta_{min}} \right] +$$

where v_{max} is the maximum speed of the ego vehicle. The corresponding enforcement rule is reported in Code 1. The rule is triggered when the actual longitudinal distance to the front vehicle (the 0-ary function `actual_distance`)[4] is less than `dRSS_upper_bound`. In this case, the enforcement model prescribes slowing down. An alternative way to achieve G1 is by maintaining the RSS distance (*Go safe* strategy) as specified by the enforcement rule reported in Code 2, where

[3] In a self-adaptive system, it is usually assumed that the target system is in a steady state before an adaptation is triggered in response to environmental changes [23].

[4] In all models, the `actual_distance` is a derived function defined using the X-axis positions of the vehicles: `actual_distance = x_front - x_self - l_vehicle`.

the (0-ary) function dRSS is calculated from the observations of the current cycle using the formula described in Sect. 2.1.

```
macro rule r_unsafeDistanceSuperSafe =
  if actual_distance <= dRSS_upper_bound
     then outAction := SLOWER endif
```

Code 1: Enforcement rule for goal G1, strategy *Go super safe.*

```
macro rule r_unsafeDistanceSafe =
  if actual_distance <= dRSS
     then outAction := SLOWER endif
```

Code 2: Enforcement rule for goal G1, strategy *Go safe.*

```
macro rule r_goFast =
  if actual_distance > dRSS * gofast_perc
     then outAction := FASTER endif
```

Code 3: Enforcement rule for goal G2, strategy *Go fast.*

```
macro rule r_keepRight = if rightLaneFree
  then outAction := LANE_RIGHT
  endif
```

Code 4: Enforcement rule for goal G3, strategy *Take the rightmost free lane.*

To achieve goal G2, we introduce the enforcement rule shown in Code 3 that prescribes to speed up safely, i.e. when the front vehicle is more than a certain percentage of the dRSS distance (e.g., 70%).

Case Multi-lane. Enforcement rules introduced for goals G1 and G2 in the single-lane case can be used also in the multi-lane setting, where each vehicle can also change lanes. Additionally, we introduce the enforcement rule shown in Code 4 to achieve goal G3, namely to promote a virtuous driving style by preferring the lane directly right when free (as by our assumption 11). We postpone dealing with more complex multi-lane scenarios to future work (**step 5** of the RSE process). framework. Note that the enforcement model can evolve and be re-engineered separately, and re-deployed easily without re-building the component framework. This is the main flexibility of using runtime models that are causally linked to the target system, rather than integrated into the system via embed code or model synthesis.

To combine enforcement rules we use the ASM par-rule constructor in the main rule (entry point of execution) of an Asmeta model as shown in Code 5, where we select one rule per each goal. Moreover, since the main rule consists of guarded parallel updates of the same out function outAction, in order to avoid inconsistent function updates we applied the semantic pattern *mutual exclusive guards*[5] by making the guards of the enforcement rules mutually exclusive. As an example, Code 6 shows how the r_unsafeDistance rule has been restructured after applying such a pattern. Note that in the proposed rule scheduling, we prioritize the change to the right lane rather then other actions, whenever it is possible to do it safely (i.e., the lane directly right is free).

[5] The workflow of the machine follows only one of the possible parallel execution paths.

```
main rule r_Main = par
  r_unsafeDistance[]
  r_goFast[]
  r_keepRight[]
 endpar
```

Code 5: Main rule of the `Asmeta` enforcement model

```
macro rule r_unsafeDistance =
  if actual_distance <= dRSS
     if not rightLaneFree then
           outAction := SLOWER
  endif endif
```

Code 6: Enforcement rule for goal G1, strategy *Go safe* (refined).

3.3 RSE Framework for Driving Agents on a Simulated Highway

According to **step 3** of the RSE process, we designed the enforcer mechanism to act as a proxy system which wraps the controlled AI driving agent. We developed it using the Python programming language and embedded it into a closed loop setting with the AI agent in the simulated highway environment of AVs.

Figure 1 shows an overview of the architecture of the enforcer component (the subsystem `Enforcer Framework`) once instantiated and bound to the simulated highway environment, using a UML-like notation. The I/O interfaces[6] used by the ego AI agent (the subsystem `Autonomous Driving System`) and by the `Enforcer` are as follows: the input interface `I` corresponds to the AVs observations as provided by the simulated environment, while the output interface `O` is the action decided by the ego autonomous agent. The `Observation Processor` is responsible for de-normalizing run-time observations and making them absolute (see assumption 3 of Sect. 3.1). The interface `I'` corresponds to the de-normalized and absolute observations and the interface `O'` corresponds to the sanitized action to actuate. The `Configuration Manager` initializes the environment and framework using the configuration file `Config.json`, setting parameters like the number of highway lanes and the vehicle's policy frequency. The `Model Uploader` and the `Enforcer` interact with the `ASM@run.time Simulator` via its `AsmetaS REST API`. The `Model Uploader` is responsible for uploading the proper `Asmeta` enforcement model into the online simulator, while the `Enforcer` is in charge of starting, executing (one single step per cycle), and stopping the `Asmeta` model. Finally, the `Experiment Data Exporter` and the `Logging Manager` collect quality metrics and logging data for debugging/manual inspection, respectively.

4 Evaluation

In this section, we evaluate our proposed approach. Our benchmark contains 4 enforcement models, listed in Table 2 along with the strategies they implement and the goals they address. The first three models (`SafetyEnforcerSuperSafe`, `SafetyEnforcerSlower`, and `SafetyEnforcerFaster`) were applied on a single-lane highway. The fourth model, `SafetyEnforcerKeepRight`, was applied on a 3-lane highway where all vehicles travel in the same direction. We start by presenting the offline validation and verification activities and, then, we discuss the experiments we run to assess the efficiency and efficacy of our framework.

[6] The circle (or ball) indicates input events or data that the component can handle; the semi-circle (or socket) indicates output events or data from the component.

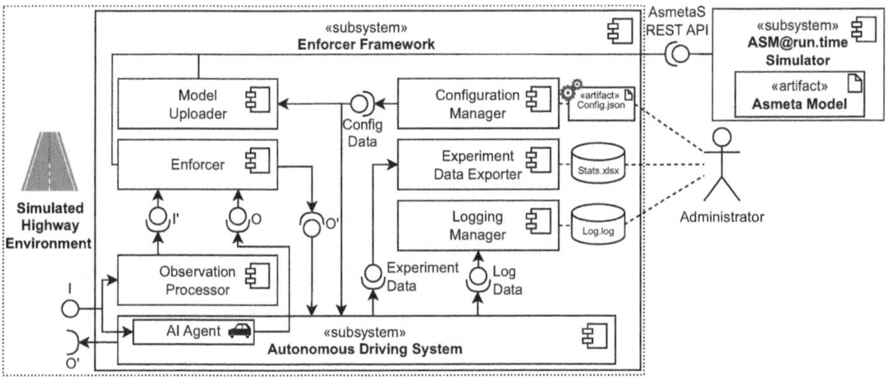

Fig. 1. RSE framework for simulated AVs driving on a highway.

Table 2. Mapping of `Asmeta` models to driving strategies and safety goals.

`Asmeta`Enforcement Model	Strategies	Goals
SafetyEnforcerSuperSafe.asm	Go super safe	G1
SafetyEnforcerSlower.asm	Go safe	G1
SafetyEnforcerFaster.asm	Go safe, Go fast safely	G1, G2
SafetyEnforcerKeepRight.asm	Go safe, Go fast safely,	G1, G2
	Take the rightmost free lane	G3

4.1 Offline Validation and Verification

We here report on the validation and verification results (analysis task of **step 2** of the RSE process) for the functional correctness of the enforcement models. This stage is carried out offline (i.e., at design-time) before releasing the `Asmeta` enforcement model in production with the enforcer framework and letting them co-operate at runtime. To ensure that an enforcement model behaves as expected, i.e. it achieves the enforcement goal(s) for which it was designed, we carried out both model validation by scenarios using the validator `AsmetaV`, and property verification using the `Asmeta` model checker `AsmetaSMV`.

We run different scenarios on each model to cover all rules. In Fig. 2 we report an example of scenario execution on the `SafetyEnforcerFaster.asm` specification. After a few steps, where the safety distance was violated and the enforcer forces the ego vehicle to go slower (`outAction=SLOWER`), once the front vehicle is far enough the strategy G2 is implemented (`outAction=FASTER`). Note that `AsmetaV` does not support natively approximate comparison among real numbers, so we had either to specify the values with all decimal digits (like in Fig. 2) or use the `abs` function explicitly.

Type	Functions	State 1	State 2	State 3	State 4	State 5
C	actual_distance_contr	26.539108276367188	24.996673583984375	24.808074951171875	27.736114501953125	34.50360107421875
C	currentAgentAction	FASTER	FASTER	FASTER	FASTER	FASTER
C	dRSS_contr	123.37380284196115	99.0896848983306	64.4047825463155	33.154612475462876	8.34258452798628
C	inputAction	FASTER	FASTER	FASTER	FASTER	FASTER
C	outAction	SLOWER	SLOWER	SLOWER	SLOWER	FASTER
C	result	1	1	1	1	1
C	step_	1	2	3	4	5
C	v_front	18.887428283691406	16.612892150878906	15.222702026367188	14.304786682128906	13.669296264648438
C	v_self	20.854446411132812	16.000450134277344	11.025405883789062	6.029670715332031	9.321517944335938
C	x_front	229.99667358398438	229.80807495117188	232.73611450195312	239.50360107421875	245.46859741210938
C	x_self	200.0	200.0	200.0	200.0	200.0

Fig. 2. Scenario execution for the `SafetyEnforcerFaster.asm` specification.

Regarding the verification process, we have used `AsmetaSMV` by invoking `NuXmv` [12], the symbolic model checker to analyze synchronous finite-state and infinite-state systems. This choice became necessary because the specification in `Asmeta` makes use of real, hence infinite, domains. At first, we started by proving Linear Temporal Logic (LTL) properties, with these general forms:

LTLSPEC g(ϕ implies φ)
LTLSPEC g(ϕ implies x(φ))

However, the model checker was not able to prove their correctness. Due to their form, we expressed properties as invariants, propositional formulas that must always hold in the model. As an example, we report the invariants of the model `SafetyEnforcerFaster` we have verified using IC3 engines [13].

```
/*If the ego vehicle is close to the front vehicle, break (go SLOWER)*/
INVARSPEC NAME invar_01 := (actual_distance<=dRSS) -> next(outAction=SLOWER)

/*If the front vehicle is far enough from the ego vehicle, increase the speed (go FAST)*/
INVARSPEC NAME invar_02 := (actual_distance>(dRSS*gofast_perc)) -> next(outAction
    =FASTER)

/*If there is no risk of collision, keep the action decided by the agent*/
INVARSPEC NAME invar_03 := (actual_distance>dRSS and actual_distance<=(dRSS*
    gofast_perc)) -> next(outAction=currentAgentAction)
```

4.2 Online Validation

Once in operation in the simulated highway (**step 4** of the RSE process), we check whether our enforcement framework, based on the enforcement rules as served at run-time by the `Asmeta` model, is able to ensure under change the required safety and the other considered driving requirements. Specifically, we address the following Research Questions (RQs):

RQ1 *How effective is the enforcer in ensuring safety while adjusting speed and driving style?*

RQ2 *What is the computation overhead of running the enforcer in combination with the simulated system?*

RQ1 investigates how well the corrective measures of our enforcement framework are able to deliver the intended behavior by enhancing three key outcomes: It ensures safety by avoiding collisions, travels a significant distance, and spends a significant time on the rightmost lane. RQ2 is regarding the cost, in terms of computation time (the wall-clock time), of the enforcement software. This section reports on the design of the evaluation and the major results.

4.3 Design of the Evaluation

To answer RQ1 and RQ2, we compared the enforced driving agent of the controlled vehicle with the non-enforced one (baseline system). Both RQs are addressed with the same setup. The experiments were performed on a PC with Intel(R) Core(TM) i7-8550U CPU @ 1.80 GHz and 16 GB RAM, running Windows 11. The server exposing the Spring REST API of `AsmetaS` was executed natively on Windows 11, while the enforcement framework was executed on the same machine via WSL (Windows Subsystem for Linux) running Ubuntu 24.04, within a Python virtual environment using Python 3.11 as the runtime platform.

For both lane configurations (single-lane and multi-lane), the case study [18] provides two agents trained using Deep Q-learning (DQN): A *base agent*, which receives penalties for collisions and rewards for maintaining high speed and staying in the right lane, and an *adversarial agent*, which is rewarded for collisions, high speed, and frequent lane changes. This setup results in 8 different configurations for the single-lane scenario: no enforcement and 3 enforcement models applied to both the base and adversarial agents; and 4 configurations for the multi-lane scenario: no enforcement and the multi-lane enforcement model applied to both agent types.

The experiments were conducted extending the test run duration from 40 simulation seconds, as defined in the case study, to 100 simulation seconds. This duration was chosen based on manual observations of the agent's behavior executing without the enforcer. In the single-lane configuration, the base (non-adversarial) agent's performance deteriorates due to poor decision-making. A longer duration allows us to quantitatively assess this decline in performance. A test run concludes in one of two cases: either the ego vehicle crashes or the simulation duration ends. The experiments were initially conducted with a *policy frequency* of 1 Hz, which means that the agent made one decision per simulation second, resulting in a response time of 1 s. The experiments were then repeated with a doubled policy frequency (2 Hz), reducing the response time to 0.5 s. The simulation frequency was set to the default value of 15 Hz. Therefore, a total of 24 configurations were tested, with 50 test runs each, and metrics were recorded during every run.

Our efforts to introduce enforcement techniques aims to enhance the safety of autonomous vehicles. To evaluate this in RQ1, we meticulously record the *number of crashes* that occurred in various scenarios and with different enforcement models. More specifically, for each simulation run, we recorded whether it terminated because of a crash or because the simulation duration expired. Considering that one of our objective, beyond the safety, is to let the vehicle travel the longest distance, we also recorded the *distance* traveled by the ego vehicle during the test run, expressed in kilometers and computed by multiplying speed by the simulation time. Furthermore, in our experiments we favor scenarios in which the vehicle travels in the rightmost lane. Thus, we record (only when multiple lanes are available) the *distance traveled on the rightmost lane* by the ego vehicle during the test run, expressed in kilometers.

Additionally, in RQ2, we are interested in evaluating the overhead introduced by the enforcement framework. To measure the impact of *enforcer interventions* on output sanitization, we calculated the percentage of times the interventions changed the agent's action compared to the total number of actions performed by the ego vehicle (i.e., the product of the effective durations by the policy frequency). Moreover, we collected, for each test run, the total *execution time* and the *enforcement overhead* introduced by the enforcer, consisting of the time required to start and stop the execution of the `Asmeta` model and the time required to perform all output sanitizations. Both times are measured in wall-clock seconds. The overhead measurements include the time associated with the HTTP request and the execution time of the `Asmeta` model, which serves as the run-time model for enforcement. To collect the wall-clock time we used `time.perf_counter()` to capture high-precision timestamps.

4.4 Results

Table 3 reports the results of our statistical tests. In the following, we discuss them for the two proposed research questions separately.

Table 3. Effectiveness and efficiency of the safety enforcement models.

Policy Freq. [Hz]	Lane Config.	Agent	Enforc. Model	Number of Crashes	Distance [km]	Distance on Right Lane [km]	Enforc. Interventions [%]	Execution Time [s]	Enforc. Overhead [s]
1	Single-lane	Base	—	0	0.97 ± 0.17	—	—	11.34 ± 1.52	—
			SuperSafe	0	0.08 ± 0.00	—	14.70 ± 0.58	12.21 ± 1.30	0.70 ± 0.50
			Slower	0	0.89 ± 0.09	—	21.14 ± 0.93	13.94 ± 0.95	2.23 ± 0.28
			Faster	0	1.44 ± 0.02	—	40.28 ± 1.53	14.10 ± 1.59	2.42 ± 0.37
		Adversarial	—	50	0.08 ± 0.01	—	—	0.29 ± 0.06	—
			SuperSafe	0	1.34 ± 0.04	—	63.04 ± 1.48	13.47 ± 0.60	1.93 ± 0.18
			Slower	0	1.47 ± 0.02	—	51.00 ± 0.00	14.53 ± 0.32	2.92 ± 0.06
			Faster	0	1.47 ± 0.02	—	51.00 ± 0.00	13.89 ± 0.39	2.33 ± 0.06
	Multi-lane	Base	—	4	1.97 ± 0.46	1.79 ± 0.58	—	13.61 ± 3.14	—
			KeepRight	0	2.01 ± 0.07	1.34 ± 0.87	48.62 ± 5.15	17.53 ± 0.75	2.21 ± 0.26
		Adversarial	—	50	0.35 ± 0.18	0.09 ± 0.08	—	1.46 ± 0.73	—
			KeepRight	1	1.97 ± 0.26	0.83 ± 0.97	50.15 ± 2.55	17.46 ± 2.37	2.23 ± 0.31
2	Single-lane	Base	—	0	0.99 ± 0.15	—	—	11.99 ± 0.46	—
			SuperSafe	0	0.06 ± 0.00	—	14.56 ± 0.41	13.98 ± 0.40	1.02 ± 0.05
			Slower	0	0.98 ± 0.11	—	15.53 ± 2.48	18.71 ± 0.77	4.88 ± 0.44
			Faster	0	1.45 ± 0.02	—	32.51 ± 1.45	18.55 ± 0.55	4.87 ± 0.13
		Adversarial	—	50	0.08 ± 0.01	—	—	0.28 ± 0.06	—
			SuperSafe	0	1.32 ± 0.03	—	59.02 ± 0.73	17.47 ± 0.32	3.65 ± 0.08
			Slower	0	1.48 ± 0.02	—	50.50 ± 0.00	19.78 ± 0.17	6.07 ± 0.06
			Faster	0	1.47 ± 0.02	—	50.50 ± 0.00	19.04 ± 0.48	4.85 ± 0.13
	Multi-lane	Base	—	6	1.96 ± 0.41	1.58 ± 0.72	—	15.83 ± 3.25	—
			KeepRight	0	2.03 ± 0.05	1.49 ± 0.82	46.53 ± 8.78	22.85 ± 1.13	4.53 ± 0.74
		Adversarial	—	50	0.44 ± 0.20	0.09 ± 0.11	—	2.01 ± 0.93	—
			KeepRight	0	2.04 ± 0.06	0.89 ± 0.96	48.21 ± 6.08	22.22 ± 0.37	4.67 ± 0.15

RQ1 - Effectiveness. To assess the effectiveness of our enforcement approach, we have measured, for each test run, the number of crashes, the traveled distance and, in case multiple lanes were available, the distance traveled on the rightmost lane (see Table 3). The box plot depicted in Fig. 3 visually shows the results.

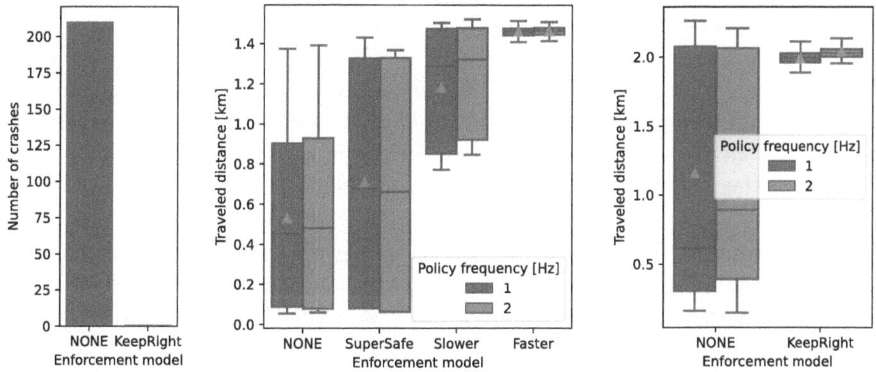

(a) # Crashes (b) Distance with Single-lane (c) Distance with Multi-lane

Fig. 3. Effectiveness analysis.

Regarding the number of crashes (see Fig. 3a), our results confirm the positive impact of enforcement techniques: regardless of the enforcement model, only one crash were registered when the enforcer was activated, while 210 happened if no enforcer was used. The only crash reported when using the enforcement framework happened in the multi-lane scenario with adversarial agents, when using the lowest policy frequency (i.e., 1 Hz). A manual inspection revealed that the limited observation interface that allows to observe only the four closest front vehicles, as described in assumption 2 of Sect. 3.1, made it possible to observe the nearest vehicle on the same lane only when overtaking a vehicle in a different lane. This limitation, combined with a high response time, ultimately resulted in a crash. Increasing the policy frequency, i.e., reducing the response time, allowed us to solve this limitation and to avoid any crash. To further validate this finding, we ran 50 additional experiments with the *KeepRight* model for the multi-lane scenario with the adversarial agent and a policy frequency of 2 Hz, which resulted in no occurrence of crashes. However, we acknowledge that rare failure cases may still be possible. Interestingly, reducing the response time never reduced the number of crashes when no enforcement was used. Overall, we can state that adopting our `Asmeta`-based enforcement framework is effective in reducing the number of crashes of the considered agent.

When it comes to the traveled distance (see Figs. 3b and 3c) we can see that its value increases as the goal moves from G1 to G2/G3, i.e., from *Super safe* to the *Go fast safely*/*Take the rightmost free lane* strategy. As for the number of crashes, using our proposed solution allows for improving the measured results. Moving towards G2/G3 increases the speed of the vehicle, but this does not influence its safety. Interestingly, when considering the distance traveled on the rightmost free lane, using the safety enforcement strategy leads to different results depending on the agent type. On the one hand, when the agent is *non-adversarial*, using a safety enforcement model leads to a decrease in the distance traveled on the rightmost lane, while still traveling a higher total distance. This is because the agent was trained with a reward for staying in the right lane, whereas the safety enforcer prioritizes the driving safety, changing to the right lane only when it is completely free. Consequently, the vehicle may spend less time in the rightmost lane when doing so helps to avoid crashes. On the other hand, if the agent is *adversarial* (trained without a reward for staying in the right lane), the vehicle spends more time on the rightmost lane when under enforcement.

RQ1 Summary. **The `Asmeta`-based RSE framework effectively reduces the number of collisions, while favoring the right lane (when safe) and often achieving a higher distance traveled within the simulation time than driving without safety enforcement.**

RQ2 - Efficiency. To assess the efficiency of the proposed enforcement framework and models, we have recorded (see Table 3), for each test run, the percentage of enforcer interventions (i.e., the number of times in which the enforcer changed the decision previously made by the agent divided by the total number of decisions), the total execution time, and the overhead due to the use of the enforcer. The overhead does not include the time to de-normalize and convert the observations to absolute values, as this computation is also necessary to collect metrics when the enforcer is not running. For the sake of completeness, we report that this computation is approximately 70–80% less costly than the enforcement overhead.

For what concerns the number of interventions we can observe that, both in single-lane and multi-lane scenarios, the number of interventions is greater with the adversarial agent. This is because the adversarial agent makes more dangerous decisions, which must be sanitized to return the AV to a safe state. Furthermore, in the single-lane scenario, we can observe two different trends, depending on the agent type. On the one hand, when the agent behaves as non-adversarial, we can see that the number of interventions increases as the goal moves from G1 to G2, i.e., from *Super safe* to the *Go fast safely* strategy. This is due to the fact that, if no front vehicle is observed, the enforcer is not activated, as described in assumption 9 in Sect. 3.1, and the agent slows down until the vehicle stops. In such a case, both the *Super safe* and *Go safe* strategies do not intervene, but the *Super safe* strategy brings the simulation to such a case earlier, resulting in fewer interventions. Meanwhile, the *Go fast safely* strategy actively intervenes even when the front vehicle is far, resulting in an increased number of interventions. On the other hand, with an adversarial agent, the number of enforcement interventions decreases when switching from the *Super safe* to the *Go safe* strategy and remains stable when adding the *Go fast safely* strategy. This is due to the fact that such an agent always tries to increase the speed.

Therefore, at the beginning of the simulation, the *Super safe* strategy requires more interventions to ensure a safe state compared to the *Go safe* strategy and, after that, the two strategies will behave very similarly. In addition, the *Go fast safely* strategy is never activated, therefore it does not increase the number of interventions. In all cases, however, using one of the enforcement models allows for higher execution time w.r.t. the baseline scenario in which no enforcer is used. This result is compliant to what we observed in RQ1: with the enforcer active, the number of crashes is lower, and the AV can proceed more often till the end of the simulation time. Furthermore, the overhead introduced by the enforcer is negligible in all analyzed scenarios and does not exceed an average of 6.07 s in any configuration.

RQ2 Summary. The `Asmeta`-based RSE framework does not introduce significant time overhead compared to driving without safety enforcement.

5 Related Work

The complexity of AI-based systems can hinder safety assurance for testers and developers. Some literature suggests using simple techniques to control these systems. For instance, [20] proposes leveraging a simple and verified controller taking control over an unverified system to enforce safety properties. Similarly, in this paper, we use a simple `Asmeta` model to force unsafe AI-based agents to behave in a safe and predictable manner. Our approach, presented in [7], is inspired by the RSS properties suggested in [21] and acts as a safety shield.

Runtime assurance for neural controllers is crucial in software engineering. In [19], the authors introduce *Neural Simplex Architecture* for potentially unsafe neural controllers, improving safety through online retraining without significantly impacting performance. Two different approaches are analyzed in [1], in which the safety shield is placed either before (pre-shielding) or after the system under control (post-shielding), and our approach is comparable with this last post-shielding technique. In the future, we may explore if corrective actions from an `Asmeta` model can aid in retraining AI-based controllers.

The approach in [22] uses a ProB specification alongside a reinforcement learning (RL) agent as a safety shield. Unlike this solution implemented in ProB, which requires the RL agent to receive a set of enabled operations and to chose among them, our approach uses an `Asmeta` model for correcting the output of the agent. The formulas we adopted are derived from those presented in the case study description and in [14], where the authors used them to prove safety properties through model-based assurance cases in Isabelle, or in Event-B [16].

In [7], we proposed a gray-box approach to safety enforcement. In addition to the I/O, this mechanism can observe specific system's operational changes and compute more effective enforcement actions to maintain safety through probing and effecting interfaces provided by the target system. This mechanism uses `Asmeta` enforcement models and the MAPE-K feedback loop [15] to architect the enforcer as an autonomic manager for self-adaptation. We here adopted a black-box enforcement mechanism instead, as no probe/effector interfaces (and/or explanation facilities about the agent behavior [3,11]) are available to monitor and adapt the AV; we treated it as a black box by observing only its I/O.

6 Conclusion

We presented a RSE framework for the output sanitization of the AI-based ego AV of the highway simulation environment [17] for the ABZ 2025 case study [18]. The main enforcement goals consist in maintaining safety while achieving good performance in terms of total distance traveled and time spent on the right-most free lane. The enforcer wraps the ego vehicle agent and, using decisions made by an `Asmeta` runtime model, adjusts the agent's control action to meet enforcement goals and, possibly, overrides agent's decisions when they are considered to be unsafe. Though the case study is based on a simulated environment and we considered a limited number of scenarios, the two forms of analysis we conducted, @design.time and @run.time, suggest a new way of analyzing safety-critical software. This new approach combines the rigor of formal safety-critical analysis environments during system design or development with the benefits of run-time analysis when the system is in operation and more realistic evidence is available.

Acknowledgments. This work has been partially funded by PNRR - ANTHEM (AdvaNced Technologies for Human-centrEd Medicine) - Grant PNC0000003 - CUP: B53C22006700001 - Spoke 1 - Pilot 1.4. and by project SERICS (PE00000014) under the NRRP MUR program funded by the EU - NGEU and by the European Union - Next Generation EU. We also acknowledge financial support of the project PRIN 2022 SAFEST (Trust assurance of Digital Twins for medical cyber-physical systems), funded by the European Union - Next Generation EU, Mission 4, Component 2, Investment 1.1, CUP F53D23004230006, under the National Recovery and Resilience Plan (NRRP) – Grant Assignment Decree No. 959 adopted on 30 June 2023 by the Italian Ministry of University and Research (MUR).

Disclosure of Interests. The authors have no competing interests to declare that are relevant to the content of this article.

References

1. Alshiekh, M., Bloem, R., Ehlers, R., Könighofer, B., Niekum, S., Topcu, U.: Safe reinforcement learning via shielding. In: Proceedings of the AAAI Conference on Artificial Intelligence, vol. 32, no. 1 (April 2018). https://doi.org/10.1609/aaai.v32i1.11797
2. Arcaini, P., Bombarda, A., Bonfanti, S., Gargantini, A., Riccobene, E., Scandurra, P.: The ASMETA approach to safety assurance of software systems. In: Logic, Computation and Rigorous Methods - Essays Dedicated to Egon Börger on the Occasion of His 75th Birthday. LNCS, vol. 12750, pp. 215–238. Springer, Cham (2021). https://doi.org/10.1007/978-3-030-76020-5_13

3. Bersani, M.M., Camilli, M., Lestingi, L., Mirandola, R., Rossi, M.G., Scandurra, P.: Architecting explainable service robots. In: Tekinerdogan, B., Trubiani, C., Tibermacine, C., Scandurra, P., Cuesta, C.E. (eds.) Software Architecture - 17th European Conference, ECSA 2023, Istanbul, Turkey, September 18-22, 2023, Proceedings. LNCS, vol. 14212, pp. 153–169. Springer, Cham (2023). https://doi.org/10.1007/978-3-031-42592-9_11
4. Blair, G., Bencomo, N., France, R.B.: Models@ run.time. Computer **42**(10), 22–27 (2009). https://doi.org/10.1109/MC.2009.326
5. Bombarda, A., Bonfanti, S., Gargantini, A., Pellegrinelli, N., Scandurra, P.: Replication Package for the Paper: Safety Enforcement for Autonomous Driving on a Simulated Highway Using Asmeta models@run.time. https://github.com/foselab/abz2025_casestudy_autonomous_driving (2025)
6. Bombarda, A., Bonfanti, S., Gargantini, A., Riccobene, E., Scandurra, P.: ASMETA tool set for rigorous system design. In: Formal Methods - 26th International Symposium, FM 2024, Milan, Italy, 9–13 September 2024, Proceedings, Part II. LNCS, vol. 14934, pp. 492–517. Springer (2024). https://doi.org/10.1007/978-3-031-71177-0_28
7. Bonfanti, S., Riccobene, E., Scandurra, P.: A component framework for the runtime enforcement of safety properties. J. Syst. Softw. **198**, 111605 (2023). https://doi.org/10.1016/j.jss.2022.111605
8. Börger, E., Raschke, A.: Modeling Companion for Software Practitioners. Springer, Berlin, Heidelberg (2018). https://doi.org/10.1007/978-3-662-56641-1
9. Börger, E., Stärk, R.: Abstract State Machines: A Method for High-Level System Design and Analysis. Springer Verlag, Cham (2003). https://doi.org/10.1007/978-3-642-18216-7
10. Calinescu, R., Kikuchi, S.: Formal methods @ runtime. In: Calinescu, R., Jackson, E. (eds.) Foundations of Computer Software. Modeling, Development, and Verification of Adaptive Systems. Monterey Workshop 2010. LNCS, vol. 6662. pp. 122–135. Springer, Berlin, Heidelberg (2011). https://doi.org/10.1007/978-3-642-21292-5_7
11. Camilli, M., Mirandola, R., Scandurra, P.: XSA: explainable self-adaptation. In: 37th IEEE/ACM International Conference on Automated Software Engineering, ASE 2022, Rochester, MI, USA, 10–14 October 2022, pp. 189:1–189:5. ACM (2022). https://doi.org/10.1145/3551349.3559552
12. Cavada, R., et al.: The nuXmv symbolic model checker. In: Biere, A., Bloem, R. (eds.) CAV. LNCS, vol. 8559, pp. 334–342. Springer, Cham (2014). https://doi.org/10.1007/978-3-319-08867-9_22
13. Cimatti, A., Griggio, A.: Software model checking via IC3. In: Madhusudan, P., Seshia, S.A. (eds.) Computer Aided Verification, pp. 277–293. Springer, Berlin, Heidelberg (2012). https://doi.org/10.1007/978-3-642-31424-7_23
14. Crisafulli, P., Taha, S., Wolff, B.: Modeling and analysing cyber-physical systems in HOL-CSP. Robot. Auton. Syst. **170**, 104549 (2023). https://doi.org/10.1016/j.robot.2023.104549
15. Kephart, J.O., Chess, D.M.: The vision of autonomic computing. Computer **36**(1) (2003). https://doi.org/10.1109/MC.2003.1160055
16. Kobayashi, T., Bondu, M., Ishikawa, F.: Formal modelling of safety architecture for responsibility-aware autonomous vehicle via Event-B refinement. In: Chechik, M., Katoen, J.P., Leucker, M. (eds.) Formal Methods, pp. 533–549. Springer International Publishing, Cham (2023). https://doi.org/10.48550/arXiv.2401.04875
17. Leurent, E.: An Environment for Autonomous Driving Decision-Making (2018). https://github.com/eleurent/highway-env

18. Leuschel, M., Vu, F., Rutenkolk, K.: Case Study: Safety Controller for Autonomous Driving on Highways – Specification document v3 (2025). https://abz-conf.org/case-study/abz25/
19. Phan, D.T., Grosu, R., Jansen, N., Paoletti, N., Smolka, S.A., Stoller, S.D.: Neural simplex architecture. In: Lee, R., Jha, S., Mavridou, A., Giannakopoulou, D. (eds.) NASA Formal Methods, pp. 97–114. Springer International Publishing, Cham (2020). https://doi.org/10.1007/978-3-030-55754-6_6
20. Sha, L.: Using simplicity to control complexity. IEEE Softw. **18**(4), 20–28 (2001). https://doi.org/10.1109/MS.2001.936213
21. Shalev-Shwartz, S., Shammah, S., Shashua, A.: On a Formal Model of Safe and Scalable Self-driving Cars (2018). https://doi.org/10.48550/arXiv.1708.06374
22. Vu, F., Dunkelau, J., Leuschel, M.: Validation of reinforcement learning agents and safety shields with ProB. In: NASA Formal Methods: 16th International Symposium, NFM 2024, Moffett Field, CA, USA, 4–6 June 2024, Proceedings, pp. 279–297. Springer-Verlag, Berlin, Heidelberg (2024). https://doi.org/10.1007/978-3-031-60698-4_16
23. Weyns, D.: Introduction to Self-Adaptive Systems: A Contemporary Software Engineering Perspective. Wiley, Hoboken (2020)
24. Weyns, D., et al.: Perpetual assurances for self-adaptive systems. In: Software Engineering for Self-Adaptive Systems III. Assurances - International Seminar, Dagstuhl Castle, Germany, 15-+19 December 2013, Revised Selected and Invited Papers. LNCS, vol. 9640, pp. 31–63. Springer, Cham (2013). https://doi.org/10.1007/978-3-319-74183-3_2

Enhancing Decision-Making Safety in Autonomous Driving Through Online Model Checking

Duong Dinh Tran(✉), Akira Hasegawa, Peter Riviere, Takashi Tomita, and Toshiaki Aoki

Japan Advanced Institute of Science and Technology, Nomi, Ishikawa 923-1292, Japan
{duongtd,akira.hasegawa,priviere,tomita,toshiaki}@jaist.ac.jp

Abstract. While artificial intelligence (AI) offers promising approaches for developing intelligent autonomous driving (AD) agents, ensuring the safety of these AI-driven AD systems is a critical challenge. This paper proposes an approach to enhancing AD safety through the development of a safety shield based on online model checking. The safety shield acts as a real-time verification layer, monitoring and validating the actions proposed by the AI agent before execution. We demonstrate the practicality and efficiency of our approach through a highway driving case study with different AI agents trained. We construct a formal model of the driving environment, capturing the states and behaviors of the ego vehicle and surrounding traffic, and specify the safety requirements within this model. For each proposed action, we leverage Maude's invariant model checker to determine if executing the action would violate the safety requirements. Our experimental results demonstrate the capability of online model checking to enhance the safety of AI-driven autonomous vehicles.

Keywords: safety shield · autonomous driving · model checking · reinforcement learning · AI

1 Introduction

Autonomous driving (AD) represents a paradigm shift in transportation, promising increased efficiency, accessibility, and potentially increased safety. Achieving this vision requires the development of sophisticated systems capable of navigating complex and dynamic environments. The rise of artificial intelligence (AI) and machine learning (ML) has demonstrated their capabilities in developing intelligent controllers for such AD systems. Techniques like reinforcement learning (RL) [22], with algorithms like Deep Q-Networks (DQN) [15] and Proximal Policy Optimization (PPO) [20], have enabled the creation of AD agents capable of learning diverse driving behaviors [11,18]. These learning-based approaches

This work was supported by JST, CREST Grant Number JPMJCR23M1.

M. Leuschel and F. Ishikawa (Eds.): ABZ 2025, LNCS 15728, pp. 231–248, 2026.
https://doi.org/10.1007/978-3-031-94533-5_14

offer advantages in efficiency and robustness compared to traditional rule-based methods. However, despite their potential, ensuring the safety of decision-making in these AI-driven AD systems remains a critical challenge [3]. The inherent complexity of RL models, coupled with the stochastic nature of their learning process, makes it difficult to provide rigorous guarantees of safe operation.

One promising approach to mitigate this challenge is the concept of a *safety shield* [2]. This shield acts as an intermediary layer between the AI agent's decision-making process and the actual control of the vehicle. Its primary function is to monitor and validate the actions proposed by the AI agent to prevent dangerous situations. Typically, a set of safety rules, which can encompass different aspects of safe driving, such as maintaining safe distances from other vehicles, are defined in advance, and once the AI agent's proposed action violates any of these safety rules, the safety shield intervenes, either by modifying the action to a safe alternative or by preventing its execution altogether.

In this paper, we propose leveraging *online model checking* [24] to develop a safety shield for AD. Online model checking is a lightweight runtime verification technique designed to ensure the correctness of a system's execution trace as it runs. Unlike traditional model checking, which exhaustively explores the entire state space, online model checking operates incrementally by analyzing only a partial model space corresponding to the system's current execution. Thus, it mitigates the state space explosion problem that often hinders the application of model checking to complex systems. This characteristic makes online model checking particularly well-suited for developing a safety shield in AI-driven AD. At each verification cycle, by synchronizing the current state of the formal model with the driving environment, irrelevant states can be eliminated from the search state space. Furthermore, since it suffices to ensure safety only until the next verification cycle, we can limit the search depth, ensuring that the model-checking process always succeeds within a short amount of time. To the best of our knowledge, this work represents the first application of online model checking to safety verification in the AD domain.

In this work, we demonstrate our approach through a highway AD case study [13], which is the challenge proposed for the ABZ 2025 conference. A safety shield is developed and evaluated with several RL agents. Specifically, we construct a formal model that captures the real-time driving environment, including the statuses and behaviors of the ego vehicle and surrounding Non-Player Characters (NPCs). The desired safety requirements are formally specified with respect to (w.r.t.) this model. For each action proposed by the RL agent, we leverage the Maude tool [4] to perform online model checking with a bounded depth, determining whether executing the action would violate safety constraints. To mitigate the state space explosion issue, we introduce several optimization techniques in the formal model, such as abstracting NPC kinematics and preventing unnecessary interleaving. The experimental results demonstrate that our safety shield effectively prevents collisions and maintains compliance with the specified safety requirements. While minor performance trade-offs exist, their impact on overall efficiency is negligible.

The formal model, shield implementation, RL agents, experiment traces, and other supporting materials are available at https://github.com/fomaad/OnlineMC-SafetyShield.

Organization. The remainder of this paper is organized as follows. Section 2 briefly introduces background information. Section 3 presents an overview of the proposed safety shield based on online model checking and describes the highway AD case study. Section 4 details the construction of the formal model, while Sect. 5 reports the experimental results. Section 6 discusses closely related work and Sect. 7 summarizes our study.

2 Background

2.1 Maude in a Nutshell

Maude [4] is a high-performance reflective language and system based on rewriting logic, allowing both functional and concurrent system specifications. Maude offers a variety of formal analysis tools, including reachability analysis (searching) and LTL model checking, making it ideal for specifying and analyzing various systems. In the following, we briefly introduce some of the core concepts of Maude that are relevant to this work.

Modules. Maude's primary unit of specification and programming is the *module*. Maude has two types of modules. A *functional module* $\mathcal{M}$ specifies an order-sorted equational logic theory (Σ, E) with the syntax: **fmod** $\mathcal{M}$ `is` (Σ, E) **endfm**, where Σ and E are an order-sorted signature and set of equations, respectively. In Σ, we can declare *sorts* (or types), *operators*, and importations of previously defined modules. A *system modules* $\mathcal{R}$ specifies a rewrite theory (Σ, E, R) with the syntax: **mod** $\mathcal{R}$ `is` (Σ, E, R) **endm**, where Σ and E are the same as those in an equational theory, while R is a set of *rewrite rules*, which describe dynamic system behavior.

Operators and Equations. In Maude, operators (or function symbols) are declared with the **op** keyword. They define functions and constants in the system and specify their input and output sorts. Equations can be unconditional or conditional with the **eq** and **ceq** keywords, respectively.

The following functional module `VECTOR2` defines the 2D vector data structure with the addition function:

```
fmod VECTOR2 is
  pr FLOAT .
  sort Vector2 .
  op vector2 : Float Float -> Vector2 [ctor] .
  op _+_ : Vector2 Vector2 -> Vector2 [assoc comm] .
  vars X X2 Y Y2 : Float .
  eq vector2(X, Y) + vector2(X2, Y2) = vector2(X + X2, Y + Y2) .
endfm
```

It first imports the predefined module `FLOAT`, introduces sort `Vector2`, and defines the constructor of `Vector2` (lines 2–4). Line 5 declares the signature of the addition, while line 7 defines its semantics.

Rewrite Rules. Rewrite rules in system modules specify state transitions and allow dynamic behaviors to be modeled. Rewrite rules are non-deterministic and describe how the system evolves. An unconditional rewrite rule is in the form of **rl** [*label*] : u => v ., where *label* is a name (can be omitted), u and v are terms.

Model Checking Invariants. Model checking of invariants can be done through the **search** command. The following command searches for a state reachable from state t such that the state matches pattern p and satisfies condition c:

search [n,m] **in** MOD : t =>* p such that c .

where `MOD` is the name of the Maude module concerned, and `n` and `m` are optional arguments specifying a bound on the number of desired solutions and the maximum depth of the search, respectively.

Given an invariant property, we can verify it using the **search** command, where t represents the initial state of the state machine formalizing the system and p is the negation of the property. While Maude also includes an LTL model checker, we do not discuss it here, as invariants are sufficient to express the safety requirements in this work.

2.2 Reinforcement Learning and Safety Shields

Reinforcement learning (RL) [22] is a machine learning paradigm where an agent learns to interact with an *environment* by taking *actions* and receiving *rewards* (or penalties) as feedback. The agent's goal is to learn a *policy*—a mapping from states to actions—that maximizes its cumulative reward over time. Unlike supervised learning, which relies on labeled data, RL learns through trial and error, exploring different actions and refining its policy based on the resulting rewards. In the context of AD, the RL agent may still make dangerous decisions despite the reward function usually being designed to promote safety.

Safety Shields. Safety shields can serve as an additional layer of safety in autonomous systems by preventing the system from executing unsafe actions that could lead to hazardous situations. Depending on when they intervene in the decision-making process, safety shields can be classified into pre-shields and post-shields [9]. Pre-shields enforce safety by filtering a set of safe actions, from which the AI agent selects an action for execution. Post-shields, on the other hand, evaluate the agent's chosen action after selection but before execution, intervening if it is unsafe by modifying or replacing it. Our proposed shield in this work belongs to the post-shields.

3 Decision-Making Safety Shield Based on Online Model Checking

In an RL-based AD system, the RL agent controls the ego vehicle by continuously selecting and executing actions in a *cycle-based process*. A *cycle* refers to the

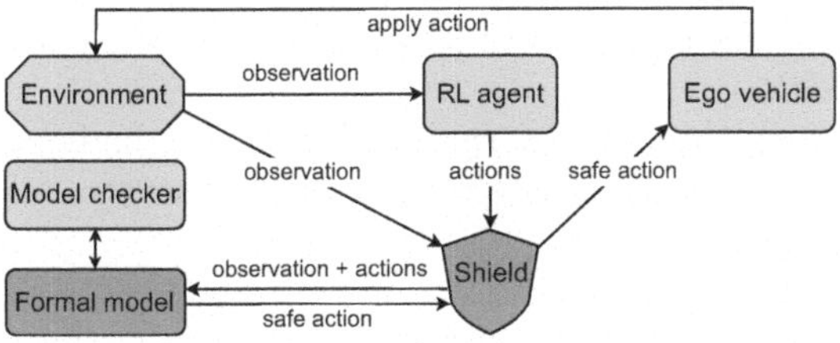

Fig. 1. Decision-making safety shield for autonomous driving based on online model checking.

time interval in which the vehicle observes its environment, makes a decision, and executes an action until the next observation occurs.

Specifically, at the beginning of each cycle, the driving environment is observed, generating a state representation known as an *observation*. This observation includes key information about nearby vehicles, such as their positions and velocities, which can be collected through onboard sensors like radar and LiDAR. In a standard RL-based decision-making process (without shielding), the trained RL agent then selects an action, such as accelerating or braking, based on the current observation and sends it to the ego vehicle. The chosen action is then applied to the ego vehicle, updating its state, while the environment naturally progresses, initiating the next cycle.

3.1 Safety Shield Overview

We propose an online model-checking-based safety shield to enhance the decision-making safety of RL-based AD systems. Figure 1 provides an overview of our approach, illustrating how the shield operates at each cycle.

In essence, the safety shield intervenes before executing the RL agent's chosen action. Instead of blindly applying the top-ranked action, our shield validates and selects the safest option from a ranked list of candidate actions proposed by the RL agent. To achieve this, a formal model is maintained, specifying the environment's state, including the status of the ego and NPC vehicles, as well as vehicle kinematics that govern their motion (e.g., speeding up and slowing down). Safety requirements for AD can be expressed as invariant properties w.r.t. this model.

Specifically, at each cycle, our method follows these steps:

1. The RL agent generates a ranked list of candidate actions, sorted from high to low (ordinarily, the first action in this list would be executed directly), passing to the shield.
2. The shield updates the encoded system state within the formal model based on the current observation and the RL agent's proposed actions.
3. For each candidate action (starting from the highest-ranked one), we perform online model checking against the negation of the invariant property specifying the safety concerned. If a counterexample is found, it indicates that

executing this action may lead to an unsafe state (w.r.t. the safety requirements concerned).
4. The shield iterates through the ranked list until it finds an action with no counterexample—this action is then passed to the ego vehicle as the safe action for execution.

Safety Requirements. In the context of AD, safety requirements must go beyond simply avoiding collisions. A common approach to enhancing safety is to enforce the ego vehicle to maintain a safe distance from surrounding vehicles. This can be quantified using metrics such as Time-To-Collision (TTC) and models like Responsibility-Sensitive Safety (RSS) [21] (will be discussed in Sect. 6). In this work, we define the safety requirements for AD based on TTC as follows:

SR: The TTC with any other vehicle must never be lower than 2 seconds.

The two-second threshold aligns with the safety standard [7], and the United Nations Regulation (UNR) collision warning guidelines, which define the boundary for emergency action at a TTC of two seconds. This guideline establishes a standardized risk evaluation boundary for maintaining safe distances from other vehicles. By adopting this criterion, we ensure that the ego vehicle has sufficient reaction time to avoid hazardous situations in dynamic driving environments.

3.2 Highway Autonomous Driving Case Study

In this paper, we demonstrate the efficiency and practicability of our proposed approach with the highway AD case study [13]—the challenge proposed for the ABZ 2025 conference. In the following, we borrow some description from [13] to elaborate on this case study.

This case study focuses on a mechanism for the safe operation of AD on a highway. Two different environments are considered: a single-lane highway where each vehicle can accelerate and brake, and a multi-lane highway where each vehicle can also change lanes. The AD system is RL-driven, i.e., a trained RL agent controls the ego vehicle's operation. A *cycle* duration is set to 1 s. The perception system is abstracted away, assuming that the agent has access to the ego vehicle's position as well as the positions of all nearby vehicles. The safety goal is to ensure that the ego vehicle avoids collisions and dangerous situations. The environment assumes that all vehicles drive in the same direction without reversing and that there are no obstacles other than vehicles. Each vehicle has a length of 5 m, a width of 2 m, a maximum speed v_{max} of 40 m/s, and maximum acceleration and deceleration a_{max} of 5 m/s^2. Highway-env [11] is provided as the simulated 2D environment to execute the experiments.

In the single-lane environment, there are three possible actions for the ego vehicle as follows:

- **ACT1** (FASTER): This action increases the speed (up to v_{max}) with an acceleration up to a_{max}.

- **ACT2** (SLOWER): This action brakes with a deceleration up to a_{max}.
- **ACT3** (IDLE): This action reduces the (braking) acceleration close to 0.

In the multi-lane environment, in addition to the three actions above, the ego vehicle can also perform the following two actions:

- **ACT4** (LANE_LEFT): This action changes the current lane of the vehicle to the adjacent lane on the left within the current cycle.
- **ACT5** (LANE_RIGHT): This action changes the current lane of the vehicle to the adjacent lane on the right within the current cycle.

NPC vehicles also perform these actions, but potentially at a higher frequency. For instance, an NPC vehicle might brake during the first half of a cycle and then accelerate in the second half.

4 Formal Model

The formal model is designed to capture the state and behavior of the ego vehicle and surrounding NPCs in the highway driving scenario. It serves as the foundation for online model checking, enabling the safety shield to verify the safety of proposed actions in real time.

4.1 Model Construction

We formally specify the ego vehicle, the NPC vehicles, and their behaviors as a state machine, specified in Maude. Each state captures the status of the ego vehicle and all NPC vehicles, while transitions specify their motions. In the following, we describe how vehicles are encoded, how states are represented, and how vehicle motions are specified.

Vehicle Encoding. Vehicles are represented using the sort `Vehicle`, which captures key attributes such as the identifier, position, velocity, and heading angle (in degrees). The following code snippet declares the sort `Vehicle`, defines its constructor and a projection function to extract the vehicle's position:

```
sort Vehicle .
op veh : Int  Vector2  Vector2  Float  -> Vehicle [ctor] .
op position : Vehicle -> Vector2 .
--- ID, POS, VEL, ANGLE are variables of the corresponding sorts
eq position(veh(ID,POS,VEL,ANGLE)) = POS .
```

The term `veh(ID,POS,VEL,ANGLE)` represents a vehicle object with its unique identifier (`ID`), current position (`POS`), velocity (`VEL`), and heading angle (`ANGLE`). The `POS` attribute refers to the middle center point of the vehicle, which serves as the reference point for position calculations. Here, vehicle positions and velocities are represented in 2D, as the highway AD case study considers a two-dimensional space, not 3D. Note that `---` denotes a Maude comment.

Given two vehicles, we implement a collision detection function that determines whether the two vehicles collide based on their positions, heading angles, and sizes. In this implementation, Maude is used as a functional programming language. Given two vehicles, our formal model also implements a TTC calculation between them, based on the algorithm [8].

For the ego vehicle, we additionally encode its current action and the remaining duration of the current cycle, making its representation in the form of `VEH # ACTION # T`.

State Representation. The formal model encodes a concrete state as a tuple: `ID | EGO | NPCs`, where `ID` is the ID of the last NPC vehicle that took an action, `EGO` represents the ego vehicle's state, and `NPCs` denotes a set of NPC vehicles.

Since the safety requirement considered in this work are defined in terms of TTC, which depends solely on the positions, velocities, and heading angles of the vehicles, our formal model does not require encoding other information, such as lane making and road geometry. Consequently, while demonstrated in a highway setting in this paper, the formal model and our approach are not tied to this environment and could be generalized to other driving scenarios.

NPC Vehicle Action Specification. In our formal model, an NPC can take three actions **ACT1**–**ACT3** without changing its current direction of motion. Direction changes are not specified in the formal model for a reason that will become clear later (Sect. 4.2).

Maude rewrite rules are used to specify the vehicle's actions. For instance, the action **ACT3** (`IDLE`) is specified by the following rewrite rule:

```
rl [npc-idle] :
   ID | EGO          | (veh(ID, P, V, ANGLE) & VEHs)
=> ID | advance(EGO) | (veh(ID, P + V * simulationStep, V, ANGLE) & VEHs) .
```

Here, `simulationStep` represents the time interval between two consecutive simulation steps (it is different from the cycle duration). In this work, we configure it as 0.25 s. The rule says that in the successor state, the position of the NPC vehicle identified by `ID` is updated based on its current position and velocity as well as the simulation step size, while its velocity and heading angle remain unchanged. Other NPC vehicles (`VEHs`) are unaffected. The symbol `&` acts as the concatenation symbol of the vehicle set and variable `VEHs` represents other NPC vehicles. In the source state pattern of the rewrite rule, the variable `ID` constraints that only the last vehicle that executed an action can proceed with the specified action. This constraint prevents unnecessary interleaving, which will be discussed in Sect. 4.3.

The ego vehicle kinematic should be updated simultaneously with that NPC motion, and it is achieved using the function `advance(EGO)`. Specifically, this function computes the next state of the given ego vehicle `EGO` according to its encoded action.

4.2 Model Checking and Integration with the Shield

Online model checking w.r.t. the formal model is used to verify that a proposed action from the RL agent does not violate the safety requirement at each cycle.

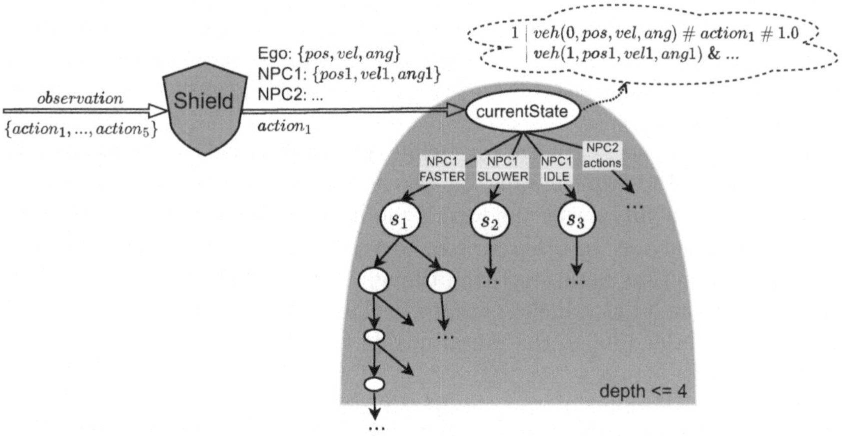

Fig. 2. State synchronization and Search state space with bounded depth 4.

The safety shield leverages this verification process to ensure that only safe actions are executed.

Safety Requirement Checking. The formal model provides a function `ttc`, which computes the minimum TTC between the ego vehicle and all NPC vehicles in a given state, provided that all vehicles keep going with their current velocities. The function returns a tuple `< T ; ID >`, where `T` is the smallest TTC value, and `ID` identifies the NPC vehicle associated with this value. This function is a key to specify **SR**—the safety requirement considered in this work.

Figure 2 illustrates how the formal model is synchronized with the simulated environment and how the search space is explored with a bounded depth. At each cycle, the safety shield updates the encoded system state within the formal model based on the latest observation and the RL agent's proposed actions. The updated state (`currentState` in Fig. 2) serves as the initial state for invariant model checking, which verifies whether any reachable state within a predefined depth violates **SR**. This model-checking process is conducted using the following Maude command:

```
search [1, depth] in PROPOSITIONS : currentState =>* S:Sys
  such that < T:Float ; ID:Int > := ttc(S:Sys) /\ T:Float < 2.0 .
```

Here, `Sys` and `PROPOSITIONS` are the sort of states and the name of the module containing the formal model, respectively. `depth` is the desired bounded depth for the search (set to 4 in this study). The command tries to find a state `S:Sys` reachable from the current state with a depth up to the given `depth` such that in that state, the minimum TTC between the ego vehicle and NPC vehicles is less than two seconds. As explained above, `T:Float` and `ID:Int` are the minimum TTC value and the ID of the NPC vehicle associated with this value. Note that the symbols `:=` and `/\` represent pattern matching and Boolean conjunction in Maude, respectively.

If such a state is not found, the candidate action under consideration is regarded as safe and it passes the shield. Otherwise, the action is deemed unsafe and rejected. The shield iterates through the remaining candidate actions until it finds one that is safe.

During state space exploration, while the ego vehicle's action is predetermined, each NPC vehicle can *non-deterministically* select any action from **ACT1–ACT3**. In this sense, the formal model provides an *over-approximation* of the NPC's behavior. In other words, there are cases where the safety shield may classify an action as unsafe, even though it would be safe if executed. This occurs because the NPC vehicles' actions in the actual execution may differ from those in the path leading to the found unsafe state.

Fallback Action. If none of the candidate actions pass the safety shield, the shield selects `SLOWER` as the fallback action. While abrupt braking on highways can increase rear-end collision risk, the following vehicle is primarily responsible for maintaining a safe distance. In our case study, the ego vehicle's maximum deceleration is limited to $5\,\mathrm{m/s^2}$, which does not constitute sudden braking. We emphasize that more sophisticated and/or heuristic-based fallback strategies can be implemented and incorporated into the shield.

Ignoring NPC Direction Changes. Our formal model omits direction-changing behaviors of NPC vehicles to avoid overly conservative AD strategies. Encoding such behaviors would restrict the ego vehicle from accelerating whenever an NPC is present in adjacent lanes, reducing efficiency. Instead, we assume that NPCs do not make abrupt steering maneuvers when the ego vehicle approaches, aligning with typical real-world behavior. Note, however, that unchanging direction does not imply never changing lanes. For instance, if an NPC's velocity is currently directed diagonally to the left, it will eventually move into the left lane.

Integration of the Shield with the Formal Model. The connection between the safety shield, implemented in Python, and the formal model, specified in Maude, is established through the Python bindings for Maude [19]. This tool provides a general programming interface to Maude from Python as well as several other programming languages. It allows loading Maude specifications, manipulating Maude terms and modules, and performing various Maude functionalities, including term rewriting, searching, and LTL model checking, directly from Python code.

4.3 Techniques for Mitigating State Space Explosion

State space explosion is widely known as the most challenging issue in model checking. In the context of online model checking, this challenge becomes even more pronounced due to the stringent time constraints imposed on each verification cycle. To mitigate the state space explosion issue, we incorporate several techniques in the formal model construction and the model-checking process.

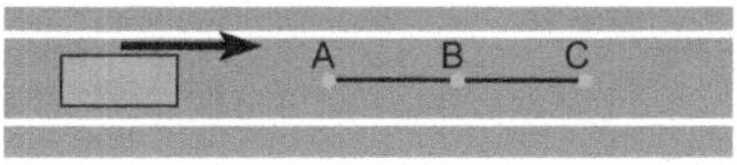

Fig. 3. Kinematic abstraction results in only three discrete positions of an NPC vehicle.

Table 1. Number of reachable states w.r.t. our formal model and two other variants up to depths 2–5 when there are 4 NPC vehicles. With depth 4 (used in our shield), the times to solely iterate all states and to model check **SR** are also recorded.

Model	Depth 2	Depth 3	Depth 4	Depth 5
Our optimized model	53	145	314, 11 ms, 118 ms	705
Adding two rules	125	593	2541, 86 ms, 868 ms	7841
Interleaving relaxing	103	627	3190, 134 ms, 1091 ms	14174

NPC Kinematic Abstraction. In fact, an NPC vehicle's acceleration can take continuous values within the range $[-a_{max}; a_{max}]$. However, in our formal model, we discretize this range to only three values: $\{-a_{max}$, 0, and $a_{max}\}$ (i.e., $\{-5, 0, 5\}$). This abstraction in the modeling process reduces the number of possible successor states, making state exploration more efficient.

As illustrated in Fig. 3, the vehicle's next position in the successor state is restricted to three discrete points: A (`SLOWER`), B (`IDLE`), and C (`FASTER`). In contrast, the actual position could be anywhere within the continuous range between A and C. Note that abstraction based on the upper and lower bounds (like points A and C in the figure) may omit critical intermediate states, potentially missing cases where a collision/dangerous situation could occur between these points.

To assess the impact of this technique, we tried to modify the formal model to include two additional rewrite rules, allowing acceleration and deceleration at an intermediate value of $2.5\,\mathrm{m/s^2}$. Using an initial state extracted from the experiments reported in Sect. 5, we measured the resulting increase in the number of states and model-checking time, as shown in Table 1. The third row presents another variant of the model, which will be described shortly.

Up to depth 4, there are 314 reachable states in total in the original formal model. It takes 11 and 118 milliseconds (ms) to solely iterate and to model check the TTC constraint **SR**, respectively. Meanwhile, if the two rewrite rules were added, the number of reachable states and the time required for model checking increased nearly eightfold. In the context of AD, 868 ms is unacceptable for real-time decision-making.

From a kinematic perspective, this abstraction in the modeling process results in an *under-approximation* of NPC's motions. However, as demonstrated in Sect. 5, the shield still works effectively in avoiding dangerous situations. Recall that the formal model provides an *over-approximation* of the NPC's behaviors in terms of the actions they can take. Consequently, the formal model represents a combination of *under-approximation* and *over-approximation*.

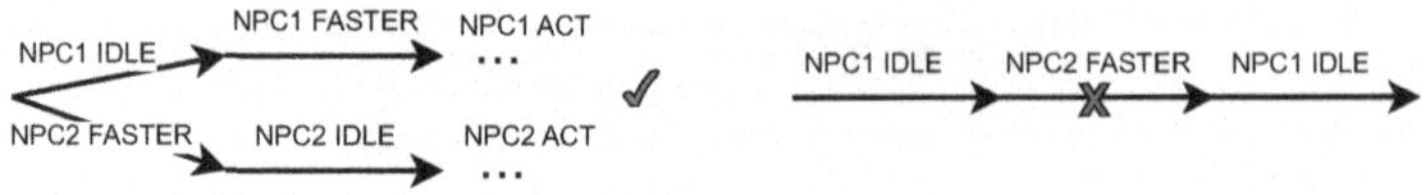

Fig. 4. Transitions on the left are allowed, while transitions on the right are not allowed.

Preventing Unnecessary Interleaving. We are only concerned about the collisions and/or dangerous situations between the ego vehicle and some NPC vehicle. Since NPC vehicles do not interact with each other, their actions can be modeled independently.

To minimize unnecessary interleaving of actions from different NPC vehicles, our formal model includes a vehicle ID constraint (the first entry in the model's state representation), which ensures that only the last NPC vehicle that executed an action can proceed in the next transition (see an illustration in Fig. 4). This constraint effectively reduces the number of interleaved transitions between NPCs, significantly limiting redundant state combinations.

To quantify the efficiency gain, we conducted another experiment where we modified our model to relax this constraint, allowing unrestricted interleaving (the transition sequence like on the right-hand side of Fig. 4 will become valid). The results in Table 1 indicate that, at depth 4, the number of reachable states and model checking time increased nearly tenfold compared to our optimized model, highlighting the importance of limiting unnecessary interleaving. Note that the state space also grows as the number of NPC vehicles increases. However, this can be effectively managed by ignoring NPCs that are too far from the ego vehicle.

State Synchronization and Bounded Search Depth. By synchronizing the current state of the formal model with the simulated environment at each cycle, the model-checking process does not need to explore the entire state space but only the sub-state space expanded from the current state (see Fig. 2). Additionally, since it is sufficient to ensure safety only until the next cycle, we limit the search depth to an appropriate value. In our implementation, a search depth of 4 and the simulation step of 0.25 s were determined to provide a practical balance between computational efficiency and verification accuracy, ensuring that online model checking can meet the strict constraints of real-time decision-making.

5 Experiments

We conducted a series of experiments in the simulated environment [11] with two different road configurations: a single-lane highway and a three-lane highway.

5.1 RL Agent Training and Experiment Setup

To evaluate the effectiveness of the safety shield, we trained a total of eight RL agents by combining two environment settings (single-lane and three-lane), two

RL models (DQN and PPO), and two types of agent behaviors, which are as follows:

- **Good agent** (GA): Trained to drive safely. During training, the agent receives penalties for collisions and rewards for maintaining high speed and driving in the right-most lane (the reward configuration is available in the supplementary material on GitHub repository: https://github.com/fomaad/OnlineMC-SafetyShield).
- **Adversary agent** (AA): Trained to behave adversarially. The agent is rewarded for causing collisions, performing lane changes, and driving at high speeds, while no reward is given for staying in the right-most lane.

We selected DQN and PPO algorithms because they represent two fundamentally different RL paradigms—DQN as a value-based approach and PPO as a policy-based approach. Evaluating both ensures that the safety shield's effectiveness is not limited to a specific type of RL agent and can be generalized across different decision-making models used in AD. Note, however, that this study does not aim to compare the performance of these two algorithms in the AD domain. For the training process, we leverage the Stable Baselines3 (SB3) [18], a collection of pre-implemented RL algorithms. To train the DQN agents, we adopted the script provided in [13], while for the PPO agents, we adapted the script from [10]. We also note that tuning hyperparameters to maximize the performance of RL agents for AD is beyond the scope of this work.

Experiment Setup. We conducted 1000 tests for each combination of agent, environment (single-lane and three-lane), and safety shield status (enabled and disabled). Each test lasted for 30 s unless a collision occurred. The simulation execution traces, including vehicle trajectories, were logged and are available at our GitHub repository.

5.2 Results and Analysis

Table 2 presents the experimental results for the three-lane environment. The results for the single-lane environment are available in the supplementary material. The table includes the number of collisions, the average per test of the travel distance, speed, and reward received, the percentage of environment observations where the TTC between the ego vehicle and an NPC was below 2 s, the approval ratios of `LANE_RIGHT` and `FASTER` actions by the shield. Recall that each test lasts for 30 s and environment observations are made every second; thus, a total of 30 observations were recorded per test. Since the AAs were not trained to avoid collisions or drive on the right lane, their reward and right lane change approval ratio are not shown in the table.

Unshielded GAs exhibited collisions in the three-lane environment. The introduction of the safety shield completely eliminated collisions across all tests. Interestingly, in the experiments with the PPO-based agents, the shielded GA achieved even higher travel distance and reward than unshielded ones, suggesting that enforcing safe decision-making did not necessarily reduce driving performance. With the DQN-based GA, the shield contributed to a slight increase

Table 2. Three-lane experiment results. $x \pm y$ denotes the average value and standard deviation.

		DQN model	PPO model
Unshielded GA	Collisions	38/1000	34/1000
	Distance (m)	648.01 ± 60.64	623.41 ± 84.05
	Speed (m/s)	21.84 ± 1.23	21.20 ± 1.10
	Reward	23.01 ± 1.86	22.78 ± 2.94
	TTC < 2 (%)	1.31	1.00
Shielded GA	Collisions	0/1000	0/1000
	Distance (m)	647.32 ± 33.65	630.52 ± 37.10
	Speed (m/s)	21.58 ± 1.12	21.02 ± 1.24
	Reward	23.04 ± 0.57	23.08 ± 0.57
	TTC < 2 (%)	0.48	0.30
	Right lane change approval (%)	64.48	44.19
	Faster approval (%)	55.05	69.83
Shielded AA	Collisions	2/1000	9/1000
	Distance (m)	675.70 ± 45.85	678.73 ± 62.06
	Speed (m/s)	22.57 ± 1.48	22.80 ± 1.67
	TTC < 2 (%)	0.89	0.96
	Faster approval (%)	25.18	31.43

in the agent's reward, while its impact on the travel distance was very minor (reduced by 0.11%).

The safety shield also significantly improved TTC performance. The percentage of observations where TTC fell below 2 s was noticeably lower in shielded tests, confirming that the shield effectively maintained safer driving distances.

The right lane change and faster approval rates in the shielded tests confirm that the shield still permitted a significant number of these actions, ensuring a balance between safety and maneuverability.

A total of 11 collisions were observed in shielded AA tests, a significantly lower rate compared to unshielded tests, where collisions occurred in approximately 97% of cases (not shown in the table). Analyzing the vehicle trajectories from these 11 collisions, we found that 7 collisions occurred despite at least three consecutive `SLOWER` actions being applied immediately beforehand, while 4 collisions resulted from NPC vehicles spawning within the ego vehicle's occupied region. Our shield was not responsible for all of these collisions. A more detailed discussion is provided in the supplementary material.

A closely related work is [23], which presented a safety shield using the B method and ProB [1,12] (their approach is discussed in Sect. 6). Their experimental results showed that the safety shield prevented collisions in 91.8% of 1000 tests when used with a DQN agent trained to drive safely, similar to our GAs. To measure our shield's performance against theirs, we conducted additional experiments. We cloned their DQN agent and ran 1000 tests under the same conditions but with our shield. The results revealed that our shield prevented 98% of collisions and achieved a higher average reward per test (45.48 vs. 42.88).

5.3 Validity and Trade-Offs

The experimental results highlight several key insights. First, the safety shield successfully eliminated collisions for GAs across all test scenarios, demonstrating its effectiveness in enforcing safe driving, which would not be achieved without the shield. Second, the shield proved robust against adversarial behaviors, preventing AAs from causing collisions despite their incentive to do so. This is particularly important since RL agents may sometimes fail to make optimal decisions or behave unpredictably. Third, the shield played a crucial role in maintaining the predefined safety requirement, which is usually stricter than collision avoidance, ensuring that the ego vehicle always kept a safe TTC or distance from surrounding traffic.

While the shield significantly improves safety, it introduces a slight trade-off in driving efficiency. When enabled, the total distance traveled and the total reward received were slightly reduced in some cases. This reduction tends to be attributed to the shield restricting certain high-risk actions, such as accelerations or lane changes that could lead to unsafe situations. However, the impact on efficiency was minimal, indicating that the shield does not overly constrain the ego vehicle's ability to progress effectively. The non-conservativeness of the safety shield is further evidenced by the right lane change and speeding up approval rates.

6 Related Work

Vu et al. [23] presented an approach to validating RL-based autonomous agents and a safety shield using the formal method tool ProB [12]. Similar to our approach, they constructed a formal model of the environment using the B method [1]. However, unlike our work, they encoded many specific safety rules as *guards* in their formal model, such as prohibiting the ego vehicle from changing lanes to the left if a vehicle is present in the left lane within 10 m behind and 10 m ahead. While these rule-based constraints enforce safety, they also increase model complexity and limit generalizability, as the predefined distances may be too short at high speeds or too long at low speeds. In contrast, our approach defines safety requirements based on the TTC metric, which provides an adaptable safety criterion applicable across various driving environments. Additionally, unlike our online model-checking approach with Maude, their method did not use the ProB model checker for verification. Instead, safety assessment was performed by directly evaluating the encoded guards, which can be implemented in any programming language without the need for formal verification techniques. Our approach, however, leverages reachability analysis, a technique that cannot be efficiently replicated within conventional programming languages.

Fulton and Platzer [6] presented an approach that combines formal verification with runtime monitoring to ensure the safety of RL-based controllers in safety-critical systems including AD. They used Differential Dynamic Logic [16] to model the hybrid system (discrete decision-making of the RL agent and continuous dynamics of the driving environment) and prove safety properties like collision avoidance. Their method integrated formal proofs from the hybrid system verification with real-time monitoring using ModelPlex [14] to check whether the observed system behavior aligns with the verified model. Compared to our work, their approach relies on offline formal verification and runtime monitoring, whereas we employ online model checking to verify actions dynamically. The runtime monitor continuously checks system behavior but reacts after a violation is detected, whereas our online model-checking approach verifies one step ahead, determining whether a candidate action would lead to an unsafe state before execution. Furthermore, their method follows a pre-shielding strategy, where verification produces a set of safe actions from which the RL agent selects an action for execution. In contrast, our approach functions as a post-shield.

In addition to manual implementation, a shield can also be *synthesized* from a formal abstraction of the environment and a safety specification [9]. In this approach, the shield is precomputed offline and used to prevent unsafe actions during both the training and execution phases. In contrast, our online model-checking approach dynamically verifies actions at runtime without interfering with the training phase. As a result, our shield can be applied to existing RL agents without requiring retraining. Shield synthesis is particularly useful when safety requirements are defined by a set of specific rules, as in [23]. However, in our work, we adopt a more general TTC-based safety criterion that is applicable across various environments. This eliminates the need for manually specifying numerous safety rules, as the only requirement is the implementation of the TTC calculation. Thanks to Maude's powerful functional programming capabilities, this can be done efficiently and seamlessly.

RSS [21] is a rigorous mathematical model that defines the safety distance that the ego vehicle needs to maintain in order to achieve safety. Five safety rules are defined for five different scenarios, such as when two vehicles traveling on the same lane or when a vehicle traveling on the adjacent lane cuts into the ego vehicle. This means that RSS requires explicit encoding of further information like vehicle lanes, adding complexity to the formal modeling process. In contrast, we adopt the TTC metric as our safety criterion because it can be computed solely based on vehicle positions, velocities, and heading angles, without the need to explicitly model lane structures. This allows for a more general and flexible formal model, making it applicable to a wider range of driving scenarios beyond highway environments.

Online model checking has been explored in prior studies [17,24]. However, these studies primarily focused on demonstrating its applicability to some mutual exclusion algorithms and communication protocols. Our work explores this lightweight verification technique in the AD domain.

7 Conclusion

This paper has presented an online model-checking-based safety shield to enhance the decision-making safety of RL-based AD systems. The proposed approach integrates a formal model that captures the real-time driving environment and verifies each RL-proposed action against predefined safety requirements using Maude-based model checking. To address the state space explosion problem, we have introduced some optimization techniques such as NPC kinematic abstraction and restricted interleaving.

Experimental results have demonstrated that the safety shield effectively prevents collisions and improves adherence to safety constraints. By validating actions before execution, the safety shield ensures that decision-making remains within predefined safety requirements. While minor trade-offs in driving efficiency were observed, their impact was minimal, and the shield successfully balanced safety and maneuverability.

To the best of our knowledge, this study is the first to demonstrate the online model-checking technique's applicability as a practical and effective safety mechanism in the AD domain. Future work will extend this approach beyond highway driving to further environments, such as merging regions and intersections, which are supported by the Highway-env [11], making this exploration a natural next step. Additionally, we plan to explore alternative formal methods, such as narrowing [5], as a potential replacement for the invariant model-checking approach used in this work. As described in [4, Chapter 20], narrowing-based reachability analysis is considered a more powerful technique than search-based reachability analysis, offering greater expressiveness and the potential for improved verification efficiency.

References

1. Abrial, J.: The B-Book - Assigning Programs to Meanings. Cambridge University Press (1996). https://doi.org/10.1017/CBO9780511624162
2. Alshiekh, M., Bloem, R., Ehlers, R., Könighofer, B., Niekum, S., Topcu, U.: Safe reinforcement learning via shielding. In: 32th AAAI Conference on Artificial Intelligence, pp. 2669–2678 (2018). https://doi.org/10.1609/AAAI.V32I1.11797
3. Amodei, D., Olah, C., Steinhardt, J., Christiano, P., Schulman, J., Mané, D.: Concrete problems in AI safety (2016). https://arxiv.org/abs/1606.06565
4. Clavel, M., et al. (eds.): All About Maude (2007). https://doi.org/10.1007/978-3-540-71999-1
5. Escobar, S., Meseguer, J., Thati, P.: Narrowing and rewriting logic: from foundations to applications. In: Proceedings of the 15th Workshop on Functional and (Constraint) Logic Programming WFLP, vol. 177, pp. 5–33. Elsevier (2006). https://doi.org/10.1016/J.ENTCS.2007.01.004
6. Fulton, N., Platzer, A.: Safe reinforcement learning via formal methods: toward safe control through proof and learning. In: 32th AAAI Conference on Artificial Intelligence, pp. 6485–6492 (2018). https://doi.org/10.1609/AAAI.V32I1.12107
7. Japan Automobile Manufacturers Association: Automated driving safety evaluation framework ver 3.0. Technical report (2022). https://www.jama.or.jp/english/reports/docs/Automated_Driving_Safety_Evaluation_Framework_Ver3.0.pdf
8. Jiao, Y.: A fast calculation of two-dimensional Time-to-Collision (2023). https://github.com/Yiru-Jiao/Two-Dimensional-Time-To-Collision

9. Könighofer, B., Lorber, F., Jansen, N., Bloem, R.: Shield synthesis for reinforcement learning. In: Margaria, T., Steffen, B. (eds.) ISoLA 2020. LNCS, vol. 12476, pp. 290–306. Springer, Cham (2020). https://doi.org/10.1007/978-3-030-61362-4_16
10. Leurent, E.: PPO-based agents for autonomous driving. https://github.com/Farama-Foundation/HighwayEnv/blob/master/scripts/sb3_highway_ppo.py
11. Leurent, E.: An environment for autonomous driving decision-making (2018). https://github.com/eleurent/highway-env
12. Leuschel, M., Butler, M.: ProB: a model checker for B. In: Araki, K., Gnesi, S., Mandrioli, D. (eds.) FME 2003. LNCS, vol. 2805, pp. 855–874. Springer, Heidelberg (2003). https://doi.org/10.1007/978-3-540-45236-2_46
13. Leuschel, M., Vu, F., Rutenkolk, K.: Case study: safety controller for autonomous driving on highways. In: Leuschel, M., Ishikawa, F. (eds.) ABZ 2025. LNCS, vol. 15728, pp. 195–203. Springer, Cham (2025)
14. Mitsch, S., Platzer, A.: ModelPlex: verified runtime validation of verified cyber-physical system models. In: Bonakdarpour, B., Smolka, S.A. (eds.) RV 2014. LNCS, vol. 8734, pp. 199–214. Springer, Cham (2014). https://doi.org/10.1007/978-3-319-11164-3_17
15. Mnih, V., et al.: Human-level control through deep reinforcement learning. Nature **518**(7540), 529–533 (2015). https://doi.org/10.1038/NATURE14236
16. Platzer, A.: A complete uniform substitution calculus for differential dynamic logic. J. Autom. Reason. **59**(2), 219–265 (2017). https://doi.org/10.1007/S10817-016-9385-1
17. Qanadilo, M., Samara, S., Zhao, Y.: Accelerating online model checking. In: Sixth Latin-American Symposium on Dependable Computing, LADC 2013, pp. 40–47. IEEE Computer Society (2013). https://doi.org/10.1109/LADC.2013.20
18. Raffin, A., Hill, A., Gleave, A., Kanervisto, A., Ernestus, M., Dormann, N.: Stable-baselines3: reliable reinforcement learning implementations. J. Mach. Learn. Res. **22**(268), 1–8 (2021). http://jmlr.org/papers/v22/20-1364.html
19. Rubio, R.: Maude as a library: an efficient all-purpose programming interface. In: Bae, K. (eds.) WRLA 2022. LNCS, vol. 13252, pp. 274–294. Springer, Cham (2022). https://doi.org/10.1007/978-3-031-12441-9_14
20. Schulman, J., Wolski, F., Dhariwal, P., Radford, A., Klimov, O.: Proximal policy optimization algorithms (2017). https://arxiv.org/abs/1707.06347
21. Shalev-Shwartz, S., Shammah, S., Shashua, A.: On a formal model of safe and scalable self-driving cars (2018). https://arxiv.org/abs/1708.06374
22. Sutton, R.S., Barto, A.G.: Reinforcement Learning - An Introduction. Adaptive Computation and Machine Learning. MIT Press (1998). https://www.worldcat.org/oclc/37293240
23. Vu, F., Dunkelau, J., Leuschel, M.: Validation of reinforcement learning agents and safety shields with ProB. In: Benz, N., Gopinath, D., Shi, N. (eds) NFM 2024. LNCS, vol. 14627, pp. 279–297. Springer, Cham (2024). https://doi.org/10.1007/978-3-031-60698-4_16
24. Zhao, Y., Rammig, F.J.: Online model checking for dependable real-time systems. In: 15th IEEE International Symposium on Object/Component/Service-Oriented Real-Time Distributed Computing, ISORC 2012, pp. 154–161 (2012). https://doi.org/10.1109/ISORC.2012.28

Polychronous RSS in a Process-Algebraic Framework - A Case Study

Paolo Crisafulli[1], Adrien Durier[2], Benjamin Puyobro[3], and Burkhart Wolff[2](✉)

[1] IRT SystemX, Palaiseau, France
paolo.crisafulli@irt-systemx.fr
[2] LMF, Université Paris-Saclay, Paris, France
{adrien.durier,wolff}@lmf.cnrs.fr
[3] LMF, Université Paris-Saclay, IRT SystemX Paris, 91120 Palaiseau, France
bpuyobro@lmf.cnrs.fr

Abstract. The ABZ 2025 conference case study focuses on developing a safety controller for autonomous highway driving. Within this context, we present a model of interacting agents that synchronize with a global state at specific points in time. These agents follow the differential equations of standard kinematics, operating within a physical environment. They can make non-deterministic decisions regarding acceleration and follow strategies to avoid collisions.

We instantiate our model according to the Responsibility-Sensitive Safety (RSS) setting. By defining agent properties such as extensions, cycle times, and acceleration limits, we concentrate on the single-lane model specified in the case study requirements document.

We also consider a polychronous setting, i.e. we demonstrate that the safety invariants still hold if agents have mutually independent and unknown clocks. This enhances the model's realism and makes it well-suited for refinement into implementations using synchronous languages.

Keywords: Process-Algebra · Semantics · Concurrency · Computational Models · Theorem Proving · Isabelle/HOL

1 Introduction

As Cyber-Physical Systems (CPS) such as robots or Autonomous Vehicles (AV) are a developing industrial field, the need for safety certification is widening. Therefore, there is an important opportunity for formal methods to address this type of systems and a need to meet the respective scientific challenges.

Recently, a process-algebraic approach to verify various properties of CPSs has been proposed [10]. Based on HOL-CSP [39–41], an embedding of the process algebra CSP [36], this approach allows for the modeling of the dynamics of physical states in dense time, exploring uncountably many possible accelerations for the cyber-agents, *as well* as digital communication between *actors* (other vehicles, gates, traffic-lights, ...).

M. Leuschel and F. Ishikawa (Eds.): ABZ 2025, LNCS 15728, pp. 249–268, 2026.
https://doi.org/10.1007/978-3-031-94533-5_15

A global system state (called *scene*) is constructed via synchronization of local actor states. Exploiting CSP's *compositional* view on non-deterministic processes and their interaction, actors can be specified and analyzed in a modular way. The diagram Fig. 1 (left) introduces some of the key concepts:

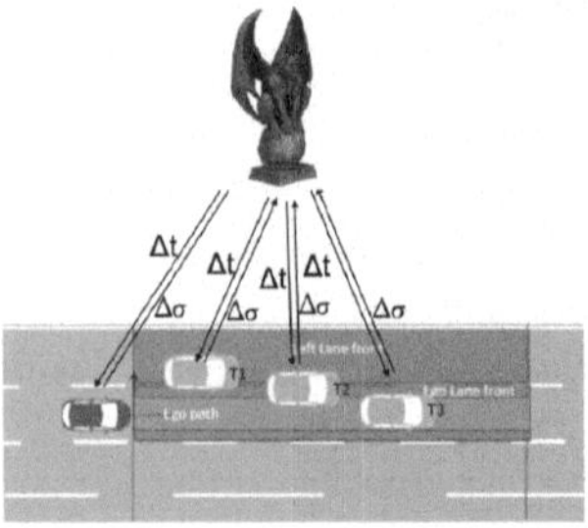

(a) Demon, actors, ...

$$demon \equiv \sqcap \Delta t \in \mathbf{R}_+ \rightarrow \Box \sigma_g \in \Sigma \rightarrow demon$$

$$actor_{id}\ ds\ \sigma_g \equiv \Box\ \Delta t \in \mathbf{R}_+ \rightarrow \sqcap\ \sigma'_g \in \{\Sigma \mid \Sigma[id] \in moves\} \rightarrow actor_{id}\ ds\ \sigma'_g$$

(b) ... and their formalization.

Fig. 1. The overall Process Architecture

The demon process emits repeatedly arbitrary time-intervals δt and forces the actors to agree on a global state after δt. The actors are also CSP processes, parameterised by a *driving strategy*. This abstract control algorithm proposes, depending on the current scene, a set of possible accelerations that are constant during δt. Then, the proposed acceleration and current physical state allow the computation of the actor's next state (i.e. position, speed, acceleration, etc.). This creates a set of possible futures, and, inductively, sets of traces, capturing the possible *runs* of a given scenario. The right part of Fig. 1 shows the corresponding CSP formalization, as detailed in Sect. 3.

In this paper, we instantiate the formal theory of [10] to meet the requirements of the "Safety Controller for Autonomous Driving on Highways" case study for ABZ 2025. We consider a single-lane scenario where an AI component proposes acceleration values, verified by a formally proven safety controller to ensure non-collision. The requirements, inspired by [37], assume perfect sensor accuracy, absence of external forces, and constant acceleration effects. They also emphasize a key feature: actors operate on independent schedules. Our model builds on this by allowing different, unsynchronized cycle times, resulting in a polychronous system [16,17,25]. Our formal proof confirms that independent cycle times do not compromise collision avoidance.

The paper proceeds as follows: after a background chapter introducing to CSP and its formalized theory HOL-CSP, we outline our CPS framework, and come to our safety controller instances and proofs of non-collision. In a final section, we inject the formally proven driving strategy into the simulation environment provided by the organizers of the ABZ 2025 case study, evaluating its shielding effectiveness and impact on vehicle performance.

2 Background

2.1 Classic CSP Syntax and Semantics

At a glance, the syntax of the classical CSP core language reads as follows:

$$P ::= SKIP \mid STOP \mid P \,\Box\, P' \mid P \sqcap P' \mid P \,[\![A]\!]\, P' \mid P \,;\, P' \mid \\ P \setminus A \mid a \rightarrow P \mid \Box a{\in}A \rightarrow P(a) \mid \sqcap a{\in}A \rightarrow P(a) \mid \mu\, X.\, f(X)$$

SKIP signals termination, *STOP* denotes a deadlock. CSP possesses two distinguished choice operators:

1. the *external choice* -$\Box$-, which forces a process "to follow" whatever its context requires,
2. the *internal choice* -$\sqcap$-, which imposes on the context of a process "to follow" the non-deterministic choices made.

With the prefix operator $a \rightarrow P$ which signals a and continues with P (where a is an element of a set Σ of *events*), generalized choices of the form $\Box a{\in}A \rightarrow P(a)$ resp. $\sqcap a{\in}A \rightarrow P(a)$ are constructed (A is originally a finite set). When events are tagged with *channels*, i. e. $\Sigma = CHANNELS \times DATA$, syntactic sugar like $c?x{\in}A{\rightarrow}P(x)$ or $c!!x{\in}A{\rightarrow}P(x)$ is added; the former reads intuitively as "x is read from channel c" while the latter means "x is arbitrarily chosen from A and sent into c" (where $c \in CHANNELS$ and $x \in DATA$).

CSP describes all communication with one single primitive: the synchronized product written $P \,[\![A]\!]\, P'$. Note that interleaving $P \,|||\, P'$ stands for $P \,[\![\{\}]\!]\, P'$, whereas the parallel operator $P \,||\, P'$ is a shortcut for $P \,[\![\{x.\ True\}]\!]\, P'$.

2.2 Classic CSP Semantics

The traditional denotational semantics (following [36]) comes in three layers: the *trace model*, the *failures model* and the *failure/divergence model*.

In the trace semantics model, the behaviour of a process P is denoted by a prefix-closed set of traces (i.e., sequences of events), denoted $\mathcal{T}\ P$. Since traces are finite lists, and infinite behaviour is thus represented via the set of approximations, an additional element *tick* (written $\checkmark$) is used to represent explicit termination (signalized by *SKIP*).

In order to distinguish external and internal non-determinism, [5] proposed the failure semantics model, where traces were annotated with a set of *refusals*, i. e. sets of events a process can *not* engage in. This leads to the notion of a *failure* $(t,\ X) \in \mathcal{F}\ P$ which is a pair of a trace t and a set of refusals X. Consider for example the process $P = (a \rightarrow SKIP) \,\Box\, (a \rightarrow STOP)$. The traces $\mathcal{T}\ P$ will non-deterministically lead to a situation where the process accepts termination (but refuses everything else) or just refuses everything. So, if we assume $\Sigma = \{a,\ \checkmark\}$, then the traces $\mathcal{T}\ P$ will be $\{[],\ [a]\}$. The failures $\mathcal{F}\ P$ are then $\{([],\ \{\{\checkmark\}\}),\ ([a],\ \{\Sigma,\ \{a\}\})\}$ (plus all subsets of the respective refusal sets, which is required for the recursion ordering).

Finally, [5] enriched the semantic domain of CSP with one more element, the set of *divergences* (written $\mathcal{D}\ P$), in order to distinguish deadlocks from lifelocks.

CSP comes with a refinement notion: P refines Q iff P is more deterministic and more defined [36]. Depending on the semantic model, this results in the following formal definitions: the *trace refinement* is defined by $P \sqsubseteq_T Q \equiv \mathcal{T}\ P \supseteq \mathcal{T}\ Q$, and the *failures refinement* $\sqsubseteq_F$ and *failure-divergence refinement* $\sqsubseteq_{FD}$ are constructed analogously. It turns out that beyond common protocol refinement proofs and test-problems, many properties such as deadlock or lifelock freeness can be expressed via a refinement statement. This is also the case for the desired safety of autonomous vehicles.

2.3 Isabelle, HOL, and HOL-CSP

Isabelle is a major interactive proof assistant implementing higher-order logic (HOL). The Isabelle distribution comes with a number of library theories constructed solely from definitional axioms; among them basic data-types for sets, lists, arithmetics, analysis and - particularly relevant here - Scott domain theory (HOLCF) [33]. HOLCF provides the concept of a *complete partial ordering* -$\sqsubseteq$-, *continuity*, and *admissibility*, for the fixed-point induction principle. In particular, this gives semantics to the fixed-point $\mu\ X.\ f(X)$ verifying the property $(\mu\ X.\ f(X)) = f\ (\mu\ X.\ f(X))$. Basic key theorems of the HOL-CSP theory include the continuity of the CSP operators.

Of course, except in foundational proofs, the denotational semantics of HOL-CSP is not used directly: rather, about 200 rules derived from the denotational semantics are together with the fixpoint induction the weapons to reason 'algebraically' over infinite processes. Just for one example out of many, the basic synchronization rule looks as follows:

$$(\forall y.\ c\ y \in S) \Longrightarrow c?x \rightarrow P\ x\ [\![S]\!]\ c?x \rightarrow Q\ x = c?x \rightarrow (P\ x\ [\![S]\!]\ Q\ x)$$

The interested reader is referred to [36], or [40] for their formal proofs in HOL.

3 The Framework and its Rationale

In Fig. 1, we introduced the key-concepts of our framework: the *demon*, the *actors* with their *dynamics* captured in *motions* and the non-deterministic *driving-strategy*, a specification of an algorithm that computes the set of possible accelerations. In this section, we will explain in more detail the right part of Fig. 1: how these concepts were formalized in HOL-CSP, how they combine to a process architecturef, and the proof technique establishing non-collision in all possible scenarios.

3.1 Discretization and Decision Points: The Demon

Models for cyber-physical systems, be them time- or event-triggered, alltogether insist on a discretization of the timeline, on concrete decision points of the agents. This snapshot view of the system model is captured by a process that we call the 'Demon'[1]. This demon makes an arbitrary, non-deterministic and unilateral

[1] ... inspired by "Maxwell demon" of thermodynamics who knows everything.

choice of the time-step δt and forces individual actors to agree with each other's local physical state within a global state $\sigma_g \in \Sigma$ (also called the *scene*). The time-step δt is a strictly positive real, and is upper bound by the model parameter Δt, useful for forcing finer discretizations.

$$demon\ \Delta t \equiv \sqcap \delta t \in]0, \Delta t[\ \rightarrow \Box \sigma_g \in \Sigma \rightarrow demon\ \Delta t$$

3.2 An Extensible Model of Scenes

We formalize the basic *actor state* via the **record** construct, similar in Isabelle/HOL to its homonymous in other programming languages; the *actor state* contains fields for the position, the speed, and the acceleration of the agent.

Actor states are explicitly parameterized by the type variable $'\upsilon$ which is constrained by the type-class *real-normed-vector* (from the HOL library). This class provides a theory for vector spaces such as,e. g., $\mathbb{R}^n$, that possess a scalar product in $\mathbb{R}$. HOL also supports *extensible* records which allow to refine actor states at need. It is thus possible to give an actor an extension field, a set of possible accelerations, or a specific reaction time.

Repeated extensions allow for building up an actor family with different characteristics and specific elements in their local state.[2] We define the concept of a *global state* σ of the cyber-physical system (or *scene*) as a map from the set *actor identifiers* to the actor state space:

type-synonym $('\upsilon,'\alpha)\ scene = \langle id_{actor} \Rightarrow ('\upsilon,'\alpha)\ as_{ext} \rangle$

3.3 Formally Defining Actor Behaviour

We can now describe the definition from the introduction in more detail:

$$actor_{id}\ ds\ \sigma_g \equiv \Box \delta t \in \mathbb{R}_+ \rightarrow \Box \sigma'_g \in \{\Sigma \mid \Sigma[id] \in motion\} \rightarrow actor_{id}\ ds\ \sigma'_g$$

where a *motion* is constructed as a composition of the *driving strategy ds*, which computes a set of possible accelerations, and the *kinematics*, which translates this into the future actor states: $motion \equiv (kinematics\ (\sigma_g[id])\ \delta t) \circ (ds\ id\ \sigma_g)$. (Both driving strategies and kinematics will be discussed later in detail).

Actually, motions are a fairly general concept in our theory, which can be combined by a number of elementary operators to more complex *motions*:

type-synonym $('\upsilon,'\alpha) motion = time \Rightarrow ('\upsilon,'\alpha) scene \Rightarrow id_{actor} \Rightarrow ('\upsilon,'\alpha)\ as_{ext}$ *set*

[2] Such subclass hierarchies are used in common simulator technology in the autonomous car domain for the modeling of so-called "ontologies" for the actor states in, e. g., the MOSAR platform[3] or ASAM's OpenSCENARIO 2.0[4].

Recall that $'v$ are usually restricted to *real-normed-vector*'s and $'\alpha$ are the possible extensions of actor-states and therefore $('v,'\alpha)$ *scenes*. In particular, we optionally allow *motions* to produce the empty set of local states in order to delete impossible branches of the scenario (such as, for instance, not allowing an agent to react within its allowed time reaction – although this does not need to happen in the models presented in this paper).

3.4 Kinematics

Since the HOL-Analysis-library provides the theory for the derivation and integration operators, written *deriv* and *integrate*, it is perfectly possible to define the concept of a kinematics as the solution of a differential equation system:

$$SOME\ X.\ deriv\ X = F\ t\ X \wedge X(0) = X_0$$

where $SOME$ is the Hilbert choices operator that just returns a solution of a vector X of functions over a matrix F whenever it exists.

In the concrete application of our theory, i.e. the requirements stated in the ABZ case-study such as *no external forces* and *constant acceleration* in Δt, this leads to a kinematics that we call *standard kinematics*:

$$\begin{aligned} pos' &= pos + \delta t * speed + (\delta t^2/2) * a_0, \\ speed' &= speed + \delta t * a_0, \\ acc' &= a_0 \end{aligned}$$

Since the local physical state consists of a triple of the real-vector functions $(pos,speed,acc)$, then the future state $(pos',speed',acc')$ can be computed via the chosen constant acceleration a_0. The astute reader will recognize the usual Newtonian laws underlying the RSS driving strategy. We actually prove that these laws follow from the instantiation of the above concept of kinematics. Note, however, that it is perfectly possible to model accelerations like, e.g., air-resistance (depending on $speed^2$) or slopes (depending on pos) in our framework.

3.5 Actors and Demon Combined

Since any real positive value (smaller than Δt) can be non-deterministically chosen by the Demon for the time-step δt, all possible discretizations are considered. Different parameters correspond to different execution traces within a single *scenario*, i.e., a combined process that integrates Demon and actors.

Definition 1 (Scenario). *A scenario is defined as the parallel composition of the demon and actors, synchronized over scenes and timing choices:*

$$scenario\ ds\ \Delta t\ \sigma_0 \equiv (demon\ \Delta t\ ||\ (||\ id \in\#\ SID.\ actor_{id}\ ds\ \sigma_0))$$

This definition gives access to the usual process-algebraic definitions like "the set of traces" $\mathcal{T}(scenario\ ds\ \Delta t\ \sigma_0)$ or the theory over refinement.

3.6 Safety-Proofs by Refinement

Safety properties are a well-known class of trace properties (originating from concurrency theory), which can be described as sets of authorized traces [8]. For instance, in the case of autonomous vehicles, the 'non-collision' *safety property* can be described as the set of all traces that do not contain any collision, for any possible discretization of time (be aware that 'safety', in the general sense, may have a very different meaning than what is implied by a *safety property*, although in our case, 'non-collision' is indeed a *safety property*).

We abstract this notion of *safety properties* as a fully non-deterministic process, defined relative to subsets of actors, that can pick, at any step and for any δt, all possible scenes that do not contain collision (with no regard to any kinematics, driving strategy, or even any degree of spatial or physical consistency).

Definition 2 (Safety Process). *The safety process is recursively defined as:*

$$\textit{safety-process}\ P\ SID = \Box \delta t {\in} \mathbb{R} \rightarrow \Box \sigma_g \in (P\ \sigma_g\ SID) \rightarrow \textit{safety-process}\ P\ SID$$

A typical instance of P in our application scenario RSS is that the positions of actors are distinct, their extension fields do not overlap pairwise, etc. We instantiate the *safety property* P as the desired non-collision property.

Inclusion of trace properties and the ensuing lattice therefore translates to the refinement pre-order over safety processes. This motivates the following:

Definition 3 (Safe). *Safety of a scenario or a driving strategy can thus be described as a trace refinement over processes. More formally, we will define the concept safe-scenario by:*

$$\textit{safety-process}\ P\ sid \sqsubseteq_{DT} \textit{scenario motion}\ \Delta t\ g_0$$

Note that we restrict ourselves to the 'Divergence-Trace' pre-order over processes $\sqsubseteq_{DT}$ defined by $P \sqsubseteq_{DT} Q \equiv \ \mathcal{T}\ Q \subseteq \mathcal{T}\ P \wedge \mathcal{D}\ Q \subseteq \mathcal{D}\ P$. The reason for this is that the synchronization between *demon* and *actor*'s is inherently deadlocking: any global state where the actors did not agree represents a deadlock. This is the price we have to pay for the fact that the execution of *demons* represents some form of "true concurrency". However, agents can communicate along protocols with each other over own channels, which can be analysed with the full machinery of the failure divergence refinement ($\sqsubseteq_{FD}$).

The *safety-process*-predicate enjoys a number of useful properties such as monotonicities between them. In the context of the ABZ-Case-Study, the most relevant is the following theorem, which allows to break down a reasoning over refinements into the (more conventional) reasoning over state-invariants:

Theorem 1 (Safety Proof By Invariant). *Assuming the following holds:*

1. $P_{inv}\ \sigma_0\ sid$: *P_{inv} is true for the initial scene,*
2. $P_{inv}\ \sigma\ sid \Longrightarrow P\ \sigma\ sid$: *$P_{inv}$ implies the safety property we aim to prove,*

3. $P_{inv}\ \sigma\ sid \Longrightarrow \forall\, \sigma' \in move\text{-}sid\ \mathcal{M}\ \delta t\ \sigma\ sid.\ P_{inv}\ \sigma'\ sid$: *the invariant is preserved by any single motion step,*
4. and $sid \neq \emptyset$: *actors exist*

Then the resulting scenarios are P-safe: $safe\text{-}scenario\ P\ sid\ \mathcal{M}\ \Delta t\ \sigma_0$

4 A Safety Controller for Single Lane Scenarios

In this section, we will present our solution to the ABZ case study challenge [28], which focuses on designing a formally verified safety controller to prevent collisions in autonomous highway driving. The controller must ensure safety in both single-lane and multi-lane environments, functioning as an AI safety shield [1]. We focus on the single-lane scenario, demonstrating how our framework is particularly well-suited to the case study's requirements.

4.1 Safety Requirements and Assumptions

The ABZ case study challenge [28, Section 2.4], suggests the use of the Responsibility-Sensitive Safety (RSS) model [37] in order to provide a verified safety shield for autonomous vehicles, assuring the primary safety requirement of this case study: "All controlled vehicles must avoid collisions" (**SAF**).

The chosen set of parameters, assumptions, and vehicle behavior requirements align closely with the RSS safety distance and prescribed behavior for longitudinal single-lane scenarios, as defined in [37]. In Sect. 4.2, we will present an specialized version of our work [10], which satisfies the primary requirement **SAF**. Then, we will shift our focus to a secondary yet fundamental requirement stated in [28, Section 2.1]:

> *Note that the other vehicles also perform* [...] *actions, but at different times.*

In other words, we must account for the coexistence of multiple independent clocks – a requirement which is referred to as polychrony. Finally, we demonstrate how our formal model provides a verified safety shield for single-lane scenarios.

4.2 A First Safety Controller Formal Model

In this section, we will build upon the results presented in [10] to address the main safety requirement **SAF**: "All controlled vehicles must avoid collisions". As previously stated, our approach is grounded in the RSS model. It asserts that when vehicles follow the standard kinematics of piecewise constant acceleration motions, a minimal distance exists that guarantees collision-free safety. This principle serves as the foundation for designing our safety controller model.

Vehicles Requirements. [28, Section 2.1] defines the dimensioning requirements for the case study, including dynamics (*VEH3* to *VEH7*), and the response

```
locale ABZ_parameters =
  fixes a_max::‹nat⇒real› —‹This is ‹a_max› as defined in specification document.›
    and b_min::‹nat⇒real› —‹This is ‹b_min› as defined in specification document.›
    and b_max::‹nat⇒real› —‹This is ‹b_max› as defined in specification document.›
    and ρ::‹nat⇒real› —‹This is the boundary of the cycle time of the vehicle.›
    and N::nat —‹This is the number of vehicle in the scenario.›
  assumes a0:‹∀i∈{0..N}. 0 < a_max i› —‹‹a_max› is strictly positive›
    and a1:‹∀i∈{0..N}. b_min i > 0› —‹‹b_min› is strictly positive›
    and a2:‹∀i∈{0..N}. b_max i ≥ b_min i› and a2':‹∀i∈{0..<N}. b_max (i+1) ≥ b_min i›
—‹‹b_max› is strictly positive, it is needed to have ‹b_max› of other greater than ‹b_min› of ego›
    and a3:‹∀i∈{0..N}. ρ i > 0› —‹cycle time is strictly positive.›
    and a5:‹N > 0› —‹The number of vehicle is positive.›
```

Fig. 2. Formalization of the Vehicles Requirements

time of the controlled vehicle (*CON1*). In Isabelle/HOL, provides a mechanism for parameterized theories [21]. The parameters for our case study theory are shown here:

In Fig. 2, we capture most of the aforementioned dimensioning requirements, while adhering to the case study naming conventions. We will later instantiate the more general theorem proved in [10] in this locale, showcasing the modularity that locales bring to our framework.

Choosing a Safety Model. The RSS is our selected safety model because it is grounded in worst-case considerations ([37, Definition 1]: In this always achievable worst-case scenario, vehicles initially exactly distant by the RSS safety distance come to a stop with their separation reduced to zero. Thus, if the RSS driving strategy is not adhered to at any point, a collision will not necessarily occur in the actual continuation of the scenario; however, from that moment onward, an inevitable collision scenario can always be constructed based on the worst-case assumptions defined by RSS. In conclusion, deviations from the safety envelope established by the RSS driving strategy can be considered a definitive measure of unsafety.

RSS-Related Distances. We can now proceed to formalize the RSS distance-thresholds definitions (Fig. 3):

```
definition d_real:‹d_real car i ≡ pos(car (i+1)) - pos(car i)›

definition no_collision : ‹no_collision car sid ≡  ∀j∈{0..<N}. 0 < pos(car (j+1)) - pos(car j)›

definition d_rss:
‹d_rss car i ≡ [ρ i * speed (car i) + (((ρ i)²)/2) * a_max i +
                (speed (car i) + ρ i * a_max i)² / (2 * b_min i)
                - (speed (car (i+1)))² / (2 * b_max (i+1))]₊›

definition d_min:
‹d_min car i ≡ [(speed (car i))² /(2 * b_min i)-(speed (car (i+1)))²/(2 * b_max (i+1))]₊›
```

Fig. 3. Distance definitions in the RSS environment.

- d_{real} is the difference between the positions of two consecutive vehicles.
- d_{rss} is the RSS safe distance over which braking is not necessary [37].

- d_{min} is the required minimal distance at the end of the cycle time. This corresponds to the to the difference between the distances traveled by the two vehicles in case of braking until they come to a stop.
- $no\text{-}_{collision}$ expresses the safety criterion: the distance between consecutive vehicles remains strictly positive.

The Safety Controller. We define the kinematics of our vehicles as described in Sect. 3. The controller is formally defined as follows (Figs. 4 and 5):

```
definition driveRSS:
‹driveRSS i car ≡ if drss car i ≤ dreal car i
                then {-bmax i .. amax i}
                else {-bmax i .. -bmin i}›
```

Fig. 4. Formal model of the controller

```
definition standard_kinematics where
‹standard_kinematics δt car i a ≡
    if speed (car i) + (δt * a) > 0
    then car i ⦇pos:= pos (car i) + δt * speed (car i) + ((δt^2)/2) * a,
               speed := speed (car i) + (δt * a),
               acc := a⦈
    else car i ⦇pos := pos (car i) - (speed (car i))² / (2 * a),
               speed := 0,
               acc := a⦈›
```

Fig. 5. Standard kinematics

$drive_{RSS}$ is our driving strategy; it essentially serves as the controller of the vehicle. It must be interpreted as follows:

- If the vehicle is closer than d_{rss}, braking is enforced. The applied acceleration will be chosen non-deterministically within $\{-b_{max}\ i\ ..\ -b_{min}\ i\}$. This corresponds to the controller *SLOWER* action.
- Otherwise, we let the vehicle choose non-deterministically within $\{-b_{max}\ i\ ..\ a_{max}\ i\}$. Both *IDLE* and *FASTER* actions are encompassed within this choice, along with non required actions (negative accelerations): non-deterministic choice allows for simpler models by subsuming a broader range of behaviors without requiring additional proof effort.

Our goal is to determine the minimal condition for a scenario to evolve while remaining refined as a safety process (as defined in Definition 3).

A common formal method is to reason via invariant over the state of an evolving system as seen in Theorem 1 (Figs. 6 and 7):

```
definition Synchronousinv where
‹Synchronousinv car ≡ (∀i ≤ N. 0 ≤ speed (car i)) ∧ (∀i < N. dmin car i < dreal car i)›
```

Fig. 6. The synchronous safety invariant

```
locale Safe_Synchronized_scenario = ABZ_parameters +
  fixes car::"nat ⇒ real actor_state"
  assumes a: ‹(∀i∈{0..<N}. dmin car i < dreal car i) ∧(∀i∈{0..N}. 0 ≤ speed (car i))›
begin
```

Fig. 7. Locale Safe Sync, can be used as instantiation

We now aim at establishing that the scene defines a safe scenario regarding collision, as explained in Theorem 1. The property *safe-scenario* is a safety property that ensures that "something bad never happens" concerning the proposition $no\text{-}_{collision}$, meaning that no collision can occur, and thus satisfying **SAF**.

```
theorem rss_is_safe_N_cars:
  assumes b: ‹∀i∈{0..N}.0 < Δt ∧ Δt ≤ (ϱ i)›
    shows ‹safe_scenario (no_collision 0) (nat_fset N) (kinematicsfw (drivesafe ε')) Δt car›
```

Fig. 8. The refinement theorem

This generalizes a two-car scenario into a formal model involving N vehicles. The key idea of the proof is to show that the minimum distance d_{min} is preserved between successive vehicles when all follow the RSS driving strategy, which we establish in the following theorem:

The proofs of Figs. 8 and 9 are available at [9, Sections 4.1 4.2]

```
lemma d_min_2cars:
  fixes car' car::‹(real, 'α) scene› assumes cc:‹δt ≤ Δt›
    and  b: ‹0 < Δt ∧ Δt < ϱ i› and c:‹i∈{0..<N}› and d:‹ 0 ≤ speed (car i)›
    and e:‹0 ≤ speed (car (i+1))› and f:‹dmin car i < dreal car i› and g:‹ 0 < δt›
    and imp:‹ (car' i) ∈ (standard_kinematics δt car i) ` (driveRSS i car)›
    and imp2:‹ (car' (i+1)) ∈(standard_kinematics δt car (i+1)) ` (accrange (i+1))›
  shows ‹dmin car' i < dreal car' i›
```

Fig. 9. The preservation of d_{min} through time.

The technical aspect of demonstrating theorem 8 is to show that if the invariant holds at initialization, it still holds after evolving the physical state of the agents. The challenging is ensuring that the safety distances are maintained within a given time step, which is precisely what 9 establishes.

By proving this, we validate Theorem 8 and guarantee that the safety condition **SAF** is satisfied.

Numerical Application. The locale environment allows us to simulate simple scenarios. As an example, we can analyze what happens when two vehicles travel at 130 km/h with parameters *VEH3-VEH7*, as described in [28, Section 2.1] (Fig. 10).

```
locale VEH_ENV_130_KMH =
  fixes car::‹nat⇒real actor_state› and amax bmin bmax ϱ::‹nat⇒real› and N::nat
  assumes pos_car_0:‹pos(car 0) = 0› —‹Position of car 0 is 0›
    and speed_car_0:‹speed (car 0) = 36› —‹Speed is ‹36 m.s-1› or ‹130km.h-1››
    and pos_car_1:‹pos(car 1) = 144› —‹Position of car 1 is 144 meters away from car 0›
    and speed_car_1:‹speed (car 1) = 28›
    and bmax:‹bmax i ≡ 5› and bmin:‹bmin i ≡ 3› and amax:‹amax i ≡ 5› and ϱ:‹ϱ i ≡ 1› and N:‹N≡1›
```

Fig. 10. An example for vehicles going at 36 m.s^{-1}

We compiled some relevant data from our calculations over safe distances in the following tables:

Table 1. Safe distances at initialization - *CON1-ENV*

Ego ↓ Other→	50 ($km.h^{-1}$)	100 ($km.h^{-1}$)	130 ($km.h^{-1}$)
50	20 m	6 m	6 m
100	117.5 m	60 m	7.1 m
130	203 m	144 m	92.5 m

Table 2. Safe distance at initialization

cycle time↓ speed→	50 $km.h^{-1}$	100 $km.h^{-1}$	130 $km.h^{-1}$
0.5 (s)	20 m	60 m	92.5 m
1 (s) - *CON1-ENV*	20 m	60 m	92.5 m
1.5 (s)	20 m	60 m	92.5 m

In Table 1, we observe that the safe distance strongly depends on the speed of both vehicles. The distance evolves intuitively: the faster the ego vehicle is, the larger the safe distance becomes, while the faster the front vehicle is, the smaller the safe distance gets.

In Table 2, we see that the cycle time has no effect on safe distances. This suggests that the model is not sufficiently realistic, as both intuition and mathematical analysis indicate that the safe distance for a car making decisions ten times per second should differ from that of a car making decisions once per second. This limitation motivates an improvement to our model, leading us to the next version that we will now introduce.

4.3 A Refined Safety Controller: Achieving Polychrony

In this section, we introduce a polychronous time-triggered scenario for autonomous cars. This approach considers autonomous cars as systems that complete a full sense-plan-act sequence within the constraints of a fixed periodic cycle. Our model does not require these cycles to be aligned, making it inherently polychronous [42,43].

```
record ('v::real_normed_vector) as_polychronous =
  ‹'v actor_state› +
  deadline  ::real
  cycle_time::real
```

Fig. 11. Extending *actor-state* record with time parameters

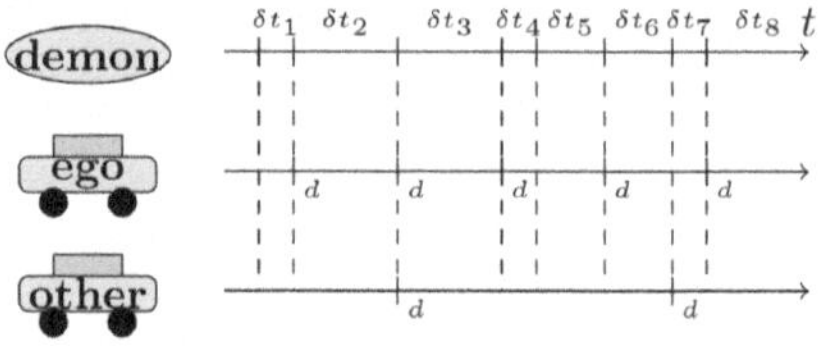

Fig. 12. A polychronous scenario.

In order to be able to model time we add the parameters 11 to the cars.

In the synchronized scenario described in Sect. 4, actors were required to make a decision after every δt elapsed. In contrast, in this scenario, actors are expected to make decisions only when they have reached the end of their *cycle-time*, indicated by their *deadline* reaching 0. This removes the restrictive assumption that actors are synchronized at every new time interval defined by the demon, as illustrated in Fig. 12. The primary objective of this analysis is to demonstrate that the corresponding driving strategy continues to ensure car safety (Fig. 13).

```
definition k0_async:
  ‹polychronous_kinematicsRSS ℳ δt car i ≡
   if (some_deadline_will_be_missed δt car)
   then {}
   else update_deadline δt `
        (standard_kinematics δt car i ` ℳ i car)›
```

(a) Polychronous kinematic

```
definition r0_async:
  ‹polychronous_driveRSS i car ≡
    if deadline (car i) = 0
    then driveRSS i car
    else {acc (car i)}›
```

(b) Polychronous driving strategy

Fig. 13. Polychronous driving strategy

- *polychronous-drive$_{RSS}$* is the new controller, our polychronous driving strategy:
  - If the vehicle is at deadline, it selects an acceleration based on the driving strategy, using the controller defined in the previous section Sect. 4.1.
  - If the vehicle has not yet reached its deadline, it continues with the last chosen acceleration, as given by the function *acc* (*car i*).
- *polychronous-kinematics* is the function that describes the movement of the vehicle:
  - If a deadline is missed, it returns an empty scene[5].
  - Then, it applies the kinematics function to a driving strategy $\mathcal{M}$, which, in this case, is specifically *polychronous-drive$_{RSS}$*.
  - It also updates the actor's deadline using the *update-deadline* function, which computes *deadline* (*car i*) = *deadline* (*car i*) − δt if *deadline* $\neq 0$, or *cycle-time* (*car i*) − δt otherwise. This modeling approach satisfies requirement *CON1*, as it accommodates varying *cycle-time* values, enabling vehicles to respond at their own pace.

The Invariant

```
definition Poly_inv where
‹Poly_inv car ≡ (∀i ≤ N. 0 ≤ speed (car i)) ∧ (∀i < N. dmin car i < dreal car i)
∧(∀i<N. deadline (car i) ≠ 0 ⟶ (∀t∈{0<..deadline(car i)}.
  pos (standard_kinematics t car (i+1) (-amaxbrake (i+1)))
  - pos (standard_kinematics t car i (acc (car i))) >
  [(speed (standard_kinematics t car i (acc(car i))))² / (2 * aminbrake i)
  - (speed (standard_kinematics t car (i+1) (-amaxbrake (i+1))))² / (2 * amaxbrake (i+1))]+))
∧ (∀i∈{0..N}. 0 ≤ deadline (car i) ∧ deadline (car i) < cycle_time (car i)
∧ cycle_time (car i) > 0   ∧ cycle_time (car i) < ϱ i) ∧ (∀i∈{0..N}. acc(car i) ∈ accrange i)›
```

Fig. 14. The safety invariant for polychronous model

- *deadline* (*car i*) $\neq 0$: If the deadline is 0, the model falls back into the synchronous case (Fig. 14).
- *standard-kinematics t car* $(i+1)$ b_{max}: This accounts for the worst-case scenario where other is braking at maximum capacity.
- *standard-kinematics t car i* (*acc* (*car i*)): The state of ego at time t.

[5] such cases are not treated in our analysis.

- The right-hand side of the inequality is d_{real} but its definition is unfolded.
- The left-hand side of the inequality is d_{min} but its definition is unfolded. Ultimately, this states that $d_{min} < d_{real}$ for the remaining time until the deadline. The synchronous model already implied this property but did not formalize it due to the absence of clock management.

A polychronous locale that gathers *ABZ-parameters* and time-related definitions is defined, and the following locale inherits from it while asserting that *Poly-inv* holds (Fig. 15).

```
locale SAFE_Poly_scenario = RSS_Ncars_polychronous_longitudinal +
  fixes car::‹nat ⇒ (real, 'α) as_polychronous_scheme›
  assumes a: ‹Poly_inv car›
```

Fig. 15. The locale for polychronous case

This provides the appropriate context to prove the polychronous scenario safety theorem which also satisfies the **SAF** requirement.

```
theorem RSS_polychronous_is_safe:
  assumes b: ‹∀i∈{0..N}.0 < Δt ∧ Δt < (ϱ i)›
  shows ‹safe_scenario no_collision (N vehicles)
                   (polychronous_kinematicsRSS polychronous_driveRSS) Δt car›
```

Fig. 16. The safety theorem for polychronous case

The proofs of 16 is available at [9, Sections 5.1]

Since our invariant relies only on the ego vehicle's parameters (other's parameters are generic, such as b_{max}), we can conclude that the safe distance depends only on the ego vehicle's cycle time. This is a key aspect of our model, as it is more realistic to assume that vehicles do not have knowledge of other vehicle's cycle times. Our model does not require this information, making it more aligned with real-world expectations.

Numerical Application. Our goal is to compare 2 from the previous section with the results obtained using our new model. We replaced cycle time with deadline in the table, as it is actually this parameter that matters (Table 3).[6]

[6] A deadline of 1.5 s implies that the cycle time is at least 1.5 s, since the deadline cannot exceed the cycle time.

Table 3. Safe distance at initialization, depending on speed and cycle times

deadline ↓ speed →	50 ($km.h^{-1}$)	100 ($km.h^{-1}$)	130 ($km.h^{-1}$)
0 (s)	20 m	60 m	92.5 m
0.5 (s)	40 m	98 m	148 m
1 (s) - *CON1-ENV*	64 m	140 m	196 m
1.5 (s)	91 m	186 m	252 m

This time, we can observe that the safe distance varies with the deadline, and therefore the cycle time, as the cycle time is the maximum value the deadline can take. Allowing a cycle time of 0.5 s caps the safe distance to 148 m at 36 m/s, whereas allowing a cycle time of 1.5 s caps it to 252 m[7].

Finally, we can see that if the deadline is equal to 0, we return to the values seen in 1, which tends to verify that our polychronous model is consistent with our synchronous model. In fact, our synchronous model is a specific case of the polychronous model, where the deadline is always 0 and actors must react every time they are state-checked. In contrast, in the polychronous case, this is not necessary. However, we did not add anything beyond a "clock manager", and thus our model was already "polychrony-ready".

5 Simulation and Evaluation

The case study specifications included the configuration of a simulation environment [27], designed for experimenting with the safety shield. This environment builds upon the highway-env reinforcement learning framework [26], which was specifically created to train and test autonomous vehicle agents within a simplified yet representative model of the environment of road vehicles.

We implemented the safety shield as a straightforward method call, overriding the model's returned action whenever it deviates from the behavior prescribed by RSS. The implementation and documentation are available in our fork of the case study GitHub repository [29].

Table 4. Comparison of different agents performance

	Crashes (%)	Unsafe steps (%)	Min. net safe d. (m)	Travelled d. (m)
Base	0	65.1	−13.4	614
Base + shield	0	0	0.77	575
Adv.	100	0	N/A	273
Adv. + shield	0	0	0.77	575

[7] These values are rounded.

The data in Table 4 were obtained through:

- 100 test runs, each consisting of 30 steps per agent configuration.
- Two types of agent models: both are rewarded for high speed, with *Base* penalized for collisions, while *Adversarial* is rewarded.
- Computed metrics: percentage of runs ending in a crash, percentage of unsafe steps, minimum achieved safe net distance (both explained below), and average traveled distance per run.

Unsafe steps account for deviations from the RSS safety envelope, which serves as a reliable measure of unsafety, as explained in Sect. 4.2.

The "safe net distance" ($d_{real} - d_{min}$) represents the remaining distance after both the ego and front vehicles brake to a complete stop. Its minimum value indicates the most hazardous situation the ego vehicle encountered, with negative values signaling a potential crash.

The measurements indicate that:

- The *Base* agent, while never crashing, frequently places the ego vehicle at risk.
- The *Base* agent with the shield never puts the ego vehicle at risk. The minimum achieved safe net distance (77 cm) suggests that the RSS safety distance is not overly conservative, at least within this simulation. Additionally, it attains 94% of the distance covered by its unshielded counterpart.
- The *Adversarial* agent, as expected, performs poorly in all aspects, including traveled distance.
- Notably, when the shield is activated, the *Adversarial* agent achieves performance comparable to the *Base* agent with the shield.

Table 5. The *Base* agent vs. Aggressive vehicles

	Crashes (%)	Unsafe steps (%)	Min. net safe d. (m)	Travelled d. (m)
Base	65	51.5	−16.9	356
Base + shield	0	0	0.47	478

The data in Table 5 were obtained by evaluating the *Base* agent against a different behavior of surrounding vehicles, using the *AggressiveVehicle* class.

The results further support the idea that the risk identified in the initial experiments (negative values of the "net safe distance") can materialize in practice but can also be compensated by the RSS safety shield.

6 Related Work

There are numerous approaches to model and analyse CPSs in general, and autonomous vehicles in particular, from simulation-based approaches to model-checking approaches, for which tools include [2,14,15,20], or more recently [7,

13,23] (see [18] for a survey). Proof-based approaches, similar to ours, include Differential Hoare Logics [12], also using Isabelle/HOL, but being *event-triggered* rather than *time-triggered* as we are; Event-B and the Rodin platform have also been proposed to formalize CPSs as abstract machines [6,11,38]. Last but not least, Platzer [4,35] uses a version of Differential Hoare Logics to implement the specialized KeyMaera and KeyMaera X systems. As for car control and collision avoidance specifically, existing approaches include discrete time point based temporal logics and discrete time automata [3,31]; reachable sets in ODE's [22,32]; RSS is also tackled from a testing perspective in [19]; lastly, [30] treats the problem of distributed car control system.

These approaches each have their advantages and drawbacks. While a lot of these are more tractable than formal proofs, they are limited by complexity barriers, and necessitate important and often ad-hoc abstractions. On the other hand, our approach allows us to cover the *complete* set of possible scenarios; computations are made symbolically on mathematical real numbers; we also profit from (and contribute back to) the open platform Isabelle/HOL and its fairly extensive libraries in the Isabelle Archive of Formal Proofs, in particular $HOL\!-\!Analysis$, and its ODE formalization. Because it is time-triggered, it is more directly implementable (contrary to event-based models). Lastly, our use of CSP would make it possible to model communications between actors, reusing the vast literature on CSP processes and its implementation in $Isabelle$ [41].

7 Conclusion

In this paper, we introduced a framework for CPS based on a process algebraic modeling, instantiated it on scenarios for autonomous vehicles, meeting the requirements specified in [28]. We refined the abstract concept of a driving strategy to a concrete controller satisfying the safety property **SAF**, based on RSS, and also considered an extension to polychrony. We provided formal proof that requirements **CON1** and **CON1-ENV** are satisfied, and injected the resulting code by hand into the Single-Lane highway environment given by the ABZ case study challenge. Our evaluations allow for the following conclusions: Firstly we observe that our model is roughly coherent with conventional driving regulations, however they predict larger safety distances as prescribed by law. The good news is that our derived controller is an effective watchdog that avoids collision even in the presence of extremely aggressive actors, while still preserving liveness. Secondly, while polychrony is a relevant phenomenon in a realistic system, its impact is small. In this sense our study yields evidence that we have a controller that is closer to reality. Thirdly, the instantiation by Isabelle/HOL locales creates a relatively easy interface to study the impact of model parameters changes.

As future work, we envision the following directions:

- Prove the safety of the RSS driving strategy in two (or more) dimensional scenarios, including multi-lanes and cutoffs.

- Answer the criticism raised in [24], exploring more flexible driving strategies.
- Utilize the IsabelleVODEs [34] environment to support advanced kinematics described by elaborate systems of ODEs.

Acknowledgements. This work has been supported by the French government under the "France 2030" program, as part of the SystemX Technological Research Institute.

References

1. Alshiekh, M., Bloem, R., Ehlers, R., Könighofer, B., Niekum, S., Topcu, U.: Safe Reinforcement Learning via Shielding. AAAI Press (2018) https://doi.org/10.1609/aaai.v32i1.11797
2. Asarin, E., Dang, T., Maler, O.: The D/DT tool for verification of hybrid systems (2002)
3. Bannour, B., Niol, J., Crisafulli, P.: Symbolic model-based design and generation of logical scenarios for autonomous vehicles validation. In: IEEE Intelligent Vehicles Symposium, IV 2021, Nagoya, Japan, 11–17 July 2021, pp. 215–222. IEEE (2021). https://doi.org/10.1109/IV48863.2021.9575528
4. Beckert, B., Platzer, A.: Dynamic logic with non-rigid functions. In: Furbach, U., Shankar, N. (eds.) IJCAR 2006. LNCS (LNAI), vol. 4130, pp. 266–280. Springer, Heidelberg (2006). https://doi.org/10.1007/11814771_23
5. Brookes, S.D., Hoare, C., Roscoe, A.W.: A theory of communicating sequential processes. J. ACM **31**(3), 560–599 (1984)
6. Butler, M.J., Abrial, J., Banach, R.: . https://doi.org/10.1201/b20053-5
7. Chen, X., Ábrahám, E., Sankaranarayanan, S.: Flow*: an analyzer for non-linear hybrid systems (2013)
8. Clarkson, M.R., Schneider, F.B.: Hyperproperties. J. Comput. Secur. **18**(6), 1157–1210 (2010). https://doi.org/10.3233/JCS-2009-0393
9. Crisafulli, P., Durier, A., Puyobro, B., Wolff, B.: HOL-CyberPhi: a process-algebraic framework for cyber-physical systems. Technical report, IRT SystemX; LMF - Laboratoire Méthodes Formelles (2024). https://hal.science/hal-04803841
10. Crisafulli, P., Taha, S., Wolff, B.: Modeling and analysing cyber-physical systems in HOL-CSP. Robot. Auton. Syst. **170**, 104549 (2023) https://doi.org/10.1016/J.ROBOT.2023.104549
11. Dupont, G., Ameur, Y.A., Singh, N.K., Pantel, M.: Formally verified architectural patterns of hybrid systems using proof and refinement with Event-B. Sci. Comput. Program. **216**, 102765 (2022) https://doi.org/10.1016/j.scico.2021.102765
12. Foster, S., Huerta y Munive, J.J., Struth, G.: Differential hoare logics and refinement calculi for hybrid systems with Isabelle/HOL. In: Fahrenberg, U., Jipsen, P., Winter, M. (eds.) RAMiCS 2020. LNCS, vol. 12062, pp. 169–186. Springer, Cham (2020). https://doi.org/10.1007/978-3-030-43520-2_11
13. Fränzle, M., Herde, C., Teige, T., Ratschan, S., Schubert, T.: Efficient solving of large non-linear arithmetic constraint systems with complex Boolean structure. J. Satisf. Boolean Model. Comput. **1**(3–4), 209–236 (2007). https://doi.org/10.3233/sat190012
14. Frehse, G.: PHAVer: algorithmic verification of hybrid systems past HyTech. **10**(3), 263–279 (2008). https://doi.org/10.1007/s10009-007-0062-x

15. Frehse, G., et al.: SpaceEx: scalable verification of hybrid systems. LNCS. Springer (2011)
16. Gamatié, A., Gautier, T., Le Guernic, P., Talpin, J.P.: Polychronous design of embedded real-time applications (2007). https://doi.org/10.1145/1217295.1217298
17. Gautier, T., Le Guernic, P., Talpin, J.P.: Polychronous design of real-time applications with signal (2008). https://hal.science/hal-00549814. aRTIST Survey of Programming Languages, Alan Burns, Ed. http://www.artist-embedded.org/artist/ARTIST-Survey-of-Programming,1489.html
18. Geretti, L., et al.: ARCH-COMP22 category report: continuous and hybrid systems with nonlinear dynamics. EasyChair (2022). https://doi.org/10.29007/fnzc, https://easychair.org/publications/paper/JrQ4
19. Hekmatnejad, M., Hoxha, B., Fainekos, G.: Search-based test-case generation by monitoring responsibility safety rules (2020). https://doi.org/10.48550/ARXIV.2005.00326, https://arxiv.org/abs/2005.00326
20. Henzinger, T.A., Ho, P.H., Wong-Toi, H.: HyTech: a model checker for hybrid systems (1997)
21. Kammüller, F., Wenzel, M., Paulson, L.C.: Locales a sectioning concept for Isabelle (1999)
22. Kochdumper, N., Gassert, P., Althoff, M.: Verification of collision avoidance for commonroad traffic scenarios. EasyChair (2021). https://doi.org/10.29007/1973
23. Kong, S., Gao, S., Chen, W., Clarke, E.: dReach: δ-reachability analysis for hybrid systems (2015)
24. Koopman, P., Osyk, B., Weast, J.: Autonomous vehicles meet the physical world: RSS, variability, uncertainty, and proving safety (expanded version) (2019). https://arxiv.org/abs/1911.01207
25. Le Guernic, P., Gautier, T., Talpin, J.P., Besnard, L.: Polychronous Automata (2015). https://doi.org/10.1109/TASE.2015.21, https://hal.science/hal-01240440
26. Leurent, E.: An environment for autonomous driving decision-making (2018). https://github.com/eleurent/highway-env. GitHub repository
27. Leuschel, M., Vu, F., Rutenkolk, K.: ABZ 2025 Case Study: Training and testing of agents (2024). https://github.com/hhu-stups/abz2025_casestudy_autonomous_driving. GitHub repository
28. Leuschel, M., Vu, F., Rutenkolk, K.: Case study: safety controller for autonomous driving on highways. Technical report. Heinrich-Heine-Universität Düsseldorf, Institute of Computer Science (2025). https://github.com/hhu-stups/abz2025_casestudy_autonomous_driving/blob/main/case_study/specification_v3.pdf
29. Leuschel, M., Vu, F., Rutenkolk, K., Crisafulli, P.: ABZ 2025 Case Study: training and testing of agents (2024). https://github.com/paolo-crisafulli/abz2025_casestudy_autonomous_driving. GitHub repository
30. Loos, S.M., Platzer, A., Nistor, L.: Adaptive cruise control: hybrid, distributed, and now formally verified. In: Butler, M., Schulte, W. (eds.) FM 2011. LNCS, vol. 6664, pp. 42–56. Springer, Heidelberg (2011). https://doi.org/10.1007/978-3-642-21437-0_6
31. Maierhofer, S., Moosbrugger, P., Althoff, M.: Formalization of intersection traffic rules in temporal logic. IEEE (2022). https://doi.org/10.1109/IV51971.2022.9827153
32. Manzinger, S., Pek, C., Althoff, M.: Using reachable sets for trajectory planning of automated vehicles. IEEE Trans. Intell. Veh. **6**(2), 232–248 (2021). https://doi.org/10.1109/TIV.2020.3017342
33. Müller, O., Nipkow, T., von Oheimb, D., Slotosch, O.: HOLCF = HOL + LCF. J-FP **9**(2), 191–223 (1999). https://doi.org/10.1017/S095679689900341X

34. y Munive, J.J.H., Foster, S., Gleirscher, M., Struth, G., Laursen, C.P., Hickman, T.: IsaVODEs: interactive verification of cyber-physical systems at scale. J. Autom. Reason. **68**, 21 (2024). https://api.semanticscholar.org/CorpusID:273492134
35. Platzer, A.: Logical Foundations of Cyber-Physical Systems. Springer, Cham (2018). https://doi.org/10.1007/978-3-319-63588-0
36. Roscoe, A.: Theory and Practice of Concurrency. Prentice Hall (1997)
37. Shalev-Shwartz, S., Shammah, S., Shashua, A.: On a formal model of safe and scalable self-driving cars. arXiv e-prints arXiv:1708.06374 (2017)
38. Su, W., Abrial, J., Zhu, H.: Formalizing hybrid systems with Event-B and the Rodin platform. Sci. Comput. Program. **94**, 164–202 (2014). https://doi.org/10.1016/j.scico.2014.04.015
39. Taha, S., Wolff, B., Ye, L.: The HOL-CSP refinement toolkit. Arch. Formal Proofs **2020** (2020). https://www.isa-afp.org/entries/CSP_RefTK.html
40. Taha, S., Ye, L., Wolff, B.: HOL-CSP version 2.0. Archive of Formal Proofs (2019). http://isa-afp.org/entries/HOL-CSP.html
41. Taha, S., Wolff, B., Ye, L.: Philosophers may dine - definitively! In: Dongol, B., Troubitsyna, E. (eds.) IFM 2020. LNCS, vol. 12546, pp. 419–439. Springer, Cham (2020). https://doi.org/10.1007/978-3-030-63461-2_23
42. Nguyen Van, H., Balabonski, T., Boulanger, F., Keller, C., Valiron, B., Wolff, B.: On the semantics of polychronous polytimed specifications. In: Bertrand, N., Jansen, N. (eds.) FORMATS 2020. LNCS, vol. 12288, pp. 23–40. Springer, Cham (2020). https://doi.org/10.1007/978-3-030-57628-8_2
43. Van, H.N., Boulanger, F., Wolff, B.: TESL: a model with metric time for modeling and simulation. Schloss Dagstuhl-Leibniz-Zentrum für Informatik (2020). https://doi.org/10.4230/LIPIcs.TIME.2020.15, https://drops.dagstuhl.de/opus/volltexte/2020/12983

On The Road Again (Safely): Modelling and Analysis of Autonomous Driving with STARK

Sebastián Betancourt(✉) and Valentina Castiglioni

Eindhoven University of Technology, Eindhoven, The Netherlands
j.s.betancourt.arias@tue.nl

Abstract. STARK has been introduced for the specification, analysis and verification of cyber-physical systems operating under uncertainty. In this paper, we apply it to the modelling and safety analysis of several instances of a highway environment with autonomous vehicles: One vehicle will be controlled by a STARK agent, while the others are modelled as part of a STARK environment. Given the unpredictable behaviour of the environment, we analyse some safety guarantees on the behaviour of the agent in terms of its robustness against perturbations by means of the temporal logic RobTL and statistical model checking. We then discuss the use of STARK for the validation of the behaviour of reinforcement learning agents in the highway environment with the temporal logic DisTL.

1 Introduction

Human error is the main cause of accidents on the road: several physical and psychological factors (such as high speed, impairing substances, stress, and fatigue) can alter the driver's perception of the environment and invalidate their ability to react promptly and correctly to events. For this reason, since the mid-1980s, researchers have been studying and developing *autonomous driving systems* (ADS) that can support drivers and reduce the number of accidents. As an outcome, the majority of drivers can nowadays benefit from the assistance of a number of devices, like ABS, parking and lane assistants, cruise controllers, etc. In this setting, the driver still needs to ensure the safe behaviour of the vehicle, as those devices are only meant to support them. The advent of new technologies, such as learning methods and artificial intelligence, has raised expectations about autonomous vehicles: The goal is now to develop an ADS that can replace the driver [1,21].

There are numerous challenges to overcome before we can achieve such a goal, ranging from liability [15] to the integration of numerous heterogeneous devices [2]. From the point of view of formal methods, the main challenge is to provide the means to guarantee the correctness and safety of the ADS before they can be deployed. Specifically, we need to develop verification techniques that allow us to deal with the unpredictable and uncontrollable behaviour of the environment in which the system is deployed. Despite the wealth of methodologies and tools that can be found in the literature for verification of safety-critical systems, autonomous vehicles are still involved in several accidents that are caused by faulty decisions taken by their controllers. These

M. Leuschel and F. Ishikawa (Eds.): ABZ 2025, LNCS 15728, pp. 269–287, 2026.
https://doi.org/10.1007/978-3-031-94533-5_16

Table 1. Parameters for vehicles.

Physical parameter	Value	Unit	Action	Value
$v_{\max}$	40	m/s^2	FASTER	1.0
$a_{\max}$	5.0	m/s^2	IDLE	0.0
$b_{\max}$	5.0	m/s^2	SLOWER	−1.0
$b_{\min}$	3.0	m/s^2	LANE_LEFT	1.0
l	5.0	m	LANE_RIGHT	−1.0
w	2.0	m		
TIMER	t	s		

can be due to altered sensing due to adverse weather conditions [31], training data that do not cover rare events [10], delays in communication between all components of the vehicle [19], sensor and actuator failures [20], etc.

Therefore, it is fundamental to provide the tools for verifying *robustness* of an ADS against uncertainty and perturbations [11,12,17,22,24,29].

In this paper, we use the case study proposal from [18] on autonomous driving on the highway environment from [16], to show how we can use the STARK tool [9] to analyse the robustness of ADS against perturbations.

STARK has been initially developed for the specification, analysis, and verification of robustness properties of cyber-physical systems operating under uncertainty, but has also seen some recent successful applications in the analysis of digital twins [3] and biological systems [7]. Moreover, in [4,6,9] the tool has been applied to study various ADS case studies: obstacle avoidance with one [9] or two [6] autonomous vehicles, and a control system that assists the driver in reaching a tollbooth [4].

We note that STARK is a tool for testing and verifying systems, rather than their design. Hence, our approach is meant to be complementary to controller synthesis. For this reason, in this paper we will not discuss safe design principles for controllers but provide a quantification of safety guarantees on their behaviour expressed in terms of their robustness against perturbations. These are obtained through formal verification of the requirements in *Robustness Temporal Logic* (RobTL) [8] and in *Distribution Temporal Logic* (DisTL) [4]. Specifically, we will consider four instances of the proposed highway environment. In all of those, we consider a single controlled vehicle with one or more uncontrolled ones, the difference being that we model the controller of the former, whereas the latter vehicles are modelled within the environment. We will then use RobTL to analyse the robustness of the controlled vehicles in the following scenarios: 1. Single lane with one uncontrolled vehicle; 2. Single lane with two uncontrolled vehicles; 3. Two lanes with one uncontrolled vehicle. As a fourth case study, we use RobTL and DisTL to validate the controller of a reinforcement learning agent in a three-lane highway environment with several uncontrolled vehicles.

2 Autonomous Driving on Highways

In this section, we summarise the design and specification requirements for the highway environment from [16,18]. All vehicles move in a 2D plane that consists of a straight highway with one or more lanes. There are no obstacles on the road and all the vehicles are moving in the same direction. We assume that each vehicle has access to the positions and speed of all other vehicles, and we abstract away from the perception system acquiring this information. The only distinguishing feature of vehicles is whether they are controlled or not. They are identical in all physical aspects: they are l metres long and w meters wide; their speed range is $[0, v_{\max}]$ m/s, which means they cannot move backward, and the acceleration range is $[0, a_{\max}]$ m/s^2 if the vehicle is not moving; otherwise, the range is $[-b_{\max}, a_{\max}]$ m/s^2. Specifically, when braking, the acceleration range is in $[-b_{\max}, -b_{\min}]$ m/s^2, since a minimum deceleration of $b_{\min}$ m/s^2 is guaranteed. The values of these parameters, taken mainly from [16, 18], are reported in Table 1. In addition, all vehicles are characterised by a *cycle*, or `TIMER`, expressing the frequency at which they can observe the environment and make decisions on which action to take until the next cycle. In all scenarios, and thus regardless of the number of lanes, vehicles can choose among the following three actions:

- `FASTER`: This action increases the speed up to $v_{\max}$ with an acceleration *up to* $a_{\max}$. If the car speed is $v_{\max}$, the acceleration is 0.
- `SLOWER`: This action decreases speed with a braking deceleration *between* $b_{\min}$ and $b_{\max}$. If the car speed is 0, the braking deceleration is 0.
- `IDLE`: This action sets the current (braking) acceleration *close to* 0, that is, between $[-\Delta_{idle}, \Delta_{idle}]$, for some small $\Delta_{idle} > 0$.

We note that the choice of an action does not guarantee a determined value of acceleration. We will show how this uncertainty can be easily modelled in STARK.

When a multilane scenario is considered, the number of lanes does not change over time, and in each cycle, the vehicles can decide to take action `FASTER`, `SLOWER`, `IDLE`, or to change lanes by means of actions:

- `LANE_LEFT`: This action sets the acceleration to `IDLE`, and changes the current lane of the vehicle to the lane directly left of it within the current cycle.
- `LANE_RIGHT`: This action sets the acceleration to `IDLE`, and changes the current lane of the vehicle to the lane directly to the right of it within the current cycle.

Actions `LANE_LEFT` and `LANE_RIGHT` are automatically performed by a steering controller, managing the operational details of the lane change that are abstracted away.

We note that the `TIMER` of the vehicles are not necessarily synchronised. Hence, although all vehicles can observe the environment at the same frequency, they can make decisions and move between lanes, at different moments.

Safety Requirements. The principal safety requirement, over which we will focus our analysis in the paper, is collision avoidance.

SAF. *All vehicles must avoid collisions.*

SAF can be achieved by maintaining a safety distance. On a single lane, the *Responsibility-Sensitive Safety* (RSS) model [23] defines the safety distance between a rear and a front vehicle, with speed v_r and v_f respectively, both having response time σ, as:

$$\text{RSSgap}(\sigma, v_r, v_f) = \max\left\{0, \sigma \cdot v_r + \frac{a_{\max}}{2}\sigma^2 + \frac{(v_r + \sigma \cdot a_{\max})^2}{2b_{\min}} - \frac{v_f^2}{2b_{\max}}\right\} \tag{1}$$

In the multi-lane environment we will combine RSS with other requirements based on safety rules and common sense (see Sect. 5 for a detailed discussion). Specifically, we will check whether the controlled vehicle adheres to the following requirements:

R2L *A vehicle in the rightmost (respectively, leftmost) lane cannot perform action* `LANE_RIGHT` *(respectively,* `LANE_LEFT`*).*
KIR *Always occupy the rightmost free lane.*
SO *Overtake only when it safe to do so.*

The main objective of our analysis will be to study *robustness* of such a safe controller against unexpected events. The scripts for the case studies are available at https://github.com/quasylab/jspear/blob/ABZ_2025/examples/ABZ2025/.

Remark 1. According to the design requirements, the response time σ in (1) is equal to the duration of a cycle, and in the models we use the parameter `TIMER` to represent both. The issue is to find a suitable value for it: in fact, one requirement is that lane changes are completed within a cycle. In real life, the frequency with which a controller can react to the environment and the time required to safely change lane are incomparable (on the order of milliseconds [13] versus seconds [25]). Therefore, we had two possibilities: either to adhere to the standard frequency of controllers and accept to have vehicles almost teleporting from one lane to another, or to follow a more realistic kinematic model and work with slower than human controllers. We opted for the latter option because we find it more insightful from the point of view of safety analysis (if a slower controller is robust, so is a faster one). Hence, in our case studies `TIMER` is a natural number $t \geq 1$.

Remark 2. Given the strong dependency on initial conditions and parameter values, it would be absurd to claim that we can guarantee that the vehicles will behave safely in *all* possible scenarios. In fact, there are cases where it is not possible to avoid collisions, no matter how well the controller is designed. For example, on a single lane with the controlled vehicle in between the other two, the controlled vehicle cannot do anything to avoid collisions if the rear vehicle never brakes. Similarly, if the controlled vehicle initially has the accelerator at $a_{\max}$ and is positioned at a distance of 5m from the preceding vehicle that is braking, the collision is inevitable. Hence, in our studies, we will always start simulations in safe conditions, with uncontrolled vehicles showing reasonable behaviour.

3 Modelling the Highway Environment with Stark

Stark offers the evolution sequence model [5] for the representation of systems behaviour, and the Robustness Temporal Logic (RobTL) [8] and Distribution Temporal Logic (DisTL) [4] for the specification of requirements on such behaviour.

In this section, we make use of a simple instance of the highway environment to showcase the features of the tool and to give the reader a grasp on how to build models

Table 2. Parameters and variables for modelling the one lane two vehicles scenario.

Name	Description	Initial value
TIMER	Time interval between actions of vehicles	1
IDLE_OFFSET	When action IDLE is selected, acceleration is set within [−IDLE_OFFSET, IDLE_OFFSET]	1
intent	Value representing the action to be performed by the controlled vehicle (−1.0 = SLOWER, 0.0 = IDLE and 1.0 = FASTER)	0.0
v(i)	Physical speed of vehicle $i \in \{1, 2\}$	15.0
a(1)	Physical acceleration of vehicle 1	0.0
a(2)	Physical acceleration of vehicle 2	5.0
gap	Distance between the front-most point of vehicle 1 and the rear-most point of vehicle 2	100.0
safe_gap	Safety gap distance $RSSgap(\rho, v(1), v(2))$ between vehicles	66.67

with it. Specifically, we consider a highway scenario consisting of a single lane with two vehicles driving on it, one following the other. We assume that, initially, the vehicles have the same speed, the accelerator of the rear vehicle is set to IDLE and that of the front vehicle to FASTER, and the vehicles are at a distance compatible with the initial RSS gap (Remark 2). The objective of the case study is to model a controller of the rear vehicle (index 1) that is robust against unsafe, perturbed, behaviour of the vehicle in front (index 2). See the script at https://github.com/quasylab/jspear/blob/ABZ_2025/examples/ABZ2025/src/main/java/Scenarios/SingleLaneTwoCars.java for the implementation.

The Model. The evolution sequence model [5] follows a discrete-time, data-driven approach: the behaviour of the system is modelled in terms of the modifications that the interaction of a set of *agents* with a *environment* induces in a data space, containing the values assumed by *variables*, representing physical quantities, sensors, actuators, and internal variables of agents. The parameters and variables of the considered case study, in addition to the physical values in Table 1, are listed in Table 2. We call *data state* the current state of the data space, and we represent it by mapping $\mathbf{d}$ from variables to values. Due to the unpredictability of the environment and the potential approximations in the specification of agents, these modifications are modelled as continuous *distributions* on the attainable data states. The *evolution sequence* of a system is then defined as the sequence of the distributions over data states that are obtained at each time step. Given an evolution sequence $\mathcal{S}$, $\mathcal{S}^{\tau}$ denotes the distribution reached at time τ in $\mathcal{S}$.

The separation between agents and environment is ideal for the highway case study: we can model the controller of the chosen vehicle as a STARK agent and use a STARK environment to model the uncontrolled vehicle(s) and all physical events. Moreover, as we can specify uncertainties within the models, we can easily account for the noise on the accelerator actuator as given in the specification. We note that in this instance of the case study, we set TIMER $= 1$. Hence, following the discrete-time approach, we assume the duration of a computation step in the simulation to be 1 s, so that both the agent and the environment observe and modify the data at each step.

The Controller. STARK agents are specified as processes in a generative probabilistic process calculus [5] that includes, among other operators, action prefixes of the form

Algorithm 1 One lane, two vehicles: STARK agent for controlled vehicle

Control $\stackrel{\text{def}}{=}$ if [gap > safe_gap] (FASTER → intent).Control ▷ do action FASTER
else if [gap < safe_gap] (SLOWER → intent).Control ▷ do action SLOWER
else (IDLE → intent).Control ▷ do action IDLE

Algorithm 2 One lane, two vehicles: Environment

if intent = FASTER **then**
  a(1) $\sim U[0, a_{\max}]$; ▷ uniformly distributed in the interval
else if intent = SLOWER **then**
  a(1) $\sim -U[b_{\min}, b_{\max}]$;
else a(1) $\sim 0.5 * U[-\text{IDLE\_OFFSET}, \text{IDLE\_OFFSET}]$;
a(2) $\sim U[0, a_{\max}]$; ▷ accelerator of uncontrolled vehicle
gap = gap − (a(1)/2 + v(1)) + (a(2)/2 + v(2));
v(1) = min{max{0, v(1) + a(1)}, $v_{\max}$};
v(2) = min{max{0, v(2) + a(2)}, $v_{\max}$};
safe_gap = RSSgap(TIMER, v(1), v(2)); ▷ see Equation (1)

$(\overline{e \to x}).P$, with e ranging over expressions over values and variables, x ranging over variables, and $\bar{\cdot}$ denoting a finite sequence of elements; conditional processes of the form if$[e]P_1$ else P_2; and process variables. Here, we recall that, in a single step, a process can read and update a set of state variables. This is done by the process $(\overline{e \to x}).P$ that modifies the current data state $\mathbf{d}$ by applying the sequence of assignments $\overline{e \to x}$ to it. The modified data state will then change according to the environment, and, in the next step, the process will behave like P on the (distribution over) data states.

In Algorithm 1 we report the process Control that models the vehicle controller in the case study considered. The decision on which action to take among FASTER, SLOWER and IDLE is based on the comparison of the current distance from the preceding vehicle, with the value of the RSS gap.

The Environment. A STARK environment consists of a set of (randomised) functions that model the effects of physical phenomena and events on data. These also include the update of the variables that represent the physical aspects of the agents STARK. As shown in Algorithm 2, once agent Control has set variable intent, the environment will first update the accelerator value with the corresponding noisy acceleration value a(1). Given the simplicity of the case study, we have taken this noise to extreme values: for example, when the controller selects the action FASTER, the actual value of the acceleration is drawn uniformly from $[0, a_{\max}]$. Then, the environment will compute the distance that the vehicle will cover in one step given the acceleration and the new speed v(1). The environment is also responsible for updating the behaviour of the uncontrolled vehicle. In the absence of perturbations, this follows a regular behaviour: since there are no obstacles on its way, it will continue to select action FASTER. Also in this case, the actual value of the acceleration is noisy.

Verification: RobTL. It is quite straightforward to conclude that, as long as we consider the specified (ideal) behaviour of the agent and the environment, **SAF** is satisfied: the vehicle in front never brakes and the controlled vehicle brakes as soon as the RSS gap is violated. In fact, classic model-checking techniques can be used to formally verify that this is the case. However, we find it more interesting to check whether the controller is robust, namely, it is able to maintain this safe behaviour even in situations that are not ideal, that is, even if the uncontrolled vehicle is not behaved as expected, because, for example, the driver is drunk or *brake checker*. The analysis of robustness properties boils down to being able to measure both the effects of perturbations on the behaviour of a system and the capability of a (perturbed) system to fulfil its original tasks. To this end, STARK exploits RobTL [8], which allows us to express the temporal properties of distances over system behaviours, and consists of a language $\mathtt{P}$ to specify *perturbations*; a language $\mathtt{DE}$ to specify *distance expressions*; classic Boolean and temporal operators to specify requirements on *evolution of distances in time*.

A perturbation is the effect of unpredictable events on the current state of the system that can be repeated or different in time. Hence, we model it as a time-dependent function that maps a data state into a distribution on data states. Specifically, a perturbation $\mathrm{p} \in \mathtt{P}$ is a list of mappings in which the i-th element describes the effects of p at time i. The language $\mathtt{P}$ is defined by:

$$\mathrm{p} ::= \quad \mathsf{id} \quad | \quad \mathfrak{f}@\tau \quad | \quad \mathrm{p}_1 \,;\, \mathrm{p}_2 \quad | \quad \mathrm{p}^n$$

where p ranges over $\mathtt{P}$, n and τ are finite natural numbers, and: 1. id has no effects and behaves like the identity function; 2. $\mathfrak{f}@\tau$ applies a function $\mathfrak{f}$, mapping a data state to a distribution over data states, after τ time steps from the current instant; 3. $\mathrm{p}_1 \,;\, \mathrm{p}_2$ applies p_1 and p_2 sequentially; 4. p^n applies p, sequentially, for a total of n times. For instance, we can capture the behaviour of a drunk driver by means of perturbation

$$\mathrm{p}_{\mathrm{dd}}(\tau, n, \mathrm{DD}) = (\mathfrak{f}_{\mathrm{DD}}@\tau - 1)^n$$

that applies function $\mathfrak{f}_{\mathrm{DD}}$ every τ steps for a total of n times, where $\mathfrak{f}_{\mathrm{DD}}(\mathbf{d}) = \mathbf{d}'$ with

$$\mathbf{d}'(\mathsf{a}(2)) = \begin{cases} \mathrm{a}_{\mathrm{dd}} \sim U(X) & \text{if } \mathrm{u} \sim U[0,1] \leq \mathrm{DD} \\ \mathbf{d}(\mathsf{a}(2)) & \text{otherwise} \end{cases}$$

expressing that with probability DD variable $\mathsf{a}(2)$ assumes a value a_{dd} drawn uniformly from $X = [0, a_{\max}] \cup [-b_{\max}, -b_{\min}]$, regardless of safety conditions. Although not reported here, due to space limitations, the atomic function $\mathfrak{f}_{\mathrm{dd}}$ also updates the values of $\mathtt{v}(s)$, $\mathtt{gap}$ and $\mathtt{safe\_gap}$ in $\mathbf{d}'$, using the new value of $\mathsf{a}(2)$. Similarly, we can model a brake checker by means of $\mathrm{p}_{\mathrm{bc}}(\tau, n, \mathrm{BC}) = (\mathfrak{f}_{\mathrm{BC}}@\tau - 1)^n$, where $\mathfrak{f}_{\mathrm{BC}}$ differs from $\mathfrak{f}_{\mathrm{DD}}$, in that $\mathrm{a}(2)$ assumes the value $-b_{\max}$ with probability BC.

Once we have the two behaviours, nominal and perturbed, we use the expressions in $\mathtt{DE}$ to define distances over them. These are based on a distance from the ground over the distributions of data states measuring their differences with respect to a given task. Firstly, to capture a particular task, we use a *penalty function* ρ assigning to each data state $\mathbf{d}$ a penalty in $[0, 1]$. For instance, the penalty function

$$\rho_{\mathrm{crash}}(\mathbf{d}) = \begin{cases} 1 & \text{if } \mathbf{d}(\mathtt{gap}) \leq 0 \\ 0 & \text{otherwise} \end{cases}$$

assigns the maximal penalty 1 to those data states in which the two vehicles collided (their distance, $\mathtt{gap}$, is 0 or less). We then use penalty functions to define a ground distance m_ρ on data states. For the case studies in this article, it suffices to consider the

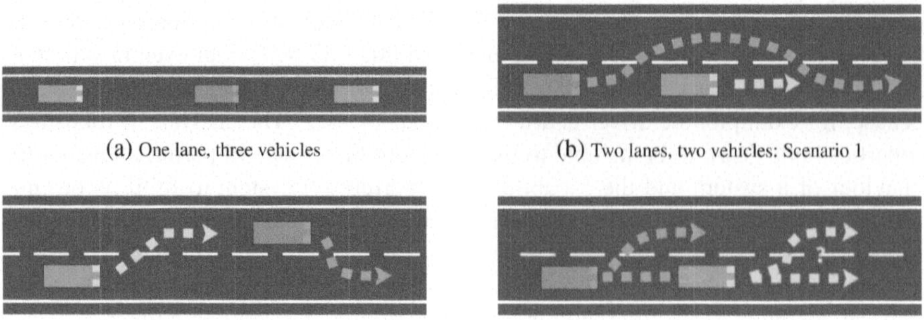

(a) One lane, three vehicles

(b) Two lanes, two vehicles: Scenario 1

(c) Two lanes, two vehicles: Scenario 2

(d) Two lanes, two vehicles: Scenario 3

Fig. 1. Scenarios considered in Sects. 4 and 5. The controlled vehicle is depicted in green. (Color figure online)

metric m_ρ as the Euclidean distance on $[0, 1]$. Then, we make use of the *Wasserstein lifting* [28] to lift m_ρ to a metric $\mathbf{W}(m_\rho)$ over distributions over data states. For instance, assuming that $\mathcal{S}$ is the nominal behaviour and $\mathcal{S}_{\mathtt{p_{dd}},t}$ is its perturbation obtained by applying $\mathtt{p_{dd}}$ to $\mathcal{S}$ as step t, we have that $\mathbf{W}(m_{\rho_{\mathrm{crash}}})(\mathcal{S}^\tau, \mathcal{S}^\tau_{\mathtt{p_{dd}},t})$ gives us the probability of a collision occurring at step τ in the perturbed system (as $\rho_{\mathrm{crash}}(\mathbf{d}) = 0$ for all $\mathbf{d}$ in $\mathcal{S}^\tau$). In the language DE, this distance is expressed by means of the atomic distance expression $<^{\rho_{\mathrm{crash}}}$ evaluated at step τ on $\mathcal{S}$ and $\mathcal{S}_{\mathtt{p_{dd}},t}$. The language DE provides, among others, three temporal expression operators, namely $\mathtt{F}^I$, $\mathtt{G}^I$ and $\mathtt{U}^I$, allowing the evaluation of minimal and maximal distances over time. Specifically, the evaluation of the distance expression

$$\mathrm{M_{crash}} = \mathtt{G}^{[0,300]} <^{\rho_{\mathrm{crash}}}$$

in $\mathcal{S}$ and $\mathcal{S}_{\mathtt{p_{dd}},t}$ gives us the maximum evaluation of $<^{\rho_{\mathrm{crash}}}$ in the time interval $[0, 300]$, that is, the maximum probability of a collision occurring in $[0, 300]$.

To complete the specification of the desired robustness property, we use formulae in RobTL, that are defined by:

$$\varphi ::= \top \mid \Delta(\mathtt{de}, \mathtt{p}) \bowtie \eta \mid \neg\varphi \mid \varphi \wedge \varphi \mid \varphi\, \mathcal{U}^I\, \varphi$$

where φ ranges over formulae, de ranges over expressions in DE, p ranges over perturbations in P, $\bowtie \in \{<, \leq, \geq, >\}$, $\eta \in [0, 1]$, and I is a bounded time interval.

Formulae are evaluated in an evolution sequence and a time instant. The semantics of the classic Boolean and temporal operators is standard and is based on the evaluation of atomic formulae $\Delta(\mathtt{de}, \mathtt{p}) \bowtie \eta$. The pair $\mathcal{S}, \tau$ satisfies $\Delta(\mathrm{M_{crash}}, \mathtt{p_{dd}}(3, 20, 0.8)) \leq 0.1$ if the distance $\mathrm{M_{crash}}$ between $\mathcal{S}$ and $\mathcal{S}_{\mathtt{p_{dd}},\tau}$ is ≤ 0.1. Then, formula

$$\varphi^{\mathbf{SAF}} = \Box^{[0,100]}(\Delta(\mathrm{M_{crash}}, \mathtt{p_{dd}}(3, 20, 0.8)) \leq 0.1)$$

expresses that regardless of when $\mathtt{p_{dd}}$ is applied to the system in the first 100 steps, it is always the case that the maximum probability of a collision to occur within 300 steps following the initial application of $\mathtt{p_{dd}}$ is at most 0.1.

Table 3. Additional variables for one lane and three vehicles, $i \in \{1, 2, 3\}$.

Name	Description	Initial value
v(i)	Physical speed of car i.	0.0
a(i)	Physical acceleration of car i.	1.0
gap(1)	Distance between the front-most point of car 1 and the rear-most point of car 2.	300.0
gap(2)	Distance between the front-most point of car 2 and the rear-most point of car 3.	300.0
safe_gap(1)	Safety gap distance $RSSgap(\rho, v(1), v(2))$ between car 1 and 2.	11.67
safe_gap(2)	Safety gap distance $RSSgap(\rho, v(2), v(3))$ between car 2 and 3.	11.67

Algorithm 3 Single lane three vehicles: process Control

```
Control ≝ if [gap(1)=safe_gap(1) ∧ gap(2)=safe_gap(2)] (IDLE → intent).Control
              else if [gap(1) < safe_gap(1) ∧ gap(2) < safe_gap(2)]
                     if [gap(1) < gap(2)](FASTER → intent).Control
                     else (SLOWER → intent).Control
                 else if [gap(2) < safe_gap(2)](SLOWER → intent).Control
                 else (FASTER → intent).Control
```

4 One Lane, Three Vehicles

We consider a single-lane highway with a controlled vehicle (index 2) driving between two uncontrolled ones (index 1 for the rear one and 3 for the front one); as depicted in Fig. 1a. See the script at https://github.com/quasylab/jspear/ABZ_2025/examples/ABZ2025/src/main/java/Scenarios/OneLaneThreeCars.java for the implementation. The variables specific to this scenario are listed in Table 3.

The objective of the controlled vehicle is to keep the front (respectively rear) distance bigger than the front (respectively rear) safety gap distance, to ensure **SAF**. The challenge is to decide whether to accelerate or brake in case one or both RSS gaps are violated. In Algorithm 3 we implement a STARK agent to tackle this challenge by prioritising the riskier gap: if both RSS gaps are violated, the vehicle chooses action FASTER if it is closer to vehicle 1, and SLOWER otherwise. In the other cases, the RSS gap with vehicle 3 determines the choice of action as in Algorithm 1.

The environment takes charge of the kinematics and uncontrolled cars. To make the case study more demanding and relevant from the perspective of robustness analysis, we enable only action FASTER for vehicles 1 and 3, and only perturbations can make them decelerate. The other physical quantities are updated as in Algorithm 2.

Analysis. We note that in this scenario the likelihood of collision is highly dependent on the initial values of variables such as gap(i) and v(i). Hence, we set those values in such a way that **SAF** is satisfied in the nominal system and focus on the robustness analysis (cf. Remark 2). Specifically, we evaluate the robustness of the controller against perturbations p_{dd} and p_{bc} with respect to RSS violations. In Fig. 2, we report the average values of gap(i) and safe_gap(i) ($i = 1, 2$) over the first 200 time steps

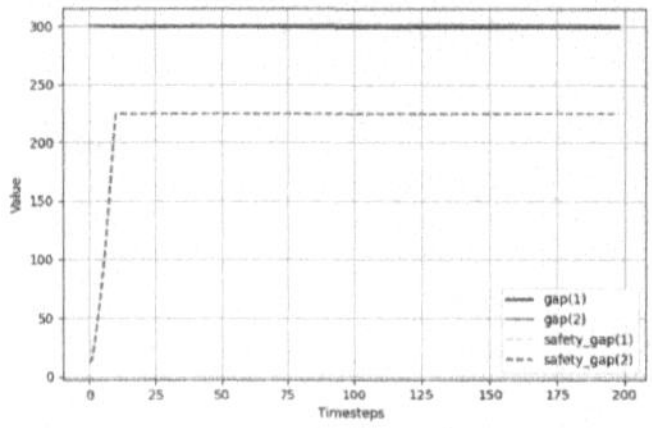

(a) Average gap and safe_gap with no perturbation

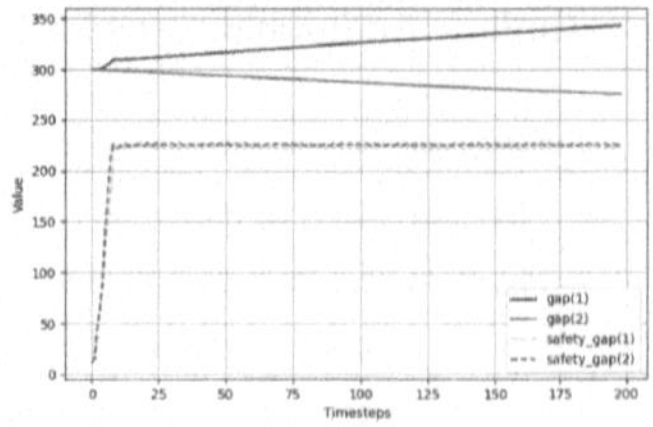

(b) Average gap and safe_gap with $p_{dd}(3, 20, 0.2)$

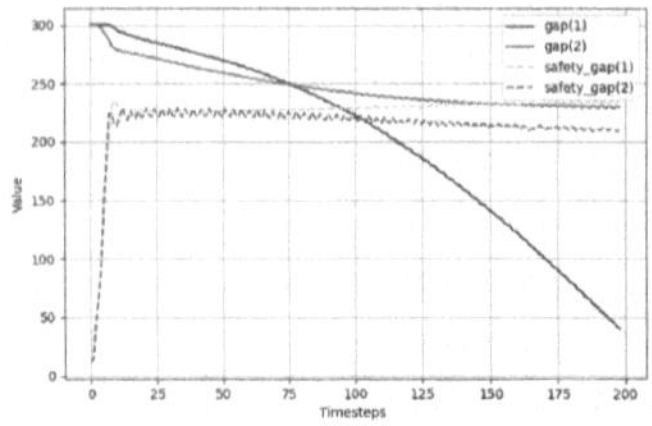

(c) Average gap and safe_gap with $p_{bc}(3, 20, 0.2)$

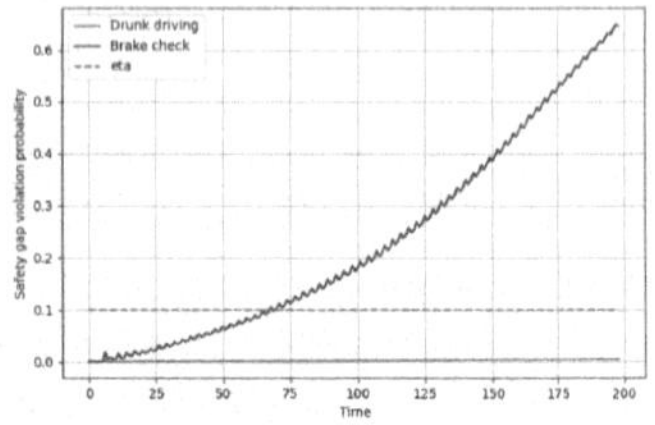

(d) Pointwise evaluation of $\lessdot^{\rho_{sgv}}$, $\eta_{sgv} = 0.1$

Fig. 2. Simulations for scenario 1 lane 3 cars (200 steps, 10^4 samples).

in a simulation with 10^4 samples. In Fig. 2a we consider the nominal behaviour of the system; in Fig. 2b $p_{dd}(2, 20, 0.2)$ is applied; and in Fig. 2c we apply $p_{bc}(2, 20, 0.2)$. In all cases, the closer the value of $\mathtt{gap(i)}$ to the value of $\mathtt{safe\_gap(i)}$, the more likely a violation of the RSS gap (and thus a collision) will occur. We are interested in quantifying the severity of such a violation. To this end, the following penalty function measures the (normalised) maximum violation in the RSS gap with the two uncontrolled vehicles:

$$\rho_{sgv}(\mathbf{d}) = \left[\max\left\{\frac{\mathbf{d}(\mathtt{safe\_gap(1)}) - \mathbf{d}(\mathtt{gap(1)})}{\mathbf{d}(\mathtt{safe\_gap(1)})}, \frac{\mathbf{d}(\mathtt{safe\_gap(2)}) - \mathbf{d}(\mathtt{gap(2)})}{\mathbf{d}(\mathtt{safe\_gap(2)})}\right\}\right]_0^1$$

with $[r]_0^1 = \min(\max(r, 0), 1)$ for every $r \in \mathbb{R}$. Then, the distance expression $\mathrm{M}_{sgv} = \mathtt{G}^{[0,200]} \lessdot^{\rho_{sgv}}$ gives the maximum pointwise distance, with respect to severity of violation, between the distributions that are reached in the first 200 computation steps in $\mathcal{S}$ and $\mathcal{S}_{p_{dd},0}$ (respectively, $\mathcal{S}_{p_{bc},0}$). Figure 2d shows the pointwise evaluation of $\lessdot^{\rho_{sgv}}$ over the nominal and perturbed evolution sequences.

Given a maximum acceptable severity of violation of the RSS gap of $\eta_{sgv} = 0.1$, the formula

$$\varphi_{sgv,dd} = \Delta(\mathrm{M}_{sgv}, p_{dd}(3, 20, 0.2)) \leq 0.1$$

is satisfied by the pair $\mathcal{S}, \tau$ if the controller manages to keep the entity of the violation of the RSS gaps below the 10%, over the interval $[\tau, 200 + \tau]$, when $p_{dd}(3, 20, 0.2)$ is applied at step τ. A similar formula, $\varphi_{sgv,bc}$, can be constructed for the perturbation p_{bc}. In our experiments, the evaluations of $\varphi_{sgv,dd}$ and $\varphi_{sgv,bc}$ show that the system is robust against p_{dd} but it is not robust enough against p_{bc} (cf. Fig. 2d).

Algorithm 4 Multiple lanes controller: process Idling

```
1: Idling ≝ if [timer(1) > 0] √.Idling      ▷ √.P idles for one step and then behaves like P
2:          else Control
```

5 Modelling Multiple Lanes

We now consider three instances of a highway environment with two lanes and two vehicles, one controlled by a STARK agent (index 1) and one by the environment (index 2). The reader may see illustrations for these instances in Fig. 1. In scenario 1, both vehicles are initially placed on the rightmost lane, with vehicle 1 following the other. The objective of vehicle 1 is to continue in the rightmost lane unless it is possible to overtake in a safe manner (**R2L,SO**). Vehicle 2 respects the safety distance from the other vehicle and proceeds in the rightmost free lane. In Scenario 2, vehicle 1 is initially positioned on the leftmost lane, preceding vehicle 2 that is moving from the rightmost to the leftmost lane. The objective of vehicle 2 is to occupy the leftmost lane and never leave it. Vehicle 1 has to leave the leftmost lane free as soon as it is necessary and safe to do so (**R2L,KIR**). In Scenario 3, the initial condition is as in Scenario 1. However, vehicle 2 is now free to change lane and overtake vehicle 1, as long as those manoeuvres are performed when it is safe to do so. Vehicle 1 has to adapt to its behaviour and comply with the following directives: proceed in the rightmost lane whenever possible and overtake only when it is safe to do so (**R2L,KIR,SO**).

We give only a high-level overview of the models and analysis performed in the case study. All details can be found at https://github.com/quasylab/jspear/blob/ABZ_2025/examples/ABZ2025/src/main/java/Scenarios/TwoLanesTwoCars.java.

The Model. To keep track of the position of a vehicle on the highway, we will use variables x(i), y(i). We assume $x \geq 0$, as the origin of the x axes can always coincide with the initial position of the rear vehicle, and $y \in [0, 8]$, as we consider two lanes, each 4 m wide. The distance between the two vehicles is then given by their Euclidean norm on $\mathbb{R}^2$. The main differences from the previous sections are that we consider a cycle of length TIMER > 1, and that actions LANE_LEFT and LANE_RIGHT are now enabled. Each vehicle is equipped with a timer (timer(i)) that is decreased by 1 at each step, and the vehicle can perform an action only when the timer is equal to 0, and idles otherwise (see Algorithm 4). The timer is reset to TIMER once an action is selected. By setting the initial values of the two timers at different values in [0, TIMER] we can interleave the decisions taken by the two vehicles. As a consequence, the conditions under which the STARK agent Control takes a decision, might be invalidated by the choices taken by the other vehicle during the idling time. In the following, we discuss the relation between the value of TIMER and the robustness against perturbations. Regarding lane changes, the choices made by Control are based on the safety and driving regulations **SAF**, **R2L**, **KIR**, and **SO**. We remark that, given the limitations in kinematics imposed by the specification, we cannot properly model and quantify the lateral speed of vehicles. Hence, the RSS formula for safe lateral distance [23] cannot be used in vehicle decision-making. Hence, we design the controller so that the safe behaviour is enforced

Algorithm 6 Multiple lanes controller: process Moving_right

Let $(\mathtt{fast}) = (\mathtt{FASTER} \rightarrow \mathtt{intent}, 0 \rightarrow \mathtt{move(1)}, 0 \rightarrow \mathtt{lane(1)}, \mathtt{TIMER} \rightarrow \mathtt{timer(1)})$
Let $(\mathtt{slow}) = (\mathtt{SLOWER} \rightarrow \mathtt{intent}, 0 \rightarrow \mathtt{move(1)}, 0 \rightarrow \mathtt{lane(1)}, \mathtt{TIMER} \rightarrow \mathtt{timer(1)})$
Let $(\mathtt{nul}) = (\mathtt{IDLE} \rightarrow \mathtt{intent}, 0 \rightarrow \mathtt{move(1)}, 0 \rightarrow \mathtt{lane(1)}, \mathtt{TIMER} \rightarrow \mathtt{timer(1)})$
Moving_right $\stackrel{\text{def}}{=}$ if $[\mathtt{timer(1)} > 0]$ $\surd$.Moving_right
    else if $[\mathtt{pos(1)} = 1 \vee \mathtt{gap} > \mathtt{safe\_gap}]$ $(\mathtt{fast})$.Idling
        else if $[\mathtt{gap} = \mathtt{safe\_gap}]$ $(\mathtt{nul})$.Idling
            else $(\mathtt{slow})$.Idling

Algorithm 5 Multiple lanes controller: process Control (snippet)

Let $(\mathtt{go\_right}) = (\mathtt{IDLE} \rightarrow \mathtt{intent}, \mathtt{LANE\_RIGHT} \rightarrow \mathtt{move(1)}, \mathtt{TIMER} \rightarrow \mathtt{timer(1)})$
Control $\stackrel{\text{def}}{=}$ if $[\mathtt{timer(1)} > 0]$ $\surd$.Control
    else if $[\mathtt{lane(1)} = 1]$ ▷ if vehicle on the leftmost lane
        if $[\mathtt{gap} > \mathtt{safe\_gap}]$ $(\mathtt{go\_right})$.Moving_right
        else if $[\mathtt{pos(1)} = 1]$ ▷ if vehicle precedes the other
            if $[\mathtt{lane(2)} = 1]$ $(\mathtt{go\_right})$.Moving_right ▷ on the same lane
            else $(\mathtt{FASTER} \rightarrow \mathtt{intent}, \mathtt{TIMER} \rightarrow \mathtt{timer(1)})$.Idling
...

by means of evaluations of (1) combined with specific requirements based on the relative position of the vehicles. Due to space limitations, we only report process snippets related to the LANE_RIGHT action (Algorithm 5). Vehicle 1 can move from the leftmost to the rightmost lane either if its distance from vehicle 2 is larger than the RSS gap, or in case both vehicles are on the leftmost lane and vehicle 2 is approaching vehicle 1 at a high speed. To avoid zigzag behaviour, agent Moving_right can only decide, once the timer allows it, how to set the accelerator, by means of actions FASTER, IDLE, SLOWER, based on the relative position of the two vehicles and the RSS gap (Algorithm 6). Vehicle 1 is allowed to move from the right to the left lane only when it is possible to safely perform an overtake. This means that both vehicles are in the right lane, vehicle 1 follows the other, and the distance between them is at least 80% of the RSS gap. Otherwise, the controller will choose among actions FASTER, IDLE, SLOWER as in Algorithm 1.

Given that vehicle 2 behaviour differs in the three scenarios, we have modelled an environment for each. In all of those, the variables that represent the behaviour of vehicle 1 are updated as in Algorithm 2. The only difference is in the update of the vehicle's position, which has to take lane changes into account. Since it takes a whole cycle for vehicles to change lane, regardless of their current speed, at each step we let $\mathtt{x(1)} = \mathtt{x(1)} + (\mathtt{a(1)}/2 + \mathtt{v(1)}) * \cos((\pi/9) * \mathtt{move(1)})$ and $\mathtt{y(1)} = \min\{8, \max\{0, \mathtt{y(1)} + \mathtt{move(1)} * 4/\mathtt{TIMER}\}\}$. The choice of a steering angle of $\pi/9$ is based on mean values and studies on safety control [30]. The factor $4/\mathtt{TIMER}$ follows by the assumption that the vehicle will keep the centre of each lane. In the environments, the behaviour of vehicle 2 follows the description given above: always keeping the rightmost lane in Scenario 1; always trying to occupy the leftmost lane in Scenario 2; a randomised behaviour in Scenario 3. In all cases, the actions taken by the vehicle are subject to safety checks based on the RSS gap and the relative position of the vehicles. However, to favour lane changes, in Scenarios 1 and 3 we limit the maximal speed

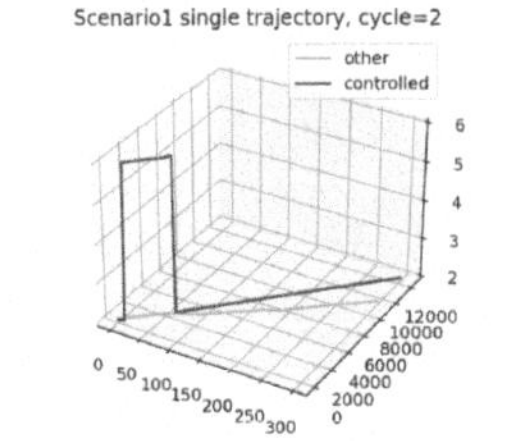

(a) Scen. 1 (1 sample)

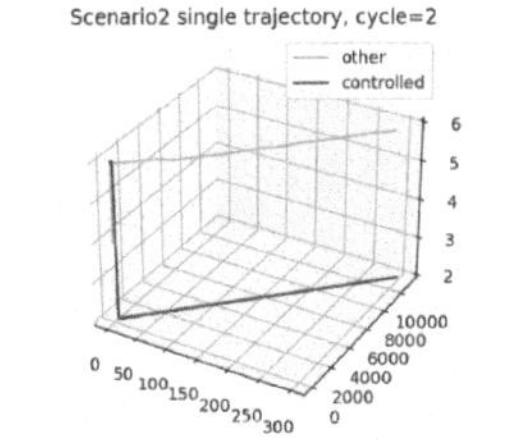

(b) Scen. 2 (1 sample)

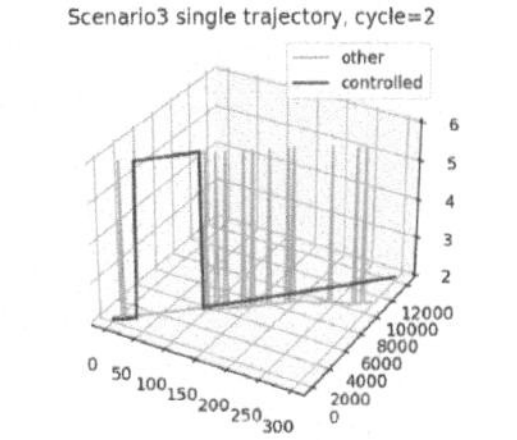

(c) Scen. 3 (1 sample)

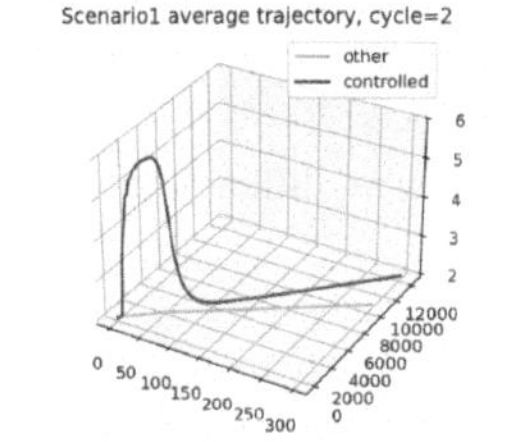

(d) Scen. 1 (10^5 samples)

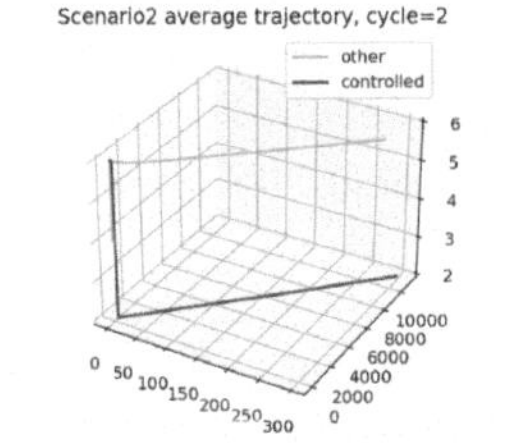

(e) Scen. 2 (10^5 samples)

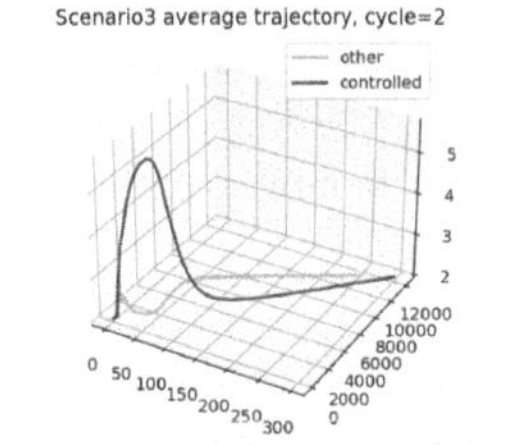

(f) Scen. 3 (10^5 samples)

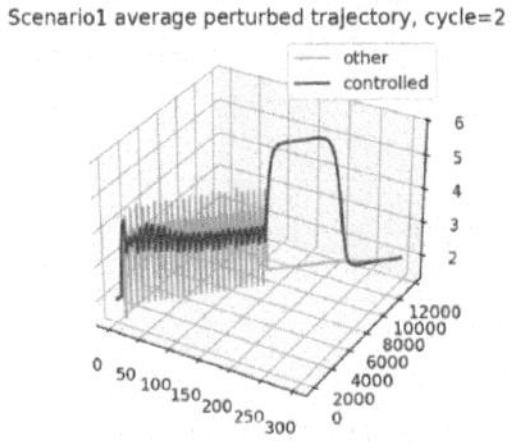

(g) Scen. 1 perturbed (10^5 samples)

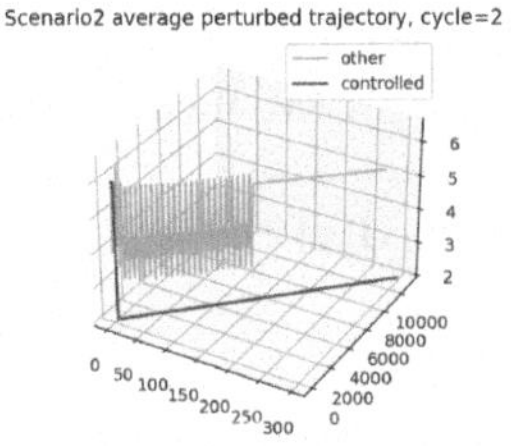

(h) Scen. 2 perturbed (10^5 samples)

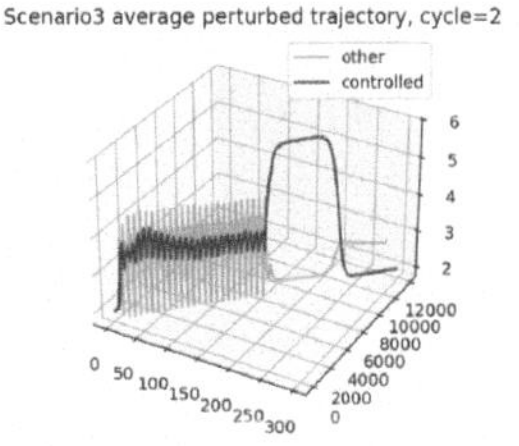

(i) Scen. 3 perturbed (10^5 samples)

Fig. 3. Nominal and perturbed trajectories of the two vehicles in the three scenarios.

of vehicle 2 to 35 m/s^2, and in Scenario 2 we limit the maximum speed of vehicle 1 to the same value. Moreover, vehicle 2 randomly selects an action among those that can be performed safely. Hence, for instance, there is a (small) chance that vehicle 2 will brake even if it is not necessary. In Fig. 3 we report the trajectories in the first 300 steps of the two vehicles in the three scenarios, with `TIMER` $= 2$. In the upper part, we report a single trajectory, whereas in the central part, we report the average trajectories.

Analysis. We consider the *reckless driver* perturbation p_{rd}, which takes advantage of the possibility of changing lanes. Formally, $\mathrm{p}_{\mathrm{rd}} = \mathsf{id}@5; (\mathfrak{f}_{\mathrm{rd}}@2)^{50}$, which means that after 5 steps the perturbation applies the function $\mathfrak{f}_{\mathrm{rd}}$ every 3 steps for 50 times. Briefly, the function $\mathfrak{f}_{\mathrm{rd}}$ is such that, whenever the distance between the two vehicles is at least 25% of the RSS gap, vehicle 2 changes lane with probability 0.6. Otherwise, the value of the gap between vehicles is perturbed by a random value in $[0, l \times w]$. In the bottom part of Fig. 3, we report the mean trajectories under the effect of p_{rd} in the three scenarios.

In fact, one can perform an analysis of robustness against p_{rd} with respect to the probability of collision, as done in Sect. 3. To make full use of the features of STARK

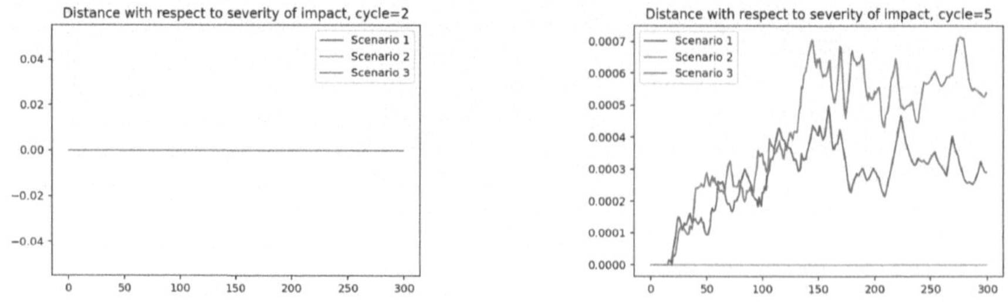

(a) $\texttt{TIMER} = 2$. (b) $\texttt{TIMER} = 5$.

Fig. 4. Pointwise evaluation of $<^{\rho_{\mathrm{SI}}}$ over $[0, 300]$ in the three scenarios w.r.t. different timers.

and RobTL, we combine this requirement with robustness with respect to *severity of impact*. This is determined by taking into account the speed of vehicles when an impact occurs: the higher the speed, the more severe the consequences of the collision [26]. Given the limitations in our kinematics model, we measure the severity of the impact by $\mathrm{SI}(\mathtt{v}(1), \mathtt{v}(2)) = 0.5 * |\mathtt{v}(1) - \mathtt{v}(2)|$. We then use the penalty

$$\rho_{\mathrm{SI}}(\mathbf{d}) = \begin{cases} \mathrm{SI}(\mathbf{d}(\mathtt{v}(1)), \mathbf{d}(\mathtt{v}(2)))/v_{\max} & \text{if } \mathbf{d}(\mathtt{crash}) = 1 \\ 0 & \text{otherwise} \end{cases}$$

to obtain the normalised value of the severity of impact when a collision occurs. The variable $\mathtt{crash}$ is set to 1 if there is a collision, that is, if the $l \times w$ rectangle centred on $(\mathbf{d}(\mathtt{x}(1)), \mathtt{y}(1))$ intersects the $l \times w$ rectangle centred on $(\mathbf{d}(\mathtt{x}(2)), \mathtt{y}(2))$. The distance expression $\mathrm{M}_{\mathrm{SI}} = \mathtt{G}^{[0,300]} <^{\rho_{\mathrm{SI}}}$ then allows us to evaluate the maximum value of the pointwise distance between distributions with respect to severity of impact over the interval $[0, 300]$. We remark that here we use the Wasserstein distance to quantify the magnitude of the event weighted by its likelihood to occur. Specifically, we can use the atomic formula $\varphi_{\mathrm{SI}} = \Delta(\mathrm{M}_{\mathrm{SI}}, \mathtt{p}_{\mathrm{SI}}) \leq 0.01$ to check whether impacts at high speed are very unlikely (high value of ρ_{SI}, but negligible probability of having $\mathtt{crash} = 1$), or if collisions are inevitable, at least they occur at low speed ($\mathtt{crash} = 1$ with high probability, but really small value of ρ_{SI}). By combining this formula with $\varphi_{\mathrm{crash}} = \Delta(\mathrm{M}_{\mathrm{crash}}, \mathtt{p}_{\mathrm{SI}}) \leq 0.01$ which limits the probability of collisions, we obtain a strong requirement of the robustness of the system against perturbation $\mathtt{p}_{\mathrm{rd}}$

$$\varphi^{\mathbf{SAF}}_{\mathrm{crash\&SI}} = \Box^{[0,200]}(\varphi_{\mathrm{crash}} \wedge \varphi_{\mathrm{SI}}).$$

A similar analysis can be carried out for the safety requirements **R2L**, **KIR**, and **SO** (see https://github.com/quasylab/jspear/blob/ABZ_2025/examples/ABZ2025/src/main/java/Scenarios/TwoLanesTwoCars.java for details).

For $\texttt{TIMER} = 2$, the system is robust against $\mathtt{p}_{\mathrm{rd}}$ in all three scenarios. In fact, the distances considered are compared to 0 (Fig. 4a). As one can expect, if we increase the value of TIMER, i.e. the time interval between the decision of the controllers, then the safety guarantees decrease. Figure 4b shows the pointwise evaluation of $<^{\rho_{\mathrm{SI}}}$ (with $\mathtt{p}_{\mathrm{SI}}$ applied at step 0) when $\texttt{TIMER} = 5$. Then, in Fig. 5 we report the point-wise evaluations

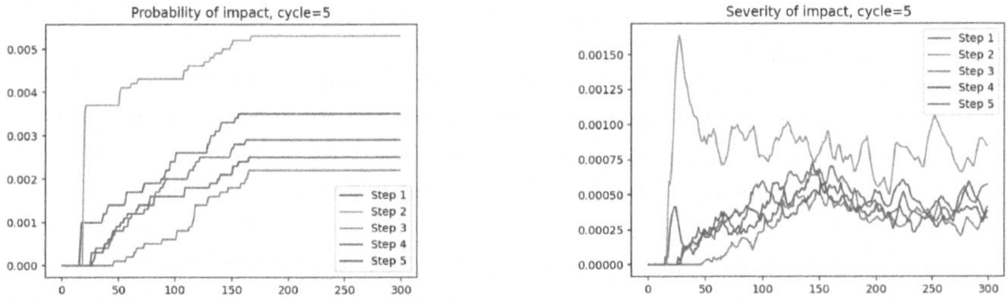

(a) $<^{\rho_{\mathrm{crash}}}$.

(b) $<^{\rho_{\mathrm{SI}}}$.

Fig. 5. Pointwise evaluation of $<^{\rho_{\mathrm{crash}}}$ and $<^{\rho_{\mathrm{SI}}}$ over $[0, 300]$ in Scenario 3, with the first application of $\mathtt{p}_{\mathrm{rd}}$ at step varying from step 1 to step 5.

of $<^{\rho_{\mathrm{crash}}}$ and $<^{\rho_{\mathrm{SI}}}$ in Scenario 3, with respect to the variation of the first step in which $\mathtt{p}_{\mathrm{rd}}$ is applied. Variations in the evaluations show that the perturbation can be more or less disruptive, depending on when it hits the system and how fast the controllers can react to it. Interestingly, the system still satisfies $\varphi^{\mathbf{SAF}}_{\mathrm{crash\&SI}}$ for $\mathtt{TIMER} = 5$, since the maximum values of the distances are still bounded by the tolerance 0.01.

6 Robustness of AI Agents

Ensuring the safety and reliability of AI-driven systems is crucial, particularly in dynamic and uncertain environments such as autonomous highway driving. In this section, we present a validation framework that leverages the STARK *Distribution Temporal Logic* (*DisTL*) [4] to assess the robustness of AI agents in a simulated highway environment. DisTL allows us to specify the desired, ideal behaviour of AI agents, and quantify deviations between the actual behaviour of the AI agent and this ideal reference, enabling thus a systematic evaluation of its safety properties. Moreover, we also analyse the robustness of the AI system against sensors failure by using RobTL. This section details the methodology used to define ideal behaviour, measure deviations, and integrate formal verification techniques into the road simulation environment.

The AI Environment. The AI system provided in [18] includes several reinforcement learning (RL) agents trained in the *highway-env* project [16]. We are interested in the *highway* environment, were the controlled vehicle (index 1) is driving on a three-lane highway populated with other vehicles. The controller's objective is to reach a high speed while avoiding collisions with neighbouring vehicles. Driving on the right side of the road is also rewarded. Uncontrolled vehicles follow a simple and predictable behaviour based on the IDM [27] and MOBIL [14] models. The agents provided were trained for runs of 30 time steps of duration.

The controller is modelled according to the design requirements given in Sect. 2. An *observation* of the environment is a 5×5 matrix that has columns for the presence, positions $\mathtt{x}, \mathtt{y}$ and speeds $\mathtt{v_x}, \mathtt{v_y}$ of vehicle 1 and the four vehicles closest to it. The position and speed of vehicle 1 are given in absolute terms, whereas those of other

	$\mathtt{Presence}(i)$	$\mathtt{x}(i)$	$\mathtt{y}(i)$	$\mathtt{v_x}(i)$	$\mathtt{v_y}(i)$
Vehicle 1 (controlled)	1.0	0.74	0.66	0.31	0.0
Vehicle 2	1.0	0.12	-0.66	-0.02	0.0
Vehicle 3	1.0	0.24	-0.66	-0.04	0.0
Vehicle 4	1.0	0.35	0.00	-0.04	0.0
Vehicle 5	1.0	0.48	0.00	-0.03	0.0

Fig. 6. Example observation matrix in the highway environment.

vehicles are relative to it. For any vehicle within a range of 100 m from vehicle 1, we have $\mathtt{Presence}(i) = 1$, otherwise $\mathtt{Presence}(i) = 0$. All values are normalised to $[0, 1]$. Figure 6 shows an example of an observation matrix.

Interaction with STARK. We set up a framework where STARK obtains the observation matrix, uses it to compute distances, and (possibly) applies perturbations to it before feeding it to the RL agent, which decides what action to take. The simulation then proceeds in accordance. The implementation can be found at https://github.com/quasylab/jspear/blob/ABZ_2025/examples/ABZ2025/src/main/java/Scenarios/AIMultipleLanes.java.

The variables in the data states are then those in the observation matrix in Fig. 6, with the addition of the variable `crash` that is initially set to 0, and assumes the value 1 when a collision occurs, as described in Sect. 5.

Robustness with RobTL. We simulate a failure of proximity sensors: each neighbouring vehicle has probability $\mathfrak{a}_{\text{inv}}$ of not being detected. This could prevent the controller from performing collision avoidance manoeuvres, which poses a safety risk. The system is then robust against this failure if vehicle 1 can limit the risk of collision. First, we model the failure by means of an *invisibility* perturbation $\mathfrak{p}_{\text{inv}}(\mathfrak{a}_{\text{inv}}) = id@0; (\mathfrak{f}_{\mathfrak{a}_{\text{inv}}}@2)^{14}$, which has no effect on the initial step, and then apply the function $\mathfrak{f}_{\mathfrak{a}_{\text{inv}}}$ every three steps for 14 times. For each data state $\mathbf{d}$, we define $\mathfrak{f}_{\mathfrak{a}_{\text{inv}}}(\mathbf{d}) = \mathbf{d}'$ with

$$\mathbf{d}'(\mathtt{Presence}(i)) = \begin{cases} 0 & \text{if } u_i < \mathfrak{a}_{\text{inv}} \\ \mathbf{d}(\mathtt{Presence}(i)) & \text{otherwise} \end{cases}$$

where $i \in \{2, 3, 4, 5\}$, $\mathfrak{a}_{\text{inv}} \in [0, 1]$, and u_i uniformly distributed in $[0, 1]$; $\mathbf{d}'(x) = \mathbf{d}(x)$ for all other variables $x \in \mathcal{V}$. We use the penalty function $\rho_{\text{coll}}(\mathbf{d}) = \mathbf{d}(\mathtt{crash})$ and the distance expression $\text{M}_{\text{coll}} = \mathtt{G}^{[0,30]} <^{\rho_{\text{coll}}}$ to quantify the maximal probability of a collision along the time interval $[0, 30]$. We express the robustness of the system against $\mathfrak{p}_{inv}$ using the RobTL formula $\varphi^{\mathbf{SAF}}_{\mathfrak{a}_{\text{inv}}} = \square^{[0,30]} \Delta(\text{M}_{\text{coll}}, \mathfrak{p}_{\text{inv}}(\mathfrak{a}_{\text{inv}})) \le \eta_{\text{coll}}$. In our analysis, we considered the initial parameters generated by the *highway-env* environment, and we analyse the impact of $\mathfrak{p}_{\text{inv}}(\mathfrak{a}_{\text{inv}})$ on the system, with different values for $\mathfrak{a}_{\text{inv}}$. We set the acceptable collision risk $\eta_{\mathtt{coll}}$ to 0 and evaluated $\varphi^{\mathbf{SAF}}_{\text{inv}}(\mathfrak{a}_{\text{inv}})$ for $\mathfrak{a}_{\text{inv}} \in \{0.01, 0.05, 0.1, 0.25, 0.5\}$. The formula is not satisfied as soon as $\mathfrak{a}_{\text{inv}} \ge 0.05$. Figure 7a shows the pointwise evaluation of $<^{\rho_{coll}}$ when $\mathfrak{p}_{\text{inv}}(\mathfrak{a}_{\text{inv}})$ is applied in the first step, varying $\mathfrak{a}_{\text{inv}} \in \{0.01, 0.05, 0.1, 0.25, 0.5\}$.

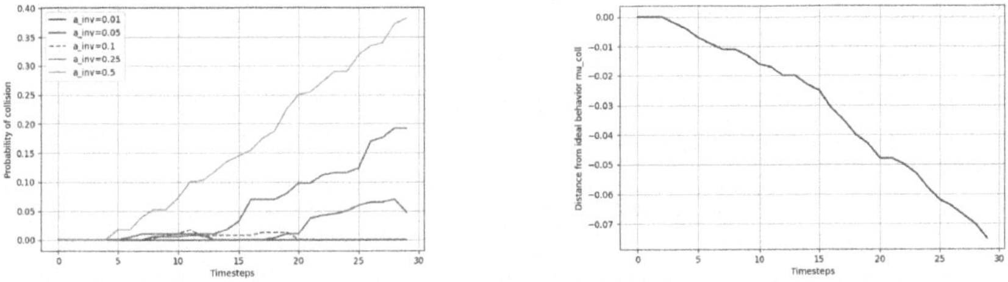

(a) Point-wise evaluation of $<^{\rho_{\mathrm{coll}}}$ when $\mathtt{p}_{\mathtt{inv}}$ is applied at the first step, with increasing values of $\mathtt{a}_{\mathtt{inv}}$.

(b) Step-wise evaluation of the DisTL formula $\mathbf{target}(\mu_{coll})_{0.0}^{\rho_{coll}}$.

Fig. 7. Simulation results of validating the AI environment with STARK.

Validation with DisTL. In [3] we implemented a *feedback mechanism* in STARK as an abstraction of the communication between a digital and a physical twin. Unfortunately, in its current version, the feedback is not expressive enough to allow us to create a safety shield for the RL agents. We leave this challenge as an avenue for future research. However, we can give some insight on how we can use STARK for model validation. STARK includes the temporal logic DisTL that allows us to analyse the robustness of systems. whose complete specification is unavailable. This is the case of AI agents, as they may make decisions that are not explainable and cannot thus be modelled. The idea is to use DisTL to specify the desired, ideal behaviour of the system and to compare it with the actual behaviour shown by the AI agent. DisTL offers the atomic proposition $\mathbf{target}(\mu)_q^{\rho}$, where μ is a distribution over data states that represent some desired or expected behaviour, $q \in [0, 1]$ is the *maximal acceptable distance* between the desired behaviour μ and the current behaviour, and ρ is a penalty function. By combining atomic propositions with temporal and classic boolean operators, one defines an evolution sequence of system requirements, i.e., the ideal behaviour of a system. Then, we use the real-valued semantics of DisTL to quantify the *degree of robustness* of the AI agent with respect to those requirements. Specifically, the degree of robustness of a system $\mathtt{s}$ with respect to $\mathbf{target}(\mu)_q^{\rho}$ is expressed as a real number $⟦\mathbf{target}(\mu)_q^{\rho}⟧_{\mathcal{S}}^{\tau} = q - \mathbf{W}(\mathtt{m}_{\rho})(\mathcal{S}^{\tau}, \mu) \in [-1, 1]$. If $⟦\mathbf{target}(\mu)_q^{\rho}⟧_{\mathcal{S}}^{\tau} = k$, then $k \geq 0$ indicates that the behaviour of $\mathtt{s}$ is at distance k from the set of behaviours that violate the formula; symmetrically, $k \leq 0$ means that $\mathtt{s}$ is at distance k from the set of behaviours that satisfy $\mathbf{target}(\mu)_q^{\rho}$.

To express the degree of robustness with respect to **SAF**, first we define the distribution $\mu_{\mathrm{coll}} = \mathtt{crash} \sim \delta_0$, where δ_0 is the Dirac delta distribution at 0, representing an ideal behaviour that avoids all collisions. Given the penalty function ρ_{coll} defined above and a tolerance $\varepsilon \geq 0$, the formula $\varphi_{\varepsilon}^{\mathbf{SAF}} = \square^{[0,30]}\mathbf{target}(\mu_{\mathrm{coll}})_{\varepsilon}^{\rho_{\mathrm{coll}}}$ captures the **SAF** requirement. The results of the evaluation of $\varphi_0^{\mathbf{SAF}}$, starting from the initial parameters generated by the *highway-env* environment, are presented in Fig. 7b.

References

1. Bachute, M.R., Subhedar, J.M.: Autonomous driving architectures: insights of machine learning and deep learning algorithms. Mach. Learn. Appl. (2021). https://doi.org/10.1016/j.mlwa.2021.100164
2. Badue, C., et al.: Self-driving cars: a survey. Expert Syst. Appl. (2021). https://doi.org/10.1016/j.eswa.2020.113816
3. Castiglioni, V., Lanotte, R., Loreti, M., Tini, S.: Evaluating the effectiveness of digital twins through statistical model checking with feedback and perturbations. In: Haxthausen, A.E., Serwe, W. (eds.) Formal Methods for Industrial Critical Systems. FMICS 2024. LNCS, vol. 14952, pp. 21–39. Springer, Cham (2024). https://doi.org/10.1007/978-3-031-68150-9_2
4. Castiglioni, V., Loreti, M., Tini, S.: DisTL: a temporal logic for the analysis of the expected behaviour of cyber-physical systems. In: Proceedings of ICTCS 2023. CEUR Workshop Proceedings (2023). https://ceur-ws.org/Vol-3587/4168.pdf
5. Castiglioni, V., Loreti, M., Tini, S.: A framework to measure the robustness of programs in the unpredictable environment. Log. Methods Comput. Sci. (2023). https://doi.org/10.46298/LMCS-19(3:2)2023
6. Castiglioni, V., Loreti, M., Tini, S.: STARK: a software tool for the analysis of robustness in the unknown environment. In: Jongmans, SS., Lopes, A. (eds.) Coordination Models and Languages. COORDINATION 2023. LNCS, vol. 13908, pp. 115–132. Springer, Cham (2023). https://doi.org/10.1007/978-3-031-35361-1_6
7. Castiglioni, V., Loreti, M., Tini, S.: Bio-Stark: a tool for the time-point robustness analysis of biological systems. In: Gori, R., Milazzo, P., Tribastone, M. (eds.) Computational Methods in Systems Biology. CMSB 2024. LNCS, vol. 14971, pp. 62–70. Springer, Cham (2024). https://doi.org/10.1007/978-3-031-71671-3_5
8. Castiglioni, V., Loreti, M., Tini, S.: RobTL: robustness temporal logic for CPS. In: Proceedings of CONCUR 2024. LIPIcs, Schloss Dagstuhl - Leibniz-Zentrum für Informatik (2024). https://doi.org/10.4230/LIPICS.CONCUR.2024.15
9. Castiglioni, V., Loreti, M., Tini, S.: STARK: a tool for the analysis of CPSs robustness. Sci. Comput. Program. (2024). https://doi.org/10.1016/j.scico.2024.103134
10. Fremont, D.J.: Scenic: a language for scenario specification and data generation. Mach. Learn. (2022). https://doi.org/10.1007/s10994-021-06120-5
11. Ghosh, S., Bansal, S., Sangiovanni-Vincentelli, A.L., Seshia, S.A., Tomlin, C.: A new simulation metric to determine safe environments and controllers for systems with unknown dynamics. In: Proceedings of HSCC 2019 (2019). https://doi.org/10.1145/3302504.3311795
12. Gruteser, J., Geleßus, D., Leuschel, M., Roßbach, J., Vu, F.: A formal model of train control with AI-based obstacle detection. In: Milius, B., Collart-Dutilleul, S., Lecomte, T. (eds.) Reliability, Safety, and Security of Railway Systems. Modelling, Analysis, Verification, and Certification. RSSRail 2023. LNCS, vol. 14198, pp 128–145. Springer, Cham (2023). https://doi.org/10.1007/978-3-031-43366-5_8
13. Katrakazas, C., Quddus, M., Chen, W.H., Deka, L.: Real-time motion planning methods for autonomous on-road driving: state-of-the-art and future research directions. Transp. Res. Part C: Emerg. Technol. (2015). https://doi.org/10.1016/j.trc.2015.09.011
14. Kesting, A., Treiber, M., Helbing, D.: General lane-changing model MOBIL for car-following models. Transp. Res. Rec. (2007)
15. Kubica, M.L.: Autonomous vehicles and liability law. Am. J. Comp. Law (2022). https://doi.org/10.1093/ajcl/avac015
16. Leurent, E.: An environment for autonomous driving decision-making (2018). https://github.com/eleurent/highway-env

17. Leurent, E., Blanco, Y., Efimov, D.V., Maillard, O.: Approximate robust control of uncertain dynamical systems. CoRR (2019). http://arxiv.org/abs/1903.00220
18. Leuschel, M., Vu, F., Rutenkolk, K.: Case study: safety controller for autonomous driving on highways (2024). https://github.com/hhu-stups/abz2025_casestudy_autonomous_driving/blob/main/case_study/specification_v2.pdf
19. Li, W., Rios-Torres, J., Wang, B., Khattak, Z.H.: Experimental assessment of communication delay's impact on connected automated vehicle speed volatility and energy consumption. Commun. Transp. Res. **4** (2024). https://doi.org/10.1016/j.commtr.2024.100136
20. Matos, F., Bernardino, J., Durães, J., Cunha, J.: A survey on sensor failures in autonomous vehicles: challenges and solutions. Sensors (2024). https://doi.org/10.3390/s24165108
21. Plebe, A., Svensson, H., Mahmoud, S., Da Lio, M.: Human-inspired autonomous driving: a survey. Cogn. Syst. Res. (2024). https://doi.org/10.1016/j.cogsys.2023.101169
22. Polymenakos, K., et al.: Safety guarantees for iterative predictions with gaussian processes. In: Proceedings of CDC 2020. IEEE (2020). https://doi.org/10.1109/CDC42340.2020.9304029
23. Shalev-Shwartz, S., Shammah, S., Shashua, A.: On a formal model of safe and scalable self-driving cars (2018). https://arxiv.org/abs/1708.06374
24. Shivakumar, S., Torfah, H., Desai, A., Seshia, S.A.: SOTER on ROS: a run-time assurance framework on the robot operating system. In: Deshmukh, J., Ničković, D. (eds.) Runtime Verification. RV 2020. LNCS, vol. 12399, pp 184–194. Springer, Cham (2020). https://doi.org/10.1007/978-3-030-60508-7_10
25. Toledo, T., Zohar, D.: Modeling duration of lane changes. Transp. Res. Rec. (2007). https://doi.org/10.3141/1999-08
26. Tolouei, R., Maher, M., Titheridge, H.: Vehicle mass and injury risk in two-car crashes: a novel methodology. Accident Anal. Prevent. (2013). https://doi.org/10.1016/j.aap.2012.04.005
27. Treiber, M., Hennecke, A., Helbing, D.: Congested traffic states in empirical observations and microscopic simulations. Phys. Rev. E (2000). https://doi.org/10.1103/PhysRevE.62.1805
28. Vaserstein, L.N.: Markovian processes on countable space product describing large systems of automata. Probl. Peredachi Inf. (1969)
29. Wicker, M., Laurenti, L., Patane, A., Paoletti, N., Abate, A., Kwiatkowska, M.: Probabilistic reach-avoid for bayesian neural networks. Artif. Intell. **334**, 104132 (2024). https://doi.org/10.1016/J.ARTINT.2024.104132
30. Yang, Q., Lu, F., Wang, J., Zhao, D., Yu, L.: Analysis of the insertion angle of lane-changing vehicles in nearly saturated fast road segments. Sustainability (2020). https://doi.org/10.3390/su12031013
31. Zhang, Y., Carballo, A., Yang, H., Takeda, K.: Perception and sensing for autonomous vehicles under adverse weather conditions: a survey. ISPRS J. Photogramm. Remote. Sens. (2023). https://doi.org/10.1016/j.isprsjprs.2022.12.021

Verification of Autonomous Neural Car Control with KeYmaera X

Enguerrand Prebet(✉), Samuel Teuber, and André Platzer

Karlsruhe Institute of Technology, Karlsruhe, Germany
{enguerrand.prebet,teuber,platzer}@kit.edu

Abstract. This article presents a formal model and formal safety proofs for the ABZ'25 case study in differential dynamic logic (dL). The case study considers an autonomous car driving on a highway with a neural network controller avoiding collisions with neighbouring cars. Using KeYmaera X's dL implementation we prove collision-freedom on an infinite time horizon which ensures that safety is preserved independently of trip length. The safety guarantees hold for time-varying reaction time and brake force. Our dL model considers the single lane scenario with cars ahead or behind. We demonstrate dL and its tools are a rigorous foundation for runtime monitoring, shielding, and neural network verification. Doing so sheds light on inconsistencies between the provided specification and simulation environment `highway-env` of the ABZ'25 study. We attempt to fix these inconsistencies and uncover numerous counterexamples indicative of issues in the provided reinforcement learning environment.

Keywords: Differential dynamic logic · Hybrid systems · Formal verification · Highway car control · Neural Network Control Systems

1 Introduction

This paper contributes a comprehensive study of formal safety proofs for the ABZ'25 highway case study of straight-line driving on highways with a neural network (NN) control system for the ego car based on the rigorous foundations of differential dynamic logic [25,26,28,29] (dL). Given the interest in highway driving, the contributions to the ABZ'25 case study challenge stand a more general appeal. While the specific outcomes focus on the ABZ'25 case study, the generality of the underlying tools could help make other applications safe.

Contributions. To tackle ABZ's case study we provide: *i)* A formal, provably safe dL [25,26,28,29] model of the hybrid systems dynamics of straight-line driving described by ABZ'25 [16]. We identify the control constraints required for safe driving. *ii)* A derivation of real arithmetic constraints that serve either as sandbox/shield for the black-box NN or for the *gapless* rigorous white-box verification of concrete NNs. *iii)* A verification-based, exhaustive characterization

M. Leuschel and F. Ishikawa (Eds.): ABZ 2025, LNCS 15728, pp. 288–307, 2026.
https://doi.org/10.1007/978-3-031-94533-5_17

of all unsafe behaviours in two NNs trained using the `highway-env` environment provided by ABZ'25. *iv)* An empirical validation of the derived sandbox and shield.

Importantly, our safe controller and the derived monitoring/verification conditions are fully symbolic and proved safe for arbitrary parameter choices making the model, controller, sandbox and NN verification technique useful for future endeavours. Additionally, reaction time and braking power may vary (within bounds) during execution. The results underscore that safety guarantees in dL are practically applicable to (neural) real-world systems – either through monitoring/shielding or via verification of the NN w.r.t. dL derived constraints.

While we demonstrate that dL and implementation monitoring/verification can be *gaplessly* integrated, we observe the existence of a significant *model-to-simulation* (*model2sim*) gap between the specification and the simulator provided by ABZ [16]. The well-known *sim2real gap* leads to decreased performance when simulation-trained agents are deployed in the real world. Similarly, the *model2sim* gap induces unsafe behaviour of an agent if the simulation insufficiently matches the model's assumptions about the real world. We identify this gap as an important roadblock on the highway to safe NN controllers.

Related Work. Prior work analysed safe car control in dL [18,27,33] (in one instance using refinement [17]). Unlike prior case studies applying dL guarantees to NN control [8,35], this work has a more complex environment (e.g. variable speed for surrounding cars) which increases the complexity of safety criteria. Car control (with different dynamics [36]) has also been studied by numerous closed-loop NN verification tools (see e.g. the ARCH competition [19–21]). Unlike the closed-loop approaches, our work can provide guarantees on an infinite-time horizon, i.e. independent of the car's trip length. Event-B [1] has also been used to model automotive applications [2] without application to NNs. Unlike a `highway-env` ProB model [38] we explicitly model the environment's continuous dynamics and support NN verification. Unlike another shielding approach [34] we characterize safe behaviour a priori instead of learning from catastrophic behaviour.

2 Background

This section provides an overview of differential dynamic logic (dL). Before presenting results on highway car control, we first illustrate the concepts of this section using a cartoonishly simplified application: We consider a car that starts at a one-dimensional, positive position p and pretend the car's controller can influence the car's position by directly choosing the car's velocity v with immediate effect. The safety requirement of the controller is to keep the car at a positive position, i.e. $p > 0$. We first present dL in general, then the ModelPlex technology for the derivation of runtime monitors and three applications of these formulas.

2.1 Differential Dynamic Logic for Hybrid Systems

dL is a program logic for reasoning about cyber-physical systems given as *hybrid programs*. On a high level, dL is a first-order multi-modal logic where modalities are parameterized with programs and the first-order formulas are interpreted w.r.t. real arithmetic. Formulas of dL have the following structure:

Definition 1 (Formulas). Formulas *are defined by the grammar below where* θ, η *are terms,* ϕ, ψ *are formulas and* α, β *are hybrid programs (Definition 2):*

$$\phi, \psi ::= \theta \leq \eta \mid \neg\phi \mid \phi \wedge \psi \mid \forall x\, \phi \mid [\alpha]\phi \mid \alpha \leq \beta$$

While the first four elements of the grammar correspond to logical structures known from first-order real arithmetic formulas, the latter two are specific to differential dynamic logic [25,26,28,29] and differential refinement logic [17,30].

Unlike first-order formulas which are usually evaluated in a fixed structure, dL evaluates formulas w.r.t. states that assign values to variables. The programs (which will be discussed in greater detail below) then induce a state transition relation which is integrated into the logic via the grammar's fifth formula: $[\alpha]\phi$ is true in a state ω iff *after every program run* of α the formula ϕ is satisfied, i.e. if for all state transitions of α from the current state ω the formula ϕ holds in the resulting state. If ϕ is a property that indicates safety of the system, then $[\alpha]\phi$ expresses that the system always remains safe (see Sect. 3.5). Finally, $\alpha \leq \beta$ expresses that the program α *refines* the program β in the current state, i.e. $\alpha \leq \beta$ holds in a state ω iff all states reachable from ω via the transitions of α are also reachable via β's state transition relation. Refinements are used to transfer safety properties between hybrid programs (see Sect. 4.1). A formula is called *valid* if it is satisfied in all states. We now turn to dL's *hybrid programs* which allow discrete and continuous actions and are formally defined as follows:

Definition 2 (Hybrid Programs). Hybrid programs α, β *are defined by the grammar below where* x *is a variable,* θ *is a term and* ψ *is a formula:*

$$\alpha, \beta ::= ?\psi \mid x := \theta \mid x := * \mid x' = \theta \& \psi \mid \alpha \cup \beta \mid \alpha;\beta \mid \alpha^*$$

The first program primitive $?\psi$ (check) only proceeds if formula ψ is satisfied in the current state. The second and third primitive are assignments, either w.r.t. a term ($x := \theta$) or nondeterministically to an arbitrary value ($x := *$). The fourth primitive ($x' = \theta \,\&\, \psi$) describes the continuous, nondeterministic evolution of variable x along the differential equation $x' = \theta$ within the domain constraint ψ. The next two primitives allow the composition of programs by either nondetermnistically choosing one of two ($\alpha \cup \beta$) or by executing them sequentially ($\alpha;\beta$). The final primitive α^* nondeterministically runs the program α for 0 or more iterations. The support of hybrid programs for continuous evolution and discrete as well as continuous nondeterminism is e.g. crucial for the analysis of cyber-physical systems without a fixed clock cycle. Many classical program constructs can be translated into the primitives of hybrid programs. For example, if-then-else can be rewritten as follows: $\texttt{if}\,(\psi)\ \alpha\ \texttt{else}\ \beta \stackrel{\text{def}}{=} (?\psi;\alpha) \cup (?\neg\psi);\beta$. Similarly, we can represent while loops: $\texttt{while}\,(\psi)\ \alpha \stackrel{\text{def}}{=} (?\psi;\alpha)^*;?\neg\psi$.

Example. We now explain how our simple cyber-physical system (the velocity-controlled car) can be modelled in dL. All variables, $p, v, \ldots$, that evolve along the execution are in lower-case, while constants like T are in upper-case. As outlined above, the car's position is described by a real-valued position p. The car's dynamics are then described by the differential equation $p' = v$ where v is the velocity determined by the controller. To derive safety guarantees we assume that our controller is invoked at least every T seconds. Hence, we model the physical part of our example as $\alpha_{\text{plant}} \stackrel{\text{def}}{=} t := 0; p' = v, t' = 1 \,\&\, t \leq \text{ T}$. Here, p evolves as outlined above and we additionally introduced a clock variable t which guarantees that the evolution runs for at most T seconds via the domain constraint $t \leq T$. We already formulated the car's safety condition as $p > 0$ at the beginning of this section. The final ingredient for our dL model is a *control envelope* that provides a nondeterministic description of allowed behaviour which keeps the system safe. Using dL to verify control *envelopes* rather than one concrete controller is quite a common approach as it allows the verification of a whole family of possible controller implementations at once [11]. It is generally preferable to design very general control envelopes that encompass the largest possible range of behaviours that can be certified as safe. In our example, we can formulate the control envelope as the nondeterministic program $\alpha_{\text{ctrl}} \stackrel{\text{def}}{=} v := *; ?(p + Tv > 0)$. This control envelope ensures that we only choose velocities v that avoid negative positions. Indeed, we can use dL's proof calculus (and its implementation in KeYmaera X) to prove the validity of the following dL formula $T > 0 \wedge p > 0 \rightarrow [(\alpha_{\text{ctrl}}; \alpha_{\text{plant}})^*]p > 0$. This formula expresses that (assuming an initial state with $T > 0$ and $p > 0$) we can run this system for arbitrarily long (note the nondeterministic loop) and the safety condition $p > 0$ will always be satisfied afterwards. This can be proven inductively through the invariant $T > 0 \wedge p > 0$. The ability to perform inductive, infinite time horizon reasoning for dL models is one of the major advantages of dL over many reachability-based analyses.

The formula above also exhibits a very common pattern in dL models where we provide a safety guarantee over the execution of a nondeterministic loop which consists of the sequential execution of a control envelope (α_{ctrl}) and an environment model (α_{plant}). However, while we have verified an infinite class of potential controllers, we have not yet verified any concrete given controller implementation. In the remainder of this section, we will present dL-based technologies that allow us to bridge the gap between a verified control envelope and a concrete controller implementation.

2.2 ModelPlex for Verified Runtime Monitoring

In the previous section, we saw how dL can be used to model cyber-physical systems and to verify control envelopes. However, the verified control envelopes differ from the control systems we would like to use in practice: Concrete, real-world controllers will often be implemented in compilable programming languages or, as in the case of the highway case study, the controller's behaviour might even be determined by an NN. This raises the question how this challenge can be overcome. On the one hand, it is possible to embed the behaviour of more complicated programming languages into dL [10,12], however, such approaches are always tailored to specific programming languages and require that we perform interactive proofs on the concrete controller's behaviour. On the other hand, we can use a verified control envelope to derive runtime monitoring conditions that can subsequently be checked on a concrete system – possibly even in a black box fashion. This technique to derive correct-by-construction runtime monitoring conditions from a given control envelope α_{ctrl} is called *ModelPlex* [22].

Based on a given control envelope α_{ctrl} over variables $V\alpha_{\text{ctrl}}$, ModelPlex uses dL 's calculus rules to derive a first-order real arithmetic formula ψ over variables $V(\alpha_{\text{ctrl}}) \dot{\cup} \{x^+ | x \in V(\alpha_{\text{ctrl}})\}$ where x^+ indicates the value of x in the next state. For instance assuming $V(\alpha_{\text{ctrl}}) = \{x\}$, if the formula ψ is satisfied by $x = v_1$ and $x^+ = v_2$ for some v_1, v_2, then there exists a state transition for α_{ctrl} where the value of x changes from v_1 to v_2. Since we have a safety proof for α_{ctrl} this implies the safety guarantees for our control envelope carry over to a system where x's value changes from v_1 to v_2. Hence, the formula ψ can be used to monitor the safety of a (black-box) controller implementation by checking whether a concrete assignment of the implementation's pre- and post-values satisfies ψ.

For the velocity-controller car, the variables $V(\alpha_{\text{ctrl}})$ are the position and the velocity: $\{p, v\}$, and the formula given by ModelPlex is $\psi \stackrel{\text{def}}{=} p^+ = p \wedge p + Tv^+ > 0 \wedge t^+ = 0$. Thus, any concrete implementation of such a controller will be safe if this formula is satisfied during execution, i.e. if the controller does not change the position ($p = p^+$) and sets some velocity v^+ that respects $p + Tv^+ > 0$. Additionally, it requires that the clock variable t be reset to 0.

2.3 Applications of ModelPlex

The formula computed by ModelPlex [22] tells us which control actions come with a dL safety guarantee. As explained below, this formula can be used in at least three manners to derive safety guarantees for controller implementations.

Monitoring (VeriPhy). First and foremost, we can use the derived formula to check the actions computed by the controller implementation at runtime via a runtime monitor. To this end, we assign the formula's variables with the implementation's input and output values and check whether the action is provably safe according to the ModelPlex runtime monitor. In case the implementation chooses an action violating the runtime monitor, we overwrite the action using a fallback controller. This approach comes with a formally verified code generation pipeline called VeriPhy [3] which serves as a sandbox for a given controller and comprises provably correct machine arithmetic.

Shielding (Justified Speculative Control). One drawback of VeriPhy in the context of NN Control is its conservatism: While traditionally programmed controllers usually return exactly one action that must be overwritten if unsafe,

NNs often return a probability distribution over actions. However, it is not necessarily reasonable to entirely overwrite the NN's action if its most likely action is unsafe. Instead Justified Speculative Control [8,9] (JSC) *shields* the NN using runtime enforcement technique [14,22] that constrain the action space to known-safe options. Thus, JSC can still treat the concrete controller as a black box but allow for more flexibility in the chosen actions. To this end, JSC checks for possible actions whether they satisfy the ModelPlex condition. JSC then chooses the allowed action with the highest probability according to the reinforcement learning agent. Additionally, JSC only performs a safety check in situations where the environment behaves as modelled in dL (this is achieved via ModelPlex's environment monitoring technology which goes beyond the scope of this exposition). Importantly, this technique can be applied both during training and at runtime.

Verification (VerSAILLE and NCubeV). The previous approaches only provide *a posteriori* guarantees by restricting or overwriting the controller's actions at runtime. Alternatively, we can also use the monitoring condition derived by ModelPlex for *a priori* verification of the NN. This is achieved via the VerSAILLE approach [35]: In essence, we verify whether there exists a state inside the dL model's invariant state space where the NN's action violates the ModelPlex controller monitor. For this section's running example, we would verify that an NN (with input p and output v^+) satisfies the following specification [35, Thm. 2]:

$$\underbrace{p > 0}_{\text{Invariant}} \rightarrow \underbrace{p + Tv^+ > 0}_{\text{Controller Monitor}} .$$

This is achieved by a compute-intensive numerical analysis of the NN that mathematically proves the absence of such counterexamples. As our running example has a simple, linear controller monitor and invariant, most modern NN verifiers (as reported in recent surveys and competitions [4,5,13]) can be used. However, for realistic dL models, the ModelPlex conditions usually have a significantly more complicated propositional structure with nonlinear real arithmetic. Neither of these features is supported by "classical" NN verifiers nor by their common specification language [6]. To this end, we recently proposed the NCubeV tool [35] supporting both arbitrary propositional structure and polynomial arithmetic.

The usage of NN verification has multiple advantages. First, it allows the deployment of autonomous, unmonitored NN Control Systems. Second, it allows the usage of NNs in applications without an obvious fallback strategy or for cases with continuous action spaces. Finally, it can also serve for diagnostics: Either to estimate how often a given NN performs (un)safe actions or to discover unsafe behaviour that is empirically invisible, e.g. due to simulator limitations.

3 A Verified dL Model for the ABZ Highway Case-Study

This section presents the verified dL model developed for this case study. We start by introducing the cyber-physical system of interest (Sect. 3.1). After giving the general structure and how it interleaves the discrete and continuous actions that can occur between each control cycle (Sect. 3.2), we focus on the plant (Sect. 3.3) and the controller (Sect. 3.4). Finally, we express safety conditions in dL for the model and verify them using the theorem prover KeYmaera X [7,24,28] (Sect. 3.5). Our proofs are reproducible via an artifact [31].

3.1 A Safe Autonomous Driving System

The model is about a safe autonomous driving system, referred to as the ego car, that should prevent collision with another car on a single straight lane. All constants, $A_{\max}, V, T, \ldots$, must be positive except for braking deceleration, $B_{\min}, B_{\max}$, which are negative. Both cars have length L but are modelled as single points: with position x_e, speed v_e, and acceleration a_e for the ego car, and with position x_o, speed v_o, and acceleration a_o for the other. Thus, absence of collision is ensured by maintaining a distance of at least L between the two cars. No car moves backwards and their speed is at most V. The cars have a maximum acceleration of $A_{\max}$ and a maximum braking deceleration of $B_{\max}$. Additionally, the ego car may not always draw the maximum power of the brake or the engine. It will however always be able to brake with deceleration at least $B_{\min} \geq B_{\max}$ and accelerate with acceleration at least $A_{\min} \leq A_{\max}$. These constraints are imposed on the cars themselves, so even if they are trying to brake or accelerate, they cannot go backward or exceed speed limit V. The ego car observes the environment at least every T seconds, whereas the other car may react more often without restriction. No regularity or periodicity is assumed in the reaction time of the ego car as long as it always remains below T seconds.

Overall, the constants are constrained by the formula: $\mathtt{ctx}_C \stackrel{\text{def}}{=} T > 0 \wedge L > 0 \wedge V > 0 \wedge B_{\max} \leq B_{\min} < 0 < A_{\min} \leq A_{\max}$. It can be extended by bounds on speed and acceleration: $\mathtt{ctx} \stackrel{\text{def}}{=} \mathtt{ctx}_C \wedge B_{\max} \leq a_e, a_o \leq A_{\max} \wedge 0 \leq v_e, v_o \leq V$.

3.2 Overall Structure of the dL Model

The general structure of the model is as follows:

$$\mathtt{model(c)} ::= \Big(\underbrace{\mathtt{ctrl}_o; (\mathtt{c} \cup ?t < t_e + T)}_{\text{control}}; \underbrace{\mathtt{accelCorr}; \mathtt{dyn}}_{\text{plant}}\Big)^*$$

The model is parametric in the controller of the ego car $\mathtt{c}$ to handle both the generic controller $\mathtt{ctrl}_e$ (see Sect. 3.4) and the NN controller $\mathtt{ctrl}_{\text{NN}}$ (see Sect. 4.1). In this section, we write $\mathtt{model}$ for $\mathtt{model(ctrl}_e\mathtt{)}$.

$\mathtt{ctrl}_o$ models the controller of the other car. It does not assume any minimal time between each execution of $\mathtt{ctrl}_o$. Then $\mathtt{c}$ models the controller of the ego car and sets t_e to t. If it has been less than T seconds since t_e was last set, the nondeterministic choice allows $\mathtt{c}$ to be skipped. Thus, the controller is only assumed to run at least once every T seconds. Having the possibility of skipping the controller allows discrete events, e.g. the other controller, to still occur without the ego car reacting. `accelCorr` (defined in Sect. 3.3) models the acceleration correction when reaching the speed boundaries. It ensures that a braking car, with negative acceleration, does not go backwards by changing its acceleration to zero. This is a discrete change but happens independently of any controller. In particular, the ego car does not notice the change before its next control cycle. Finally, `dyn` models the continuous dynamics of the system, i.e. the actual motion of the car evolving with time. These execute in a loop so that the system alternates between the control and the plant arbitrarily many times. We elaborate the details of each component, starting with the plant.

3.3 Modelling the Physical Plant

$$\begin{array}{r|l}
\texttt{accelCorr} & \texttt{if}\ (v_o = 0 \wedge a_o < 0) \vee (v_o = V \wedge a_o > 0)\ a_o := 0 \\
& \texttt{if}\ (v_e = 0 \wedge a_e < 0) \vee (v_e = V \wedge a_e > 0)\ a_e := 0 \\
\texttt{dyn} & {x_e}' = v_e, {v_e}' = a_e, {x_o}' = v_o, {v_o}' = a_o, t' = 1 \\
& \qquad \& \ t \leq t_e + T \wedge 0 \leq v_e \leq V \wedge 0 \leq v_o \leq V
\end{array}$$

The plant is composed of a discrete part, `accelCorr`, and a continuous part, `dyn`. First, if any car has come to a stop or reached their speed limit, then their acceleration is set to 0 for saturation. Then the continuous dynamics follows the ODEs specifying for both cars, that speed is the derivative of the position, ${x_i}' = v_i$, and that acceleration is the derivative of speed, ${v_i}' = a_i$. Time is explicit with constant derivative. The domain constraints ensure that the dynamics always stop before a discrete event must be executed, whether it is a controller event – if $t = t_e + T$ – or a plant event – if a car stops, or reaches their speed limit.

3.4 Modelling the Car Controllers

$$\begin{array}{r|l}
\texttt{ctrl}_o & a_o := *; ?(B_{\max} \leq a_o \leq A_{\max}); \\
\texttt{ctrl}_e & a_e := *; ?(B_{\max} \leq a_e \leq A_{\max}); t_e := t; \\
& \texttt{if}(\neg(\texttt{safeBack} \vee \texttt{safeFront})) \\
& \quad \texttt{if}(x_e \leq x_o) \\
& \qquad a_e := *; ?(B_{\max} \leq a_e \leq B_{\min}); \\
& \quad \texttt{else} \\
& \qquad a_e := *; ?(A_{\min} \leq a_e \leq A_{\max});
\end{array}$$

The control consists of the controllers for the two cars. The controller $\texttt{ctrl}_o$ for the other car isn't concerned about safety so it just selects any acceleration within the limitation of the vehicle. As the assignment is nondeterministic, all choices of acceleration are taken into account for the safety proof. Then the controller for the ego car also selects an arbitrary acceleration. It however performs an additional check. If the chosen acceleration does not satisfy one of the safety conditions, `safeBack` or `safeFront` discussed below, then a fallback procedure overrides the acceleration. The fallback simply tries to increase the distance with the other car. If the ego is behind, it brakes with $a_e \leq B_{\min}$, and accelerates, $a_e \geq A_{\min}$, if ahead. Finally, t_e is set to t to record the last time the controller ran.

Safety Condition When Behind. We focus on `safeBack` shown in Formula (1). It expresses when an acceleration guarantees safety when the ego car is behind the other car. First, the two cars should be at a distance of at least L from each other, as that would correspond to a collision otherwise. Additionally, if both cars were to brake, there should still be a distance at least L when they stop. For a braking ego car with acceleration $a_e < 0$, it stops at position $\text{pos}_e(a_e) \stackrel{\text{def}}{=} x_e - \frac{v_e^2}{2a_e}$ meters. For the other car, we assume the worst case. This happens when the other car's acceleration is directed towards the ego car, that is when it is braking at maximum force, $a_o = B_{\text{max}}$, in which case it stops at position $\text{pos}_o \stackrel{\text{def}}{=} x_o - \frac{v_o^2}{2B_{\text{max}}}$. With constant acceleration, if the current position of the cars and their stopping position are both at safe distance, then these properties are invariants of the dynamics and thus ensure collision-freedom. Changing acceleration for the other car can only increase its distance to the ego car and so does not risk collision.

$$\begin{aligned} x_e + L \leq x_o \wedge \big(&a_e \leq B_{\text{min}} \wedge \text{pos}_e(B_{\text{min}}) + L < \text{pos}_o \\ &\vee B_{\text{min}} \leq a_e \wedge v_e + a_e T < 0 \wedge \text{pos}_e(a_e) + L < \text{pos}_o \\ &\vee B_{\text{min}} \leq a_e \wedge v_e + a_e T \geq 0 \wedge \text{pos}_e(B_{\text{min}}) + \text{corrDist} + L < \text{pos}_o\big) \end{aligned} \tag{1}$$

To handle the ego car's change of acceleration, this idea is refined further and split in three scenarios:

1. Since the ego car is only assumed to be able to brake with $a_e = B_{\text{min}}$ for sure, even if it is currently braking more, we still must rely on the minimum braking deceleration for checking the distance, so we use $\text{pos}_e(B_{\text{min}})$.
2. If $a_e \geq B_{\text{min}}$ but the car will stop before T seconds, then the acceleration a_e can be used directy. Once stopped, the car remains safe, so we use $\text{pos}_e(a_e)$.
3. Otherwise, we must check that the car can start braking at the next control cycle, after at most T seconds, and stop before crashing. This reuses the first case, with a correction term to account for the distance travelled and the speed change before the next cycle: $\text{corrDist} \stackrel{\text{def}}{=} (\frac{-a_e}{B_{\text{min}}} + 1)(\frac{a_e}{2}T^2 + Tv_e)$.

Safety Condition When Ahead. If the ego car is ahead, the setting is similar when changing the frame of reference. From the perspective of an observer moving at constant speed V, the two cars are moving at speed $\widetilde{v}_i \stackrel{\text{def}}{=} v_i - V$ in the opposite direction. Their positions are now $\widetilde{x}_i \stackrel{\text{def}}{=} x_i - V \times t$, and the worst case occurs when the other car approaches the ego car with maximal acceleration (i.e. $a_o = A_{\text{max}}$). Reusing the insight for the previous case, we consider their stopping position in that new frame of reference ($\widetilde{v}_i = 0$), which amounts to reaching maximum speed ($v_i = V$). This gives the following distances updated with the new variables: $\widetilde{\text{pos}}_e(a_e) \stackrel{\text{def}}{=} \widetilde{x}_e - \frac{\widetilde{v}_e^2}{2a_e}$ for the ego car, and $\widetilde{\text{pos}}_o \stackrel{\text{def}}{=} \widetilde{x}_o - \frac{\widetilde{v}_o^2}{2A_{\text{max}}}$ for the other. The resulting formula `safeFront` is given in [32].

3.5 Safety Proofs

Now that the model is defined comes the actual verification. Since the goal is to prevent collisions, the safety condition is simply that the two cars have at least a distance L between them. Being on a single lane, they cannot cross each other, so the order of the cars remains the same, so the two cases when the ego car is behind or ahead can be proved independently. Due to their similarity, we again focus on the case where the ego car is behind. The general assumptions include the constraints from the specifications from Sect. 3.1, i.e. `ctx`, and assume the controller of the ego car has last been run T seconds ago so that it must run initially, i.e. $t_e = t - T$. The only other requirement is that initial states where a crash is unavoidable are prohibited, in which case, no controller can guarantee safety. This initial condition correspond to the first case of Formula (1): the fallback action should give enough distance before stopping.

Theorem 1. *Formulas* (2) *and* (3) *are valid and guarantee the absence of collision.*

$$\texttt{ctx} \wedge x_e + L \leq x_o \wedge \text{pos}_e(B_{min}) + L < \text{pos}_o \wedge t_e = t - T \rightarrow [\texttt{model}]\, x_e + L \leq x_o \quad (2)$$
$$\texttt{ctx} \wedge x_o + L \leq x_e \wedge \widetilde{\text{pos}}_o + L < \widetilde{\text{pos}}_e(A_{min}) \wedge t_e = t - T \rightarrow [\texttt{model}]\, x_o + L \leq x_e \quad (3)$$

The theorem is proved using KeYmaera X. The proof relies on invariants that generalise of `safeBack` and `safeFront` where T is replaced by $T + t_e - t$ to account for the time elapsed since the last run of $\texttt{ctrl}_e$, extended with the specification constraints `ctx`. The evaluation of the two verifications is given in [32].

4 Safeguarding Neural Control

The previous section derived a dL model for the highway environment as specified in ABZ's case study document [16] and proved its safety. As a next step, we connect these (abstract) safety guarantees to the concrete control system implementation running inside the `highway-env` simulation [15]. To this end, we use the techniques described in Sect. 2.3. In contrast to the dL controller $\texttt{ctrl}_e$ that chooses a (continuous) acceleration value $B_{\max} \leq a_e \leq A_{\max}$, the trained reinforcement learning agent for the single-lane case of `highway-env` consists of an NN outputting one of three discrete actions (brake, idle, accelerate). The NN outputs three values and determines its action via an argmax operation (e.g. brake is chosen whenever the NN's first output is maximal), prioritising lowest speed in case of ties. Hence, we must first extend our dL controller model to account for the NN's three outputs (Sect. 4.1). Subsequently, we can use ModelPlex and the refined controller to derive a formula that can be used for verification, shielding and monitoring (Sect. 4.2). While our methodology is general, this section focuses on the case where the ego car drives behind another car and must ensure safety.

4.1 Refining the dL Controller

To account for the concrete NN, we transform the controller's action space from choosing an acceleration a_e to choosing an action via three outputs y_1, y_2, y_3:

$$
\begin{array}{l|l}
\texttt{ctrl}_{\text{NN}} & y_1 := *; y_2 := *; y_3 := *; \\
& \texttt{if}(y_1 \geq y_2 \wedge y_1 \geq y_3)\ \{a_e := *; ?(B_{\max} \leq a_e \leq B_{\min})\}; \\
& \texttt{if}(y_2 > y_1 \wedge y_2 \geq y_3)\ \{a_e := 0\}; \\
& \texttt{if}(y_3 > y_1 \wedge y_3 > y_2)\ \{a_e := *; ?(A_{\min} \leq a_e \leq A_{\max})\}; \\
& \{\ \ ?(x_e \leq x_o \wedge B_{\max} \leq a_e \leq B_{\min}) \\
& \ \cup\ ?(x_e \geq x_o \wedge A_{\min} \leq a_e \leq A_{\max}) \\
& \ \cup\ ?(\texttt{safeBack} \vee \texttt{safeFront})\ \}; t_e := t
\end{array}
$$

Based on the NN's outputs y_1, y_2, y_3 the program determines the corresponding acceleration value a_e and then ensures safety via the checks we already know from the dL model for $\texttt{ctrl}_e$. To recover the formal guarantee from Formula (2), we show that $\texttt{model}(\texttt{ctrl}_{\text{NN}})$ refines $\texttt{model}(\texttt{ctrl}_e)$, i.e. $\texttt{model}(\texttt{ctrl}_{\text{NN}})$'s transitions are included in $\texttt{model}(\texttt{ctrl}_e)$'s. In fact, we prove a slightly relaxed refinement to ignore the variables y_1, y_2, y_3 that are modified by $\texttt{ctrl}_{\text{NN}}$ and not $\texttt{ctrl}_e$.

Lemma 1. *The following refinement is valid:*

$$\texttt{ctx}_C \rightarrow (\texttt{model}(\texttt{ctrl}_{NN}) \leq (y_1 := *; y_2 := *; y_3 := *; \texttt{model}(\texttt{ctrl}_e))) \tag{4}$$

Using this refinement, it is then trivial to extend the proof of Formula (2) to $\texttt{model}(\texttt{ctrl}_{\text{NN}})$. The proof of refinement is done using KeYmaera X's differential refinement logic implementation[1] and is based on a proof of refinement between $\texttt{ctrl}_{\text{NN}}$ and $y_1 := *; y_2 := *; y_3 := *; \text{ctrl}_e$.

4.2 ModelPlex for Safe Neural Network Control

We have now shown that any action taken by $\texttt{ctrl}_{\text{NN}}$ keeps the system safe on an infinite-time horizon. Using ModelPlex we derive a controller monitor for $\texttt{ctrl}_{\text{NN}}$ that we can use w.r.t. a concrete NN. To this end, we note that according to the specification [16] the NN has (among other inputs) a vector $\overline{\texttt{in}} = (x_e, v_e, x_o, v_o)$ and the NN's only output is a vector $\overline{\texttt{out}} = (y_1^+, y_2^+, y_3^+)$. Besides the variables in $\overline{\texttt{in}}$, $\overline{\texttt{out}}$ the controller monitor derived via ModelPlex also constrains the acceleration variables a_e and a_e^+ (as $\texttt{ctrl}_{\text{NN}}$ modifies a_e) as well as the clock variables t, t_e^+ (required for book-keeping on control cycles). We denote this ModelPlex condition for $\texttt{ctrl}_{\text{NN}}$ as $\texttt{mon}(\overline{\texttt{in}}, \overline{\texttt{out}}, a_e, a_e^+, t, t_0^+)$. As described in Sect. 2.3, VerSAILLE allows us to use the monitor $\texttt{mon}$ to verify the safety of an NN by additionally exploiting the dL model's loop invariant which tells us what states are reachable (and thus for which states the NN must exhibit safe actions). We denote this invariant as $\texttt{inv}(\overline{\texttt{in}}, a_e, a_o, t, t_0)$. In addition to the two cars' positions and velocities, the invariant also mentions the cars' accelerations and the clock variables t, t_e. As explained in Sect. 2.3 we can prove the infinite-time horizon safety of an NN by showing that all inputs inside the invariant $\texttt{inv}$ lead to outputs satisfying the controller monitor $\texttt{mon}$. Formally, this can be expressed as the following Theorem which follows from [35, Thm. 2]:

[1] https://github.com/LS-Lab/KeYmaeraX-release/tree/dRL-ABZ'25.

Theorem 2 (NNCS Safety Criterion). *Let g be an NN for highway car control as modeled in Sect. 3. If Formula* (5) *is satisfied for all $\overline{\mathtt{in}}$ and $\overline{\mathtt{out}} = g\left(\overline{\mathtt{in}}\right)$ then the safety guarantees derived in Theorem 1 apply to* $\mathtt{model}(g)$.

$$\forall a_e, a_e^+, a_o, t, t_e, t_e^+ \underbrace{\mathtt{inv}(\overline{\mathtt{in}}, a_e, a_o, t, t_0)}_{\textit{system invariant}} \rightarrow \underbrace{\mathtt{mon}(\overline{\mathtt{in}}, \overline{\mathtt{out}}, a_e, a_e^+, t, t_e, t_0^+)}_{\textit{monitoring formula}} \quad (5)$$

While this work omits the precise formulation, it is worth noting that the safety guarantees for g are rigorously founded in dL via a reconstruction of g inside dL through the notion of *nondeterministic mirrors* [35, Def. 16].

$$\begin{aligned}&\mathtt{nnCtx}(\overline{\mathtt{in}}, \overline{\mathtt{out}}, a_e^+, t_0, t_0^+, t) \stackrel{\text{def}}{=}\\ &y_1^+ \geq y_2^+ \wedge y_1^+ \geq y_3^+ \rightarrow B_{\max} \leq a_e^+ \leq B_{\min} \wedge\\ &y_2^+ > y_1^+ \wedge y_2^+ \geq y_3^+ \rightarrow a_e^+ = 0 \wedge\\ &y_3^+ > y_1^+ \wedge y_3^+ > y_2^+ \rightarrow a_e^+ = A_{\max} \wedge\\ &x_e + L \leq x_o \wedge t_e^+ = t \wedge t_e \leq t \leq t_e + T \wedge \mathtt{ctx}_C\end{aligned}$$

Fig. 1. Context assumptions for simplification

Unfortunately, Formula (5) cannot effectively be used for the NN verification directly as the NNs do not set the ego-cars acceleration (a_e^+) but rely on surrounding software which computes a_e^+ based on y_1, y_2, y_3 (and resets the clock variable t_e). Moreover, a_e, a_o, t and t_e are not inputs to the NN and would thus need to be quantified over. To make our verification condition practical, we derive a simplified version that we prove equivalent to Formula (5). To this end, we begin by axiomatizing our assumptions on the NN's surroundings. We assume the software correctly assigns a_e based on y_1, y_2, y_3, correctly manages clock variables and that we drive behind the other car (as mentioned above, we focus on this case). We also set $A_{\min} = A_{\max}$ (as done in the official ABZ specificaton [16]) and assume the known ranges of constants as formalized in Fig. 1. Assuming nnCtx, the system's invariant can then be simplified as follows:

$$\mathtt{inv}_{\text{simp}} \stackrel{\text{def}}{=} 0 \leq v_o \leq V \wedge 0 \leq v_e \leq V \wedge x_e + L \leq x_o \wedge \text{pos}_e(B_{\min}) + L < \text{pos}_o$$

The simplified invariant makes sense intuitively as it matches the initial condition constraints in Formula (2) on the variables in $\overline{\mathtt{in}}$. Similarly, we simplify mon by removing cases irrelevant to the ego-car driving behind, the management of clock variables and explicit mentions of a_e^+. This yields a simplified formula $\mathtt{mon}_{\text{simp}}(\overline{\mathtt{in}}, \overline{\mathtt{out}})$ [32]. For these simplifications, we prove equivalence to Formula (5) in KeYmaera X under the assumption of nnCtx:

Lemma 2 (Simplified NN Verification). *The following formula is valid:*

$$\mathtt{nnCtx}(\overline{\mathtt{in}}, \overline{\mathtt{out}}, a_e^+, t_0, t_0^+, t) \rightarrow$$
$$\left(\underbrace{\begin{pmatrix}\mathtt{inv}_{simp}(\overline{\mathtt{in}}) \rightarrow\\ \mathtt{mon}_{simp}(\overline{\mathtt{in}}, \overline{\mathtt{out}})\end{pmatrix}}_{\textit{simplified}} \leftrightarrow \underbrace{\begin{pmatrix}\forall a_e \forall a_o \Big((\mathtt{inv}(\overline{\mathtt{in}}, a_e, a_o, t, t_0))\\ \qquad \rightarrow \mathtt{mon}(\overline{\mathtt{in}}, \overline{\mathtt{out}}, a_e, a_e^+, t, t_0^+)\Big)\end{pmatrix}}_{\textit{Formula}(5)}\right)$$

This serves as justification for verifying the simplified condition $\texttt{nnSpec}_{\text{simp}} \overset{\text{def}}{=} \texttt{inv}_{\text{simp}}\left(\overline{\texttt{in}}\right) \rightarrow \texttt{mon}_{\text{simp}}\left(\overline{\texttt{in}}, \overline{\texttt{out}}\right)$ on our NNs as we can assume nnCtx. While $\texttt{nnSpec}_{\text{simp}}$ is free of quantifiers, it still contains polynomial arithmetic (e.g. in $\text{pos}_e(B_{\text{min}})$). In addition to the two cars modelled in dL , the NN controller gets as input the states of up to three more cars (we will call these cars car 1 to car 5 with car 1 being the ego car). For the single-lane case, the ego car's influence on crashes with cars 3–5 is very limited. However, we know that car 2 can avoid a crash with car 3 if the velocity of car 3 is larger than the velocity of car 2 (e.g. by performing an emergency brake). For now, we thus assume that for the extra cars $3 \leq i \leq 5$ it is guaranteed that car $i-1$ is slower than car i. We thus encode these additional constraints on the state of cars 3–5 in a predicate $\texttt{nnSpec}_{\text{add}}$ [32] and then verify the NN w.r.t. to the specification $\texttt{nnSpec}_{\text{add}} \rightarrow \texttt{nnSpec}_{\text{simp}}$. $\texttt{nnSpec}_{\text{add}}$ also contains constraints on the encoding of (non-)presence of cars and the NN's input space normalisation described in ABZ's specification [16]. In Sect. 5 we will see concrete examples for verifying NNs with respect to the full specification $\texttt{nnSpec}_{\text{add}} \rightarrow \texttt{nnSpec}_{\text{simp}}$, but we will first demonstrate that similar formulas can also be used for monitoring and shielding.

Justified Speculative Control and VeriPhy. Assuming nnCtx and $\texttt{inv}_{\text{simp}}$, it also holds that $\texttt{mon}_{\text{simp}}(\overline{\texttt{in}}, \overline{\texttt{out}}) \leftrightarrow \texttt{mon}(\overline{\texttt{in}}, \overline{\texttt{out}}, a_e^+, a_e^-, t, t_0^+)$. Consequently, we can use the simplified monitoring condition not only for verification, but also for the construction of shields (JSC) and runtime monitors (VeriPhy). JSC is meant to only check the runtime monitor when the observed behaviour matches the model. To this end, JSC usually has a model monitor that checks whether a given state transition is explainable by the dL environment model. However, early experiments showed divergence in the simulation's environment and the dL environment model which would effectively deactivate JSC in most of the state space (these observations will be discussed in more detail in the latter sections). Consequently, we relaxed the model monitor to its "most" safety-critical parts and only check whether a given state is inside the invariant state space.

In this section, we have seen how ModelPlex conditions and invariants can be applied even if they contain unobservable variables [23]. This allows us to apply dL -based monitoring, shielding and verification techniques independently of whether some variables (e.g. time or effective acceleration) are measurable or not.

5 Verification Results

A manual analysis of the agents in ABZ's case study uncovered that the agents' action space is different from its formal specification [16]: The highway-env simulator configuration admits different action spaces. The

Table 1. Results of NN verification.

NN	Time	# Crashes	
		default	braking
Sect. 5.1	3.6 h	538	3,593
Sect. 5.2	1.9 h	4,852	8,713

provided agents used `DiscreteMetaAction` configuring the agent's action space as decreasing/increasing a *reference velocity* $v_r \in \{0, 5, \ldots, 35, 40\}$ achieved via a low-level proportional controller. This can lead to very different action outcomes compared to the specified action space. For example, the *brake* action as described in the formal specification *always* leads to a deceleration (unless v_e is zero already). In contrast, the "brake" action with the `DiscreteMetaAction` configuration can even lead to an *acceleration* (e.g. if $v_e = 10$ and $v_r = 20$, "braking" sets v_r to 15 and the proportional controller accelerates so that $v_e = 15$ is reached). The safety guarantees and verification conditions derived in Sects. 3 and 4 thus only apply to the written specification, but not to the simulator's default configuration violating its own description. We trained a new NN using `highway-env`'s `DiscreteAction` configuration option[2] (otherwise using the default configuration) that can brake, idle or accelerate *directly* ($a_e \in \{B_{\max}, 0, A_{\max}\}$). We discuss verification of this NN (Sect. 5.1) and an improved version (Sect. 5.2). Results are reproducible via our artifact [31].

5.1 A First Attempt at Verification

As a first step we attempted to verify the NN for two cars w.r.t. the specification derived in Sect. 4 using NCubeV [35] which supports polynomial arithmetic specifications. In case a specification cannot be proven, NCubeV is also capable of enumerating *all* counterexample regions (represented as polytopes) to a given specification. Notably, successful verification would, by construction, guarantee that the two cars on the highway will never crash – independently of trip time. The trained NN instead turned out to be unsafe: NCubeV returned **14,917 counterexample regions**. Computing these counterexamples took 3.6 h (see Table 1). However, verifying safety is often quicker than enumerating all counterexamples for NCubeV [35]. Each counterexample region has a representative input violating the specification. These inputs can be used to sample trajectories from the simulator to find concrete crashes. Figure 2 shows one of 538 concrete crashes we observed when the front car is controlled by the *Intelligent Driver Model* [37] (IDM). Importantly, these crashes could have all been avoided by braking. When the front car is configured to perform an emergency brake, our sampling strategy yielded 3,593 crash trajectories.

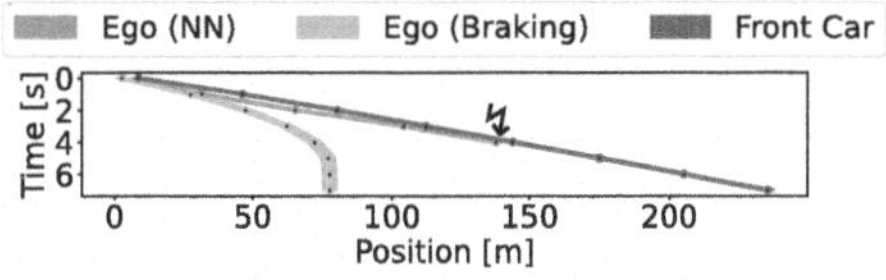

Fig. 2. One of 538 examples of unsafe NN behaviour in `default` environment (x-axis shows position, y-axis shows time). Braking could have avoided a crash (↯).

These observations raise two questions: 1. Why did the NN not learn to brake in time? 2. Is there nonetheless a way to safely deploy the NN at hand? One

[2] Python's weak type system makes the configuration especially error-prone: The `acceleration_range` is configured via a *2-tuple* (`min,max`). Accidentally providing a *list* of actions interpolates discrete accelerations between the list's first two elements.

answer to the former question can be found in the IDM. While originally derived as a means to understand traffic congestion, `highway-env` uses the model to control the environment's cars. Due to the way IDM is set up, the ego-car rarely experiences emergency brakes of front cars and thus does not learn to account for them (as indicated by over 3,000 crash trajectories for emergency braking front cars). The `highway-env` simulation environment is thus another example of a previously observed phenomenon that worst-case scenarios which occur with low probabilities during training are typically not learned by reinforcement learning agents and that these errors can be uncovered by formal verification [35]. In the present environment, this issue is exacerbated by the fact that the agent learns that it can brake with acceleration $a_e = B_{\max}$ although (according to the specification) the acceleration can be as little as $B_{\min}$.

We now turn to the question of how the NN can be safeguarded under the given conditions. To this end, we evaluated the NN's empirical performance (reward) and crash behaviour w.r.t. the IDM front-car (`default`) as well as w.r.t. an environment where the front car performs emergency brakes and the ego car can only decelerate with $B_{\min}$ (`braking`). We evaluate the stand-alone NN, a monitored version using a Python implementation of the VeriPhy approach (this implementation comes without the rigorous compilation guarantees of VeriPhy [3]) and a shield for the NN using JSC [8]. We evaluate w.r.t. initial conditions satisfying the invariant over 1000 sampled trajectories[3]. The results are in Table 2 and indicate relatively consistent behaviour w.r.t. to the reward standard deviation. Empirically, we observe that the agent trained w.r.t. to the IDM model (`default` environment) crashes in 996 out of 1000 cases when evaluated w.r.t. a braking front car (`braking` environment). Our investigation indicates that the dynamics in `default` lack diversity in at least three dimensions: First, the environment assumes maximal braking power (contradicting the formal specification [16]); Secondly, the environment very rarely simulates braking front cars. Finally, we posit that `default` only samples initial conditions from a small subset of admissible initial conditions as our verifier found many concrete initial conditions that lead to crashes in `default`. Importantly, VeriPhy and JSC allow us to (provably!) avoid these crashes by intervening when the model chooses unsafe actions. We observe that, based on the reward function, JSC matches the best results across both environments while leading to 0 crashes. VeriPhy's and JSC's behaviour differs in their statistics on taken actions: For example, JSC chooses the idle action in 6.3% of time steps while VeriPhy never chooses this action.

5.2 An Improved NN Controller

Based on the results from Sect. 5.1 we attempted to train a second agent. To this end, we also modified the training. First, we enforce that 80% of initial states satisfy the invariant (like above, we achieve this by sampling with reduced

[3] Initial conditions are generated via rejection sampling. For a sufficiently high success rate, we had to reduce the simulator's car density parameter.

Table 2. Empirical results for the original, monitored (VeriPhy) and shielded (JSC) controller given initial conditions *inside* the safely controllable (i.e. invariant) state space. The velocity bounds of JSC's invariant check had to be modified as the simulator occasionally produces velocities outside $[0, V]$ which would otherwise deactivate JSC.

Env	Original NN		VeriPhy		JSC*	
	Reward	Crash	Reward	Crash	Reward	Crash
`default` (IDM)	$\mathbf{17.63} \pm 0.21$	**0 %**	16.72 ± 0.32	**0 %**	$\mathbf{17.63} \pm 0.21$	**0 %**
`braking`	5.44 ± 1.27	99.6%	$\mathbf{16.47} \pm 0.05$	**0 %**	$\mathbf{16.47} \pm 0.05$	**0 %**

car density). Second, we modified the behaviour of environment variables: In each control round a car initiates (and then continues in subsequent steps) an emergency brake with 15% probability. Our objective is to increase the likelihood of the agent experiencing worst-case behaviour of the environment as a learning opportunity – especially in situations where crashes can be avoided. Finally, as NN verification and counterexample region enumeration scales exponentially with the NN's size, we reduce the NN to two layers with 16 neurons each. Unlike the provided environment (20k steps) we train for up to 40k steps and choose the best-performing model (achieved after 22k steps). To simplify the task, we furthermore assume $B_{\min} = B_{\max} = -5.0$. An evaluation across 1,000 initial conditions for `braking` (with $B_{\min} = -5$) yielded a reward of 16.08 ± 0.07 with 0 crashes. Compared to the first NN's performance for the `braking` environment in Table 2 this is a notable performance improvement. Given these promising results, we attempted verification w.r.t. the full NN specification (2 to 5 cars).

Verification took 1.9 h and still returned **11,059 counterexample regions**. Simulations with the representative inputs for the returned regions uncovered 4852 crashes in the `default` simulation (using IDM) and 8713 crashes in the `braking` simulation (with $B_{\max} = B_{\min} = -5$; see Table 1). Surprisingly, for the two simulations we resp. found 181 and 40 cases that even produced a crash when the ego-car performed an emergency brake! This is surprising as our dL proof states that braking should keep our system safe. A closer examination uncovered that these are *Euler Crashes*, i.e. the occurrence of a crash depends on the resolution of the Euler approximation. For a finer step size of the Euler approximation, the spurious crash disappears. Importantly, in almost all cases the crash produced by the NN remained. An example for an Euler Crash (evaluated with 10 and 100 Euler steps per second of evolution) can be found in Fig. 3.

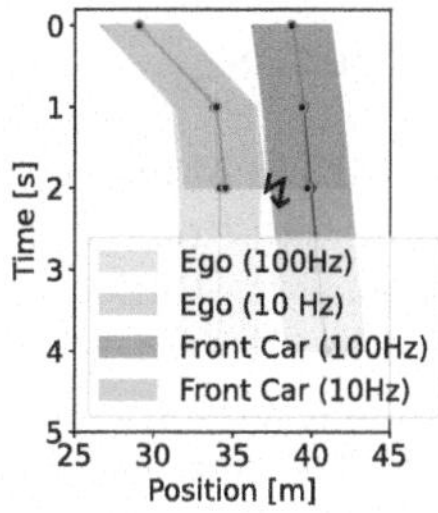

Fig. 3. An *Euler Crash* (↯): Occurrence depends on Euler approximation resolution.

6 The Model2Simulation Gap

Overall, this work has not only derived an abstract dL model, but also demonstrated in practice that verification can serve as a powerful tool to detect flaws in reinforcement learning systems. Across two NNs our analysis uncovered numerous concrete counterexamples for NNs even though they performed *flawlessly* in their respective simulations. Throughout, we attempted to trace these faults to design choices in the simulator such as the intelligent driver model or the sampling method for choosing initial conditions. Overall, our results provide strong evidence that *as is* the `highway-env` simulator provides no reliable basis for the training of safe car control NNs. However, we believe the detected issues point to a larger issue concerning inconsistencies between models and simulators in general. While we consistently took the stance that our model is correct and the simulation is to blame, in reality, this is not always the case: For example, was it justified that we changed the NN's action space or should we have built an entirely different KeYmaera X model? Here, we believe our choice was justified by ABZ's specification document [16], but such documentation may not always be available. While this work demonstrates how far dL -based safety certification for NN Control Systems has come, it also underscores the intricate issues of interlinking simulation-based evaluation with a symbolic, dL -based analysis.

Acknowledgements. This work was supported by funding from the pilot program Core-Informatics of the Helmholtz Association (HGF) and by an Alexander von Humboldt Professorship.

References

1. Abrial, J.: Modeling in Event-B - System and Software Engineering. Cambridge University Press, Cambridge (2010). https://doi.org/10.1017/CBO9781139195881
2. Banach, R., Butler, M.J.: Cruise control in hybrid Event-B. In: Liu, Z., Woodcock, J., Zhu, H. (eds.) Theoretical Aspects of Computing - ICTAC 2013 - 10th International Colloquium, Shanghai, China, 4–6 September 2013. Proceedings. LNCS, vol. 8049, pp. 76–93. Springer, Cham (2013). https://doi.org/10.1007/978-3-642-39718-9_5
3. Bohrer, R., Tan, Y.K., Mitsch, S., Myreen, M.O., Platzer, A.: VeriPhy: verified controller executables from verified cyber-physical system models. In: Foster, J.S., Grossman, D. (eds.) Proceedings of the 39th ACM SIGPLAN Conference on Programming Language Design and Implementation, PLDI 2018, Philadelphia, PA, USA, 18–22 June 2018, pp. 617–630. ACM (2018). https://doi.org/10.1145/3192366.3192406
4. Brix, C., Bak, S., Johnson, T.T., Wu, H.: The fifth international verification of neural networks competition (VNN-COMP 2024): summary and results. CoRR **abs/2412.19985** (2024). https://doi.org/10.48550/ARXIV.2412.19985
5. Brix, C., Müller, M.N., Bak, S., Johnson, T.T., Liu, C.: First three years of the international verification of neural networks competition (VNN-COMP). Int. J. Softw. Tools Technol. Transf. **25**(3), 329–339 (2023). https://doi.org/10.1007/s10009-023-00703-4

6. Demarchi, S., Guidotti, D., Pulina, L., Tacchella, A.: Supporting standardization of neural networks verification with VNNLIB and coconet. In: Narodytska, N., Amir, G., Katz, G., Isac, O. (eds.) Proceedings of the 6th Workshop on Formal Methods for ML-Enabled Autonomous Systems, FoMLAS@CAV 2023, Paris, France, 17–18 July 2023. Kalpa Publications in Computing, vol. 16, pp. 47–58. EasyChair (2023). https://doi.org/10.29007/5PDH
7. Fulton, N., Mitsch, S., Quesel, J.-D., Völp, M., Platzer, A.: KeYmaera X: an axiomatic tactical theorem prover for hybrid systems. In: Felty, A.P., Middeldorp, A. (eds.) CADE 2015. LNCS (LNAI), vol. 9195, pp. 527–538. Springer, Cham (2015). https://doi.org/10.1007/978-3-319-21401-6_36
8. Fulton, N., Platzer, A.: Safe reinforcement learning via formal methods: toward safe control through proof and learning. In: McIlraith, S.A., Weinberger, K.Q. (eds.) Proceedings of the Thirty-Second AAAI Conference on Artificial Intelligence, (AAAI-18), New Orleans, Louisiana, USA, 2–7 February 2018, pp. 6485–6492. AAAI Press (2018).https://doi.org/10.1609/aaai.v32i1.12107
9. Fulton, N., Platzer, A.: Verifiably safe off-model reinforcement learning. In: Vojnar, T., Zhang, L. (eds.) TACAS 2019. LNCS, vol. 11427, pp. 413–430. Springer, Cham (2019). https://doi.org/10.1007/978-3-030-17462-0_28
10. Garcia, L., Mitsch, S., Platzer, A.: HyPLC: hybrid programmable logic controller program translation for verification. In: Bushnell, L., Pajic, M. (eds.) ICCPS, pp. 47–56 (2019).https://doi.org/10.1145/3302509.3311036
11. Kabra, A., Laurent, J., Mitsch, S., Platzer, A.: CESAR: control envelope synthesis via angelic refinements. In: Finkbeiner, B., Kovács, L. (eds.) TACAS. LNCS, vol. 14570, pp. 144–164. Springer, Cham (2024). https://doi.org/10.1007/978-3-031-57246-3_9
12. Kamburjan, E., Mitsch, S., Hähnle, R.: A hybrid programming language for formal modeling and verification of hybrid systems. Leibniz Trans. Embed. Syst. **8**(2), 04:1–04:34 (2022). https://doi.org/10.4230/LITES.8.2.4
13. König, M., Bosman, A.W., Hoos, H.H., van Rijn, J.N.: Critically assessing the state of the art in neural network verification. J. Mach. Learn. Res. **25**, 12:1–12:53 (2024). https://jmlr.org/papers/v25/23-0119.html
14. Könighofer, B., Bloem, R., Ehlers, R., Pek, C.: Correct-by-construction runtime enforcement in AI - a survey. In: Raskin, J., Chatterjee, K., Doyen, L., Majumdar, R. (eds.) Principles of Systems Design - Essays Dedicated to Thomas A. Henzinger on the Occasion of His 60th Birthday. LNCS, vol. 13660, pp. 650–663. Springer, Cham (2022). https://doi.org/10.1007/978-3-031-22337-2_31
15. Leurent, E.: An environment for autonomous driving decision-making (2018). https://github.com/eleurent/highway-env
16. Leuschel, M., Vu, F., Rutenkolk, K.: Case study: Safety controller for autonomous driving on highways (v2) (2024). v2. https://raw.githubusercontent.com/hhu-stups/abz2025_casestudy_autonomous_driving/refs/heads/main/case_study/specification_v2.pdf. Accessed 11 Feb 2025
17. Loos, S.M., Platzer, A.: Differential refinement logic. In: Grohe, M., Koskinen, E., Shankar, N. (eds.) LICS, pp. 505–514. ACM, New York (2016). https://doi.org/10.1145/2933575.2934555
18. Loos, S.M., Platzer, A., Nistor, L.: Adaptive cruise control: hybrid, distributed, and now formally verified. In: Butler, M., Schulte, W. (eds.) FM 2011. LNCS, vol. 6664, pp. 42–56. Springer, Heidelberg (2011). https://doi.org/10.1007/978-3-642-21437-0_6

19. Lopez, D.M., et al.: ARCH-COMP24 category report: AINNCS for continuous and hybrid systems plants. In: Frehse, G., Althoff, M. (eds.) Proceedings of the 11th Int. Workshop on Applied Verification for Continuous and Hybrid Systems. EPiC Series in Computing, vol. 103, pp. 64–121. EasyChair (2024). https://doi.org/10.29007/mxld
20. Lopez, D.M., et al.: ARCH-COMP22 category report: AINNCS for continuous and hybrid systems plants. In: Proceedings of 9th International Workshop on Applied, vol. 90, pp. 142–184 (2022). https://doi.org/10.29007/wfgr
21. Lopez, D.M., Althoff, M., Forets, M., Johnson, T.T., Ladner, T., Schilling, C.: ARCH-COMP23 category report: (AINNCS) for continuous and hybrid systems plants. In: Frehse, G., Althoff, M. (eds.) Proceedings of 10th International Workshop on Applied Verification of Continuous and Hybrid Systems (ARCH23), San Antonio, Texas, USA, 9 May 2023. EPiC Series in Computing, vol. 96, pp. 89–125. EasyChair (2023). https://doi.org/10.29007/X38N
22. Mitsch, S., Platzer, A.: ModelPlex: verified runtime validation of verified cyber-physical system models. Form. Methods Syst. Des. 33–74 (2016). https://doi.org/10.1007/s10703-016-0241-z
23. Mitsch, S., Platzer, A.: Verified runtime validation for partially observable hybrid systems (2018). CoRR **abs/1811.06502**, http://arxiv.org/abs/1811.06502
24. Mitsch, S., et al.: LS-Lab/KeYmaeraX-release: Version 5.1.1 (July 2024). https://doi.org/10.5281/zenodo.13380145
25. Platzer, A.: Differential dynamic logic for hybrid systems. J. Autom. Reas. **41**(2), 143–189 (2008). https://doi.org/10.1007/s10817-008-9103-8
26. Platzer, A.: Logical Analysis of Hybrid Systems: Proving Theorems for Complex Dynamics. Springer, Heidelberg (2010). https://doi.org/10.1007/978-3-642-14509-4
27. Platzer, A.: A complete axiomatization of quantified differential dynamic logic for distributed hybrid systems. Log. Meth. Comput. Sci. **8**(4:17), 1–44 (2012). https://doi.org/10.2168/LMCS-8(4:17)2012, special issue for selected papers from CSL'10
28. Platzer, A.: A complete uniform substitution calculus for differential dynamic logic. J. Autom. Reason. **59**(2), 219–265 (2016). https://doi.org/10.1007/s10817-016-9385-1
29. Platzer, A.: Logical Foundations of Cyber-Physical Systems. Springer, Cham (2018). https://doi.org/10.1007/978-3-319-63588-0
30. Prebet, E., Platzer, A.: Uniform substitution for differential refinement logic. In: Benzmüller, C., Heule, M.J., Schmidt, R.A. (eds.) IJCAR. LNCS, vol. 14740, pp. 196–215. Springer, Cham (2024). https://doi.org/10.1007/978-3-031-63501-4_11
31. Prebet, E., Teuber, S., Platzer, A.: LS-Lab/verified-neural-highway-control: 1.0 (March 2025). https://doi.org/10.5281/zenodo.14959858
32. Prebet, E., Teuber, S., Platzer, A.: Verification of autonomous neural car control with KeYmaera X (2025). https://arxiv.org/abs/2504.03272
33. Renshaw, D.W., Loos, S.M., Platzer, A.: Distributed theorem proving for distributed hybrid systems. In: Qin, S., Qiu, Z. (eds.) ICFEM 2011. LNCS, vol. 6991, pp. 356–371. Springer, Heidelberg (2011). https://doi.org/10.1007/978-3-642-24559-6_25
34. Shperberg, S.S., Liu, B., Allievi, A., Stone, P.: A rule-based shield: accumulating safety rules from catastrophic action effects. In: Chandar, S., Pascanu, R., Precup, D. (eds.) Conference on Lifelong Learning Agents, CoLLAs 2022, 22–24 August 2022, McGill University, Montréal, Québec, Canada. Proceedings of Machine Learning Research, vol. 199, pp. 231–242. PMLR (2022)

35. Teuber, S., Mitsch, S., Platzer, A.: Provably safe neural network controllers via differential dynamic logic. In: Globerson, A., et al. (eds.) Advances in Neural Information Processing Systems. Curran Associates, Inc. (2024). https://doi.org/10.48550/arXiv.2402.10998
36. Tran, H., Cai, F., Lopez, D.M., Musau, P., Johnson, T.T., Koutsoukos, X.D.: safety verification of cyber-physical systems with reinforcement learning control. ACM Trans. Embed. Comput. Syst. **18**(5s), 105:1–105:22 (2019). https://doi.org/10.1145/3358230
37. Treiber, M., Hennecke, A., Helbing, D.: Congested traffic states in empirical observations and microscopic simulations. Phys. Rev. E **62**(2), 1805 (2000). https://doi.org/10.1103/PhysRevE.62.1805
38. Vu, F., Dunkelau, J., Leuschel, M.: Validation of reinforcement learning agents and safety shields with prob. In: Benz, N., Gopinath, D., Shi, N. (eds.) NASA Formal Methods - 16th International Symposium, NFM 2024, Moffett Field, CA, USA, 4–6 June 2024, Proceedings. LNCS, vol. 14627, pp. 279–297. Springer, Cham (2024). https://doi.org/10.1007/978-3-031-60698-4_16

Short Papers

State-Based Modelling with a Concept DSL

Nikolaj Kühne Jakobsen(✉)

Aarhus University, Nordre Ringgade 1, 8000 Aarhus C, Denmark
nkj@ece.au.dk

Abstract. Concept-based design is a new emerging formalism that uses *concepts* to facilitate the construction of modular and reusable software. Concepts are independent and generic units of functionality that can be composed to form complex applications. This work presents *Conceptual*, a domain-specific language for defining and composing concepts. A compiler from this language to Alloy6 is implemented, establishing a way to model and validate concept specifications of software formally. The practical application of Conceptual is examined qualitatively by leveraging Alloy's analysis tools to reason about existing concept specifications in the literature.

Keywords: Concepts · DSL · Alloy · Compiler · Formal methods · LTL

1 Introduction

Every developer recognizes the value of good abstractions [7,9]. Yet, such abstractions are nontrivial to come up with, promoting reuse [14]. Consequently, considerable work has gone into figuring out how to write effective and reusable code. Dijkstra famously advocated for separation of concerns and simplicity [2,3], and similar principles are abundant in other work [7,22].

However, even when adhering to such principles or following idiomatic design patterns [5], diverse requirements tend to necessitate unique implementations. Despite seemingly sharing common functionality, features are often customized uniquely across different applications. For example, tagging someone in Gmail highlights their name in the email, automatically adds them to the list of recipients, and clicking their highlighted name generates a new draft email for that person. The same feature on X (formerly Twitter) creates a link to their profile, notifies them about a post, and may indirectly impact the ranking algorithm with an increase in engagement. While developers may attempt to repurpose such components or functionality, it is not always effective [1], may increase technical debt [16] and decrease modularity [21].

In his latest book, *The Essence of Software: Why Concepts Matter for Great Design* [10], Daniel Jackson scrutinizes software from industry giants such as Apple, Dropbox, and Google, showing unintuitive behavior in even their most popular products. The claim is that many such problems stem from poor design

M. Leuschel and F. Ishikawa (Eds.): ABZ 2025, LNCS 15728, pp. 311–321, 2026.
https://doi.org/10.1007/978-3-031-94533-5_18

decisions that do not accurately reflect the conceptual model of the users or developers. He rethinks software design using mutually independent and free-standing *concepts*.

Essentially, concepts are abstract entities that describe some familiar behavior. Like how microservices are combined to contribute to an overall system, concepts can be composed to form complex applications. Although the concepts exist independently, their internal states are observable, creating a dependency graph once concretely *instantiated* [10]. The nodes are the concepts, and each edge represents a synchronization of actions. For example, email clients often have the ability to add a special label to deleted emails, and emails with this label automatically appear in a special *trash* folder. That is, the action of deleting an email triggers another action that labels the email (and vice versa).

As the notion of concept-centric design is fairly new, existing work on the topic is scarce. Perez De Rosso has used concepts to redesign and remedy well-known difficulties of git [20]. Moreover, he has created a platform, **Déjà Vu** [19], for assembling full-stack applications by combining concepts from a centralized catalogue using an HTML-like template language. Similarly, Namazov developed a framework, **Kodless** [18], which leverages concept specifications to more efficiently generate and deploy simple, full-stack web applications. Palantir has published a holistic experience report [23], highlighting their successes and challenges of using concept-centric design methodologies in a larger organization.

However, the primary focus of this research appears to be on practicality and real-world application, emphasizing *low-code* development processes, integration with LLMs, and organizational challenges, rather than formal methods.

This work presents *Conceptual* [12], a new external domain-specific language (DSL) for describing and composing concepts, formalizing the proposed syntax in [10]. Additionally, a compiler is implemented from this language to Alloy [8]. Using the compiler, various concept specifications from [10] are translated and analyzed using Alloy's analysis tools.

2 Concepts

In his book on concept-centric design [10], Daniel Jackson describes a concept as follows:

> A concept is a particular solution to a particular design problem - not a large and vague problem but a small and well-defined need that arises repeatedly in many contexts.

That is, concepts are invented by someone at a certain point in time to fulfill a particular purpose. Concepts should be one-to-one with this purpose: for every concept, there should only be one purpose that motivates it, and vice versa. A reader might question how concepts differ from the traditional object-oriented design pattern [5]. Both solve particular design problems, provide a common vocabulary, and provide basic building blocks for constructing reusable software through abstraction. However, design patterns are often categorized into different types (e.g. structural, behavioral, and creational) and aim to reduce internal coupling, whereas concepts are designed to be user-facing and strictly behavioral.

In a more formal sense, a concept can be modeled using a deterministic state machine: given a state and a set of argument values for an action, at most one state can result from executing it. In [10], a concept definition includes a name, a purpose, a state, a set of actions, and *operational principles.* In particular, only the declarations of name, state, and actions functionally affect the behavior of the action system. With the name declaration, concepts are typically made generic with polymorphic subentities. The state encompasses the concept's internal memory, and actions define state transitions for the dynamic behavior. However, concepts are not just semantic entities. Operational principles teleologically describe how a concept fulfills its intended purpose and core functionality through archetypical scenarios and linear temporal logic (LTL) [15]. This notion of operational principles may resemble an LTL extension of axioms in algebraic specification languages, e.g. CASL [17], or property-based testing approaches [4].

A system can be composed of several concepts. Concepts cannot directly alter another concept's state or influence the behavior of its actions, but its state can be observed. When a system integrates various concepts, it coordinates their actions using a CSP-like [6] synchronization mechanism. Each concept runs autonomously, determining when its actions may occur and the impact of the said actions on its own internal state. Structurally, each synchronization consists of a trigger action and accompanying response actions that occur when the trigger is executed. Semantically, synchronizations are transactional, meaning that they are assumed not to happen when a response action is impossible; either every action occurs or none do. Importantly, such a composition does not introduce new actions to any particular concept. Moreover, as any trace of the composed system is an interleaving of traces of individual concepts, any property that holds for a particular concept holds for the system trace as a whole [11].

2.1 Reservation Concept

Figure 1 expresses the reservation concept from [10] in Conceptual. The reservation concept is defined using parametric polymorphism, naming two type parameters *User* and *Resource.* The concept attempts to optimize resource when resources are limited. It maintains two sets in its state: the *available* resources that are currently not reserved, and a set of user *reservations* of said resources. These sets (and any sets defined in the state) are empty at the time of *initialization* unless declared with multiplicity *one.* This ensures that the concept is not initially in an erroneous state that can produce traces violating the defined properties. Actions modify the concept state, providing ways to add or remove resources from the available pool and create or cancel reservations.

The *use* action verifies a user has reserved a resource without modifying state. "When" clauses act as firing conditions and resemble preconditions, but (unlike a precondition) they ensure that the action cannot happen unless a particular boolean expression holds. The operational principle ensures users can use resources continuously between reservation and cancellation, though it arguably omits an essential property related to double-booking of resources.

```
concept reservation [User, Resource]
purpose "use a limited pool of resources efficiently"
state
 available: set Resource
 reservations: User → set Resource
actions
 provide(r: Resource)
  available += r
 retract(r: Resource)
  when r in available and r not in reservations
   available -= r
 reserve(u: User, r: Resource)
  when r in available
   u.reservations += r
   available -= r
 cancel(u: User, r: Resource)
  when r in u.reservations
   u.reservations -= r
   available += r
 use(u: User, r: Resource)
  when r in u.reservations
principle
  reserve(u,r) then can use(u,r) until cancel(u,r)
```

Fig. 1. The *reservation* concept from [10] expressed in Conceptual.

2.2 Label Concept

Figure 2 describes a state machine for associating labels with some abstract items. Two properties are expressed in the operational principle, conveying how

```
concept label [Item, Label]
purpose "organize items into overlapping categories"
state labels: Item → set Label
actions
 affix(i: Item, l: Label)
  i.labels += l
 detach(i: Item, l: Label)
  i.labels -= l
 find(l: Label) : Item
  l.~labels
 clear(i: Item)
  i.labels := {}
principle
 affix(i,l) then i in find(l) until detach(i,l),
 no affix(i,l) or detach(i,l) then i not in find(l)
```

Fig. 2. The *label* concept from [10] expressed in Conceptual.

a *find* action can be used to locate items with specific labels and how items remain findable only while their labels are attached.

2.3 Composition of Concepts

Figure 3 depicts a simple composition of the todo and label concepts in Conceptual. Whereas the label concept has already been discussed, an account of the todo concept can optionally be found in [13]. However, beyond knowing that this concept has actions for moving tasks between two sets *done* and *pending*, the details are not essential for understanding the composition itself.

```
app todo_label
include
 todo
 label [todo.Task, string]
sync todo.delete(t)
 label.clear(t)
sync todo.add(t)
 label.affix(t, "pending")
sync todo.complete(t)
 label.detach(t, "pending")
sync label.detach(t, "pending")
 todo.complete(t)
```

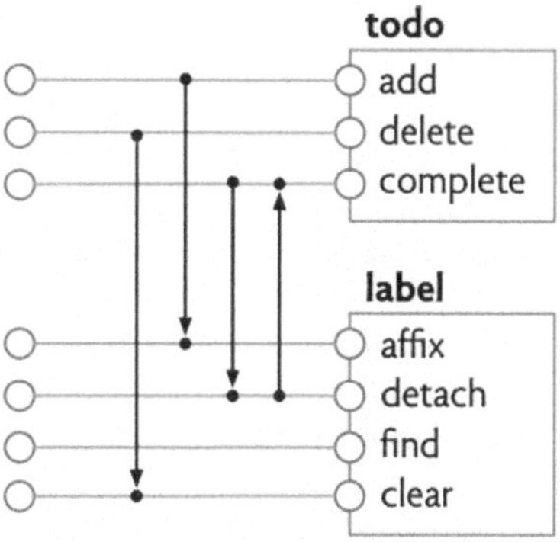

Fig. 3. An application from [10] synchronizing the label and todo concepts.

A strength of this composition is that it is synergistic; it provides new functionality for querying whether tasks are pending or not using the find action within the label concept. Moreover, suppose that a richer version of the *label* concept was used. If it had logical querying capabilities, it would be possible to query for high-priority tasks that are labeled both as *pending* and *urgent*. Richer concepts increase functionality not just within the particular concept but also in its various applications.

3 Translating Conceptual to Alloy

The syntax is illustrated through examples, with a complete account of the abstract syntax available in [13]. The expression-level semantics closely match the first-order logic of Alloy. While a formal account of the foundational elements is not provided explicitly, their meaning can be inferred implicitly from the translation of the high-level language constructs presented below.

Concepts: Each concept is translated into its own Alloy module (with the same name) to emulate the mutual independence of concepts. These modules are named and can be parameterized over arbitrary signatures, adequately capturing even generic concept declarations. A concept's **purpose** is embedded into the module as a verbatim comment.

State: A global singleton signature, *State*, with mutable fields for each variable, is used to model the changing state of a concept. State variables can be mutually recursive, becoming dependent fields in Alloy. Additionally, state variables can optionally be declared with an expression constraining the universe of possible values, represented with a *fact* in Alloy. Custom types (used in the state or the declaration of a generic concept) are mapped to empty top-level signatures, which are inherently disjoint.

Actions: Conceptual distinguishes between actions that mutate the state and query the state for information. The action types are translated into predicates and functions, respectively. Mutations are modeled using state transitions. In Alloy, mutable variables and fields may evolve freely across transitions unless explicitly specified not to. Consequently, Conceptual keeps track of which variables are being mutated, instructing unused variables to remain the same (frame conditions). Another detail is that Alloy's *always* operator, used for analysis, will test an assertion at every state, and so desired properties must crucially be true even in intermediate states. Actions are translated to be atomic, allowing at most one state transition to simplify this.

Operational Principle: The operational principle is translated into assertions that can verify whether the desired properties of the concept logically follow from the definition of its behavior. These properties are expressed in LTL, must evaluate to truth values, and are checked across all possible concept traces. Only a small subset of the LTL operators introduced with Alloy6 is needed to express the desired semantics of the operational principle in Conceptual. Specifically, Conceptual has an operation for sequential composition using ';' or "then". For example, an expression *a;b* means immediately after *a*, then *b* holds. In addition, *a until b* is a boolean expression stating that *a* is true until *b* becomes true. Finally, a unary operator *no* can be used to signify that something has not been true historically. For example, *no a* is true if *a* has not been true prior to this point and false otherwise.

Apps: Apps (or applications) are named entities composing various concepts. Each app must explicitly declare the concepts it depends on and instantiate any generic type. Subsequently, apps specify their synchronizations. Both trigger and response actions are essentially regular action calls, except that the trigger may define new variables usable by the response with its arguments (similar to the operational principle). These calls can also access and utilize the state of the concepts. In addition, arguments may appear with a multiplicity, restricting the synchronization to execution with select inputs rather than all inputs. Each synchronization is translated into a *fact*-clause in the shape of an implication. The trigger action is the antecedent, and the consequent is a conjunction of all response actions. In Alloy, concept inclusions are essentially equivalent to opening and specializing the corresponding module with appropriate types.

4 Analysis Using Conceptual

In [10], Daniel Jackson defines a number of concepts using an informal pseudocode that relies on natural language descriptions of actions and operational principles. However, this introduces ambiguities in the specification. For instance, what does it mean to "use a reservation"? Is this a one-time event that consumes the reservation? Or perhaps the reservation persists and the resource can be used continuously? Both interpretations can be reasonable in practice. Moreover, since the behavior of many of these concepts is so intuitive and familiar to us, we may become overly reliant on the conceptual model in our minds rather than the written specification in front of us, leading us to forget or inadvertently overlook certain assumptions that we take for granted or find self-evident.

This section does not argue for or against concept-centric design, but it uses Conceptual and some of the existing concepts from [10] to demonstrate the usefulness of integrating formal methods in such a design process. Specifically, the specifications are translated to Alloy and validated using Alloy's powerful analysis tools, catching some inconsistencies and bugs. In hindsight, many of the design issues that were found are trivial and sometimes appear harmless. However, experience dictates that such trivial issues have a nasty habit of becoming nontrivial, if they are not caught and addressed early.

4.1 Analysis of the Label Concept

A simple flaw appears in the label concept's first operational principle (Fig. 2):

```
affix(i,l) then i in find(l) until detach(i,l)
```

The compiler translates the principle into an assertion, testing the formula:

```
all l : Label, i : Item | { always (
    affix[i, l] ⇒ after (
      detach[i, l] releases i in find[l]  ))}
```

When checking the assertion above under a reasonable scope, a violating execution trace is indeed found. Specifically, an item i may be affixed a label l, but this does not imply that $i \in find[l]$ (even without using *detach*), since the *clear* action can also be used to remove labels. The operational principle should have added a guard against this, as seen below:

```
affix(i,l) then i in find(l) until detach(i,l) or clear(i)
```

Issues of this type likely stem from the designer's conceptual coupling of operations, focusing on the symmetrical and natural pairing between *affix* and *detach*. Notably, a faulty operational principle does not affect the model's behavior but misrepresents the concept's properties, risking misuse in other contexts.

4.2 Analysis of the Reservation Concept

The reservation concept (Fig. 1) contains a critical and inconspicuous design flaw. Moreover, this flaw is not discoverable solely from the specification and the generated assertions. In fact, a developer may even be misguided into believing that the concept is well-functioning, given that the assertion derived from the operational principle holds universally. Using the translated Alloy model, however, one may express and attempt to validate a formula such as the one below:

```
always ( no r : Resource, u : User |
    r in State.reservations[u] and r in State.available )
```

This formula states that a resource r cannot be reserved by a user u and simultaneously be in the pool of available resources. In other words, this expresses a fundamental property of the desired reservation concept: double-booking should never be possible. Nevertheless, the analyzer can find a counterexample ín which a resource is being provided to the pool of available resources, despite already being reserved by a user. This type of behavior is allowed because the specification unintentionally assumes that every resource being provided is fresh. In the model, however, the action of *providing* a resource r is always valid, even if that resource is already reserved. This effectively allows double-booking, defeating the entire purpose of the concept. The problem can be addressed by including a firing condition that prevents resources from being arbitrarily provided:

```
provide(r : Resource)
  when r not in reservations
    available += r
```

The designer seems to have defined actions in isolation, rather than considering the system state holistically. This type of mistake is particularly insidious because the operation correctly conveys the design intent but fails to properly enforce it. The operational principle itself could be augmented to include a property that detects such instances of double-booking.

```
reserve(u,r) then can not reserve(u2,r) until cancel(u,r)
```

4.3 Analysis of a Concept Composition

The synchronizations in Fig. 3 seem incomplete. A straightforward assertion shows that items with the 'pending' label may not always be in the todo concept's pending set. Therefore, until the formula below is satisfied, the label concept's *find* action cannot reliably identify pending tasks within the todo concept.

```
all t : todo/Task |
  t in label/find["pending"] ⇒  t in todo/State.pending
```

The formula can be satisfied by including an additional synchronization, ensuring that when a "pending" label is affixed to an item, the item is also added as a todo-task.

```
sync label.affix(t, "pending")
 todo.add(t)
```

Although this concrete problem revolves around achieving exhaustiveness, it highlights a fundamental challenge for synergistic compositions as a whole. Specifically, gaps can occur inadvertently when cross-concept invariants are not properly maintained. Moreover, Conceptual does not currently have a way of expressing and verifying synergistic effects from the interaction between concepts.

5 Future Work

Conceptual represents a first step toward establishing tool support based on formal methods for concept-centric software design. As such, the tool remains somewhat primitive. Preliminary language support and syntax highlighting is established in Visual Studio Code, but no external language server is implemented for more sophisticated IDE features. Moreover, errors located using Alloy's analysis tools are not traced directly back to the Conceptual source code but to the Alloy translation. Due to the one-to-one nature of the translation, manually inferring this should be simple, but it is still an additional step. Recent work with concept pseudocode [11] uses a slightly different syntax and certain features that are not currently supported in Conceptual. This includes on-the-fly variable declarations, which were not used in Conceptual to allow code blocks to be read in a declarative manner. However, such features might be useful when modeling certain problems. Applications were also only explored to a limited extent, and further work remains to examine how the composition could be done more effectively. A current concern is that the synchronization mechanism and parameterization of concepts may not be adequate or too rigid to mitigate small compositional side-effects, especially when integrating closely related but non-identical concepts or handling naming conflicts. In particular, sets and actions tend to be named uniquely across concepts, which is difficult to capture.

6 Conclusion

This work introduced Conceptual, a DSL for defining and composing concepts, with a formal mapping to Alloy6 for validation. By leveraging formal methods, Conceptual aimed to ensure that concept specifications are precise, analyzable, and free of unintended interactions. Case studies from the literature were used to demonstrate how Conceptual could help uncover bugs and to refine concept specifications. As concept-centric design gains traction, formal methods and tools like Conceptual can play a role in enhancing the quality of concept specifications.

Acknowledgments. I thank Professor Daniel Jackson for hosting me at MIT and discussing this work. I am grateful to Stibofonden, Aarhus University, Reinholdt W. Jorck og Hustrus Fond, Jyske Bank, IDA, and It-vest for providing travel grants. I also thank Nuno Macedo for help with Alloy6 and Peter Gorm Larsen for his feedback.

Disclosure of Interests. The author has no competing interests to declare.

References

1. Digkas, G., Nikolaidis, N., Ampatzoglou, A., Chatzigeorgiou, A.: Reusing code from stackoverflow: the effect on technical debt. In: 2019 45th Euromicro Conference on Software Engineering and Advanced Applications (SEAA), pp. 87–91 (2019). https://doi.org/10.1109/SEAA.2019.00022
2. Dijkstra, E.W.: The humble programmer. Commun. ACM **15**(10), 859–866 (1972)
3. Dijkstra, E.W.: On the role of scientific thought. Selected writings on computing: a personal perspective, pp. 60–66 (1982)
4. Fink, G., Bishop, M.: Property-based testing: a new approach to testing for assurance. ACM SIGSOFT Softw. Eng. Notes **22**(4), 74–80 (1997)
5. Gamma, E., Helm, R., Johnson, R., Vlissides, J.: Design Patterns: Elements of Reusable Object-Oriented Software. Addison-Wesley Longman Publishing Co., Inc., USA (1995)
6. Hoare, C.: Communicating Sequential Processes. Prentice-Hall International Series in Computer Science, Prentice Hall, Hoboken (1985)
7. Hunt, A., Thomas, D.: The Pragmatic Programmer: From Journeyman to Master. Addison-Wesley, Harlow, England (1999)
8. Jackson, D.: Alloy: a lightweight object modelling notation. ACM Trans. Softw. Eng. Methodol. **11**(2), 256–290 (2002). https://doi.org/10.1145/505145.505149
9. Jackson, D.: Software Abstractions: Logic, Language, and Analysis. The MIT Press, Cambridge (2012)
10. Jackson, D.: The Essence of Software: Why Concepts Matter for Great Design. Princeton University Press, Princeton (2021)
11. Jackson, D.: A concept-oriented approach to software development. In: The Practice of Formal Methods: Essays in Honour of Cliff Jones, Part I, pp. 216–235. Springer (2024)
12. Jakobsen, N.K.: Conceptual (2024). https://github.com/TheRealNestor/Conceptual/
13. Jakobsen, N.K.: Establishing tool support for a concept dsl (2025). https://arxiv.org/abs/2503.05849
14. Krueger, C.W.: Software reuse. ACM Comput. Surv. **24**(2), 131–183 (1992)

15. Lamport, L.: The temporal logic of actions. ACM Trans. Program. Lang. Syst. **16**(3), 872-923 (1994). https://doi.org/10.1145/177492.177726
16. Li, Z., Liang, P., Avgeriou, P., Guelfi, N., Ampatzoglou, A.: An empirical investigation of modularity metrics for indicating architectural technical debt. In: Proceedings of the 10th International ACM Sigsoft Conference on Quality of Software Architectures, pp. 119–128. QoSA '14, Association for Computing Machinery, New York, NY, USA (2014). https://doi.org/10.1145/2602576.2602581
17. Mosses, P.D. (ed.): CASL Reference Manual. LNCS, vol. 2960. Springer, Heidelberg (2004). https://doi.org/10.1007/b96103
18. Namazov, A.B.: Kodless (2024). https://github.com/BarishNamazov/kodless
19. Perez De Rosso, S.: Declarative Assembly of Web Applications from Predefined Concepts. Ph.D. thesis, MIT, USA (2020)
20. Perez De Rosso, S., Jackson, D.: What's wrong with git? A conceptual design analysis. In: Proceedings of the 2013 ACM International Symposium on New Ideas, New Paradigms, and Reflections on Programming & Software, pp. 37–52. Onward! 2013, Association for Computing Machinery, New York, NY, USA (2013). https://doi.org/10.1145/2509578.2509584
21. Skiada, P., Ampatzoglou, A., Arvanitou, E.M., Chatzigeorgiou, A., Stamelos, I.: Exploring the relationship between software modularity and technical debt. In: 2018 44th Euromicro Conference on Software Engineering and Advanced Applications (SEAA), pp. 404–407 (2018). https://doi.org/10.1109/SEAA.2018.00072
22. Sullivan, K.J., Griswold, W.G., Cai, Y., Hallen, B.: The structure and value of modularity in software design. In: Proceedings of the 8th European Software Engineering Conference Held Jointly with 9th ACM SIGSOFT International Symposium on Foundations of Software Engineering, pp. 99–108. ESEC/FSE-9, Association for Computing Machinery, New York, NY, USA (2001)
23. Wilczynski, P., Gregoire-Wright, T., Jackson, D.: Concept-centric software development (2023)

Towards an End-to-End Toolchain for Traceable and Verifiable Railway Signalling Specifications

Frederic Reiter[1](✉), Roman Wetenkamp[2], Robert Schmid[3], Richard Kretzschmar[1], and Lukas Iffländer[4]

[1] Deutsches Zentrum für Schienenverkehrsforschung, Dresden, Germany
{ReiterF,KretzschmarR}@dzsf.bund.de

[2] Saarland Informatics Campus, Universität des Saarlandes, Saarbrücken, Germany
roman.wetenkamp@uni-saarland.de

[3] Hasso-Plattner-Institut, University of Potsdam, Potsdam, Germany
Robert.Schmid@hpi.de

[4] Fakultät Informatik/Mathematik, Hochschule für Technik und Wirtschaft Dresden, Dresden, Germany
lukas.ifflaender@htw-dresden.de

Abstract. Specifications for safety-critical railway signalling systems have traditionally been expressed in natural language. Due to a lack of traceability features, these requirements are difficult to reason about and thus very resistant to change. Validation and verification processes of cyber-physical components based on such specifications require extensive manual review and are prone to inefficiencies.

This paper describes our work towards a comprehensive methodology for deriving formal specifications for railway signalling and generating verified software for it. Our method focuses on accessibility for domain experts and industrial applicability. To this effect, we integrate established techniques into a unified tool chain comprising (1) fault tree analysis, (2) the goal-oriented requirements engineering method KAOS, and (3) formal modeling with AdaCore SPARK. We aim to facilitate end-to-end traceability of requirements through all artifacts. Currently, we are applying our methodology to a case study that involves the specification of a new ETCS-based moving block signalling system.

Keywords: Railway signalling · Moving block · Domain modeling · Requirements engineering · KAOS · SPARK

1 Introduction

Cyber-physical systems with critical safety concerns necessitate complex sets of requirements. For railway signalling in Germany, these requirements are issued in the form of a multitude of natural language documents, which are interpreted by domain experts for design, construction, and certification purposes.

M. Leuschel and F. Ishikawa (Eds.): ABZ 2025, LNCS 15728, pp. 322–329, 2026.
https://doi.org/10.1007/978-3-031-94533-5_19

Approach. Previous academic work suggests that the development and certification of innovative digital interlocking systems would benefit from incorporating two approaches already well established in other domains: (1) Goal-oriented requirements engineering, which improves traceability and helps experts reason about requirements [15,19], and (2) formal methods, which provide mathematical validation and support verification processes [9,10,16]. Formally specified requirements will not only help automate the certification process, but also provide feedback to the requirements engineering teams and increase safety by supporting the auditing experts with mathematical proofs. They might also help facilitate the safety case of the new interlocking paradigm of moving blocks, which entails a significant increase in capacity for the rail network, but so far has seen no utilization – mostly due to safety concerns [5,23].

Regulation. The use of safety-critical components is regulated by national and international laws. Standardization bodies have agreed that perfect safety for cyber-physical systems cannot realistically be achieved. Instead, regulation defines safety integrity levels (SIL) which, for software, translate to qualitative requirements in the form of software fault-tolerance measures and design disciplines [17]. For the rail sector, they are issued in EN 50716 [2]. This norm is of special interest for the selection of software tools, as it defines functional tiers for them: Most importantly, *T3* for tools that create output that directly contributes to executable code, such as compilers [1,9].

ETCS Specification. The literature base for most works has been the specification of the European Train Control System (ETCS) level 2 with Train Integrity Monitoring System (TIMS)[1]. The specification has been shown to allow implementations with compromised interoperability to each other, include ambiguities [6,8], seem incomplete [22], and difficult to read [3]. Most works conclude that the ambiguities are due to the informal natural language phrasings, which call into question the merits of such methods. The justification for leaving that space for interpretation is to not restrict vendors in their implementations unnecessarily [8]. It appears that for a railway signalling system, the benefits of such individual implementations are heavily outweighed by interoperability issues, so much so that interoperability served as the main reason for the inauguration of the ERTMS project itself. We conclude that a natural language specification intended to solve interoperability will impose limits on that goal, if not outright fail by design. If possible, formal methods should be used instead [12,16].

Related Work. Although many previous works deal with the formalization of interlocking logic, a recent systematic literature review conducted by Ferrari and ter Beek showed a lack of studies on formal approaches in later development phases [16].

Fotso et al. proposed an approach using the goal-oriented requirements engineering method SysML/KAOS to develop a formal model in a dialect of Event-B,

[1] formerly known as ETCS level 3

which they applied to ETCS Level 3 in the ABZ2018 case study [25]. In a paper by Abrial the informal descriptions of the ETCS Level 3 specification were completely rewritten and simplified for the creation of their own Event-B model [3]. Both papers used Rodin to discharge their respective model's proof obligations. Hansen et al. described a successful field demonstration of a formal B model of ETCS Level 3 being used as an interlocking [18]. Their model was not proven, but animated in ProB with a custom interface to the trains. Unlike prior efforts using Event-B, our approach prioritizes industrial adoption via SPARK and EN 50716-compliant tooling.

Aim. In this paper, we describe our attempt to integrate these approaches into a unified tool chain while considering the relevant regulation in the choice of tools and methods. The result is a binary for a digital interlocking system that is trustworthy, as it has been formally verified to behave as specified. As an intermediate step, our specification should be developed in a way that ensures the absence of redundant rules and every object should be traceable from the stakeholder needs to the source code.

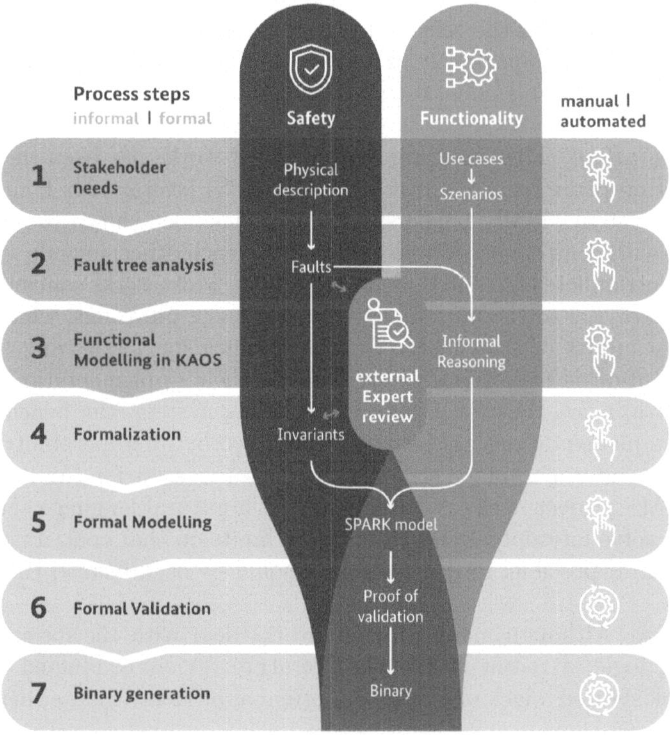

Fig. 1. Structure of the developed methodology.

2 Methodology

To develop a moving block specification with the highest possible degree of traceability, we opt to not use previously published ETCS specifications. By this, we avoid adopting redundant or contradictory requirements and eliminate the effort to reverse engineer the reasoning behind unclear rules. Instead, we construct our specification from the ground up without assumptions on the environment other than the physical properties of the railway system, technical compatibility with ETCS components and the basic stakeholder use cases. In the following, we describe the steps of our methodology as pictured in Fig. 1.

2.1 Stakeholder Needs

Our goal was to find the smallest set of rules needed to satisfy the needs of the stakeholders safely. To this effect, we start with a bare-bones physical description of the railway system without assumptions regarding existing interlocking logic. The stakeholder needs were derived from the use cases included in the operational objectives of the German national railway operator [21]. To systematically structure informal needs into traceable artifacts, we adapt the *OTHELLO* method [13]. It groups requirements into categories that define how they are processed in later steps. Example categories are *glossary*, for all domain elements ("Trains are formed from one or more connected rail vehicles"), *configuration*, for properties of these elements ("Trains have a specific length"), and *scenario*, for use case descriptions ("Trains should be able to move from one location of the track topology to a specific other location").

2.2 Fault Tree Analysis and Expert Review

Unsafe states of the interlocking logic are captured as invariants, which are logical conditions that must hold in every possible state of the system. Formulating these invariants is the most important step in the approach, as it marks the translation from safety-relevant faults in natural language to formally modeled safety properties.

To build the safety case for certification, domain experts need to verify the correctness of the formal transformation as well as the completeness of the chosen set of safety properties. We used fault tree analysis to derive these properties, as this method is able to systematically identify failures and is well known in the domain [1,5]. Following the methodological framework established by Borälv et al. [7], we collected top-level faults, e.g., "Train collides with another train". They were decomposed until all conceivable causes of a potential fault were covered and each cause could be attributed either to the interlocking logic or to the operating environment. Faults caused by the operating environment ("The train broke apart") constitute assumptions about auxiliary systems, e.g., "Trains need to be manufactured in a way to permit safe operation". The faults of the interlocking logic ("The interlocking allowed a train to go to an already occupied location") finally make up the requirements, e.g., "Each train's assigned area must be disjoint from every other train's assigned area".

This approach makes it possible to trace each specified rule to either a top-level fault or a scenario (see Sect. 2.4).

2.3 Invariants

The informal requirements are transformed into invariants formalized in a first-order logic expression. To formalize the last example above, we assign to every train the set of track segments it occupies. Let t_A, t_B be two trains, $Trains$ be the set of all trains that are in operation, and $TrainAreas\colon Trains \rightarrow \mathbb{P}(Locations)$ is a total function that assigns every registered train a subset of the interlocking system's track segments. Equation (1) shows the mathematical representation.

$$\forall t_A, t_B \in Trains\colon \quad t_A \neq t_B \Rightarrow TrainAreas(t_A) \cap TrainAreas(t_B) = \emptyset \quad (1)$$

2.4 Functional Modeling

While fault tree analysis is used to make safety properties traceable, methods of goal-oriented requirements engineering facilitate traceability for decisions about the functionality of a system. We adapted the KAOS-method (Keep All Objects Satisfied) [20] which has been successfully applied to the railway domain before.

In place of a top-level fault as an event that should *not* occur, the starting point for a KAOS tree is a goal which describes what the system *is* supposed to do. Whereas the leaves of the fault tree are invariants, the leaves of our goal tree are the actors responsible for the realization of the respective goal. Starting with a scenario from Sect. 2.1 as the top-level goal ("Trains should be able to move from one location in the track topology to a specific other location"), the decomposition is performed as follows:

- Subgoals are added until their combined satisfaction is sufficient to achieve the parent goal, e.g. "Send a new set of locations to the train that it is allowed to occupy".
- Every invariant derived from the fault tree analysis is added to the KAOS tree as an obstacle. Obstacles are decomposed into subgoals with the aim of satisfying both the parent and the invariant. For example, the invariant from above ("The interlocking allowed a train to go to an already occupied location") would spawn the subgoals "The interlocking monitors each train's occupied location" and "The interlocking commands each train its allowed locations".
- Subgoals are further decomposed until their satisfaction can be accomplished by a specific variable or method, which is established as the actor object for the fulfillment of this goal. For example, "The interlocking monitors each train's occupied location" would spawn a variable *trainAreas*.

2.5 Formal Modeling, Implementation and Proof

In the next step, we create a formal specification based on the list of invariants, as well as the variables and methods in the leaves of the KAOS tree. This specification is used to prove the conformance of an implementation of the system in a (semi-)automated fashion as provided by the utilized tools. While the method we describe in this work is not limited to a specific choice of tools, we require the existence of a certified compiler according to tool class T3 of EN 50716 [2]. Crucially, this certification assures auditors that binaries compiled by the tool behave exactly as specified, rendering further testing other than final integration tests redundant.

An example of a tool that fulfills this requirement is AdaCore *SPARK*. *SPARK* is a formal Ada-based software development technology [4]. A *SPARK* specification file contains *contracts* that comprise pre- and postconditions for every operation. Using AdaCore's GNATprove tool, the conformance of a *SPARK package body* with its specification can be proven. As *SPARK* is a subset of the Ada programming language, no further transpilation to another language is required [4]. The GNATprove compiler has a T3 certification [11].

In order to model a property like Eq. (1) in *SPARK*, we have decided to transform the sets into arrays. Sets are available in *SPARK* as abstract mathematical data types useful for reasoning, but are neither a default feature of Ada nor will they be a part of the final binary [14].

In Listing 1.1, an implementation of this property is given in a specification function. This function will be used as part of the pre- and postconditions of each procedure to ensure that the property is fulfilled in all possible states of the system. `RegTrains` is an array of trains. `TrainAreas` is an array of locations arrays, indexed equivalent to `RegTrains`. We iterate over `RegTrains` and require that all locations in one train's area are different from all locations in another train's area.

Listing 1.1. Implementation of the disjointness property in AdaCore SPARK.

```
function EnsureDisjointAreas return Boolean is
  (for all Train1 in RegTrains'Range =>
    (for all Train2 in RegTrains'Range =>
      (if RegTrains (Train1) /= RegTrains (Train2) then
        (for all Loc1 in TrainAreas (Train1)'Range =>
          (for all Loc2 in TrainAreas (Train2)'Range =>
            TrainAreas (Train1) (Loc1)
              /= TrainAreas (Train2) (Loc2))))));
```

3 Conclusion and Ongoing Work

Formal methods offer a framework to address interoperability and complexity challenges in railway signalling specifications. While academic experiments [18] have shown promise, industrial applicability remains an ongoing research focus [24]. Our primary contribution is a novel toolchain to enforce end-to-end traceability and compliance with EN 50716, demonstrated by an ongoing ETCS moving block case study. To support the requirements engineering process, we are developing an accompanying tool which integrates our KAOS adaption, stakeholder needs collection process, and fault tree analysis. Interfaces between method steps and full validation results will be detailed in a follow-up publication, currently under preparation.

References

1. EN 50126-1:2017. Railway Applications - The Specification and Demonstration of Reliability, Availability, Maintainability and Safety (RAMS) - Part 1: Generic RAMS Process. CENELEC (2017)
2. EN 50716:2023. Railway Applications - Requirements for software development. CENELEC (2023)
3. Abrial, J.R.: The ABZ-2018 case study with Event-B. Int. J. Softw. Tools Technol. Transf. **22**(3), 257–264 (2020)
4. AdaCore, Thales: Implementation Guidance for the Adoption of SPARK (2020). https://www.adacore.com/uploads/books/pdf/Spark-Guidance-1.2-web.pdf
5. Aoun, J., Goverde, R.M.P., Nardone, R., Quaglietta, E., Vittorini, V.: Towards a fault tree analysis of moving block and virtual coupling railway signalling systems. In: 2022 6th International Conference on System Reliability and Safety (ICSRS), pp. 69–74. IEEE, Venice, Italy (November 2022)
6. Arcaini, P., Kofroň, J., Ježek, P.: Validation of the Hybrid ERTMS/ETCS Level 3 using Spin. Int. J. Softw. Tools Technol. Transf. **22**(3), 265–279 (2020)
7. Borälv, A., Schwencke, D., Mejia, L.F.: X2Rail-5 Deliverable D10.4 Verification Report (June 2023)
8. Bartholomeus, M., Luttik, B., Willemse, T.: Modelling and analysing ERTMS hybrid level 3 with the mCRL2 toolset. In: Howar, F., Barnat, J. (eds.) FMICS 2018. LNCS, vol. 11119, pp. 98–114. Springer, Cham (2018). https://doi.org/10.1007/978-3-030-00244-2_7
9. Basile, D., Ter Beek, M.H., Ferrari, A., Legay, A.: Exploring the ERTMS/ETCS full moving block specification: an experience with formal methods. Int. J. Softw. Tools Technol. Transf. **24**(3), 351–370 (2022)
10. Borälv, A.: Deliverable D10.9 Formal Methods (FMs) Guidebook. Shift2Rail (2023)
11. Boulanger, J.L., Ochem, Q.: AdaCore Technologies for CENELEC EN 50128:2011. AdaCore (2018)
12. Bruel, J.M., Ebersold, S., Galinier, F., Mazzara, M., Naumchev, A., Meyer, B.: The role of formalism in system requirements. ACM Comput. Surv. **54**(5), 1–36 (2022)
13. Cimatti, A., Roveri, M., Susi, A., Tonetta, S.: Validation of requirements for hybrid systems: a formal approach. ACM Trans. Softw. Eng. Methodol. **21**(4), 1–34 (2012)
14. Dross, C.: Containers for specification in SPARK. ACM SIGAda Ada Lett. **42**(2), 62–68 (2023)
15. Letier, E.: Reasoning about Agents in Goal-Oriented Requirements Engineering. Ph.D. thesis (2002). http://hdl.handle.net/2078.1/5139
16. Ferrari, A., Beek, M.: Formal methods in railways: a systematic mapping study. ACM Comput. Surv. **55**(4), 1–37 (2023)

17. Gabriška, D.: Software requirements for the control systems according to the level of functional safety. J. Appl. Math. Stat. Inform. **12**(1), 25–32 (2016)
18. Hansen, D., et al.: Validation and real-life demonstration of ETCS hybrid level 3 principles using a formal B model. Int. J. Softw. Tools Technol. Transf. **22**(3), 315–332 (2020)
19. Kadakolmath, L., Ramu, D.U.: Goal-oriented modeling of an urban subway control system using KAOS. Indones. J. Comput. Sci. **12**(3) (2023)
20. Lamsweerde, A.V.: Goal-oriented requirements engineering: a guided tour. In: Proceedings of the Fifth IEEE International Symposium on Requirements Engineering, p. 249. IEEE Computer Society (2001)
21. Kopitzki, M., Nenke, T., Möller, P., Braun, W., Menne, D.: Das Betriebliche Zielbild als Basis für ein modernes und anwenderfreundliches Regelwerk. Deine Bahn (Oktober), 6–11 October 2021. https://www.system-bahn.net/wp-content/themes/systembahn/includes/readpdf.php?file=33016
22. SaddemYagoubi, R., Beugin, J., Ghazel, M.: Verification framework for moving block system safety: application on the loss of train integrity use case. Mauritius Island (April 2022)
23. Saddem-Yagoubi, R., Beugin, J., Ghazel, M.: A methodology framework for modelling a rail moving block system. Transp. Res. Procedia **72**, 1576–1580 (2023)
24. Ter Beek, M.H., et al.: Formal methods in industry. Form. Aspects Comput. **37**(1), 1–38 (2025)
25. Tueno Fotso, S.J., Frappier, M., Laleau, R., Mammar, A.: Modeling the hybrid ERTMS/ETCS level 3 standard using a formal requirements engineering approach. In: Butler, M., Raschke, A., Hoang, T.S., Reichl, K. (eds.) ABZ 2018. LNCS, vol. 10817, pp. 262–276. Springer, Cham (2018). https://doi.org/10.1007/978-3-319-91271-4_18

A Reasoning and Explicit Algebraic Theory for BBSL in Event-B: EB4BBSL Framework

Peter Riviere(✉), Duong Dinh Tran, Takashi Tomita, and Toshiaki Aoki

Japan Advanced Institute of Science and Technology, Ishikawa, 923-1292 Ishikawa, Japan
{priviere,duongtd,tomita,toshiaki}@jaist.ac.jp

Abstract. Automated Driving Systems (ADS) are major engineering and research topics, and ensuring the safety of such a critical system becomes crucial. Nevertheless, ADS are inherently complex, with many of their components, particularly sensors, relying on Artificial Intelligence. In addition to traditional environment data, ADS now processes object recognition outputs. To handle this new type of information, the Bounding Box Specification Language (BBSL) has been formalised to capture the relation between the abstraction of the image with the bounding box and the correct action to be performed. However, this language has a lightweight semantics, leading to multiple interpretations when no tools are available and its semantics remain implicit. In this paper, we propose a framework that fully formalises the language and allows the manipulation of the elements of the language as a first-class citizen in algebraic theory. We introduce three BBSL proof obligations and a mechanism to automatically generate and discharge the proof obligation. We also propose an extension of BBSL by explicitly formalising the semantics and behaviour of external interactions, such as importing information from outside sources. Furthermore, we also propose two instantiation mechanisms, deep-modelling and shallow-modelling, and we use an interpretation of BBSL in an Event-B machine.

Keywords: BBSL · New proof obligation · Refinement and proof · Model instantiation · Algebraic theories · Event-B

1 Introduction

Context: Several manufacturers are actively working on Automated Driving Systems (ADS), which show the potential to enhance transport mobility. The emphasis on ADS safety is paramount, as any malfunction can lead to accidents with severe consequences [6]. The complexity and dynamic environments in which ADS operate present significant safety hurdles. ADS comprise interconnected components such as sensing, perception, planning, and control; a fault

This work was supported by JST, CREST Grant Number JPMJCR23M1.

M. Leuschel and F. Ishikawa (Eds.): ABZ 2025, LNCS 15728, pp. 330–338, 2026.
https://doi.org/10.1007/978-3-031-94533-5_20

in any of these could affect the whole system. The perception module is vital, interpreting data from cameras, radar, and LiDAR for obstacle detection, traffic sign recognition, and road condition assessment, which are imperative for safe operation. Our research centres on the perception module's image recognition systems, which analyse images to create bounding boxes for object location identification, and the planning module, which processes this data to instruct the control module correctly. This component is critical in interpreting the complex environmental data encountered by ADS. The ADS camera captures environmental data as input. Objects are represented with bounding boxes, and events are defined by their spatial relationships. To fill the gap between the complexity of the world visualised through the image recognition, the Bounding Box Specification Languages (BBSL) [11] have been proposed to specify the relation between the object and the events of the system. The particularity of BBSL is to abstract the object with a bounding box and a label system that is currently information provided by ADS and is equipped with a high level operator based on spatial relation directly expressed on the bounding box to ease the specification and provide an expression language easier for the engineer to understand. However, the semantics of BBSL and the integration of domain knowledge are implicit and lightweight.

Our Contribution: In this paper, we present the EB4BBSL framework, which focusses on the formalisation of BBSL and expresses explicitly the semantics and its relation to the application domain, and also propose a logical framework for reasoning in BBSL. We take advantage of Event-B [1] and its extension for defining algebraic theories [4] to articulate a meta-model. Through the use of a deep embedding, a BBSL specification is represented as instances of algebraic data types that encapsulate the diverse BBSL operators, while the shallow modelling delivers a state-based interpretation. This metamodel captures the semantics of BBSL, its attributes, and the proof system used to validate these properties. The instantiation maintains the structure of BBSL models, facilitating the traceability of identified errors back to BBSL itself. Furthermore, we emphasise that by enhancing the core metamodel, additional proof obligations can be appended to the EB4BBSL framework. Due to space limitations, the models are not presented in the paper, but they are all available at https://github.com/fomaad/EB4BBSL.

Organisation of the Paper: Sect. 2 provides an overview of the features of BBSL used in this paper. Sections 3 present the EB4BBSL framework we designed to develop specific BBSL models, the definitions, the generation of BBSL proof obligations, and the instantiation mechanism. Finally, the assessment and conclusion are presented along with future work in Sect. 4 and Sect. 5.

2 BBSL

Many systems incorporate image recognition to capture environmental information and apply control regarding this information. For this purpose, an architecture is common [2,7] in the fields of autonomous drive systems. This architecture is composed of three modules: **Perception modules**: Use the information obtained from all the sensors and provide useful information about the environment; **Planning modules**: Use the information from the perception modules and decide on the order, according to multiple factors such as safety, goals, or comfort; **Control modules**: Apply to the system the right control according to the order.

The main focus of the bounding box specification (BBSL) [11] is to provide a logical framework for specifying the planning modules. The first feature of BBSL is to propose a logical framework to reason on a bounding box. This corresponds to an abstraction of objects that can appear in an image or on Lidar, and it is mainly the new information that can appear in the ADS system from the perception modules, along with the usual information such as speed and position. The second feature is to propose a framework to specify the planning modules, so it proposes a set of rules described from the output of the perception module, represented as a bounding box and the order sent by the planning modules.

3 EB4BBSL Framework

3.1 Methodology

The purpose of our framework is to fully formalise BBSL, to manipulate any element as a first-class citizen, and to express new properties inspired by the work presented in EB4EB [8,9] and EB[ASTD] [5]. However, the Bounding Box Specification Language semantics for all components are not fully established, compared to Event-B and ASTD. In addition, the incorporation of autonomous vehicle knowledge into the semantics is not established. In the EB4BBSL framework, we also explicitly formalise the semantics and the dynamics aspect of BBSL, i.e. its interaction with the environment and integration into the planning modules. Figure 1 shows the architecture of the framework. The framework has three parts:

- **BBSL Meta level** ($\mathcal{M}$) – It formalises the structural syntax and semantics of BBSL with new data types and operators in the `BBSL core` ($\mathcal{M}$.1) algebraic theory, and the ability to manipulate BBSL to express the high level reasoning mechanism in `BBSL PO` ($\mathcal{M}$.2) theory.
- **Bounding Box Expression** ($\mathcal{E}$) – It formalises all the mathematical background necessary to express high-level reasoning to manipulate expression in BBSL. Three kinds of expressions are essential in BBSL: Set, Interval, and Bounding Box. Only the set is native in the Event-B expression. To complete the BBSL expression language, the `Interval` ($\mathcal{E}$.2) and `Bounding Box` ($\mathcal{E}$.3) theories are developed to extend the Event-B expression. Both theories are grounded in a theory of `Comparable` ($\mathcal{E}$.1).
- **Instantiation mechanism** ($\mathcal{I}$) – It defines two mechanisms of instantiation, similar to the instantiation presented in [8,9], the *deep modelling* ($\mathcal{I}.\mathcal{D}$), which consists of expressing concrete BBSL models as FOL and set theory formulae

in an Event-B context ($\mathcal{I.D}$.1) by instantiating `BBSL Meta Level (`$\mathcal{M}$`)`. The shallow modelling ($\mathcal{I.S}$) uses a generic machine that interprets the semantics defined in the theory using an Event-B machine ($\mathcal{I.S}$.1) and the planning module, and the concrete BBSL model is described in an Event-B machine ($\mathcal{I.S}$.2) that refines the generic machine. Both modellings use comprehension axioms to transform the predicate to set and the `Bounding Box Expression (`$\mathcal{E}$`)` to express BBSL case rule.

Note that all parts in blue in Fig. 1 are described once and for all. To exploit our framework to reason on BBSL, only the instance is needed.

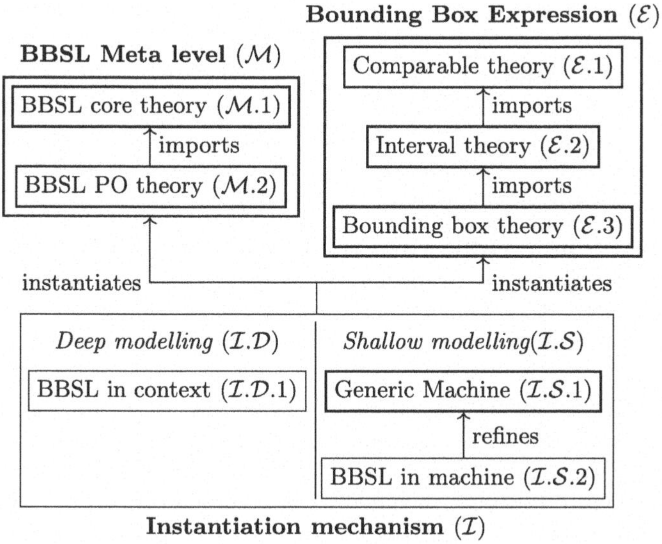

Fig. 1. EB4BBSL Framework

3.2 Formalisation of BBSL ($\mathcal{M}$)

BBSL Core Theory ($\mathcal{M}$.1): To capture and manipulate BBSL components as first-class citizen elements, a data-type `BBSL` has been defined. Based on BBSL grammar, BBSL specification has three main parts: the external function, the precondition, and the case block. The basic elements are the actions defined by the case block and the variables expressed with the external function. BBSL's primary function is to outline the actions of the planning modules within a case block governed by a precondition clause. Initially, the external function delayed the linkage semantics with the perception modules.

In our framework, instead of relying on external functions to express all the information needed to express the rule and precondition, an abstract representation of the variables is used. As a consequence, the data-type takes two type parameters, `Act` to represent the action case of the case block and `Var` to represent the elements accessible by the external function and used in the precondition and the case block. The data type has many destructors to access different constituents of BBSL: `actions` – set of all possible actions addressed in BBSL models; `variables` – set of possible variables addressed in BBSL models; `hyp` – set of the variables that verify the precondition; `bbslcase` – relation between the valuation of the variables and the applicable action. The data type definition provides only the type information of all the constituents of BBSL. To complete the formalisation, additional predicate operators are presented to capture the structural properties between BBSL elements and ensure a correct definition of BBSL metamodels. The predicate operator `ActionsWellCons` and respectively `VarWellCons` ensure that `hyp` and `bbslcase` when they refer to the actions, and respectively to the variables, use only the possible values defined in `action`, respectively `variables`. Another predicate operator such as `NotHypCase` is also formalised to capture the semantics of the implicit semantics of BBSL. This operator captures the default relation when the variables do not belong to the precondition, and then any actions can be performed $(Var \cap variables(bbsl)) \setminus hyp(bbsl) \leftrightarrow actions(bbsl)$.

Proof Obligations ($\mathcal{M}$.2): From the formalisation of BBSL, the property can be expressed and used to formalise the proof obligation on BBSL models following the methodology in [10]. Three properties are not mandatory in the formalisation of BBSL specifications but can be required in some applications and are defined [12,13]. We have formalised these properties in EB4BBSL in a theory. The first property is *exhaustivity*: for any variable that satisfies the precondition, an action is associated. This property is captured by the predicate operator `Exhaustive`, which takes a BBSL model *bbsl* and is defined with the set of precondition values included in the domain of the case rule of BBSL $hyp(bbsl) \subseteq bbslcase(bbsl)$. The second property is *exclusionary*: for any value of the variables, at most one action is specified. `Exclusionary` predicate operator is defined for this property. The operator takes a BBSL model *bbsl* and is defined as the case block of BBSL model being a partial function between the variables and the actions of BBSL. The last property is *non-redundancy*: for all actions, at least one valuation of variables can trigger the action. The predicate operator `non_redundant` takes BBSL models *bbsl* and verifies that the case block is a surjective relation between the variables and actions of BBSL $(hyp(bbsl) \lhd bbslcase(bbsl)) \in variables(bbsl) \twoheadleftrightarrow action(bbsl)$.

3.3 Instantiation Mechanism ($\mathcal{I}$)

To obtain a specific BBSL model, two instantiation mechanisms are identified, the *deep modelling* and *shallow modelling*. Inspired by the deep and shallow embedding [3], the two mechanisms instantiate BBSL meta-theory, with a context for the *deep modelling* and using only the elements defined in the theory. Or with a machine in the *shallow modelling* using refined events to describe the model.

Deep Modelling ($\mathcal{I}.\mathcal{D}$): The principle of *deep modelling* is to represent BBSL model in a context by instantiating the data type and the concrete value of each field. For this, two concrete sets must be provided to instantiate the type parameters of the meta-theory. One concrete set for the action label *Act*, and the cartesian product of the type of variable to instantiate *Var*. The fields of the data type are defined by a set where all the elements verify the definition of the related clause, i.e. hyp is a set where all elements verify the hypotheses of BBSL specification, and bbslcase is all the pairs act and var that verify the clause rule of BBSL specification. For example, the stop rule and precondition of Listing 1 will lead to the instantiation of Listing 2 The proof obligation is generated on a theorem clause, where the concrete BBSL model is in argument of the related predicate operator of the meta-theory.

```
precondition
 [objectExists() = true]
endprecondition
case Stop
 let object: bb = object(), stopping_order:interval = stopping_order()
  in PROJ_y(object) ≈ stopping_order ∨ PROJ_y(object) < stopping_order
endcase
...
```

Listing 1: An extract of a specification of ADS to response to the distance to a detect element

$$
\begin{aligned}
\textbf{axm5}:\ & bbslcase(ads) = \{(object \mapsto stopping\_order) \mapsto act \mid \\
& \quad ((act = Stop \land (IoverlapInt(projy2d(object), stopping\_order) \ldots\} \\
\textbf{axm6}:\ & hyp(ads) = \{object \mapsto stopping\_order \mid \\
& \quad NotEmpty2DInt(object) \land ItoSetInt(stopping\_order) \neq \emptyset\}
\end{aligned}
$$

Listing 2: A deep modelling of the braking systems example

Shallow Modelling ($\mathcal{I}.\mathcal{S}$): The shallow modelling consists of representing BBSL model directly using an Event-B machine. For this, we first need to provide a state-based semantic interpretation of BBSL, using a generic machine based on the definition of the planning modules. Then, describe the concrete BBSL model by refining the generic BBSL. The benefit of shallow modelling is the use of the refinement process to compose BBSL specifications or to use BBSL models as an abstract model to define the autonomous driving system.

Similarly to deep modelling, the type parameter must be instantiated with a concrete set; at the generic level, only a symbolic set is provided, and the content of the set will be described at the level of the refines machine. This machine was designed to represent an abstract planning module that satisfies BBSL specifications. Two variables *st* to represent the variables of BBSL, and *act* the action to send to the control modules. The initialisation of the variables is non-deterministic, assigned to one element of $action(bbsl)$ and $variables(bbsl)$.

Two kinds of events are defined: the event that occurs to update the variables from the perception modules and to update the actions. The assignment of the action can occur in two cases. The first case is the event *Apply_rule* that can trigger when the state *st* checks the preconditions. The state *st* must also verify the case definition of the event parameter, the new action *new_act*. The action

```
MACHINE GenericMchBBSL
SEES GenericBBSL
VARIABLES st , act
INVARIANTS
  inv1−2: st ∈ S ∧ act ∈ Action
EVENTS
INITIALISATION
 THEN
  act1: st :∈ variables(bbsl)
  act2: act :∈ actions(bbsl)
 END
NotHyp
 WHERE grd1: st ∉ hyp(bbsl)
 THEN act1: act :∈ NotHypCase(bbsl)
 END
```

```
ApplyRule
 ANY new_act
 WHERE
  grd1: st ∈ hyp(bbsl)
  grd3: new_act ∈ actions(bbsl)
  grd2: st ∈ bbslcase(bbsl)⁻¹[{new_act}]
 THEN act1: act := new_act
 END
Update
 WHERE grd1: st ∉ hyp(bbsl)
         ∨st ∈ bbslcase(bbsl)⁻¹[{act}]
 THEN act1: st :∈ variables(bbsl)
 END
END
```

Listing 3: Generic machine for BBSL

variable act is assigned the new value new_act. The event $NotHyp$ occurs when the variables do not belong to the precondition, and the variables relying on the `NotHypCase` define in the Meta-theory. The last event is related to the assignment of variables; this is defined in the event $Update\_Var$. This event occurs when the variables verify BBSL specification, or the precondition does not hold and assigns a new value to the variables in $variables(bbsl)$.

The concrete BBSL model ($\mathcal{I}.\mathcal{S}.2$) is described within a machine that refines the generic one. The syntactical description of BBSL needs to be expressed in the context, in the same manner as deep modelling. The initialisation and update events do not need additional information. Each case is described within an event that refines *ApplyRule* with two guards. Guard $grdHyp$ ensures that the variables are in the precondition, and $grdCase$ instantiates one case and verifies that the variables belong to it. The shallow modelling of the specification for the stop rule is shown in Listing 4. The preconditions rule is expressed in the same manner as the deep modelling in a context.

```
Stop REFINES ApplyRule
 WHERE
  grdHyp: object ↦ stopping_order ∈ hyp(BBSL1)
  grdCase: (IoverlapInt(projy2d(object), stopping_order)
 WITH new_act: new_act = Stop
 THEN act1: act := Stop
 END
```

Listing 4: A Shallow modelling of the braking systems example

4 Discussion

This paper is focused on the formalisation of BBSL; our approach used many different Event-B techniques to formalise the concept of BBSL and its semantics, as well as to efficiently use the native proof obligations to support the properties of BBSL. During the process, we identified two key points of discussion that appear in this work in comparison to EB4EB and EB[ASTD]:

Semantics: The formalisation of the EB4BBSL framework has raised many issues regarding the semantics of BBSL for many parts of it. A trade-off occurs between the expressiveness capabilities and the elements with concrete semantics to perform reasoning. The decision process is based on information from the ADS domain and the initial purpose of BBSL. One significant decision is to use the external function as variables to represent all the information provided by the perception modules, without restraint on the expressiveness capabilities, and to incorporate the notion explicitly inside BBSL. Another decision concerns the semantics of the state-based interpretation of BBSL in shallow modelling. The choice to design the planning module instead of only the rules of BBSL has multiple consequences; it links BBSL component directly to the planning in a shallow manner and makes the further development straightforward by refining to concrete planning modules or by introducing the other modules by refinement.

Deep vs Shallow: In the deep modelling, BBSL model is designed using only the elements of the meta-theory. The advantage of this modelling is the generation of proof obligations, but all the descriptions of BBSL models are done in one block, and no composition and refinement processes are available. However, shallow modelling proposes splitting the case description into multiple events that make it easier to read and validate the model. It allows us to use the invariant clause to prove some properties or the refinement of Event-B between machines to support a refinement process between BBSL specifications or between BBSL specifications and concrete models. The interest in the generation of the proof obligation on the machine side will be to use the induction principle built inside the Event-B machine; however, all the BBSL proof obligations are not based on an induction schema; they are fully deductive.

5 Conclusion

This paper proposes a formal technique that allows an engineer to define specific bounding box specifications and verify properties such as exhaustivity, exclusionary, and non-redundancy on concrete specific BBSL models. This work also shows the capabilities of EB4BBSL, on the one hand, to formalise and manipulate elements of BBSL as first-class citizens to express new proof obligations for BBSL, and on the other hand, extends the expression of Event-B with a theory of comparable, interval, and bounding boxes with all the reasoning operators associated and proof rules to simplify the proof process. Combined, both parts propose two instantiation mechanisms, with their pros and cons. Deep modelling is used to generate proof obligations for BBSL models, and shallow modelling is used to integrate with the refinement process into a complete development of ADS. This paper also proposes another formalisation of a formal method that consolidates the embedded capabilities of Event-B. All theories are done once and for all and can be reused, and the theorem does not need to be proved again; only the instantiation is required.

We believe that the formalisation of EB4BBSL is an improvement to the semantics of BBSL and its formal verification. This framework opens the path to extending BBSL in many types of extensions. The first path is to include an internal state to the bounding box, or to describe a data flow semantics to allow the formalisation of ADS and BBSL in a framework similar to Simulink. Another path is to express standard conformance operations in BBSL, or to define a specification operation to refine directly on concrete models.

References

1. Abrial, J.R.: Modeling in Event-B: System and Software Engineering. Cambridge University Press, Cambridge (2010)
2. Baidu Apollo team (2017): Apollo: Open Source Autonomous Driving. https://github.com/ApolloAuto/apollo. Accessed 25 Sep 2024
3. Boulton, R.J., Gordon, A.D., Gordon, M.J., Harrison, J., Herbert, J., Van Tassel, J.: Experience with embedding hardware description languages in hol. In: TPCD, vol. 10, pp. 129–156. Citeseer (1992)
4. Butler, M.J., Maamria, I.: Practical theory extension in Event-B. In: Liu, Z., Woodcock, J., Zhu, H. (eds.) Theories of Programming and Formal Methods - Essays Dedicated to Jifeng He on the Occasion of His 70th Birthday. LNCS, vol. 8051, pp. 67–81. Springer, Cham (2013). https://doi.org/10.1007/978-3-642-39698-4_5
5. Chen, C., Riviere, P., Singh, N.K., Dupont, G., Ait Ameur, Y., Frappier, M.: A proof-based ground algebraic meta-model for reasoning on ASTD in Event-B. In: FormaliSE 2025 (2025)
6. Devi, S., Malarvezhi, P., Dayana, R., Vadivukkarasi, K.: A comprehensive survey on autonomous driving cars: a perspective view. Wirel. Pers. Commun. **114**(3), 2121–2133 (2020)
7. Kato, S., et al.: Autoware on board: enabling autonomous vehicles with embedded systems. In: Proceedings of the 9th ACM/IEEE International Conference on Cyber-Physical Systems, ICCPS 2018, pp. 287–296 (2018). https://doi.org/10.1109/ICCPS.2018.00035
8. Riviere, P., Singh, N.K., Aït Ameur, Y.: EB4EB: a framework for reflexive Event-B. In: ICECCS 2022, pp. 71–80. IEEE (2022)
9. Riviere, P., Singh, N.K., Aït Ameur, Y.: Reflexive Event-B: semantics and correctness the EB4EB framework. IEEE Trans. Reliabil. 1–16 (2022)
10. Riviere, P., Singh, N.K., Aït Ameur, Y., Dupont, G.: Standalone event-b models analysis relying on the EB4EB meta-theory. In: ABZ. LNCS, vol. 14010, pp. 193–211. Springer (2023)
11. Tanaka, K., Aoki, T., Kawai, T., Tomita, T., Kawakami, D., Chida, N.: A formal specification language based on positional relationship between objects in automated driving systems. In: COMPSAC, pp. 950–955. IEEE (2022)
12. Tanaka, K., Aoki, T., Kawai, T., Tomita, T., Kawakami, D., Chida, N.: Specification based testing of object detection for automated driving systems via BBSL. In: ENASE, pp. 250–261. SCITEPRESS (2023)
13. Tanaka, K., Aoki, T., Tomita, T., Kawakami, D., Chida, N.: Specification-based testing of the image-recognition performance of automated driving systems. IEEE Access **13**, 6321–6349 (2025)

Model-Based Testing of Non-deterministic Systems

Alexander Onofrei, Marc Frappier(✉), and Émilie Bernard

University of Sherbrooke, Sherbrooke, Canada
{onoa2801,marc.frappier,emilie.bernard4}@usherbrooke.ca

Abstract. Testing non-deterministic systems is challenging due to unpredictable behaviours arising from timing, concurrency, and random inputs. This paper explores the application of model-based testing (MBT) to tackle these challenges, leveraging formal methods and tools to ensure systematic test coverage. We employ ProB, a model checker for the B method, to analyse a formal model of the system under test (SUT) and generate test scenarios from the formal B model. As a proof of concept, we apply MBT to the TLS 1.3 protocol, a widely used complex cryptographic standard, and test one of its implementation using the BouncyCastle OpenSSL Java API. While the TLS handshake is primarily deterministic, it includes non-deterministic components like cipher selection and random value generation, making it an excellent candidate for evaluating MBT's effectiveness. We present the design and logic of our proof of concept, showcasing its flexibility to support various models and SUTs. This study demonstrates that combining formal methods, non-deterministic analysis, and state-based testing can effectively address the challenges of non-deterministic systems, enabling improved testing strategies and greater system reliability.

1 Introduction

Models are essential in software development, particularly as system complexity increases. They abstract intricate architectures, employing tools like graphs and finite state machines (FSMs) to predict behavior [2]. Ideally, a model fully represents the implementation under test (IUT), yet non-deterministic FSMs remain constrained [14]. While effective for systematic testing, real-world systems-especially distributed architectures and protocols like TLS—introduce external dependencies that complicate verification [10].

This paper presents a proof of concept: testing non-deterministic systems using B, a model-based specification method [1]. We construct an abstract B machine to model key behaviors of the system under test and develop a test generator using ProB [15] to verify the correctness of the SUT. To validate this approach, we apply it to the TLS 1.3 session protocol [21], a highly complex standard. Using a simplified model of TLS, we test the BouncyCastle OpenSSL Java API implementation [24]. The challenge in MBT of non-deterministic systems is that the test scenario is constructed online during the execution of a test, since

M. Leuschel and F. Ishikawa (Eds.): ABZ 2025, LNCS 15728, pp. 339–346, 2026.
https://doi.org/10.1007/978-3-031-94533-5_21

the next event to generate depends on the output that was non-deterministically chosen by the SUT. For example, in TLS, the response of the client depends on the response chosen by the server.

Testing, model checking, and formal proofs each offer distinct advantages and limitations. Formal proofs provide mathematical certainty but struggle with scalability and practical implementation. Model checking systematically explores all possible states but is constrained by state-space explosion [8]. Testing, while less exhaustive, remains the most practical method for verifying real-world implementations. Model-based testing bridges these approaches by automating test generation from formal models, reducing human error and increasing coverage compared to manually derived test cases. This makes MBT particularly valuable for testing non-deterministic systems.

2 Related Work

Research on testing nondeterministic systems remains limited, with few studies examining model-based approaches in this context. Key challenges include test model coverage under uncertainty, scenario generation via model checkers, and efficient testing strategies. [11] provides foundational insights, highlighting methods for handling concurrency, randomness, and the selection of test conditions. We tackle these issues using ProB, which offers greater expressiveness than FSMs, because of their lack of state variables-allowing the extraction of specific paths that satisfy a given predicate.

In MBT, nondeterministic models arise from abstraction or inherent software behavior. A single test case may follow multiple paths due to internal system decisions [12,13]. Techniques such as probabilistic model checking and transition annotations mitigate this problem, but ensuring sufficient test coverage remains a challenge [4,20]. By deriving tests directly from the model within the model checker, we ensure comprehensive scenario handling. To improve testing efficiency, innovative techniques have been proposed. For example, integrating model checkers with mutation analysis enables the generation of systematic tests by injecting faults into the system models [5]. We address this by leveraging the ProB API to generate abstract test cases based on specific test criteria and analyze logical operations within the model. Other approaches, such as [17], optimize state graph-based test generation to balance coverage and test set size, critical for multi-threaded and distributed systems. Providers, such as Entrust [9], offer SSL/TLS tools to help organizations assess and enhance digital security by evaluating configurations on both client and server sides, including verifying compliance with encryption algorithms.

Combinatorial testing has been used for TLS [16,23], and several errors were found. We hope that a ProB MBT approach will enable us to find interesting combination of parameters using predicate analysis and logic solving that are not covered by traditional combinatorial testing, as shown in [22].

3 Foundations

3.1 B and ProB

B is a formal method for system specification, design and implementation, providing precise modeling through abstract machines and refinement [1]. It ensures correctness and reliability, making it essential for safety-critical systems. In this project, B is used to formally model the SUT. ProB, a model checker and animator, enables dynamic analysis, model execution, and real-time verification [15]. The ProB Java API [3] is integral to our proof of concept, facilitating interaction with the B model. It is used to generate targeted test cases for specific traces while also identifying states that satisfy given predicates.

3.2 TLS Protocol

TLS (Transport Layer Security) is a widely adopted cryptographic protocol designed to ensure secure communication over computer networks. It guarantees data integrity, confidentiality, and authenticity between a client and a server. TLS is a cornerstone of secure online interactions, used extensively in web browsers, email systems, and various online services due to its ability to prevent eavesdropping, tampering, and forgery.

The TLS handshake, which is the first phase of communication between a client and server, plays a crucial role in establishing a secure session. This process involves authentication, key exchange, and negotiation of session parameters. While largely deterministic, the handshake includes non-deterministic choice of elements such as cipher selection and initial random values. These steps can be summarized with the sequence diagram provided in Fig. 1. The Client Hello and Server Hello messages, along with the encrypted extensions, contain the essential parameters required to establish a basic TLS communication. These parameters include the supported versions, cipher suites, signature algorithms, supported groups, and shared keys, among others [21].

These nondeterministic factors necessitate careful testing to confirm the protocol's reliability and security. Thus, testing TLS for its non-deterministic components is essential to ensure it can correctly handle unexpected behaviors.

4 Methodology and Design

Our MBT approach for non-deterministic systems relies on black-box testing. This means we evaluate whether a system adheres to a predefined model based on its specification and rules, without considering its internal implementation. To achieve this, we integrate our Java implementation with the ProB model checker via the ProB Java API. This integration allows us to control, execute, and retrieve information from the model checker directly within our application, streamlining test selection and execution. The SUT in our study is the BouncyCastle OpenSSL Java Library, which will be evaluated based on model-derived tests.

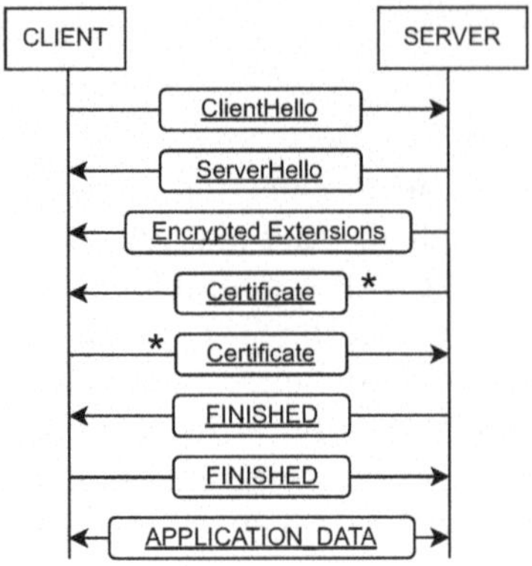

Fig. 1. TLS 1.3 Sequence Diagram

This methodology enables testing of both the client and server sides of a TLS implementation. When testing the server, ProB generates a client message, which is sent to the server. The server's response is then compared against the expected output defined by the specification. A match indicates a successful test, while any deviation results in a failed test. To test the client, the process is reversed, with the server-side behavior being modeled and validated against expected responses.

The sequence diagram provided in Fig. 2 illustrates the interactions between our application components during server-side testing. Notably, the same diagram applies to client-side testing, with the only modification being the entity that initiates the first message. This implementation is designed for flexibility, facilitating adaptation to any SUT. To achieve this, we structured each component in a generalized framework, enabling adaptation based on the specific requirements of the SUT. Since our specification abstracts from implementation details, we developed a test instantiator to convert abstract tests-generated by the test scenario generator—into concrete, executable tests. The scenario generator performs operations such as state predicate satisfaction and random trace generation. Each test consists of a sequence of events and corresponding operations with assigned parameters. An Information Capture module collects the SUT's outputs, feeding them back to the Test Instantiator, which converts them into abstract results for comparison against the specification's expected results. If the result is one of them, the test is passed and the next operation is executed. Otherwise, the test case is marked as a failure.

As a proof of concept, we test the implementation of the ClientHello and ServerHello messages in TLS 1.3. Each message is represented by a send operation for the issuer of the message, and a receive operation for the recipient, which will enable us to model man-in-the-middle attacks. The model initially generates the ClientHello message, using the SendClientHello operation, in an abstract format, which is then translated into a concrete TLS ClientHello message. The ServerHello response from the SUT is converted back into an abstract

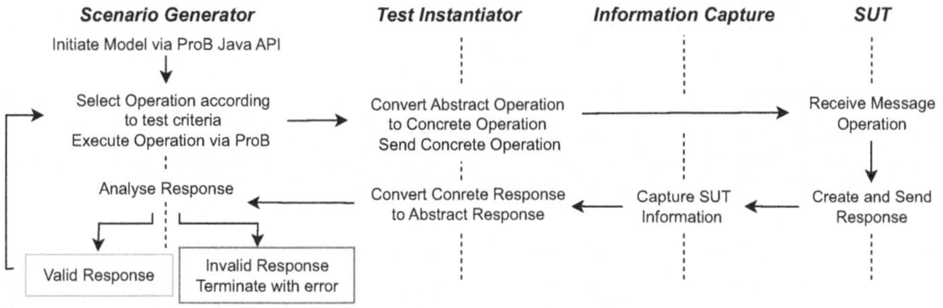

Fig. 2. Architecture of our MBT testing approach

representation and compared against the expected abstract message generated by the model.

For our proof of concept, we selected a typical sequence of operations within the model: SendClientHello, ReceiveClientHello, SendServerHello, ReceiveServerHello. The Send operations include parameters corresponding to those in a concrete TLS message, as specified in [21]. The specification enforces basic parameter validation to ensure that values are within acceptable bounds. The RFC allows for interpretation by using terms such as "SHOULD", "SHOULD NOT" and "MAY" [6], which introduce flexibility in compliance. As a result, different implementations of the TLS protocol can be derived from the same RFC, leading to variations in behavior. This might also be a source of bugs and non-interoperability, since one party's implementation may take a "SHOULD" as a practical "MUST", and the other party's implementation taking "SHOULD" as something really optional as stated in [6] ("SHOULD ... *mean that there may exist valid reasons in particular circumstances to ignore a particular item, but the full implications must be understood and carefully weighed before choosing a different course.*").

5 Results

After testing and comparing BouncyCastle's server response to specific Client Hello messages generated by our model checker, we successfully generated 16 distinct ClientHello messages with varying parameters to evaluate the corresponding ServerHello responses. The generated messages included 5 cipher suites, 8 signature algorithms, 2 supported groups, 1 supported versions TLS 1.3, and 2 compression methods. The complete results are available in our GitHub [19] repository. In all 16 test cases, the server responses were consistent with the model's predictions, confirming that our specification accurately represents the SUT and that the SUT exhibits no flaws within the tested parameters.

Given the complexity of the task, we focused solely on modifying the Client Hello parameters, limiting our scope to analyzing the server's response. Nevertheless, this study demonstrates the feasibility and effectiveness of our test generation approach. Furthermore, it highlights the potential for expanding test coverage to more intricate aspects of TLS, such as certificate validation and key exchange mechanisms.

6 Discussion

Our approach opens-up new possibilities for systematically testing complex system like TLS. This becomes particularly important since TLS will have to support in the near future new quantum resistant cryptographic primitives, called post-quantum cryptography [18]. A transition period, where both classic and quantum resistant interactions must be supported by clients and servers, will induce new possibilities for attacks, bugs and interoperability issues. Model checkers can systematically explore possible input combinations to produce expected outputs, uncovering test cases that might otherwise be overlooked. However, our approach comes with certain limitations. MBT is easier to achieve if the SUT has a modular design that allows for an easy re-use of methods that send and receive messages between the SUT and the tester. For instance, BouncyCastle provides a method to send a ClientHello to the server. However, this method cannot be reused easily, because it is highly dependent on the state of the protocol, and it has several dependencies with other methods that must be executed before, but that we do not want to execute, since we use ProB to model and analyse the protocol state and drive the test generation. Sending and receiving TLS messages in the proper format is not an easy task. We had to recode these methods, with very low-level handling of the messages as bit streams, and little code could be re-used from the BouncyCastle implementation. We capture messages from the server on the communication port and manually decode them, thus we must ignore TCP messages and other irrelevant information for just testing the TLS part of the communication. We also considered to reuse the widely used OpenSSL implementation of TLS, but it was not easier, because it is written in very old-school C and harder to understand. It makes heavy use of function pointers and macros, instead of using modern object-oriented programming concepts. Unfortunately, writing the code to send and receive messages in TLS was the most difficult and time-consuming part of our work. In the next version of our implementation, we will explore the TLS-Attacker framework [7], a fuzzy-testing tool, to try to streamline this step. Additionally, refining translation methods between abstract and concrete messages will be crucial for improving automation. By incorporating test criteria, we aim to selectively generate test cases that target specific needs, ensuring comprehensive test coverage and deeper insights into system behavior. Our approach differs from the testing offered by industrial providers, as we specifically test each step of the TLS handshake implementation rather than only analyzing its overall configuration and final communication result [16].

References

1. Abrial, J-R.: The B-book - assigning programs to meanings (2005). isbn: 978-0-521-02175-3
2. Beizer, B.: Software Testing Techniques (2nd ed.) USA: Van Nostrand Reinhold Co., (1990). isbn: 0442206720
3. Bendisposto, J., et al.: ProB2-UI: a java-based user interface for ProB. In: Lluch Lafuente, A., Mavridou, A. (eds.) FMICS 2021. LNCS, vol. 12863, pp. 193–201. Springer, Cham (2021). https://doi.org/10.1007/978-3-030-85248-1_12
4. Bertrand, N., et al.: Off-line test selection with test purposes for nondeterministic timed automata. In: Logical Methods in Computer Science, vol. 8, no. 4 (2012). issn: 1860-5974. https://doi.org/10.2168/LMCS-8(4:8)2012. https://lmcs.episciences.org/1037
5. Boroday, S., Petrenko, A., Groz, R.: Can a model checker generate tests for non-deterministic systems? Electron. Notes Theor. Comput. Sci. **190**(2) (2007). Proceedings of the Third Workshop on Model Based Testing (MBT 2007), pp. 3–19. issn: 1571-0661. https://doi.org/10.1016/j.entcs.2007.08.002. https://www.sciencedirect.com/science/article/pii/S1571066107005373
6. Bradner, S.O.: Key words for use in RFCs to Indicate Requirement Levels. RFC 2119 (1997). https://doi.org/10.17487/RFC2119. https://www.rfc-editor.org/info/rfc2119
7. Bäumer, F., et al.: TLS-attacker: a dynamic framework for analyzing TLS implementations. In: Proceedings of Cybersecurity Artifacts Competition and Impact Award (ACSAC 2024) (2024)
8. Clarke, E., et al.: Model checking and the state explosion problem, pp. 1–30 (2012). isbn: 978-3-642-35745-9. https://doi.org/10.1007/978-3-642-35746-6_1
9. Entrust Corporation. Entrust SSL/TLS Tools (2025). https://www.entrust.com/knowledgebase/ssl/ssl-tls-tools. Accessed 24 Feb 2025
10. Firesmith, D.: Testing in a non-deterministic world. In: SEI Conference (2017)
11. Graham, D.: Foundations of Software Testing: ISTQB Certification. Course Technology Cengage Learning (2008). isbn: 9781283285186. https://books.google.ca/books?id=h6h2AQAACAAJ
12. Kushik, N., Yevtushenko, N., López, J.: Probabilistic approach for minimizing checking sequences for non-deterministic FSMs. In: Bonfanti, S., Gargantini, A., Salvaneschi, P. (eds) Testing Software and Systems, pp. 237–243. Springer, Cham (2023). isbn: 978-3-031-43240-8
13. Kushik, N., Yevtushenko, N., López, J.: Testing against non-deterministic FSMs: a probabilistic approach for test suite minimization. In: Clark, D., Menendez, H., Cavalli, A.R. (eds.) Testing Software and Systems, pp. 55–61. Springer, Cham (2022). isbn: 978-3-031-04673-5
14. Lee, D., Yannakakis, M.: Principles and methods of testing finite state machines-a survey. In: Proceedings of the IEEE, vol. 84. no. 8 (1996). https://doi.org/10.1109/5.533956
15. Leuschel, M., Butler, M.: ProB: an automated analysis toolset for the B method. In: Int. J. Softw. Tools Technol. Transf. **10**(2), 185–203 (2008). issn: 1433-2779
16. Maehren, M., et al.: TLS-anvil: adapting combinatorial testing for TLS libraries. In: 31st USENIX Security Symposium (USENIX Security 22). Boston, MA: USENIX Association, pp. 215–232 (2022). isbn: 978- 1-939133-31-1. https://www.usenix.org/conference/usenixsecurity22/presentation/maehren

17. Nachmanson, L., et al.: Optimal strategies for testing nondeterministic systems. SIGSOFT Softw. Eng. Notes **29**(4), 55–64 (2004). https://doi.org/10.1145/1013886.1007520. issn: 0163-5948
18. Näther, C., et al.: Migrating software systems toward post-quantum cryptography-a systematic literature review. IEEE Access **12**, 132107–132126 (2024). https://doi.org/10.1109/access.2024.3450306. issn: 2169-3536
19. Onofrei, A.: MBT TLS using ProB. https://github.com/ohnoitsalex/TLSModeling.git
20. Prasetya, I.S.W.B., Klomp, R.: Test Model Coverage Analysis Under Uncertainty. In: Ölveczky, P.C., Salaün, G. (eds.) SEFM 2019. LNCS, vol. 11724, pp. 222–239. Springer, Cham (2019). https://doi.org/10.1007/978-3-030-30446-1_12. isbn: 9783030304461
21. Rescorla, E.: The Transport Layer Security (TLS) Protocol Version 1.3. RFC 8446 (2018). https://doi.org/10.17487/RFC8446. https://www.rfceditor.org/info/rfc8446
22. Savary, A.: Détection de vulnérabilités appliquée à la vérification de code intermédiaire de Java Card. Theses. Université de Limoges ; Université de Sherbrooke (Québec, Canada) (2016). https://theses.hal.science/tel-01369017
23. Simos, D.E., et al.: Testing TLS using combinatorial methods and execution framework. In: Yevtushenko, N., Cavalli, A.R., Yenigün, H. (eds.) ICTSS 2017. LNCS, vol. 10533, pp. 162–177. Springer, Cham (2017). https://doi.org/10.1007/978-3-319-67549-7_10
24. The Legion of the Bouncy Castle, Inc. Bouncy Castle Java Library. https://www.bouncycastle.org/download/bouncy-castle-java/. Accessed: 2025-02-25. 2025

PhD Symposium Papers

Weakening Goals in Logical Specifications

Ben M. Andrew(✉)

University of Manchester, Manchester, UK
benjamin.andrew@manchester.ac.uk

Abstract. Logical specifications are widely used to represent software systems and their desired properties. Under system degradation or environmental changes, commonly seen in complex real-world robotic systems, these properties may no longer hold and so traditional verification methods will simply fail to construct a proof. However, weaker versions of these properties do still hold and can be useful for understanding the system's behaviour in uncertain conditions, as well as aiding compositional verification. We present a counterexample-guided technique for iteratively weakening properties, apply it to propositional logic specifications, and discuss planned extensions to state-based representations.

1 Introduction

Software systems, along with properties that we are interested in proving about them, are often specified in logics such as first-order or temporal logic. Many verification techniques exist for automatically checking whether desired properties hold in a system, but in complex systems that interact with the real world, unexpected environmental conditions or system degradation can cause these properties to no longer hold [9].

In these cases traditional formal verification techniques will simply report property violations, leaving us unable to say anything about the system's behaviour. However, for many applications we may be interested in weakened forms of the property that do hold in the system.

As an example, consider a quadrotor drone that we have proven can only safely land when the wind speed is below a certain threshold, and now imagine that this property does *not* hold when one of the rotors has failed. There may still be a weaker version of this property, for example with a lower threshold on the wind speed, that does hold for the degraded drone. Being able to automatically deduce this weakened property may be crucial for regulatory approval or understanding how the system properties change under uncertain conditions.

To be precise, a weakening of a property P is any property that specifies a superset of the behaviours of P. For example, we can logically specify the above example as weakening $HighWind \vee LowWind \rightarrow CanLand$ to $LowWind \rightarrow CanLand$. (Note that strengthening the antecedent weakens the implication.)

Automatic deduction of weakened properties is also useful in compositional assume-guarantee reasoning [8], where our system is an individual component

M. Leuschel and F. Ishikawa (Eds.): ABZ 2025, LNCS 15728, pp. 349–353, 2026.
https://doi.org/10.1007/978-3-031-94533-5_22

providing guarantees that feed into the assumptions of other components' specifications [11], and aid proofs of the composed system's global properties.

This PhD project currently aims to answer two core research questions:

RQ1: How can a system property, normally holding but invalidated by system degradation or environmental changes, be automatically weakened so that it both holds in the degraded system and is still useful?

RQ2: In compositional assume-guarantee reasoning, how does the weakening of a component's guaranteed properties affect other components or system-level properties?

Related Work. Goal weakening has been explored in requirements engineering [12]. However, conflicts are only handled between goals because the weakening is done at requirements engineering-time, whereas our approach is concerned with inconsistencies between the requirements and the implementation, which occur at a later stage in the development lifecycle.

Belief revision [6] is a technique where a belief set is updated when new information conflicts with existing beliefs, removing those that conflict. However, this is a coarse approach that does not weaken the individual beliefs themselves, and so can be overly conservative.

Counterexample-guided techniques have been applied to areas like abstraction refinement [3], inductive synthesis [1], and control [7]. However, they have not yet been applied to the problem of weakening goals in specifications.

2 Counterexample-Guided Weakening

Our approach finds counterexamples that show that the property doesn't hold in the system, integrates them into the property, and repeats. By integrating counterexamples we iteratively weaken the property until it holds in the system.

Our algorithm, initially applied to propositional logic, is implemented in OCaml, using the Why3 [5] platform with Alt-Ergo [4], a tableau-based solver. The code is hosted publicly on GitHub[1].

Not all weakenings of the desired property are useful, as evidenced by the trivial property $\bot$ that any system guarantees. Thus, along with our desired property we also specify a *critical* property P_C that our system must satisfy, as the minimum weakening of P_D that we allow.

Our specifications are triples $\langle A, P_D, P_C \rangle$ of propositional formulae, where A represents the internal structure of the system and the environment, P_D represents the desired property of the system, and P_C represents the critical property of the system. $\langle A, P_D, P_C \rangle$ is well-formed if and only if P_D implies P_C, i.e. $P_D \rightarrow P_C$. We begin the proof process by checking whether the iterative algorithm is necessary:

1. Check that $A \rightarrow P_D$. If true, then finish successfully with P_D as the property; otherwise,

[1] https://github.com/benmandrew/prop-goal-weakening.

2. Check that $A \rightarrow P_C$. If false, then finish unsuccessfully, as our critical property does not hold; otherwise,
3. Find an intermediate property P_I between P_D and P_C such that $A \rightarrow P_I$.

(By P_I being *between* P_D and P_C, we mean that $P_D \rightarrow P_I$ and $P_I \rightarrow P_C$, considering propositional formulae to be partially ordered by implication.)

Algorithm. The algorithm uses a counterexample-guided approach, iteratively computing counterexamples using a SAT solver and integrating them back into the candidate property until it is satisfied. It is detailed below as well as in Fig. 1.

The i-th candidate property is denoted by P_I^i, for $i \in \mathbb{N}$, and we begin by initialising $P_I^0 = P_D$. We then construct a formula $F(i)$ that is a conjunction of the following:

1. $A \rightarrow P_I^i$, the candidate property must hold in the system,
2. $P_D \rightarrow P_I^i$, the candidate property must be weaker than or equivalent to the desired property, and
3. $P_I^i \rightarrow P_C$, the candidate property must be stronger than or equivalent to the critical property.

We check the validity of $F(i)$ using a SAT solver. If $F(i)$ is valid, then P_I^i holds in the system and we are finished. Otherwise, the SAT solver gives us a counterexample model that holds in A but does not in P_I^i. This model may contain assignments to *hidden* variables that occur in A but not in P_D or P_C. Including them would expose the inner logical workings of the system which may sometimes be desirable, but for the purposes of overapproximating the weakened property, we remove all hidden variables from the counterexample.

From this overapproximated counterexample we construct a formula C_i which is a conjunction of positive or negative propositional variables. For example, the model $\{X = \text{true}, Y = \text{false}, Z = \text{false}\}$ corresponds to the formula $X \wedge \neg Y \wedge \neg Z$.

The next iteration of the candidate property is then

$$P_I^{i+1} = P_I^i \vee C_i$$

and we repeat the loop by constructing and checking $F(i+1)$.

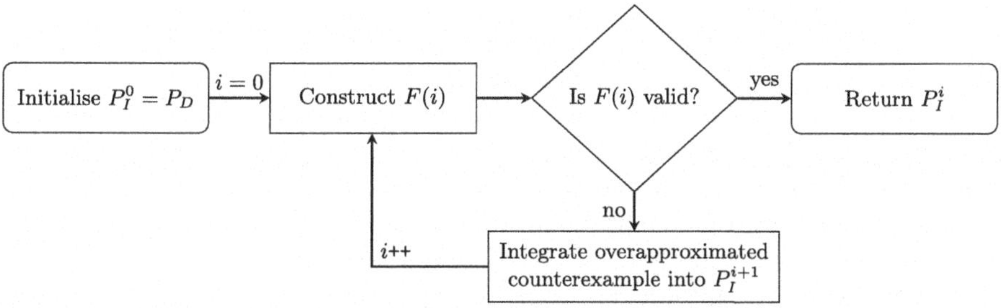

Fig. 1. Overview of the algorithm, which iteratively weakens the candidate property P_I^i until it is satisfied by the system representation A.

The algorithm is complete for systems with finite numbers of variables. As each step adds at least one complete interpretation to the candidate property, the number of iterations is bounded by 2^N, where N is the number of unique propositional variables in P_D and P_C combined.

Example. We use the example from the introduction concerning a quadrotor drone. Our propositional variables are R_4, that all four rotors work; R_3, that only three rotors work; W_H, that windspeed is high; W_L, that windspeed is low; and L, that the drone can land.
The system is modelled by three assumptions,

$$A = \underbrace{R_3}_{\text{(3a)}} \wedge \underbrace{(R_4 \wedge (W_H \vee W_L) \to L)}_{\text{(3b)}} \wedge \underbrace{(R_3 \wedge W_L \to L)}_{\text{(3c)}}$$

which specify (3a), that only three rotors work (i.e. one rotor has failed); and (3b, 3c), the conditions for the drone being able to land. Our desired goal property is $P_D = (W_H \vee W_L) \to L$, but this is not satisfied by the assumptions, so we must weaken it. (For the purposes of demonstration we let our critical property $P_C = \top$.)

We construct the initial $F(0)$ with $P_I^0 = P_D$, and check for validity with the SAT solver, receiving a negative answer with the counterexample $\neg L \wedge W_H \wedge \neg W_L \wedge R_3 \wedge \neg R_4$. This counterexample contains the 'hidden' variables R_3 and R_4, and as we would prefer not to expose the inner state of our system, we remove them, resulting in the overapproximated counterexample $\neg L \wedge W_H \wedge \neg W_L$. Integrating this into our candidate property results in

$$\begin{aligned} P_I^1 &= ((W_H \vee W_L) \to L) \vee (\neg L \wedge W_H \wedge \neg W_L) \\ &= W_L \to L \end{aligned}$$

Which is a valid property of the system and so we are done.

3 Future Work

To answer **RQ1**, we are investigating how to extend weakening to properties expressed in state-based specification languages, such as Deterministic Finite Automata (DFAs), Buchi automata (which commonly correspond with LTL formulae), and Abstract State Machines (ASMs). We are currently exploring how these properties can be automatically weakened, based on the framework of automata learning with the L^* algorithm [2].

Weakening goals is not the only way to weaken a specification: in contract-based reasoning [11], strengthening the corresponding assumption serves the same purpose, and may be a more natural solution for changes in the environment. This will contribute to answering **RQ2**. It remains to be seen when this would be appropriate, and how exactly it would be done.

It may be more suitable to frame weakening as an interpolation problem [10]—that is, finding a suitable interpolant between the desired and critical properties, subject to the constraint of being a valid property of the system. This approach requires investigation.

References

1. Alur, R., et al.: Syntax- guided synthesis. In: Formal Methods in Computer-Aided Design, pp. 1–8. IEEE (2013). https://doi.org/10.1109/FMCAD.2013.6679385
2. Angluin, D.: Learning regular sets from queries and counterexamples. Inf. Comput. **75**(2), 87–106 (1987). https://doi.org/10.1016/0890-5401(87)90052-6
3. Clarke, E., Grumberg, O., Jha, S., Lu, Y., Veith, H.: Counterexample-guided abstraction refinement. In: Emerson, E.A., Sistla, A.P. (eds.) CAV 2000. LNCS, vol. 1855, pp. 154–169. Springer, Heidelberg (2000). https://doi.org/10.1007/10722167_15
4. Conchon, S., Coquereau, A., Iguernlala, M., Mebsout, A.: Alt-Ergo 2.2. In: International Workshop on Satisfiability Modulo Theories (2018). https://inria.hal.science/hal-01960203
5. Filliâtre, J.-C., Paskevich, A.: Why3 — where programs meet provers. In: Felleisen, M., Gardner, P. (eds.) ESOP 2013. LNCS, vol. 7792, pp. 125–128. Springer, Heidelberg (2013). https://doi.org/10.1007/978-3-642-37036-6_8
6. Gärdenfors, P.: Belief Revision. Cambridge Tracts in Theoretical Computer Science. Cambridge University Press, Cambridge (1992). https://doi.org/10.1017/CBO9780511526664
7. Henzinger, T.A., Jhala, R., Majumdar, R.: Counterexample-guided control. In: Baeten, J., Lenstra, J.K., Parrow, J., Woeginger, G.J. (eds.) ICALP 2003. LNCS, vol. 2719, pp. 886–902. Springer, Heidelberg (2003). https://doi.org/10.1007/3-540-45061-0_69
8. Jones, C.B.: Tentative steps toward a development method for interfering programs. ACM Trans. Program. Lang. Syst. **5**(4), 596–619 (1983). https://doi.org/10.1145/69575.69577
9. Luckcuck, M., Farrell, M., Dennis, L.A., Dixon, C., Fisher, M.: Formal specification and verification of autonomous robotic systems: a survey. ACM Comput. Surv. **52**(5), 100:1-100:41 (2019). https://doi.org/10.1145/3342355
10. McMillan, K.L.: Applications of craig interpolants in model checking. In: Halbwachs, N., Zuck, L.D. (eds.) TACAS 2005. LNCS, vol. 3440, pp. 1–12. Springer, Heidelberg (2005). https://doi.org/10.1007/978-3-540-31980-1_1
11. Meyer, B.: Applying design by contract. Computer **25**(10), 40–51 (1992). https://doi.org/10.1109/2.161279
12. van Lamsweerde, A., Letier, E.: Handling obstacles in goal-oriented requirements engineering. IEEE Trans. Softw. Eng. **26**(10), 978–1005 (2000). https://doi.org/10.1109/32.879820

Formal Modelling and Reasoning on Assurance Cases Expressed with GSN in Event-B

Christophe Chen(✉)

INPT-ENSEEIHT/IRIT, University of Toulouse, Toulouse, France
christophe.chen@toulouse-inp.fr

Abstract. An Assurance Case (AC) is a structured argumentation for certification describing how industrial activities support system requirements. The most widely used notation for AC is the Goal Structuring Notation (GSN), which provides a graphical representation of argument structures. Despite the advances in the definition of a methodology for developing AC using the GSN, establishing the soundness of ACs relies essentially on experts reviews. Indeed, the lack of rigorous semantics for the GSN hinders the application of formal methods to check the consistency of ACs. The objective of our work is to design a logical (i.e., proof-based) framework supporting the definition of formalised ACs, in order to assist system designers and certification authorities in building goal structures and checking their consistency with respect to the formalised semantics and domain knowledge model that formalises system-specific concepts. The proposed framework will be grounded in the Event-B method and associated algebraic theories.

1 Context

Critical systems must meet several types of requirements including safety, security and process-related constraints. Once formalised, several formal techniques such as testing, proof, model-checking, model animation, simulation, static analysis, and so on are set up. Due to the guarantees they offer, they play the role of supporting evidence to show that requirements are fulfilled. However, keeping track of the relationship between requirements and supporting evidence is often unclear, informally stated, not explicit or even not expressed at all. The relationship between the evidence and a high-level goal is usually expressed through arguments expressed using natural language.

In order to provide an explicit link between high-level requirements or goals or claims and evidence provided by system models analyses, structured documentation models based on goal/claim decomposition have been proposed [7]. Such a model is useful not only for requirement validation but also for certification purposes. This structured documentation model enables recursively breaking down high-level goals into smaller sub-goals, until a level where the evidence

M. Leuschel and F. Ishikawa (Eds.): ABZ 2025, LNCS 15728, pp. 354–358, 2026.
https://doi.org/10.1007/978-3-031-94533-5_23

becomes directly relevant and sufficient for validation is reached. The decomposition mechanisms rely on an implicit logical framework that helps establish connections between requirement goals and the supporting evidence.

Such a structured documentation model is called an **Assurance Case** (AC) [10]. When the Assurance Case regards safety (resp. security) goals or requirements, then it is also called safety (resp. security) case.

The most common notation for Assurance Case is the **Goal Structuring Notation** (GSN) [6,12], supported by a graphical language. An AC represented using GSN has a *hierarchical goal structure* describing goal decomposition. *Strategies* define decomposition or inference rules that produce sub-goals and *justifications* provide explanations for the adopted strategies producing these sub-goals. *Assumptions* may be introduced to define hypotheses associated to a goal. *Contexts* in which goals are expressed are also described, and contribute to defining the scope in which claims are stated. In most cases, such GSN features are described using natural language statements, referring to system and safety engineering concepts.

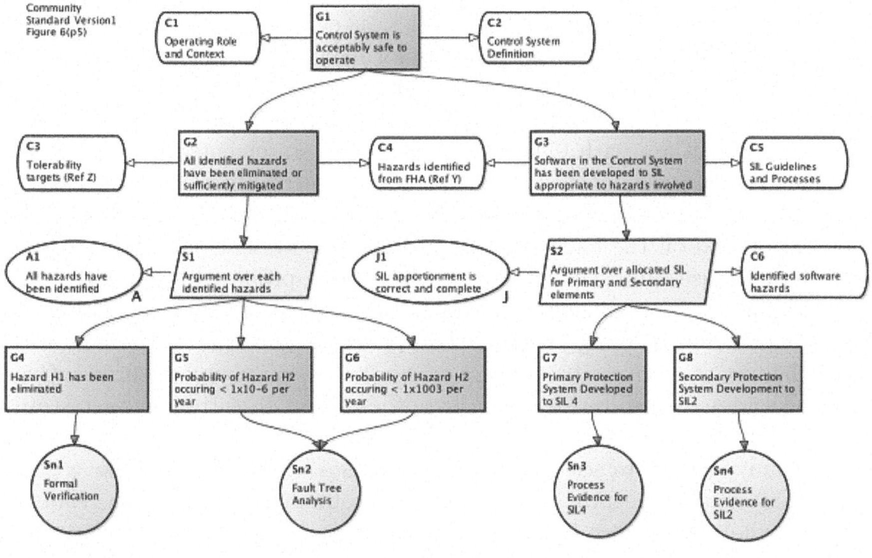

Fig. 1. A safety argument from the community standard

Figure 1 is an example of a goal structure taken from the GSN community standard [1,5]. The main goal G1 (safety) is broken into two sub-goals G2 (hazards mitigation) and G3 (standard SIL compliance), while making explicit the definition of terms (C2, C3, C5) and their origins (C1, C4). Sub-goal G2 (resp. G3) is furthermore decomposed according to strategy S1 (resp. S2), using assumptions (A1) and justifications (J1). When goals are clearly defined at a low level by employing decompositions, they are directly backed by *evidence* (solutions) that reference various activities (Sn1..4) carried out by industries to fulfil the requirements.

2 Motivation and Objectives

From Fig. 1, we observe that the concepts (goal, context, justification, evidence, etc.) of a goal structure graph are described using natural language, and the links between these concepts are modelled using arrows. Despite the advances in the definition of a methodology for developing AC using the GSN, establishing the soundness of ACs relies essentially on expert reviews. The semantics of GSN describing such goal structure construct is given using natural language and semi-formal notations [5].

The lack of rigorous semantics for the GSN hinders the application of formal methods to check the consistency of Assurance Cases which can be a subject of study to ensure their correctness. Reasoning on Assurance Cases requires their formalisation, but most provided formalisms only check structural well-formedness, and do not control the content of the AC building blocks, nor the link between evidences in terms of semantics, as evidences may rely on domain-specific knowledge. A recent contribution formalises a subset of GSN in Lean [8], modelling goal contents as *propositions* and generating proof obligations (POs) for the correctness of the deductive reasoning. Another contribution considers Assurance Case with CAE notation. Claim statements about *properties* of an *object* in a given *environment* are transformed into clauses in a logical programming language, making it possible to query the flattened AC [9]. Other approaches based on the formalisation of deductive systems allowing to reason on Assurance Cases in a sequent calculus have been proposed by [2,11].

We claim that formal methods can be applied to assist in reasoning and to speed up the engineering process. More generally, we want to mechanise the implicit human reasoning on assurance cases, that is, supplying Assurance Cases with a reasoning system by clarifying hypotheses and objectives at each step.

An usual concern with Assurance Cases is the *propagation effect* on node change. Many suggest to see Assurance Cases as a whole [5] (more like a graph than a tree) so asserting the impact on their soundness requires the reader to study the whole Assurance Case again which is a repetitive and laborious task.

The objective of our work is to design a logical (i.e., proof-based) framework supporting the definition of formalised Assurance Cases, in order to assist system designers and certification authorities in building goal structures and check their consistency with respect to the formalised semantics and domain knowledge model formalising system specific concepts. The proposed framework will be grounded on the Event-B method and associated algebraic theories.

3 Next Steps

First of all, our bibliographic work will be continuously updated in order to follow the different contributions in the area of AC formalisation. As part of the thesis work, and with the goal of producing a formal framework offering the possibility to reason about ACs while preserving their consistency, the approach we propose is based on different stages.

Formalising Assurance Cases Expressed with GSN. First, we propose to formalise the GSN as a parameterised algebraic theory offering all the constructors needed to build ACs in this notation. Well-definedness conditions will be associated with these constructors. The content of the different concepts of an AC, which can be goals, assumptions, evidences, etc., generally expressed in natural language, will be formalised as statements in the chosen logical framework.

Modelling Domain Knowledge. At the same time, a domain knowledge model, conforming to a knowledge representation language, will be formalised. This shall describe all the domain-specific information, together with the constraints that apply, related to the system for which an Assurance Case is being proposed. The previously mentioned statements will refer to this domain knowledge via an annotation mechanism to be defined. This annotation relationship must maintain the Assurance Case's consistency by taking into account the associated knowledge and its related constraints. At this point, consistency proof obligations will be generated and checked. Note that the domain knowledge model is independent of the AC, and thus may be reused for another AC and as well as help reducing *confirmation bias* [3]. However, we are aware that knowledge is debated and continually evolving.

Designing a Formal Reasoning Mechanism. At this stage, the logical reasoning mechanism on Assurance Cases remains to be set up. We therefore plan to define a reasoning mechanism to guarantee the consistency of an Assurance Case. For example in the case of goal decomposition, the deduction rule

$$\frac{G1 \quad G2}{G}$$

meaning that sub-goals $G1$ and $G2$ entail main goal G, is one of several possible goal decomposition reasoning rules.

Other strategies than deduction, like abduction or induction can be envisioned. In addition to consistency, relevant properties, to be defined and formalised, associated to an Assurance Case could be checked using the defined reasoning mechanism. The reachability of a goal based on evidences, taking into account assumptions, is an example of such properties.

Linking Systems Artefacts to Engineering Concepts. System models are one of the main design artefact essential for building Assurance Cases. Linking systems artefacts to engineering concepts is helpful for validation. Therefore, it is desirable to formalise references to a specific part of the system model like [4] which increase traceability and help the validation process. Additionally, we would like to generate proof obligations that verify whether or not the developed model indeed possesses the artefact in question.

Support of Impact Analysis. Last, but not least, impact analysis on argument modification will be the subject of a further study. Indeed, checking the consistency of an Assurance Case after a change or among a set of Assurance Cases will be addressed as well. Changes may occur in all the features and concepts of the designed framework: Assurance Cases, system models, domain knowledge, used reasoning rules, etc.

Case Studies. All the points mentioned above will be driven by a set of case studies formalised with Event-B and its associated algebraic theories and developed on the Rodin platform.

References

1. Cabot, J.: https://modeling-languages.com/goal-structuring-notation-introduction/
2. Cassano, V., Maibaum, T.S.E., Grigorova, S.: Towards making safety case arguments explicit, precise, and well founded, pp. 227–258. Springer, Singapore (2021)
3. Dekker, S.: The Field Guide to Understanding 'Human Error'. CRC press (2017)
4. Foster, S., Nemouchi, Y., O'Halloran, C., Stephenson, K., Tudor, N.: Formal model-based assurance cases in Isabelle/SACM: an autonomous underwater vehicle case study. In: Proceedings of the 8th International Conference on Formal Methods in Software Engineering, FormaliSE 2020, pp. 11–21. ACM (2020)
5. Working group, T.G.: https://scsc.uk/gsn
6. Kelly, T., Weaver, R.: The goal structuring notation–a safety argument notation. In: Proceedings of the Dependable Systems and Networks Workshop Assurance Cases (2004)
7. van Lamsweerde, A.: Requirements Engineering: From System Goals to UML Models to Software Specifications, 1st edn. Wiley Publishing (2009)
8. Murphy, L., Viger, T., Sandro, A.D., Chechik, M.: PLACIDUS: engineering product lines of rigorous assurance cases. In: Integrated Formal Methods: 19th International Conference, IFM 2024, 2024, pp. 87–108. Springer (2024)
9. Murugesan, A., et al.: Semantic analysis of assurance cases using S (CASP). In: ICLP Workshops (2023)
10. Rhodes, T., Boland, F., Fong, E., Kass, M.: Software assurance using structured assurance case models. J. Res. Natl. Inst. Stand. Technol. **115**, 209 (2010)
11. Rushby, J.: Logic and epistemology in safety cases, pp. 1–7 (2013)
12. Toulmin, S.E.: The uses of argument. Philosophy **34**(130), 244–245 (1958)

Author Index

M. Leuschel and F. Ishikawa (Eds.): ABZ 2025, LNCS 15728, pp. 359–360, 2026.
https://doi.org/10.1007/978-3-031-94533-5